Decline and Fall of the Roman City

J. H.W. G. LIEBESCHUETZ

OXFORD
UNIVERSITY PRESS

OXFORD
UNIVERSITY PRESS

Great Clarendon Street, Oxford OX2 6DP
Oxford University Press is a department of the University of Oxford.
It furthers the University's objective of excellence in research, scholarship,
and education by publishing worldwide in
Oxford New York
Athens Auckland Bangkok Bogotá Buenos Aires Calcutta
Cape Town Chennai Dar es Salaam Delhi Florence Hong Kong Istanbul
Karachi Kuala Lumpur Madrid Melbourne Mexico City Mumbai
Nairobi Paris São Paulo Shanghai Singapore Taipei Tokyo Toronto Warsaw
and associated companies in Berlin Ibadan

Oxford is a registered trade mark of Oxford University Press
in the UK and certain other countries

Published in the United States
by Oxford University Press Inc., New York

First published 2001

British Library Cataloguing in Publication Data
Data available

Library of Congress Cataloging-in-Publication Data
Liebeschuetz, J. H. W. G. (John Hugo Wolfgang Gideon)
The decline and fall of the Roman city / J.H.W.G. Liebeschuetz.
p. cm.
Includes bibliographical references and index.
ISBN 0-19-815247-7
1. Cities and towns, Ancient–Rome. 2. Rome–History–Empire,
284-476. 3. Byzantine Empire–History. 4. Europe–History–392-
814. I. Title.
DG70.A1 L54 2000 937'.009732–dc21 00-059815

ISBN 0–19–815247–7

1 3 5 7 9 10 8 6 4 2

Typeset in Caslon by Regent Typesetting, London
Printed in Great Britain by
Biddles Ltd., Guildford and King's Lynn

To Margaret

PREFACE

Ever since I finished *Antioch* I have felt that I ought to write a sequel dealing with what happened to the cities of the Empire after the fourth century. This is the sequel, though it has become rather a different kind of book. Many friends and colleagues have helped to bring it into being. Some years ago John Matthews asked me to write a chapter on cities for volume xiv of the new edition of the *Cambridge Ancient History*. In 1992 John Rich needed an introductory chapter for the volume *The City in Late Antiquity*, which he was then editing. I was fortunate to be elected to a fellowship at the Princeton Institute of Advanced Study, that scholars' paradise, for the autumn semester 1993. There I got through more reading than I have ever been able to manage within a comparable period. Chapter 7 started as a seminar paper at Princeton, Chapter 3 as a lecture at a conference organized by C. Lepelley in 1993 at the University of Paris X-Nanterre. Subsequently, I regularly attended meetings of Walter Pohl's team of the Transformation of the Roman World project of the European Science Foundation, and invariably returned home with new ideas and new perspectives. Euangelos Chrysos instigated the paper which eventually became Chapter 11 of this book. Gisela Ripoll and Javier Arce supplied me with offprints, and bibliographical information, and answered many questions about Late Roman Hispania. Fortified with an introduction from Arce, I was welcomed, and shown over the villa La Olmeda by J. Cortes, its proprietor and excavator. I have learnt much about the settlement of barbarian federates from the books and articles of Maria Cesa. Gian-Pietro Brogiolo showed me over the site of his excavation at Brescia. Beat Brenk sent me offprints of reports of his excavation on the cathedral-site at Gerasa. Zbigniew Fiema has kept me informed about the progress of the important Petra project. He has also kindly allowed me to cite still unpublished work. Ken Holum and Yossi Patrich have answered questions and sent me offprints about the work of the Combined Caesarea Expeditions, and Yoram Tsafrir has brought me up to date on Scythopolis/Bet Shean. I want to thank everybody who answered letters of enquiry over the ten years or so that I have worked on the book: Manfred Klinkott for his views on the dating of the walls of Pergamum; Mark Humphries for information about Aquileia; John Kent and Peter Lampinen for their opinions on the so-called Arab-Byzantine coins of Syria and Palestine; Archie Dunn and Helen Saradi for papers, both published, and not yet published, on the archaeology of the Balkans and related topics; Ariel Lewin for his two books on, respectively, the cities of the Late Roman Empire in the East, and Late Roman popular politics; Linda Jones Hall for a stream of news about Beirut; Roberta Tomba for information about excavations at Berenike, Charlotte Roueché and Stephen Mitchell for sharing their wide knowledge of developments in Anatolia. Michael Whitby wrote a report on the typescript for Oxford University Press, which alarmed the author, but probably benefited the text. Lynn Childress, copy-edited the typescript, and in the process removed numerous mistakes and inconsistencies. If any are left she is certainly not to blame. David Taylor of the Nottingham Department of Archaeology drew the maps. The *Decline and Fall of the Roman City* is essentially a work of my retirement, and I am grateful to all those who have kept me in touch with the subject in conversations about Ancient History over the years, and above all to Averil Cameron, and to John Drinkwater and his two visitors from Germany, Werner Lütkenhaus and Hartmut Leppin, to Luke Lavant, and to Carlo Noethlichs, and last but far from least to Robert Markus, who also wrote critical but helpful annotations to the first six chapters of the text, and to Andrew Poulter. I know that some of these people are not happy with the book's insistence on the relevance of 'decline', but without them the book might not have been written at all.

J.H.W.G.L.

CONTENTS

List of Illustrations x
List of Maps and Plans xi
Abbreviations xiii

1. Introduction 1

PART I. THE END OF CLASSICAL URBAN POLITICS

2. The Survival of the Cities 29
3. Post-curial Civic Government 104
4. The Rise of the Bishop 137
5. Civic Finance in the late Late Roman Cities of the East, with Special Reference to Egypt 169
6. Shows and Factions 203

PART II. A SOCIETY TRANSFORMED

7. Transformation of Greek Literary Culture under the Influence of Christianity 223
8. Conflict and Disorder in the East 249
9. Decline and the Beginnings of Renewal in the East, including the Eastern Balkans 284
10. The Transformation of Literary Culture in the West under the Influence of Christianity 318
11. The Decline of Classical Citizenship and the Rise of Ethnic Solidarity in the West 342
12. Decline and the Beginnings of Renewal in the West 369
13. Summary and Conclusions 400

Bibliography 417
Index 463

LIST OF ILLUSTRATIONS

Nicopolis ad Istrum: reconstruction 80
From A. Poulter, *Nicopolis ad Istrum*, i (London, 1995)

Mosaic from Madaba showing 1. personifications of Rome, Gregoria, and Alexandria; 2. Aphrodite and Adonis; 3. Phaedra and Hippolitus 227
From M. Piccirillo, *I Mosaici di Giordania* (Rome, 1986), p. 78, tav. IV

Dionysus mosaic from Nea Paphos, Cyprus 229
From W. A. Daszewski, *Dionysos der Erlöser* (Mainz, 1985), abb. 3

LIST OF MAPS AND PLANS

1. The Roman Empire and principal regions 28
2. Cities in the East 31
3. Ephesus: the late ceremonial centre, and the late walls 33
   From S. Karwiese, *Gross ist die Artemis von Ephesus* (Vienna, 1995)
4. Aphrodisias: the late ceremonial centre 35
   From R. R. R. Smith and C. Ratté, 'Archaeological research at Aphrodisias in Caria 1995', *AJA* 101 (1997), fig. 1
5. Pergamum: the move into the plain and late fortifications 47
   From K. Rheidt, *Die Altertümer von Pergamum*, XV.2 (1991), end-plan and p. 42, abb. 47, by U. Wulf
6. Miletus: the so-called Justinianic wall 50
   From W. Müller Wiener, 'Von der Polis zum Kastron', *Gymnasium*, 93 (1986), 435–75, abb. 4
7. Gerasa in Late Antiquity 60
   From F. Zayadine, *Jerash Archaeological Project*, i (Amman, 1986)
8. Cities in the West 75
9. Old *civitates* and new fortified hill settlements in south eastern Macedonia 78
   From A. Dunn, 'Was there a militarisation of the Southern Balkans in Late Antiquity?', Acts of the XVIIth International Congress of Roman Frontier Studies at Amman 2000 (forthcoming)
10. Nicopolis ad Istrum: resistivity survey and interpretation 79
    From A. Poulter, *Nicopolis ad Istrum*, i (London, 1995), p. 41, fig. 10; p. 261, fig. 104; plate 1
11. Justiniana Prima: a late Late fortified centre of civil and ecclesiastical administration with few inhabitants 81
    From V. Kondic and V. Popovic, *Caricin Grad* (Belgrade, 1977), fig. 4; and from B. Bavant, V. Kondic, and M. Spiesser, *Caricin Grad*, ii, Collection de l'école française de Rome75 (Belgrade/Rome, 1990), pp. 312 and 314

12. Recopolis: a Visigothic version of a Byzantine administrative centre type city? 82
From H. Schlunk and T. Hauschild, *Hispania Antiqua*, ii (Mainz, 1978), p. 169, abb. 97a
13. Angers and Reims: late Roman walls and extramural churches 83
From P. A. A. Février, M. Fixot, and C. Godineau, *Histoire de la France urbaine*, ii (Paris, 1980), pp. 406 and 407
14. Tours and Metz: late Roman walls and extramural churches 87
From P. A. A. Février, M. Fixot, and C. Godineau, *Histoire de la France urbaine*, ii (Paris, 1980), pp. 437 and 446
15. Cities in North Africa 98–9
16. Cities in Egypt 261
17. Cities and villages in Syria, Palestine, and Arabia 296
18. Scythopolis (Bet Shean) 301
From Yoram Tsafrir and Gideon Foerster, 'Urbanism at Scythopolis', *DOP* 51 (1997), figs. C and D
19. Anjar, an Umayyad settlement 309
Qasr al-Hayr, Umayyad settlement described as madīna
From G. R. D. King and Averil Cameron, *Land Use and Settlement Patterns* (Princeton, 1994), fig. 29
20. Damascus: classical into Arab city 312
From D. Sack, *Damaskus* (Mainz, 1989), p. 13, abb. 4
21. Harat Bain: a quarter of Damascus 313
From D. Sack, *Damaskus* (Mainz, 1989), p. 71, abb. 12
22. Visigothic cemeteries in Hispania and 'seventh'-century churches 359
From P. de Palol, 'Demography and Archaeology in Roman, Christian and Visigothic Spain', *Classical Folia*, 23.1 (New York, 1969), 32–114, pl. 6; and H. Schlunk and T. Hauschild, *Hispania Antiqua*, ii (Mainz, 1978), p. 88, abb. 64

The plans of town centres have been simplified and redrawn by David Taylor of the Department of Archaeology of Nottingham University from the sources indicated for each plan.

ABBREVIATIONS

ABSOR	*Annual of the American School of Oriental Research*
ABSA	*Annual of the British School at Athens*
ACO	*Acta Conciliorum Oecumenicorum*, ed. E. Schwartz (Berlin/Leipzig, 1914–40)
ADAJ	*Annual of the Department of Antiquities of Jordan*
AE	*Anné Epigraphique*
AHR	*American Historical Review*
AJA	*American Journal of Archaeology*
AJP	*American Journal of Philology*
Annales ESC	*Annales, économies, sociétés, civilisations*, ed. Lucien Febvre *et al.* (Paris, 1946–)
ANRW	*Aufstieg und Niedergang der römischen Welt*
Anz Wien	*Anzeiger der Akademie der Wissenschaften in Wien*
ASR	*Archivio della Società Romana de Storia Patria*
BAR Brit.	British Archaeological Reports, British Series
BAR Int	British Archaeological Reports, International Series
BASOR	*Bulletin of the American School of Oriental Research*
BASP	*Bulletin of the American Society of Papyrologists*
BBA	*Berliner byzantinistische Arbeiten*
BCH	*Bulletin de correspondance hellénique*
BCTH	*Bulletin archéologique du Comité des travaux historiques et scientifiques*, Paris
BGU	*Aegyptische Urkunden aus den staatlichen Museen zu Berlin*
BICS	*Bulletin of the Institute of Classical Studies of the University of London*
BIFAO	*Bulletin de l'Institut Français d'Archéologie Orientale*
BMB	*Bulletin du musée de Beyrouth*
BMGS	*Byzantine & Modern Greek Studies*
Breviarium	*Breviarium Alaricianum* also known as *Lex Romana Visigotorum*, ed. G. Haenel (Berlin, 1849)
BZ	*Byzantinische Zeitschrift*
CAH	*Cambridge Ancient History*
CCL	Corpus Christianorum Series Latina
CE	*Chronique d'Égypte*
CIG	*Corpus Inscriptionum Graecarum*
CIL	*Corpus Inscriptionum Latinarum*

CJ	*Codex Justinianus*
Const. Prag.	*Constitutio Pragmatica*
CPR	*Corpus Papyrorum Raineri* (Vienna, 1895–)
CRAI	*Comptes rendus de l'Académie des Inscriptions et Belles-Lettres*, Paris
CSCO	*Corpus Scriptorum Christianorum Orientalium*
CSEL	*Corpus Scriptorum Ecclesiasticorum Latinorum*
CT	*Codex Theodosianus*, ed. Th. Mommsen and P. Meyer (Berlin, 1905)
C Tol III	*Concilium Toletanum III* (AD 589), *Mansi* 977–99
DACL	*Dictionnaire d'archéologie chrétienne et de liturgie*, by F. Cabrol and H. Leclercq
DAI	*De Administratione Imperii*
DHGE	*Dictionnaire d'histoire et de géographie ecclésiastique*
DOP	*Dumbarton Oaks Papers*
EcHR	*Economic History Review*
Edict	*Edict of Justinian*, published with Justinian's *Nov*
EHR	*English Historical Review*
ESI	*Excavations and Surveys in Israel*
FJRA	*Fontes Iuris Romani ante-Iustiniani*, ed. S. Riccobono *et al.*
GRBS	*Greek, Roman and Byzantine Studies*
HE	*Historia Ecclesiastica*
HF	Gregory of Tours, *History of the Franks, MGH SS R Mer*, vol. i
HG	*Historia Gothorum*
HTR	*Harvard Theological Review*
IEJ	*Israel Exploration Journal*
IG	*Inscriptiones Graecae*
IGLS	*Inscriptions grecques et latines de la Syrie*
IGSK	*Inschriften griechischer Städte Kleinasiens*
ILS	*Inscriptiones Latinae Selectae*, ed. H. Dessau
JAC	*Jahrbuch für Antike und Christentum*
JHS	*Journal of Hellenic Studies*
JJP	*Journal of Juristic Papyrology*
JNG	*Jahrbuch für Numismatik und Geldgeschichte*
JÖAI	*Jahreshefte des österreichischen archäologischen Instituts*
JÖB	*Jahrbuch der österreichischen Byzantinistik*
JRA	*Journal of Roman Archaeology*
JRS	*Journal of Roman Studies*
L Eur	*Leges Eurici*
Lib Pont	*Liber Pontificalis (pars prior), MGH Gest Pont Rom I*

LIGMC	*Lexicon Iconographicum Mythologiae Classicae*
LSJ	H. G. Liddell, R. Scott, and H. S. Stuart Jones, *A Greek–English Dictionary* (Oxford, 1925–40)
LV	*Leges Visigothorum*
MAMA	*Monumenta Asiae Minoris Antiquae*
MEFR	*Mélanges d'archéologie et histoire de l'école française de Rome*
MGH AA	*Monumenta Germaniae Historica, Auctores Antiquissimi*
MGH LL	*Monumenta Germaniae Historica, Leges*
MGH SR Mer	*Monumenta Germaniae Historica, Scriptores Rerum Merovingarum*
MÖG	*Mitteilungen des Instituts für Österreichische Geschichtsforschung*
MPER NS	*Mitteilungen aus den Papyrusurkunden der Nationalbibliothek in Wien,* Neue Serie (Vienna, 1932–64), 5 parts
Nov	*Leges Novellae*
Nov App	*Novellarum Appendices*
OCP	*Orientalia Christiana Periodica*
OMS	L. Robert, *Opera minora selecta* (Amsterdam, 1969–90)
P Amh	*Amherst Papyri*, ed. B. P. Greenfell and A. S. Hunt, 2 vols. (London, 1900–1)
P Apoll	*Papyrus grecs d'Apollōnus Anō*, ed. R. Rémondon (Cairo, 1953)
PBSR	*Papers of the British School at Rome*
P Cair	*Catalogue général des antiquités égyptiennes du Musée du Caire, papyrus grecs d'époque byzantine,* ed. J. Maspero (Cairo, 1911–16), 3 vols.
PCPS	*Proceedings of the Cambridge Philological Society*
P Edfou	*Tell Edfou: Les Papyrus et les ostraca grecs*, ed. J. Manteuffel (Cairo, 1937)
PEQ	*Palestine Exploration Quarterly*
P Flor	*Papiri greco-egizii*, ed. D.Comparetti and G. Vitelli (Milan, 1906–15), 3 vols.
P Freer	*Greek and Coptic Papyri in the Freer Gallery*, ed. L. MacCoull (Washington, 1973)
P Fuad	*Fuad University I Papyri*, ed. D. S. Crawford (Alexandria, 1949)
PG	*Patrologia Graeca*, ed J.-P. Migne
PGM	*Papyri Graecae Magicae*, ed. K. Preisendanz *et al.*
P Goth	*Papyrus grecs de la bibliothèque municipale de Gothem-*

	bourg, ed. H. Frisk (Göteborg, 1929)
P Hamb	*Griechische Papyrusurkunden der hamburger Staats- und Universitätsbibliothek*, ed. P. M. Meyer (Leipzig/Berlin, 1911–24)
P Harr	*The Rendel Harris Papyri*, ed. J. E. Powell (Cambridge, 1936)
P Haun	*Papyri Graecae Haunienses*, ed. T. Larsen (Copenhagen, 1942)
P Ital	*Die nichtliterarischen Papyri Italiens*, ed. J.-O.Tjäder (Lund, 1955–82), 3 vols.
P kl Form	*Studien zur Paleographie und Papyruskunde III and VIII*, ed. C. Wessely (Leipzig, 1904–8)
PL	*Patrologia Latina*, ed. J.-P. Migne
P Landlisten	*Zwei Landlisten aus dem Hermupolites*, ed. P. J. Sijpesteijn and K. A. Worp (Zutphen, 1978)
P Laur	*Dai Papiri della Biblioteca Medicea, Laurenziana*, ed. R. Pintaudi and others (Florence, 1976–)
P Lips	*Griechische Urkunden aus der Papyrussammlung zu Leipzig*, i, ed. L. Mitteis (Leipzig, 1906)
P Lond	*Greek Papyri in the British Museum*, ed. F. G. Kenyon and H. I. Bell (London, 1893–1917), 7 vols.
PLRE	*Prosopography of the Later Roman Empire*, ed. J. Morris, A. H. M. Jones and others (Cambridge, 1970–92), 3 vols.
P Lugd Bat	*Papyrologica Lugduno-Batava* (Leiden, 1941–)
P Michael	*The Greek Papyri in the Collection of G. A. Michailidis*, ed. D. S. Crawford (London, 1955)
P Nessana	*Excavations at Nessana*, iii. *Non-literary Papyri*, ed. C. J. Kraemer (Princeton, 1958)
PO	*Patrologia Orientalis* (Paris, 1903–)
P Oxy	*The Oxyrhynchus Papyri*, ed. B. P. Greenfell and A. S. Hunt and others (London, 1898–)
P Princ	*Papyri in the Princeton University Collection*, ed. A. C. Johnson and others (Princeton, 1931–)
PSI	*Papiri greci e latini*, ed. G. Vitelli, M. Norsa *et al.*, Publicazioni della società italiana per la ricerca dei papiri greci e latini in Egitto (Florence, 1912–)
P Tebt	*Papyri from Tebtunis in Egyptian and Greek*, ed. W. J. Tair (London, 1977)
P Thead	*Papyrus de Théadelphie*, ed. P. Jouguet (Paris, 1911)
P Turner	*Papyri Turner*
P Warren	*The Warren Papyri* (*Papyrologica Lugd.-Bat.*, vol. i), ed.

	M. David and others (Leiden, 1941)
P Wisc	*The Wisconsin Papyri*, ed. P. J. Sijpesteijn (Leiden, 1967–)
P Würzb	*Mitteilungen aus der würzburger Papyrussammlung*, ed. U. Wilcken (Berlin, 1934)
RA	*Revue archéologique*
RAC	*Reallexikon für Antike und Christentum*
RE	*Real-Encyclopädie der klassischen Altertumswissenschaft*, ed. A. Pauly, G. Wissowa, and W. Kroll
REA	*Revue des études anciennes*
REB	*Revue des études byzantines*
REG	*Revue des études grecques*
RH	*Revue historique*
RIC	*Roman Imperial Coinage*
R Ph	*Revue de philologie*
SB	*Sammelbuch griechischer Urkunden aus Ägypten*, ed. F. Preisigke and others (Strasbourg, later Berlin and Leipzig, 1913–)
SHAJ	*Studies in the History and Archaeology of Jordan*, Amman
St Pal	*Studien zur Paleographie und Papyruskunde*, ed. C. Wessely (Leipzig, 1901–22; repr. 1965–7)
TAPA	*Transactions of the American Philological Association*
TIB	*Tabula Imperii Byzantini*
Var	Cassiodorus, *Variae*, ed. Th. Mommsen *MGH AA* XII
VJESNIK	*Vjesnik za arheogiju i historiju dalmatisku* = Bulletin d'archéologie et d'histoire dalmate, Split
V Porph	Marc le diacre, *Vie de Porphyre, évêque de Gaza*, ed. and tr. H. Grégoire and M.-A. Kugener (Paris, 1930)
V Théod	*La Vie de Théodore de Sykéon*, ed. and tr. A.-J. Festugière (Brussels, 1970)
WB	*Wörterbuch der griechischen Papyrusurkunden*, ed. F. Preisigke and others (Berlin, 1926–)
ZPE	*Zeitschrift für Papyrologie und Epigraphik*
ZRG GA	*Zeitschrift der Savigny-Stiftung für Rechtsgeschichte (Germanische Abteilung)*
ZRG RA	*Zeitschrift der Savigny-Stiftung für Rechtsgeschichte (Römische Abteilung)*
ZRVI	*Zbornik Radova* (Belgrade)

I

Introduction

1. *The late Late Roman City*

This book is about the transformation of cities and life in cities during what is sometimes known as the age of Migrations or the Dark Ages, that is the years from *c*.400 to *c*.650 AD, the period when the classical Roman world was changing into the world of the Middle Ages. At the centre of the investigation is the development of urbanism over the whole area, East as well as West, of what had been the Roman Empire.

Part I of the book begins with a survey of the survival of the physical structures of classical cities in different parts of the Empire over the fifth and sixth centuries. Chapters 3 to 6, which are in a sense the core of the book, are about forms of administration that succeeded curial government. Of these chapters, only Chapter 6, dealing with the reorganization of the public spectacles, is without a Western section. That is because in most Western cities this feature of classical urbanism had already faded out in the course of the fifth century.

Part II of the book deals with wider aspects of urban transformation, the Christianization of education, the simplification of social and economic life, the extent and significance of deurbanization. While the focus is on the running down of the classical world, there is a glimpse at the emerging worlds of Byzantium and Islam and the new kingdoms of the West. East and West are treated in parallel: Chapters 7 to 9, which discuss Eastern topics, are followed by Chapters 10 to 12, which are concerned with related topics in the West. The object of the arrangement is to bring out both differences and similarities. The divergence of subject matter is greatest between the Eastern Chapter 8 and the Western Chapter 11. Both are concerned with what might be called changing political mentality. In the Eastern chapter, the topic examined is the growth of diversity and discord, represented by the circus factions, doctrinal conflicts, and developing regionalism. The Western chapter traces the shrinking significance of Roman citizenship and relates it to the growth of new loyalties and feelings of identity in the successor kingdoms. This chapter is written from an imperial rather than a civic point of view. A corresponding chapter about the East ought perhaps to have been included. But the author does not feel ready to tackle this very large topic at this stage. Chapter 13 summarizes the book. It also discusses the interrelation of the decline of the classical city and the decline of the Empire.

The city (or town) as a social institution can be defined in various ways; most naively perhaps as a concentration of buildings, housing a large population and catering for its needs. But then the question arises how large a population has to be before it becomes entitled to be called a city. Alternatively, a town can be defined by the occupation of its inhabitants. For instance: a town is a settlement, having a certain density of population, with a significant proportion of its inhabitants not engaged in agricultural work, but following a diversity of occupations, including those of craftsmen and traders. All occupations should be represented in sufficiently large numbers to distinguish a town from a village, even though it is impossible to set a minimum level for any category in order to draw a sharp line between town and non-town.[1]

But the city of the Greco-Roman world (Latin: *urbs*, Greek: *polis*) was more than simply a town in the modern sense, however defined. For it always and by definition consisted of an urban centre together with a rural territory which was administered from it. The territory might be large or small. It might include towns as well as villages. The villages and towns in the territory were subject to government from the city centre, and their inhabitants formed a single community, the city state. So the elements that defined an ancient city were many and varied, political and cultural, as well as demographic and economic. For the Roman administration however the difference between a city and a mere town or large village was simple—a settlement was a city if the Roman government had entrusted it with a city's role in the administration of a territory.[2] So in the Roman Empire city status could be quite independent of the size, or indeed the occupations, of a city's population. It was by no means necessary for a Roman city to have a large urban population, or for a significant proportion of that population to be engaged in trading or manufacture. No doubt a mere town (*oppidum*), or even a large village (*vicus*) might have a larger population or manufacturing base than many a city—although normally the city was the largest settlement in its territory, and as the administrative centre might be expected to draw economic activities to itself.

A classical city possessed almost by definition a set of institutions of self-government. The city state had been an essential element of Greco-Roman civilization from its earliest beginnings. When the Romans took over, they almost invariably encouraged control by the wealthy at the

[1] Various definitions of 'town': J. de Vries 1984: 21–2.

[2] Rodríguez, Molinos, and López 1991: 29–36, esp. 35: whether a pre-Roman *oppidum* became *vicus* or an *urbs* was decided by the Roman government.

expense of the popular assembly. This meant that government of the cities of the Empire was in the hands of the local senates, the city councils (*curiae* or *boulai*), and councillors (*decuriones* or *bouleutai*). By the end of the second century these were hereditary bodies. The Roman authorities kept them in power, and in return required them to run the administration of city and territory, and they were held responsible for law and order, and for the due performance of all obligations imposed by the imperial government, above all the collection of the taxes. The ability of the councillors to fulfil the requirements of the Empire depended on their authority being broadly accepted by their fellow citizens, or, to put it slightly differently, on their remaining in a position to put a functioning administration at the disposal of the imperial authorities. This was the case well into the third century. Civic pride, the cohesion of the city's social order, the munificence of its propertied classes, and the citizens' loyalty to the Empire were given symbolic expression at great religious festivals, and by the construction of the spectacular public buildings, which still impress today even though in ruins.[3] Civic pride and civic cohesion made the city organization a useful prop for the Empire.

The situation changed with the so-called 'Crisis of the Third Century'. The Empire as reorganized by Diocletian and Constantine made heavier demands on the taxpayers of the Empire, and hence on the decurions who had to collect the taxes. Subsequently, the councillors had to be compelled to perform their duties. The round of festivals expressing civic solidarity was reduced by shortage of money, and the hostility of Christianity to ceremonies which were closely linked with the traditional religion. A system of administration that had almost run itself, now required a great deal of bureaucratic supervision. The cities of the Later Empire were changed in many ways from what they had been under the High Empire. The condition of the cities of the fourth century is well known. This stage of the evolution of the ancient city has been described and analysed in books, which if not yet very old, are nevertheless already classics. Outstanding among them are Petit's book on Antioch,[4] Lepelley's on the cities of North Africa,[5] and the great syntheses of A. H. M. Jones, *The Greek City* and *The Later Roman Empire*.[6]

But the evolution of the city continued. There has been much less work on the later Late City, the city of the fifth and sixth centuries, and its special characteristics have not yet been fully defined. The best overall

[3] On the link between incorporation into the Roman system and spectacular monumental building, see Patterson 1991: 147–68.

[4] Petit 1955.

[5] Lepelley 1979–80.

[6] A. H. M. Jones 1940, 1964. On A. H. M. Jones: Liebeschuetz 1992*a*: 1–8. The most recent survey: Ward-Perkins 1998: 371–410.

survey is still that of Claude.[7] Since then there has been some interesting work on aspects of the later Late City. Patlagean has written a very important book on poverty. She has drawn attention to the introduction into social discourse under the influence of Christianity of the concept of 'the poor', and has shown how the Christian precept of charity took the place of the traditional system of mutual obligations linking patron and client and city and citizen.[8] Peter Brown has explained how well publicized championing of the poor helped bishops to achieve a dominating position in many cities.[9] Alan Cameron's two books on the circus factions have revolutionized our understanding of these organizations, and of the rioting of which they were the cause.[10] But these are all specialist investigations. The new overall view of the late Late Roman city is still missing. I do not claim to have provided the needed new synthesis, but hope that this book will make some contribution towards it.

The book's principal theme is political change. The discussion focuses on the end of city-government by the *curia*, and its replacement by another looser, and much less transparent form of oligarchical control. The change involved the end of open politics, and it can also be seen as the end, at least for some centuries, of the political culture which had been classically analysed by Aristotle in the *Politics*. The same period saw the Christianization of the city. This meant the separation of religious and secular spheres of administration, the creation of a distinction between the claims of God and the claims of Caesar, followed by the gradual expansion of the religious sector at the expense of the secular one. In terms of power the beneficiary of this trend was the bishop, who tended to become the most powerful figure in the city. Christianization in turn had a gradual but very profound impact on all aspects of culture, on the appearance of cities, on the forms of public entertainment, and last but far from least, on education, that is the institution by which the values and experiences of past generations are passed on to the young. These and related changes affected the relations between city and Empire. It is argued that the post-curial form of municipal government, because in it ultimate responsibility was not defined, was much more difficult to control by the agents of the central administration than the old city councils had been. Weakening of civic administration was only one of a number of factors that weakened the control of the city over the countryside, and eventually led to the countryside's emancipation.

[7] Claude 1969.

[8] Patlagean 1977.

[9] P. Brown 1992. This is of course only one of many contributions by Peter Brown. For a bibliography and a discussion of the significance of his work, see Bowersock *et al.* 1997: 5–90.

[10] Alan Cameron 1973, 1976.

At the end of our period, around AD 650, life in most areas of what had been the Roman Empire was very different from what it had been at its beginning, around AD 400. The change can be summed up as a process of simplification. In many regions the appearance of cities had changed beyond recognition. The built-up areas had shrunk, secular monumental buildings were abandoned or neglected. Churches had replaced temples. Populations in the built-up core were much reduced. In the West probably only a very small number of cities retained a fully urban population-profile, that is a propertied class together with a sizeable population of shopkeeper-traders, and a 'proletariat' of unskilled labourers, seasonal workers, and beggars. Changes in the countryside, that is in the rural territory of the city, were just as great; and as in the urban centre they involved a simplification of the everyday life of all classes, and indeed of the whole system of economic relations. In the East many cities did retain a large urban population together with a flourishing surrounding countryside for much longer than in the West. But in the seventh century the cities of Anatolia underwent a transformation quite comparable to that suffered by cities in the West from the third century onwards.

The book covers both the Eastern Empire and the Western Empire and its successor states; and the chapters are arranged to stimulate comparisons of the two areas. From the late fourth century the Western Empire experienced barbarian invasions and settlement; and in the various Germanic successor kingdoms the relatively uniform environment that had existed under the imperial administration was replaced by a great variety of conditions. The Eastern Empire however remained intact until the seventh century, with only its Balkan provinces suffering invasions. In view of the diverging histories of East and West, it is surprising to what extent the evolution of cities in East and West continued to follow parallel lines, and that comparable developments can be observed in the new barbarian kingdoms and in areas which remained under imperial control, regional differences often being a matter of timing rather than substance.[11]

The sharp distinction between East and West is however to some extent artificial. For the two zones overlap: Greece and the eastern Balkans, and Sicily and Byzantine Italy, were neither wholly of the East, nor of the West. Furthermore, neither in the East nor in the West was change monolithic. Most notably, at least in my view, there was a considerable difference between the development of cities in Anatolia, on the one hand, and in Syria, Palestine, and Egypt, on the other.

There has been debate whether in spite of their reduced state, the cities of the West after the third century, of the East from the early seventh, still

[11] General surveys: Rich 1992; Dölger 1959.

deserved to be called cities. This debate is really a question of definition.[12] The fact that these places were now so much smaller, less spectacular to look at, and housing a much narrower range of urban activities than in the golden age of the second century, does not mean that we must cease to regard them as cities. For even in their shrunken condition they continued to fulfil a large number of functions which can only be classified as 'urban'. They remained administrative centres, both in the Empire and in the successor kingdoms. Emperors and kings continued to reside in cities. Imperial and royal officials, such as provincial governors, continued to have their headquarters there. Tax collection was administered on a city basis. Judges held court in cities. Charters were issued and coins minted there. Cities were garrisoned, and the conduct of wars centred on the defence and capture of cities.

Moreover the city had acquired a new function as the residence of a bishop. The growth of the Church brought the accumulation of wealth, the establishment of charitable institutions, the foundation of monasteries, which all gave employment, not only to different grades of clerics, but also to lay-workers in ecclesiastical enterprises. Bishops often were great builders, and so gave work to masons, carpenters, and craftsmen of every kind. The tombs of saints attracted pilgrims, and these in turn required hostels and other services.

But performance of all these functions was compatible with a very small population, such as we would today associate with a village rather than a town. Take the example of Tours.[13] Throughout our period Tours was important. While the Empire lasted, it was the capital of a large province. Subsequently, it was the residence of a royal count, and of a metropolitan bishop. The city became an important centre of pilgrimage. It provided contingents for the Merovingian army. It was frequently defended, sometimes captured. The name recurs again and again in the history of the times—admittedly much of that history was written by its bishop. Yet Tours was a very small place. The city of the Early Empire had covered around forty hectares, the walled enclosure of Late Antiquity no more than nine. There was in addition a new suburb which had grown up around the abbey of St Martin. But suburb and city were not united by any sense of shared Touraine citizenship. Eventually, in AD 918/19, the suburb became a separate little town ruled by its abbot and directly subject to the king, while the old city was ruled by count and bishop. If the inhabitants of the old *civitas* still shared a common loyalty it was not

[12] For continuity in the West: e.g. Ward-Perkins 1984; Wickham 1981: 80–92; against: Brogiolo 1987: 27–46, 1993; Hodges and Whitehouse 1983. For the East, the discussion and its literature are comprehensively summarized by Brandes 1989: 17–22.

[13] Piétri 1983. Gallinié 1988: 57–62.

to any secular community, but to their heavenly patron, St Martin of Tours.

The population of the built-up area of Tours and its suburbs in Late Antiquity was probably very small, perhaps a few thousand. Political, administrative, military, and ecclesiastical arrangements have left evidence in written sources. Fortifications and ecclesiastical buildings, whether still intact, or reduced to archaeological remains, bear witness to the activities of soldiers and bishops. Economic conditions are much more difficult to assess. But it is certain that in Western Europe around AD 600, far more of the places described as cities resembled Tours than resembled Milan or Rome.[14] It would be quite wrong to refuse to consider an important centre a city because it had only 3,000 inhabitants, or indeed fewer still.

Some classical cities did cease to perform any urban functions, or were even left totally uninhabited for a shorter or longer number of years, and in some cases permanently abandoned. It is however clear that some extraordinary and sustained run of unfavourable developments was needed to bring about the cessation of all urban activities in what had been a city. The complete abandonment of a city was a comparatively rare phenomenon. In the numerous upheavals of Late Antiquity cities were destroyed, plundered, starved, and suffered every kind of damage. But the effects of war, and indeed of barbarian settlement, were as a rule not permanent, unless reinforced and prolonged by other factors.[15] The coincidence of a large number of factors hostile to urbanization was a regional not an Empire-wide phenomenon. Accordingly, a high death-rate among cities tends to be peculiar to a particular region; and the death of cities occurred in different areas, at different times, and from different causes.[16]

The period covered in this book saw great economic changes, which affected city and country alike, even if in different ways. In both city and country the change was in the direction of impoverishment. I do not take the view that the prosperity of the cities of the High Empire was made possible only by exploitation at the expense of the countryside. On the

[14] To perform important administrative functions a city need not have more than a few thousand inhabitants. Distributive and manufacturing functions did not employ very large numbers of people, numbers depending on the size of the area serviced. It is agreed that distribution and manufacture were relatively much more important for 'the medieval town' than they had been for the 'ancient city'. Yet most medieval towns were very small. Around 1300, at the height of the medieval population boom, a population of more than 10,000 was large. It was only in regions at the centre of an exceptionally wide network of trade, notably Flanders and Northern Italy, that there were clusters of cities of 30,000 or more inhabitants. See Ennen 1975: 199–204.

[15] High mortality of towns in Piedmont: Ward-Perkins 1988: 16–27, esp. fig. 6, p. 17.

[16] In Britain after 400: Millett 1990: 221–3. The causes are still far from clear. In Gascony the abandonment of cities was probably due to Basque raids, see Rouche 1979: 271–7. On the inland cities of Syria-Palestine (Chalcis, Apamea, Gerasa, etc.): see below, pp. 303–14. On cities of Balkans and western Greece, see below, pp. 248–91.

contrary, the prosperity of town and country rose and fell together. It follows that most cities performed functions which might in a broad sense be called economic. To varying degrees, and according to their geographical situation, they provided markets for the surrounding countryside and for local, or long-distance trade. They housed craftsmen, who made goods not only for town-dwellers but also for the peasantry of the neighbourhood. The amenities of city life attracted the greater landowners of the neighbourhood, who continued to spend a part of their rents in the city.

That the Ancient city made a positive contribution to the economy of which it was part, has of course been denied. First Max Weber, and then A. H. M. Jones and Moses Finley, have argued that it was essentially a centre of consumption, whose relation to the productive economy was parasitic. There can of course be no question but that the typical classical city was a place where landowners lived in comfort on rents largely drawn from the countryside. But this fact does not mean that the relationship of such a city to the countryside was necessarily entirely parasitic. Heavy consumption has been known to have acted as an incentive to economic development in its own right. It is likely enough that it had this effect in Antiquity.[17] After all Classical Antiquity, and especially the period of the Early Empire, was enormously more productive of objects for human use of every kind, than the periods that preceded, and indeed those that followed it. For the story of Late Antiquity is, among other things, one of greatly reduced production of manufactured objects.

The negative view of the economic role of the city is partly based on an implicit bilateral classification of urban activities into basic, essential, and productive ones, and others which are luxurious and unproductive. The division is largely arbitrary: it depends on the assumption that religion, education, management, political arrangements, and justice are in some basic sense superfluous, and do not ever facilitate economic growth and development, or indeed a better life. In fact they might not do these things, but it is at least equally possible that they might. It depends on circumstances. Scholars have argued that the consumption by the inhabitants, and particularly the court, at Madrid placed a real burden on the rural areas of Castille. But London too was a consumer city, and London has been called the engine of growth for the English economy.[18] The difference between a parasitic and a generative city is not the source of its income but the pattern of its expenditure.[19]

This book registers some of the economic accompaniments of the

[17] Wallace-Hadrill 1994: 142–74 on diffusion of 'luxury' downwards through society.
[18] F. J. Fischer 1971: 3–16. The same claim is made for ancient Rome by Morley 1996.
[19] J. De Vries 1984: 248.

decline of the ancient city. The author has not attempted to write an economic history of the late Late Roman period. The scale of the economic change, and the relationship of economic cause and effect are difficult enough to assess in the classical period, in spite of its relative abundance of literary and epigraphic evidence, and its solidly built urban remains.[20] It is very much more difficult in this late period. The evidence of written sources relevant to economic activity is at best incidental. The archaeological evidence is inconspicuous, and of a kind that can be accumulated only by numerous small discoveries over a long period of time. The houses of the bulk of the population, including those of craftsmen and traders and craftsmen-traders, have often been ignored by older generations of archaeologists.

Moreover when describing economic change it is more enlightening to look at all the centres of population in a particular region rather than to study specimens selected from the whole, huge expanse of the Empire. The emergence of an urban system is a crucial step in regional development, that is the process whereby regional resources of all kinds, social and cultural, as well as economic and political, are multiplied and deployed with greater effectiveness, and exploited with increased efficiency.[21] Similarly the reduction or simplification of economic exchanges is a regional development also. Significant developments in urbanization cannot therefore be identified by looking at one 'typical' city or even at a selection of 'typical' cities. It is necessary to look at the regional network as a whole, and also at its interaction with other networks. A historian of urbanism in the early modern period notes that

> when one focuses attention on cities in the aggregate, the assessment tends to lean more heavily on the internal structure of the urban system, and how a city functions within that system . . . it allows us to portray the history of urbanisation in the early modern era as the dismantling of an old urban structure and its replacement by a new one. An important feature of this process was that the constituent cities of the two structures remained the same.[22]

This approach can be applied to the study of the Roman world.[23] Certainly such political developments as the setting up of a capital at Constantinople, the loss of North Africa, the setting up of several *regna* within the boundaries of what had been a single Empire, and the decline followed by the collapse of long-distance trade in the western Medi-

[20] Hence the controversy over the Weber–Jones–Finley theory of the 'consumer city', on which Parkins 1997.

[21] J. De Vries 1984: 10, citing from Skinner 1977: 211: 'This work based on non-western urbanisation carries the ironic implication that the era of the . . . parasite city, simultaneously marked the emergence of the "generative urban system", that is the efficient articulation of regional economies by networks of cities, which makes possible . . . the mobilization of labour, capital and information.'

[22] J. De Vries 1984: 254.

[23] Morley 1997: 42–58.

terranean in the course of the fifth and sixth centuries, must have had a profound influence on different regional urban networks. But in the present state of the subject such changes are difficult to map in detail because generally our information comes from only a small proportion of the cities of any one 'network'. So it can easily escape our notice that what looks like decline, on the evidence of the cities about which we happen to have evidence, was in fact balanced by urbanization elsewhere in the same region.[24] At any rate the study of urban systems would require a different kind of book from the present one.

There is however no shortage of evidence bearing on one factor which had a very great impact on the economy, as on every other aspect of city life: that is the rise and fall of the Roman Empire. The Empire did not create the classical city, but its administration depended on cities, and Roman occupation was followed by urbanization in many areas. It is a safe assumption that the urban governing class, the *curiales*, owed the security of their position to Roman protection, and a great part of their wealth to the perquisites of tax collection.[25] At the same time Roman rule involved transport of natural products over long distances on a huge scale by the standards of the ancient economy, in the first place to feed the population of Rome, but also to supply the frontier armies whether in garrison or on campaign. At the same time imperial taxation and expenditure had the effect of transferring and redistributing large amounts of money, creating new centres of purchasing power, and stimulating the provision of goods and services for purchase.[26] All of this had a positive impact on cities. With the Crisis of the Third Century this process began to go into reverse, though the running down of the Empire-wide economic system was a process of long duration which proceeded at quite different speeds in different parts of the Empire.[27]

The mere fact of barbarian rule did not necessarily harm cities. Certainly Visigoths, Vandals, and Ostrogoths seem not to have signifi-

[24] On different forms of urbanization, see J. De Vries 1984: 254–5: urbanization can be *demographic*, i.e. it can involve the growth of the percentage of population of an area living in cities. This is of course almost impossible to prove in Late Antiquity. But European urbanization 1500–1800 shows that demographic urbanization is not needed for *structural urbanization*, that is of organizational innovations that 'increase the range of urban activities and increase the need for coordination and communications . . . affecting the nature of inter-urban links and hence of the system of cities'. Again this is very difficult to trace in Late Antiquity except where it took the form of building of roads and bridges. *Behavioural urbanization*, i.e. the diffusion of an urban way of life, was clearly in regression in Late Antiquity—except inasmuch as Christianization can be thought a form of behavioural urbanization.

[25] Corbier 1991: 211–40.

[26] I take Hopkins 1980 to be essentially correct, see also Hopkins 1978.

[27] For my views on the effect of the Crisis, see Liebeschuetz 1992*b*: 4–25. On detrimental effect on cities of Late Roman taxation, see also Millett 1990: 48–51. On the final stages of the Roman imperial system in the West, see the essays in Hodges and Bowden 1998.

cantly accelerated the decline of cities in the territories governed by them. But in lands settled by Anglo-Saxons, Basques, or Slavs, there was no role for cities for a considerable time. It is not a coincidence that these peoples were pagans when they settled. For Christianity was a city-centred religion, and very many Roman cities survived precisely because they were the residence of a bishop. At the same time it can be argued that the ascetic and other-worldly ethos of Christianity made it easier for people to accept, and perhaps in some cases even to welcome, the simplified and impoverished life that circumstances were forcing upon them. But paradoxically the area where it is least appropriate to talk of the decline of cities is in the provinces occupied by the Muslim Arabs.

2. *The Evidence*

The study of the administrative and political development of the Late City makes use of three kinds of evidence: epigraphy, legislation, and papyri. For economic history, coins are an essential source. The quantity of evidence available under each of these heads changes very considerably in the course of the period studied. But the rise and fall of the quantity of different kinds of evidence is in itself evidence of social change. In the second part of this chapter the significance of these fluctuations will be examined for each category of evidence in turn.

INSCRIPTIONS

Compared with the Early Empire, Late Antiquity produced fewer inscriptions. The epigraphic habit was on the wane.[28] To start with the East: very many smaller cities have left no Late Empire inscriptions of any kind, or only very few. Not only are civic inscriptions and monuments to civic or imperial dignitaries conspicuously lacking, but there is a similar absence of inscriptions recording the building of churches, and even of inscribed tombstones. The fact that many of these sites have not been excavated may partly explain the shortage of late inscriptions.[29] The pattern is however too consistent to be simply due to lack of excavation.

It is difficult to avoid the conclusion that in many cities of Asia Minor very few inscriptions were carved in Late Antiquity. If this was so, it will not do—at least in my opinion—to explain what is a highly conspicuous transformation of public behaviour simply in terms of taste or fashion. The decline of the epigraphic habit does after all coincide with a profound

[28] See Mrozek 1973: 355–68; Mac Mullen 1982: 243–5, 1986: 237–8; Mann 1985: 204–6; Meyer 1990: 74–96.

[29] e.g. *IGSK* 32 (1987), ed. T. Corsten: Apamea, Bithynia. *IGSK* 1 (1972), ed. H. Engelmann, R. Merkelbach: Erythrai and Klazomenai. *IGSK* 3 (1975), ed. P. Frisch: Ilion. *IGSK* 5 (1976), ed. H. Engelmann: Kyme. *IGSK* 27 (1985), ed. W. Ameling: Prusias ad Hypium.

cultural change: the decline of the city as a political community and of the institutions and social and political attitudes which had found expression in the putting up of public monuments. As the council and other institutions of the self-governing city state declined in authority and prestige, people ceased to care whether acts like decisions of the council, the names of individuals honoured by the city, or of victors in the public games, or of munificent citizens were commemorated, or not. It is notable that in a large number of cities the latest emperors to be commemorated are Diocletian and his colleagues, or Constantine.[30] One might conclude that the reforms of Diocletian and Constantine confirmed rather than reversed the political decline of these cities.

The state of affairs described is particularly conspicuous in the old provinces of Pontus, Bithynia, and Asia where Greek cities had been established for a very long time. It was not however universal. A number of cities have left a significant number of late Roman inscriptions, even if their numbers are much smaller than those from the Early Empire and Hellenistic times. Among these are Aphrodisias, Ephesus, Side,[31] and Corinth.[32] Excavation may in time add to the list significantly.

Meanwhile it is perhaps not a coincidence that each of these cities was the residence of a provincial governor. For it could be that the classical forms of commemoration survived best in provincial capitals. There is reason to believe that in the Later Empire the administration came to regard provinces, which were smaller and more numerous than under the principate, as the basic units of administration rather than cities.[33] In Late Antiquity provincial assemblies, meeting in the largest cities in the province, and normally in the provincial capital, were attended by all *honorati* and senior *decuriones*, that is by everybody that mattered in the province.[34] This made them the natural forum for voicing complaints, and for publishing new imperial legislation subsequently put on permanent public record in the provincial capital.[35] The acclamations of the assembly

[30] e.g. at Klaudiopolis *IGSK* 31; Kios *IGSK* 29; Kyme *IGSK* 5; Stratonikaia *IGSK* 22.1; Klazomenai *IGSK* 2. Sometimes Julian is the last, so at Iasos *IGSK* 14; Ilion *IGSK* 100; Magnesia on the Mäander: Kern 1900: 227–8. Embassies by individual cities discouraged: *CT* XII.12.7 (380).

[31] Side *IGSK* 43, ed. J. Nollé (Bonn, 1993).

[32] J. H. Kent 1966: 220 inscriptions of Late Empire out of total 720. See also Feissel 1985: 267–383.

[33] C. Roueché 1989*a*: 33–4.

[34] Place of meeting: *CT* XII.12.1 (392), ibid. 12.13 (392). Attendance: *CT* XII.12.1, qui primatum honorantur insignibus, with exception of *praefectorii* who are consulted in their homes. Fines for not attending on the part of *honorati* and *curiales*: *MGH* (*Ep.*) III.13–15 (418 addressed to seven provinces of Gaul).

[35] At any rate Justinian seems to have legislated for provinces (e.g. *Nov* XXIV–XXXII), and the Empire as a whole, rather than to have responded to the problems of individual cities. Eventually candidates for governorships were proposed by the notables of the province: *Nov* (Justin II) 149 (569); *Nov App* 7, *Const. Prag.* 12 (554). This could surely only have been done at a provincial assembly. See also below, pp. 38–39, and nn. 43–51.

were taken down in writing, and sent to Constantinople to inform the emperor of public opinion in his cities.[36] But if in Asia Minor the inscriptional habit, like the conservation of monumental public buildings still flourished in some provincial capitals, it did not do so—at least judging by the evidence available today—in all, and probably not even in a majority of provincial capitals.[37] It does however seem that along the south-eastern coast of Asia Minor, in Pamphylia and Cilicia[38] inscriptions of every kind were produced in much larger numbers, and in a much larger proportion of cities than in the rest of Asia Minor. This also holds for Syria, Palestine, and Arabia, a region where the epigraphic habit had come relatively late.

In Late Antiquity not only were fewer inscriptions produced, but the relative abundance of different types of inscription changed also. The number of epigraphic monuments that commemorate living individuals, or record the decisions of civic institutions, was very much reduced both absolutely and proportionally. However, the proportion of tombstones and the like was greatly increased—even though the custom of setting up inscribed tombstones was current only in some regions, and not in others where one might have expected to find it. Among grave inscriptions a significant proportion commemorate clerics. From the early fifth century a very high proportion of building inscriptions record the building or embellishment of churches, often paid for by clerics.[39] So the appearance of inscriptions now marks the progress of Christianization, and the increasing power and prestige of Church and clergy.

It is a feature of the Eastern epigraphy that villages become articulate from say, the later second century. This is particularly marked in the villages of central Asia Minor which have produced an abundance of inscribed monuments, their production reaching a peak in the late fourth and early fifth century. The inscriptions are mainly funereal, and overwhelmingly Christian. An interesting and significant development is that tombstones cease to mention the deceased's kin. The dead are commemorated as individuals whose family background, and public position are unimportant. On the Christian tombstone the only tie that really matters is that between the dead person and God.[40]

If one compares the number of inscriptions produced at successive

[36] *CJ* I.40.3, but without specification of the provincial assembly. The law applies to acclamations wherever made.

[37] Inscriptions were part of the ceremonial not of the functional instruments of the Empire. Written copies of decrees were certainly sent wherever the need of administration required them to be known. But a reduction in the number of centres of the 'ceremonial of monuments' may itself be significant.

[38] Dagron and Feissel 1987.

[39] e.g. see Donceel-Voûte 1988.

[40] Mitchell 1993: ii. 119–21.

periods from a sufficiently large number of Late Roman urban sites,[41] a definite pattern emerges. After the carving of inscriptions had almost come to end in the third quarter of the third century, there was a modest revival in the early fourth century. Then the decline resumes. A nadir is reached in the third quarter of the fifth century. After that there is a revival which lasts up to say AD 550. Subsequently the decline resumes, with inscriptions practically coming to an end around AD 600. The basic pattern rise/fall, rise/fall, is generally recognizable—wherever there are enough inscriptions for any trend to be visible at all. It surely reflects fundamental changes in the cities.

The inscriptions themselves throw light on the nature of the changes. The traditional local magistrates disappear from inscriptions early in the fourth century.[42] Before the end of the century the councils (*curiae-boulai*) too have ceased to appear. We know that councils were still functioning, but their disappearance from inscriptions suggests that they had lost a great deal of status. Individuals were no longer eager to publicize their membership of the council to fellow citizens, and council business was no longer thought sufficiently important to merit permanent commemoration on stone. When and where they occur in the fourth century, civic inscriptions suggest that public life was now dominated by the imperial governor.[43] But the epigraphic prominence of the governor did not last, at least not outside a limited number of provincial capitals, for instance Ephesus.[44] Most provincial cities simply ceased to put up inscribed stone monuments, even to the reigning emperor.

There was a revival of building inscriptions in the last quarter of the fifth century. They now mainly commemorate the building of churches, but not entirely. There was again some secular construction. Most of this was military, but there is evidence of a limited amount of secular monumental building of the classical kind. This, as indeed the whole pattern of rise, fall, rise, is witnessed most clearly in the cities which have left the fullest sequence of inscriptions over the whole period, i.e. at Aphrodisias,[45] Ephesus,[46] Gerasa,[47] and Bostra,[48] but the boom in epigraphic

[41] Village inscriptions do not necessarily follow the same pattern. The villages of the central Anatolian plateau produced plenty of inscriptions in the 3rd cent: Mitchell 1993: i. 239–40. But unlike village inscriptions from Syria, Palestine, and Arabia, they seem to decline from the 3rd cent. See *MAMA* X. 1993, p. 197: of the dated inscriptions from the Upper Tembris Valley, the latest is from AD 337. Also *MAMA* IX. 1988, pp. lvii–lviii, of inscriptions from Aezanitis, the latest is from AD 487/8.

[42] See evidence for local officials in C. Roueché 1989*a*: 321–2.

[43] Robert 1948: 34–114. The dominance of the governors at Antioch is very clear in the speeches of Libanius: Liebeschuetz 1972: 110–14.

[44] Foss 1983: 196–219.

[45] C. Roueché 1989*a*.

[46] *Die Inschriften von Ephesos*, *IGSK* 11–17.2 (Bonn, 1979–84).

[47] Kraeling 1938.

[48] *IGLS* XIII.1, ed. M. Sartre (Paris, 1982); Sartre 1985.

commemoration from the late fifth century can be observed elsewhere too.[49] This revival did not however last beyond the middle years of Justinian. One factor that made building again possible was the expenditure of imperial money in major cities. Justinian's achievement as a builder has been given a lasting, though somewhat exaggerated, record in the *Buildings* of Procopius, which in the manner of panegyrical writings fails to give credit where it is due to Justinian's predecessors.[50] Procopius lists far more Justinianic building activity in the provinces along the eastern frontier than in western or central Asia Minor. However the period also saw the resumption of public building by wealthy laymen, often men bearing titles of real or honorary imperial rank.[51] It was presumably the same class of wealthy city-based magnates that provided both pupils and teachers for the contemporary revival of higher education at Athens, Alexandria, Berytus, and Gaza.[52]

The pattern of Late Roman inscriptions in the West is more difficult to establish because of the number and variety of modern works in which they have been published. My impression is that, while there is of course great regional variation, the overall pattern of rise and fall is similar to that of the East. In the West too there was a dramatic decline in the production of inscriptions in the third century, and some recovery in the fourth. But it was only in Africa, and to a lesser extent in Italy (and there only south of Rome), and in Greece (which politically and linguistically formed part of the East) that there was a significant revival of secular civic building and monumental commemoration. Elsewhere such secular building inscriptions as were produced were imperial. Everywhere, whether the territory was under barbarian occupation or not, civic inscriptions had come to an end by the second quarter of the fifth century. There was a marked recovery early in the sixth century in Ostrogothic Italy, and later in Merovingian Gaul, and above all in Visigothic Spain.[53] But the late building inscriptions overwhelmingly commemorate the building of churches or the donation of church furnishings.

[49] See for instance most of the volumes of *IGLS*. In Syrian small towns and villages the epigraphic habit flourished to the end of the 6th cent., and in what is now Jordan even into the 8th: *IGLS* XXI.2, *Inscriptions de la Jordanie* (Région centrale: Amman, Hesban, Main, Dhiban), ed. P.-L. Gatier (Paris, 1986), p. 251 (list of dated inscriptions).

[50] Procopius' accuracy has been much debated. Up to a point, it can be checked against the finds of archaeology, e.g. Michael Whitby 1986*a*: 713–35, 1986*b*: 737–83.

[51] C. Roueché 1989*a*.

[52] Glucker 1978; Duneau 1971; Seitz 1892; Sorabji 1987; also Sorabji 1983.

[53] On the whole subject of late epigraphy in the West, see Galvao-Sobrinho 1995: 431–62. Spain has left scarcely any civic inscriptions even from the 4th cent. The classical tradition of epigraphic commemoration survived in tomb inscriptions, but on the whole only in the areas which had been most thoroughly Romanized, Lusitania and Baetica in the south and Tarraco and its hinterland in the north (Vives 1969: 1–267).

Bryan Ward-Perkins has analysed urban building in northern and central Italy, AD 300–850, making full use of Late Antique inscriptions of that area. His study clearly shows how the output of inscriptions reflects the decline of civic[54] institutions. The fourth century saw a recovery in the epigraphic habit, but spending by private individuals on secular buildings had ended for good. Spending on building by civic magistrates has become extremely rare. There is no spending on new buildings by cities. Some new public buildings were paid for by senatorial patrons of cities,[55] and that mainly in Campania and Samnium, regions where senators had estates. It looks as if Roman senators were the strongest upholders of the traditional patterns of urban life. Some major public works were directed by provincial governors, again most often in Samnium, but occasionally elsewhere.[56] The continued existence and functioning of city councils is witnessed in a large number of cities by inscribed monuments they dedicated to governors or senatorial patrons.

But in the first decade of the fifth century, after Alaric's Gothic invasion, all epigraphic commemoration of secular activities in cities came to an end. The events of the first decade of the fifth century produced a shock comparable to that of the 'Crisis of the Third Century'. Of course the cities as cities survived. So did their councils which continued to be responsible for collecting taxes and for maintaining basic civic services and public buildings. We have some information, from sources other than inscriptions, about the repair of palaces, aqueducts, and above all city walls, but not of *fora*, *basilicae*, *curiae*, porticoes, markets, theatres, or amphitheatres.[57] We are short of archaeological evidence, but it is likely that in many cities the decay of these structures had begun in the fourth century, and accelerated in the course of the fifth century.[58] The end of civic inscriptions did not involve the end of the inscriptional habit, quite the reverse. The output of inscriptions continued to increase, as did the area in which they were produced but the increase was limited to two specific contexts: tombs and churches. The overwhelming majority of late Late Roman inscriptions is funereal and Christian.[59] While the production of inscribed tombstones at Rome peaked around AD 400, and sub-

[54] The following paragraph is not concerned with inscriptions from the city of Rome itself, where Christian epitaphs peaked around AD 400, to decline to almost nothing by AD 600, see fig. 1 in Galvao-Sobrinho 1995.

[55] Harmand 1957: 432–9.

[56] Ward-Perkins 1984: 14–31. See also Mrozek 1978: 355–68.

[57] Ward-Perkins 1984: 118–19.

[58] See below, pp. 94–6.

[59] Tomb inscriptions had of course always been by far the most numerous. The significant thing is that at a time when most kinds of secular inscriptions were disappearing funereal inscriptions were actually on the increase. On this the comprehensive and thoughtful survey of Galvao-Sobrinho 1995: 431–62.

sequently fell into a slow decline, elsewhere the setting up of inscribed funereal monuments seems to have been on the increase, even though many of the stones were humble, and clumsily inscribed.[60] Absolute numbers vary greatly from area to area, but Galvao-Sobrinho has shown that over a sharply diverse range of localities, that is on two sites in Carthage,[61] at Haïdra,[62] Maktar,[63] and Sbeitla[64] in North Africa, at Tarraco in Spain,[65] at and around Vienne in Provence,[66] in the area of Trier on the Moselle,[67] and in Macedonia,[68] a peak was reached during the sixth century.[69] The custom of putting up inscribed monuments to the dead was not of course specifically Christian, but rather just one aspect of Romanization, and in the Early Empire its prevalence provides a measure of the degree of Romanization of an area. But funerary epigraphy was given a new lease of life by the spread of Christianity, at a time when the epigraphic habit in other fields was in decline. The relative abundance of Christian tombstones should not however be taken as evidence of intense competition between Christianity and the traditional religion. The conflict of religions had long been won and lost, and paganism had been driven underground, by the time that Christian tomb epigraphy reached its peak. Christian burial was expected to improve the dead person's prospects in the afterlife. But also, and perhaps most of all, the Christian tombstone proclaimed membership of the community of the Church. In this way its function was quite comparable to that of the thousands of provincial Roman tombstones of earlier times, which proclaimed the deceased's membership of the Roman *res publica*, his or her citizenship and family descent, and if he had served the state, a summary of the man's career in the administration, the army, or in local government. In the fifth century and after, Christian tombstones almost invariably show a cross or other Christian symbol. They may bear a Christian formula expressing hope of eternal life, or a quotation from the Bible, but they generally give no hint of the deceased's family background. The *gentilicium* had been abandoned by all but senators, and most people were now known

[60] Galvao-Sobrinho 1995: 449–50 is surely right to insist that the social range of Christian funereal inscriptions was wider than that of pagans had been. But it is also the case that there were fewer skilled stonemasons in late Late Antiquity (see below, pp. 387–8) and that literacy was declining (see below, pp. 318–20).

[61] Galvao-Sobrinho 1995: 441 and fig. 2.

[62] N. Duval and F. Prévot 1975; Galvao-Sobrinho 1995: 438–9 and fig. 3.

[63] Prévot 1984.

[64] N. Duval 1987: 385–414.

[65] Vives 1969: 61–72; Alföldy 1975; Fabre, Mayer, and Rod 1984–91; Knapp 1992.

[66] Descombes 1985; Guyon 1985.

[67] Gauthier 1975: 103: more inscriptions were produced at Trier in the 5th cent. than when it was an imperial capital.

[68] Feissel 1983.

[69] Galvao-Sobrinho 1995: figs. 2–8.

by only one name.[70] Nor do these late Christian tombstones as a rule indicate a dead man's secular achievements. If rank is recorded, it is almost invariably ecclesiastical. In fact epigraphy like classical rhetoric has been appropriated by the Church.

From the second half of the fifth century there is a modest recovery also of building inscriptions. They are now almost entirely ecclesiastical, and they reflect monumental church building. The progress of church building is not at all easy to date, because the remains of the churches are more often than not without dating evidence, and often can be dated only very approximately.[71] But the impression is that the process gathered pace towards the end of the fourth century, and with setbacks due to wars and Germanic settlements, resumed in Vandal North Africa, in Ostrogothic Italy, in Merovingian Gaul, and last of all in Spain after the religious reunion, to continue right though the sixth century and beyond.[72] Inscriptions commemorate the donor of the church, also the very much more numerous contributors to its furnishing, especially of mosaic floors.[73] Inscriptions honour martyrs.[74] Verse inscriptions preserve the memory of the holiness and devotion of bishops[75] and help to build up a succession linking the most recent holder of the office to revered predecessors, to saints and martyrs. This gave cities a Christian sense of identity which replaced the older civic pride based on secular history and links with Rome. A fairly large number of inscriptions commemorate the donors of blocks of mosaic floor. It was most usual for lay donors to have only their name inscribed, without any reference to rank or office. But in the sixth century in the north-east corner of Italy at Grado, San Canzian D'Isonzo, and Trieste, which were under Byzantine rule, rank and profession appear on a number of floor inscriptions: a few *clarissimi*, a few imperial office holders in civil service or army, a few *notarii*, a number of lectors and deacons.[76] No civic dignities are recorded at all. There are some of craftsmen: two shippers, a cobbler, a barber, a tailor and an officer of a guild of weighers (*primicerius pensorum*). The relative prominence of craftsmen can be observed elsewhere in late Late Roman cities, for instance at Ravenna, and on tomb inscriptions at Corinth, and at Corycus in Cilicia.

[70] Galvao-Sobrinho 1995: 452 n. 95.

[71] For Africa: N. Duval, J.-P. Caillet, and I. Gui 1992. For Italy: Caillet 1993.

[72] e.g. Vives 1969: nos. 337–60.

[73] See Ward-Perkins 1984: 236–49: survey of church-building in Rome, Ravenna, Pavia, and Lucca. Diehl 1924–31: nos. 1752–1979 (tituli aedificiorum et operum sacrorum).

[74] Diehl 1924–31: nos. 1986–2125.

[75] Spain: Vives 1969: nos. 272–9 (bishops), also 280–5 (abbots). Verse epitaphs of others, nos. 286–300. Vienne: Descombes 1985: 199–201 on verse *elogia*, by no means only of bishops, the last *c.*580. Italy: Picard 1988.

[76] Caillet 1993: 451–65.

The late flowering of epigraphy went into sharp decline everywhere in the seventh century. Even in its Christian form, it belonged to the Roman or sub-Roman world rather than to that of the barbarian kingdoms.

LEGISLATION

When we look at the output of legislation at different periods, we find a pattern which is very like that of inscriptions. There is a great deal of fourth-century legislation. Relatively few laws were issued in the third quarter of the fifth century. Legislation again becomes more abundant towards the end of the century under Anastasius.[77] It is difficult at this stage to say how far Anastasius took the initiative, and how far he merely reacted to critical events: at any rate seen in retrospect his laws amount to a programme of administrative reform. Legislation continues to be abundant in the reigns of Justin I and Justinian. Justinian was not only responsible for the codification of the legal rulings of previous rulers and of jurisconsults over centuries of Roman history, he was no mean legislator himself. Much of his legislation is preserved in the *Novellae*, the third volume of the *Corpus Juris Civilis*. Many of the *Novellae* are themselves a kind of codification, in that their object seems to be to summarize and tidy up a confusing mass of earlier imperial rulings in a particular field of administration, such as for example the procedure for the appointment of a provincial governor,[78] or the standing instructions for a governor setting out to take over a province, the so-called imperial *mandata*,[79] or the rules governing the ordination of a bishop,[80] or whatever. The *Novellae* are on the whole very generally phrased. They do not go into details. In fact from time to time the emperor alludes to alternative procedures in the administrative arrangements at provincial and civic level—of which there seem to have been significantly more than in the fourth century. So we have considerable difficulty in matching the view from the capital as conveyed by the *Novellae* with the evidence of provincial sources and especially of the papyri. But in spite of, or perhaps even because of this, the *Novellae* of Justinian offer a conspectus of the administrative developments of the early sixth century comparable only to that offered by the *Theodosian Code* for the fourth century.

We have only a small number of laws issued by the successors of Justinian. This could reflect a decision by the editors of the *Novellae* to include only a minimum of post-Justinianic legislation, rather than the absence of such legislation. But it is the case that the decline in the volume of legislation surviving from the middle of the sixth century is strictly paralleled by a decline in the number of surviving inscriptions and

[77] See legislation year by year in Seeck 1919.
[78] *Nov* 8.
[79] *Nov* 17.
[80] *Nov* 6.

of secular literary texts, just as earlier, in the mid-fifth century, a decline in the volume of legislation in the mid-fifth century followed by an upswing up to around AD 550 had coincided with parallel developments in the field of inscriptions.

For the West, the laws published by the Germanic kings provide an important source. The oldest of the Germanic Codes is that of Euric. This was compiled as the law book for Euric's Gothic kingdom in Gaul. We are told that it put the unwritten custom of the Goths into writing for the first time.[81] The *Code of Euric* has survived only in fragments. We can however make some deductions about the general character of the lost sections of Euric's *Code* because it certainly provided the foundation and framework of the surviving Visigothic Code, the *Liber Iudiciorum*.[82] The *Code of Euric*, was certainly not simply a written compilation of Germanic custom. The laws employ scarcely any Germanic legal terms. Even concepts that may be Germanic in origin have been translated into Latin legal vocabulary, and thereby inevitably Romanized. In detail the *Code of Euric* was not a collection of ancestral Germanic folk custom, but rather a set of laws designed for contemporary conditions by men trained in Roman law. Many of its rulings were derived from vulgar Roman law, that is the simplified version Roman law practised in the provincial courts.[83] But it does incorporate some Germanic custom, for instance, in the area of the compensation of victims of violence and in the law of inheritance.[84]

The Goths who settled in Aquitaine in AD 418 certainly had their traditional customary law. But the custom was unwritten. It had not been applied in sedentary conditions for more than twenty years. It is far from certain and even unlikely that all the individuals who were settled as Goths in Aquitaine in AD 418 were used to exactly the same custom. Furthermore, the Goths did not settle in virgin territory but were fitted into a land system already governed by a sophisticated body of law. So a great deal of adaptation was inevitable which could only come from the king. The *Code of Euric* surely represents a compilation of royal rulings of this kind. But a king who was the head of state of both peoples is not likely to have spoken with two voices about the same legal issue. Euric's law book was certainly not a complete statement of the law of either people, but on the matters it dealt with it must have been authoritative for both.

A parallel to the *Code of Euric* is provided by the *Edict of Theoderic*.[85]

[81] Isidore *HG* 35. I take the view that the code was territorial from the first.

[82] Still basic: F. Zeumer 1898: 419–516, 1899: 39–122, 571–630, 1901: 91–149.

[83] Wieacker 1955.

[84] See the thorough discussion of one area of the Code: Nehlsen 1972: 153–250. P. D. King 1972: 222–50 (the family), 251–8 (theft and robbery), 259–63 (killing and misuse of person).

[85] *MGH LL* V (Hanover, 1868), 145 ff. Various suggestions that the *Edict of Theoderic* was not

The author of this *Edict* was almost certainly the Ostrogothic king of Italy, and he proclaimed explicitly that the *Edict* was intended for all his subjects, Romans as well as barbarians.[86] The greater part of the *Edict* simply restates Roman legislation,[87] but, as in the *Code of Euric*, some rules seem to be derived from Germanic custom.[88] We know from Cassiodorus' *Variae* that Theoderic was anxious to demonstrate that Romans and Goths were living under the same rights.[89] His legal rulings were evidently meant for both peoples.

In AD 506 the Visigothic king Alaric II published a law book, the *Lex Romana Visigotorum* or *Breviarium Alarici*. This essentially consists of extracts from earlier Roman collections of laws, especially the *Codex Theodosianus*, and the *Novellae* of Theodosius and of his immediate successors. Most of the extracts are accompanied by an *interpretatio* which is not simply a paraphrase of the legal text, but introduces modifications adjusting the law to changes in society.[90] As a source for the social history of Visigothic Gaul, the *Breviarium* of Alaric has the serious disadvantage that, while it provides information about surviving Roman institutions, and, thanks to the *interpretationes*, about the modifications which they have undergone, it does not inform us about institutions introduced by the Gothic kings themselves.

Visigothic rule in Gaul came to an end soon after the publication of the *Breviarium*, but the *Code* remained in force in the Visigothic kingdom of Spain together with the *Code of Euric* until both were superseded at the latest by the *Code of Recessuinth* in AD 654.[91] Moreover the fact that the *Code* has been preserved in thirteen manuscripts of Gallic origin, against one from Spain, suggests that it continued to be used under the Merovingian kings as a source of Roman law for litigation of Romans, and of ecclesiastics who continued to be subject to it.[92] But the fact that the *Breviarium* was found useful as a collection of Roman law for centuries after its promulgation does not change its essential character, that of a shortened version of the *Theodosian Code*, with a commentary updating it to around AD 500. This means that its rulings concerning administrative detail can be assumed to give a fairly accurate picture of arrangements in

issued by the Ostrogothic king are refuted by Nehlsen 1972: 120–3 and in *ZRG GA* 86 (1969), 246–60, a review of Vismara 1967.

86 Edict of Theoderic, *praef.*: quae barbari Romanique sequi debeant.

87 *Epil.*: quae ex novellis ac veteris iuris sanctimonia . . . collegimus.

88 von Halban 1899: i. 117 ff.

89 *Variae* III.13.2 nec permittimus discreto iure vivere quos uno voto volumus vindicare; ibid. 8.3.4. ius et Gothis Romanisque apud nos esse commune.

90 The *interpretationes* are cited below by page references to Conrat 1903 and then by the laws as numbered in Mommsen's edition of the *Theodosian Code* and the associated *Novellae.*

91 *LV* II.1.10, but quite likely already in the first version of the Spanish *Leges Visigothorum*, published by Leovigild (AD 568–86).

92 I. Wood 1993: 159–77.

Late Roman and Visigothic Gaul, but not of the administration of Visigothic Spain, and even less of that of Gaul under the Merovingians.[93]

PAPYRI

As in the cases of inscriptions and laws, so also in that of papyri there is great variation in the number of documents that has reached us from different periods. The rate of production of papyrus documents seems to have risen through the fourth century until *c.*370. Then a steady decline sets in which lasts for around 100 years. After *c.*470 numbers increase again, and continue to rise for most of the sixth century. The pattern of rise, fall, rise is therefore parallel to that of the other two bodies of evidence, with the difference that the production of papyri does not appear to have fallen drastically before the seventh century, if it did then.

Rémondon has drawn attention to a qualitative change in the documentation of the sixth century when compared with that of the fourth which provides a pointer to the nature of the intervening social development. The later period has produced relatively few fiscal documents, and few documents related to municipal administration. The late papyri include few documents of the kind formerly sent by the imperial administration to city councils, and none issued by the councils themselves. There are few edicts of governors, public announcements, or documents relating to civic liturgies. The documents of the later period seem to be derived not from civic archives, but from the archives of large, sometimes very large, estates. Rémondon explains the change in documentation as a result of a decline in municipal political life and in the administrative importance of the council, developments which were paralleled by the growth of large estates, whose owners took over many of the functions of the councillors. It is significant that the latest minutes of a meeting of a council dates from AD 370, and the last reference to the election of a councillor known to Rémondon writing in 1966, is dated to AD 426.[94] We have not yet got a clear picture of the sixth-century system of administration, although Gascou has made a very interesting start to working it out. He has certainly shown that the new system relied to a considerable extent on the great 'houses', that is on large complexes of property including land belonging to churches or monasteries.[95] It is pretty clear that the heads of the 'houses' are identical with the munificent notables of the late inscriptions, and the 'leading citizens' of the laws. The three kinds of evidence illustrate different aspects of the same development.

[93] On the coexistence of laws, see below, pp. 357–8.

[94] Rémondon 1966: 135–48. Bagnall and Worp (1980) show that more recent publications have not essentially changed the picture.

[95] Gascou 1985: 1–90. For some modifications of Gascou's view, see below, pp. 181–6.

COINAGE

Coinage shows a fifth-century nadir like epigraphy and legislation but even more striking. Between the end of the reign of Arcadius and the coinage reform of Anastasius (AD 498) silver was only coined rarely and for distribution by the emperor on special occasions. Bronze coins shrank to very small sizes—so that they have often been missed by archaeologists, and were also produced very irregularly. Was the near abandonment of the coining of bronze and silver a consequence of the coins being no longer needed—for whatever reason—to pay troops?[96] Regular production of ranges of bronze and silver coins was resumed in the East only after Anastasius' reform.[97] In the West the silver and bronze coinages of the Vandals and Ostrogoths preceded the reform of Anastasius.[98]

Considering how much excavation there has been, the number of published lists of coin finds from excavated sites—and these almost exclusively of copper coins—is remarkably small.[99] This is probably a consequence of the way the sites were excavated rather than reliable evidence of a genuine scarcity of sixth-century coins on particular sites. It is more significant that a shortage of coins dating from the reigns of the emperors Theodosius II to Zeno is almost universal. On a majority of sites, the number of coin finds rises very significantly from the reign of Anastasius, that is from the time of his creation of a stable bronze coinage to supplement the high-value coinage in gold.[100] The number of coins from the late Late Antique period nowhere reaches the level of the fourth century, but the individual coins were of greater value. The recovery was probably weakest in inland Anatolia.[101] At Sardis the number of coins per regnal year rises steadily from Anastasius to reach a first peak with the reign of Justin II. There follows a decline during the reigns of Tiberius Constantine and Maurice, with growth resumed under Phocas and Heraclius. A new peak was reached AD 610–16. After that there is a gap. It is generally assumed that around this time the city was destroyed by the

96 See Duncan 1993.

97 Grierson 1961: 411–53.

98 Morrisson 1989: 239–60, relevant 240–4.

99 Generally numbers are too small to allow significant conclusions about the relative abundance of coins of different reigns. So in Voegtli 1993: 54ff. Goldman 1950 (no coins later than three of Theodosius II).

100 On the reform, see Grierson 1961: 410–53, esp. 431–6. The very small badly struck 'nummi', which were the only bronze coins struck in any quantity in the decades before the reform, have probably often been missed by archaeologists. The Eastern emperors from Theodosius II to Zeno did however mint a variety of silver coins in small numbers and erratically, see J. P. C. Kent 1994: 73–121; Hendy 1985: 474–5.

101 B. Levick, S. Mitchell, J. Potter, M. Waelkens, D. Nash (coins) *MAMA* IX, Monuments from the Aezanitis recorded by C. W. M. Cox, A. Cameron, and J. Cullen (London, 1988): 4th cent.: 31 coins; 5th cent.: 5; 518–65: 5; 566–616: 4; next coin 886/912. Devreker and Waelkens 1984: i. 210–13: 518–65: 2; 566–16: 23.

Persians. Eighty-six coins date from the reign of Constans II (AD 641–68). After that there is very little. At Ephesus coin finds per regnal year seem to have peaked in the reign of Justinian.[102] At Antioch too, far more coins have been found dating from the fourth century than from subsequent periods. 'The Anastasian recovery' reaches a peak under Justin I. There is a dip in the reign of Justinian—when Antioch was destroyed by the Persians, and a strong recovery under Justin II and Tiberius Constantine, followed once again by a fall in the reigns of Maurice and Phocas. There are again abundant coins from the early years of Heraclius. There was a gradual recovery under the Arabs, especially AD 695–750 under the Umayyads.[103] But at the village site of Déhès in the limestone massif of northern Syria, though the total number of coins is small, the chronological pattern is remarkable. There are 15 coins from the fourth century. As usual there are very few coins from fifth century later than the reign of Theodosius II, in fact only one of Leo. More unusually there are no coins of Anastasius or Justinian, but an increase subsequently: 11 coins from AD 582–641, 13 genuine and 13 imitation coins of Constans II (AD 641–68), 9 Umayyad and 7 Abbasid coins. But no coins from ninth century. The three buildings were occupied until the early ninth or perhaps even into the tenth century.[104] At Emesa in the Orontes valley excavators have found approximately half a coin per year for the period AD 491–641 against one per year in AD 300–491.[105] In Palestine, the port of Caesarea continued to produce relatively many coins into the seventh century, and into the Arab period.[106] At Scythopolis (Bet Shean) about 1,000 coins were found dating from the fourth century, over 2,500 but mostly *minimi* from the fifth, less than 1,000 from the sixth and *c.*1,750 from AD 635–750.[107] There were few coins subsequent to 750. At Gerasa in Arabia the coin finds of excavation of the 1920s were consistently high throughout the fourth century peaking around AD 400. As elsewhere there are very few coins from the mid-fifth century. A second peak occurs in the reign of Justinian. This is followed by a marked decline.[108] The significance of the rise and fall of bronze currency remains uncertain. Was a reduction in the coining of bronze a response to a lower demand for coins of low denominations in ordinary life? If so, it can be used as an index for the extent of market economy. On the other hand, it is quite

[102] See below, p. 44, but in the 'Byzantine shops' at Sardis coin finds peak in the reign of Heraclius.

[103] Waage 1952: 408–50: 23 coins per year; 450–98: 1.6 per year; 498–565: 29 per year; 565–602: 11 per year; 602–41: 2.3 per year; 695–75: (Umayyads) 9 per year.

[104] Morrison 1980: 273.

[105] Christensen, Thomsen, and Ploug 1931–8: 68–9.

[106] Hohlfelder 1992: 167–8; Lampinen 1992: 169–72. Levine and Netzer 1986: 146.

[107] Tsafrir and Foerster 1991: 120–8.

[108] Kraeling 1938: 502–3.

likely that whether or not the government coined money of low denominations, depended mainly on how it chose to pay its soldiers and officials. In that case the increase in the number of such coins in circulation would be a stimulus to the market economy rather than a response to it.[109]

There is not going to be a section on literary evidence. This is simply because such an account would have to be disproportionately long. It does in fact make an enormous difference to our understanding of cities whether we have literary evidence or not. A few examples will make the point. We know far more about the late Late Roman cities of Gaul than those in Spain, about cities in the North of Italy than those in the South, about Antioch in the fourth century than Antioch in the sixth. The fate of most of the Balkan cities is still perfectly obscure. All this because of the availability or absence of literary sources.

[109] Cf. Metcalfe 1967: 270–310.

PART I

The End of Classical Urban Politics

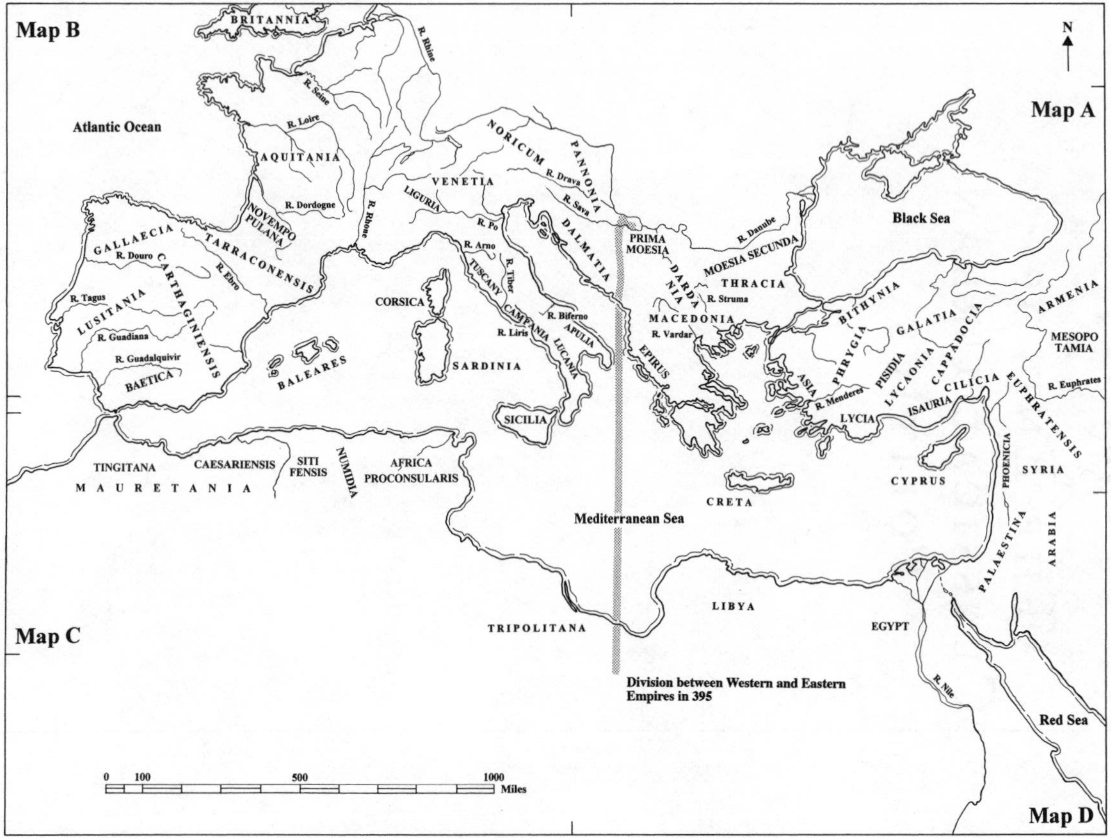

1. The Roman Empire and principal regions

2

The Survival of the Cities

1. *Problems of Interpretation*

What happened to the physical structures of the cities of the Roman Empire in the Late Roman period? Archaeology has by now provided a great amount of evidence. But the story of urban evolution is still very, very incomplete. It is also unfortunately true that a great deal of the evidence is not dated. Another difficulty is that archaeological results are published in a wide range of periodicals, many of which are not at all easily accessible. Moreover the very bitty evidence we have is not at all easy to synthesize into a clear and convincing panorama. Classical urbanism certainly did not everywhere go into terminal decline, though decline is, emphatically, the only word to express what happened in large areas in the West and eventually in the East too.[1] Cities sometimes did decline catastrophically to the point of extinction, in the sense that there was very little social activity of any kind left on the site of what had been a city. But more often an important range of urban activities continued on the site, but in a transformed environment. So what seems evidence of decline could be merely a symptom of change. Occupation might have shifted from the area we know because it has been excavated to another which archaeologists have not yet found.

Abandonment or downgrading of buildings may not reflect de-urbanization, but only a transformation of the character of urban life, as for instance the change from government by the *curia* to government by notables, or the rise of the bishop. So buildings which had served local self-government, for example the *curia* (*bouleutērion*), the prytaneion, or the civic basilica might be allowed to fall into decay, or be adapted to serve a different purpose, or simply quarried for building materials. There are many indications that attitudes to public space were changing. What had been a public square might be built over with houses. Shops might be constructed between the pillars of a monumental colonnade. New building might ignore the traditional rectangular street plan. Much of this could be—and has been—interpreted as a symptom of urban decline and demoralization, but in fact it may often represent simply a more 'laissez-

[1] Of course, urban change after the 3rd cent. was a complex process, not everywhere at the same rate and not all in one direction. On the state of play in the 4th cent., see Ward-Perkins 1998.

faire' attitude to the development of cities. Since we can date the successive stages of this process in only very few cities, we are still far from being in a position to write a comprehensive history of late Late Roman urbanism, which would relate changes in urban structure to other long-term developments, whether political, economic, demographic, or military.

Christianization meant the building of churches and charitable institutions. Temples were destroyed or more often simply left to decay.[2] Theatres and amphitheatres fell into decay or were adapted to new uses. Huge imperial baths might be wholly or partly abandoned, but often only to be replaced by smaller and more utilitarian structures. Different combinations of all these developments were happening at different times in different parts of the Empire. For Late Antiquity saw the relative uniformity of classical urban civilization breaking up into regional diversity. To assemble the evidence systematically city by city, region by region, as B. Ward-Perkins has done for Italy,[3] would certainly be useful. It would help to map the spreading of different kinds of change, religious, cultural, and economic over the vast area, and would allow us to trace in detail the developments which are the subject of this book. A corpus of urban archaeology would throw much new light on topics such as the decline of curial institutions, the rising power of the bishop, the Christianization of culture, the changing relationship of town and country, and also in many areas the declining importance of urbanization as such.[4]

In this book no attempt will be made to give a complete presentation of the material. My aim has been to provide examples rather than to offer comprehensive coverage, and, by comparing and contrasting in a general way the process of urban change in East and West, to show that not even these two major divisions were monolithic in their evolution.

2. *Cities of the Greek East: Pattern I. Western and Central Anatolia*

THE DECLINE OF CLASSICAL MONUMENTALITY

Taking the cities of the second century AD as a standard of comparison, it is clear that the classical type survived better in the East[5] than the West, but not uniformly well even there. To anticipate: in Syria, Arabia,

[2] Brenk 1993.

[3] Ward-Perkins 1984.

[4] At present the most complete assembly of material (for the East) is to be found in the volumes of the *Tabula Imperii Byzantini* = *TIB*, although in general the articles are insufficiently detailed to answer questions of this kind.

[5] Claude 1969; Brandes 1989; Kirsten 1958.

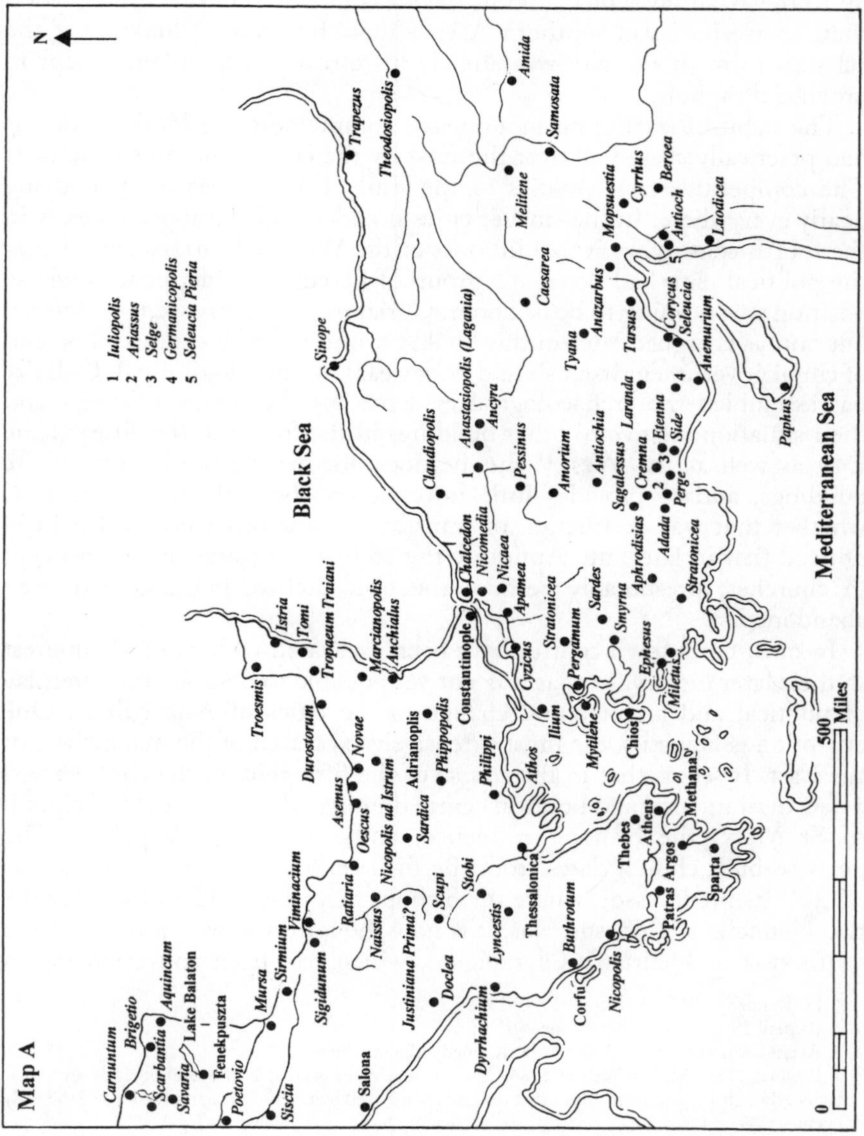

2. Cities in the East

Palestine,[6] and Egypt[7] the classical city, with an urban population, monumental buildings, games, and a highly literate upper class, survived right up to the Arab invasions,[8] and in the areas under Arab rule even beyond that. In western and southern Asia Minor[9] however, it looks as if the classical form of the city was already in retreat much earlier, except in provincial capitals.[10]

The habit of setting up monuments commemorating local politicians had practically ceased all over the East by the end of the fourth century. The competitive civic politics of the Early Empire was dead or dying nearly everywhere. In the smaller cities it had already disappeared early in the fourth century, as it had in most of the West. Decurions from being the political elite had become a group of hereditary functionaries whose position was nothing to boast about. Curial responsibility went on longer, but not, as is argued later in this book, beyond the fifth century. The end of curial government itself should be traceable archaeologically. J. C. Balty has assembled the archaeological evidence for the design of *curiae* and their situation relative to other buildings in the forum in the cities of the East as well as the West.[11] But he does not discuss the history of the buildings, and so provides little information about their ultimate fate, whether that was destruction or transfer to some other use. It has been noticed that in late Late Antiquity the archives of some cities were kept in churches: presumably because the civic archive building had been abandoned.[12]

In most cases town centres have been excavated with too little interest in their later history, so that it is not yet possible to describe the interplay of political and architectural change in the cities of Asia Minor. One exception is Ephesus, the most extensively excavated of the major cities of the East. It seems that in the course of the fifth century the city received a new monumental and political centre dominated by the cathedral church of St Mary, the bishop's residence, and the governor's palace. The purpose-built church dates from the fifth century AD, perhaps as late as *c.*500.[13] Its predecessor, where the bishops met in AD 432 and 439 for the two Councils of Ephesus, was, it is now thought, the western part of the south stoa of Hadrian's Olympieion, which had been converted into a

[6] H. Kennedy 1985*a*; Whittow 1990: 13–20.

[7] Bagnall 1993—much, but mainly 4th cent.

[8] Averil Cameron 1993*b*: 158–66; H. Kennedy 1985*a*, 1992.

[9] Brandes 1989; Müller-Wiener 1986. The writings of Foss cited in the Bibliography are indispensable, though I argue against him that decline started well before the Persian invasions of the early 7th cent.

[10] For the qualification, see C. Roueché 1989*b*: 218–20, 1989*a*: 34.

[11] J. C. Balty 1991.

[12] Saradi 1988*b*. See also below, p. 122.

[13] At any rate, Karwiese regards this as proved.

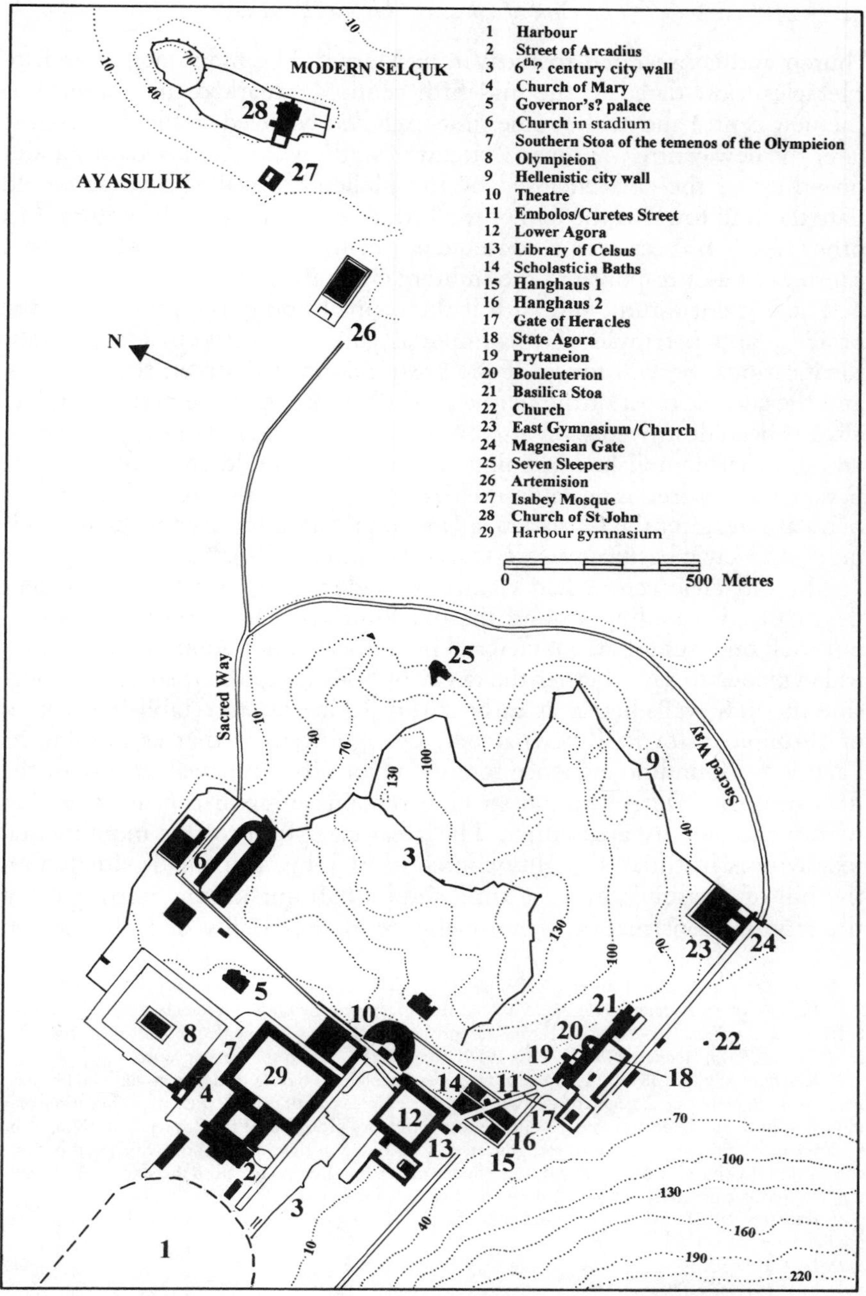

1 Harbour
2 Street of Arcadius
3 6th? century city wall
4 Church of Mary
5 Governor's? palace
6 Church in stadium
7 Southern Stoa of the temenos of the Olympieion
8 Olympieion
9 Hellenistic city wall
10 Theatre
11 Embolos/Curetes Street
12 Lower Agora
13 Library of Celsus
14 Scholasticia Baths
15 Hanghaus 1
16 Hanghaus 2
17 Gate of Heracles
18 State Agora
19 Prytaneion
20 Bouleuterion
21 Basilica Stoa
22 Church
23 East Gymnasium/Church
24 Magnesian Gate
25 Seven Sleepers
26 Artemision
27 Isabey Mosque
28 Church of St John
29 Harbour gymnasium
0
500 Metres
MODERN SELÇUK
AYASULUK
N
Sacred Way
Sacred Way

3. Ephesus: the late ceremonial centre, and the late walls

church and consecrated to the Virgin Mary.[14] The monumental arch of Heracles, now dated to the mid-fifth century,[15] marked the entrance to the new centre and at the same time excluded wheeled traffic. Some time later the new centre was given a circuit of walls, which enclosed only about one-third of the area enclosed by the Hellenistic wall. Karwiese would date the wall towards the end of the fifth or early in the sixth century.[16] In other words he sees it as a consequence of the restructuring of the town centre, not as a response to the military crisis after AD 600.[17]

The ancient forum, and with it the council house, the prytaneion, the basilica, and a temple of the imperial cult were left outside the new fortifications. So was much of the great colonnaded street, the embolos, and the sites of most of the temples. The temples and the prytaneion had already been destroyed soon after AD 400.[18] The material of the prytaneion and of other demolished buildings was used to rebuild and embellish the new civic centre, especially the baths now known as the Baths of Scholasticia, after the Christian lady who provided money for the rebuilding.[19] The civic basilica was destroyed around AD 500.[20]

The old civic centre had clearly been devalued, and to some extent deurbanized. Building around the old forum was no longer continuous, but took on a suburban character. There is as yet not enough archaeological evidence to say whether the decay of housing in the quarters left outside the new walls began as early as this, or indeed to establish any kind of chronology for it. But what may be significant is that archaeologists have so far found no evidence for any major urban renewal later than the fifth century.[21] There are no striking remains of sixth-century churches within the old city area either. The great exception to this monumental inactivity is Justinian's mighty church of St John. But this is situated on the hill of Ayasuluk, at least a mile and a half outside the north gate of the city. Its construction is not evidence of the vitality of Ephesus. On

14 The interpretation of Karwiese 1986: 85–91.

15 P. Scherrer in Koester 1995: 21 n. 109. A. Bammer dates the Gate of Heracles to AD 459 on the basis of *Incr. of Eph.* II (= *IGSK* XII), 588, identifying Fl Konst [. . .] with the consul of that year, *JÖAI* 51 (1976–7), Beiblatt 119–22. Foss 1979: 103–5 dates wall to the Persian wars.

16 Karwiese 1995*b*: 138–40. There is so far no archaeological dating evidence at all. The problem here, as at Pergamum and Miletus, is whether the 'early Byzantine wall' with its implication of a reduction in the built-up area was a response to the military problems of the 7th cent., as thought by C. Foss, or whether it represents a recognition of a shrinking of the built-up area which had become conspicuous by the early or middle 6th cent., more than a hundred years before the start of Arab raiding. Sooner or later archaeology will surely provide a definite answer.

17 Karwiese 1995*b*: 140. On the general problem of dating such Early or Middle Byzantine walls, see below, p. 51.

18 Ibid. 129–30.

19 Foss 1979: 70, 80.

20 Ibid. 81. See also Scherrer 1995: 1–25; Karwiese 1995*a*: 311–19.

21 See list of secular building in Bammer 1988: 156–7.

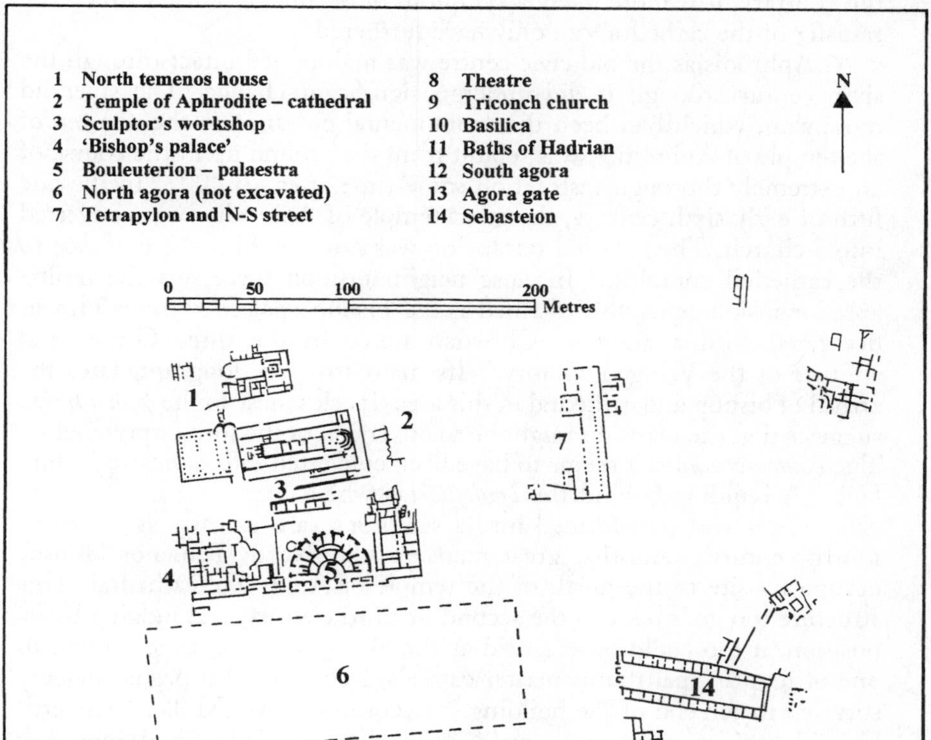

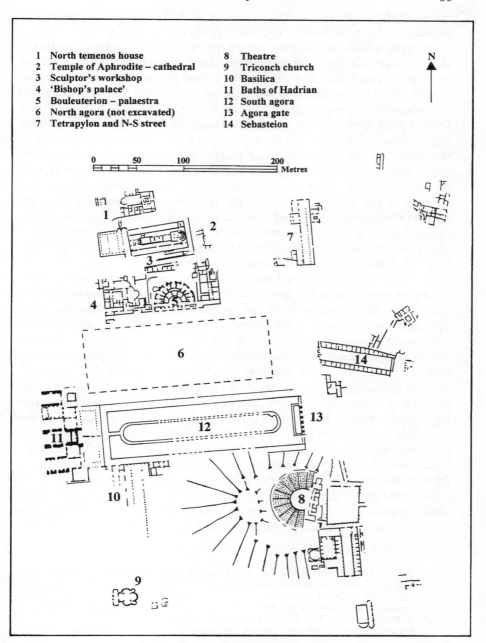

4. Aphrodisias: the late ceremonial centre

the contrary, it is more likely a symptom of decline, a process which the transfer of the cathedral can only have furthered.

At Aphrodisias the old civic centre was maintained intact through the sixth century though it did undergo significant change. The splendid tetrapylon, which had been the monumental entrance to the *temenos* of the temple of Aphrodite, was rebuilt from the ground up in the course of an extremely thorough restoration some time after AD 400.[22] In the late fifth or early sixth century, the great temple of Aphrodite was converted into a church. The restored tetrapylon was now in effect the entrance to the cathedral complex.[23] In close neighbourhood there was the multi-apsed mansion generally described as the 'bishop's palace',[24] though it was decorated with a quite un-Christian fresco of the three Graces and another of the Winged Victory.[25] Its main structure long antedates the arrival of bishop and cathedral in this area. Its closeness to the *bouleutērion* suggests that the mansion might be a conversion of the former prytaneion. The *bouleutērion* itself seems to have been converted into a theatre/lecture hall.[26] A building behind the *bouleutērion* which may once have housed civic offices was transformed into a sculptor's yard as early as the mid-fourth century.[27] Another great mansion, the 'North Temenos House', occupies a site to the north of the temple of Aphrodite/cathedral. This structure too goes back to the second or third century, and judging by its position, it too could have served as the bishop's palace, even though in one of its principal rooms plaster capitals decorated with pagan imagery survived to the end of the building.[28] According to W. Müller-Wiener,[29] bishop's residences were normally comparatively modest buildings, not planned on a monumental scale, but extended as the need arose; so avoiding visual competition with the cathedral. In fact it is not necessary that either of the two mansions excavated in the neighbourhood of the cathedral was the palace of the bishop. One of the two could well have been the residence of the governor. In any case it is clear that the transformed town centre reflected the decline of curial government.

So Aphrodisias throughout the sixth century retained a large monumental civic centre, comparable to the monumental zone within the inner wall at Ephesus. The old agora of Aphrodisias immediately to the south

[22] Paul 1996: 202–14, relevant 213.

[23] Cormack 1990: 26–41.

[24] C. Roueché 1989*a*: nos. 31 and 32 honouring governors of late 4th/early 5th cent. stood in front of the palace in the south colonnade of the north Agora.

[25] Campbell 1996: 187–200.

[26] C. Roueché 1989*a*: no. 43, of mid-5th cent.? Discussion of 'palaestra', ibid. 78–9.

[27] R. R. R. Smith and C. Ratté 1996: 5–33, esp. 9–13; also 1997: 1–22.

[28] Dillon 1997: 731–33. C. Roueché 1989*a*: no. 8, honouring a governor in Latin was found inside it.

[29] Müller-Wiener 1989: 651–709.

of the odeon/*bouleutērion* has not yet been excavated, but the agora of Tiberius and the adjoining baths of Hadrian, only 100–200 metres from the cathedral, kept its representative function: in the middle or late fifth century its eastern gate was carefully restored and remodelled into a nympheum with a large ornamental pool, a project which strongly recalls the contemporary remodelling of the Library of Celsus and the square in front of it at Ephesus.[30]

The 'bishop's palace' and the north *temenos* mansion, with their pillared peristyles, fountains, and apsed reception halls are a type of mansion characteristic of Late Roman cities in the East.[31] Palaces of this kind have been excavated in many places,[32] including well-published examples at Apamea in Syria.[33] At Ephesus the so-called 'Hanghäuser 1 and 2', which are in fact adjacent *insulae*, are made up of respectively five and six houses of various sizes but of the same elegant type.[34] Other mansions of this kind have been excavated at Athens,[35] Sardis, Erythrae, and Arycanda.[36] These were the houses of the notables who now dominated the political life of the cities.[37] The apsed halls were the setting for the private political manoeuvring which had replaced the open politics of forum or agora.[38]

Great centres like Ephesus and Antioch, and smaller capitals like Corinth or Aphrodisias, retained their classical monumentality into the mid-sixth century and beyond,[39] but ordinary cities lost their classical appearance much more rapidly.[40] Provincial governors strove to preserve

[30] C. Roueché 1989*a*: 67–73 and nos. 38–40, and summary of building inscriptions, ibid. 329.

[31] Campbell 1996: 187–99. J. Balty 1984*a*: 471–86. The great houses at Apamea (as also the Hanghäuser at Ephesus), originated in the late 2nd cent. but they were several times rebuilt after destruction, and more or less kept their original shape until the 7th cent.

[32] Sodini 1984: 375–8, 1995, 1997; J. C. Balty 1984.

[33] J. Balty 1984*a*.

[34] The houses were almost all built for well-to-do owners, with peristyles, paintings, and mosaic pavements. The largest in H1 covers 1,400 square metres, in H2 950 square metres: 300–400 square metres is more typical. The 1,400 square metre house is thought to have been built for representation rather than living. So Vetters 1997: 12–28. Lang-Auinger 1996: 26–7 (chronology). The latest coin on the site is dated AD 612–16.

[35] Frantz 1975: 31–6, figs. 10–12, though they are not necessarily the houses of philosophers.

[36] Mitchell 1989–90: 96 Sardis, 97 Erythrae, 115 Aphrodisias, 119 Arycanda.

[37] See below, pp. 111–15.

[38] It is a question whether the prominence of these houses is something new or whether they are simply more conspicuous in the more modest context of a late city, cf. n. 31 above.

[39] The argument for undiminished secular monumentality and continued secular building in the writings of C. Foss (see Bibliography) is based mainly on cities like these, which are also the cities which in the 6th cent. had a financial official entitled 'father of the city', see C. Roueché 1979: 173–85.

[40] See below, pp. 46–8, 49–51, for Pergamum and Miletus. The differences in the development of provincial capitals and ordinary cities however requires further research; e.g. against C. Roueché 1979 it now seems that the office of *patēr civitatis* was not restricted to provincial capitals. See Dagron and Feissel 1987: nos. 24, 89, 104?, and the list in appendix 1, 215–20.

the monumental appearance of their capitals, and took personal credit for the public works involved.[41] The beautification of the capital of the province might be at the expense of other cities. At first the imperial government opposed this, but eventually sanctioned the transfer of civic funds, statues, and even building materials from ordinary cities to the provincial capital.[42]

A factor favouring provincial capitals over other cities of the province was the changed composition and function of late Roman provincial assemblies. As we have seen, these bodies were no longer made up of delegates, with each city of the province being represented by one or two individuals. Instead, these gatherings now brought together all the notables of the province. Normally they met in the provincial capital,[43] where they received instructions from the governor, and discussed the affairs of the province.[44] The acclamations of the assembly were taken down in shorthand and sent to the emperor.[45] That the same development took place also in the West is witnessed by the imperial letter setting up the Council of Seven Provinces of Gaul,[46] and by some official letters addressed to inhabitants of provinces, that is surely to assemblies of provincial notables, in Ostrogothic Italy.[47]

If the administration was now treating provinces rather than cities as the basic administrative units of the Empire,[48] it was only logical to have imperial constitutions published at the provincial assembly, and subsequently placed on permanent display in the provincial capital.[49] At the same time the traditional diplomacy by embassy, panegyric, and inscribed statue seems to have ceased to operate between provincial cities and the emperor, and even between the governor and the ordinary cities of his province. At any rate after the first decades of the fourth century, it was rare for run-of-the-mill cities to put up an inscribed monument to the

41 Robert 1948.

42 *CT* 15.1.1. (357), 18 (374), 26 (390), 37 (398).

43 See J. A. O. Larsen, *Representative Government in Greek and Roman History* (Berkeley, 1996), 145–57. See also above, pp. 12–13.

44 e.g. *IG* VII.24 (401/2) found at Megara, records the decision reached by representatives of cities and the proconsul meeting at Corinth to agree how much corn each city was to supply to the *praepositi horreorum*, and which cities would have to supply which granary.

45 See below, p. 209.

46 *MGH (Ep.)* III.13–15 (418).

47 e.g. Cassiodorus, *Variae* III. 17 (inhabitants of Gaul), XI.16 (Ligurians), XII.22 *provincialibus Histriae*. Other examples of collective action by provinces: Epiphanius of Pavia gets requests from landowners of Liguria, see below, p. 000. In the Gothic war, provinces collectively submit to one or the other of the combatants (e.g. Proc. V.16.4). See also Cecconi 1994: 83–106). In Gallaecia there was collective action and negotiation by 'Gallaecians' (Hydatius, ed. R. W. Burgess (1993), 181, 192). For Procopius the names of Italian provinces are not only administrative designations but the names of actual 'peoples' (V.15.16–250).

48 C. Roueché 1989*a*: 33–4, 1989*b*: 218–21.

49 Surely the destination of the provincial reforms of Justinian, e.g. *Nov* XXIV–XXXI.

emperors. Such cities continued to honour governors with inscribed monuments for a little, but not much, longer. Non-capital cities seem also to have given up the practice of displaying inscribed copies of new imperial decrees. In provincial capitals however, or at least in some of them, statues of emperors and governors, and inscribed imperial decrees continued to be set up right through the fifth century. At Ephesus new imperial decrees, together with older inscriptions collected from the old agora and other parts of the city, were displayed together in the so-called Stoa of the Alytarch, a colonnade on the lower end of the Embolos.[50] At Aphrodisias too, monuments to emperors,[51] and to governors continued to be set up.

The downgrading of cities that were not provincial capitals was not, of course, the only reason for the retreat from classical monumentality. Since the imperial crisis of the middle of the third century, cities had begun to build walls against the threat of hostile attack. This meant that there was less money to spend on maintenance of public buildings. Sometimes indeed the public buildings were demolished to provide material for fortifications. In the first half of the fifth century Isaurian raids once more reminded cities of the need to see to their defences.

How these developments affected ordinary cities is being revealed by archaeology. The decline of a monumental centre is strikingly illustrated at Pergamum where the whole monumental area on the hill was abandoned in the course of the fourth century. Everywhere gymnasia went out of use, and were built over, or fell into ruin. Frequently public spaces such as theatres or colonnaded streets were invaded by shoddy structures.[52] The agora might be built over, and sometimes even aqueducts were allowed to decay, although it appears that of the classical amenities baths were maintained longest. A new baths complex might even be built, when other public buildings had already been abandoned.[53] Eventually in the seventh century classical urbanism collapsed over much of Anatolia: cities shrank to fortresses, were re-sited on more easily defended sites, or even disappeared altogether. The eventual outcome is clear.[54]

[50] Foss 1979: 69.

[51] C. Roueché 1989*a*: 343.

[52] Crawford 1990: 107–25, in a survey of colonnaded streets, refers to encroachment at Anemurium, Pergamum (on which, see also Rheidt in Koester 1998: 400 and 415, fig. 2; 4th cent. according to de Luca 1984: 154–6), Selge, Side, Corinth, and Stobi. On encroachment at Sagalassus, see Waelkens and Poblome 1995: 29–30 (5th/6th cent.), at the Syrian Apamea: J. Balty and J. C. Balty 1972: 17–18; elsewhere in Syria: Sauvaget 1949 and H. Kennedy 1985*a*. See also below, p. 61 (Gerasa) and p. 302 (Bet Shean). The list is far from exhaustive.

[53] Yegül 1986, 1992: 313–49 (on baths and bathing in Late Antiquity and Early Islam, esp. in Syria); Nielsen 1990: esp. 114–18 (late *balnea* in the East).

[54] Evidence summarized in Brandes 1989: 80–141, e.g. 88 (Priene), 95 (Hierapolis), 108 (Caesarea in Cappadocia), 110 (Pergamum), 115 (Cyzicus), 120 (Anemurium). On Sardis, Foss 1980, but also Rautman 1986. See also Russell 1982 and 1987.

The street plan of the typical late Roman city was changing, but changing slowly. The imperial government tried in vain to maintain the classical structure of cities.[55] Unfortunately, it is not yet possible to tell the story of the decline of classical urbanism in detail region by region, or even, except in the case of a very few cities, to provide a chronology of the crucial changes. Too few of the older excavations have been directed to finding an answer to this kind of question. But the story of the decline of classical urbanism must be kept separate from that of urban depopulation. The building on previously open spaces implies that there was need for more houses and shops.[56] The restating of older laws shows that pressure to occupy public space was nothing new.[57] The laws give the impression that the building by private individuals on public space was not itself an offence. The object of the legislation was not so much to return every piece of usurped public space to public ownership, as to give the civic administration legal authority to pull down such private building on publicly owned land as it judged against the public interest.[58] Actually these structures were a source of public revenue. So the shopkeepers who had put up wooden shacks in the monumental colonnades at Antioch paid rent to the city council.[59] No wonder wooden shacks were sometimes consolidated as permanent structures in stone.[60] Councils were always short of money, and glad both to save on the upkeep of old buildings, and to obtain income from new ones. But I suppose that it is also true that as civic governments weakened—the theme of this book—they also became less able to enforce building regulations[61] in the face of pressure to infringe them.

It must however be borne in mind that pressure on public spaces need not represent 'growth'. It was easier to build on previously open sites, or to occupy disused but solidly constructed public buildings, than to redevelop derelict sites which had to be cleared before building could start. At Alexandria there is evidence of encroachment onto the road while housing in the interior of the *insula* became ruinous and uninhabitable.[62]

'Taste' had of course changed, although that word trivializes the

55 *CT* XV.1.1 (357), 14 (365), 37 (398); XV.5.1. (372), 3 (409).

56 On building on public spaces at Sagalassus: Waelkens and Poblome 1995: 29. The city did not fully recover from earthquakes of AD 518 and 528. Waelkens 1993: 48–9. Areas outside new walls abandoned in 5th cent.: Waelkens and Poblome 1993: 16–17. 'Infilling' at Ephesus: Bammer 1988: 159 ff., illus. 47–8.

57 *CT* XV1.9 (362); 22 (383); 25 (389); 38–9 (398); 46 (406); 50 (412). See Saradi 1994: 295–308.

58 *Digest* XLIII.17; *CJ* VIII.11.3 (Julian), 11.6 (383), 11.14 (396). *CJ* VIII.10.12 (Zeno), states the principle that streets and stoai are the property of the people, but allows shacks in colonnades to be legalized retrospectively if they are dressed with marble.

59 Libanius, *Or* XXVI.2–2; 23 same at Berytus.

60 See Müller-Wiener 1989: 439 n. 13.

61 Saliou 1994. The treatise on 'urbanism' of Julian of Ascalon, edited, translated into French, and explained by C. Saliou (1996) shows that building regulations were still observed in at least some cities in the 6th cent.

62 Majcherek 1997: 133–45, relevant 144.

profound cultural change involved in Christianization. From perhaps the last quarter of the fourth century the building of churches gathered pace. As churches became the symbols of civic identity and civic cohesion, there was ever less incentive to maintain the old symbols, and to resist pressures that unless resisted would inevitably transform the classically planned city into something else.[63] The development was in the direction of the Islamic town. To quote P. Pentz, 'in the long history of urbanism in the East, the Graeco-Roman town was nothing more than a long digression; when possible the towns reestablished their old oriental plan, with larger strictly planned streets, combined with narrow winding alleys.'[64]

In most cities of central Anatolia, a region where the emergence of classical cities had been closely linked with Roman rule under the Early Empire,[65] there is very little evidence, either of inscriptions,[66] or of remains of public buildings, to suggest monumental secular activity after, say, the early fourth century. Antioch in Pisidia is an exception in that it clearly benefited from becoming a provincial capital around AD 300.[67] The theatre was actually enlarged. At some late stage housing intruded onto the *cardo maximus* of the old Roman colony, but the city received a triumphal arch in the fourth century and a new—or restored—aqueduct, thanks to private munificence in the fifth or sixth century. Bishop Optimus built a large church *c*.375 and another was later erected in the heart of the old civic centre. Three churches are known in all.[68] There is no evidence of abandonment of residential areas before the sixth century. A loss of civil monumentality can only be observed in the sixth century when columns from the imperial temple area were reused for domestic housing.

The smaller cities of this region, as elsewhere, lost their classical appearance more quickly. For instance at the small city of Ariassus the forum was demolished and replaced by a church surrounded by crudely built churchyard walls.[69] But regardless of their changed appearance these

[63] e.g. the supplementation and superseding of the rectangular grid of streets by dead-ended alleyways and courtyards to form neighbourhoods that could be shut off: Y. Porath in Raban and Holum 1996: 176 (Caesarea); Haas 1997: 194, pl. 2 (Polish excavation – Kôm el-Dikka, Alexandria; Rodziewicz) 1984: 59–61, 252–6, Plans I and III.

[64] Pentz 1992: 49; on 'Arab city', cf. Wirth 1975: 49–54, Wirth 1974: 203–60, 1975: 6–46, also Glaube and Wirth 1984, on urban structure of an 'Arab town', and the economics of caravan trading.

[65] On urbanization in the first century of the imperial period: Mitchell 1993: i. 81–98.

[66] See *MAMA* IX Monuments from Aezanitis, ed. B. Levick, S. Mitchell, J. Potter, M. Waelkens (London, 1988), pp. lvii–lviii, list of dated inscriptions. *MAMA* X, Upper Tembris Valley, Cotiaeum, Cadi, Synaus, Ancyra Sidera, Tiberiopolis, recorded by C. W. M. Cox, A. Cameron, J. Cullen, ed. B. Levick, S. Mitchell, J. Potter, M. Waelkens (London, 1993), 197.

[67] T. Drew Bear in D. M. Robinson 1924: 435–44; Mitchell and Waelkens 1998: 14, 109–10, 195, 217, 226–7.

[68] Mitchell and Waelkens 1998: 201–18; Brandt 1992: 178.

[69] Schulz 1992: 29–41.

places regained city status, and continued to have bishops, who are duly listed as having attended ecclesiastical councils.[70] It is even likely that new bishoprics were still being created.[71] Surface remains—there has been very little excavation—suggest that by, say, AD 500 many bishops must have presided over what were visually little more than large fortified villages.[72] But these usually possessed a number of monumental intramural churches, and perhaps some burial churches and/or monasteries beyond the walls.[73] Moreover, there is no evidence that these places were becoming depopulated. Housing at Cremna, Ariassus, and Sia seems to have been continuously occupied and modified until the sixth century. At Anemurium by the sea in Cilicia an artisans' quarter was built into what had been a large classical *palaestra*.[74] The countryside too was probably more densely populated than ever before. Overall there seems to be more and larger sites from this late period than from the Early Empire. This is vividly illustrated at Ceraitae, north-west of Cremna and legally a village of that city, where sherds dating from Late Antiquity are scattered far beyond the fortified hill which was the old settlement.[75]

Isauria enjoyed a great boom of mainly ecclesiastical building under the emperors Leo and Zeno. But the region does not appear to have recovered from the consequences of the ruthless suppression by Anastasius of the Isaurian rebellion of AD 491–8.[76]

In the coastal belt of Lycia, and even in inland areas with reasonably easy communications with the coast, settlements of every kind seem to have flourished until the Persian invasion inaugurated the 'dark age' of the seventh century.[77] Meanwhile impressive churches were built both in historic cities and in quite remote villages. In the cities the new building involved the destruction of old monuments and the reuse of their materials.[78] M. Harrison has argued that the reuse of building material was evidence of general economic regression.[79] This has been refuted by Foss as far as the coastal belt is concerned; it could however be true of central and north Lycia. Along the densely settled coast, settlements grew

[70] Mitchell 1993: ii. 120–1; Chrysos 1966; *Le Synecdémos d'Hiéroclés*, ed. E. Honigmann (Brussels, 1939).

[71] Belke 1994: 179–82.

[72] Mitchell 1993: ii. 120–1.

[73] In Pisidia: Cremna 8, at Sagalassus 4, Ariassus 3, Sia 2, Adada 2 or 3, Etenna 3, a *mansio* in pass between Pamphylia and Pisidia 8, Brandt 1992: 177–81.

[74] F. Hild and H. Hellenkemper, *TIB* V: 187–91.

[75] Information of Mitchell: the entries of *TIB* are generally too brief and too little concerned with dates of visible remains to allow judgements about the condition of settlements at different times.

[76] S. Hill 1996: 5–10.

[77] See report of six-week survey of Kyaneai and its territory in *Istanbuler Mitteilungen*, 41 (1991), 187–263.

[78] Hellenkemper 1994: 213–38; 215–17 on Lycia. On use of spolia, see Saradi 1997.

[79] R. M. Harrison 1963: 117–51, 1979: 222–39.

up which resemble the better known contemporary villages of Syria in that they show no trace of a geometrical street plan. But late Late Roman building in Lycia, unlike building in Syria, produced very few inscriptions.[80] Urbanism in Lycia, as in Asia Minor as a whole, was to collapse in the seventh century.

Summing up it would seem that all over central Anatolia cities, even when they had lost their classical appearance, remained densely populated, in many cases certainly up to the second half of the sixth century. The teeming populations of the towns reflected a densely populated countryside. In large areas of rural Asia Minor in Isauria, Cilicia Tracheia,[81] Phrygia,[82] Pisidia, and rural Galatia around Ancyra (Ankara), the population as judged by the size and density of archaeological sites appears to have been greater in the fourth to sixth centuries than it had been under the Early Empire.[83] This of course raises the question why the state of apparent prosperity should so soon have changed to one of rapid and calamitous decline.

THE ONSET OF URBAN DECLINE IN WESTERN AND CENTRAL ANATOLIA

Some scholars, for instance Foss and Whittow,[84] have argued that in general cities flourished up to around AD 600, and that the collapse was caused precisely by destructive raiding, sustained over many years, first by the Persians, then by the Arabs. This theory is attractive, but it does not account for evidence which, to this author at least, suggests that stagnation followed by decline set in half a century before the great Persian invasion, and in some areas perhaps even earlier.[85]

In fact it is still very difficult to establish a conclusive chronology of the decline of urbanism in Anatolia. Comparison of the number of coins from different reigns has been used to assess changing economic conditions over a period of time.[86] But the interpretation of coin evidence is far from straightforward. Sardis was a provincial capital which certainly flourished for many years in Late Antiquity.[87] The coin finds in the so-called

80 Foss 1996.

81 *TIB* V.

82 *c.*1,000 funerary inscriptions from around Laodicea Catacecaumene C3–C5 (*MAMA* I and VII). The buildings, probably of mud-brick on stone foundations, have left no standing remains.

83 Just. *Nov* XXIV.1 'quoniam vici maximi in ea [i.e. Pisidia] sunt et populosi et crebro et contra ipsa resultantes tributa fiscalia'.

84 Foss 1975, 1977*a*, 1979; Whittow 1996.

85 Mid-6th cent. date for beginning of decline agreed by Russell 1986, esp. 145; Saradi 1988*a*.

86 Whittow 1996: 60: 'The continued appearance of copper coins in quantity on Roman sites in the eastern heartlands . . . up to 600 and beyond is . . . evidence for the prosperity of that economy and its continued avoidance of recession.'

87 J. A. Scott 1987: 74–87.

Byzantine shops, which are thought to have been occupied from the early fifth century to the destruction of the town in the reign of Heraclius, confirm this impression of late prosperity. Of 1,065 coins listed (all bronze) 47 per cent are later than AD 491, and of these a high percentage belong to the reigns of Maurice, Phocas, and Heraclius, that is the last forty or so years of the shops' existence.[88] These coins presumably represent coins lost by shoppers or change kept by the shopkeepers. So there can be no doubt that in this shopping-centre plenty of money was changing hands in return for pots, glassware, textiles, or dyestuffs,[89] right up to the destruction of the city. It is a notable feature of the coin evidence from the Byzantine shops at Sardis that 50 per cent of the coins are what the editors call 'Roman', i.e. earlier than AD 491, and overwhelmingly from the fourth century. This suggests that the coins of the fourth century remained in circulation irrespective of changes in imperial coinage policy such as Anastasius' reform. Moreover, if these coins represent survivors that were still circulating two hundred years after they had gone into circulation, that would suggest that they were originally issued in much larger numbers than the bronze coins of the sixth century. In fact taking the coin evidence from all sites at Sardis we find that for the years AD 294–491 the average number of coins per regnal year unearthed in the excavations is 16.9 per annum; if we take only the coins minted in the fourth century, the number of coins per regnal year is much greater still, but for the years 491–616 it is only 8.[90]

At Ephesus comprehensive coin lists have been published in connection with the excavation of the elegant residential area overlooking the 'Embolos', the so-called 'Hanghäuser'. On the site of 'Hanghaus 2', at Ephesus there were far more coins of the first than of the second half of the sixth century, but the coins of the fourth century were far more numerous still.[91] Of course the decline of coin finds from the 'Hanghäuser' after the last quarter of the sixth century may well only reflect the progressive depopulation of that particular district.[92]

If we look for evidence further inland and further east, we find that among the coins found in the extensive gymnasium complex at Ankara the great majority date from the fourth century, but there is a small

[88] Crawford 1990: 12 and 126–8.

[89] Ibid. 13–17.

[90] Buttray *et al.* 1981: 122, table v. Bates 1971: 6–7, table iii. But it is necessary to compare not only numbers but also value. The bronze of the late 4th cent. had a lower value than the bronze issued after Anastasius' reform, but the second half of the 6th cent. saw a progressive loss of value of the follis, see Morrisson 1989: 248, table 2.

[91] See below p. 49 n. 111.

[92] Foss 1979: 197–8, Byzantine coins from Selcuk area of Ephesus (around St John's church), has 0.8 coins per year of Justinian; 2.5 per year of Justin II; 0.5 for Maurice; 2.6 for Phocas. Numbers of coins are small.

number of coins from each of the emperors of the sixth century with the years AD 610–16 of Heraclius most abundantly represented.[93] But a survey in the rural territory of Aezanitis in Pamphylia found 31 coins from the fourth century, 5 from the fifth, and 7 from the sixth, of which 5 are from the first half of the century.[94] In Egypt the papyrus evidence leaves no doubt that the economy was as highly monetarized around AD 600 as it ever had been. Yet in the Red Sea port of Berenice archaeologists have found hardly any sixth-century coins at all.[95]

The precise implications of this for the economy are difficult to deduce. Above all there are still far too few coin lists from far too few sites. The evidence of a small number of places from which we have a significant number of coins—and of the Egyptian papyri—is that the money economy was not in retreat in the sixth century, if anything the reverse was true. But there are places where the evidence, such as it is, suggests that regression set in earlier, there are vast areas from which we have no evidence at all. It may be the case that while in some regions there was an abundance of currency, both in copper and gold, in others there was a shortage of coin.[96] If in Tripolitania landowners compelled their tenants to pay in coin, that suggests that coins were in short supply in the province. If the government thought it necessary to prohibit the transport of coin for the purpose of sale, this suggests that the availability of coin, and hence its value, varied sufficiently from region to region to encourage speculation.[97] It is also a problem whether the coin evidence can reflect such a thing as 'the state of the economy'. It is more likely that abundance of coins in a particular place, at a particular time, reflects not so much local boom conditions as the fact that the government was spending a lot of money in the area, whether in grants to local causes, or in salaries to officials, and above all to soldiers.

There is another point. The coins of the sixth century from the shops at Sardis have overwhelmingly been minted in Asia Minor, the great majority at Constantinople, some at Nicomedia and Cyzicus, none at Alexandria, and only a few at Antioch. As we are dealing with what is

[93] Foss 1977*c*: 29–87. See also Kienast 1962: 65–112.

[94] Aezanitis: C. W. M. Cox, A. Cameron, J. Cullen, *MAMA* IX: Monuments from Aezanitis, ed. B. Levick, S. Mitchell, J. Potter, M. Waelkens (London, 1988), 196–9: 39 coins (AD 285–450), 7 (AD 498–618). The area has also produced only 9 Christian inscriptions altogether. See also coins from Limyra, Gorecki 1991/2: 185–7: 186 coins (AD 294–498), 45 (Byzantine).

[95] S. E. Sidebotham and W. Z. Wendrich (eds.), *Berenike 1995*, Preliminary Report of the 1995 Excavations at Berenike (Egyptian Red Sea Coast) and the Survey of the Eastern Desert, Research School CNWS (Leiden, 1996). Dr Roberta Tomber informs me that while the excavators found a great deal of pottery (both amphorae and other wares) which is common in the 5th cent. and could easily continue into the 6th, they found no types restricted to the 6th cent.

[96] On barter as an alternative to money in a much later period, see Saradi 1995: 405–18.

[97] *CJ* XI.48.5 (Valentinian I), *CT* IX.23.1 (356), and Hendy 1985: 289–91.

in effect a collection of change, it would be wrong to use it to draw far-reaching conclusions about interprovincial trade. Nevertheless as far as it goes this evidence suggests a regional circulation of coins. Very tentatively one might identify the early symptoms of the breaking up of the unified imperial economy into regional economies which would become evident in the course of the seventh century.[98] Now this phenomenon has been observed in hoards of the Early Empire.[99] It would be interesting to compare the evidence for mobility or immobility of coins at different periods. This would help to establish the relative importance of trade at different times and in different places. For it is trade above all that causes coins to move away from the region where they first came into circulation, and to mix with coins whose circulation started elsewhere. Meanwhile it would seem that the evidence of coins does not yet give a clear answer to our question as to the beginning of the decline of cities in Asia Minor.

This leaves the evidence of archaeology. There has been so far too little excavation of residential areas to make any judgement more than provisional. Take the example of Pergamum. Archaeologists have been working on the city for more than a century, though they have left many problems still to be solved. One thing seems certain: the spectacular monumental quarter on the hill, the area that had been the city in Hellenistic times received a new wall, 'the late Roman wall', in the third century, but was largely abandoned by the fourth. This is an extreme example of the discarding of its classical town centre by a city which failed to become a provincial capital. It does not necessarily mean that the city was becoming depopulated. In fact the population had been shifting from the hill into the plain throughout Roman times, and the 'Roman city' in the plain had its own theatre, amphitheatre, and agora. The fourth and fifth century merely saw the completion of this shift of population. The city now centred on the Red Hall, that is the huge sanctuary of the Egyptian gods, which had been converted into the cathedral, and the Lower Agora, now the site of a purpose-built church. The area of occupation in the plain alone amounted to something like 140 hectares.[100] The

[98] See Crawford 1990: 126–8 (compiled by M. D. Weishan). The great dominance of coins from Constantinople over those from other mints of the region (Cyzicus, Nicomedia), a progressive concentration of coining at the capital was a long-term trend. See C. Morrisson, 'La Diffusion de la monaie', in Mango and Dagron 1977: 77–89, esp. 78–81.

[99] Duncan Jones 1994: 172–9. But it may be significant that compared with the composition of coin hoards from Asia Minor AD 318–64 (J. P. C. Kent 1981: 95, 109) there has been a sharp reduction in the proportion of coins from Alexandria (none) and from Antioch. The progressive reduction of coins from Antioch and Alexandria has also been noted at Sagalassus: Waelkens and Poblome 1997: 342, table 3.

[100] Wulf 1994: 135–74. Note that the principal church in the plain was not purpose-built but a conversion of the monumental sanctuary of the Alexandrian gods (i.e. the 'red hall', see Deubner 1977–8: 227–50). Altogether three early Byzantine churches: Rheidt 1991: 223, fig. 43; 187, fig. 37.

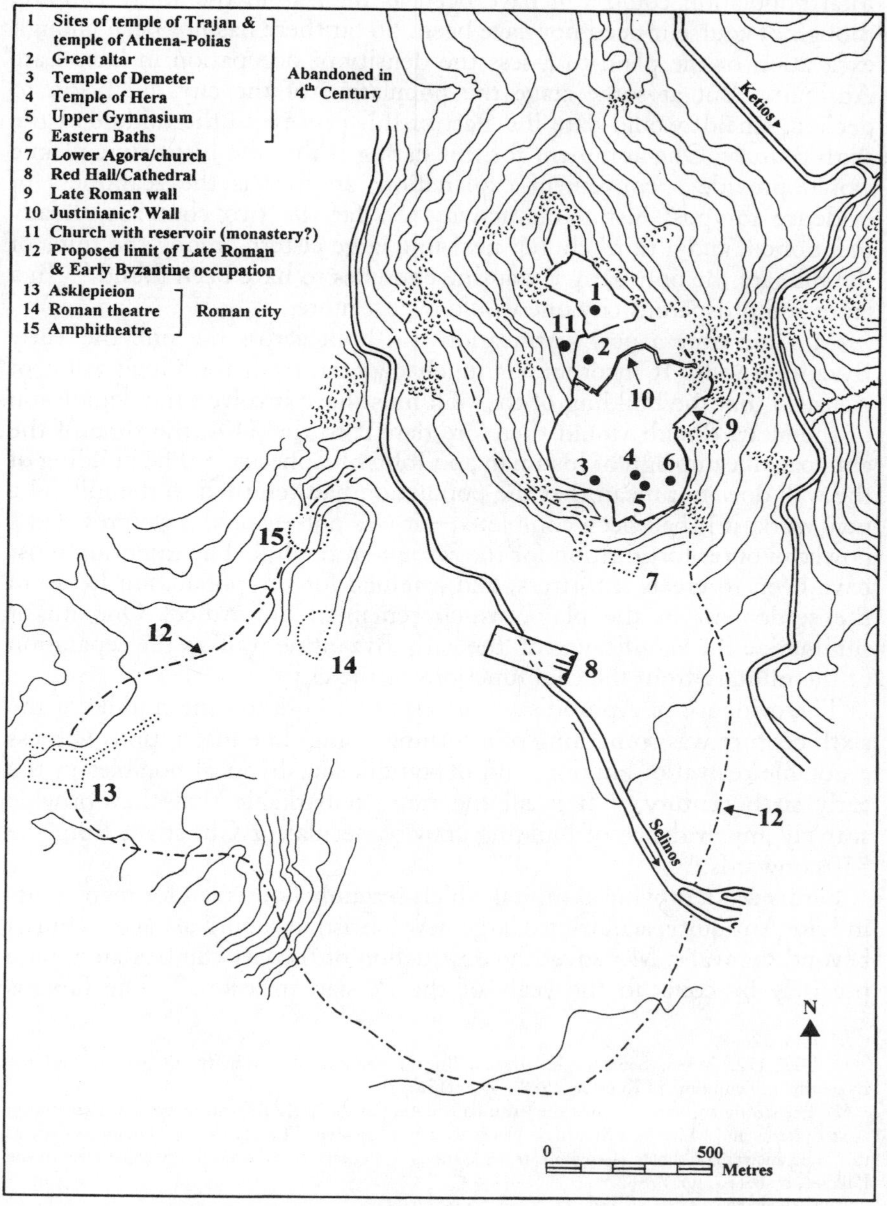

5. Pergamum: the move into the plain and late fortifications

total population could still have been as high as in the Early Empire, though of course it need not have been. So far there has not been enough excavation of the plain to assess the density of occupation in later Late Antiquity. But at some stage the population of the city did begin to decline. Rheidt would date the start of this process to the middle of the sixth century. One argument for this dating is that the Justinianic plague would provide a convenient explanation; another is the scantiness of evidence for post-Justinianic activity. So far the two churches already mentioned, and a third church next to a large cistern among the ruins of the hill, are the only early Byzantine churches to have been found.[101] In a large and prosperous city one would expect more.

At some time a new fortification was built across the hill, the 'early Byzantine wall'. It incorporates much material from the Great Altar of Zeus, so that the building of the wall must have involved the demolition of the altar. Rheidt would therefore date it to the 540s, the time of the anti-pagan campaign of Justinian and John of Ephesus.[102] The building of the wall does not mean that the population had returned to the hill. The new work, if it had been completed—it was not—would have provided a powerful outer fortification for the *castron* on the hill. The intention must have been to create a fortress, and a refuge for the population living in the settlement in the plain, which remained unfortified. One might summarize the significance of 'the early Byzantine wall' as the separation of the military from the civil functions of the city.[103]

The evidence of Aphrodisias suggests that here too the middle of the sixth century was something of a turning point. The inscriptions witness a notable revival of building and of munificence by local notables in the early sixth century.[104] It is all the more remarkable that they provide scarcely any evidence of building activity, secular or Christian, from the 550s onwards.[105]

Sardis was a provincial capital which certainly flourished for many years in Late Antiquity, acquiring a large new Christian suburb around a church beyond the walls. Moreover the destruction of the city can be dated quite precisely by coins to the years of the Persian invasion.[106] The famous

[101] Ibid. 226–8.

[102] Ibid. 172, 243–5. See also K. Rheidt, 'In the shadow of Antiquity: Pergamum and the Byzantine millennium', in Koester (1998), 395–413.

[103] The strong argument against the Justinianic dating of the 'early Byzantine walls' at Pergamum, as at Ephesus and Miletus, is that these places were not threatened by any external enemy as early as this. The answer could be a change in strategic thought, perhaps based on military experience in the Balkans, cf. below, pp. 77–82.

[104] C. Roueché 1989*a*: 86 and nos. 53–4, 55–8, 66–80.

[105] Ibid., secular, 148–52; Christian, 153–90. The Triconch Church (159–61) would be an exception if it should not be dated, as now seems more likely, to around the 10th cent.

[106] J. A. Scott 1987: 74–87.

synagogue-gymnasium complex and the 'Byzantine shops' were occupied until their violent destruction.[107] But it is by no means certain that they are representative. An area of large houses, dating from the early fifth century seems to have fallen into decay in the second half of the sixth century.[108] Rooms filled with rubble. In some cases residential accommodation came to be used industrially. Houses appear to have been cleared of furnishings before the final destruction. The latest layers of the filling of a well have very little imported pottery in contrast to an abundance in earlier layers.[109]

At Ephesus the fact that large parts of the old city were left outside the new fortification need not mean that these districts were now wholly or partially depopulated: the elegant houses on the slope overlooking the embolos provide evidence of occupation, though by less wealthy owners, living more simply, at least up to AD 600.[110] However, the reduction of coin finds suggests that decline had started at least twenty years earlier.[111] So either the number of inhabitants had shrunk well before the Persian war, or the last inhabitants had grown very short of coins. Karwiese certainly is under the impression that the areas outside the new wall were no longer fully urbanized.[112] But so far too little of the residential areas of Ephesus has been excavated to establish with any degree of precision when any of the quarters of the city became depopulated. But even if a large number of people continued to live outside the new wall, the fact that so much of the old city was left outside the fortifications must be significant.

At Miletus the so-called 'Justinianic wall' girds only about one-quarter of the Roman city. In the reign of Justinian the city had a remarkable benefactor in the *illustris* Hesychius. He restored the baths, regulated the course of the Maeander, and erected a large church.[113] But the archaeo-

[107] See above pp. 43–4, nn. 87–90.

[108] Rautman 1986 compactly, but systematically and clearly argues for widespread decay in Sardis from the later 6th cent. So also specifically for the residential area south of the gymnasium-synagogue complex: Rautman 1995*a*: 49–65. See also Greenwalt, Ratté, and Rautman 1993: 1–43, esp. 6, 39 n. 10, 1995: 1–36, esp. 8–10. Rautman 1995*b*: 37–84.

[109] Greenwalt, Ratté, and Rautman 1993: esp. 6 and 39 n. 10, 1995: esp. 8–10; Rautman 1995*b*: esp. table 1, p. 79, table 2, p. 81.

[110] On the so-called *Hanghäuser*, see above, p. 37 n. 34.

[111] Coins found in House II in 1983 include only 8 coins from AD 550–600. Coins from 490–550 are far more numerous, and 4th-cent. coins more numerous still: Karwiese 1986: 111–23. The list of coin finds in 1982 (Karwiese 1985) has a much higher proportion of coins *c.*550–79, but it too has very few of Maurice or later. A fair proportion of coins found in the street running above *Hanghaus* 2 (Stiegengasse 3), date from the years before 580, but very few are later than that. The *Hanghäuser* themselves were partly abandoned as early as the 3rd cent. The site was eventually occupied by water-driven corn mills.

[112] Karwiese 1995*b*: 141: 'die Stadt war deutlich kleiner geworden.'

[113] von Gerkan and Krischen 1928: 164–6; Foss 1977*a*: 477.

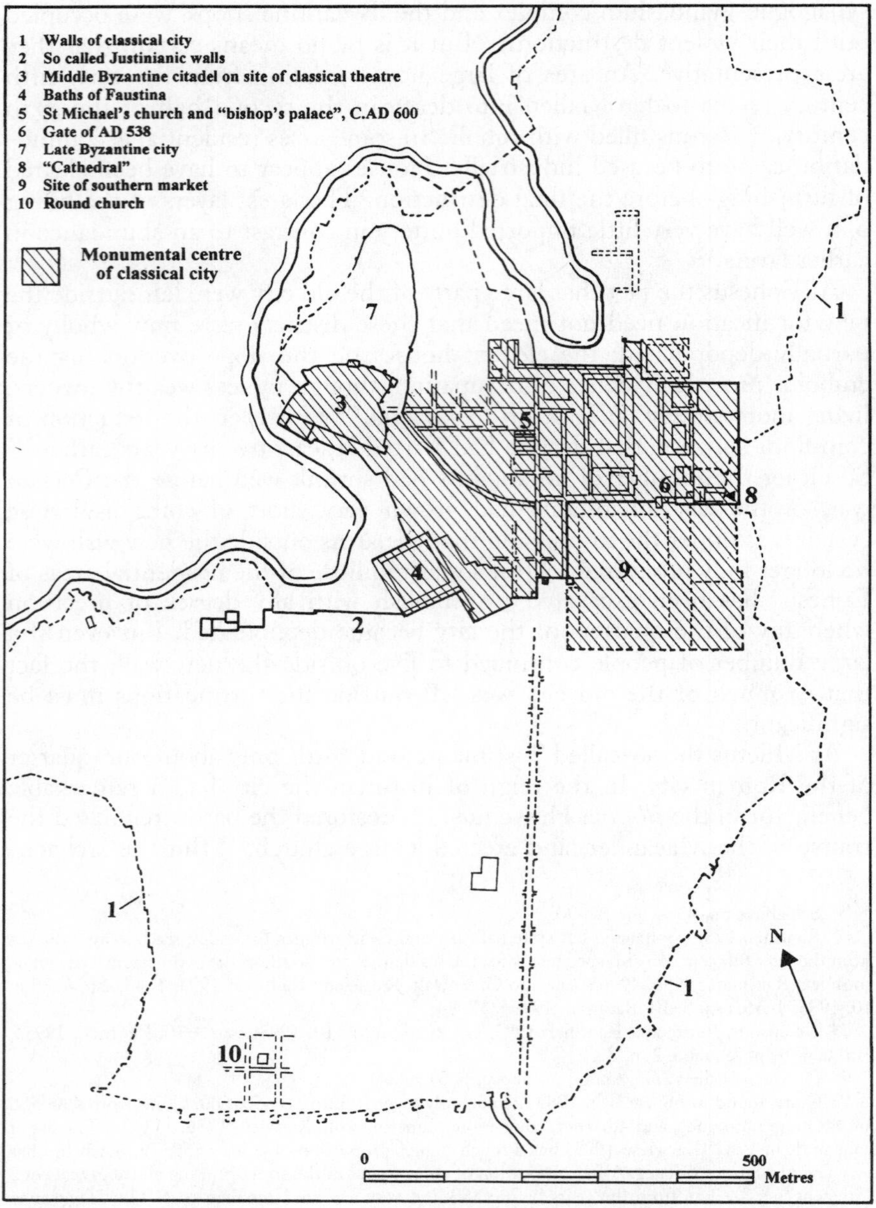

6. Miletus: the so-called Justinianic wall

logical evidence for building in the sixth century is not impressive. Even though the church of St Michael was completely rebuilt as late as AD 595–606,[114] and the cathedral complex was rebuilt and extended early in the century,[115] this is not very much compared with the secular building of the Early Empire, or sixth-century church building at Gerasa, or urban renewal at Scythopolis and elsewhere in Palestine. Moreover, if the late wall was indeed Justinianic that would imply that the great southern market had already been demolished.

Any attempt to assess the condition of the famous cities of Asia in later Late Antiquity must involve a decision about the dating and purpose of their 'early Byzantine walls'.[116] None of these fortifications has up to now been given a reliable archaeological date,[117] though in the case of Ephesus,[118] Pergamum,[119] and Miletus[120] a date in the middle, or even the early, sixth century has been favoured by a director of the relevant excavation. The excavator of Sardis is uncertain.[121]

The objection to the early dating of these walls is that western Anatolia was under no threat of invasion before the Persian war early in the seventh century. There was therefore no obvious need for costly fortification. It is however possible that military thought had come to favour shorter wall-circuits. In the Balkans the sixth-century cities of Nicopolis ad Istrum and Justiniana Prima were large fortresses rather than fortified cities. Many shortened circuits were constructed in the reign of Justinian in reconquered North Africa, and more relevantly for the present argument, at Caesarea in Cappadocia and at Antioch in Syria.[122] Justinian justified his

[114] W. Müller-Wiener, *Is Mitt.* 27–8 (1977–8), 94–125; 29 (1979), 162–73.

[115] Ibid. 23–4 (1973–4), 131 ff.; 32 (1982), 5–14.

[116] Brandes 1989: 82–111. For plans, see Müller-Wiener 1986: 435–75, esp. figs. 2, 4, 7.

[117] M. Klinkott is preparing a monograph.

[118] See above, p. 34.

[119] Rheidt 1991: 170 ff., 197; but Radt (1988: 80) argued in favour of a 7th-cent. date. M. Klinkott, in a letter to the author, argues that the military situation in 672–8 provides the most likely setting for the construction of a powerful outwork for the *castron* on the hill, as well as for the failure to complete the work.

[120] H. Knackfuss, Milet I.7, *Der Südmarkt und benachbarte Bauten*, 303–4, inscr. 206 records date 538 (= P. Hermann (ed.), *Die Inschriften von Milet,* Pt. I, nos. 187–406 (Berlin, 1997), p. 35, no. 206). The excavators thought that the inscription (on a reused block from a temple of Serapis) formed the lintel of the middle passage of the Roman market gate, after this had been converted into a fortress gate through the wall which now blocked the other two passages (ibid. 154; photographs of site: Abb. 41–2, pp. 47–8; of inscribed stone: Abb. 170, p. 154); plan of wall and gate: Abb. 3. If the excavators were right to associate the inscription with the fortress gate, and not with a last renovation of the ceremonial market gate, which they have reconstructed with arched (and not rectangular) openings, the fortress gate is firmly dated to 538, then the wall, and the demolition of the south market must date to this time too. Foss (1977*a*: 478 n. 49) and Brandes (1989: 90) assign the stone to a last restoration of the ornamental gate.

[121] Hanfmann 1983: 143–4: 'the riddle of the city wall'.

[122] *CJ* I.27.2.14 (precept for reconquered North Africa); Procopius *Aed.* V.4.7 (Caesarea in Cappadocia). At Antioch the 'island' on which palace and cathedral were situated was left outside the new fortifications, ibid. II.10.3, Downey 1961: 546–9.

instructions for Africa with the argument that shorter walls required fewer defenders, and this was also the reason for the shortening of the wall at Caesarea. At Antioch the population had certainly been greatly reduced by a terrible earthquake, and the deportation of many inhabitants by the Persians. But readiness to leave large areas and important buildings undefended suggests either that these districts were no longer fully inhabited, or that the government had lost confidence in its ability to defend them in the face of a serious invasion. Either reason would imply that something was going seriously wrong quite early in the sixth century.

As far as building activity in the second half of the sixth century is concerned evidence from the smaller inland cities supports the view that the 'Late Roman boom' had been checked, if not even reversed long before the end of the century. At Anemurion in Cilicia many churches were built in the fifth century, but two of them partly collapsed around AD 580 and were not repaired.[123] At Antioch in Pisidia, Sagalassus, Cremna,[124] and Ariassus a careful survey has shown no new building that is clearly later than AD 500; and more casual observation by S. Mitchell at Selge, Etenna, Pednelissus, and Adana has found the same absence of evidence for building in the sixth century. At the time of writing very little positive evidence for occupation after AD 600 has been identified at any of these places.[125] Sagalassus was an important centre for the production of a local ware of pottery which was traded widely in inland areas.[126] But the site seems to have been greatly weakened after an earthquake between AD 518 and 528. This destroyed among other things the aqueduct which was not rebuilt.[127] However, coins and pottery found in private dwellings occupying structures on the old forum into the seventh century show that the site was not abandoned.[128] On the roads of Pisidia, French found no milestones later than the reign of Julian, and no evidence of construction or even repair later than AD 476.[129]

If one looks for some development to explain decline, or at least stagnation, setting in fifty or more years before the Persian war of Phocas

[123] Hild and Hellenkemper 1990: 187–91.

[124] Mitchell 1995: 232: no pottery or architecture that requires dating after 5th cent.

[125] This is the assessment of S. Mitchell in a letter to the author. Waelkens and Poblome (1997: 101) consider that the number of settlements diminished somewhat in the 5th cent., perhaps as a result of Isaurian raids, but in general the 5th and 6th cent., triggered by an earthquake in the early part of the century.

[126] On Sagalassus, see Waelkens 1993 and Waelkens and Poblome 1993, 1995, and 1997. Mitchell, Owens, and Waelkens 1989: 63–77; M. Waelkens, 'Sagalassos', in Schwertheim 1992: 45–60.

[127] Waelkens and Poblome 1993: 16–17.

[128] See coins of Heraclius and Constans II in list of coin finds in Waelkens and Poblome 1997: 315–50. There are no coins of Heraclius in corresponding lists in Waelkens 1993: 198–200, Waelkens and Poblome 1993: 249–55, or 1995: 197.

[129] French 1992: 167–75.

and Heraclius, the most obvious candidate is the plague of AD 542, whose effects have been graphically described by Procopius, and which recurred regularly in the following decades. If this disease brought about a significant fall of the population it could well have marked the turning point from steady growth to rapid demographic decline, a decline which had not been checked by AD 603 when the Persian war triggered another series of disasters. The effect of the plague is the subject of scholarly controversy. Durliat has pointed out that there is little archaeological, epigraphic, or papyrological evidence to support the literary accounts. He argues that the descriptions of vast mortality are rhetorically exaggerated, or at least not to be made the basis for generalizations about the scale of the epidemic over the Near East as a whole.[130] Some have accepted this argument,[131] others not.[132] The present author thinks that Durliat has not made his case. The evidence that the plague was devastating, widespread and, what must have magnified its long-term effect, regularly recurring, is however very strong[133]—at least by standards of proof normally accepted by Ancient historians. Furthermore the fact that other evidence would seem to require a disaster of some kind at just about the time of the first visitation of the plague by itself makes it more likely that acceptance of the literary evidence is justified.[134] A possible scenario is that after perhaps a century and a half of continued population growth had resulted in a density of population that was historically exceptional, the plague of AD 542, and subsequent outbreaks, reversed the process and produced a sustained population decline.[135] In the absence of other adverse factors populations recover surprisingly rapidly from the losses caused by epidemics. Even so recovery from the ravages of the Black Death of 1346 seems to have taken at least 100–130 years, and probably considerably longer.[136] In Macedonia the Black Death greatly reduced the population

[130] Durliat 1989: 107–19.

[131] Whittow 1996: 66–8.

[132] J. N. Biraben, 'La Peste du VIe siècle dans l'empire byzantin', in *Hommes et richesses*, i. 121–5.

[133] For references, see Stein 1949: 759 n. 1. The most important: Procop. II.22.1–21; Evagrius *HE* IV.29 with commentary in Allen 1981: 190–4; Agathias V.10; John of Ephesus, *Lives of Eastern Saints* 36; the same author's *Ecclesiastical History* preserved in Pseudo-Dionysius of Tel-Mahrē, *Chronicle*, Part III, tr. W. Witakowski, Liverpool Translated Texts for Historians 22 (Liverpool, 1996), 73–98; Mich. Syr. IX.28.32; *Chron Min* II.313–14; *La Vie ancienne de S. Syméon le Jeune*, ed. P. Van den Ven (Brussels, 1962), 69 (AD 542), 126–9 (AD 554). Conrad 1994: 12–58. On the prevalence of both plague and famine in 6th cent., see Patlagean 1977: 77–92.

[134] That there was a demographic calamity in Syria and Palestine is supported by Arab sources: see Conrad 1986: 143–63; also Conrad 1994: 12–58. Further literature cited by Haldon 1990: 111 n. On effect of Palestine, see also Dauphin 1998: ii. 511–18.

[135] The Black Death of 1348 also came at the end of a long period of sustained growth of population: McNeill 1976: 146–7.

[136] See Bridbury 1973: 573–93; ibid. 590–1: wages did not rise. But Ormrod and Lindley (1996: 26–45) argue for a very much slower rate of recovery and discuss reasons for that.

for at least fifty years.[137] But in the case of sixth-century Anatolia the Persian invasion and sustained Muslim raiding intervened before there could have been any significant recovery. These very destructive wars, involving as they did the plundering of livestock and the deportation of inhabitants, must have greatly increased the momentum of the decline.

But the plague cannot be the only explanation. High mortality leaves the survivors richer. So while it is not surprising that a severe visitation of plague should have left some urban areas depopulated, one would also expect the living to have thanked God for their survival by building churches. Churches certainly continued to be built in the hill-villages of northern Syria; so why not in Anatolia? Moreover, as we have seen, there are indications that the decline in some areas may have started before AD 542. At Miletus a gatehouse in a greatly shortened circuit of wall may well date from AD 538. So we must look for some additional factor or factors. Some suggestions are made in the last chapter, but essentially what is needed are more excavations and surveys.

3. *The Greek East: Pattern II. Syria, Palestine, and Arabia*

In the eastern areas of the Hellenistic classical world the evidence for urban development in late Late Antiquity falls into a different pattern. This can be observed at Side in Pamphylia,[138] further east in Cilicia-Isauria,[139] at Apamea[140] and other sites in eastern Syria, and finally in Palestine and in Arabia,[141] where Gerasa and Bostra[142] are the most fully documented sites. In sites all over this area there is an abundance of evidence, not only surface remains but also inscriptions, bearing witness to great activity in cities in the fifth, and also in the sixth century. It is the evidence from the sixth century that is particularly significant, for it gives the impression that in this century there was more building, and more ambitious building, not only of churches, but also of secular edifices in the cities of this region than in the cities of western and central Anatolia.

The evidence comes not only from cities, but also from numerous remains of villages, for instance in Cilicia, eastern Phrygia, the limestone massif in northern Syria, the Hauran, and the Negev.[143] A common

137 Lefort 1991: esp. 78–82 and J. M. Martin's comment, ibid. 84–5.

138 Robert 1958: 15–53.

139 *MAMA* III; Dagron and Feissel 1987.

140 J. Balty and J. C. Balty 1972; J. Balty 1984*a*; J. C. Balty 1989.

141 *IGLS* XI (*Inscriptions de la Jordanie*); X (*Inscriptions de Bostra*); Dentzer 1985.

142 Kraeling 1938; Sartre 1985.

143 Survey in Patlagean 1977: 307–13; Dentzer 1985; Tchalenko 1953–8; Dauphin and Schonfield 1983; Evenari 1971. Mitchell 1993: ii. 122–34: account of villages in western Galatia drawn from informative life of the abbot Theodore of Sykeon.

feature of all these areas is that the inscriptional habit came relatively late, and that late Roman inscriptions form a much higher proportion of surviving inscriptions than in the core lands of classical civilization. Moreover the epigraphic habit remained strong through most of the sixth century. With some regional exceptions this area seems to have prospered right up to the end of the sixth century. Furthermore buildings that imply prosperity are found in towns of every kind. The distinction between provincial capitals and ordinary provincial cities is much less sharp than in Anatolia. Splendid late Late Antique building schemes, both secular and ecclesiastical, have been excavated not only at Apamea, capital of Syria II,[144] Scythopolis, capital of Palestina II,[145] at Caesarea capital of Palestina I,[146] at Bostra capital of Arabia,[147] but also in the provincial cities of the Decapolis, east of the river Jordan, at Pella,[148] Gadara, Capitolias,[149] and Gerasa.[150] Among the smaller cities, the Cilician port of Korykus is remarkable for the number of its inscriptions. They are overwhelmingly funereal. A high proportion are late imperial and Christian, dating from the fourth to sixth centuries, and they provide us with something like the social profile of a small late Roman town.[151] Among 591 inscriptions no fewer than 408 commemorate craftsmen, with the great majority working in trades providing for the subsistence of their fellow townsmen. There are seventy-four members of the clergy or employees of the Church. The town had at least nine ecclesiastical institutions for looking after the poor. In format the inscriptions are remarkably egalitarian. The higher ranks of society did not receive significantly more elaborate epitaphs than craftsmen. There are five members of the council, one *illustris*, two *comites*, one *protector*, five *privatarii*, a *censitor*, a *censualis*. These were the notables, the *honorati*, of the place. They were not numerous nor particularly prominent, but they were no doubt among the *ktētores* (κτήτορες) who together with clergy and bishop elected the *defensor* and the *curator*.[152] The procedure for election was laid down in an edict of Anastasius, issued in reply to a petition by bishop, clergy, landowners, and inhabitants, who were

[144] J. C. Balty 1989: 89–96; J. Balty and J. C. Balty 1981: 41–75.

[145] Tsafrir and Foerster 1997.

[146] Vann 1992; on coins, see esp. Hohlfelder 1992: 167–8 and above, p. 24.

[147] Sartre 1985.

[148] McNicoll, Smith, *et al.* 1982; McNicoll, Edwards, *et al.* 1992; R. H. Smith, Day, *et al.* 1989.

[149] Gadara: Holm Nielsen *et al.* 1986; Boll, Hoffmann, and Weber 1990; Mulder and Guinée 1992; Vriezen 1992. Capitolias: Merschen and Knauf 1988; Lenzen and Knauf 1987. See also on Sepphoris: Netzer and Weiss 1995 and the general survey of cities in Byzantine Palestine and Arabia in Whittow 1990: 15–17, and in Walmsley 1996.

[150] Kraeling 1938; Zayadine 1986*a*.

[151] *MAMA* III. 197–788; Patlagean 1977: 158–69; Trombley 1987. For a social profile of an unknown proportion of the taxpaying landowners at Hermopolis in Egypt, see Gascou 1994: 60–4 and the tax register itself.

[152] *MAMA* III. 197A.

concerned that elections should not be fixed in advance by members of the provincial *officium*.[153] So this little town had a council, but its role was subordinate. It was no longer the voice of the city. Craftsmen and small traders are more prominent than they would have been in the epigraphy of a classical city.[154] Leading silversmiths (*argentarii*) like the *collectarii* at Rome may have had the important role of buying back solidi for the government with bronze coins which they thus helped to bring into circulation.[155]

To the east of Cilicia, in Syria and Arabia, villages have produced a very large number of late inscriptions.[156] Much less is known about the major cities. Epiphania (Hama)[157] and Emesa (Homs) have left few archaeological or epigraphic remains, principally because their sites are still densely built up. Late Roman Antioch is deeply buried.[158] Apamea however was abandoned in the Middle Ages. This has given the Baltys the opportunity to excavate the city which achieved the status of provincial capital around AD 415, and subsequently flourished exceedingly. After the earthquakes in AD 526 and 528 had destroyed much of Apamea, monumental colonnades, mansions, and churches were rebuilt, even though the agora was progressively abandoned. In AD 573 the city was burnt by the Persians and a large part of its population deported. From this date there is evidence of decline and impoverishment, though the destroyed monuments were rebuilt once more. It was only in the second quarter of the seventh century that the character of the city began to change radically, great mansions being clumsily remodelled into working farms.[159] There is considerable evidence that the cities of northern Syria were already weakened before the last and most destructive Persian war (AD 602–29). The coastal cities did not really recover before the coming of the Egyptian Fatimid dynasty in AD 969.[160] Nevertheless the seventh century did not bring about a collapse of urbanism in Syria comparable to that which happened in Asia Minor.[161]

[153] At Korykus there are 38 inscriptions of government officials, military or civil, against 5 of councillors. Similarly the tax register from Hermopolis lists 50 officials against only 3 councillors and 4/5 *defensores*, 2 *riparii*, 2 *nuctostrategoi* (νυκτοστράτηγοι), each of whom could have been a councillor, but need not have been (Gascou 1994: 61–2).

[154] Not only at Korykus: *IGLS* XIII.1, 9129, 9134 gold and silversmiths supervise building work at Bostra; at Constantinople money dealers formed a serious conspiracy, Malalas XVIII.493–4.

[155] See A. H. M. Jones 1964: 442 n.79 and Hendy 1985: 242–51 on Symmachus *Relatio* XXIX, also Carrié 1998*b*.

[156] Published in the series *IGLS*.

[157] But see now Pentz 1997.

[158] Downey 1961; Lassus 1977.

[159] J. C. Balty 1989: 79–96.

[160] Trombley 1997; H. Kennedy 1985*b*: 141–83; H. Kennedy 1992: 181–98; Conrad 1986.

[161] H. Kennedy 1992: 196–7. On urbanism in Syria, Palestine, and Arabia at the time of the Arab invasion and after, see also below, p. 313ff.

Penz has suggested that economic regression in northern Syria had a serious effect on the livelihood of the caravan trading tribes of Arabia in the late sixth and early seventh centuries, and that the resulting hardship was a principal motive for their invasion of the settled lands of Syria and Palestine under Islam.[162] This is an interesting hypothesis, but to date nothing more.

A number of the cities of Palestine evidently increased their populations in later Late Antiquity. The walled area of Caesarea was extended in the fifth century to enclose about 95 hectares, that of Tiberias in the sixth to enclose around 75 hectares.[163] Twenty-two towns of Byzantine Palestine and Arabia measured over 30 hectares, of which six ranged between 80 and 100 hectares, three being larger than 100 hectares. Jerusalem, the largest city, covered 120 hectares.[164] The archaeological evidence for flourishing urban life is parallelled by the findings of area surveys of rural districts: there too the late Late Roman period appears to have been a time of peak activity.[165]

Cities were of course changing. Churches rather than temples came to dominate the townscape.[166] Some temples were destroyed. We know most about a wave of destruction of temples in Syria around AD 390. This was instigated by the monks in the countryside, cooperating with bishops in the cities, among whom Marcellus of Apamea was the most active and fanatical.[167] Yet more often temples were simply allowed to decay, and their ruins, like that of the precinct of Artemis at Gerasa, and of a second-century temple in the very centre of Scythopolis, must have long continued to tower impressively over what were now Christian cities. Over the years an enormous number of churches were built in cities, towns, and villages.[168] But church building started quite slowly. Comparatively few churches were built in the fourth century. Construction gathered pace in the early fifth and reached a peak in the late fifth and early sixth centuries.[169] Eventually churches were extremely numerous. Fifteen have been identified at Gerasa, ten at Caesarea, five at Bostra, and no less than fifteen at Umm al-Jimal, which was in law only a village.[170]

162 Penz 1992: 68–73.

163 Walmsley 1996: 126–58, esp. 147–50.

164 Broshi 1979: 1–10.

165 Christie and Loseby 1996: 152, fig. 6.8 Esbus (Hesban), Kerak plateau, Ghor and Araba, Wâdî Yâbis; Dauphin 1998: 77–121 and maps of Byzantine sites, ibid. vol. ii, figs. 1–23; see also below, p. 299.

166 Schick 1995. A special case: Brenk 1995 on Christianization of Jewish city centre at Capernaum. The Christianization of Palestine is mapped in Dauphin 1998: vol. ii, figs. 43–107.

167 Libanius *Or.* XXX. *Pro templis*, text and English tr. by F. Norman, *Libanius Selected Works*, ii. 92–151; Sozomen *HE* VII.15; cf. Trombley 1993–4: ii. 283–9.

168 Ovadiah 1970; Donceel-Voûte 1988. Ulbert 1989: 429–57. Piccirillo 1989: 459–502. Dufay 1989: 637–50.

169 N. Duval 1994: 149–212.

170 Figures from Walmsley 1996: 138; B. De Vries 1998.

In the course of our period, and well before there was a real threat of invasion, most cities had been given a circuit of walls.[171] Caesarea, Scythopolis,[172] and Jerusalem received new colonnaded streets.[173] Walls, colonnaded streets, and churches were now the defining feature of urban civilization. Floors with mosaic representations of local cities became popular in Syria and Arabia at this time, and their simplified and schematic design emphasizes above all walls, gates, colonnaded streets, and churches. Theatres, amphitheatres, and agoras, on the other hand, were often abandoned.[174]

Infilling of public spaces, and the building of more or less permanent commercial structures between the columns of monumental colonnades, occurred here, as it did in Asia Minor. The installation of more or less permanent shops in the colonnades of monumental streets is particularly well evidenced at Scythopolis/Bet Shean. The occupation of what had been a monumental gateway to a temple complex by industrial structures happened as early as the fourth century. Infilling of colonnades and extensive encroachment on to the roadway by more or less makeshift structures became increasingly prevalent towards the end of the sixth century, though it is evidently difficult to date in detail.[175] This is likely to reflect a decline of the city itself, as well as a weakening of its administration.[176]

At Caesarea the building of shops into the colonnades of the monumental streets has not been observed, though building did encroach on the pedestrian way of Decumanus 3.[177] At some time a large zone in the south of the city was abandoned, and subsequently laid out in garden plots with irrigation channels.[178] Unfortunately, the date when the Late Antique buildings of this area were abandoned is still uncertain. It could be that the ruralization of part of Caesarea only occurred well into the seventh century, but it seems that no Arabic pottery has so far been found in the building remains of that area.[179]

One would not have expected significant urban decline at Caesarea

[171] J. Wood 1992: 125–7.

[172] See also below, pp. 300–3.

[173] Holum and Hohlfelder 1988: 175–6. Tsafrir and Foerster 1997: 101–2. Avigdad 1984: 213–46.

[174] Images of cities: see Avi-Yonah 1954; Dekkers 1989; Bertelli 1999. Theatres, amphitheatres, and hippodromes: Segal 1995; Tsafrir and Foerster 1997: 131–5.

[175] For references to preliminary reports, see Tsafrir and Foerster 1997: nn. 17–18. For current interpretations, ibid. 116–26 ('boom' of late 5th and early 6th cents.), ibid. 140–6 (infilling and encroachment in last decade of Byzantine rule). The so-called 'Byzantine shops' in 'Sylvanus Street' are now thought to be Umayyad (ibid. 138–9).

[176] Cf. below, p. 302.

[177] Porath 1996: esp. 116–17.

[178] Vann 1992: 99–100.

[179] Information from K. G. Holum, A. Raban, and J. Patrich (eds.), *Caesarea Papers*, ii, Herod's temple, the praetorium and granaries, the later harbour, a gold coin hoard, and other studies, Journal of Roman Archaeology Supplement (Ann Arbor, forthcoming).

since the city remained the most important military base and centre of administration in Palestine right up to the Arab conquest. So why did it happen? Explanations vary according to the dating favoured by the explainer. Lasting damage resulting from the Samaritan revolts of AD 529–30 and 556 has been one suggestion. The reduction of the city's water supply when an aqueduct was interrupted through subsidence on marshy ground has been another. Holum is of the opinion that the major destructive layer is more likely to date from the seventh than the sixth century, and could indeed be later still, and need not by any means be interpreted as evidence of hostile attack.[180] The fact that Caesarea lost its function as the principal link between the imperial capital and its Palestinian provinces must have inflicted lasting damage on the city. But there seems to be evidence that a decline in trade set in well before the Arab conquest. Judging by ceramic evidence, imports at Caesarea peaked in the fifth century and had shrunk to almost nothing by the seventh.[181] A probable explanation would be that the harbour walls were subsiding and the inner harbour silting up, making the port unattractive for shipping. So any decline of the Caesarea probably had local causes, and need not reflect deteriorating conditions in the region of Palestine as a whole.

Among the Arabian sites, Bostra[182] and Gerasa[183] are exceptionally informative because they not only have extensive remains of buildings, but have also yielded many late inscriptions. In both places there was considerable building activity in Late Antiquity, reaching a peak in each city in the first half of the sixth century. At Bostra most of the building was military or ecclesiastical. The walls were maintained, and many churches built, some to a sophisticated design, but generally, as is characteristic of building in this period, using spolia rather than stone cut for the purpose. Political life shows the same trends as elsewhere. The civic magistrates are last mentioned, in connection with building projects in AD 320 and 325.[184] The council does not figure in late inscriptions at all, but there is reference to a decurion supervising work on the governor's palace as late as AD 490.[185] Some building work was financed by individuals who were neither decurions nor officials.[186] Goldsmiths and silversmiths are mentioned as taking part in the administration of building. Most secular work was ordered by the military commanders.[187] Some work was ordered by the

180 Holum 1992.

181 Oleson 1996: 359–80, esp. summary 363–5, see also Blakely 1996: 327–45, esp. fig. 3, p. 338: few amphorae imported AD 525–75; Oleson *et al.* 1994: esp. 79 and 159.

182 Sartre 1982, 1985.

183 Kraeling 1938.

184 Sartre 1982 = *IGLS* XIII.1, no. 9111–12. Unfortunately many Bostra inscriptions were found out of their original context.

185 Ibid. 9123.

186 9124, church or chapel built by a *notarius*.

187 Goldsmiths and silversmiths: 9129, 9134; *duces:* 9115–16, 9127.

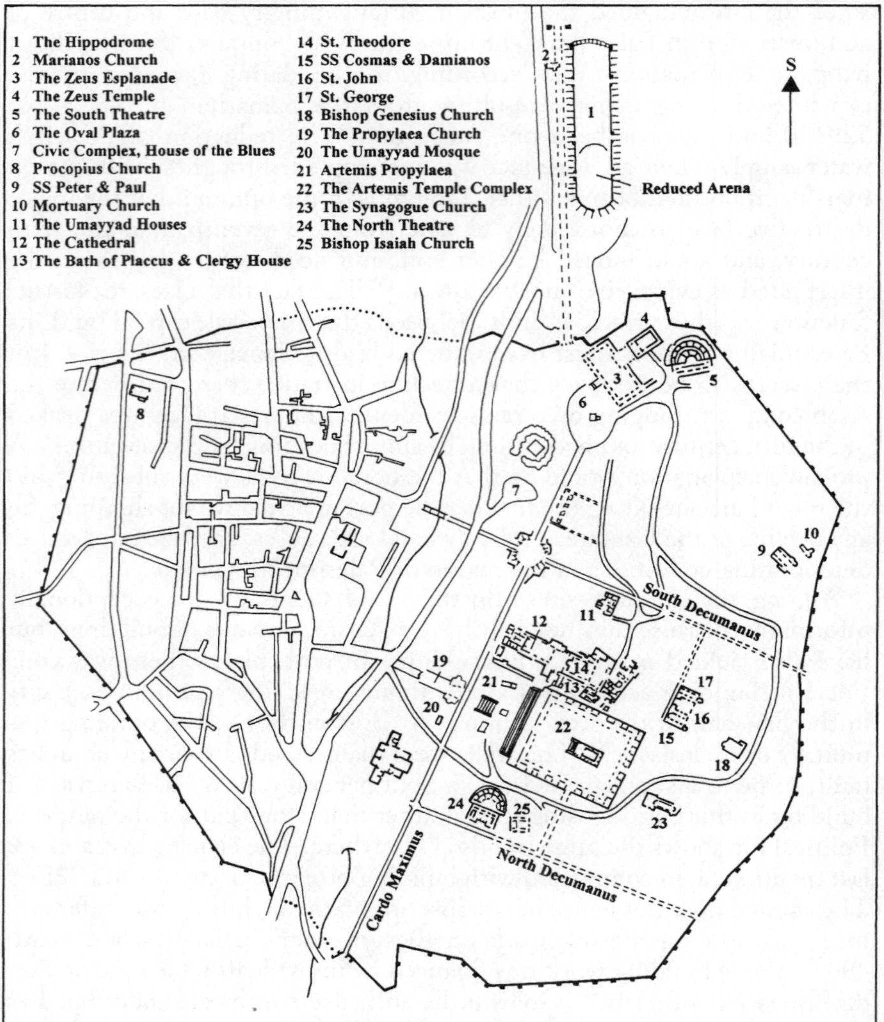
1 The Hippodrome
2 Marianos Church
3 The Zeus Esplanade
4 The Zeus Temple
5 The South Theatre
6 The Oval Plaza
7 Civic Complex, House of the Blues
8 Procopius Church
9 SS Peter & Paul
10 Mortuary Church
11 The Umayyad Houses
12 The Cathedral
13 The Bath of Placcus & Clergy House
14 St. Theodore
15 SS Cosmas & Damianos
16 St. John
17 St. George
18 Bishop Genesius Church
19 The Propylaea Church
20 The Umayyad Mosque
21 Artemis Propylaea
22 The Artemis Temple Complex
23 The Synagogue Church
24 The North Theatre
25 Bishop Isaiah Church
S
Reduced Arena
South Decumanus
North Decumanus
Cardo Maximus
0
500
Metres
After R.E. Pillen

7. Gerasa in Late Antiquity

magister militum per Orientem.[188] The emperor Justinian provided financial support for a great deal of building at Bostra, for restoration of an aqueduct, for work on fortifications, for at least one church and for an almshouse.[189] It is significant that the bishop was involved in the administration not only of the building of churches, but also of secular and military work: a subsidy for fortification had been urged to the emperor by the bishop on an embassy,[190] and he played some part—though short of actually supervising the work—in the construction of the city's new defences.[191]

The pattern of activities witnessed by inscriptions from Gerasa is very similar to that at Bostra, though here the epigraphic evidence has been supplemented by the evidence of excavation.[192] Temples were abandoned but not systematically destroyed: much of the temple of Zeus survived until the early twentieth century. In the second half of the sixth century what had been the lower terrace of the temple was occupied by workshops and rural housing.[193] The two theatres decayed. Part of the former hippodrome ceased to be used for public entertainment, and the disused area came to be occupied by simple houses, workshops, and even burials. Parts of the cavea of the hippodrome collapsed.[194] There was encroachment of various kinds on the monumental colonnades. Makeshift structures invaded the south *cardo* and the oval forum.[195] They are now no longer visible since their remains were removed in the course of the excavations in the early 1930s.[196] There was a considerable amount of new building in the later fifth and early sixth centuries. This included work on fortification, ordered by a military commander, but also non-military building. A bathhouse was constructed at the expense of an *agens in rebus*. A portico was put up by a *scholasticus* and the *defensor* in AD 447.[197] In 454/7 bishop Placcas paid for a small baths complex next to the cathedral.[198] No fewer than thirteen churches are known. At least eight of them date from the sixth century: five from the years 526–33,[199] and

188 9118 of 438.

189 9127–37, Procop. *Aed.* V.9.

190 9134.

191 9130, 9135, 9136.

192 Kraeling 1938; Zayadine 1986*a*.

193 Seigne 1986*a* and *b*, 1989; Rasson and Seigne 1989.

194 Ostrasz 1989: 51–77.

195 Kraeling 1938: 103–5, 113–15; and C. S. Fisher, 'the forum'; ibid. 152–8. Harding 1949 dates the encroachment on the forum as late as the 8th cent.

196 Gawlikowski 1992: 357–61.

197 Kraeling 1938: no. 275.

198 Ibid., no. 296.

199 On churches, see Crowfoot 1931 and 1938; on their mosaics, F. M. Biebel in Kraeling 1938: 297–352.

four others are dated by mosaic inscriptions to respectively, 559,[200] 565, 570,[201] and 611. The latest year in which building is recorded at Gerasa is AD 629.[202] No doubt the Church made a major contribution to the expense, but individual donors, lay and clerical, are mentioned too. So much activity, in what was not a provincial capital, points to a generally flourishing condition of this region.[203]

Nevertheless a qualification must be made. Building on public space need not be proof that the population of the city was still growing. In fact there is evidence that large areas around the northern decumanus and the north theatre were abandoned around the end of the fifth century.[204] The houses and workshops that had sprung up in part of the hippodrome were already abandoned in the middle of the sixth century, and those on the terrace of Zeus in the middle of the seventh.[205] The cathedral, in the centre of the town, was badly damaged by fire in the late sixth, or early seventh century, and in the subsequent restoration five western bays were not rebuilt.[206] At Bostra the apparent cessation of building around AD 540–1, that is just before the plague, may suggest that the city did not fully recover from that disaster.[207] At Petra the agora was destroyed in an earthquake in 363, and it appears never to have been rebuilt.[208] So while in the later sixth century the cities of Arabia and Palestine were certainly in a much better state than those of northern Syria it may be that they too had passed their peak of population and prosperity. Nevertheless, it does seem to be the case unlike northern Syria, Palestine and Arabia appear to have continued to enjoy much of their Late Antique prosperity through the sixth century to the time of the Arab conquest, and even beyond that.[209] Village churches were still being built after churches had ceased to be erected in cities. To the south of Gerasa, church building continued into the seventh century, and in villages around Madaba until AD 756 and

200 V. A. Clark in Zayadine 1986*a*: 303–18.

201 M. Gawlikowski and A. Musa in Zayadine 1986*a*: 137–62.

202 Zayadine 1986*a*: 16–18, 137–62, 303–41. Judging by available evidence the church building at Gerasa in the 6th cent. was much more impressive than that of the famous cities of Asia, e.g. Sardis, Miletus, Pergamum, and even Ephesus—apart from the church of St John.

203 As summarized by Walmsley 1996; Whittow 1990: 14–18; and H. Kennedy 1985*a*.

204 W. Ball, J. Bowsher, I. Kehrberg, A. Walmsley, P. Watson in Zayadine 1986*a*: 351–93, summary 392–3. Cf. Watson 1992*a*: 163–81 on Pella.

205 Rasson and Seigne 1989: 117–67, esp. 149–51; Ostrasz 1989: 51–77, esp. 74–7.

206 Brenk, Jäggi, and Meier 1995 and 1997.

207 The latest inscriptions: *IGLS* XIII.1, 540–1, but Bostra has not been excavated.

208 Koenen 1996: 177–91, relevant 187; see also Fiema 1995: 1–3: the ecclesiastical complex was destroyed after AD 582, the latest date on a papyrus from the archive, and it was not rebuilt. See also Fiema, 'The church, the papyri, and the late Byzantine-Early Islamic Petra: Historical notes', ch. 22 in the Petra Church Project Publication (forthcoming).

209 Crowfoot 1931: 4, iconoclastic mutilation of mosaics in all but one of the churches suggests that they were still standing and in use in AD 717–20. See also below, p. 295ff.

785.[210] Looking at the evidence available at the time of writing, it still seems that on the whole,[211] it was the end of the Umayyad dynasty in AD 750 and the transfer of the capital of the caliphate from Damascus to Bagdad which marked a turning point in the condition of both towns and villages in Syria, Palestine, and Arabia—and not only there.[212]

4. *Greater Prominence of Villages and the Ascetic Movement*

A feature of Late Antiquity is the greater prominence of villages.[213] Of course, the word 'village' covers a great variety of settlements ranging from what we might describe as small towns to hamlets of only a few houses. What distinguished a city from a village in Roman law was that a city had been declared a unit of administration by the Roman government, and made responsible for the administration of all settlements, large and small, in a territory assigned to it.[214] The character of villages and their relationship to their city differed from region to region, and was influenced perhaps more than anything by the size of a city's territory and the distance between city and village. In inland Anatolia, i.e. in Phrygia, Lydia, Galatia, and Pisidia, small cities had huge territories, and villages were the dominant form of settlement. In many areas the villages had existed since time immemorial, in others agriculture and sedentary life was a consequence of Roman occupation, and villages as well as towns owed their existence to Roman rule.[215] Subordination to a city or to a great landlord did not necessarily mean poverty and oppression for the villages. It is clear that some villages flourished under Roman rule, and managed to maintain a culture of their own, which was independent of that of their ruling city.[216] The evidence is almost entirely epigraphic, but it enables us to see some aspects of village society very clearly, above all the role of the traditional religion in upholding law and order, and the early and rapid spread of Christianity in the course of the second and third centuries.[217]

[210] While in northern Syria there was little building in villages after AD 600, cf. below, p. 71.

[211] This is the impression left by Zayadine 1986*a* and 1989 for Gerasa. But see Walmsley 1992*a* and Whitcomb 1992, and below, pp. 304–5.

[212] See below, p. 314.

[213] P.-L. Gatier explains ('Villages du proche-orient protobyzantin (4ème–7ème)' in G. D. R. King and Cameron (1994), 25): the defining characteristic of a city is that it has subject villages. The large settlements in the Negev (e.g. Esbeita 390 m. x 290 m. or Nessana) though often described as cities were, in law, villages subject to the cities of Elusa or Mampsis. So were the large settlements in the limestone massif, like el-Bara in the Djebel Zawiyé (1 km. × 2 km.) or Brad (about 700 m. × 500 m.), or in Jordan Umm al-Jimal about the same size as Brad. A large village might well have more inhabitants than a city, and might have as important, or more important, an economic role. But both secular and ecclesiastical administration was centred in the city.

[214] A. H. M. Jones 1964: 712–18.

[215] Mitchell 1993: i. 148–62.

[216] Ibid. 176–96.

[217] Ibid., ii. 100–8.

On the other hand, except in Rough Cilicia and Isauria, the houses of villages of the Early Empire have left few visible remains, and the literary sources are very little concerned with village life.

In Late Antiquity villages became more prominent in several ways. The remains of stone-built, almost monumental, villages have been found east of the Orontes in Syria, in the Hauran, in Galilee, Judaea, and the Negev in Palestine,[218] and around Bostra and Amman in Arabia.[219] There are remains of Late Roman villages in the hills of Cilicia,[220] and along the coast of Lycia.[221] In the pre-desert of Tripolitania where settlements reached a maximum density as early as the second century the picture was different. From the third century there is a shift away from the southern reaches of the cultivated wadis, and a tendency for dwellings to cluster around fortified farmhouses (*gasr,* plural *gsur*) further north. This change did not necessarily result in a fall in population, at least not in the short run.[222] The 'gsur system' does however strongly suggest that there had been a change in social structure, with the effect that leadership together with responsibility for defence, was taken over by the owners of the fortified farms.[223]

The conspicuous remains of villages are mostly in areas that have been scantily inhabited in later times. It remains an open question whether comparable Late Roman villages once existed, for instance, in western Syria or the coastal belt of Asia Minor, that is in areas which have been continuously inhabited, so that remains of Late Antiquity have been obscured by later constructions. But in some of these areas too, for instance in Palestine and Lebanon, archaeologists have uncovered foundations of substantial churches with elaborate and artistic mosaic floors. This suggests that monumental village architecture was not restricted to marginal land and the desert fringe.[224] In Syria and Palestine the areas where mosaics have been found do not overlap with those that have monumental remains of rural temples.[225] In Egypt villages have left no stone remains, and there has so far been very little excavation.[226] However, it is evident from papyrus documents that large villages with

218 See above, p. 57 n. 165; also Dauphin 1987; Sodini and Tate 1980.

219 Donceel-Voûte 1988. Building in villages goes on longer than in cities: Sartre 1985: 136–8.

220 See *MAMA* III and *TIB* V.

221 See above, p. 42.

222 Though it does look as if the whole province was beginning to run down from the late 4th cent., see D. Mattingly in Barker (ed.) and others 1996: 337–42. The whole volume is an important in-depth examination of the history of life in the Tripolitarian pre-desert in the light of remains of buildings, irrigation works, animal and plant remains, and historical texts.

223 Mattingly 1995: 203–9.

224 See maps in Donceel-Voûte 1988: 14, 442.

225 D. Krenker and W. Tschietzschman, *Römische Tempel in Syrien* (Berlin/Leipzig, 1938), map.

226 Bagnall 1993: 6–7: many mounds have been destroyed this century, metres of silt cover Roman levels of occupation. But see plan of Early Empire Karanis in the Fayum, ibid., plate 4.

elders, craftsmen, and prosperous peasants did exist there.[227] Aphrodito in the territory of Antaeopolis was probably larger than its city. It certainly had many characteristics of a city, including some highly literate inhabitants.[228]

City and village continued to be linked administratively, but this does not mean that their relations were unchanged. There is some evidence for greater independence of villages, though on a secular level this is difficult to prove. There is for instance no clear evidence that in the East landowners transferred their principal residence to the country in significant numbers.[229] In Egypt some villagers obtained the privilege of *autopragia*, that is the right to collect the imperial taxes of the village themselves.[230] Outside Egypt the political and administrative relations between villages and the city are far from clear. How were the villages administered, how were the taxes collected, and how were law and order maintained? If the administration of taxes, justice, and police was not in the hands of officials from the local city, it must have been in that of village officials. There is in fact very little epigraphic evidence from the Syrian villages for activity by officials, whether civic or imperial or even ecclesiastical, from the city. The bishop is occasionally mentioned on donors' inscriptions of rural churches in Syria and Palestine, but in the great majority of such inscriptions all the names, whether cleric or lay, are those of villagers.[231]

Villages had headmen, but only relatively very few inscriptions in the villages on the North Syrian massif mention them.[232] In the hill districts of the Hauran villages have left very many inscriptions which bear witness to the existence of institutions of local self-government. However, these cease in the fifth and sixth centuries,[233] and this fact needs to be explained. Gatier has suggested alternative explanations.[234]

[227] Bagnall 1993: 133–8: in the 4th cent. village officials and communal organization in Egypt were almost exclusively concerned with the performance of obligations imposed by the metropolis or the imperial administration.

[228] MacCoull 1988: 5–9.

[229] P.-L. Gatier, 'Inscriptions métrique de Jordanie', *SHAJ* 4 (1992), 291–4, argues that the presence of metrical tombstones in villages around Madaba implies the movement of some of the educated well-to-do to the villages.

[230] See below, p. 67.

[231] In Donceel-Voûte 1988 most inscriptions naming the bishop are from cities in the Orontes valley.

[232] *Pentaprōtoi* (πεντάπρωτοι): *IGLS* 684 (Kafr Lata AD 449). D. Feissel, 'Bull epigr', *REG* 102 (1989), 498, no. 972 (not localized). 4 *gerontes* (γέροντες) and *pentaprōtoi* at Haouarte: J.-P. Rey-Coquais in *Huarte: Sanctuaire chrétien d'Apamène*, ed. P. Canivet and M. T. Canivet (Paris, 1987), 53–4. Dekaprōtoi (δεκάπρωτοι) at Has, AD 338, Tchalenko (1953–8): iii. 35–6. *Kōmarch* (κωμάρχης) at el-Meshréfé, *IGLS* 908, cf. 1905. Hir esh Sheikh (n. of Apamea) *pentaprōtoi* Donceel-Voûte 1988: 118 n. 11. *Prōtos* (πρῶτος) at Soughan'e (n. of Djebel Sem'an), ibid. 314.

[233] Sartre 1991: 328–32.

[234] 'Villages du proche-orient protobyzantin (4ème–7ème)', in G. R. D. King and Cameron (1994), 39–40.

(1) When Jerusalem became a patriarchate a number of large villages were given city status and bishops so that the new patriarch should have subordinates. This development destroyed the autonomy of the remaining villages.

(2) Gradually all collective functions in the villages came to be undertaken by the local clergy.

Gatier favours the second option, proposing that the church eventually took charge of all collective activities in most of the villages in the Hauran and elsewhere in the Near East.[235] This remains to be proved. It would be very important if true. But is it right? The argument is based on the silence of inscriptions. But this could be misleading. After all secular public inscriptions cease in cities too, and there the church did not take over routine administration.

The village of Nessana in the Negev certainly had corporate identity in law, seeing that tax demands were addressed to the villagers collectively. We have one document dating from after the Arab conquest, acknowledging the receipt of taxes by a group of inhabitants of the village led by an 'archon'.[236] This body looks like a committee of village headmen responsible for the collection of taxes. We also hear of an administrator (*dioikētēs*/διοικητής) who received orders from Gaza to collect levies, and of a 'public place' (*dēmosios topos*/δημόσιος τόπος), perhaps the village office, where heirs make public declaration of the division of an inheritance.[237] The fact that the surviving administrative documents of Nessana come from the archive of the abbots of a local monastery, who were all members of the same family,[238] need only show that the abbot was involved in village administration as one of the local magnates, not that he ran the administration by virtue of his monastic office. If there was a sizeable monastery in a village, the abbot could hardly fail to have been one of the most influential villagers, the equal at least of the leading local landowners.[239]

In Egypt the great landowners, the 'houses', performed important administrative functions; and churches and monasteries were subjected to public duties such as the transport of tax-corn for other landowners.[240] At the same time the villages did have their own leaders, and a large village might have leading men of some stature and education, such as the poet

[235] Ibid. 42.

[236] Kraemer 1958: 168–71, no. 58.

[237] See Kraemer 1958: 202–3, no. 70; 209–11, no. 74; both of AD 695. The 'public place', ibid. 91–3, no. 30.

[238] Ibid. 6–8.

[239] Ibid. 160–7, no. 57 of AD 689 records a divorce negotiated in front of the head of the monastery, two priests, and four laymen.

[240] See below, p. 190.

and lawyer Dioscoros of Aphrodito.[241] At Aphrodito the larger peasants evidently enjoyed some self-government, and as the village was *autopract*, they were responsible for collecting the taxes from some of the land in the village territory. In strict law they were outside the authority of the pagarch in the city of Antaeopolis: they were liable to receive orders from him nevertheless.[242] All in all one gets the impression that village officials of Egypt were more concerned with fiscal and other duties owed by the villages to the imperial administration than with village self-government.[243]

It is significant that the inscriptions of lay donors of a mosaic floor for the village church do not normally record secular rank—though some of them must surely have had it. The hierarchical rank of clerical donors was regularly recorded.[244] The vast majority of collective building projects in villages were ecclesiastical. It looks as if the secular village authorities hardly every initiated public building schemes, and rarely even participated in the building or decorating of churches. If villagers possessed a sense of collective identity it was as members of the Church. Moreover his literacy and his links with the wider ecclesiastical organization as well as the prestige of his calling made the village priest the natural spokesman for ordinary villagers.[245] In fact many will not previously have had so influential a patron—but this does not mean that village government was a standard part of the priest's duty.[246]

The position of the village vis-à-vis the city was strengthened by the success of the ascetic movement. Monasteries were mostly situated in the countryside,[247] and even though they might be situated on the edge of the desert, they were generally not very far from inhabited localities. In some areas, for instance the Tur Abdin in Mesopotamia, in northern Syria,[248] and in Palestine on the edge of the desert to the east of Jerusalem,[249] there were large concentrations of monasteries. Elsewhere, as in western Galatia, the setting of the *Life* of Theodore of Sykeon, monasteries

241 About Dioscorus, see below, p. 230; but *P. Haun* III.58 of AD 439 shows twelve *presbyteroi* (πρεσβύτεροι) and five deacons heading a statement forbidding the interception of water at Karanis. In this case, leadership was clearly with the clergy.

242 G. Poethke, 'Metrocomiae und Autopragie in Ägypten', in P. Nagel (ed.), *Graeco-Coptica* (Halle, 1984), 37–44.

243 See articles of J. G. Keenan 1981: 479–85, 1984: 557–83, 1985: 137–69. For a systematic view, but mainly based on 3rd-cent. evidence, see Drecoll 1997: 201–7 and 274–5.

244 Donceel-Voûte 1988: *passim*.

245 A few examples in Bagnall 1993: 224–5; see also the dossier of *hiereis* (ἱερεῖς), Gascou 1994: 66–70.

246 See below, pp. 151–53, for the same argument applied to the office of the bishop in the city.

247 Vööbus 1958–60; Tchalenko 1953–8: iii. 63–106; P. Brown 1971; Hirschfeld 1992; Palmer 1990.

248 Tchalenko 1953–8: iii. 86–106.

249 Hirschfeld 1992: pp. xviii–xix; Patrich 1995.

were more widely dispersed, but still quite numerous. In Asia Minor monasteries tended to be concentrated in particular areas, notably in the neighbourhood of Constantinople, in western Cappadocia, and in Lycaonia north of Laranda.[250] It is likely that there was some continuity between Late Antique and Byzantine monasticism, but more often than not the Byzantine monasteries represent a new start, a revival of the Late Antique forms of religious life without any institutional continuity. Most of the known Byzantine monasteries were founded in the Middle Byzantine period from the seventh century onwards.[251] In Egypt monasteries were very numerous indeed, around Aphrodito for instance there were no fewer than forty monasteries.[252] Some of the Pachomian monasteries were very large.[253] All these institutions benefited from donations and legacies,[254] not only from villagers but also from townspeople and pilgrims.[255] Much of this went into buildings of a solidity and quality not previously seen in the countryside. So the existence of monasteries must have diverted resources from towns. However their economic impact certainly varied considerably from place to place, according to whether they were sited within reach of a city or inaccessibly on the margin of the desert. Not a few monasteries contributed to the wealth of their region by their own agricultural production.[256]

Monasteries provided villages with patrons able to defend them against demands from the city and elsewhere. Heads of monasteries with a reputation for holiness acquired great influence and power. Their connections reached far beyond the neighbourhood of the monastery, and in a few cases to the emperor himself. Such a one was Theodore of Sykeon head of a monastery in north-eastern Galatia who was called in to solve problems in other villages, and was evidently revered over a very wide area. Theodore frequently and successfully interceded for villagers with

[250] Mitchell 1993: ii. 116–19; a monastery with large estates on military road in south-west Pisidia: *CIL* III. 13640 = Grégoire no. 314.

[251] R. Morris, *Monks and Laymen in Byzantium 843–1118* (Cambridge, 1995), 20–2. L. Rodley, *Cave Monasteries of Byzantine Cappadocia* (Cambridge, 1985): hermitages 9th–11th; monasteries late 10th–late 11th.

[252] MacCoull 1988: 7.

[253] Rousseau 1985.

[254] The monasteries of the Judaean desert, and perhaps desert monasteries elsewhere, received most of their donations in money or food: Hirschfeld 1992: 102–11.

[255] The enclosed agricultural areas associated with the monasteries on the limestone massif are small: around a dozen examined range between 0.3 to 3 ha., with one 11 ha. See J. P. Fourdrin, *Contributions françaises à l'archéologie syrienne 1969–89* (Damascus, 1989), 198–201. But monasteries are likely to have received donations of land scattered much more widely, like the *oratorium sancti apostoli Ioannis* in south-western Pisidia, *CIL* III.13640. On manner of growth of estates of later monasteries, esp. on Athos, see Morris 1995: 120–42. Wipszycka 1972: 3, 75–7: far more donations to monasteries have survived on Egyptian papyri than to churches, but this reflects the greater survival of monastic documents.

[256] Hirschfeld 1992: 104–11.

threatening potentates from the city: landlords lay and ecclesiastical, tax-collectors, and the provincial governor himself. He several times visited Constantinople and was in communication with the emperor Maurice,[257] who privileged Theodore's monastery by taking it out of the jurisdiction of the local bishop and subjecting it to that of the patriarch of Constantinople. He also gave it the right of asylum.[258] Nicholas of Sion, abbot of a monastery in the neighbourhood of Myria in Lycia, had a wide-spread practice as a miraculous healer in the hill-villages of Lycia. He rarely if ever used his powers in the city, but the authorities in the city knew about him, especially during the plague of AD 541–2. In Lycia this visitation evidently amounted to a catastrophe, a catastrophe moreover which struck cities noticeably more devastatingly than villages; so much so, that peasants ceased to bring their produce to urban markets. At Myra the authorities blamed Nicholas for this, and accused him of having organized a boycott of Myra among the peasants who normally supplied the city with its food. Men were sent to arrest him. But the villagers rallied on his behalf and prevented the arrest. Subsequently Nicholas set out on a tour of the villages, slaughtering oxen and feasting with the villagers.[259] Both Theodore and Nicholas became bishops.[260] Both preferred the monastic life, and eventually resigned, Theodore after he had been bishop for eleven years. He evidently felt an incompatibility between his new responsibility as bishop and landlord of church property, and his accustomed role as protector of villagers and rural monasteries.[261]

More formidable than either Theodore or Nicholas was Shenoute of Atripe, abbot of the White Monastery near Panopolis in Egypt, who ruled over hundreds of monks, ruthlessly suppressed pagan shrines in his neighbourhood, championed the poor, and acted as spokesman for the region to imperial officials.[262] Another powerful abbot was Sabas who in AD 483 founded the Great Lavra in Palestine on the desert fringe between Bethlehem and the Dead Sea.[263] He went on to organize four more Lavras, six coenobia, and six hospices. He became the recognized leader of all the lavrite monks in Palestine, and did more than anybody else to win Palestine for Chalcedonism. On two occasions Sabas travelled to Constantinople to request tax relief for Palestine from the emperor

257 Mitchell 1993: ii. 122–50. The anonymous *Life* of Theodore of Sykeon is cited in the edition of J. Festugière (1970), 147–8, under the title *Vie de Théodore*.

258 Ibid. 82.

259 The *Life* of Nicholas of Sion is cited in the edition of I. Sevcenko (1984) and under the title *Life of Nicholas*. On plague, chs. 47–57.

260 Ibid. 68 consecrated bishop of Pinara, 71 back in monastery at Sion.

261 *Vie de Théodore*, 75–9.

262 Leipoldt 1903; Van der Vliet 1993; Trombley 1993–4: ii. 207–19.

263 Cf. Patrich 1995; Hirschfelt 1992; Binns 1994.

Anastasius.[264] There were many other formidable abbots in Palestine, Egypt, and Mesopotamia.[265] Yet a celebrated hermit might exercise as much power as an abbot. Simeon Stylites the Elder was only the most celebrated of many. We know about these men from 'Lives' which usually, but not always, celebrate their hero from his own village-centred point of view.[266] The patronage of holy men like these must have greatly strengthened the position of villagers vis-à-vis landlord and tax-collectors.[267]

It is a feature of the monastic movement in the East that it was largely independent of the magnates, whether lay or secular, of the cities. Typically monasteries were founded by 'holy men', or at least by pious lay-men, and not by the great men of the Empire or by bishops.[268] All the names mentioned earlier were 'orthodox'. But it is significant that the Monophysite movement, which for much of the time was built up in defiance of the emperor and established orthodoxy,[269] was centred on monasteries and villages.[270] The Monophysites developed a liturgy and theology in Syriac or Coptic, the languages spoken by the majority of villagers in Syria and Egypt, but not by the upper classes in the towns, nor used in the operations of the imperial administration. This amounted to a major cultural and political change, and a challenge to the age-long cultural and political monopoly of the towns.

The question arises how the flourishing condition of villages affected cities. On the view that the Greco-Roman city was a consumer city, existing parasitically at the expense of the countryside, prosperity in cities would necessarily result in impoverished villages and vice versa. This was certainly not the case in the late Late Roman Near East. By far the best known part of the region is the North Syrian limestone massif with its hill-villages about which G. Tchalenko wrote a classic study forty years or so ago. Recent work of which that of G. Tate is the most important by

[264] K. Hay, 'The Impact of St Sabas', in P. Allen and E. Jeffreys (eds.), *The Sixth Century End or Beginning?* (Brisbane, 1996), 118–25.

[265] *Cyril of Scythopolis*, ed. E. Schwartz, Texte und Untersuchungen 49/2 (Leipzig, 1939). French trans. in A.-J. Festugière, *Les Moins d'Orient*, 7 vols. (Paris, 1961–5). English trans.: Cyril of Scythopolis, *Lives of the Monks of Palestine*, Cistercian Studies 114 (Kalamazoo, Mich., 1991).

[266] P. Brown 1971; Festugière 1959; Rousseau 1985.

[267] *Vie de Théodore* 148: peasants flee tax-collector into asylum of monastery; 147: various cases of intercession; 151: intercedes for peasants with deputy of governor; 150: settles violent dispute between two villages.

[268] Dagron 1989: ii. 1069–85, describes a comparable state of affairs in the capital. Theodore of Sykeon built his monastery and its churches at least in part out of his own inheritance (Festugière 1970: 40, 55). If the *Life* is to be believed he was the illegitimate son of the hostess of an inn (ibid. 3).

[269] Frend 1972: 136–41.

[270] Village-centred Monophysite movement: Frend 1972: 294, 325–6, 333–4. J. Meyendorf, *Imperial Unity and Christian Divisions* (Crestwood, NY, 1989).

far, has somewhat modified Tchalenko's conclusions.[271] Tchalenko's view that the 'Massif' was cultivated largely by peasant proprietors seems to have held. Few estates have been identified, either by inscriptions or by property walls. The villages were not linked by a road network, only by tracks, apart from the road from Antioch to Chalkis, which bisects the massif. The villages had neither shops nor workshops. Tchalenko's identification of specialized buildings has been disproved. The villages were simply assemblies of peasants' dwellings, the roads mere paths, the open spaces no more than unbuilt-on pieces of land. The structures identified by Tchalenko as communal were not such at all.

It has also now been established that the economy of the hill-villages did not from the start depend overwhelmingly on the monoculture of olives. The villagers engaged in arable farming and animal rearing as well as the growing of vines and olive plantations. In the course of the fifth and early sixth centuries the importance of the olive sector increased. It was this which made it possible to maintain a very much enlarged population without seemingly reducing the standard of living. But production of oil was nearly always on a farm or domestic scale, there were no large units of the kind found in North Africa.[272] The effect of this revision of Tchalenko is to make it likely that the North Syrian cities provided an adequate market for the oil produced on the massif. Development of the oil production in this area, in contrast to the production of wine around Gaza, was not driven by overseas exports. This means that the prosperity of the countryside, indeed the viability of the economy of the countryside, was closely linked to that of the North Syrian cities. It follows that far from being oppressed and exploited by the cities these villages prospered by servicing them.

The growth of population in North Syrian villages, as evidenced by the building of dwellings, came to an end in the middle of the sixth century, surely a result of the Justinianic plague and its repeated recurrences as well as of massive deportation of inhabitants by the Persians in 540, 573, and 611–13. Ambitious church building continued to the end of the century. There are practically no new inscriptions and very few signs of occupation clearly datable after AD 611. But the conclusion that the area was rapidly abandoned seems to have been a mistake. The important excavation at Déhès shows that collapse was not sudden after the Persian invasion, and Arab conquest.[273] Occupation of that site continued through the seventh

[271] Tate 1992; Gatier 1994: 17–48; supplemented by C. Foss, 'The Near Eastern countryside in Late Antiquity, a review article', *JRA Suppl.* XIV (1995), 213–34.

[272] O. Callot, *Huileries antiques de la Syrie du nord* (Paris, 1984); so also Tate 1992: 249. On Africa, see survey of work in Mattingly and Hitchner 1995: 189–95, 198–204.

[273] J.-P. Sodini and G. Tate, 'Déhès (Syrie du Nord), Campagnes I–III (1976–78)', *Syria*, 57 (1980), 1–303.

and eighth centuries. Money economy continued too. But there is no evidence of new buildings whether of secular structures, or of churches or mosques. Thicker sediments suggest an inferior quality of occupation. The impression is that the village underwent a long slow decline.[274] Clearly a great many more sites need to be excavated. It would also be worthwhile for someone to make a detailed survey of the villages on the basalt massif of the kind Tchalenko and Tate have made of the villages on the limestone hills.

So it would seem that in northern Syria the prosperity of cities and villages was closely related. Both flourished until the Persian invasions of Syria of AD 540, the capture of Antioch, and the deportation of large numbers of its inhabitants. This was followed by repeated visitations of plague, and a lasting weakening of the cities of northern Syria in the second half of the sixth century. Growth of the population of the villages, as witnessed by new domestic building had been slowing down since the 480s. It could obviously not have gone on indefinitely, but the end of growth coincided with the weakening of Antioch and the other cities of the region. The disasters suffered by Antioch and the deportation of large numbers of inhabitants by the Persians in 540 and 573 produced a progressive reduction of the population in town and country alike. Within sixty years or so there was a cessation of all building and even of the setting up of inscribed tombstones. The almost complete absence of visible remains dating after AD 600 is in the sharpest possible contrast with the abundant remains of the previous 250 years.[275]

In Arabia and Palestine too, cities and the villages situated in their large territories prospered together.[276] What is more, when after the end of the Umayyad period sedentary occupation of the territories along the whole of the desert fringe of Syria/Palestine went into decline, cities and villages were affected alike, even though here—as further north—church building continued longer in some villages than it did in towns.[277] In Tripolitania both the agricultural exploitation, and the decline, started much earlier, but here too rural and urban regression were parallel.[278]

There is no obvious reason why things should have been different in Asia Minor. It is a priori likely that here too the decline in town and

[274] The decline of this highly developed and specialized area might perhaps be compared with that of Baetica and Campania (see below, pp. 381–3), though the much more favourable conditions of soil and rainfall in those two areas limited the reduction of cultivation and population. Mosques in this area appear to be 'medieval', see Tchalenko 1953–8: iii, s.v. mosquées. Survey of 'medieval' remains, ibid. 109–29.

[275] Tate 1992: 333–42; Trombey 1997.

[276] See below, pp. 298–9.

[277] For rural decline, see survey evidence: Mittmann 1970; Ibrahim, Sauer, and Yassine 1976; Ibach 1987; Miller 1978; Macdonald 1980. For cities, see below, pp. 295–303.

[278] Mattingly 1995: 183–5, 203–9; Mattingly and Lloyd 1989: 135–53, esp. 146 and n. 222 above.

country were related. But the onset of the decline of villages in Anatolia—as that of Anatolian towns—is very difficult to date. The mud-brick walls of the villages of, say, Phrygia or Pisidia have not left substantial remains like those which are so striking a feature of eastern Syria, Arabia, and Cilicia; and the epitaphs, which give such a vivid view of a Christian society in central Anatolia in the third and fourth centuries, do not continue far into the fifth.

That villages and cities prospered together does not necessarily mean that the balance of distribution of population and wealth between city and country remained unchanged. The villages of the limestone massif in northern Syria increased the creation of wealth absolutely through increasing their production of olive oil for sale to the neighbouring cities.[279] It is conceivable, and perhaps even likely, that more wealthy people had their main residence in villages than had been the case in earlier times, and that more wealth was spent in the countryside, not least the income of monasteries. In the Oxhyrynchite nome of Egypt we hear of a large number of place names for the first time in the sixth century.[280] Similarly the names of at least 117 settlements in the Fayum do not occur on documents before the fifth century.[281] Rathbone argues that the new settlements cannot reflect an increase in population as by AD 500 Egypt already had as large a population as could be fed by its agriculture. So the inhabitants of the new settlements must have moved there from the cities. He suggests that many of the new settlements housed workers on the great estates that came into existence in late Late Antiquity.[282] If he is right, the fifth and sixth centuries in Egypt saw a reversal of the process which from the second to the fourth century had made the villages politically and economically dependent on the growing cities, the *metropoleis*. Consequently in the villages temples had decayed, literate leaders had left, and craftsmen found more profitable use for their skills in towns.[283] If this tide turned in late Late Antiquity, with the result that villages came to benefit from a redistribution of population and wealth, in their favour, archaeologists have not so far found evidence of this in the cities of Palestine and Arabia.[284] In northern Syria—as we have seen—a weakening of cities in the second half of the sixth century coincided with economic and demographic stagnation in the villages of the massif, and not

[279] Tate 1992: 315–20.

[280] P. Pruneti, *I centri abitati dell'Ossirinchite: Repertorio toponomastico* (Florence, 1981).

[281] Greenfell and Hunt, *P Tebt.* ii. 361.

[282] Rathbone 1990: 103–42, esp. 122.

[283] Bagnall 1993: 314–19.

[284] Sartre 1985: 136–8: building in cities and villages has roughly the same profile, but in villages the peak was reached later than in cities, and building went on longer—perhaps because the plague was known to hit city-dwellers more severely.

with expansion. We are of course still a very long way from being able to establish the existence of any but the very largest shifts of population from town to country, or vice versa, archaeologically.

5. *The Late Roman City in the West*[285]

The West, that is the lands ruled by the Western Emperor after the Empire had been divided in AD 395 on the death of Theodosius I, is a huge territory. Over much of this area, particularly in the Balkans, and most of Gaul, Spain, and North Africa, the majority of cities actually owed their existence to the Empire. Elsewhere, especially in southern Italy and Sicily, the cities had existed for centuries before their incorporation in the Roman system.

An account of the survival of cities in the West cannot be told in exactly the same way as the story of cities in the East because the character of the evidence is different. Generally speaking, we have far more literary evidence for the West in our period than we have for the East. On the other hand, most of the Late Antique sites of the West are still, or again, covered by buildings, and except in North Africa, the West lacks large tracts of landscape densely occupied in Late Antiquity and subsequently abandoned. As a result archaeologists have had a much more difficult task. They have developed techniques to cope with the situation, but neither the problems to which the techniques can be applied, nor the information gained by their use, precisely match those which have been the traditional concern of Mediterranean archaeologists.[286]

Generally speaking the classical city with its characteristic architecture, and its political organization uniting a rural territory with an urban core, disappeared—or was transformed into something else—much sooner in the West than in the East. But the West was far from monolithic. The Roman version of the classical ideal remained intact longest in North Africa, where monumental town-centres remained more or less intact, and classical institutions can be observed to be working up to AD 400 and longer.[287] Urban vitality and classical monumentality survived almost as long, but in a rather more dilapidated form, in many of the territories bordering on the Mediterranean, for instance in southern Spain,[288] in

[285] There is no general survey to compare with Claude's for the East, but see Février *et al.* 1980 on Gaul.

[286] K. Greene, *The Archaeology of the Roman Economy* (London, 1986) is a vivid account of what has been learnt through archaeological techniques applicable universally, but developed for Western Europe. It has very little material from the East.

[287] Lepelley 1979–80.

[288] Vitality in 6th cent.: Cordova was independent for 33 years, AD 549–72 (Isidore, *Hist. Goth.* 45, John of Biclaro 20). The rebellion of Hermenegild (AD 570) was based on Merida Italica, Seville, and Cordova (John of Biclaro 55, 66, 69; Greg T. *HF* VI.18; Thompson 1969: 71–2). The *Liber vitas*

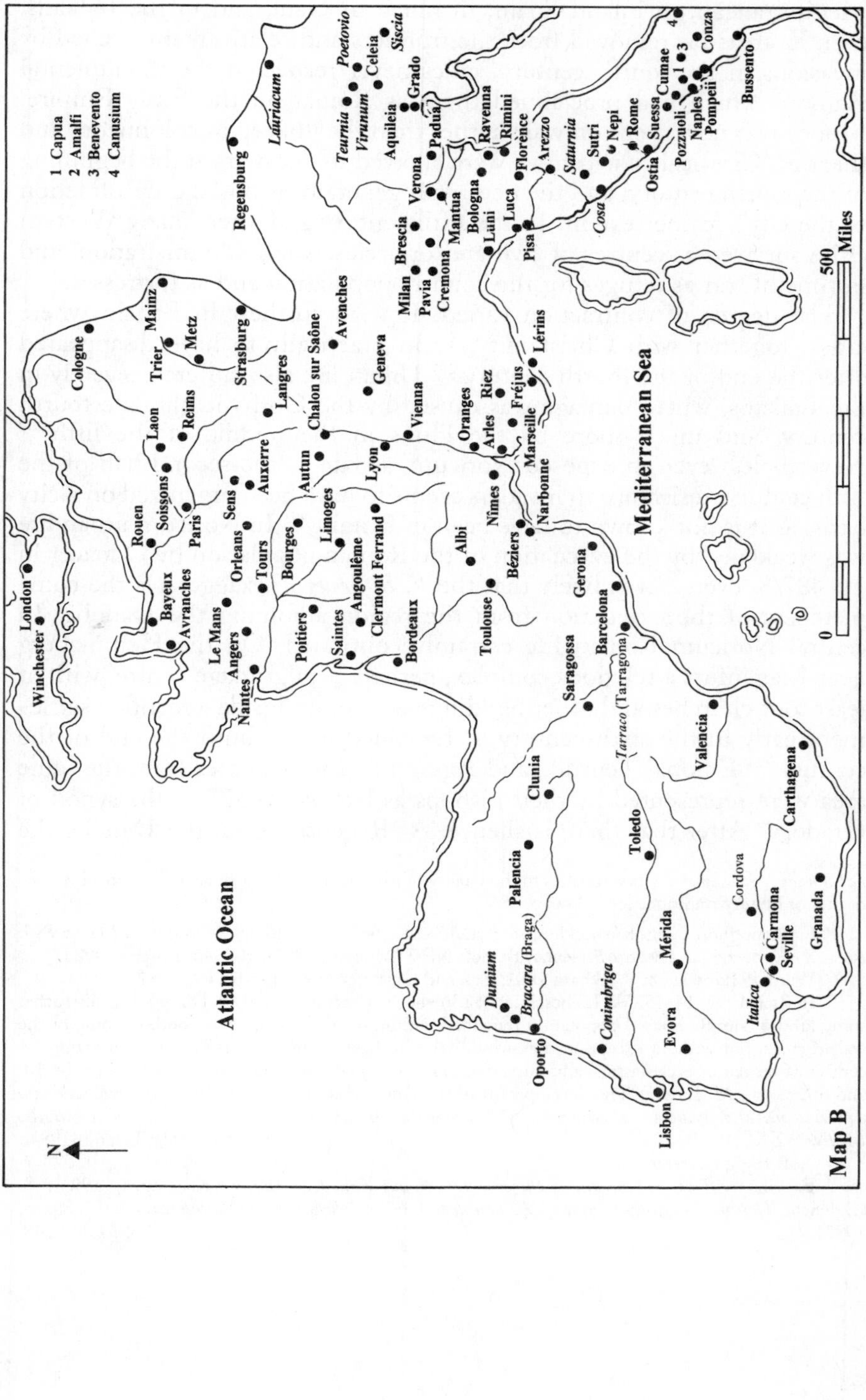

8. Cities in the West

Provence,[289] in Dalmatia, and in much of Italy.[290] Away from the Mediterranean, in inland Spain, in much of Gaul, and in the Balkans, even in areas far removed from the frontiers and relatively untouched by invasions in the fourth century, cities never recovered the monumental glamour which had proclaimed them as Roman in the Early Empire. Money was now spent on walls rather than the upkeep of colonnades and theatres. Classical civic centres were allowed to decay from the beginning of the fourth century, and the new walls generally enclosed only a fraction of the city's former extent. In the fifth century and after, many Western cities survived as centres of civil and/or ecclesiastical administration, and in time of war as refuges for the country population and as fortresses.

The degree of contraction varied. It went furthest in Britain where cities, together with Christianity, seem practically to have disappeared after the end of the fourth century.[291] Urban life also suffered severely in the Balkans, where damage was caused by the Goths in the late fourth century, and much more by the Huns in the middle of the fifth.[292] Nevertheless even in exposed Noricum, as late as the second half of the fifth century, resistance to invaders seems to have been organized on a city basis, as it is not known to have been in Britain.[293] In Noricum urban life was weakened by the evacuation of the Roman population by Odoacer in AD 487/8, even if it is likely that the *V. S. Severini* exaggerates the completeness of the evacuation from the region adjoining the Danube. In central Noricum Roman life certainly continued. On the Hemmaberg near Klagenfurt a religious complex, perhaps a pilgrimage centre, with at least four churches and other buildings was set up inside a fortified settlement early in the sixth century, it remained in use until the end of the century.[294] Emona, Teurnia, and Aguntum (Lienz), cities from the same area were represented by their bishops as late as AD 577 at the synod of Grado.[295] After that there is silence. At Regensburg on the Danube the

patrum sanctorum emeritensium testifies to the vitality of Merida in the late 6th cent. On probable continuity of literary tradition, see below, p. 336.

[289] F. Vittinghoff, 'Zur Entwicklung der städtischen Selbstverwaltung', in *Stadt und Herrschaft: Römische Kaiserzeit und hohes Mittelalter,* Beiheft NF 7 (Munich, 1982), 107–46; Loseby 1992*a*.

[290] Ward-Perkins 1978; Wickham 1981; Eck and Galsterer 1991; also below, p. 94.

[291] In Rich 1992: 14–15 (W. Liebeschuetz); 136–44 (R. Reece); 145–60 (P. Dixon). It is likely that some kind of simply housed population remained within, or in the neighbourhood, of some of the walled cities, but without exception they would seem to have ceased to perform urban functions as centres of secular or ecclesiastical administration, or as regional economic centres for most of the 5th and 6th cents. (M. Biddle, 'The development of the Anglo-Saxon town', in *Topografia urbana e vita cittadina nell'alto medioevo in occidente,* in *Settimane di Studio del Centro Italiano di Studi sull'Alto Medioevo* XXI (1973), 203–30).

[292] Poulter 1992*a*; Dagron 1984*c*.

[293] Noll 1963; Lotter 1971.

[294] F. Glaser, *Das frühchristliche Pilgerheiligtum auf dem Hemmaberg* (Klagenfurt, 1991); S. Ciglencki, *Höhenbefestigungen aus der Zeit von dem 3. bis 6. Jahrhundert im Ostalpenraum* (Ljubljana, 1987).

[295] Pohl 1988: 148.

houses inside what had been the legionary camp were deserted. The duke of the Bajuvari, and later the bishop, built castles respectively around a group of towers, and around the gatehouse, of the Roman fortification.[296] In Pannonia some town life continued in spite of invasions and barbarian settlements.[297] At Carnutum, Savaria, Aquincum, and Poetovio there is evidence of urban life, under very much simplified conditions with burials in the town area, well into the fifth century, and at Scarbantia, Siscia, Sirmium, and Carnutum into the sixth.[298] Siscia still had *curiales* in the reign of Theoderic.[299] In this region it is unlikely that civic territories survived in view of the fact of barbarian settlements in the countryside. Perhaps urban life in Pannonia received its final blow when the Lombards evacuated the population to accompany their march into Italy.[300] Cities along the coast in Dalmatia and modern Albania flourished through the fifth century. Large numbers of churches were built. It may be that the disturbed conditions inland benefited the coastal regions, so that its development was more like that of Greece than that of the Danube provinces.[301]

Further down the Danube cities had been devastated by Attila's Huns in the 440s. All the garrison towns, Viminacium, Ratiaria, Oescus, Novae, Durostorum, and Troesmus, as well as many cities further south, for instance Nicopolis ad Istrum, were destroyed. Most of them were rebuilt when the Eastern emperors, especially Anastasius and Justinian, restored imperial control in the Balkan provinces, but within a greatly shortened circuit of walls. They were no longer centres of population, but powerful fortresses and administrative centres controlling the Danube frontier.

At Nicopolis ad Istrum rebuilding took the form of a powerful circuit-wall, enclosing little more than military buildings and churches. The extensive ruins of the classical city were not reoccupied.[302] Nicopolis ad

296 W. Gauer, 'Stadtkernforschung am Beispiel Regensburg', in Jäger (1987), 161–76, esp. 170–1. H. T. Fischer and S. Rieckhoff-Pauli 1982. H. Berg, 'Bischöfe und Bischofssitze im Ostalpen und Donauraum vom. 4. zum 8. Jahrhundert', in H. Wolfram and A. Schwarcz (eds.), *Die Baiern und ihre Nachbarn*, i (Denkschriften der Östreichischen Akademie 179; Vienna, 1985), 61 ff.

297 Christie 1996: 70–98.

298 On the following, see Wolf 1991: 287–318, with lots of references.

299 Cass. *Var.* IV.49.

300 See below, pp. 378–9.

301 Saradi 1998. Churches at Salona: N. Duval, E. Mavin, C. Metzger (eds.), *Salona* I (Coll. éc. franç. de Rome 194; Rome, 1994): the episcopal group dates from third quarter of 4th cent., 6 churches before end of 5th cent., one from 6th. R. Hodges, G. Saraçi, and others, 'Late antique and Byzantine Butrint', *JRA* 10 (1997), 206–34: Butrint and territory flourished deep into the 6th cent. Churches in villages: Pascale Chevalier, *Ecclesiae Dalmatiae: L'Architecture paléochrétienne de la province romaine de Dalmatie IVe–VIIe* (Rome, 1986), 184: *c.*264 churches known, many 2nd half 5th–2nd half 6th. Many of these 6th cent.

302 Poulter 1992*a* and *b*.

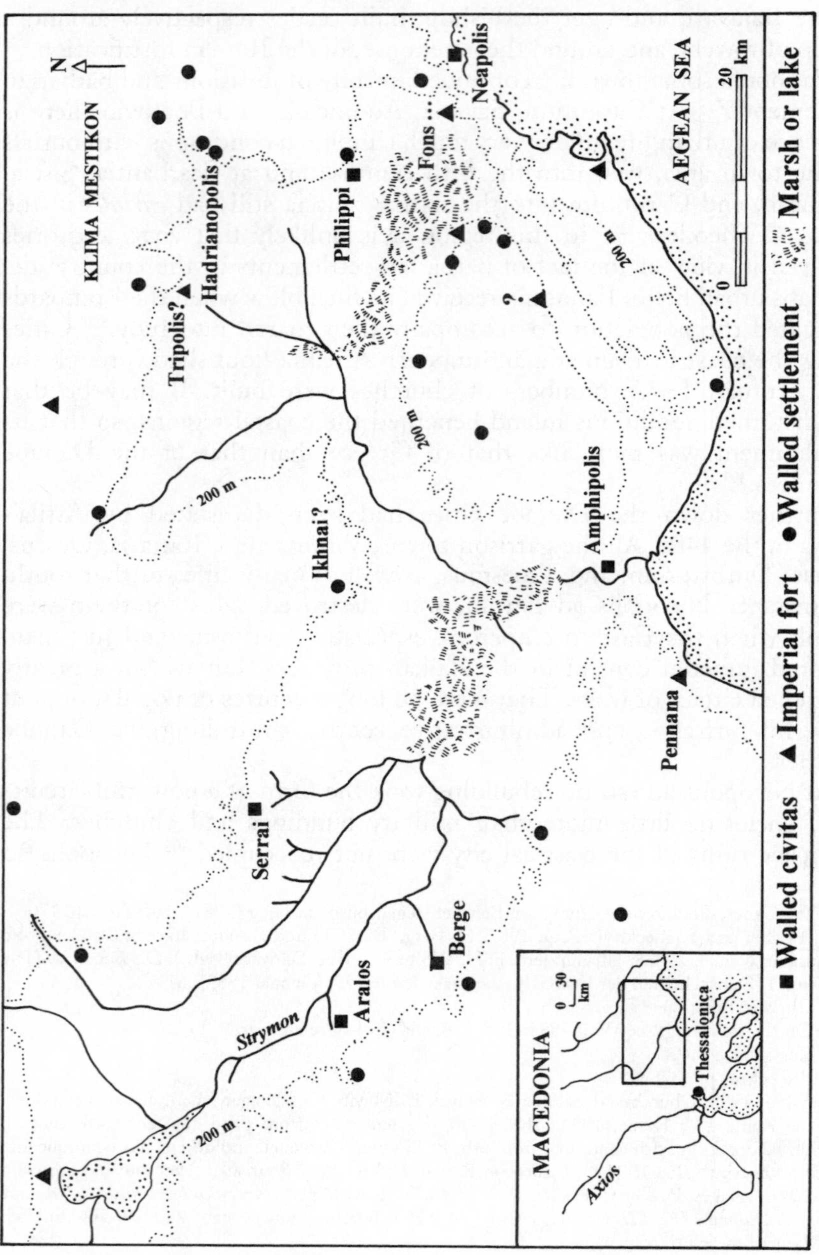

9. Old *civitates* and new fortified hill settlements in south eastern Macedonia

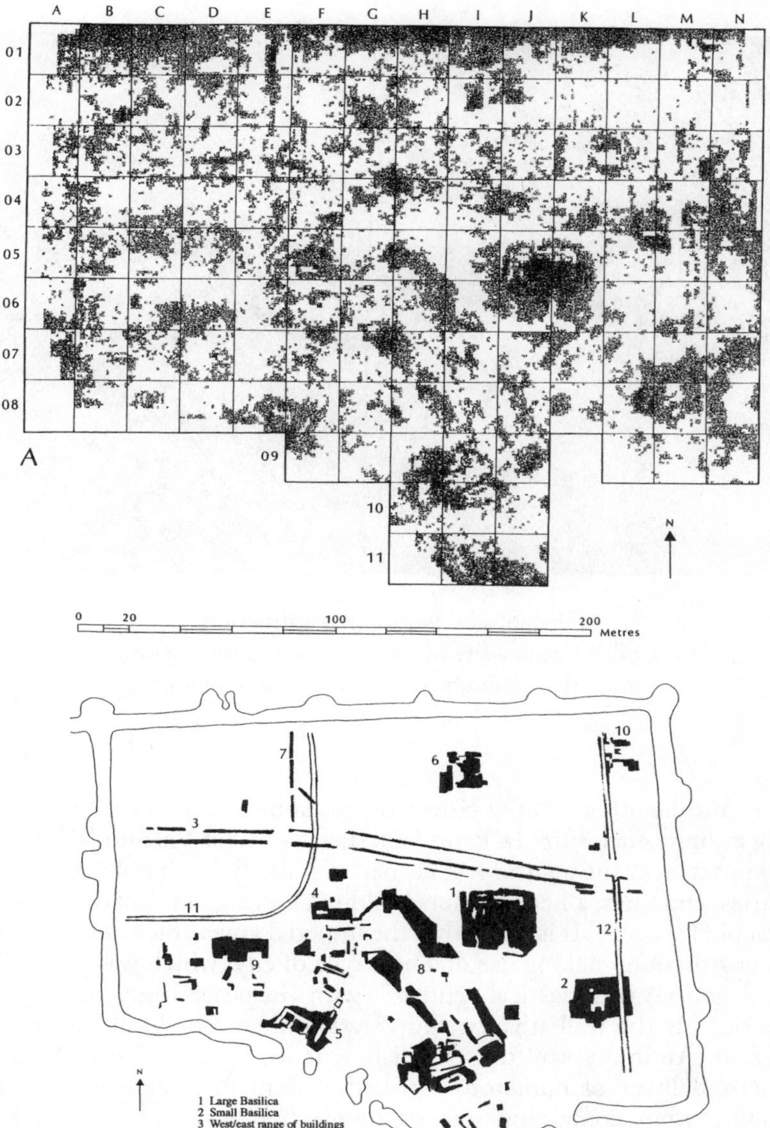

10. Nicopolis ad Istrum: resistivity survey and interpretation

Nicopolis ad Istrum: reconstruction
A 'new-model' fortress-city of late Late Antiquity, enclosing little more than military and ecclesiastical buildings

Istrum and the other frontier cities now resembled certain strongly walled purely military enclosures in Pannonia, such as that at Valcum (Keszthely-Fenékpuszta) on the south-west corner of Lake Balaton, which included granaries, churches, a headquarters building, and a great deal of seemingly unoccupied space.[303] It is likely that the imperial government's programme of reconstruction, making use of a new type of city, which was primarily a fortress and an ecclesiastical centre,[304] with (in peace time) more population outside the walls than within[305] was imitated by local leaders. For later Late Antiquity saw the establishment in Thrace, Greece, and the southern Balkans of numerous fortified settlements, sited in defensible locations, often containing one or more churches, and ranging from

303 Christie 1995*a*: 50–1.
304 See N. Duval 1984 on Tsarichin Grad = Justiniana prima; also Poulter 1992*a*: esp. 123–31, on Nicopolis ad Istrum and Tropaeum Traiani.
305 Bavant 1984: 283–4 on Justiniana prima; cf. Poulter 1995: 46 on Nicopolis ad Istrum.

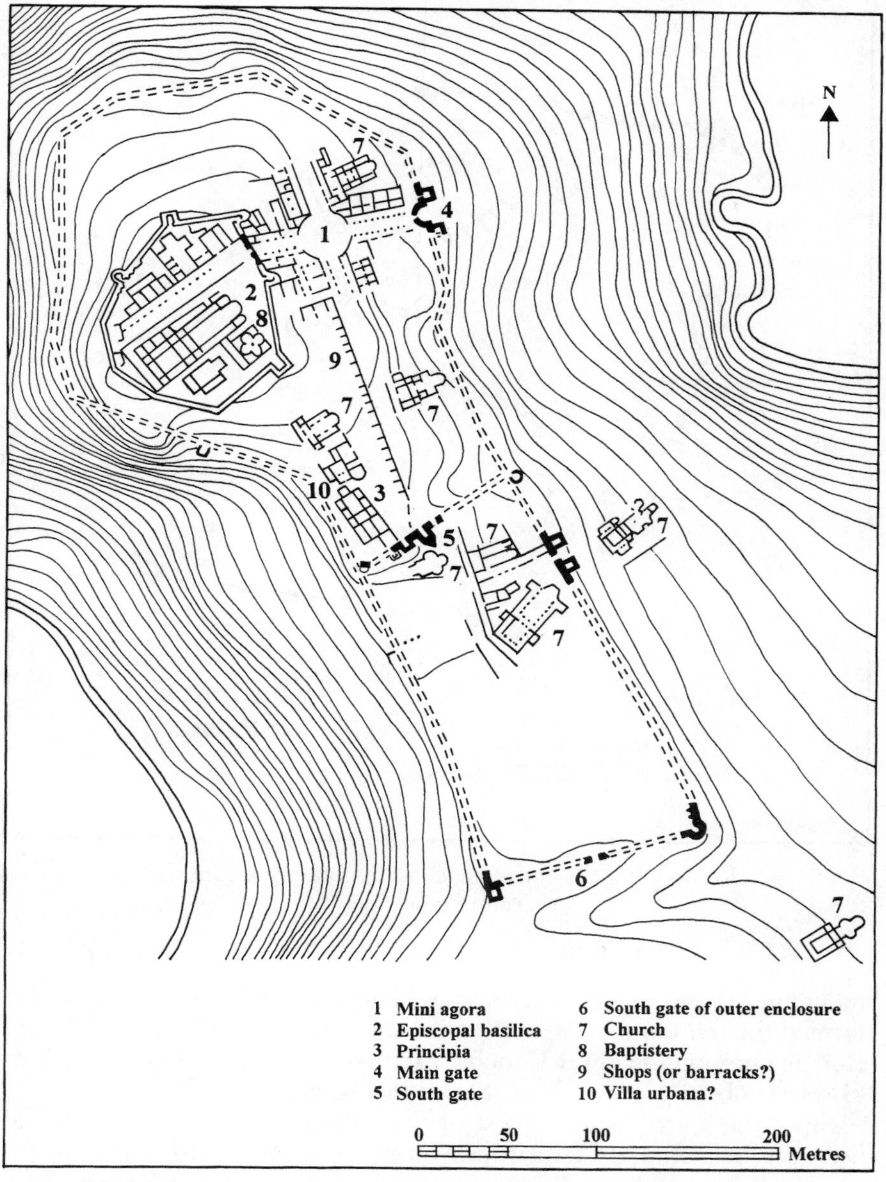

11. Justiniana Prima: a late Late fortified centre of civil and ecclesiastical administration with few inhabitants

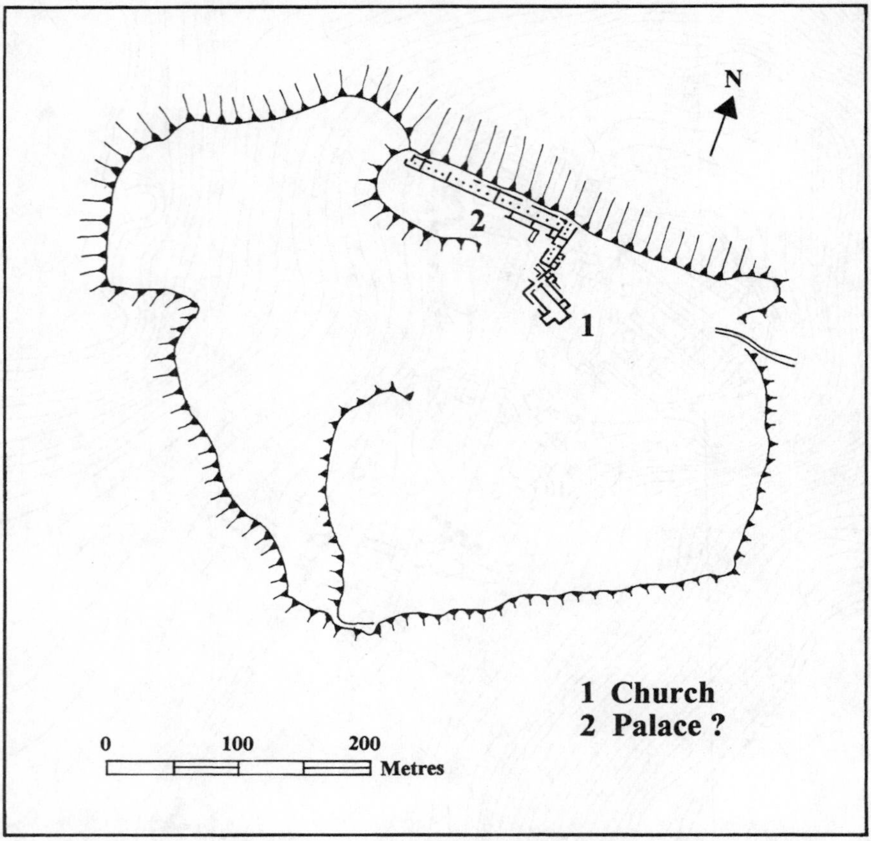

12. Recopolis: a Visigothic version of a Byzantine administrative centre type city?

mountain refuges to places of some architectural ambition.[306] These places formed the framework of a new pattern of settlement. The end of the old Roman cities on the lower Danube, like that of the cities of north-eastern Greece is obscure. It will be discussed in a later chapter.[307]

Since the fourth century most of the cities in Gaul, and in what had been the Belgian and German provinces, were defended by walls which surrounded a much smaller area than that of the classical town. Two

[306] A. G. Poulter, 'Town and country in Moesia Inferior', in A. G. Poulter (ed.) *Ancient Bulgaria*, 2 vols. (Nottingham, 1983), i. 97–9; Bavant 1984; Dunn 1994: 60–80, also a lecture at conference of ESF programme on the Transformation of the Roman World, Isernia, 1997 and above p. 78, fig. 9; Saradi 1998.

[307] See also below, p. 284ff.

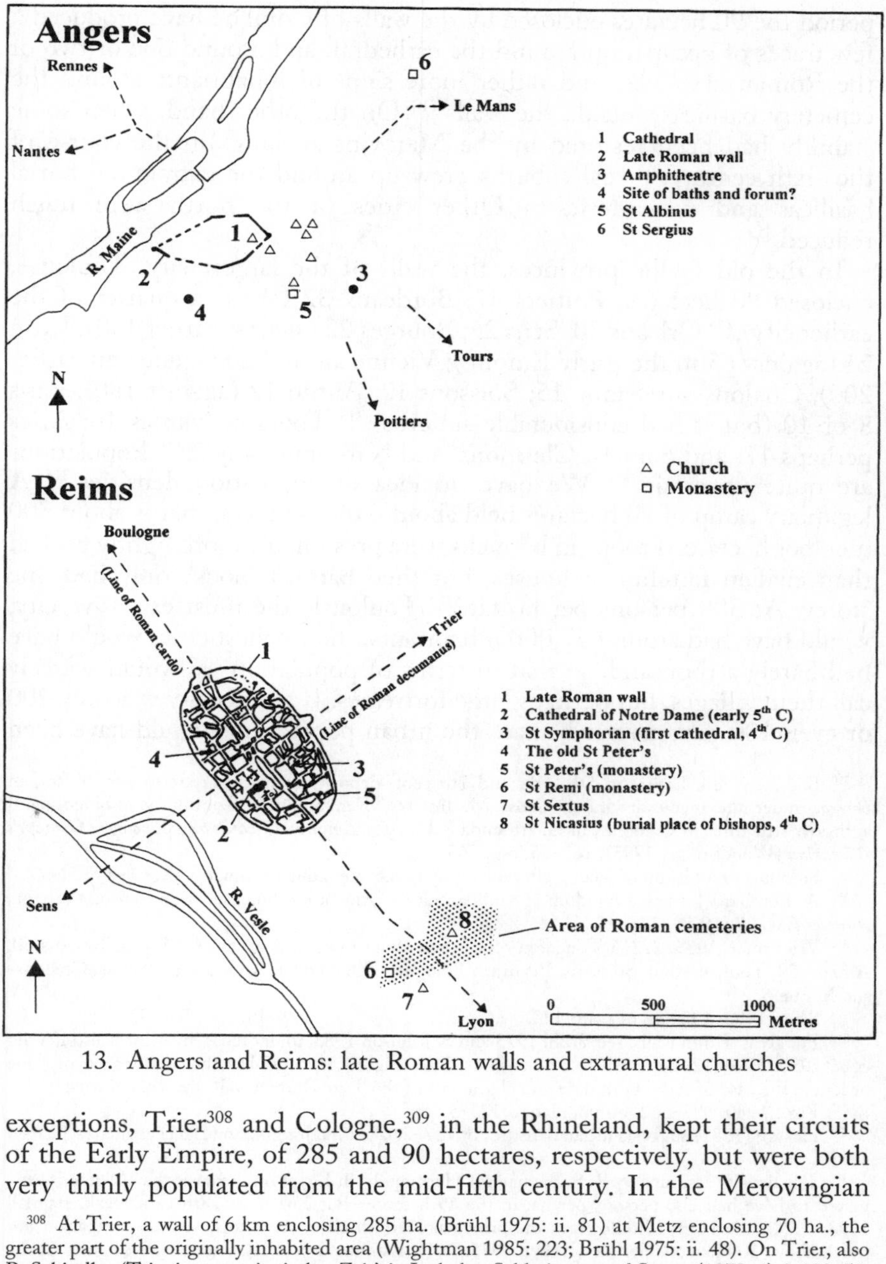

13. Angers and Reims: late Roman walls and extramural churches

exceptions, Trier[308] and Cologne,[309] in the Rhineland, kept their circuits of the Early Empire, of 285 and 90 hectares, respectively, but were both very thinly populated from the mid-fifth century. In the Merovingian

[308] At Trier, a wall of 6 km enclosing 285 ha. (Brühl 1975: ii. 81) at Metz enclosing 70 ha., the greater part of the originally inhabited area (Wightman 1985: 223; Brühl 1975: ii. 48). On Trier, also R. Schindler, 'Trier in merowingischer Zeit', in Jankuhn, Schlesinger, and Steuer (1973–4), i. 130–51.

[309] H. Steuer, 'Stadtarchäologie in Köln', in Jäger (1987), 61–102.

period the 90 hectares enclosed by the walls of Cologne have produced a few traces of occupation around the cathedral, and around one or two of the Roman churches, and rather more signs of inhabitants around the cemetery basilicas outside the walls.[310] On the other hand, when some stability had been restored by the Merovingian kings in the course of the sixth century,[311] real suburbs grew up around the extramural burial basilicas and monasteries.[312] Other cities of the north were much reduced.[313]

In the old Gallic provinces, the walls of the largest city, Toulouse, enclosed 90 hectares; Poitiers 47; Bordeaux 32 (about a quarter of the earlier city);[314] Orleans 30; Sens 25; Bourges 22 (against earlier 100); Lyon 21 (against 65 in the Early Empire); Vienne around 20 (against an earlier 200); Chalons-sur-Saône 15; Soissons 12; Autun 12 (against 180); Paris 8 or 10 (but it had considerable suburbs);[315] Tours 6; Nantes 16; Arles perhaps 17; and Saintes, Clermont, and Narbonne only 3.[316] Populations are quite uncertain.[317] We have no idea of population densities.[318] A legionary camp of 20 hectares held about 6,000 soldiers, that is about 300 men per hectare. Troops in barracks were presumably more tightly packed than civilian families in houses, but then barrack blocks only had one storey. At 300 persons per hectare[319] Toulouse, the most extensive city, would have had around 27,000 inhabitants, the smallest cities would have had barely a thousand, so that in terms of population we would scarcely call them villages, but perhaps large fortresses. If the density was only 200 or even 100 persons per hectare the urban populations would have been

310 Ibid., esp. 80. Layers of 5th, 6th, and 7th cent. deposits in market next to site of Roman *horrea*, under the medieval church Gross Martin: see Sven Schütte, 'Continuity, problems and authority structures in Cologne', in G. Ausenda (ed.), *After Empire: Towards an Ethnology of Europe's Barbarian* (Woodbridge, 1995), 163–75, esp. 165.

311 Sidonius first bishop of Mainz after a lengthy break: Venatius Fortunatus IX.9.1–2 of 566/7.

312 A. Lombard-Jordan, 'Oppidum et banlieu: Sur l'origine et les dimensions du territoire urbain', *Annales ESC* 27 (1972), 373–95.

313 Wightman 1985, 223–5 Tongeren 45–50 had about one-third of its earlier area; Rheims 60; Amiens 20; Toul, Verdun, Soissons, Beauvais, Bologne, Thérouanne, Arras 12 ha.; Senlis, Châlons-sur-Marne 6.

314 Sivan 1992: 132–43, relevant 133.

315 Fleury 1961: 77.

316 For areas within walls, see Brühl 1975 and S. Johnson 1983, under respective cities; also Février *et al.* 1980: 399–412, figs. 405–8. The authors differ slightly in detail but their figures are of same order. In the case of Arles both date and alignment of the 'Late Roman wall' are still controversial.

317 Fixot 1980: 497–562, on population 522–5.

318 Hassan (1981) suggests urban densities of 137–216 per ha. Jongmann (1991) estimates 123–84 per ha.

319 The density assumed by R. S. Bagnall for Hermopolis in Egypt on the basis that Aleppo is estimated to have had 200 persons per ha. in the 19th cent.—but 350 at its 18th-cent. peak. Bagnall 1993: 53. In the High Middle Ages the principal Flemish cities seem to have had population not much above 100 persons per ha. (Ennen 1975: 201). Estimated population densities of cities in the 15th and 14th cent. range from fewer than 100 per ha. to more than 300. In 1854 Poitiers had a population density of 119 per ha. (Claude 1960: 39).

smaller still.[320] There are many uncertainties. In the case of no city at all have we even the remotest idea of either the number of houses, or of the number of stories of a typical house, or of the number of persons occupying a typical housing unit. Nor do we know, as a rule, how much of the walled area was taken up by churches, monasteries, the residence of the *comes,* or indeed not built up at all. Within the reduced circuits, churches and chapels certainly occupied a lot of the available space, even though some large churches were generally situated outside the walls in the suburbs. By the Carolingian period Metz had 40, Claremont 25, Paris 24–6, and major towns like Rheims, Lyons, Arles, Bordeaux, Poitiers 15–20 churches.[321] There was no room for a large population.

It is likely that in time archaeology will provide us with more information relevant to demography. Meanwhile the very fact that archaeologists have so far found so little suggests that housing was not substantially built, and perhaps not very densely packed: in other words the lower estimates are the more likely. These cities were religious centres and fortresses, but not the homes of large urban populations as the cities in the East remained up to the end of the sixth century. Monasteries and burial basilicas outside the walls became the nuclei of suburban settlements, which sometimes, as for instance in the case of Paris, eventually housed a considerable number of people.[322] But we need far more archaeological information before we can estimate suburban populations.

Beyond the walls, classical monumental structures lay abandoned and were quarried for building material. In the town, monumentality was represented by churches. The second half of the fifth century and the early sixth marked a nadir in the fortune of the Gallic cities, but subsequently things improved. War and disorder did not necessarily hinder the building of churches. The late fifth and the sixth centuries were a great period of church building, not only in cities and suburbs but also in villages. Poitiers had five churches early in the fifth century. Five more were built in the course of the fifth century and nine more before 700.[323] Moreover, descriptions in the writings of Gregory of Tours and elsewhere show that some of the churches were large and richly decorated with frescoes and mosaics.[324]

[320] Mols (1954–6): iii, table 1, pp. 189–96: in general, density of persons per ha. has risen in cities in modern times. Taking only figures before 1500, density varied a great deal from city to city, from over 300 to less than a hundred, indeed density of population in the same city could change remarkably quickly. Besides there was—as there still is—variety between quarters of the same city, e.g. in Rome in 1526 from 333–5.

[321] Fixot 1980: 522–5.

[322] M. Fleury, *Paris du Bas Empire au début du XIIIe siècle* (Paris, 1961), 77. M. Roblin, 'Cités ou citadelles, les enceintes romaines du bas-empire d'après l'exemple de Paris', *REA* 53 (1951), 301–11.

[323] Claude 1960: 50; Lestocquoy 1953: 159–72.

[324] Church building in Aquitaine: Rouche 1979: 271–300. Paris, Mainz, Rheims: Ewig 1976: ii. 1–20. Generally: Lestocquoy 1953: 159–72.

The cities in the north of Gaul and the Rhineland suffered heavily during the invasions of the fifth century. The lists of bishops have long gaps, covering much of the later fifth and the first half of the sixth century. Franks settled in their territories, and the administrative link between town and territory seems in general to have been lost. The *pagus* rather than the city became the normal unit of royal administration.[325] A few cities became the residence of a Germanic king. Among the latter the most outstanding were Trier,[326] Metz,[327] Soissons, and Paris. The reviving effect of a royal residence is particularly clear at Metz. The city flourished within fortifications covering 70 hectares until the end of the fourth century. After that it appears to have been very largely abandoned. Archaeologists have found only scanty remains of occupation within the walls, and few burials that can be dated before the mid-sixth century. The city did however have an unbroken succession of bishops. After *c.*550 its fortunes improved dramatically. By AD 700 Metz had about thirty churches and ten cemeteries. Occupation was widely dispersed over the walled area and beyond: houses clustered round churches.[328]

The cities of Aquitaine[329] and of central Gaul, roughly south of a line from Avranches to Geneva,[330] were much reduced in area and population, but remained administrative centres of their old territories.[331] Gregory of Tours's *History* suggests that these *civitates* remained functional political communities. Under the Merovingians many of them were required to provide contingents of soldiers for the armies of their Frankish kings.[332] It was a peculiarity of Gaul not generally paralleled in other provinces, whether in the West or in the East, that the old senatorial aristocracy, no doubt mingling with leading families among the Franks, maintained its estates and influence, not least by managing to keep many of the bishoprics in its hands.[333] Under the Visigoths as well as under the Merovingians, Gallic *civitates* between the Seine and the Loire recovered some of the freedom of political manoeuvre of the city states of long ago, but now as bishop's republics.[334]

325 Ewig 1976: i. 456.

326 Cüppers 1977.

327 Weidemann 1970.

328 G. Halsall, 'Towns, societies and ideas: The not so strange case of Late Roman and Early Merovingian Metz', in N. Christie and S. T. Loseby (eds.), *Towns in Transition: Urban Evolution in Late Antiquity and the Early Middle Ages* (Aldershot, 1996), 235–61. See also Halsall 1995.

329 Rouche 1979; Sivan 1992; Loseby 1992*a*.

330 Ewig 1976.

331 Wightman 1978, 1985: 219–42, 305–8; H. G. Horn, *Die Römer in Nordrhein-Westfalen* (Stuttgart, 1987); Frézouls 1988.

332 D. Frye, 'Transformation and tradition in the Merovingian *civitas*', *Nottingham Medieval Studies*, 39 (1995), 1–11.

333 Heinzelmann 1976.

334 Kaiser 1987: 261, map 9.

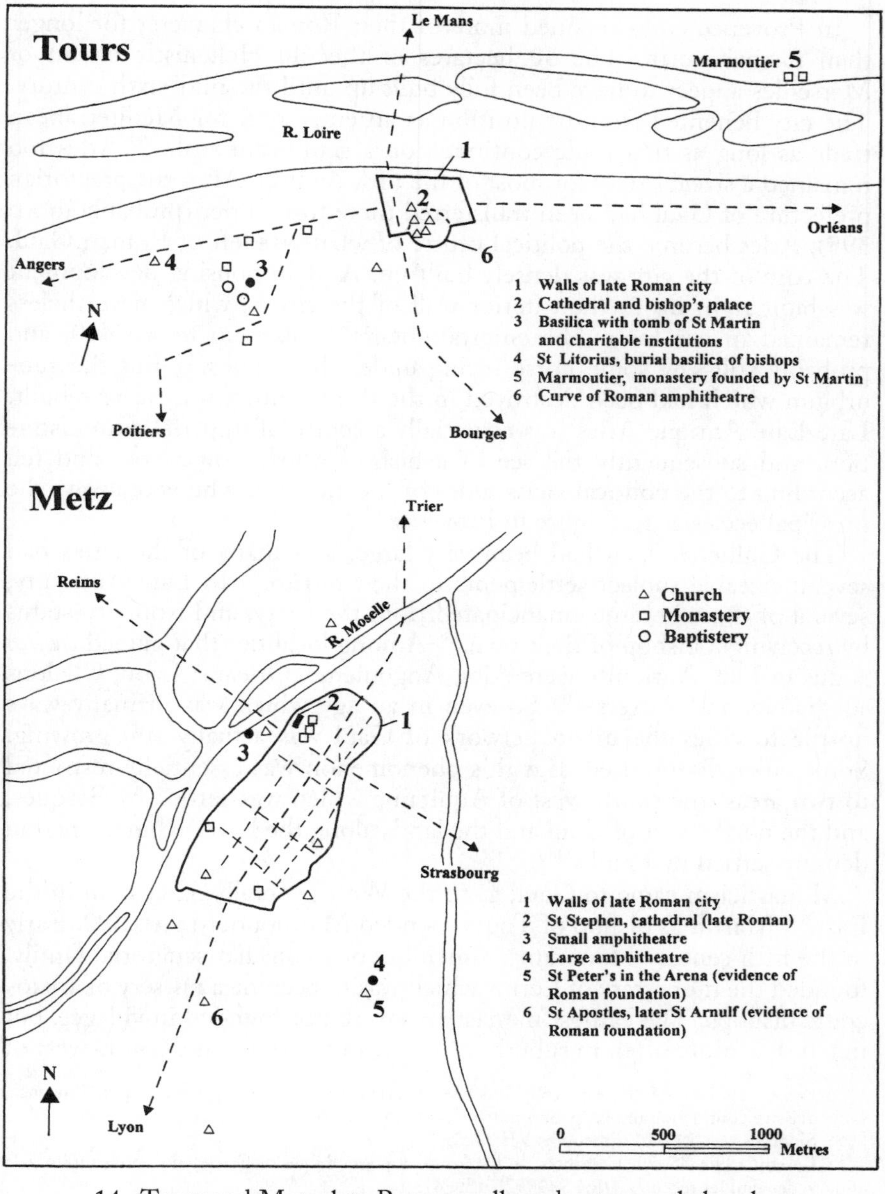
Tours
Le Mans
Marmoutier 5
R. Loire
1
2
Orléans
Angers
4
3
6
N
1 Walls of late Roman city
2 Cathedral and bishop's palace
3 Basilica with tomb of St Martin and charitable institutions
4 St Litorius, burial basilica of bishops
5 Marmoutier, monastery founded by St Martin
6 Curve of Roman amphitheatre
Poitiers
Bourges
Metz
Trier
Reims
R. Moselle
△ Church
□ Monastery
○ Baptistery
2
1
3
Strasbourg
1 Walls of late Roman city
2 St Stephen, cathedral (late Roman)
3 Small amphitheatre
4 Large amphitheatre
5 St Peter's in the Arena (evidence of Roman foundation)
6 St Apostles, later St Arnulf (evidence of Roman foundation)
4
5
6
N
Lyon
0 500 1000 Metres

14. Tours and Metz: late Roman walls and extramural churches

In Provence cities retained more of their Roman character for longer than further north. The 50 hectares of the old Hellenistic circuit of Marseilles appear to have been fully built up until the mid-sixth century. The city benefited from its position as an entry port for Mediterranean trade as long as that trade continued on a significant scale.[335] Arles too remained a sizeable city for most of the fifth century. After the praetorian prefecture of Gaul had been transferred there from Trier (probably in AD 395), Arles became the political centre of what was left of Roman Gaul. The core of the city was densely built up. A plain housing development was built right up to the exterior wall of the circus, which nevertheless remained in use for public entertainments at least up to AD 460, and probably still saw some horse racing under the Franks.[336] But the suburbium which had been destroyed in the third century was never rebuilt. Late Late Antique Arles was essentially a centre of imperial administration, and subsequently the see of a bishop whose power rose and fell according to the political vicissitudes of the area, but who was always the principal ecclesiastical figure in Provence.[337]

The Gallic *civitates* had been very large, and many of the cities had several sizeable subject settlements in their territory. In Late Antiquity, several of these became emancipated from their city, and won city-status by receiving a bishop of their own.[338] Among localities that gained *civitas* status in Late Antiquity were Albi, Angoulême, Orleans, Laon, Chalons sur Saône, and Auxerre.[339] So even in an age which was in many ways hostile to cities the urban network of Gaul was actually still growing. Some cities disappeared. But this phenomenon was essentially restricted to two areas: the south-west of Aquitaine which was settled by Basques, and the north-west of Gaul and the lands along the lower Rhine, a region densely settled by Franks.[340]

Monasticism came to Gaul, as to the West generally, later than in the East.[341] Martin as bishop of Tours founded Marmoutier in AD 390. Early in the fifth century Honoratus, a member of a consular senatorial family, founded the monastery of Lérins which was to become a nursery of aristocratic bishops. The earliest monasteries were not founded in villages, but in cities or more often in suburbs of cities, in the south and south-west of

[335] Loseby 1992*b*: 165–85, esp. 168–70. Other Provençal cities: Fréjus, Riez, Aix en Provence, show massive contraction of occupation much earlier (ibid. 169).

[336] Sidonius, *Ep.* I.11.10; Procopius VII.33.5.

[337] Loseby 1996: 45–70. C. Sintés, 'L'Évolution topographique de l'Arles du haut-empire à la lumière des fouilles récentes', *JRA* 5 (1992), 130–47.

[338] Loseby 1992*a*: 144–9. Kaiser 1987: 247–78, esp. 252–5, maps 2–4 showing *civitates* and bishoprics established in Late Antiquity.

[339] See Brühl 1975, under each city.

[340] Kaiser 1987: 260, map 8; 253, map 3.

[341] Prinz 1965, repr. 1988.

Gaul. Moreover, the earliest monasteries were founded by bishops and remained under episcopal control. So in Gaul the first stage of monasticism strengthened the position of bishops, and in so doing also that of cities. Later the foundation and patronage of monasteries was taken up by the Merovingian royal house, and subsequently by the Frankish aristocracy. Monasteries were now founded mainly in the countryside, and above all in the north and north-east of Gaul. They were important supporters of descendants of their founders, whether the royal dynasty or of a local aristocratic house. Monasteries also became important economic centres. So these other-worldly institutions paradoxically helped to consolidate the political and economic emancipation of the countryside from the old Roman cities.[342] At the same time they helped to bring about a shift of political and economic power to the north.

The development of late Roman Spain bore some resemblance to that of neighbouring Gaul, but it has produced far less literature for historians to analyse, and as a result we know much less about what was going on in its cities. Excavations have shown that urban life in Late Antiquity was everywhere much more vigorous than was believed by earlier scholars.[343] Admittedly most of the great ceremonial centres of the Early Empire, for instance the striking complexes at Italica and Tarraco,[344] were in full decay by the end of the fourth century.[345] At Clunia public buildings in the centre of the city were converted to industrial uses especially and the making of pottery, while the halls of the great baths were divided up into small private dwellings.[346] But cities continued to be inhabited. This is proved by abundant burials, which now begin to be found inside the walls,[347] as well as in large cemeteries around extramural basilicas.[348] A great deal of evidence of continuing urban life has also been provided by stray finds and unsystematic excavation. That excavation has been unsystematic is largely due to the fact that the city centres have continued to be occupied. There has been a praiseworthy reluctance to demolish later historical buildings for the sake of uncovering earlier townscapes.

In later Late Antiquity, that is in the fifth and sixth centuries, as in classical times, the more densely urbanized and more thoroughly Romanized southern provinces of Baetica and Lusitania contrasted with

[342] Ibid. 196–7; 532–40; plans XIIB–C for location of monastic foundations AD 590–768.

[343] Arce 1982: 85–105. Ripoll and Velázquez 1995: 102–10.

[344] Carreté, Keay, and Millett 1995. Keay 1991: 387–97; also 'Tarraco in Late Antiquity', in Christie and Loseby (1996), 18–44.

[345] Some references to archaeological work on late cities in Spain: Arce 1982: 91–100; Barral I Altet 1982: 105–30; de Palol 1992: 381–94; Lloret 1993: 13–35; Gurt, Ripoll, and Fernández 1994: 161–80.

[346] De Palol 1992: esp. 390–4.

[347] Examples at Barcelona, Tarraco (Tarragona), Conimbriga, Seville.

[348] e.g. at Barcelona, Tarraco (Tarragona), Mérida.

the much more thinly urbanized centre and north. The difference between the centre and north of Gaul and Provence is somewhat similar, but the contrast was much sharper in Spain. The few larger cities were in the south, above all Merida,[349] Cordova,[350] and Seville.[351] Here city life seems to have continued much as in the fourth century.[352] In the north, at Tarraco (Tarragona), a considerable population was crammed into what had been the monumental centre.[353] Spanish cities, like the cities of Gaul, were now generally fortified, or refortified. At Barcelona inscriptions from the old forum area were reused in the widening and heightening of the walls, as well as in the construction of a church and a palace in the northern corner of the city, which to the present day has been the site of the episcopal complex and of the palace of the counts.[354] At the same time private housing encroached on the public roads. Formidable new fortifications have also been found at Merida. In some cases, for instance at Conimbriga, the wall cuts through previously inhabited areas.[355] The fortified area was on average even smaller than in Gaul.[356] The largest circuits in terms of area were Saragossa (60 hectares), Cordova (50), and Merida (49).[357] At Valentia the forum area was invaded in late fourth, or early fifth century, by a Christian cemetery and by a basilica and associated episcopal buildings.[358] Altogether our picture of Spanish towns in later Late Antiquity is still extremely fragmentary.[359]

It has been suggested that in Castille cities were of no great importance after the decline of Clunia in the third century; and that in Cantabria, and perhaps over the whole of the Meseta, a tribal matriarchal society survived from pre-Roman times into the Visigothic period.[360] This was of course

349 Collins 1980: 189–219; Díaz 1997; P. Mateos Cruz, 'Arqueología de la tardoantigüedad en Mérida', in A. Velázquez *et al.* (eds.), *Los últimos romanos en Lusitania* (Mérida, 1995), 127–52. *Id.*, *Mérida Visigoda, la escultura arquitectónica y litúrgica* (Badajoz, 1983).

350 J. F. Rodríguez Neila, *Historia de Córdoba* (Cordova, 1988), 523–54.

351 A. Blanco Freijeiro, *Historia de Sevilla* (Seville, 1984), 523–54.

352 Tarradell 1977.

353 Keay 1991.

354 J. O. Granados and I. Rodà, 'Barcelone a la baixa romanitat', *III Congrès d'història de Barcelona* (Barcelona: Institut Municipal d'Història, 1993), 25–46. Banks 1984: i. 600–62.

355 J. Alarcao and R. Etienne, *Fouilles de Conimbriga*, i. *Architecture* (Paris, 1977).

356 See Barral I Altet 1982: 105–30. Fernández Ochoa, 'Fortificaciones urbanas de época bajo-imperial en Hispania. Una aproximación crítica (Segunda Parte)', *Cuadernos de Prehistoria y Arqueológica de la Universidad Autónoma de Madrid,* 19 (1992), 319–60. M. Pfanner, 'Modelle römischer Stadtentwicklung am Beispiel Spaniens und der westlichen Provinzen', in W. Trillmich and P. Zanker (eds.), *Stadtbild und Ideologie* (Munich, 1990), 59–116.

357 M. Pidal, *Historia de España,* iii (Madrid, 1991), 362. Others: Lugo 34 ha., Leon 19, Recopolis 15, Barcelona 10, Conimbriga 9, Coria 6.5, Gerona 5/6, Toledo 5.

358 V. E. Torres and R. S. Sànchez, 'El àrea episcopal de Valentia', *Archivo Español de Arqueología,* 63 (1990), 347–54, p. 351 n. 23: references to similar developments at Barcelona, Clunia, Merida, and Conimbriga. See also García Moreno 1977–8: 311–21 and Mateos Cruz 1995: 239–63.

359 e.g. Barral I Altet 1982; Lloret 1993; de Palol 1992.

360 Hillgarth 1980: 1–60, relevant 6–7, citing A. Barbero and M. Vigil, 'La organización social de

also where many Visigoths were settled, as is witnessed by some large Gothic cemeteries.[361] Toledo is situated between the main areas of Gothic settlement and the Roman cities of the south. No doubt that is why it was chosen to be the royal capital.[362] To many of the cities of the centre and north-west Christianity came very late, to judge by the fact that in many cases a bishop is not mentioned before the sixth century[363] and the countryside was converted by hermits or wandering monks sometimes in opposition to the nearest bishop.[364]

The Roman games survived in a few cities. We hear of circus games at Saragossa in AD 504.[365] In the early seventh century king Sisebut blamed bishop Eusebius for attending games at Tarraco (Tarragona).[366] The section on the games in Isidore's *Origines (Etymologiae)* suggests that chariot races, performances by 'mimes', and perhaps gladiatorial shows were still going on. Certainly Isidore thought it worthwhile to warn Christians not to have anything to do 'with the madness of the circus, the immorality of the theatre, the cruelty of the amphitheatre, the atrocity of the arena and the luxury of the games'.[367] Perhaps the bullfighting of today is descended from the Roman shows in unbroken tradition.

Spain is a very large country, and the relatively few cities had large territories. It would appear that the Gothic administration continued to be based on cities. It was in a city that there was the headquarters of the count, who seems to have been in charge of both city and territory. The laws often refer to a *iudex territorii*, but it is not clear what this functionary's duties were, or indeed whether the phrase simply refers to whatever official (*defensor, comes, dux,* or royal *villicus)* happened to perform the duties of a judge in a particular area. In spite of the abundance of surviving legislation, we have altogether very little detailed information about the practicalities of secular administration. We can only conjecture how far in practice the city's territory was still controlled by the secular administrators residing in the city, nor can we assess the degree to which great landowners exercised power independently of the administrators in the city. Under the Arabs a number of landed families were extremely powerful, and some of these were the descendants of grandees of

los cántabros y sus transformaciones en relación con los orígenes de la Reconquista', in *Hispania Antigua*, i (Madrid, 1971), 197–232.

361 See Ripoll 1989, 1991*a* and *b*, 1993; some problems discussed by Heather 1996: 203–7.

362 Ripoll and Velázquez in Gurt, Ripoll, with Chavarría (2000), 521–78.

363 De Palol 1966: 5–67; see map 10 (dates of bishoprics), map 3 (distribution of Christian remains up to end of 5th cent.). A regional study: Mateos Cruz 1995: 239–63.

364 Hillgarth 1980: 38–9.

365 *Chron. Caes. Aug.* in *Chron Min.* II.223.

366 *PL* 80, col. 370.

367 *Origines* XVIII.59. Most of the articles on technical terms of the games are in the past tense, but *auriga* (33, cf. 41) *mimi* (49), *amphitheatrum*—where gladiators fight—(52) are in present tense.

Visigothic Spain.[368] It is certain that the Roman municipal system continued to be used by the Church for its purposes, with the bishop residing in the city, and governing religious life in both city and territory. Towards the end of the Visigothic period there were seventy-five bishoprics in mainland Spain.[369] Moreover the provinces of the Spanish Church coincided more or less with the old Roman provinces, and even the old subdivisions of provinces, the assize districts (*conventus*) had a place in ecclesiastical administration up to at least the mid-sixth century, perhaps much longer.[370] It does not of course follow that the boundaries remained unchanged.

The scanty prosopographical evidence from Spain does not allow us to establish how far the bishoprics were still held by members of the class of great landowners of Roman origin, as they were in Gaul. The evidence of the *Lives* of the Fathers of Merida suggest rather that they were not. On the other hand, it is abundantly clear that bishops, and particularly assemblies of bishops at national and provincial level, played a key role in the Visigothic system of government.

Spain was a land of large and splendid villas, which have left some extraordinary mosaics. It is reasonable to ask whether in the wide rural territories of Spain some of the villas performed functions elsewhere performed by cities. As in Britain villas reached a peak of size and splendour in the fourth century, though by then there were fewer than in the second century. No new buildings of the grand villa type were constructed after the end of imperial control, but many of the existing villas appear to have continued in use considerably longer. The villa of Torre de Palma in east-central Portugal, one of the largest villas in Iberia, seems to have been occupied until the seventh or even early eighth century.[371] The same is true of villas at Centcelles (Tarraco), Els Munts (Tarraco),[372] La Cocosa (Merida), El Rabacal (Conimbriga), Sao Cucufate (Beja),[373] and Cercadilla (Cordova),[374] all of which are now thought to have been in some kind of use well into the fifth, or even sixth centuries. In fact now that archaeologists are looking for evidence of late occupation they find it on an increasing number of sites.[375] It is likely that far more villas

368 H. Kennedy 1996: 15, on the Banu Qasi of Tedela and the Banu Amrus of Huesca.

369 Orlandis 1987: 218–19.

370 Gurt, Ripoll, and Fernández 1994: 164–8. E. Albertini, *Les Divisions administratives de l'Espagne romaine* (Paris, 1923).

371 S. Maloney and J. Hall, 'The villa of Torre de Palma (Alto Alentejo)', *JRA* 9 (1996), 275–94.

372 Chavarría Arnau 1996: 165–202, relevant 182–5.

373 J. De Alcaro, R. Étienne, and F. Mayet, *Les Villas romaines de Sao Cucufate*, 2 vols. (Paris, 1990).

374 Arce 1997*a*: 293–302. R. Hidalgo, *Espacio público y espacio privado en el conjunto palatino de Cercadilla, Córdoba* (Seville, 1996).

375 J. I. R. Guillén, 'La Villa tardorromana de la Malena en Azuara y sus mosaicos', *JRA* 5 (1992),

survived into the fifth century and beyond than has been assumed by earlier scholars,[376] though not of course unchanged. In many villas, residential areas, and particularly baths, were altered to make them unsuitable for more productive use. State apartments might be used for agricultural activities or to house workshops for craftsmen. Abandoned wings came to be used for burials. The mausoleum of the landowning family might be transformed into a church for the owner and his peasants. If a village grew up within or around the remains of the villa, the estate church might remain as the village church. Medieval churches are often found on villa sites, and sometimes there is evidence of continuous occupation from Roman times.[377]

It is of course partly a question of how you define continued use. After AD 400 few landowners could probably afford to live on the scale on which their predecessors had lived in the golden days of the fourth century. The literary and documentary evidence about *villae* becomes ambiguous from say the middle of the sixth century, because the term comes to acquire a much wider meaning, after all both the modern Spanish *villa* and the French *ville* are derived from it. There is however no reason to suppose that the structure of landholding changed significantly. Large estates, whether owned by Romans or Goths, or by the church or by monasteries, continued to dominate in many parts of Spain, and especially in the Meseta, and their masters were the real holders of power in the countryside.[378] Presumably many of them continued to inhabit the old villa, if only part of it.[379]

The great estates were probably largely self-sufficient. Nevertheless the surpluses in money and kind that they produced were in all likelihood sufficiently great for their owners to dominate urban markets also. In the villas around Tarraco self-sufficiency did not preclude the consumption of imported products from North Africa and even the East, for which there is evidence up to the seventh century.[380] Though much remains obscure about the villa estates and their owners in Visigothic times, it can hardly be doubted that they remained centres of power, and moreover of power that was centred in the country.

148–61 (the villa is near Saragoza); X. Aquilué, 'Nuevas publicaciones sobre el poblamiento rural en el nordeste de la Tarraconensis', ibid. 378–85, on villas at Vilaula and Tolegassos near Ampurias.

[376] Gorges 1979 was a comprehensive summary at the time of writing, but still has very little evidence for survival into the 5th or 6th cent. or beyond. I. Velázquez Soranio and G. Ripoll, 'Pervivencias del termalismo y el culto a las aguas en época visigoda hispánica', *Espacio, Tiempo y Forma,* Serie II, 5 (1992), 550–80, esp. 572–4, refers to six villas all close to hot springs whose thermal establishments appear to have been used in Visigothic times.

[377] Chavarría Arnau 1996 and 1997.

[378] Díaz 1994*a*: 457–76, 1994*b*: 297–309.

[379] On this and the following, see J. Arce and G. Ripoll in G. B. Brogiolo (ed.) (forthcoming) and for a comparison with Gaul: Claude 1997.

[380] Carréte, Keay, and Millett 1995.

It is perhaps not a coincidence that the majority of the surviving churches of the Visigothic era are in rural situations.[381] These churches were probably estate churches, founded, maintained, and controlled by a local landed magnate.[382] In many areas, both in the East and the West, monasteries came to acquire great estates and became economic centres and centres of power in the countryside. Monasticism came to Spain only in the later sixth century. The tradition is that it was introduced by monks exiled by persecution from Byzantine Africa and that the monks brought with them the Christian literary culture of North Africa and helped to initiate a literary revival. This is almost certainly an oversimplification. But it remains the case that monasteries did not have the direct economic or political impact in Visigothic Spain which they had in Merovingian Gaul. Their educational influence was another matter.[383]

In Italy the cities of the Later Empire as a rule still occupied the extensive sites of the *principate*.[384] During the fourth century at least, the appearance of city centres, and in fact most aspects of city life, were much closer to what they had been in the Early Empire than was the case in Gaul and Spain. But the beginning of the running down of monumental civic buildings could be seen there too.[385] At Ostia, the port of Rome, parts of the monumental centre were already abandoned. Some of the characteristic Ostian blocks of apartments appear to have been pulled down and levelled. The typical new building of fourth-century Ostia was the great private residence.[386] Some of the traditional competitive munificence survived in cities of the South, where from time to time municipal grandees might still be recompensed with inscribed monuments.[387] But decurions were now hardly ever associated with new public building. Such

[381] Mateos Cruz 1995: 240–62. Recently a post-Visigothic date for these churches has been suggested by L. Caballero Zoreda, 'North and west Iberia—sixth to tenth centuries', in Keay and Díaz-Andreu (1997), 236–64. The argument is based on style. This would leave an architectural gap. One would expect the political, legal, and literary revival after AD 587 also to involve an architectural revival.

[382] Schlunk and Hauschild 1978: 88, fig. 64. Pieces of monumental ornament found at Mérida and elsewhere, and the Gothic crypt at Palencia, show that there were Visigothic urban churches which have been replaced by later structures. See also S. Fructuosus in the amphitheatre at Tarraco: C. Godoy Fernández and M. dels S. Gros i Pujol, 'L'oracional hispànic de Verona i la topografia cristiana de Tarraco a l'antiguitat tardana', *Pyrenae*, 25 (1994), 245–58; by same author: 'La *memoria* de Fructueux, Augure et Euloge dans l'arène de l'amphithéatre de Tarragone', *Antiquité Tardive,* 3 (1995), 251–62.

[383] See below, p. 336.

[384] Dates of Italian walls are with a small number of exceptions uncertain, see Wataghin 1996: 239–71, esp. 248–50.

[385] For the following, Ward-Perkins is basic, see also Brogiolo 1999. Ibid. 101–5 has evidence for early dereliction.

[386] J. Delaine, 'The insula of the paintings at Ostia I.4.2–4', in T. J. Cornell and K. Lomas (eds.), *Urban Society in Roman Italy* (London, 1995), 79–106, esp. fig. 5.10. Earlier excavators seem to have removed most traces of rebuilding on the levelled insula.

[387] Mrozek 1978: 355–68.

new buildings as were put up had either been donated by senatorial patrons, or were financed out of civic resources at the instigation of the provincial governor; and it was the latter who was given the credit and duly rewarded with a statue bearing his name.[388]

It is notable that cities of the north have produced few inscriptions of that kind. This difference between north and south should not be taken to show that the southern cities were more prosperous. Almost certainly the reverse was the case.[389] Wealth and political importance had shifted to the north.[390] It was the influence and patronage of members of the Roman senatorial aristocracy, who owned estates in the territories of the southern towns, which preserved some of the traditional civic pomp and ceremony. But all voluntary munificence everywhere, north or south, whether of governors or of private individuals, ceased early in the fifth century.

In the disturbed times that followed, the imperial government from time to time helped to finance fortifications.[391] Meanwhile the transformation of the classical city gathered pace. Temples were destroyed, or more often allowed to fall into ruins. Churches might be built on the site of a razed temple. The conversion of the actual structure of a temple into a church was exceptional before the late fifth century.[392] In many places civic buildings such as monumental fora, theatres, amphitheatres, and colonnades were allowed to fall into decay. On the whole aqueducts, baths, and bridges fared better.[393] The late fourth and early fifth century saw much building of churches. As in Gaul, there was another second great wave of church building in the late fifth and first half of the sixth century. After the Vandal conquest of North Africa, Italy was noticeably impoverished, and there is evidence in some cities that residential areas began to be abandoned.[394] Justinian's war of liberation was a disaster, and the Lombard invasion following soon after prevented recovery. The ultimate effect on cities was different in north and south. In northern Italy and Tuscany of some one hundred Roman *municipia* three-quarters still survived in AD 1000. Of those abandoned the majority were situated in Luguria and western Aemilia, inland Venetia,[395] or Picenum. Many of the

[388] Lepelley 1992: 353–71.

[389] Ruggini 1961. Cantino Wataghin 1996: 244–5: Late Roman baths at Milan, Brescia, Parma, Aosta, and Susa.

[390] Ruggini 1961.

[391] N. Christie and A. Rushworth, 'Urban fortification and defensive strategy in fifth and sixth century Italy: The case of Terracina', *JRA* 1 (1988), 73–83.

[392] Caillet 1996: 191–211. Hanson 1985: 347–58.

[393] Potter 1995: esp. 90–102.

[394] N. Christie, 'Milan as imperial capital and its hinterland', *JRA* 6 (1993), 485–7, review of *Milano capitale dell'impero Romano 286–402* (Milan, 1990). T. K. Token, 'Early medieval Florence between history and archaeology', in Ch. Redman (ed.), *Medieval Archaeology* (New York, 1988), 261–83. See also below, p. 372.

[395] Explained by cities' situation away from important lines of communication: Cantino Wataghin 1996: 254–5, with bibliography on continuity and survival of north Italian cities.

abandoned cities are not known to have ever had a bishop. The lack of a bishop considerably reduced a city's chances of survival.

In the south the survival rate of cities was much lower than in the north. Less than half of the cities of southern Italy, centres of small and infertile hill territories, survived the troubles of the sixth and seventh centuries.[396] The decline of rural settlement was quite parallel to that of the cities. From the end of the fourth century many villas were abandoned, others were partly abandoned and partly adapted to simpler forms of living. The villa system can be said to have come to an end in northern Italy by the end of the sixth century.[397]

Late Late Antiquity was not a period of decline only. In the north, particularly in the foothills of the Alps, the fifth and sixth centuries saw the establishment of many new settlements, situated in naturally defensible positions on hilltops or promontories or islands, and further strengthened by fortifications.[398] Some enclosed substantial buildings, especially churches, some were little more than refuges for the population in times of war. Some developed into cities,[399] most did not. Many are in 'strategic' situations, but by no means all. The history of these places is almost invariably obscure. Apart from a small number of fortified hill-sites established on the orders of Theoderic, we do not, as a rule, know whether a particular fort was founded by the local population or by the central government;[400] nor do we have information how they were governed. The hill-top enclosures of northern Italy have many exact parallels in Macedonia and Dalmatia. They were clearly a response to the disturbed conditions of the 'age of migrations'. They also mark the beginning of the process of *incastellamento* which eventually resulted in a large part of the rural population of Italy, both in the north and in the south living in fortified hill-top *castelli*.[401]

In Sicily we can observe contrasting change in town and country. Many cities particularly those situated inland, began to decline in the fourth century or earlier, not so the ports of Syracuse, Catania, and Massala from which the corn grown on the island was exported. The Sicilian country-

396 Wickham 1981: 80, 148–9.

397 Brogiolo 1996. Rural developments are treated more fully below, pp. 380–3.

398 Brogiolo and Gelichi 1996: general account and archaeology of Monte Barro, Castelseprio, Monselice, Castellarno, and Imola.

399 Most notably Ferrara, originally a Byzantine fortress on the border of the exarchate, Brogiolo and Gelichi 1996: 49–57; also Grado on the Venetian lagoon.

400 Cassiodorus, *Variae*, I.17, Theoderic orders Goths and Romans at Dertona (Tortona in Luguria) to build fortifications and houses in nearby fort; cf. also ibid. III.481, the king orders Goths and Romans to build houses in fort at Verruca, a strategic hill-top site in neighbourhood, perhaps above Tridentum (Trento). Ibid. V.9 order to *possessoribus Feltrinis* to build a fort near Tridentum.

401 Wickham 1981: 163–7, 173–5; also *Il problema dell'incastellamento nell'Italia centrale* (Florence, 1985); on the phenomenon of *incastellamento* in general and particularly in Spain, see Barceló and Toubert 1998.

side, in striking contrast to that of Campania and indeed most of the western side of Italy, prospered right through the fifth and sixth centuries, as can be seen from abundant evidence of buildings and cemeteries.[402] The fourth century saw the construction of new villas, which lasted well into the fifth century. It looks as if the Sicilian aristocrats had transferred their principal residence to the countryside and exported the produce of their estates through the three principal ports. When the villas were abandoned villages were established on the ruins.[403] Remains of churches are almost all later than 500, though few are securely dated.[404]

The cities of North Africa had been the most flourishing in the Latin-speaking provinces to the very end of the fourth century.[405] The decline of classical monumental urbanism, which had taken place in Gaul and Spain and much of the Balkans more than a century earlier, seems only to have begun in North Africa in the first decade of the fifth century. It has been observed that the construction cycle in North Africa was approximately a century behind that of Italy.[406] The epigraphic evidence remains extraordinarily abundant until the beginning of the fifth century, but it falls away rapidly from the first decade of the new century. This makes it difficult to trace the subsequent history of cities other than Carthage.[407] The Vandal invasion surely caused a lot of damage even if archaeologists have so far found little trace of it.[408] The Vandals confiscated many large estates, some of whose dispossessed owners fled the Vandal kingdom.[409] But evidently much of the war damage was repaired. The circus and amphitheatre continued to function. The Greens and Blues operated at Carthage, and provided mimes and charioteers. The poet Luxorius recited in the Baths of Gargilius, even though the baths of Antonius had fallen into decay and the great civil basilica on the Byrsa hill had been abandoned.

It used to be thought that production of mosaics, which had flourished in the fourth century, came to an end under the Vandals. Now a series of mosaics has been redated into the fifth century, and this and other archaeological evidence suggests that the thoroughgoing embellishment

402 Wilson 1996: 185–8, 232–6.

403 Wilson 1996: 333–6, but only two villas cited: Patti Marina and Piazza Armerina.

404 Wilson 1996: 305–8.

405 Lepelley 1979–80.

406 Jouffroy 1986: 461–2.

407 Averil Cameron 1982, 1989, 1993*a*. Bibliographies: N. Duval 1990, 1993; Mattingly and Hitchner 1995. Churches: N. Duval, Caillet, and Gui 1992; Modéran 1993. Victor de Vita's *History of the Vandal Persecutions* is the principal but enormously one-sided literary source on Vandal Africa. On Carthage: Ennabli 1997.

408 Victor de Vita I.8: at Carthage they destroyed the odeum, the theatre, the Temple of Memory, and the colonnade of the so-called Via Caelestis.

409 Proc. III.5.12–14; *Nov. Val.* 34 (451).

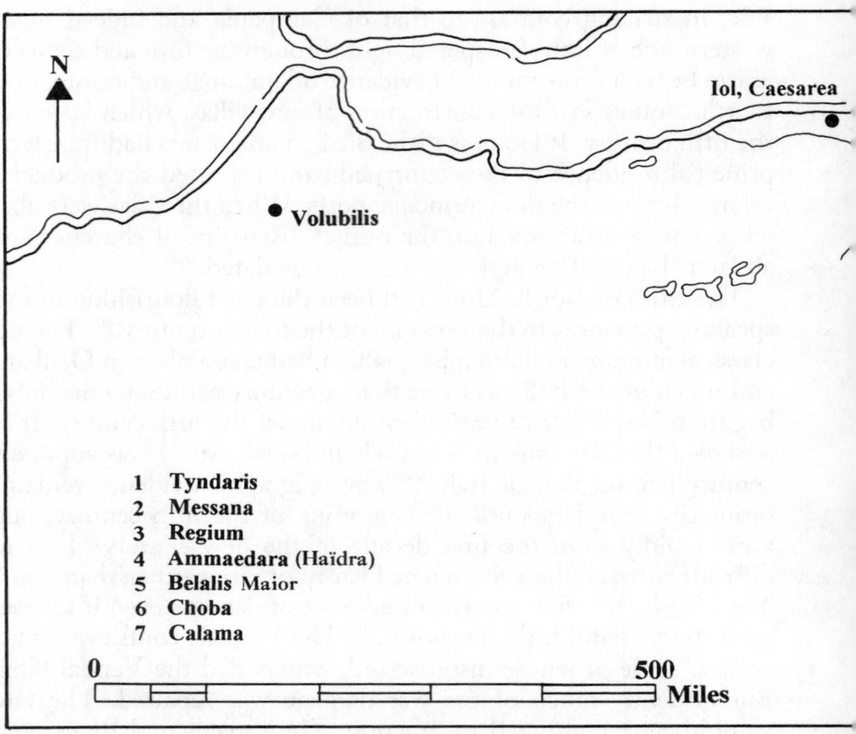

15. Cities in North Africa

of older Late Empire type mansions, and even the building on new ones, continued during the Vandal period. We do not know who owned these houses. But whether the owners were Vandals or Romans, or, as is likely, included both Vandals and Romans, it is clear that the leaders of Carthaginian society continued to enjoy a senatorial life-style.[410]

There is evidence that the city's walls were being neglected from perhaps the middle of the fifth century.[411] But the city seems to have remained peopled over its whole area.[412] So the neglect, or even abandon-

[410] Basilica: Gros 1985; hippodrome: Humphrey 1988: 1–178; circular harbour: Hurst 1994. On the villas of the Odeon quarter and the redating of mosaics, see Ben Abed and N. Duval, 'La Capitale du royaume vandale et les villes de la Tunisie', in J. M. Gurt and G. Ripoll (eds.), *Sedes Regiae* (Barcelona, 2000), 163–218. More generally, F. M. Clover, 'Carthage and the Vandals', in *Excavations at Carthage*, vii, ed. J. H. Humphrey (Ann Arbor, 1982), 1–22.

[411] Fulford and Peacock 1984: 255–62.

[412] Mattingly and Hitchner 1995: 210–11. How long the city remained fully built up is of course a question. The three small neighbourhoods whose excavation is discussed by S. T. Stevens, 'Transitional neighbourhoods and suburban frontiers in Late and Post-Roman Carthage' in Mathisen and Sivan (1996), 187–200, suggest that neighbourhoods near the wall continued to be built up well into the 6th cent. and perhaps beyond.

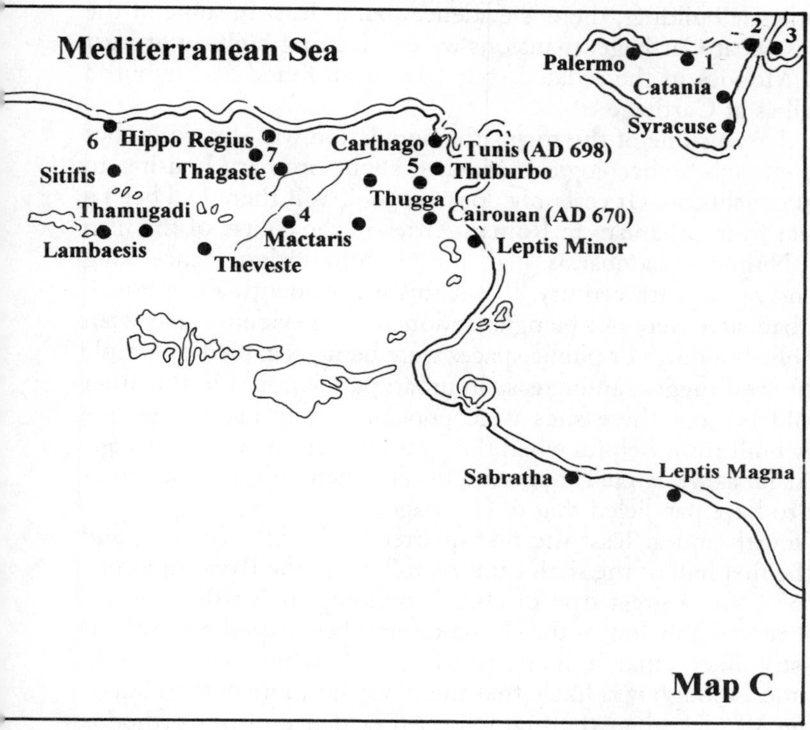

ment, of some secular communal buildings does not mean that the population was shrinking. What often seems to have happened at Carthage, and earlier and on larger scale in smaller towns, is that modest, simply constructed housing invaded what had been public spaces.[413]

Opinions differ about the evolution of cities other than Carthage. For a long time archaeologists ignored the late levels. Evidence has now been uncovered which suggests that monumental buildings, for instance, public structures around the forum,[414] theatres, amphitheatres,[415] and large bath buildings, were allowed to decline in many, but perhaps not all, cities from around the second half of the fifth century.[416]

[413] Humphrey 1980: 85–120.

[414] Potter 1995: 64–73.

[415] Augustine welcomed decay of theatres and amphitheatres, e.g. cs. 13–14 in Sermon Mayence 13, *De Psalmo* LXXXI, published B. F. Dolbeau, *Rev. des Ét. Augustiniennes,* 39 (1993), 97–106, which he dates 403–4, cited by Lepelley 1996: 12.

[416] Mattingly and Hitchner 1995: 210, 212–13. Examples: L. Maurin, 'Thuburbo Maius et la paix vandale', *Cahiers de Tunisie,* 12 (1967), 57–60, 240–50. C. Poinssot, *Les Ruines de Dougga* (Tunis, 1958). A. Beschaouch, A. Hanoune, M. Khanoussi, A. Olivier, and Y. Thébert, *Recherches archéo-*

As for domestic building, there is evidence that at least in some of the smaller towns, as at Carthage, mansions were still being built, or at least redecorated. Mosaics in the redated style have been found at Thuburbo Maius as well as at Carthage.

It may be that in some of the towns the population was shrinking, but there is not enough archaeological evidence about ordinary housing to draw general conclusions. It certainly does not look as if there had been a general retreat from urbanism in Roman Africa in the course of the fifth century. In Numidia Lambaesis had shrunk into insignificance long before the end of the fifth century.[417] But this was evidently exceptional. As a rule, urban sites were not being abandoned. The evidence that what had been public buildings or public spaces were being occupied by simple houses might even suggest an increase in urban population. On the other hand, it could be that these sites were popular simply because people found solidly built ruins helpful when they put up their own humble constructions. As far as we can tell at present, development of the minor cities would seem to have paralleled that of Carthage.

The late fourth and at least the first quarter of the fifth century, and then again the first half of the sixth century, following the Byzantine conquest (AD 533), saw a great deal of church building in North Africa,[418] even if so far remarkably few of the churches have been dated precisely. It is perhaps still likely that a majority of the churches were built in Byzantine times, though it is likely that there was far more church building under the Vandals than the highly biased evidence of our orthodox sources would lead us to believe. Some of the African churches were very large.

The massive building programme undertaken after the defeat of the Vandals by the new Byzantine authorities at Carthage, and elsewhere in the province, was financed largely but perhaps not entirely at the expense of the Empire, and it was not limited to the building of churches.[419] At Carthage there is archaeological evidence for work of roads, and on the harbour, as well as on churches. All over Byzantine Africa there was a very

logiques Franco-Tunisiennes à Bulla Regia 1–4, Collection de l'école française de Rome 28/1–28/4 (Rome, 1980–93). For other towns, see below, p. 377.

417 On mosaics redated to mid-5th cent. at Thuburbo Maius, see Ben Abed and N. Duval in Gurt and Ripoll 2000, 197–206; on end of Lambaesis: Y. Duval, *Lambèse chrétienne, la gloire et l'oublie* (Paris, 1995), 115–30.

418 Averil Cameron 1982; N. Duval *et al.* 1992; Modéran 1993. N. Duval, 'Les Églises de Haïdra III', *CRAI* (1971), 160–6. At Carthage the churches of S. Agileus and of Bir el Knissia appear to have been built during the Vandal period (Ennabli 1997: 38–9, 113–20).

419 See Procopius, *Aed* VI.5–7, which raises many questions.

extensive programme of fortifications.[420] The new circuits often enclosed a much smaller area than had been built-up in the fourth century. For instance at Calama 4.33 hectares were enclosed; at Theveste 7.50; at Leptis Magna first 40 and after a second shortening of the line, 28; at Sabratha 8.50; at Sitifis 1.69; and at Choba 5.25.[421] At Sabratha the new wall cuts right across the ruined forum. The majority of Byzantine circuit walls are fortresses, or fortified refuges rather than town-walls.[422] At Theveste the walls enclose 7.5 hectares, but an area of something like 50 hectares around the fortress shows abundant traces of fifth- to seventh-century settlement. At Ammaedara (Hadrumetum of 2.5 hectares) the remains of four churches can be seen outside the walls.[423] Clearly the populations of these cities in the sixth century cannot be assessed simply on the evidence of their walled area. But we are still very much in the dark as to the proportions of inhabitants of a city that might be found respectively within and without walls.

Byzantine rule did not bring lasting prosperity. Its story is still very obscure. But two features are certainly significant: Liberation from the Vandals, which might be described more accurately as conquest by the Byzantines, was very quickly followed by the collapse of Latin literary culture, theological as well as secular. Then, a century and a half later, the Arab conquest (Carthage fell in AD 697) rapidly led to the eclipse of African Christianity.[424] There was something rotten in the state of late Late Roman Africa. From the second half of the sixth century, or perhaps from the early seventh century, the city of Carthage was in full decay, with burials invading the intramural area, so that islands of dense building were separated by sparsely built-up zones with cemeteries. The end of Carthage cannot be dated. The whole late Late Roman layer is very thin and this makes all dating difficult.[425] In a number of places there is clear evidence that decay of the town centre was paralleled by a regrouping of urban life around the principal churches, as at Sufetula.[426] Large areas of Belalis Maior were abandoned and covered by silt in the later sixth century, but the large basilica was entirely reconstructed around AD 600, and once more thoroughly renovated in the mid-seventh century.[427] At Iol Caesarea

420 D. Pringle, *The Defence of Byzantine Africa from Justinian to the Arab Conquest,* BAR Int. 99 (Oxford, 1981).

421 Ibid. 119.

422 Fortifications in order of size, ibid. 126–7.

423 Ibid. 119.

424 See below, pp. 376–7.

425 See Hurst and Roskams 1984: 42–7. Fulford and Peacock 1984: 255–75. See also below, p. 377.

426 Potter 1995: 66–7, 73. On Sufetula, N. Duval, 'Observations sur l'urbanisme tardif de Sufetula', *Cahiers de Tunisie*, 12 (1964), 87–112; *id.*, 'L'Urbanisme de Sufetula/Sbeitla en Tunisie', *ANRW* X.2 (1982), 593–622. N. Duval and F. Baratte, *Les Ruines de Sufetula: Sbeitla* (Tunis, 1973).

427 A. Mahjoubi, *Recherches d'histoire et d'archéologie à Henchir el-Faouar (Tunisie): La Cité de Belalitani Maiores* (Tunis, 1978).

(Cherchel) the excavated forum, basilica, and church went out of use and were systematically demolished *c.*520–30. Subsequently two rather rudimentary and irregularly shaped stone buildings and two rectangular timber structures were built on part of the site. The date of these constructions was roughly around AD 640, by which time the 370-hectare site of Iol Caesarea was occupied by one, or perhaps more than one, village and cultivated fields.[428] The chronology of urban degeneration, that is the increasing prevalence of more primitive building techniques, and the appearance of large empty spaces in what had been fully built-up areas, is still very uncertain. At Rougga wooden houses were built in the forum area in the mid-sixth century, which were in their turn destroyed by fire around AD 647.[429] It may be that in North Africa as in Anatolia the decisive downturn took place from the second half of the sixth century.

When we survey the evolution of cities in East and West together we note that some basic developments occurred everywhere, though not everywhere at the same time. The Justinianic building campaign in North Africa and elsewhere was, whether Justinian was aware of it or not, part of a general revival of monumental building, not restricted to territories still governed by the Empire, and shared by East and West, though in the East the revival began a few decades earlier.[430] It everywhere involved much construction of churches. Though the Western revival produced nothing as spectacular as St Sophia, the earliest and most artistically distinguished buildings of the Western revival, which were constructed at Ravenna under the Ostrogoths and in the first decades after the Justinianic reconquest, are extremely impressive.[431] In Merovingian Gaul the second half of the sixth century saw the building of many new and impressive churches, though none of them has survived to be admired today.[432] The latest episode in this revival was the remarkable flourishing of building and related crafts early in the seventh century, in Visigothic Spain.[433]

The Western provinces did not have the monumental villages found in the East. In the West, but not as far as we can tell in the East, the grandees transferred their main residence to the countryside, though they were no longer able to live in the splendour of classical villas. But the Western countryside receives some monumental structures too, in the

[428] Potter 1995: 48–61.

[429] R. Guery, L'Occupation de Rougga (Bararus) d'après la stratigraphie du forum', *BCTH*, NS 17B (1984), 91–100.

[430] e.g. at Aphrodisias, Gerasa, Bostra, Caesarea, see above, pp. 36–7, below pp. 297–303.

[431] La Rocca 1992.

[432] Rouche 1979: table, p. 295; also Claude 1960; Dhondt 1957; Cüppers 1977; P.-A. Février 1980.

[433] Collins 1983: 51–5. On the suggestion that the buildings should be dated in the 8th or even 9th cent., see above, p. 94, n. 38. If that is correct, it would make the buildings part of the Lombardo/Carolingian renewal rather than the last of the classical revivals.

shape of monasteries. There were fewer of these in the West than in the East, but the individual monastery tended to be more wealthy and powerful, in fact a city of celebates.[434] Moreover Western monasteries were instruments of royal of aristocratic control in a way Eastern monasteries as a rule were not. In the West as in the East the administrative union of town and rural territory, the foundation of the classical city, was dissolved, though not in the same way. No Western monarchy was able to impose a theme-system. The countryside became subject to rurally based magnates.

It is not at all obvious what factors accelerated change in some regions, or slowed it down in others. Settlement of barbarians by itself was nowhere decisive. It has in fact left very little trace in the archaeological record. In Britain, where the decline and fall of the classical city was most rapid and most complete, it happened essentially before the Anglo-Saxon settlement. The end of the large-scale redistribution of money and agricultural products through imperial taxation and imperial expenditure certainly had a far-reaching impact on cities, as indeed on the whole of society.[435] But local conditions also contributed to the pace and extent of change. Above all there must have been a significant difference between the social and economic functions of cities in Western Europe and those of the older cities around the Mediterranean. Most of the changes that occurred in the West eventually happened in the East also, though the development there took considerably longer. But the collapse of the city system in Anatolia when it came seems to have been more rapid and thorough than in all but a few regions of the West.[436]

[434] Hodges, Gibson, and Mitchell 1997.
[435] See below, pp. 385–6.
[436] These topics will be discussed more fully in Chapters 9 and 12 of this book.

3

Post-curial Civic Government

1. *From Government by* Curiales *to Government by Notables in the East*

The legislation in Justinian's *Code* affecting cities still includes an abundance of laws whose object is to stop the drain of men and property from the city councils into the imperial service or the Church.[1] In fact the imperial government's struggle to keep men and wealth in the councils continued beyond the publication of the Justinianic *Code* into the subsequent *Novels*.[2] This might suggest that councils continued to play a vital role in the administration of their cities, and indeed the functioning of the Empire. That impression is misleading. Other evidence, including legislative evidence, tells a different story, that of the decline and fall of curial government.[3]

Loss of control by the councils was a gradual process. A plausible explanation was given by Libanius writing towards the end of the fourth century AD. The maintenance of curial strength depended essentially on the *curiales* themselves. If they did not keep their colleagues to their duties nobody could. But the most powerful councillors did not mind if their colleagues left the council, for this meant that they would have fewer rivals.[4] The consideration that they would now also have to bear a larger share of the financial burdens ceased to carry much weight as the civic services which councillors had to provide, that is public buildings, banquets, spectacles, and competitions came to be valued less, or were financed in new ways. On the other hand, there was little reason why an ordinary decurion should want to remain in his council. If he had the necessary connections he was likely to gain more wealth and esteem in the imperial service or the Church. In any case he would enjoy a more carefree life outside the council. Councillors always risked being beaten or bankrupted, and when the risk was no longer compensated by the prospect of high esteem in the city many councillors decided to leave. The

[1] *CJ X* 32.1–67 (AD 529); 33.1–4; 35.1–3; 38.1.
[2] Just. *Nov* 38 (536); 87 (539); 101 (439).
[3] *Nov* 38 *praef.* '. . . ut sub istos perditos conductores quos vindices vocant redacta, curia plena quidem defectibus, plena vero omni iniustitia fieret.'
[4] Libanius *Or.* XLIX.8–11, cf. XLVIII.37–41.

government did its utmost right up to the reign of Justinian to stop this trend through legislation,[5] but evidently with very limited success.

Other factors tended to undermine control of cities by their councils. Government by *curiales* was an oligarchy of the propertied: the *curiales* had achieved the leadership because they were the wealthiest inhabitants of their city. In the course of the fourth and fifth centuries they lost this position. Already in the fourth century the *curiales* of Antioch were beginning to be overshadowed by resident ex-officials of senatorial rank, who had privileged access to the governors and were exempt from curial duties and expenses. In the course of time more and more land was acquired also by the clerks and accountants of the local staff of the imperial administration. The social and economic rise of the provincial bureaucracy can be traced in considerable detail in the papyrus documents of Egypt.[6] In the fourth century *curiales* were the principal landowners in the cities of Egypt. In the fifth century landholding in city territories came to be dominated by senatorial *honorati*,[7] and also by higher ranking members of the provincial *officium* and their descendants. There was also a steady increase in the amount of land owned by ecclesiastical institutions. Among the landowners the remaining *curiales*, now generally known as *politeuomenoi* (πολιτευόμενοι), had become comparatively insignificant. Because of the absence of a rule of primogeniture, estates were normally divided between all the male heirs of the deceased owner. This meant that large blocks of property were often broken up within two or three generations. The law might up to a point succeed in preventing the land of *curiales* from passing to men who were exempt from curial duties, but it could not prevent individual *curiales* from sinking in the civic rank-order of wealth and of influence associated with wealth. The sixth century saw more and more land pass into great estates whose owners held titles of the highest grades of senatorial rank, whether honorific or acquired by holding high office in the imperial administration.[8]

The stages by which the councils lost control and responsibility for their cities can be traced to a certain extent. The last time we hear of the council of Ephesus was in AD 431, when the *comes* Candidianus

[5] Schubert 1969.

[6] See the excellent unpublished thesis of Banaji 1992: i. 134–163; ii. 51 ff.: Roman Egypt AD 100–700: a catalogue of landholders.

[7] Up to say the middle of the 5th cent. the *honorati*, i.e. ex-officials of senatorial rank, will have been a significant group only in prominent cities, but subsequently there was an inflation of senatorial rank with the result that there came into existence a hierarchically graded aristocracy at provincial level, whose members were found in greater or larger numbers in every city. See Banaji 1992: 158 ff. and pp. 279–81 below.

[8] The tax register of Hermopolis lists 40 *clarissimi* (of either sex), 12 *illustres*, over a dozen *comites*, but only 4 *politeuomenoi*, 4 or 5 *defensores*, 2 *riparii*, 2 *nuktostratēgoi* (Gascou 1994: 61–2 and index, 280–2).

summoned the councillors together with *honorati* (ἀξιοματικοί) to vote in favour of the replacement of the city's bishop, who was accused of Nestorian tendencies.[9] On that occasion the council was evidently in charge of Ephesus to the extent that its vote was required for the deposition of the bishop. The situation was somewhat different at Edessa in Mesopotamia in AD 448, when there was what can only be called a conspiracy to rid the city of its bishop Ibas, accused of the same heresy.[10] Peace and quiet of the city were disturbed by frequent demonstrations in the streets, in church, and in the governor's court calling for the bishop's deposition. Eventually the governor of Osroene, the *comes* Chaireas was prevailed upon to send successive petitions to the imperial authorities at Constantinople. A plausible attempt was made to suggest that the demand for the replacement of Ibas represented consensus of the whole city, and that all orders had participated in drawing it up. The phrasing of the document itself is conservative. It reflects the traditional constitutional order of rank in that the councillors, the *politeuomenoi* are mentioned first among the petitioners.[11] But the order of signatures is a truer reflection of the actual order of rank within the city. For clerics signed first, followed by monks, *honorati* (*axiomatikoi*) and councillors (*politeuomenoi*), and finally by representatives of the various schools at Edessa, and of the artisan guilds.[12] The implication of that order is clearly that councillors ranked below clerics, monks, and *honorati*, but above teachers and craftsmen. A number of individual councillors supported the petition, and one of them claimed that the *archontes* (ἄρχοντες) did so too.[13] But the councillors did not present the petition; it was presented to the governor sitting in his court, together with some clerics and a number of *honorati*, by a man of senatorial rank, the *comes* Theodosius.[14] The council as a constitutional body evidently played no part at all. In fact the petition had been drawn up by a pressure group of clerics and monks, with the support of some *honorati*, including the *comes* Theodosius, and of some councillors, but the council as such was simply bypassed.

A few years later, a law issued by the emperor Leo in AD 469 tacitly acknowledged that the councils had ceased to be the ruling body of their cities, for the emperor decreed that any sale of land which had been bequeathed or donated to a city must be sanctioned by a vote, not just of

[9] *ACO* Tom. I, vol. i/3, p. 47 (101). προσκαλούμενος τὸ σεμνὸν βουλευτήριον καὶ τοὺς λαμπροτάτους καὶ ἐξαιτῶν . . . φηφίματα.

[10] Flemming and Hoffmann 1917, Syriac text edited with German translation; an English translation: Perry 1881.

[11] Flemming and Hoffmann 1917: 23. Evagrius *HE* II.9 refers to a comparable petition produced at Alexandria against Timothy the Cat, a Chalcedonian bishop, in AD 457, see below, p. 258.

[12] Flemming and Hoffmann 1917: 25.31–5.

[13] Six in all, assuming that the *princeps* and the *scholasticus* are not *politeuomenoi* (ibid. 39.1–19).

[14] Ibid. 35.23–5.

the council, but of a joint gathering of decurions and *honorati* and landowners of the town.[15]

Around AD 500, that is about 50 years after the conspiracy against Ibas, the *Chronicle of Joshua Stylites* allows us another glimpse at the politics of Edessa.[16] The provincial governor now ruled the city. When he needed to consult representatives of the city he consulted the 'grandees' that is the *honorati*. These were the people whom he asked how he might raise gold to buy off the Persians.[17] Another time it was the 'grandees' who insisted that the governor must publish a tariff of what services civilian hosts were obliged to provide for the soldiers billeted on them.[18] In time of famine the 'grandees' set up infirmaries.[19] The councillors (nobles) are mentioned too. They organized the billeting of soldiers among the households of the town, and used this opportunity to enrich themselves.[20] So the councillors still had duties, even though the imperial authorities had ceased to treat the council as the voice of the city. We are told that once, in time of famine, it was the decurions (nobles) who marched at the head of a huge procession, immediately behind the bishop and the governor.[21] This suggests that the council still retained its symbolic status even after its role as the intermediary between the citizens and the governor had passed to the 'grandees'. The 'grandees' of Edessa were to have history well beyond the Arab invasion,[22] but it can be assumed that the council's formal responsibility for the city came to an end soon after AD 500.

It was in the reign of Anastasius (491–518) that the emperor ruled that *defensor* and *curator* of Corycus in Cilicia were to be elected by the bishop and *chosen* (λογάδων) inhabitants of the city. The ruling was a response to a petition sent in the name of bishop, clergy, landowners, and inhabitants. We notice that the council and the councillors are not explicitly mentioned either among the proposed electors or among the petitioners.[23] No doubt there were councillors in each group, but only as individuals. The council as a body had lost its privileged position.

15 *CJ* XI.32.3 (469), praesentibus omnibus, seu plurima parte, tam curialium, quam honoratorum et possessorum civitatis.

16 W. Wright, *The Chronicle of Joshua the Stylite*, composed in Syriac around AD 507, with a translation into English and notes (Cambridge, 1882); a new annotated translation by J. Watt and F. Trombley, in the Translated Texts for Historians Series (Liverpool), is due to appear in 2000.

17 Ibid. 63.

18 Ibid. 93.

19 Ibid. 43.

20 Ibid. 86.

21 Ibid. 43.

22 See below, pp. 305–7.

23 *MAMA* III.197A. The name is to be proposed by bishop, clergy and τῶν ἐν πᾶσι κτήτορσι κὲ οἰκήτορσι λογάδων. The law is not dated. It may be later than *CJ* I.4.19 of AD 505 which still mentions *curiales*, after bishop, clergy, *honorati*, and *possessores*, among the electors of the *defensor*. *Curiales* are not mentioned in *Nov* 15, 'de defensoribus' of AD 535.

This ruling was one of a number by which Anastasius systematically established the regime of the men whom I, following the precedent of A. H. M. Jones, describe as the 'notables', that is the men who were the actual, as opposed to the traditional, leaders of civic society. This did not mean that he abolished councils and councillors—even though some sources suggest that he did just that. In an oration of 514–15 the orator Priscian praised Anastasius for lightening the tax burden of the peasantry in consequence of all the *curiae* having abandoned their perverse habits.[24] This obscure formulation is usually taken to refer to the creation of the office of the *vindex* to supervise the collection of taxation. Malalas, writing in the reign of Justinian, is a little more precise. According to him, Marinus, praetorian prefect (512–15), 'dismissed all members of the city councils and in their place created the vindices, as they are known in each city of the Roman state'.[25] Writing around AD 555 John Lydus implies that the councils have ceased to exist and that their long history as ruling assemblies of cities had come to an end when Anastasius established the new office of *vindex*.[26] A generation or so later the ecclesiastical historian Evagrius (writing AD 593/4) appears to suggest that decurions have long ceased to exist. He confirms the testimony of Lydus and Malalas that *vindices* had replaced councillors as collectors of taxes.[27] So the end of curial government and even of the *curiae* themselves, in the reign of Anastasius appears to be well authenticated.

The testimony of these authors can nevertheless not be altogether right. Among the 68 laws of section 32 of the tenth book of Justinian's *Code*, laws 33–4 and 35–53 are concerned to ensure that councillors, and if not the councillors then their descendants, and if not the men themselves then at least their property, remain at the council's disposal to meet civic expenditure. While many of the laws date from the fourth century, legislation in this field was still issued by Anastasius and Justinian.[28] There can be no doubt that these emperors, and particularly Justinian, thought that the preservation of the numbers, and even more of the financial strength, of the councils, remained essential for the well-being of cities and empire. So Malalas, Lydus, and Evagrius have certainly exaggerated. But they can scarcely be totally wrong. A plausible compromise, and one consistent with what we know about cities in the sixth century, would be that Anastasius and Marinus did deprive councils of collective responsibility for the administration of their cities, and also of the joint liability for the collection of the imperial taxes. But this left the councillors with a

24 Chauvot 1986: 64 (194), cf. *Nov* Just. 38 *praef.* cited above, p. 104 n. 3.
25 Malalas XVI 400 (p. 225, tr. Jeffreys).
26 J. Lydus, *De Mag.* III.49 (ed. A. C. Bandy, Philadelphia, 1983, p. 208), cf. ibid. I.28 (p. 44).
27 *HE* III.42.
28 *CJ* X.32.66 (497–9), 67 (529), 35.3 (528), *Nov* 38 (536), *Nov* 87 (539), *Nov* 101 (539).

hereditary liability to perform certain *munera* of an unpleasant and expensive kind, so that even Jews, Samaritans, Montanists, and other heretics who were excluded from all public honours,[29] were not by any means to be exempted from the obligations of decurions.[30] The relevant burdens could be either personal or financial. It is however likely that financial burdens predominated, since a law of AD 539 makes curial duties a servitude on property, so that men who acquired curial property *ipso facto* became decurions.[31]

Councils continued to have some collective identity.[32] As the laws show, they might own property. Presumably they continued to meet, if only to organize the functions that were left to them. It is likely that their precise role varied considerably from area to area, and city to city. At Ombi in the Thebaid the council brought an accusation against an official late in the sixth century.[33] The early seventh-century tax register of Hermopolis names the council of Antinoopolis along with certain churches, monasteries, and secular bodies, as well as certain individuals, as intermediaries between taxpayers and the official receivers of tax.[34] Papyrus documents, dating from the sixth century, found at Petra in Arabia mention *politeuomenoi* from Petra itself, as well as the council of a neighbouring city.[35] In the papyri of the church of Ravenna, which though in Italy, was under Byzantine administration, the latest mention of *curia* and magistrates occurs in a land registration document of AD 625.[36] A decurion of Gortyn in Crete is mentioned in a letter of Pope Vitalian (657–72).[37] Leo VI (886–912) formally abolished city councils in the Byzantine Empire.[38] By then surviving councils had long become an anachronism.

[29] Just. *Nov* 37.5–7 (535).

[30] Just. *Nov* 45 *praef.* (537).

[31] Just. *Nov* 87 and 101 (539).

[32] So C. Roueché 1989*a*: no. 73 *prōtothronon anera boules* (πρωτόθρονον ἀνέρα βουλῆς) at Aphrodisias, not dated but probably late 5th–6th cent.

[33] For Egyptian evidence, see Geremek 1981: 231–47, 1990: 47–54. The existence of decurions is evidenced at Alexandria—where they received 100 solidi out of customs duties for unstated expenses (Just. *Edict* 13.12,13), and at Oxyrhynchus where a magistrate holds the *proedria* (προεδρία = office of *prytanis*/πρύτανις) jointly with office of *logistēs* (λογιστής) and that of *patēr*. *Politeuomenoi* are mentioned on a few late papyri from Oxyrhynchus. The 'budget' of Antaeopolis includes 36 solidi from taxes for expenses of *politeuomenoi* (A. C. Johnson and L. C. West 1949: 294). A few *politeuomenoi* figure among landowners on the Justinianic tax register of Aphrodito (Gascou and MacCoull 1987: 104–58); and in the early 7th-cent. register from Hermopolis (Gascou 1994).

[34] Gascou 1994: 23.5; 24.13.

[35] Koenen 1996: 183. Procop. *HA* 29.17 Anatolius first in the *album* of Ascalon under Justinian.

[36] See Stein 1968: 1–32, relevant 27–9 = *Klio* 16 (1919), 40–71, relevant 66–8.

[37] *PL* 87,1003B.

[38] Leo VI *Nov* 46–7 abolishes the laws about *curiae* and decurions and election of civic officials by them because they have become irrelevant. All is now managed by the foresight and administration of the emperor.

2. The Establishment of Government by Notables

While the decisive steps in the formal demotion of the councils were taken by the emperor Anastasius, the process had already begun in the fourth century with the disappearances of the traditional civic magistrates, that is of the traditional civic officers, who were appointed by the council from its membership, to run the internal affairs of the city, and to see to the carrying out of the orders of the imperial government.[39] During the fourth century and subsequently, these magistrates were replaced by functionaries of another type, of whom the most prominent were the *curator* (*logistēs*/*λογιστής*), the *defensor*,[40] and the corn-buyer (*sitona*/*σιτώνης*), and the *patēr* (*πατήρ*).[41] While these functionaries were normally local men, locally chosen, they were formally appointed by the imperial government. The most detailed information about their functions comes from Egyptian papyrus documents. The documents show clearly that these semi-imperial, semi-civic officials were responsible to the provincial governor rather than to the council. Their instructions came from him, and it was no doubt in his court that they had to justify their official actions. So the rise of the new type of official brought about not only the eclipse of the old civic magistrates, but also tended to concentrate political activity at the court of the governor in the provincial capital, with a corresponding loss to the authority of the local city council.

Candidates for these offices may well have been nominated by the councils,[42] but the candidates themselves were not necessarily councillors. Indeed councillors were disqualified from holding the most prominent of the new offices, that of *defensor*. But from AD 409 at the latest, *defensors* were chosen by a decree of bishop, clergy, *honorati*, *possessores*, and councillors listed in that order.[43] Henceforth councillors were only one group, and not the most important, among the electors of the secular head of the city. But when towards the end of the century Anastasius ruled that the *defensor* and the *curator* of Corycus in Cilicia were to be elected by

[39] They did not disappear everywhere at the same time: see Lewin 1995*a*: 93–7. Examples: at Iconium in Isauria Victor was archon prologos (ἄρχων πρόλογος), in reign of Valentinian I (*CIG* 4001; 3992). At Stratonicea in 5th? cent. a man has performed all magistracies (Varinhoğlu 1988: 123–4). At Athens Nicagoras was archon in AD 485 (Marinus *V. Procli* 36). At Heliopolis in Phoenicia in AD 430–1 public works paid for by Lupus a *principalis* is dated by the *stratēgia* of Serenus (*IGLS* 2831). At Patras Basileius was *quinquennalis* in 4th/5th cent. (Bingen 1954: 74–82).

[40] Rees 1952: 73–102; Rees 1953–4: 83–105. Bowman 1971: 124–5.

[41] On *sitona*, see nn. 45–6 below. On *patēr*: C. Roueché 1979: 173–85. The earliest dated evidence: *CJ* VIII. 12 (485/6).

[42] On the *defensor*: *CT* I.29.6 (387). Exclusion of decurions: *CT* I.29.1 (368); I.29.3 = *CJ* I.55.2; cf. also *CT* I.29.4–5.

[43] *CJ* I.55.8 (409). In *CJ* I.55.11 = I.4.19 of 505, the *curiales* are still mentioned among electors of the *defensor* along with *honorati* and *possessores*. In *Nov* 15.1 and epilog. (535), the *curiales* as such have no role.

bishop and chosen inhabitants of the city,[44] he did not mention council and councillors at all. Councillors had ceased to be the recognized representatives of the city. This privilege and responsibility had passed to the vaguely defined group of clerical and secular leading citizens, the 'notables'.

From the late fifth century numerous laws assign duties to the notables. Anastasius ordered that a city's corn-buyer (*sitona*) should be chosen by bishop and leading landowners from officials and ex-officials.[45] In AD 545 Justinian ruled that bishop and leading citizens *primates/prōteuontes* (πρωτεύοντες) and *possesores/ktētores* (κτήτορες) were to elect *patēr*, *sitona*, and other officers, whose accounts would subsequently be audited once a year by bishop and leading citizens.[46]

In the reign of Justinian responsibility for specific civic activities was regularly assigned to bishop and/or *defensor* and to leading citizens without council or councillors being mentioned. For instance every year the bishop and three 'in every way outstanding citizens' (καὶ ἐν ἅπασι προεχόντων) are given the duty of auditing the accounts of all individuals who had had the spending of public revenues.[47] It is the bishop who is to take the initiative against officials who demand a gratuity of more than six solidi for publishing an announcement from the emperor or other high official.[48] Officials of the central administration are not to command provincial cities to pull down private structures that infringe building regulations: the maintenance of public buildings and the preservation of civic spaces is the responsibility of bishop, *patēr*, and *possessores*.[49] So is the enforcement of regulations governing the use of water drawn from an aqueduct.[50] Bishop and leading citizens (πρωτεύοντες) are even authorized to refuse to accept orders from the central administration which infringe their prerogatives.[51]

An inscription from Hadrianopolis in Paphlagonia (Honorias) illustrates the circumstances. A *scribo* arrives from Constantinople carrying an imperial letter by which he is authorized to take action to suppress armed

[44] *MAMA* III. 197A.

[45] *CJ* I.4.17; X.27.3 (499–505). On the functions of this office and its appointment, see Sirks, Sijpesteijn, and Worp 1996, text and commentary on some extremely fragmentary papyri from Pommersfelden which seem to have set out the procedure to be followed in the appointment of a *sitona* by *ktētores*.

[46] Just. *Nov* 128.16. On the Pommersfelden papyri, the *ktētores* who sign the accounts are a *scholasticus*, a priest, and two *endoxotatoi/gloriosi* (Sirks, Sijpesteijn, and Worp 1996: 65–6, commentary on lines 32–47). In this case the *ktētores* would have included individuals who might elsewhere be classified as *habitatores*.

[47] *CJ* I.4.26 of 530; *Nov* 128.16 of 545 gives audit to bishop and five *prōteuontes* (πρωτεύοντες).

[48] *CJ* I.4.26.7.

[49] *CJ* I.4.26.8.

[50] *CJ* I.4.26.10.

[51] *CJ* I.4.26.5; 26.8.

followers of landowners, and which calls on local authorities to give him full support. The letter is addressed to bishop and landowners and it was published for the first time in the bishop's court.[52] Clearly this was a genuine mission sent to deal with a real problem and welcomed by the people of Hadrianopolis—otherwise the letter would not have been inscribed. But equally clearly the procedure would have given the bishop and the notables attending the meeting an opportunity to challenge the validity of the document, and it evidently depended on these men, that is the bishop and the *ktētores*, whether the imperial envoy would be able to carry out his mission successfully or not.

What was the process by which these notables were recognized and selected? It is significant that the authorities had no single title for the persons whom I call notables. In the laws a variety of terms are used. As we have seen the most common terms are *prōteuontes/primates* and *ktētores/possessores*, but no longer *principales*.[53] None of these terms ever receives a formal legal definition. The fact that the *possessores* of Antioch, Laodicea, and Seleucia were compensated for the damage suffered in a calamitous earthquake by the title of *illustris* shows that these *possessores* were far from being ordinary landowners.[54] They were evidently a very select group. But how then did the *prōteuontes/primates* differ from *possessores*? In *Nov.* CXXVIII.16 the *possessores* are given a part in the election of the *patēr*, but the committee of five which audits the *pater*'s accounts is said to be made up of *prōteuontes*. So it would seem that the latter were an even narrower group than the former. We are never told what qualifications entitled an individual to either description. But since *prōteuōn* is sometimes used in papyri or honorific inscriptions as if it were a definite rank,[55] the *prōteuontes* had been formally appointed by someone. In Justinian's reform of the office of *defensor*, it is the provincial governor who chooses a body of men *bonae opinionis* who are to hold the office of *defensor* in rotation.[56] The law does not use the term *prōteuontes*, but it may well be that in other contexts that is how this group would have been described. The formal appointment of a member of this rota to the office

[52] Feissel and Kaygusuz 1985: 397–419.

[53] For references to *principales* in *CT*, see A. H. M. Jones 1964: iii. 230–1 nn. 41–2. They have generally not been taken into *CJ*. It looks as if *principales*, like the councils which they led, lost their position of leadership in the late Late city. The *prōteuontes* or *prōtoi* (πρώτοι) performed a similar role, but they were not 'the first' of the council, see below, p. 113 n. 59.

[54] Malalas XVIII.444 (Jeffreys, Jeffreys, and Scott 1986: 258).

[55] *P Laur* II.27 (487–9) and *St Pal* XX.128; *P Oxy* XVI.1983.2–4 and *St Pal* XX.146; *P Lugd Bat* XIII.13.1. Whether it has a precise meaning describing a definite office is disputed. *PLRE* II.1011, s.v. Silvanus 5 (on Theod. *Ep.* 15); 1036, s.v. Strategius 9 (on *P Oxy* 2779, 1983) takes it to be a general term perhaps equivalent to *honoratus*. Monuments at Scythopolis record as supervising public building schemes, respectively, one Silvius *clarissimus comes* and *prōtos* (Tsafrir and Foerster 1987–8: 41) and Flavius Strategius *spectabilis* Father of the city and *prōteuōn* (Lifshitz 1961: 121–2).

[56] *Nov* 15. epilog.

of *defensor* was made by a decree strengthened by an oath of all *possessores* permanently resident in the city.

The relationship of *prōteuontes* and *ktētores* recalls that of *principales* and ordinary *curiales* in earlier times. Indeed Mark the Deacon describes the individuals who played a leading role at Gaza in AD 402 during the forcible suppression of paganism as *prōteuontes*.[57] These men were undoubtedly *curiales* and presumably *principales*.[58] But this was long before the reforms of Anastasius. It would be a mistake to assume that the *prōteuontes* of the sixth century were simply the old *principales* under another name.[59] A few might have been.[60] The majority were surely men of senatorial rank whose families had risen in the imperial service. However selected, they were the outstanding men among the notables.

The fact that the imperial *Code* uses certain terms to describe the notables, does not necessarily mean that the same terms were used at city level. The *Life* of Theodore of Sykeon suggests that the members of the leading group might be known by different designations in different cities. At Anastasiopolis it was the *ktētores* and the clergy who asked the archbishop at Ancyra to make Theodore their bishop, and eleven years later Theodore summoned the same two groups to inform them of his decision to resign.[61] At Ancyra however the leading group appears to have been known as *protectores*, for that is the title of the men who summoned Theodore to fight a plague that was attacking men and beasts in that city.[62] But at Pessinus, in the course of a severe drought, it was the so-called *domestici* together with the clergy who asked Theodeore to help.[63] It looks as if the notables of some cities had been collectively awarded the honorary rank of a corps of the imperial household, perhaps in recognition for some special service.

Sometimes an imperial enactment is addressed to a wider social range, targeted by the formula 'possessores (ktētores) et habitatores (oikētores/ οἰκήτορες)'.[64] Since none of these terms is defined, the precise scope of

57 *V Porph* 25.2, 28.10, 95.10.

58 Cf. Trombley 1993–4: i. 193–6, 199–200.

59 As argued by Holum 1996: 615–27. They are 'first men' of the city as in *Nov* 128,17 or even of the *ktētores* as in *CJ* X.27.3, not of the council.

60 So conceivably, but not necessarily, Anatolius whose name stood first in the album of the curia of Ascalon (Procop. *HA* 29.17–21).

61 A.-J. Festugière (ed.), *La Vie de Théodore de Sykéon*, i–ii, Subsidia Hagiographica 48 (Brussels, 1970), 57, 78. The inscription of a *protector* of Ancyra: Miltner 1936: 43 no. 47.

62 *Vie Théod* 45.

63 *Vie Théod* 101.5–6. *Domestici* were also found at Tavium: Mitchell 1982: nos. 442, 444, perhaps 463.

64 e.g. Just. *Nov* 128.16: neither *ktētores* nor *oikētores* to spend civic money earmarked for civic expenses; *MAMA* III.197: bishop, clergy, *ktētores* and *oikētores* petition emperor; *Lib Pont* 76: *habitatores* as well as *possessores* have private clergy; ibid. 78: together with people suffer under tax demands of Constans II; ibid. 86: stir up revolt at Syracuse.

this widened address is as ambiguous as the more exclusive one. The normal meaning of the word *habitatores* would include all inhabitants of a city. But the legal context usually suggests that the formula applies to a more exclusive group than that, one consisting of individuals who have a certain status in public life. This impression is confirmed by the report of a meeting of the notables of the city of Mopsuestia in Cilicia held in the *secretum* of the cathedral in AD 550. The men were assembled to receive sworn testimony that the name of Theodore bishop of Mopsuestia in the early fifth century had never been entered on the diptychs of his church.[65] Those present included both *clarissimi possessores* and *laudabiles habitatores*. At Ravenna in Byzantine Italy *laudabilis* was the title of *curiales*. I do not know what precisely this title signified in the mid-sixth century in Cilicia, but eight of the *habitatores* were officials of one kind or another, one was an architect, one a member of the ecclesiastical guild of undertakers (*lecticarii*), and three are without indication of occupational status.[66] It looks as if the *habitatores* did not include the bulk of the untitled population. The *laudabiles habitatores* were of course considerably more numerous than the fourteen witnesses at the meeting, who had been selected from a much larger body because of their age and length of memory. But it is significant that the whole ruling group, clergy, *possessores*, and *habitatores* could be accommodated in a single hall, the *secretum* of the cathedral.[67]

As neither the status of a *possessor*, nor of that of a *habitator* has ever received formal legal definition, it would seem that neither group constituted a constitutional body of defined membership. The two terms merely provided a convenient description of all the people who mattered in the city.[68] We have seen that both terms are highly ambiguous, and they are surely intentionally so. Any landowner could be described as a *possessor/ktētor*, or strictly speaking any man could be so described who was in actual control of the land, irrespective of whether he was the legal owner.

[65] Dagron 1980 on Mansi IX.275–290.

[66] Three *praefectiani*, two *agentes in rebus*, three *tabularii*. They also include one *principalis* whom Dagron is probably right to interpret as a *prōteuōn*. The Pommersfelden papyri suggest that the boundary between *ktētores* and *habitatores* was flexible. See n. 46 above.

[67] Mansi IX.276C: Adsunt nihilo minus ex vestra iussione omnes religiosissimi clerici per istam civitatem sanctae ecclesiae, nec non etiam eius defensor honestus vir, insuper et clarissimi istius possessores et laudabiles habitatores et illi quos seniores esse huius defensor putans manifestos nobis fecit. This sentence shows that all the *possessores* and *habitatores* were present at the meeting, quite apart from the *seniores* of each group who are to give sworn evidence that Theodere of Mopsuestia had not been inscribed on the diptychs of that city. Later the *seniores*, two *possessores*, and fourteen *habitatores* are asked to come forward and 'ab allis separati, sua dicant vocabula et status' (277D) where the alii presumably are the main body of the *possessores* and *habitatores*. Cf. 277A where the sixteen clerical witnesses are asked to come forward.

[68] The five *primates* (*summates*) of Alexandria *CT* XII.191 (436) = *CJ* X.57 may be a survival of an older arrangement.

Similarly any inhabitant of a city could be described as a *habitator*/*oikētor*. But we have seen that in documents dealing with city government both terms are in fact applied to much narrower groups. On the face of it, *possessores et habitatores* is a comprehensive, almost democratic, description of the whole citizen body. In practice it is nothing of the kind. These terms belong as much to the vocabulary of political double-speak as to that of constitutional law.

But then how did individuals qualify under either heading? It looks as if at Mopsuestia around AD 550 *possessores* were men of the rank of *clarissimus* and above, while *habitatores* had the rank of *laudabilis*. We know that in Byzantine Ravenna about the same time *laudabilis* was the title of the rank and file decurions. So in terms of dignity the distinction between *possessores* and *habitatores* was similar to the traditional one between *honorati* and *ordo*. But there was an important difference in that the *laudabiles* at Mopsuestia included at most only one decurion, the *principalis* Anatolius.[69]

To sum up: the *possessores* were individuals outstanding in wealth and influence, more often than not conspicuous by their senatorial titles from 'most glorious' and 'illustrious' downwards, whether these represented actual offices, offices formerly held, or honorary rank, or perhaps in some cases had simply been assumed. They included retired heads of departments of the central administration, former governors, and generals. The *habitatores* will have included mainly men with the status of lower ranking officials of the central departments or of the provincial *officium*, or lower ranking army officers as well as some leading landowners, and even traders[70] who had not held any official posts.

As *honorati*, men of the standing of *possessores* had long been privileged as a matter of right to sit with the provincial governor during sessions of his court. Others had attended regularly by invitation.[71] In the sixth century it was the same people who constituted the leading citizens, and arranged elections and made other decisions needed for the administration of the city. The part played by *habitatores* will presumably have depended on the decision of the *possessores*, and especially their leaders.

Who issued invitations to assemble the notables, and thus also decided who was to be invited, presumably differed from city to city, depending on local circumstances. There is very little evidence. In a provincial capital the initiative would presumably most often be taken by the provincial governor, as it was in the Ibas affair at Edessa. Elsewhere the

[69] This is presumably a translation of *prōteuōn*, which I would argue belongs to the post-curial arrangement.

[70] Cf. Antiochus, a Syrian trader, one of the leading notables at Naples, Procopius V.8.21.

[71] Lib. *Or.* 51 and 52.

convener might have been the bishop. At least that is what we would deduce from Justinian's legislation. In the *Novels* the bishop is regularly named first and treated as the leading notable and the most important individual in city.[72] But in Egypt, about which we have by far the most information, the bishops of cities other than Alexandria seem to have played a comparatively small part in municipal affairs.[73] Elsewhere in the East the evidence for bishops becoming involved in routine secular affairs is very limited.[74] It was only in emergencies, such as crop failure or invasion, that the bishop came into the forefront.[75] On routine occasions the role of convenor and chairman was probably performed by the *defensor* or the *patēr*. If the notables included a member, or even a dependent, of an outstandingly powerful local family like the Apions of Oxyrhynchus and Heracleopolis, he would presumably have corresponding influence.[76] In the case of the meeting at Mopsuestia, the order to hold the meeting came from the emperor. It was convened by the bishop of Anazarbus, as metropolitan of Cilicia Secunda. The lay witnesses were selected by the *defensor*. On the heavily damaged Pommersfelden papyrus the section which would have told us what functionary presided over the appointment of the *sitona* has been lost. It might have been the provincial governor.[77] Altogether it is still far from clear how coordination and leadership was achieved in post-curial government. Arrangements may well have differed from city to city.

Under notable government the mass of the people did not have a regular part in the political process. But as we have seen at Edessa, crowds did demonstrate in the streets, and petitioners might take a crowd acclaiming their cause even into the court of the governor. Moreover if the notables felt that a decision needed wide support they might invite the inhabitants of the city to express agreement or dissent by acclamation.[78] This situation might arise when a city was under attack, and its leaders had to decide whether to resist or surrender. At Naples, during the Gothic war, when Belisarius asked the authorities to open the city's gates to the imperial army a real debate ensued in which members of the public participated. In the end it was decided not to admit the army.[79]

There is not very much detailed evidence for the working of civic self-government in the sixth and seventh centuries.[80] Epigraphic evidence—

[72] e.g. Just. *Nov* 128.4, 16, 17, 23.
[73] Steinwenter 1956.
[74] Avramea 1989: i. 829–35; Feissell 1989: 801–28.
[75] Claude 1969: 123–35.
[76] See below, p. 200.
[77] Sirks, Sijpesteijn, and Worp 1996: 104–5.
[78] See below, pp. 131–3. Cf. also Fasoli 1969: 46–8, 70–6.
[79] Procopius V.8.19–42.
[80] Some references to late Late municipal officials: *defensor populi* at Syracuse (*Acta Sanctorum Mart.*

and sometimes the lack of it—throws a little light on social and political life at Thessalonica.[81] A total absence of civic inscriptions reflects the end of civic politics. There are no epigraphic references to civic institutions like the *boulē* (*βουλή*), or to civic titles, or even to the late, semi-imperial functionaries, like the *defensor* and the *patēr*. The majority of inscriptions are tombstones without any mention of rank or profession. Only two groups were at all commonly commemorated with reference to their status: former imperial officals[82] and clergy.[83] There are also a few shop-keeper-craftsmen[84] and slaves.[85] But mere civic status or civic merit was no longer thought worthy of commemoration.

There is considerably more information about Thessalonica and its notables in the decades on either side of AD 600 in the oldest collections of the miracles of St Demetrius.[86] The famous church of St Demetrius at Thessalonica was built on the site of a public bath.[87] A disused bath-building is used to house refugees.[88] Some public shows were still being offered to the inhabitants: the bishop felt embarrassed at being seen there—even if only in a dream.[89] The Blues and Greens operated at Thessalonica, but they did not riot there in the reign of Phocas when they rioted everywhere else—a blessing for which the citizens thanked the city's patron St Demetrius.[90]

Thessalonica was an important centre of imperial administration, being the headquarters of the praetorian prefect of Illyricum.[91] Among its leading inhabitants there must have been a large number of imperial officials, not to mention retired officials and officers and men holding titles of

III 843 B (between 655–662). A *patēr poleōs*, Sergios, has left a seal from the 8th cent. More examples in Longo 1990: 33–54, esp. 47. On Ravenna, long under Eastern government though not in the East, see below, p. 126, nn. 145–7. Also E. Stein, *Op. Minora,* 28 ff. = Klio 16I (1919): 40–71: Ravenna was taken out of the jurisdiction of *consularis* of Flaminia and governed, not by a prefect—like Rome and Constantinople—but by the *curator* of the city, with rank of *gloriosus*: Cass. *Var.* VII.1a. Eventually in reconquered Italy the *exercitus Ravennae* performed a political role (T. S. Brown 1984: 94).

81 Feissel 1983.

82 Ibid., nos. 132, 134, 146–51.

83 Ibid. 130, 133, 136–7, 138–44.

84 Ibid. 156–7. They are also found in other Macedonian towns. Numbers are small but relatively they are more prominent than in the cities of earlier periods. For increasing tendency for men to be identified by trade, see also *MAMA* III.200–788 (Corycus in Cilicia) and Rey-Coquais 1977, 1995.

85 Feissel 1983: nos. 158–61.

86 Lemerle 1979–81; Michael Whitby 1998*a*: esp. 201–6.

87 Spiesser 1984: 214; more references in Caillet 1996: 191–211.

88 *Miracles* I.14 (143).

89 Ibid. I.14 (132).

90 Ibid. I.10 (82).

91 As Illyricum was gradually lost to the Sclavenes (*Miracles* II.2 refers to the loss of Naissa and Serdica *c*.614), the prefect became less important, and the city seems to have been without a regular garrison, and left more or less to its own resources. So we find considerably more independence in the anonymous collection than in that of bishop John.

honorary official rank. There was a garrison and no doubt a garrison commander. The size of the population is quite uncertain, but was probably not very large.[92] The inhabitants' active contribution was needed to defend the walls against the assaults of the Sclavenes, which were both frequent and dangerous. The scale of popular participation in the defence of the city is shown by the following incident. One night while a large congregation was attending a service in the church of St Demetrius, the shrine appeared to be on fire. An anonymous official, fearing that in the ensuing confusion the treasures of the shrine might be pillaged, had it announced that the Sclavenes were about attack. Everybody rushed out of the church to man the walls. The fire was put out, and the treasure remained intact. Then it turned out that the Sclavenes were indeed attacking, and the opinion prevailed that the episode of the fire had been initiated by St Demetrius in order to get the citizens out of the church or out of bed, and on to the walls, ready to defend the saint's city.[93] That the population would take an active part in the city's defence could be taken for granted. They must have had the necessary arms. Some slaves of leading officials had even been given military training.[94] The fact that it had an armed population must have given sixth-century Thessalonica a degree of independence not enjoyed by the cities of earlier periods.

We are told something, but not very much, of the city's institutions of civic self-government. When in AD 676 the emperor wanted a Sclavene king resident in the area arrested he notified the prefect and the prefect gave orders to the civic authorities. The authorities, evidently with some reluctance, arrested the king and sent him to Constantinople, so inaugurating a long succession of troubles for the city.[95] City authorities were responsible for granaries where a great amount of publicly owned corn, presumably derived from taxation, was stored. We hear that the local notables had abused their authority by making use of an opportunity to sell the corn at an unusually favourable price even though Thessalonica was under threat of siege by the Sclavenes. The siege duly materialized, and the population was reduced to famine. The notables dared not appeal to the emperor for supplies in case their wrong-doing was revealed. Instead they ordered the requisitioning of corn from private houses, and this was duly done, with much violence and brutality.[96] They also sent

[92] *Miracles* II.4 (281), the emperor sends 60,000 modii of corn to relieve famine caused by siege. The author comments that 5,000 would have sufficed. Now 5,000 modii might have fed 319 persons for one year (Bagnall 1993: 70) or even only 111 (A. H. M. Jones 1964: 698). 60,000 modii would have fed 3,823 or 1,133.

[93] *Miracles* I.12.

[94] Ibid. I.13.

[95] Ibid. II.4.

[96] Ibid. II.4 (244, 252).

ships to buy corn from Sclavenes settled in neighbouring areas of Greece, who were at peace with the city.[97]

Who were these people in charge of Thessalonica? As so often in late Late Antiquity, the civic authorities have no title of office, and we are never told by what constitutional process they had achieved their position. The text simply describes them in terms of their situation as 'those governing' (*oi kratountes*/οἱ κρατοῦντες),[98] or as 'those holding the first positions' (*ta prōta pherontes*/τὰ πρῶτα φέροντες),[99] and in one passage the 'outstanding men among the first' (*Oi exochoi tōn prōtōn*/οἱ ἔξοχοι τῶν πρώτων).[100] Thessalonica was administered by just such an undefined group of notables as we have found elsewhere. What kind of men made up this group? We can only guess. The individuals mentioned in the *Miracles*, mostly because they had been chosen by the saint for a significant communication, were usually higher officials or ex-officials.[101] We also hear of an obviously wealthy man who gave sixty pounds of silver for the restoration of the shrine of St Demetrius, and of an ex-advocate (dikologos/δικολόγος) who gave forty pounds.[102] One might conjecture that the leading group consisted of men such as these. They were presumably laymen. But in times of emergency at Thessalonica as elsewhere the bishop would often take a leading role.

Such an emergency occurred in AD 479. The citizens (*politai*) were afraid that the prefect would hand their city over to Theoderic and his Goths. They rebelled, overthrew the statues of the emperor Zeno, and threatened to attack the prefect and to burn his palace. The clergy and the office holders (*Hoi en axiais*/οἱ ἐν ἀξίαις) pacified the citizens and asked them to take over the defence of the city themselves. So the citizens (*politai*) formed a defence force, and the prefect handed over the keys of the city to the bishop. Responsibility for surrendering the city, if that should become necessary, would be his.[103] Many years later in AD 618 Thessalonica was faced by a huge force of Avars, reinforced by Sclavenes and Bulgars. The inhabitants were panic stricken, but the bishop John led them onto the walls, patrolled the walls with them, and assured them of the support of St Demetrius. The saint did not fail them. After thirty-four days of siege and assault the enemy gave up, and withdrew in return for some unspecified concessions.[104] Clearly the bishop of Thessalonica

[97] Ibid. II.4 (254).

[98] Ibid. II.4 (252, 254, 281); I.14 (132) *archontes*.

[99] Ibid. II.1 (193).

[100] Ibid. II.4 (231).

[101] Individuals addressed by saint: ibid. I (225) high official in prefecture; I.4 (46–9) soldier; I.10 (86) relative of prefect; I.12 (106) official of prefecture; I.15 (166) holder of illustrious rank.

[102] Ibid. I.6.

[103] Malchus Fr.20.B.

[104] *Miracles* II.2.

played an important role in the city, and he was potentially the most powerful man in it. But as far as we can tell from the *Miracles of St Demetrius* he did not in normal times act as its secular head. Of course as far as this text is concerned the real head and patron of the city was St Demetrius himself, who might communicate with his citizens through the bishop, but more often than not chose somebody else.

In this account of late Late Roman civic politics I have again and again drawn attention to the absence of formal definition of constitutional institutions, rights, and duties. The cities had come to be controlled by groups of notables, made up of decurions, *honorati,* and clerics, whose membership was quite informal, and not defined by anybody other than themselves. In many cases it will have been obvious what made a man a 'leading citizen'; tenure of an imperial office, imperial rank whether earned by office holding or merely honorary, and of course wealth. But none of this seems to have given a man a constitutional obligation or even entitlement to be invited when the leaders of the city assembled to decide the affairs of the city. Nor was there any law that laid down who was to do the convening.

Lack of constitutional definition was a characteristic of the politics of the age. For instance canon law laid down that Bishops must be elected by clergy and laity, and that a bishop was needed to consecrate a bishop. But it was nowhere defined what bishops, or what members of the clergy precisely, or what laymen, were entitled to have a say in the election of a particular bishop. In practice the election was normally made by the metropolitan, with a group of local clergy and notables, and approved by acclamation of the local laity. Sometimes no doubt lay opinion or, in the case of an important see, the voice of the emperor would have a decisive say. The same lack of definition is found in St Benedict's rule for the election of an abbot.[105] The abbot may be elected by the whole congregation of monks. But election by even a fraction of the house might be valid if they have made a 'sounder choice' (*saniore consilio*). But if vicious monks should elect an abbot of similar character the election might be overruled by the diocesan bishop, by other abbots, or by neighbouring laymen. So, too, I would imagine in the cities. Normally local officials and committees were co-opted by a ruling group. These could however be overruled by the provincial governor or some higher official or even the emperor. I would suggest that the absence of constitutional definition is characteristic of the political culture of this late period which is very different from the sophisticated constitutionalism of the classical city.

[105] Benedict, *Regula*. lxiv.

3. *What difference did the end of curial government make?*

It has been suggested that the end of curial government did not in fact make any significant difference since 'élite' government continued much as before.[106] This I would argue is a mistake. First, the end of curial government also meant the end of government in accordance with a known and accepted constitution. It thus represents the end of the ancient tradition of constitutional politics going back to Solon of Athens and beyond, which had received its classic exposition in Aristotle's *Politics*. From the point of the imperial government the immediate and obvious advantage of the new arrangement was that it placed the running of the cities in the hands of the men who for over a hundred years had been the most influential and wealthiest inhabitants, whose ancestors had either never been enrolled in the *curia*, or had by one means or another obtained immunity from curial duties.[107] Besides, the new system enrolled the prestige and resources of the bishop, and gave him and his clergy a place in the administration of the city.[108]

But the reform should not be seen as merely a widening of the existing oligarchies. For the position of the notables was quite different from that of the decurions. They did not form a corporation, and they did not bear collective responsibility for the administration of the city. Individually, they were not under a hereditary duty to perform civic duties and to meet civic expenses.[109] Certainly, the imperial government was never in a position to coerce notables in the way it continued to coerce decurions. The notables' public service remained voluntary. Government by notables was also weakened by the fact that the bishop whom the emperors sometimes treated as the natural head of the new organization, in practice enjoyed a kind of 'semi-detached' relationship to secular affairs.[110]

Since end of government by the council meant that there was no public body continuously responsible for the state of the city and its public buildings and streets, one would expect it to result in neglect of public buildings and infringements of public property rights. As we have seen there is plenty of evidence of both.[111] A direct consequence of the decay of curial government was that in many towns the buildings that had served it, especially the council house itself, the prytaneion and the civic basilica, fell into decay, or were converted to other uses, or even pulled down. One civic institution whose decay is explicitly witnessed was the civic

[106] e.g. Whittow 1990: 3–29.

[107] A. H. M. Jones 1964: 740 ff.: on the government's unsuccessful struggle to check this process.

[108] See below, ch. 4.

[109] *CJ* X.33.3 (465), 4 (528) non-decurions volunteering for particular curial expenses do not thereby acquire a hereditary obligation.

[110] See below, pp. 153–5.

[111] See above, pp. 30–43.

archive.[112] Justinian noted that the public registration of property transactions was no longer taking place because cities lacked archives where the documents might be kept.[113] Consequently it had become impossible to obtain disinterested documentation of old land transactions, and information about them had to be sought from the far from disinterested present occupier of the land in question. Justinian tried to revive the public registration of transactions, by making the *defensor* responsible for the procedure. At the same time he ordered that a record office should be established in every city to house the *defensor*'s archive.[114] We cannot tell how successful Justinian's law was. It is however the case—as has been noted earlier[115]—that the papyrus documents that have survived from late Late Roman Egypt mainly come from private archives, and it is not a coincidence that two late papyrus archives found elsewhere than in Egypt, the papyri of Nessana in the Negev, and Petra in Jordan, were found in ecclesiastical buildings.[116] For the Church was stepping into the gap left by the inability of civic administration to keep records. Justinian had actually tried to stop this.[117] But like other politicians ostensibly fighting the trends of his times, Justinian himself assisted the development which he deplored. In AD 531 he had ruled that nominations of tutors should be deposited in archives of the church.[118] There is of course considerable evidence for the long-continued registration of land-transactions by the *defensor* and *curia* in the West.[119]

Civic expenses were reduced all round. But as cities in the East might still have many thousands of inhabitants there remained a need for municipal administration, and regular civic expenditure. Civic shows continued. All this required administration. But civic administration changed. How the civic administration and finance functioned under government by notables is the subject of Chapters 5 and 6. One development was the transfer of the organization of shows to the so-called circus factions.[120]

Government by notables affected the cohesion of the Empire. It was certainly more difficult to control notables than decurions. It must have

[112] On archives in Egypt (2nd–3rd cents.), see Drecoll 1997: 189–98. On decline: Saradi 1988*b*: 117–30.

[113] Just. *Nov* 15 praef. Si vero quaedam (acta). . . . conficiantur, . . . cum nullum habeant archivum, in quo gesta apud se reponant, deperit quod conficitur.

[114] Ibid. 5.

[115] See above, p. 22.

[116] So too the Ravenna papyri, but they are mostly about land eventually given to the Church.

[117] *CJ* I.3.40: Absurdum enim clericis est, immo etiam opprobrium si peritos se velint disceptationum esse forensium.

[118] *CJ* I.4.30 (531).

[119] *MGH (LL)* V.4, 28, 97, 136, 161, 170, 176, 202, 209 (Merovingian Gaul).

[120] Alan Cameron 1976: 218 ff., and below, ch. 6.

become even more so, after the designation of provincial governors had been delegated to provincial assemblies, with the effect that the official whose task it was to hold the notables to their duties was himself one of them.[121] The tax legislation of the sixth century shows quite clearly that the uniform Diocletianic procedure for collecting levies had broken down, and had been succeeded by a variety of ad hoc arrangements, no doubt suited to widely varying local conditions. Decurions still had a role, but they now were only one of several kinds of functionary on whom responsibility for collection might fall. In a law of AD 545 the men whose duty it will be to nominate tax-collectors (*hupodektai*/*ὑποδέκται*) at their own risk, i.e. who now had to bear what had formerly been the special responsibility of the *curia*, are simply described as 'landowners'.[122] In the same law the functionaries who might have to bear the financial risk of tax-collectors are listed. They comprise: 'governors, *politeuomenoi* (decurions), *exactores*, *vindices*, *canonicarii* and others'.[123] If the owner of an estate liable to pay taxes cannot be found, or is not in a position to pay the taxes, the estate is to be handed over to other taxpayers, or as a last resort to the collectors, that is *exactores*,[124] *vindices*, or members of the provincial *officium*.[125] A law of AD 556 refers to provinces in which the risk of tax collection was born by neither *vindices* nor any other functionaries. In these circumstances the governor himself would be held liable.[126] A law of Tiberius II of AD 575 remits taxes for one year in four. Instructions to this effect are given to collectors that is '*bouleutai*, *eklēptores* (ἐκλήπτορες), *scriniarii*, *taxeōtai* (ταξεῶται), *anutai* (ἀνυταί) and other *hupodektai*'.[127] Presumably these titles reflect different arrangements set up in different areas whenever the old decurion-based system broke down.

In the short run, the new system served the government well. It provided the financial resources for the ambitious policies of Justinian, enabling that emperor to finance his buildings and his wars, and to pay subsidies to the Persians and others. In the long run, the fact that it was now more difficult for the imperial administration to assign responsibility for the performance of the cities' duties to the Empire made the cities themselves less useful for the administration. That, I would suggest, is one reason why, after the disasters of the seventh century, the administrative

121 *Nov App* VII.12 (554); *Nov* 149 (569); 161 (574).

122 Just. *Nov* 128.5.

123 Ibid. 5, cf. 8.

124 *Exactores* are simply the individuals who exact the taxes. In the 4th cent. they were normally decurions. But it should not be assumed that they must be decurions in the 6th, e.g. the *exactores* who collected from the tenants of the *domus divina* in Cappadocia (Just. *Nov* 30.3) were surely not decurions, as these imperial estates were not attached to a city (A. H. M. Jones 1964: 713).

125 Just. *Nov* 30.8.

126 Just. *Nov* 134.2. In the 4th cent. the liability was the decurions'.

127 *Nov* 163.2.

system of the recovering Empire in Anatolia was based not on cities but on themes.[128] In Byzantine Italy, it was the militarization of society that put an end to government by notables, a development which is very much better documented than the beginnings of the theme organization in Anatolia.[129]

The end of government by notables can be pinpointed in the Crimea. At Cherson in the Crimea a *prōtopolitēs* (πρωτοπολίτης) Zoilos was prominent in AD 611/12.[130] A *prōteuōn* and *pateres tēs poleōs* (πατέρες τῆς πόλεως) governed Cherson and surrounding *kastra* until the reign of Theophilus (AD 829–842), when they were superseded by the creation of a *thēma* of Cherson.[131] In the areas conquered by the Arabs there was little civic self-government and cities were ruled by a centrally appointed governor,[132] unless the authority of the central administration had been weakened by civil war.

4. *Municipal Government in the West*

In the West the constitutional development of cities differed from that in the East in detail, but above all in timing. Curial government continued for longer, perhaps because the *curiales* were put under less pressure by the imperial government, and later by the Germanic kings. But if the process took longer, the outcome was the same. In the West too secular authority passed from the legally constituted and strictly regulated *ordo curialium* to an undefined group of notables. In Western cities also, the bishop became potentially the most powerful and most representative figure in the city. In fact in many cities of the West the bishop eventually achieved a position of genuine lordship, something which bishops never gained in the East.

The feature which most obviously distinguishes the history of the West from that of the East is the establishment of German successor kingdoms in Italy and the Western provinces. Yet the mere fact of the establishment of kingdoms by Goths and Vandals made little immediate difference to the condition of cities in areas under their rule.[133] Regional divergence was nevertheless a feature of political and social developments in the West.

128 It would seem that in Egypt taxes in the mid-6th cent. were significantly lower than in the early 4th, and well below those of the Early Principate: Duncan Jones 1994: 57–9 and Gascou 1989 and 1990. In my view the government tried to base its system of taxation on cities as long as that was practicable. On its subsequent policies, see Haldon 1994 and 1995; Lilie 1995: 425–60.

129 T. S. Brown 1984.

130 Theophanes (de Boer) 378.5.

131 Const. Porph. *De Admin.* 42.46.

132 Stern 1970: 26 ff.

133 Humphrey 1980; Clover 1982.

The development of civic government in Italy under the Ostrogoths (493–*c.*536) paralleled that in the East, but it was slower. Theoderic, the Ostrogothic king, was delighted when the *defensor* and the *curiales* of Catania in Sicily took the initiative of asking his permission to restore the city walls using material from the ruined amphitheatre.[134] It was to the *honorati*, *possessores*, and *curiales*, in that order, that Theoderic addressed his letters when he made demands on cities.[135] Sometimes the *defensor* is included in the address.[136] He ranked after the *possessores*, but before the *curiales*.

What does this order of rank mean in constitutional terms? By now the most influential men in Italian cities, as in cities of the East, were the *honorati*, that is those individuals who had senatorial rank of whatever kind. Next in rank came the *possessores*. These too are familiar from the East, and like the Eastern *ktētores* they are more than simple owners or controllers of land:[137] they rank above the *curiales*.[138] They are an élite among landowners. Even so they are not homogeneous: some are more powerful than others and exploit their weaker fellows.[139] Moreover the *possessores* have some corporative organization. For they voice grievances collectively,[140] and they are sometimes addressed by the central administration as a group.[141] So what is it that gives them their identity? The likeliest answer is that they are all officials, or men of official, but lower than senatorial rank. Since *possessores* could speak and be addressed as a body they must occasionally have held assemblies.[142] There is no evidence that there ever was such a thing as a council of *possessores*, but they were

[134] Cassiodorus *Var.* III.49.

[135] *Var.* IV.45 (Pavia) transport and provisions for envoys; V.14 (Syracuse), II.17 (Tridentum) tax-relief; III. 49 (Catania) permission to use material from amphitheatre for walls; III.9 (Aestusa) marble of ruins to be sent to Ravenna; IV.8 (Forli) order to transport timber; VIII.29 (Parma) order to clean sewers; VII.27 (certain cities), VI.24 (Naples) letters introducing new *comes civitatis*.

[136] Ibid. III.49, IV.45.

[137] *Possessores* are liable to taxes and compulsory services, they own *praedia*, and have subject *coloni*, they are not among *mediocres*, and may have a house in town as well as one in the country. Perhaps they correspond to the *cives* in Gregory of Tours.

[138] In this kind of context *possessor* is used in a special and restrictive sense. Ibid. XII.4 instructing *canonicarii* to buy wine for the royal table from *possessores* of Verona surely employs wider meaning. But because the word has the wider meaning all passages remain ambiguous, probably deliberately so. Cf. pp. 114–15 above.

[139] Ibid. IV.14: they shift some of their own tax liability on to the weaker *possessores*, and keep part of the tax collected for themselves.

[140] Ibid. XI.14 (Comum) burden of *cursus publicus*; IV.14 (of province of Savia) complaints about tax behaviour of certain of their number; IX.5 (locality not mentioned) complaints of profiteering in famine; IV.11 (Forli) dispute between *possessores* and *curiales*.

[141] Ibid. V.9 (Feltria) to assist in building fortifications of Tridentum; III.44 (Arles) grant of money for repair of fortifications.

[142] Gregory the Great *Ep.* I.47, IV.23, XIV.2, meetings of *possessores* and *cives* of Sardinia. For their attendance at the provincial assembly, see above, p. 12 n. 34.

entitled to attend, and probably even received summons to attend the provincial assembly.

Honorati, *possessores*, and the *defensor* have encroached on the prerogatives of the council as the governing body of the city. But the *curia* was still in a real sense a governing body.[143] Though they no longer were *the* civic authority, the city councils retained wider powers than the councils of Eastern cities. It still made sense to remind the *curiae* that they had been called 'the sinews and vital organs of their cities' before exhorting them 'to administer justice in their cities with appropriate determination'.[144] The *curia* of Ravenna still had its traditional magistrates, its *quinquennales* and its leading group of *principales*.[145] Its jurisdiction in the business of registering transactions in land still extended over the whole territory of the city.[146] We know of a number of curial families of Ravenna. Two of them can be traced for over a hundred years. As far as we can tell, they represent a social layer below, and quite distinct from, the court society of Ravenna.[147] The principal burden of the *curiae* in Ostrogothic Italy was undoubtedly still the responsibility for the collection of the taxes from the bulk of the taxpayers,[148] though some great landowners had the privilege of paying to the treasury directly.[149]

The *curia* still appointed the traditional magistrates, but their place at the head of the local administration had been taken by the *defensor*. Cassiodorus compares the *defensor*'s care for the inhabitants of his city to that of a patron for his clients.[150] Among his duties was the supervision of prices.[151] The second most important official was the *curator*.[152] The *defensor*, and probably the *curator* also, were elected by *honorati*, *possessores*, *curiales*, as well as bishop and clergy.[153] But all the local functionaries, *defensor*, *curator*, and *curia*, were now supervised by a locally resident representative of the king, the *comes civitatis*, who judged all important

[143] See also I.19 petition by *curia* of Adriana concerning taxes; II.18 *municipes Sarsinates* claim a *curialis* from clergy; IV.11 *curiales* of Velia in dispute with *possessores*; IV.14 *curiales* in province of Savia (Illyricum) involved in tax collecting; II.25.2 *curiales* liable for arrears of taxation.

[144] *Var.* IX.2 curiam . . . antiquitas non inaniter appelavit minorem senatum. . . . nervos quoque viscera civitatis. Administrate civitatum sub consentanea voluntate iustitiam.

[145] The Ravenna papyri show survival well into 6th cent. of the *defensor* (*P Ital* 31.ii.6, 32.1, 33.9); the *magistratus et quinquennalis* (P.14–15.iii.9, 10; 32.1 (540), 31.ii.6 (540)); the *principales* (29.1; 31.iii.1.2, 6).

[146] *P Ital* 10–11 (1.288 ff.).

[147] On government of Ravenna, see Deichmann 1989: 131 ff., 133–40: the *curia* and curial families; 142–63: ethnic and social structure of population. The *curial* families did not fill positions at court nor in the central administration, nor do their names appear among donors of property to the Church (ibid. 158). See also Ausbüttel 1987.

[148] *Var.* II.17, IX.4, XII.8.

[149] *Var.* XII.8.3.

[150] *Var.* VII.11: formula defensoris cuiuslibet civitatis.

[151] Cassiodorus *Var.* VII.11.

[152] *Var.* VII.12.

[153] See above, p. 110.

cases.[154] I would imagine that discussions of policy, and communication of royal wishes to the civic authorities, took place in the court of the governor or of the *comes civitatis*, in the presence of *honorati* and *possessores*, of the bishop and selected clergy rather than in the *curia*. Compared with the East municipal government in Italy was conservative, but in Italy too the 'notables', i.e. *honorati* and *possessores*, were about to replace the council as the rulers of the city. The crucial event was Justinian's Gothic war. After the Byzantine victory it was the notables variously described as the *proceres*, *primates*, *optimates*, *seniores*, or *maiores*, but never formally defined, who played a leading role.[155] This does not mean that *curiae* and *curiales* disappeared all at once. When Gregory the Great (590–604) wrote letters to cities he still addressed them to clergy, *ordo* (i.e. the *curia*), and *plebs*.[156]

In cities which still had councils their functions had become narrow and specific, as they had done earlier in the East. The principal function of the *curia* of Ravenna, as well as of some other Italian and many Gallic cities, was to register transactions in land.[157] Gregory the Great was anxious that candidates for ordination should not be liable for curial duties.[158] So these were evidently still not negligible. In Sardinia *curiales* were at this time still concerned with tax collection.[159]

From the early seventh century there is a sharp reduction of evidence. This is probably linked to impoverishment and shrinkage of the population. The latest mention of the *curia* of Ravenna occurs on a document of AD 625.[160] At Naples the council survived to the tenth century.[161] It is not certain that this represents true continuity. At Amalfi and Naples professional notaries assumed the title of *curiales* from the people who had previously performed their work.[162] In an age of unceasing wars, the notables, by now the old ruling class, were replaced by a new leading group of soldiers and descendants of soldiers.[163]

For Visigothic Gaul we have detailed evidence about administration in

[154] *Var.* VI.23, 26.

[155] T. S. Brown 1984: 128–31. More fully Ausbüttel 1988: esp. 211 ff.

[156] Gregory the Great's letters to *clerus ordo et plebs* (ed. L. M. Hartmann in *MGH*): I.58, 78; II.12, 40; III.11, 14; IV.39; V. 22; VI.26; IX.81, XI.20; XIII.17, 20. The implication of the formula, that the council (*ordo*) was still the secular civic authority, was probably in most cases anachronistic, unless *ordo* was now understood more vaguely to refer to the *maiores, seniores, cives*, etc., who constituted the leading group in the city. The formulaic character of the phrase is clear in *Ep.* IV of Gregory II (*PL* 89.502) addressed to the *clerus ordo et plebs* of the Thuringians.

[157] e.g. *acta municipalia*: *P Ital* P.14–15, 29, 31, 33.

[158] *Ep.* II.37. IV.26.

[159] Greg. I *Ep.* IV.26, cf. T. S. Brown 1984: 16–17.

[160] *P Ital* 21.

[161] Wickham 1981: 75. Frezza 1974: 99–100.

[162] Schmidt 1957: 122–4.

[163] T. S. Brown 1984: 63–81.

the *Breviarium of Alaric*, an abbreviated version of the Theodosian *Code*, published as a law book for his kingdom by king Alaric II in AD 506, and so more or less contemporary with the *Variae* of Cassiodorus. Much of the Roman administration survived, though less than in Italy. In Gaul the Gothic kings did not appoint praetorian prefects. Vicars and dioceses also disappeared, but provincial governors survived. We can however observe a reduction in the importance of the province and its governor, and a corresponding increase in that of city-based officials. Governors continued to exercise jurisdiction and to be closely associated with the collection of taxes. But the Visigothic king—like the Ostrogothic king in Italy—had a representative in the city itself, the *comes civitatis*,[164] who also acted as a judge.[165] The *comites* were appointed by the Visigothic king, but were not necessarily Goths.[166]

Decurions still had an essential role. The *Breviarium* retains many laws designed to prevent decurions from evading their duties. Decurions tried to escape into the royal service, as they had formerly escaped into the service of the emperor. But this was now much less of a problem as the German kings employed far fewer officials. The *Breviarium* anticipates other techniques of evasion. Decurions might go into hiding, move to another city,[167] marry their daughters to non-decurions,[168] refuse to have legitimate children,[169] or enter the service of a magnate.[170] It seems that all decurions now had the rank of *honorati*, and enjoyed the associated privilege of sitting with the judge when he was hearing a case.[171] The proliferation and devaluation of official titles was of course a characteristic of Late Roman society. Since the rank of an *honoratus* recognized service to the Empire, it had become meaningless in the territory of a Gothic king.[172] But the use of senatorial epithets by men who were not senators, and lived in a provincial city and had strictly speaking no claim to senatorial rank, was introduced in the East too sometime after AD 450.[173] This

164 Declareuil 1910; Spandel 1957; Claude 1964.

165 It is often not clear whether a *iudex* mentioned in the *interpretatio* of a law is a governor (*iudex ordinarius*) or a civic judge (*iudex civitatis*), who might be the *comes* or the *defensor*.

166 e.g. Attalus, *comes* of Autun: Sidonius, *Epistle* 5.18.

167 Conrat 1903: 736 = *Breviarium* XII.1.2 = *CT* XII.1.12.

168 Conrat 1903: 737 = *Breviarium* XII.1.7 = *CT* XII.1.124.

169 Conrat 1903: 737 = *Breviarium*, Nov Theodosii II, 11.1.5–9 = *CT*, Nov Theodosii II, 22.1.5–9.

170 Conrat 1903: 739–40 = *Breviarium* and *CT*, Nov Majoriani. 7.4–5.

171 Conrat 1903: 773–4 = *Breviarium* IX.15.1 and I.7.1 = *CT* IX.19.1 and I.20.1. On the privilege, see Liebeschuetz 1972: 190.

172 Of the Germanic kings only the Ostrogothic kings in Italy regularly conferred titles of senatorial rank, see Schäfer 1991: 170–84. We know of one individual, Astius Vindicianus who owed his *clarissimate* to the Vandal king early in the 6th cent., and seven individuals who received the *clarissimate* from Visigothic kings in Spain after 540, see Chastagnol 1996: 345–54, esp. 350–3.

173 C. Roueché 1989*a*: 131; A. H. M. Jones 1964: 528–9. In both East and West, Roman governments were anxious that lower-ranking *honorati* should return to the service of their city (*CT* 12.1.187 (436); *CJ* 12.1.15 (426–42)).

is yet another example of parallel development in the East and West in spite of the division of the Empire.

Apart from decurions there existed a class of powerful landowners who were not liable to curial duties, but offered themselves as patrons and protectors to fugitive decurions. This presumably included the leading Goths, but also descendants of the great senatorial families who had built up large estates in the last century of imperial rule, and were now consolidating their position in the service of the Visigothic king.[174] These men might still have town houses, but this does not mean that the city was still their principal place of residence. It is much more likely that by now they were country based as the aristocracies of Western Europe have continued to be. They did not yet build castles. On the other hand, they did sooner or later abandon their spectacular Late Roman villas, though the history of the end of the villas in Gaul and Spain is still very obscure.[175] It now looks as if many Spanish villas continued to be occupied in the fifth and even into the sixth century.[176] But the whereabouts of the great landowners of Gaul and Spain in later Late Antiquity is still something of a mystery.

Under the Visigoths the Late Roman tax system survived in Gaul, and, as long as it continued, it was necessary that the tax—which was after all a land tax—should be collected not only from the built-up area, but from the whole city territory. In this way the system of taxation preserved the unity of urban core and surrounding agricultural territory. Collection must have met with great difficulties. The big landowners were no longer able to claim privileges as members of the imperial senate—certainly these privileges have not been taken into the *Breviarium*—but their land-based power of obstruction and resistance was greater than ever: they were on the way to becoming medieval barons, even if landholding in return for military service was still centuries away. So the public revenue diminished. But the procedure of tax-collecting remained the same. There is no reference to collection other than by *curiales* in Visigothic Gaul.[177]

The sixth century saw the expulsion of the Visigoths and the establishment of the Frankish kingdom of the Merovingian dynasty in Gaul. The evolution of the late Late Roman city continued. We are particularly well informed about Gaul in the last quarter of the sixth century, the most important source by far being the remarkable writings of Gregory bishop of Tours (573–94). By now there had everywhere been a significant reduction in the classical institutions. Power in cities is wielded by the royal

[174] Rouche 1979: 327–31; Mathisen 1993: 119–31.

[175] Percival 1992; Gorges 1979. In Spain at any rate many villas seem to have been occupied considerably longer than was thought by Gorges. See above, pp. 92–3. We know very little about how or where great landowners lived after the Roman villas had been abandoned.

[176] Arce 1997*b*: 19–32; Claude 1997: 321–34.

[177] Rouche 1979: 338–46.

representative, the *comes* and by the bishop, who will normally have been by far the most powerful and influential individual in the town. The sources tell of bishops exercising jurisdiction, building fortifications, pleading on their city's behalf with the royal officials for remission of taxation, and negotiating with hostile commanders in war, civil or otherwise. Bishops provided poor relief for individuals on the church's register (*matricula*).[178] They built hospitals and ransomed prisoners. They received donations on behalf of the Church and could afford to build churches and founded monasteries, even in disturbed times.[179] As far as the cities were concerned, the competition for authority between royal count and bishop seems to have been won by the bishop. It must however be remembered that for the government of cities in the West in the sixth century our principal sources are not codes of law, but the writings of ecclesiastics, above all of Gregory of Tours, but also of various authors of Lives of saints, who tend to exaggerate the importance of bishops relative to that of lay magnates.

Curiae and *curiales* survived into the Merovingian period, but they were no longer responsible for collection of the land tax. Under a well-established king, the royal *comes civitatis* was the principal secular official, and the duty of collecting the taxes appears to have fallen to agents of the *comes*.[180] In fact taxes were no longer seen as self-evidently essential for government. Gregory of Tours could speak about the royal tax revenue as if it were a luxury. He exaggerated, to make the rhetorical point that the king did not really need the taxes he was asking the people of Tours to pay, and could safely remit them. But the argument would have been laughed out of court by a Roman emperor.

The Frankish kings had no regular army and relatively few salaried officials—but they did have some. The kings also had to reward their followers, and to show generosity to the Church. But they often met these obligations without paying wages in money by giving grants in kind, consisting either of estates or of so-called 'immunity'. The 'immune' landowner collected the royal tax together with his own rent from the tenant. This had long been a common practice among landowners in the West, as it had been in the East. But instead of having to pay the tax revenue over to the royal representative, the holder of immunity was allowed to keep it for himself.[181] So the Frankish kings had to make fewer regular

[178] Rouche 1974: 83–110.

[179] I. Wood 1994: 71–87; James 1988: 183–4; Pietri 1983.

[180] Greg. T. *HF* IV.2, V.34, IX.30.

[181] Goffart 1982, Kaiser 1979—the traditional view—rather than Durliat 1990*b*. That taxes were demanded from cities like Tours that enjoyed immunity was probably due to the fact that such immunities needed confirmation by a new king, which was sometimes withheld. See below, in Ch. 4, p. 164, n. 179.

payments in money, and had less need for a regular income. They could afford to allow the tax system which they had inherited from the Roman government to run down.[182] The development severed an important link between the city and its territory.

If *curiae* and decurions and even the *defensor* ceased to play any part in the decision-making and administration of the city,[183] they did continue to perform a function of great importance. They kept the *gesta municipalia* which provided a written record of all property transactions in the *civitas*. In fact their archive served as a communal memory of who owned what. This notarial role of the city council is attested by surviving *formulae* in Aquitaine (Bordeaux, Bourges, Cahors, and Poitiers), in Burgundy, and northern Gaul (Sens, Orleans, Tours, Le Mans, Paris).[184] In this way some city councils, sometimes with *curatores* and *defensores*, survived well into the eighth century.

The reign of a weak king, or the prevalence of civil war, a condition which was frequent in Visigothic Spain and Merovingian Gaul, offered considerable scope for self-determination by cities. In central and southern Gaul, and in some cases in Northern Gaul too, cities were still *civitates* in the old Roman sense. They were still political units made up of both a fortified urban centre and a rural territory; and the fact that the urban centres were fortified, and the *civitas* as a whole was regularly required to provide levies for the Frankish kings[185] gave them a significant degree of independence: the larger cities could not be coerced without significant military effort. Accordingly, Gallic cities regularly were in a position to decide themselves to which of competing Frankish kings they would give their allegiance.

Decision-making was therefore not monopolized by *comes* and bishop. A decree of the citizens of Bourges requests Sidonius Apollinaris to choose them a bishop.[186] The people of Angoulême swear allegiance to king Gundovald.[187] The inhabitants of Tours and Poitiers transfer their allegiance from Guntram to Childebert.[188] The inhabitants of Poitiers

[182] That in Carolingian sources the unit of land for taxation is the *mansus*, and not any longer the *iugum/caput*, suggests that the *iugatio* system had disappeared in Gaul, as it seems to have done in Spain. The *mansus*, a settlement single farm inheritance, became a new basis of taxation after stabilization of conditions from AD 550. See Herlihy 1978. Otherwise, Durliat 1990*b*.

[183] Gregory of Tours, *In Gloria Confessorum* 20, *MGH SR Mer* I.2.309 (AD 573–4). The *ordo honoratorum civium* which is part of a civic procession at Tours may be the *curia*, but more likely the notables as opposed to the ordinary people.

[184] K. Zeumer 1886.

[185] *HF* V.26 (232.10) levies from: Bayeux, Le Mans, Angers, Tours, Poitiers; VI.31 (295.15): from Tours, Poitiers, and Nantes; VII.12 the levy of Bourges is said to have been 15,000. VII.21 levies of Orleans and Blois.

[186] Sid. Ap. *Ep.* VII.5.

[187] *HF* VII.26 Gundovald receives Oath of Allegiance of Angoulême, ibid. 27 admitted by the people of Toulouse.

[188] Ibid. VII.13, cf. VII.24: Men of Bourges and Orleans force *cives* of Poitiers to recognize Guntrum.

refuse allegiance to king Sigbert and resist his general Mummolus.[189] The citizens of Angers refuse to accept a *comes civitatis*.[190] The *cives et reliqui honorati* of Poitiers ask Gregory of Tours to bless an altar in a new chapel.[191] The citizens of Tours press their bishop to accept an oath of innocence from the disreputable royal official Pelagius.[192]

Gregory distinguishes between two groups of individuals involved in making decisions on behalf of a town, the *seniores* (or *maiores*) and the *cives*. The *seniores* clearly represent the actual leaders of the town, powerful individuals who together form some kind of executive.[193] Gregory never tells us what qualifies a man for the position. In fact the *seniores* were surely an informal self-appointed and self-continuing oligarchy—like the groups we have found in charge of cities in the East, and in post-Justinianic Italy. The term *civis* is altogether ambiguous, since Gregory clearly uses it over a range of meanings. In its widest sense a *civis* is a native of a particular place. So when Gregory writes short biographies of earlier bishops of Tours he regularly mentions whether the man was a *civis* of the city or not.[194] On the other hand, when *cives* play a role in the narrative, they are usually men of property and influence.[195] In such a context the word might be translated as 'the respectable citizens', as opposed to the common crowd.[196] The 'citizens' therefore constituted those of their fellow inhabitants which the leading group might in some way consult, or whose assent they might seek for a decision which could only be carried out with wider support.

When the issue was very far-reaching, as when the question was

[189] Ibid. IV.45.

[190] Ibid. VIII.18.

[191] *Glor. Conf.* 104.

[192] *HF* VIII.40.

[193] Gregory of Tours, *In Gloria Confessorum* 58, *MGH SR Mer* I.2.331: bishop, clergy, and *seniores* of Saintes. *HF* VIII.21: bishop, duke, and *seniores* of Metz process to church of St Remigius. *HF* VI.11: Duke Gundulf assembles *seniores* of Marseilles prior to restoring its bishop. *De Virtute S. Juliani* 29, *MGH SS R Mer* 126: Germanus of Auxerre tells *seniores* of Brives the day of festival of St Julian. *HF* II.23: would-be successor of Sidonius Apollinaris shows disrespect to *seniores* of Clermont by taking first place at dinner. VIII.31: *seniores loci* at Rouen grieved at murder of their bishop. In *Gloria Confessorum* 60, *MGH SR Mer* I.2.233: blind boy deprived of his charitable sustenance by *maiores* of Lyons. None of these passages—except perhaps the last—actually shows the *seniores* taking a decision.

[194] *HF* X.31.

[195] *HF* VIII.42: houses of *cives* at Angers plundered; VIII.1: King Guntram seeks friendly relations with *cives* of Orleans, is invited to their houses for meals, exchanges gifts; II.23: the would-be successor of Sidonius Apollinaris invites *cives* of Clermont to banquet in *domus ecclesiae*; IV.45: two *cives* of Poitiers collect a mob to resist Mummolus. *Vita Caesarii Episcopi Arelatensis*, *MGH SS R Mer* III.460: *cives* distinguished from poor. *MGH LL* III.1 (*Concilia Aevi Merovingici*) 123: *cives* have duty to give alms. *HF* VIII.33: a *civis* of Paris sets fire to olive oil in his storehouse and starts a conflagration. *HF* V.49: *cives* attend the *salutatio* of Gregory of Tours.

[196] *HF* VIII.1 *populi turba*; II.23 *multitudo*; II.33 *minor populus*; also III.31; VI.31 (301.12); VII.35 (356.1).

whether to recognize a particular king or not, consultation of the *cives* might perhaps be expanded to the holding of a mass meeting in the old amphitheatre or in front of the cathedral. A meeting of that kind is surely to be envisaged when the people of Naples discussed whether to admit the Byzantine army of Belisarius. A policy adopted after such consultation could be fairly said to have been taken by the citizens of the town, and that is how Gregory of Tours regularly describes such decisions in his *History*.[197]

Gregory gives a detailed account of one such meeting. Once king Chilperic was angry with Gregory and he threatened him: 'I will call a meeting of the inhabitants of Tours and I will say to them: "Here is a slogan for you to shout about Gregory: He is an unfair man and he treats no one justly!"' To this Gregory replied: 'You can persuade my people to shout untrue things about me. What does that matter to me? they will all know that they are shouting these things to please you!'[198] No doubt this was how in many cases expression of popular protest—or indeed consent—was organized, but there were surely occasions when the shouting was spontaneous.

Gregory of Tours describes a case of 'civil war' (*bellum civile inter cives*) at Tours.[199] This was clearly nothing more than a bloody feud between two, or perhaps three,[200] powerful local families, arising seemingly accidentally out of a drunken brawl. It is also clear that there was no local authority that could coerce the two principal individuals to make peace. There was a court (*iudicium civium*)[201] which issued a judgment early in the feud, but this was ignored by both parties. Gregory summoned the parties as bishop, whose role was that of an arbitrator and honest broker rather than that of civic head who could enforce his decision. A temporary settlement was reached after a further judgment by the court in the city. Gregory made the judgment acceptable to Sichar by agreeing that the church would pay the compensation which the court had awarded to Sichar's opponent Chramnesind. Some time later Chramnesind murdered Sichar, and after various vicissitudes managed to get himself pardoned by king Guntram. It is significant that the feud seems to have started during a Christmas celebration in the *vicus* of Mantolomaus (Manthellan) where

[197] e.g. at Angers, *HF* VIII.18 (385.15); at Bourges, Sidonius Apollinaris *Ep.* VII.5, cf. VII.8.2: Simplicium . . . episcopum sibi flagitat populus Biturix ordinari. *HF* VII.24 *cives* of Poitiers forced to recognize king Guntram. IX.23 (443.5) king approves bishop of Verdun *consensu civium*.

[198] *HF* V.18.

[199] *HF* VII.47, IX.19.

[200] The feud began between Sichar and Austregesil, but then Austregesil is not again mentioned, and first Auno, and after Auno has been murdered Chramnesind (evidently Auno's son), figure as Sichar's enemies.

[201] *HF* VII.47 (366.18): *iudicium civium*; 367.24–5: a *iudex*, presumably the president of the court of *iudices* which met in the city. V.48 (258.24) in court count sits with *seniores*, both clerical and lay.

Sichar and his original antagonist Austregesil evidently lived,[202] while Chramnesind's family originated from a village in the *civitas* of Bourges.[203] These people were *cives* of the *civitas* of Tours, but their homes were in the country, where they probably spent most of their time, and they had at their disposal armed followers who would support them in what was in effect a blood feud. They were very different kind of people from the decurions of a classical Roman provincial city. They were also very unlike the notables, the *ktētores* of contemporary cities in the Greek world, even though the principal protagonists in this episode, notables, bishop, and monarch, each had an equivalent in the East.

Reliable knowledge about the government of Visigothic Spain only becomes available in the lifetime of Gregory of Tours (538–94). It is a mistake to assume that the *Breviarium of Alaric* can be relied upon as a guide to Spanish conditions.[204] Sound documentation about administration in Spain only becomes available with the laws of the late sixth and seventh centuries. Even then the evidence about Spain is very one-sided, being overwhelmingly legal. There is no Spanish historian comparable to Gregory of Tours, and only a small number of Spanish lives of saints have come down to us. The general impression is that the administration of the Visigothic kings was more 'Roman' than that of the Merovingians and that its Romananity derived not only from the remains of Roman institutions surviving in Spain but also from contemporary practice at Constantinople. The administration of Spanish cities had entered the post-curial phase. *Curiales* no longer collected the land tax.[205] Collection now was the responsibility of a city-based *numerarius*. Some detail of tax administration is given in a letter '*de fisco Barcinonensi*' (AD 592) which the bishops of the cities of Tarragona, Egara, Gerona, and Ampurias, all in the fiscal district of Barcelona, wrote to the *numerarii* who had just been appointed by the royal finance officer, the *comes patrimonii*, to supervise taxation in that tax district.[206] This is as far as I know the only reference to the existence of the tax district as a separate administrative unit comprising several cities, yet smaller than a secular or an ecclesiastical province. This system might be called 'Eastern' in its degree of centralization with the appointment of the local directors of taxation by an officer

[202] *HF* VII.47 (366.15): ad suam villam effugit; 367.22–3: the villa, which consisted of several houses, was in fact a village: domus omnes tam Sichari quam reliquorum qui participes huius villae erant incendio cremavit.

[203] *HF* IX.19 (433.16): Vosagensim territorii Biturigi pagum expetiit, in quo eius parentes degebant. Sichars's wife abandoned Sichar's sons and property in the *civitates* of Tours and Poitiers and 'ad parentes suos Mauriopes (nr. Pont-sur-Seine) vicum expetiit' (433.18–19).

[204] E. A. Thompson's (1969) reconstruction of the 'Arian Kingdom' is flawed by this assumption.

[205] Edict of Erwig of AD 683, K. Zeumer 1902: 479 ff.; cf. Thompson 1969: 215.

[206] *Mansi* X.473; Thompson 1969: 99, 127.

of the central administration. Centralization was however counterbalanced by the strong supervisory role of the bishops of the taxation districts, who were not only required to confirm the appointments made by the *comes*, but also had a strong say in the fixing of the rate of *adaeratio* of the tax in kind and of the perquisites that might be demanded by the various grades of collectors.[207]

Two laws however describe what seems to be a less centralized system. For they state that *numerarii* and *defensores* were elected by people and bishops to hold their offices for one year. It is expressly laid down that the two officials must not change places at the end of their year of office.[208] On the face of it, this arrangement is incompatible with that described in the letter *de fisco Barcinonensi*. But this is not necessarily so. It is quite possible that the role of the *comes patrimonii* was merely to make the formal appointment of the man chosen by bishop and people. In that case the position of the *numerarius* will have closely resembled that of *defensor*, *curator*, and *patēr* in the post-curial government of the East.[209] For these functionaries too were formally appointed by the emperor or his representative, after having been chosen by the local bishop and notables.[210]

It is significant that the Visigothic *Code* has altogether very few references to taxation. While laws defining the duties of the classical Roman governor dealt above all with the areas of justice and taxation, the Visigothic regulation for governors —significantly entitled *iudices*—are concerned practically only with justice.[211] If the space given to a given topic in the law code is proportional to its importance in the mind of the legislator this would suggest that income from the land tax was considered much less important by the Visigothic kings than it had been by the emperors. Visigothic Spain resembled Merovingian Gaul in its relative neglect of the revenue from the old land tax.

Curiales could be found in at least some cities of Visigothic Spain. According to a law of AD 654[212] individuals who receive property that had belonged to *curiales*, or to private individuals with liability to provide

[207] The *numerarius* might be compared to the pagarch. The bishop's supervision of the equity of taxation recalls some Justinianic legislation. Cf. below, pp. 151–2.

[208] Elected like *defensor* by people and bishops *LV* XII.1.2 (Reccared 586–601), appointed by king on commendation of bishop *LV* IX.1.21 (Wamba 672–80).

[209] See above, pp. 110–11. Vindex and pagarch too are likely to have been originally chosen—or at least 'short-listed'—by local notables and the bishop, but we have no definite evidence.

[210] Alternatively it is possible that the letter and the laws refer to alternatives found in different cities, or that one succeeded the other.

[211] But according to a decree of Reccared the *iudices locorum* together with the *actores fiscalium patrimoniorum* must attend the annual provincial synod of bishops and receive their guidance as to the forced labour services they might require from those under their administration (III Tolet. 18). *Iudices locorum* is vague. In the context of a provincial synod it should include the provincial governor—if there was one, but it would also cover the *comes civitatis* and the *defensor*.

[212] *LV* V.4.19.

horses for the *cursus publicus* or to pay taxes, must take up the duties of the previous owners. This shows that there were still some financial obligations described as *curial*, but that they were by this time attached not to individuals but to land, and moreover that '*curial*' land was just one of number of categories of land that had fiscal or other obligations attached to it.[213] There have survived two Visigothic formulae related to the registration of documents in the *gesta publica*.[214] This procedure was evidently much less widespread in Visigothic Spain than in Visigothic and Merovingian Gaul.[215] It may well have been restricted to the cities of Baetica, perhaps even to Cordova or Emerita.[216] In the *Vita Aemiliani*, set in the upper Ebro valley in the mid-sixth century, one individual is described as a *curialis*, others as senators.[217] It looks as if in this remote area Roman titles of rank survived the institutions with which they had been linked.[218] But when Aemilianus summoned the 'senate of Cantabria' to warn them that their doom was at hand, he was evidently dealing with a functioning institution, perhaps an assembly of the nobles of the *conventus* of Cantabria.[219]

213 Cf. the vestigial duties of *curiae* in Egypt, below, pp. 000–000.

214 *Formulae Visigothicae*, 21, 25.

215 Sánchez-Albornoz y Menduina 1943: 51–2 refers to procedures in *LV* which seem to replace the residual functions of *curiae*.

216 Cf. below, p. 131, for Gaul.

217 Senators: Braulio, *V. Aemiliani* XVI.24, 29 (Honorius), XV.22 (Nepotianus), XI.18 (Sicorius); a *curialis* (Maximus), ibid. XVI.23; slaughter of 'senate' of Cantabria by Leovigild in AD 574 foretold, ibid. XXVI.33. A translation of the *Life of St Aemilian*: Fear 1997: 15–41.

218 Chastagnol 1996: 345–54, esp. 351–4. Stroheker 1970: 106–36. Eventually 'senator' came to designate simply a rich and powerful individual.

219 Fear 1997: 39 n. 107. John of Biclara, *Chron.* 32 suggests that when Leovigild conquered Cantabria in AD 574, it was a political unit with Amaya as its principal town.

4

The Rise of the Bishop

Now is this golden crown like a deep well
that owes two buckets, filling one another.
(Shakespeare, *Richard II*)

1. *A Story of Desecularization*

In the loosely structured post-curial municipal administration the most permanent functionary and the only one who had achieved his position with popular consent was the bishop. The bishop would therefore seem to have been the natural leader and spokesman of his city. It is therefore not surprising that in civic emergencies we often find the local bishop in precisely that position. Moreover it is the case that as cities shrank and secular government declined, whatever administrative tasks remained tended to fall to the bishop. The outstanding example is the way the Pope took over from the senate responsibility for the administration of Rome. But the entry of the bishop into civic administration was a gradual process. In the period covered by this study secular government survived in many cities of the Empire and particularly in the East. The bishop had a role in it, but it was a special role, as befitted an officer of the Church. Generally speaking, bishops and emperors were aware that the office of a bishop was different in kind from that of a secular magistrate, and that it was wrong to fill the time of a bishop with preoccupations of this world. Neither emperors nor bishops adhered to this principle consistently. Justinian knew that bishops had the potential to make an enormous contribution to the secular well-being of cities and their inhabitants. Not a few bishops were anxious to display their talents in secular affairs. Nevertheless there remained a clear distinction between bishops and magistrates, and the involvement of bishops in the secular affairs of their cities was much more intermittent, and much more dependent on a bishop's personal predilections, than might appear from a superficial reading of the relevant legislation.

The steadily expanding influence of the bishop in urban affairs was an aspect of the desecularization of social life, one of the most extraordinary features of Christianization in Late Antiquity. In our time we are used to observing a shrinking of the area of life regulated by religion. The rise of the secular influence of the bishop involves the opposite process. This is very remarkable whether we look at it from a modern or from a classical point of view. In the modern Western world religion has become an activity which concerns mainly private life, the way individuals treat each other, birth, marriage, and death. Questions of war and peace, of taxation or diplomacy are secular activities carried out by secular ministers and their officials not by bishops or clerics. Moreover the classical world of the Roman Republic and Empire seems to have been modern in this respect. Politics and administration were carried on by secular officials and governed by considerations of secular advantage, not by religious rules. The interesting question is how did this takeover by bishops, that is of religious functionaries, of large chunks of secular business of government come about? The process can be observed all over the Empire in Syria as well as Gaul, in the Eastern Empire as well as in the Germanic successor states—even if there were significant regional differences. How then did this come about?

The first thing to note is that we are not dealing with a 'revolutionary' process.[1] The 'rise of the bishop' did not involve the deliberate overturning of secular institutions to replace them by Christian ones. Nor was it pushed forward by any social group seeking to seize power in the city from its established leaders. It was rather the case of a vigorous, creative, and forceful institution expanding under its own momentum. While some people, notably the ecclesiastical historian Socrates,[2] warned of possible dangerous consequences of the meddling of bishops in secular affairs, the growing power and influence of the bishop seems to have met with very little opposition from lay politicians. The 'rise of the bishop' was in fact the obverse of the decline of civic political institutions, and classical political culture, described earlier in this book. But its beginnings go back much further. The foundations of the power of the bishop were laid in the early Church, in the age of persecutions, long before the conversion of Constantine.

In the course of the second century the Church developed a form of leadership which gave the head of the local church, the bishop, a fullness of power without parallel in any other of the numerous voluntary societies of the cities of the Empire. This was partly a response to persecution, but it was also rooted in the nature of the Christian religion which differed from classical religion in the fact that it made high and specific moral demands on its adherents.[3] That the Christian community demanded

[1] P. Brown 1992: 77: 'We are dealing . . . with a *struggle* for a new style of urban leadership', is misleading.

[2] Socrates *HE* VII.11.

[3] It has often been thought that paganism was concerned only with ritual correctness, and had nothing to do with morality. This is a mistake, as I have argued in Liebeschuetz 1979: 39–54, 90–100.

strict observance of certain moral rules from it members gave the head of the community, the bishop, a degree of authority over the private life of believers, which was without parallel in the Roman world. At the same time weekly services and sermons put at his disposal a unique medium of publicity. The preachers exalted virginity, strongly discouraged the remarriage of widows, and ceaselessly urged donations and bequests to support the charitable work of the Church. The fact that he controlled admission to and exclusion from the Church meant that he was in a position to discipline and indeed humiliate any member of his community to whom it mattered whether he was in communion or not.[4]

2. *Bishops after the Conversion of Constantine*

The conversion of Constantine, and the fact that subsequent emperors with only one exception were Christians, inevitably increased the power of bishops. This was not only because Christian communities grew rapidly as large numbers of individuals converted to the religion of the emperor. Constantine encouraged the formal organization of the civic churches into an imperial church whose structure of provinces and dioceses paralleled the structure of the Empire. Henceforth the urban bishop was as it were an official of a second Empire-wide administration, with comparable access to the head of state. Moreover the cohesion and separateness of this structure was consolidated by privileges.[5] Bishops travelling to church councils were allowed to use the public post.[6] Clergy were given immunity from curial duties[7] and at least to some extent separated from secular jurisdiction.[8] A law of AD 384 explains the principle that bishops should not be called before secular courts: 'they have their own judges and have nothing in common with public laws, as far as ecclesiastical cases are concerned, which are properly decided by the authority of bishops'.[9] The state also gave legal validity to the settlement of civil disputes in the court of the bishop, with the provision only that the bishop's jurisdiction had

But it is true that the moral rules that regulated Roman society were not religiously based, in that they were neither derived from a holy book like the Bible, nor upheld as divine commandments.

[4] See Lane Fox 1986: 498–506.

[5] What follows is inevitably much simplified. Privileges of Constantine: Dupont 1967: 729–52. For development of privileges, including from time to time some limitation: Hunt 1993: 143–8; A. H. M. Jones 1964: 89–91, 118, 480–1, 491–2; Gaudemet 1958; Nöthlichs 1972: 136–53, 1989: 251–99. English translations of many of the texts in Coleman Norton 1966.

[6] Eusebius *HE* X.5; *CSEL* XXVI.26; Ammianus XXI.1.18.

[7] *CT* XVI.2.1 (312); 2 (313S); 7 (330); limited by 6 (326); 3 (326S).

[8] *CT* XVI.11.1 (399), 'in cases involving religion it is appropriate to trouble bishops'. XVI.2.12 (355), bishops not to be accused in secular courts, so also *Constitutiones Sirmondianae* 3 (384) and 6 (425) = *CT* XVI.2.47.

[9] *Constitutiones Sirmondianae* 3.

been recognized by both parties.[10] It was an innovation of the Christian Empire that it accepted the Church's claim that 'the poor' were a special social category, whose need it was the peculiar God-given mission of the Church to satisfy. Christian emperors starting with Constantine made numerous grants to churches to help their charitable work. It is not absolutely clear from the sources whether Constantine laid down the principle that the Church's charity must be subsidized everywhere, so that a grant from state revenue was assigned to the Church in every city, or whether he only gave grants as a special favour to chosen churches. My assessment is that grants were assigned only to some, though probably quite many, Churches,[11] and usually for specific purposes. So Constantine made certain financial arrangements to enable the Church of Constantinople to provide a free funeral service for the city's inhabitants.[12]

It is certainly not right to assume that it was the deliberate purpose of such grants and privileges to involve the Church in secular administration, and so make it easier for the emperor to govern his Empire. A number of letters, preserved in writings of Eusebius explain Constantine's strong conviction that God required him as a Christian emperor to support the work of the Church, and that in fact divine support would not be forthcoming unless he supported the Church in all its activities. Constantine and his successors accepted the fact that the Christian clergy's religious duties covered a wider range of activities than had occupied the ministers of the ancestral religion, and they supported the Church's work over the whole area, and if the Church needed privileges to enable it to do its proper work properly, the emperors felt obliged to provide them.[13]

But the primary duty of clergy always was to maintain the divine cult, and by their prayers to ensure that God would support the emperor and his subjects. Constantine felt that he had to remove any obstruction that might stand between the clergy and their work of prayer. So he wrote to Anulinus proconsul of Africa in the earliest of the letters conferring privileges on the clergy:

> Wherefore it is my wish that those persons who within the province committed to thee . . . bestow their service on this holy worship—those whom they are accustomed to call clerics—should once and for all be kept free from all public office, that they be not drawn away . . . from the worship which they owe the

[10] *CT* I.27.1 (318); 2 (408); Just. *Nov* LXXXXVI (539) treats the bishop practically as the first instance of appeal from the court of the governor. Selb 1967: 162–217. Jaeger 1960: 243 ff.; Hunt 1993: 151–4.

[11] See Appendix, below, p. 167.

[12] Just. *Nov* 59.

[13] For Constantine's feelings, see his letter: Optatus *Appendix* 37a, Eusebius *HE* X.6–7; *VC* II.46; IV.36. The genuineness and significance of these documents was demonstrated by A. H. M. Jones 1949. See now in Dagron 1996: esp. 141–54; and Averil Cameron and S. G. Hall 1999: 16–21.

divinity, but rather without any hindrance serve to the utmost their own law. For when they render supreme service to the Deity they confer incalculable benefit on the affairs of the state.[14]

Constantine very early learnt that charitable giving was an essential part of Christian worship, that it was something that God expected from Christians and that giving by the Church would make the Church's prayers more acceptable to God. In time, as we will see, successive emperors imposed various further responsibilities on bishops. But the Christian emperors from Constantine to Justinian and beyond never ceased to see it as their primary duty to make sure that nothing distracted the clergy from the vital task of praying for the Empire.[15]

If the privileging of bishops and clergy by Constantine and his immediate successors did not make them into imperial administrators, it nevertheless greatly affected the position of the bishop vis-à-vis his fellow citizens. Over the years the power and influence of the bishop grew until he was at least the equal of the most powerful individuals in many if not most cities.[16] Various factors contributed to this development. The bishop was the only authority in the city elected with some participation of the general public. His election always involved acclamation by the assembled congregation.[17] Sometimes, as in the famous case of Ambrose of Milan, it was the acclamation which decided the election.[18] Once consecrated he held the office for life as no secular civic functionary did.

As the Church grew in wealth the bishop came to control greater financial resources than all but the wealthiest inhabitants, and these enabled him to fulfil the Church's role of guardian of the poor and the sick. As guardian of the 'poor', the bishop had wider and more comprehensive clientele than any traditional civic magnate, and one which could be exploited to mount demonstrations, or to threaten or even to assault the bishop's opponents in the city. Basil's ability to resist the Arian emperor Valens was to a considerable extent based on the support he had built up among the poor and the craftsmen's guilds of Caesarea.[19] When Constantine channelled public resources, corn, oil, and probably money to the church of Alexandria to organize distributions to widows and the poor

[14] Eusebius *HE* X.7.2, tr. J. E. L. Oulton in Loeb Classical Library edition.

[15] See *CT* XVI.2.2 (319); 10 (320); 16 (361); 40 (412); *CJ* I.3.5 (531): Justinian grants monks and clergy attached to churches or monasteries exemption from guardianships so that 'when all other services have been abandoned they should adhere to the services of Almighty God'.

[16] P. Brown 1992: 46–158 is a brilliant reconstruction of the 'rise of the bishop', though the development was slower and more sporadic.

[17] This could be awkward if the people insisted on somebody whom the bishops of the province thought unsuitable, or who would have to be transferred against canon law from another city, see e.g. Aug. *Ep.* 22*.5–11.

[18] Rufinus *HE* 11.11; Paulinus, *V. Ambr.* 7–8; McLynn 1994: 43–51.

[19] P. Brown 1992: 100–3.

he significantly increased the power of the patriarch not only to do good, but also to win supporters.[20] In Alexandria and many other cities the bishop was more favourably placed than anyone else whether to start a riot or to conciliate one.[21]

In the Christian Empire a bishop was not like other men. Constantine stated that a bishop's judgement should be respected as something sacred,[22] and his words assumed to be true.[23] It is unlikely that such confidence in the moral perfection of bishops was universally held. Nevertheless the sanctity of his office made a bishop's intercession exceptionally effective. It also afforded him some protection from violence at the hands of the provincial governor, something which even men of the highest standing had to fear. So Synesius, bishop of Ptolemais, was able to excommunicate and bring about the dismissal of Andronicus governor of Libya.[24] At the same time the bishop's court, the *episcopalis audientia*, offered a valuable arbitration service to citizens. The bishop settled disputes between members of his community more quickly than any public official and without any charge. Moreover he was in position to settle a dispute involving alleged criminal acts by one or both parties without inflicting the cruel penalties which the laws laid down, and a secular judge could be expected to inflict. Not surprisingly the bishop was in great demand, not only to settle disputes in his own court, but also to intercede for individuals awaiting trial whether criminal or civil in a secular court. Bishops regularly complained of the amount of time taken up by court work, which occupied Augustine for instance, the whole of the morning right into the hours of siesta.[25]

In a large and growing number of towns the bishop became by far the most important patron, assisting a wide range of individuals in every kind of difficulty. Bishops were increasingly called upon to act as spokesmen for their city, most often to plead for relief from taxation. But in AD 388 bishop Flavian of Antioch sought and obtained the emperor Theodosius' pardon for the city after the so-called Riot of the Statues, when a mob had overturned the imperial images, a symbolic act of rebellion, and when

[20] Athanasius, *Apology* 18, *Hist. Ar.*, 10, 13, 31.

[21] Haas 1997: 295–330. P. Brown 1992: 103–17.

[22] pro sanctis habeatur quidquid ab his fuerit iudicatum (*CT* I.27.1 (318).

[23] Constantine in *Constitutiones Sirmondianae* 1 (333): a bishop's word is necessarily true and incorruptible, issuing as it does from a holy man 'in the consciousness of an undefiled mind', cited from Hunt 1993: 153.

[24] Synesius, *Ep.* 57–8, 72–3, 79.

[25] P. Brown 1992: 100; Possidius, *Life of Augustine* 17. For the scope, character, and legal professionalism of Augustine's judicial activity, see the new letters discovered by J. Divjak, edited by him in *CSEL* 88 (1981), and with French translation and commentaries by various authors in *Oeuvres de Saint Augustin* 46B, Lettres 1*–29* (Paris: Études Augustiniennes, 1987); English tr. by R. B. Enos, *Saint Augustine, Letters*, vi (1*–29*), Fathers of the Church (Washington, 1989). An example: *Ep.* 9* a dispute between a bishop and a Jew over property originally belonging to the Jew's mother.

there seemed no limit to the punishment the emperor might inflict on the city.[26] This incident became a famous example of episcopal influence and of imperial piety. It was more or less contemporary with Ambrose of Milan's celebrated confrontations of the same emperor.[27] But just as Ambrose's success in asserting his will over that of the emperor was exceptional at the time—and indeed for many years subsequently—so was Flavian's particular mission. Regular communication between city and court was still carried on through curial embassies.[28] To the end of the fourth century and beyond, the administration of almost all cities remained secular in almost all respects.

There was however one area in which bishops could—and did—use their position to coerce other than members of their proper flock. This was in the field of the enforcement of religious uniformity by the suppression of paganism and of Christian dissent. There is no doubt that in many places it was the bishop who initiated attacks on the local temples, sometimes after he had obtained an imperial order for temples in his city to be closed or destroyed.[29] From the reign of Theodosius I (379–95) the central government adopted the suppression of religious diversity as a permanent policy. Its enforcement depended largely on the active cooperation of the bishops.[30]

Some well-known cases of episcopal use of force in the field of religion involve the patriarchs of Alexandria.[31] In AD 391 Theophilus played a prominent part in the destruction of the Serapeum the principal pagan temple at Alexandria.[32] In spring 400 he expelled the so-called Long Brothers from their monasteries in the Nitrian desert.[33] In 415 Cyril, the successor of Theophilus personally led an attack on the Jews of Alexandria which ended in their expulsion from the city.[34] In the same year a mob led by a *lector* named Peter lynched the lady-philosopher Hypatia. Both Theophilus and Cyril exploited the fact that at that time the authorities at

[26] van de Paverd 1991; Browning 1952: 13–21.

[27] On Ambrose's successful confrontations of imperial power, see the somewhat revisionist account in McLynn 1994: 291–360 (Ambrose v. Theodosius), see also 158–219 (v. Valentinian II and Justina).

[28] P. Brown's generalizations from Theodosius' yielding to the pleas of Flavian after the Riot of the Statues (P. Brown 1992: 105–8) are acute, but I think anachronistic.

[29] e.g. the destruction of the temple of Zeus by Marcellus of Apamea, Sozomen VII.15; or the destruction of the Marneum at Gaza, Marc le Diacre 1930, whose historicity has been vindicated by Trombley 1993–4: i. 246–82. But sometimes lay fanatics originated attacks: Chadwick 1985: 9–26, esp. 10 and 17, and a bishop like Augustine might try to restrain them.

[30] Attacks by monks on rural temples near Antioch justified by information of prohibited sacrifices brought to Flavian, bishop of Antioch (Libanius, *Pro templis* 15); Lieu 1985: 160–4 on bishops and suppression of Manichaeism.

[31] Haas 1997: 159–69 (Theophilus), 295–316 (Cyril).

[32] Rufinus *HE* II.21–4; Socrates *HE* V.15–17; Sozomen VII.15.

[33] Palladius, *Dialog* 7; Socrates *HE* VI.7; Sozomen VIII.11–12; Kelly 1995: 191–5.

[34] Socrates *HE* VII.13; John of Nikiu LXXXIV.89–99. Dzielska 1995: 85–100.

Constantinople were encouraging the suppression of paganism.[35] The fact that the local head of the imperial administration, Orestes, the prefect of Egypt was hostile, did not deter Cyril.[36]

Bishops might feel strong enough to ignore the local secular authorities, but it was only in times of emergency that we find bishops assuming secular leadership. So for instance in AD 412 bishop Synesius of Ptolemais in Cyrenaica organized the defence of his city when it was under siege by nomads. But Synesius' pre-eminence depended on a particular constellation of local politics. It did not last.[37] Some years later bishop Appion of Syene in the extreme south of Egypt petitioned Theodosius II (AD 408–50) to send more troops to protect the inhabitants from nomad raiders and to put the troops under the bishop's own command. The request was granted.[38] In 452 Pope Leo the Great was part of a delegation which successfully interceded for Rome with the victorious Attila.[39] Three years later he pleaded with the Vandal king Geiseric in an attempt to mitigate the imminent sack of Rome.[40] In the wars of Justinian, in the mid-sixth century, it was quite normal in the frontier provinces of the East for the bishop to take a leading part in negotiations with the Persians over the surrender of his city. Procopius' history of the Persian invasion of AD 540 of Mesopotamia and Syria[41] describes a number of cases. In Procopius' account of Justinian's Italian war bishops are less prominent.[42] Around a century later, when the Arabs invaded the eastern provinces, we still hear of bishops who negotiated with the invaders, but it may be that this now happened more rarely than in the time of Justinian.[43] Even in the sixth century the fact that bishops frequently acted as civic leaders in times of crisis, does not mean that they had become an integral part of the city's regular government.[44] It will not do to ignore the wide gap between the ideal role of a bishop and that of a traditional urban magistrate. In fact the Church propagated an ideology that was incompatible with the ethos of

[35] The Serapeum was destroyed after Theodosius had issued anti-pagan legislation: *CT* XVI.10.7–12 (381–92); Cyril acted soon after Aurelian had become praetorian prefect, inaugurating a phase of religious legislation: XVI.10.21 (416); suppression of Jewish patriarchate: *CT* XVI.8.22 (415 Seeck). For a subtle study of the tension between pagans and Christians produced by a new wave of official suppression of paganism in Africa in AD 399, see Markus 1990: 112–23.

[36] For later episodes, see below, pp. 000–00.

[37] Liebeschuetz 1986: 180–95.

[38] Feissel and Worp 1988: 99, cited by P. Brown 1992: 141–2.

[39] Prosper *Chron.* Ad 452, *MGH AA* IX.482.

[40] Ibid. 484.

[41] Claude 1969: 127–9; Beroea (Procopius II.7.19 ff.), Apamea (II.11.20 ff.), Sura (II.5.13 ff.), Sergiopolis (II.20.1 ff.), and in an earlier war: Constantina (II.13.13 ff.).

[42] Claude 1969: 124 (Milan).

[43] Claude 1969: 134 (Arados), 135 (Jerusalem, Alexandria). Baladhuri 1966: 121, 186–7 (Damascus). But the Arab sources as a rule do not state who negotiated the surrender of a city: D. R. Hill 1971.

[44] See below, pp. 153–5.

traditional city politics. For the competitive giving for public entertainment and other civic purposes, which was the essence of traditional politics, was condemned as vanity and seeking after vain-glory by Christian preachers;[45] and the calendar of civic festivals was deeply suspect because of its pagan origin. Up to the end of the fourth century, the Church and its head remained altogether outside the machinery and ceremony of municipal government. Lepelley has shown that this was the situation even in the already strongly Christian cities of Africa in the age of Augustine. The situation was no different in Christian Antioch.[46] After the riot of the statues, bishop Flavian emerged as the natural spokesman of the city, and the one most capable of winning a pardon from the emperor,[47] but the speeches of Libanius which tell us a good deal about the government of Antioch give no indication that the bishop played a prominent role in it normally. It is significant that very few laws in the Codes are actually addressed to bishops.[48] When emperors sent out letters to resolve problems of secular administration they addressed them to secular officials, mostly to the provincial governor.

3. *The Position of Bishops in the East: Fifth and Sixth Centuries*

In the course of the fifth century the bishops' influence generally increased as the councils grew weaker, and as the upper classes of the cities became thoroughly Christianized. Clergy and Christian institutions came to be increasingly conspicuous in cities of the East. By the sixth century the town-like village of Aphrodito and its surrounding territory in the Thebaid of Egypt had over thirty churches and nearly forty monasteries. In addition the names of dozens of farms suggest that they had monastic owners or settlers.[49] We know the names of forty-one monasteries in the territories of Hermopolis and Antinoopolis. They were mostly small, owning only one or two farms.[50] In the same region there were fourteen hospitals, and nine 'Philoponeia', associations of laymen dedicated to assisting the Church in its work.[51] The early seventh-century tax register of Hermopolis mentions twenty-nine churches, of which eight are called

[45] See Laistner 1967, an introduction and translation of John Chrysostom's pamphlet 'On vain glory and the right way for parents to bring up their children', esp. 75–140.

[46] Lepelley 1979–80: 391–42; Liebeschuetz 1972: 239–42.

[47] *Or.* XIX.28; J. Chrys. *Hom. de statuis.* 21; cf. van de Paverd 1991; P. Brown 1992: 105–8.

[48] Hunt 1993: 151 n. 34 cites *CT* IV.7.1 (to Ossius); XVI.2.8 (to clergy); XVI.2.10 (to all bishops); XVI.2.14 (to Felix); XVI.2.20 (to Damasus); XVI.2.23 (to four bishops 'and the rest').

[49] Timm 1985: 1438–61, s.v. Kom Iŝqaw, cited by MacCoull 1988: 7.

[50] Gascou 1994: 78–9. The tax register (AD 618/19 or 633/4) mentions 25, which together make 49 payments, only 11 pay more than once. At Oxyrhynchos, 53 churches, 19 monasteries, and 8 other Christian institutions are attested. Refs: Alston 1997: 164 n. 58.

[51] Gascou 1994: 77–9; Wipszycka 1970: 511–25.

ekklēsiai (ἐκκλησίαι), and described by locality or some other external feature, while twenty-one are named after saints or martyrs. The *ekklēsiai* make 50 out of 105 payments. They were therefore considerably the wealthier of the two types of church. It is likely that the *ekklēsiai* represent congregational churches while the others are chapels (*eukētria*/εὐκτήρια) of private foundations.[52] The tax register lists 50 members of the clergy and about the same number of provincial officials and officers.[53] Among the 456 inscribed tombs naming trade or profession of the little Cilician city of Corycos 76, or 16.8 per cent, commemorate clerics or employees of the Church.[54] This compares with 38 officials and miliary men. Nine charitable institutions are mentioned. The number of foundations, and of persons in some way or other employed by them, is a measure of the Christianization of the cities. In terms of men involved, the ecclesiastical institutions of these small towns were on the same scale as the secular administration. Churches and charitable institutions were not necessarily founded by the bishop. In fact most were probably founded by private individuals, and many were small, with only small endowments, and probably not destined for a long life.[55] Some were formally linked to the episcopal church, others not. The extent of the bishop's control over various institutions their staffs, and endowments varied considerably.[56] Monasteries tended to resist the intervention by the bishop. But after AD 451 the bishop's right to supervise monasteries was established in canons of the Council of Chalcedon, and like all decisions of the Council it was upheld by imperial law.[57]

The average bishop was at the head of a considerable administrative apparatus, and controlled what were by the standards of his locality very considerable financial resources.[58] We have more detailed information about the wealth and other resources of the bishops of Alexandria than about those of any other see in the East except that of Constantinople.[59] The church of Alexandria maintained a large body of invalid attendants, the so-called *parabalani*. These included volunteers from the upper classes. Apart from their work of charity they were used to overawe sessions of the law courts or of the council. They attended the games presumably to lead demonstrations. In AD 449 they accompanied the

52 Gascou 1994: 70–6; Herman 1942: 378–442.
53 Gascou 1994: 65–6.
54 Trombley 1987: 16–23.
55 Dagron 1989: 1069–85.
56 A. H. M. Jones 1964: 899–904.
57 Dagron 1970: 229–76. Council of Chalcedon canons 4, 8, 18, 23, 24.
58 Wipszycka 1972: *passim*.
59 On the wealth, including trading ships, of the bishop of Alexandria in the early 7th cent., see Leontius of Neapolis, *Vita Sancti Ioannis Eleemosynarii*, ed. H. Gelzer (Freiburg and Leipzig, 1893), Eng. tr. in E. Dawes and N. H. Baynes, *Three Byzantine Saints* (Oxford, 1948), 207–62.

patriarch Dioscorus to the second Council of Ephesus where they cheered their leader and threatened his opponents.[60] They may well have been involved in the murder of Hypatia. At any rate it was shortly after that atrocity that the imperial government briefly tried to limit their numbers to 500 and to prevent their attendance at public meetings.[61] The *philoponoi* were another organization closely associated with the patriarchate. This was a society of Christian activists, including students of good family, who dedicated themselves to reading of Christian texts, ascetic living, and good works. We hear of them in the 480s when, at a time which was politically convenient for the orthodox patriarch Peter Mongus, they stirred up a hysterical outburst against paganism which culminated in the destruction of the temples at Canopos and Menouthis, and the ceremonial burning of a mass of pagan sacred objects.[62]

Another resource regularly exploited by the bishops of Alexandria were the thousands of monks of the many monasteries and hermitages established within thirty miles or so of the city.[63] Monks had views of their own and they could if they were so minded put considerable pressure on the bishop. So the patriarchs Theophilus and Cyril and Dioscorus were always careful to remain on good terms with the majority of monks. In return the monks were ready to physically assault the patriarch's enemies. After the Council of Chalcedon the bishops appointed by the emperors had to be even more tactful in their treatment of the monks. For many of the monasteries were Monophysite and in the later sixth century a separate Monophysite bishop of Alexandria had his headquarters in one of them.

No doubt bishop and Christian organizations were exceptionally powerful at Alexandria. But *parabalani* and *philoponoi* and similar organizations also existed at Oxyrhynchus and presumably in many other cities in Egypt, and of course elsewhere too.[64] We have a detailed account of a student-led anti-pagan witch-hunt by the *philoponoi* of Berytus very similar to the Alexandrian one.[65] We will return to the theme of the use of force by bishops to enforce doctrinal uniformity in the chapter on urban

[60] *ACO* II.1.1.179, l. 28.

[61] In AD 416 after the *parabalani* had caused trouble, possibly but not certainly connected with the lynching Hypatia, the *curia* sent an embassy of protest to Constantinople and the *parabalani* were prohibited from entering public spectacles, the *curia*, and the law-courts (ut nihil commune clerici cum publicis actibus vel ad curiam pertinentibus habeant (*CT* XVI.2.42), which was partly repealed in AD 418 (ibid. 43).

[62] Zacharias of Mytilene, *V. Severi*, ed. and tr. Kugener, *PO* 2/1 (Paris, 1903), 14–39; Haas 1997: 238–40, 327–9. Wipszycka 1970: 511–12. Trombley 1993–4: ii. 1–51, 219–25.

[63] Haas 1997: 258–67.

[64] *P Landlisten* 8.154. See Dagron 1991: esp. 161 on the 800 *lektikarioi* and *kopiatai* as well as *askētriai*, *kanonikai*, and *akolouthoi* that worked for the church in the state-financed funeral service at Constantinople (*Nov* LIX of 537).

[65] Zacharias of Mytilene, *op. cit.* 57–75.

violence.[66] What is relevant to the present chapter is that a bishop's success in forcing his version of religion on those who would not have adhered to it voluntarily, provided a demonstration which nobody could overlook of the power at the bishop's disposal, if only he decided to use it. Thus, he was inevitably a man to be reckoned with. If there was a power-vacuum in the city, the bishop was likely to be drawn into it.

But the extent to which the bishop was drawn into routine civic affairs varied very greatly from city to city and region to region, and also depended very much on the character of the individual bishop. Theodoret of Cyrrhus seems to have been very active in the affairs of his city. He used his influence at Constantinople to reduce the city's tax burden. He takes credit for building porticoes, baths, and bridges.[67] He was not alone in this. Inscriptions, mainly from the sixth century, show that in Eastern cities the bishop was sometimes responsible for the administration of public building schemes. At Gerasa the bishop built a prison.[68] At Bostra inscriptions record the name of the emperor Justinian whose generosity paid for certain fortifications, together with that of the bishop who had persuaded the emperor to be generous, and had actually supervised some of the building-work.[69] In Egypt inscriptions link bishops with public works at Kom Obo,[70] and the construction of fortifications and a harbour wall at Philae.[71] In Mesopotamia bishops are reported to have been in charge of the building of fortifications at Edessa and Birtha Castra[72] and of a granary at Arethusa. Inscriptions commemorate the supervision of building work by bishops at Trapezunt in Pontus in AD 542 and in Cilicia in AD 565–78.[73] Bishop Ibas of Edessa was said—by his enemies—to have presented chariot races.[74] The list is not exhaustive. But the number of secular building schemes and of acts of secular administration known to have been carried out or supervised by bishops are far fewer than the power and resources at the disposal of bishops would have led one to expect.[75] That a bishop should supervise the construction of fortifications

66 See below, pp. 257–60.

67 Theoderet *Ep.* 79.

68 Gatier 1985: 298–307.

69 *IGLS* 9135–6 work of fortification paid for by emperor, supervised by the bishop; 9130 paid for by the emperor at instigation of bishop, supervised by subordinate of duke; 9134 renewal of aqueduct, paid for by emperor, instigated by bishop on embassy, supervised by a silversmith.

70 H. R. Hall, *Coptic and Greek Texts of the Christian Period from Ostraca, Stelae etc. in the British Museum* (London, 1905), no. 1.

71 Lefebure 1907: no. 584 (AD 577); 592–3; 599–603.

72 Joshua Stylites, *Chron* 87 (p. 64): emperor gives Peter bishop of Edessa gold to repair walls in AD 504–5. Ibid. 91: gives money to Sergius, bishop of Birtha-Castra on Euphrates to build a wall.

73 *CIG* IV.8636; *MAMA* III.106a = *CIG* IV.8619.

74 Ibas of Edessa through an associate (J. B. Segal 1970: 131, 164).

75 Avramea 1989: 829–35, supplemented by Feissel 1989: 801–28.

was probably in the main a frontier phenomenon.[76] Certainly, the great majority of inscriptions commemorating work on urban fortifications record the names of laymen, mostly governors or generals.[77] Whether a bishop made a contribution to such activities remained a matter of individual choice, influenced no doubt by a variety of external pressures. They did not become part of the bishop's regular job, even though imperial laws might seem to make them so. In fact the rise of the bishop helped to disconnect the cities from the structure of the imperial administration.[78]

As we have seen, the bishop was regularly associated with the notables in laws setting up and regulating post-curial government. The earliest example of this association is the law of AD 409 which lays down that the *defensor* is to be chosen by a decree of bishop, clergy, *honorati*, *possessores*, and *curiales*. This was a Western law, and therefore not necessarily valid in the East; though it probably was, for it was repeated about a century later by the Eastern emperor Anastasius.[79] Since the *defensor* was by now the leading magistrate in many cities, the involvement of bishop and clergy in his election was an important step in the involvement of the bishop in secular administration.

That bishops had a special interest in the office of *defensor* is shown by the fact that it was the bishops of Africa assembled at Carthage in AD 401 who demanded that the office should be brought to proconsular Africa, thirty-three years after Valentinian I had introduced it elsewhere.[80] They asked the emperor Honorius to nominate *defensores* for their cities whose task it would be to protect not only the poor, but also the clergy from injustices at the hands of the powerful. Individuals should be nominated after consultation with the bishop.[81] This request was evidently not granted at that time; for in December 419 Augustine, as bishop of Hippo, asked his friends and colleagues Alypius and Peregrinus to support an initiative to get a *defensor* appointed at Hippo. Augustine did not know whether it was in order to appoint someone who was holding an imperial office.[82] If it was, he had a particular man in mind,[83] but in case it was not, he was putting forward the names of two men who were not office holders. Either would be suitable. Augustine's letter illustrates the

[76] So Thomas bishop of Amida together with the deputy praetorian prefect Calliopius supervised the building of the fortress-city of Daras on the Persian frontier in Mesopotamia. Ps Zacharias, *Ecclesiastical History*, tr. F. J. Hamilton and F. W. Brooks (London, 1899), vii. 6.

[77] See inscriptions assembled by Lewin 1991: 78–98.

[78] Dagron 1971: 20.

[79] *CJ* I.55.8 (409), 11 (509).

[80] *CT* I.29.1, 3 (368).

[81] *Conciliae Africae*, ed. C. Munier, Corpus Christianorum Series Latina 149 (Brepols, 1974), 202 c. 75, *defensor* to be nominated 'cum provisione episcoporum'.

[82] *Ep.* 22*.2–4.

[83] Divjak 1987: 524–5 (Serge Lancel); *PLRE* II.1192, s.v. Ursus 4.

Church's attitude to the abuses of power which it was a *defensor*'s duty to combat. The Church was very much concerned that the victims of these abuses should be helped, but it was unable to intervene directly itself because it could not afford to be seen to be obstructing the imperial administration. Besides Augustine considered it quite wrong for the Church to make accusations that could result in an individual being sentenced to punishment by a secular court. In other words Augustine thought that it was the function of the *defensor* to help victims of injustice whom the Church could not help without taking up the inappropriate role of secular prosecutor.[84]

The law of 409 was of course the first step towards the establishment of post-curial government, that is government by notables.[85] The next step, taken by the emperor Anastasius involved bishop and clergy together with secular notables in the election of *curator* and *sitona*. That bishop and clerics formed part of the electoral body obviously gave them a formal role in secular affairs. It recognized that the fact that bishop and clergy now constituted an important group in the city, a group with distinct privileges and status, in this way comparable to the *honorati* and *possessores* and the old *curiales*. As in the case of the *possessores* the state did not lay down what qualification entitled a man to be included among the clergy who participated in the election of civic functionaries. In practice only some of the local clergy will have taken part, those that were invited by the bishop and leading clerics.

That bishop and clergy were given a role in the election of civic functionaries was however not only based on a realistic assessment of the Church's secular power. It was also an act of practical Christianity. For what from a modern point of view looks like the involvement of the Church in secular politics, also represents acceptance and implementation of the Church's divinely ordained mission to right wrongs and to feed the hungry. For as it was the duty of the *defensor* to protect the (relatively) weak from injury by the strong, so it was that of the *sitona* to buy corn at public expense and to sell it at a price the ordinary people could afford.[86] Since Constantine, the state had paid subsidies to various churches to assist their charitable feeding of the poor.[87] Participation in the appointment of the *sitona* would enable the churches to perform this duty more effectively.

[84] *Ep.* 22*.3: Nam si eorum vim manu ecclesiastica pellere voluerimus, queruntur de nobis eis potestatibus a quibus mittuntur, quod per nos impediantur publicae necessitates . . . scientes nec in nostra purgatione nobis licere, ut eorum facta nudemus eis, a quibus possunt comperta puniri.

[85] *CJ* I.4.17, X.27.3 (491–505) election of *sitona* by bishop and *prōteuontes* of the *ktētores*.

[86] On *sitona*, see Sirks, Sijpesteijn, and Worp 1996.

[87] Theoderet *HE* I.11, IV.4; *CJ* I.2.12 (451); Sozomen *HE* V.5; Socrates *HE* II.17; more references in A. H. M. Jones 1964: 899 n. 66. See Appendix A below, pp. 167–8.

From the reign of Anastasius onwards, and especially under Justinian, numerous laws were issued whose effect was to involve the bishop more deeply in what we, but not necessarily the late Romans, would consider secular affairs. It is not surprising that emperors should try to do that, since as we have seen earlier,[88] the decline of the city councils had left cities without a permanent, formally defined, ultimately responsible, governing body. The bishop was ideally placed to fill the gap—and in not a few cities there will really have been no one else. For instance in Hadrianopolis in Paphlagonia towards the end of the sixth century the bishop seems to have been the only agent through whom the imperial government could communicate with the inhabitants of the city and its territory.[89] But it would be a mistake to conclude that the emperors now treated the bishop as just another imperial official.[90] They did not secularize the office of the bishop. They treated certain activities, that had previously been considered secular, as falling under the bishop's religious remit. Administration had acquired a religious aspect which it did not have before. The thinking behind this was no doubt at one level practical, but at another it was theological and it is impossible to separate state-craft and theology in the political thinking of this time. The development was part of the Christianization of social life.

These laws could in fact be seen as instructing bishops to watch over the application of Christian charity to public administration. Bishops are to remind governors that they ought to visit prisons on Sundays and acquaint themselves with the living conditions of the inmates. Bishops themselves are ordered to make regular prison-visits, and bishops are ordered to enforce the law making private prisons illegal by liberating the prisoners detained in them.[91] Bishops were given a place in the legal procedures for protecting the rights of orphans,[92] of foundlings, and of children whose fathers were not *compos mentis*.[93] Bishops are given permission to give freedom to slaves whom their masters have sent into prostitution, a right previously held only by provincial governors. They are also authorized to help slaves to abandon the stage if they had been forced by their masters to display themselves as actors or dancers.[94]

It was surely the thought that a bishop, by virtue of his holy office, could reasonably be expected to deal impartially and justly in areas where deceit and extortion were particularly rife, that at least partly accounts for

[88] See above, pp. 114–16.
[89] Feissel and Kaygusuz 1985.
[90] See Appendix B, below, p. 168.
[91] *CJ* I.4.9 (409), 22 (529), 23 (529).
[92] *CJ* I.4.27 (530), 30 (531).
[93] *CJ* I.4.22 (529), 28 (530).
[94] *CJ* I.4.14 (Leo), 33 (534).

a succession of laws requiring the bishop to supervise fair dealing in various difficult aspects of municipal administration. It had always been a weakness of the relatively interventionist imperial administration of the Later Empire that its decisions were extremely sensitive to influence and corruption. Many must have wished for an arbitrator who was above all that. The bishop seemed to be just what was needed. Of course he in his turn was influenced by interests of his own and of the Church.[95] In the long run this was very important. Meanwhile bishops were involved in the setting of the price at which the military *annona*, the tax in kind issued as salary to soldiers, was converted into money payments.[96] The bishop was brought into the enforcement of civic building regulations, and what must have been an even more delicate matter, the deciding of what to do when the regulations have been infringed.[97] Finally, the bishop was made one of a committee of notables who had the duty of auditing annually the accounts of every individual who had been responsible for spending civic money.[98]

Numerous regulations instruct the bishop to intervene in cases of extortion and other abuses of power, including the refusal by imperial officials of every rank, from members of the provincial *officium*, to provincial governors and delegates of the central administration, to pay their creditors.[99] Justinian made it part of a bishop's duty to supervise the provincial governor. On entering his province a new governor takes an oath in the presence of the metropolitan bishop and leading citizens.[100] Bishop and leading citizens are invited to bring complaints about the governor to the notice of the emperor.[101] If a citizen cannot get justice from the governor, he is to take the matter to the bishop who will take every step to see that justice is done, in the last resort informing the emperor.[102] What enabled the bishop to fill a role, which recalls that of today's ombudsman, was that he could approach successive levels of the hierarchy through other than official channels. Local grandees had always been able to do that through personal or family connections, but the bishop had at his permanent disposal an administrative structure parallel to the imperial one, with independent access to court. But it should be remembered that the

[95] P. Brown 1992: 101–2 uses Basil of Caesarea as an example.

[96] *CJ* I.4.18. An extension of this is found in Visigothic Spain, where the bishops of a fiscal district (cf. above, p. 134), not only approve the nomination of the civic directors of taxation (*numerarius*), but also approve—if indeed they do not set—the rate at which taxes in kind are to be converted into money (de fisco Barcinonensi, *Mansi* XII.473 ff.).

[97] *CJ* I.4.8–10.

[98] *CJ* I.4.26 (531); *Nov* 128.16 (545).

[99] *CJ* IV.30.5 (528).

[100] *Nov* 8.14.

[101] *Nov* 8.

[102] *Nov* 86 (539). For an excellent survey of this legislation, see K. L. Noethlichs, *RAC* 19 (1999), s.v. Justinianus (Kaiser), cols. 748–52.

bishop's effectiveness in this role depended lastly neither on his place in an administrative structure, nor on his legal prerogatives, but on the widespread belief that by virtue of his office he represented a higher moral order.

There is no doubt that these duties must have taken up much of a bishop's time, chairing meetings, interviewing individuals, investigating cases, negotiating with imperial officials, writing letters, inspecting buildings, and working through accounts. They will certainly have reduced the time that he could give to strictly ecclesiastical duties, never mind prayer, even though he had a staff to assist him. But it must be noted that all these responsibilities were supervisory, rather than executive or administrative. Very few of the activities assigned to the bishop in the imperial code would actually leave a trace in secular archives like those which fragmentarily survive as the papyri of Egypt.

The influence and power that might be achieved by a late Late Roman bishop in the East is most strikingly demonstrated by the activities of patriarch Gregory of Antioch who used to provided money, food, and clothing to recruits passing through his city on the way to the army on the eastern frontier.[103] As a result he acquired extraordinary influence over the soldiers, and in AD 589 was able to persuade a mutinous army to accept the general Philippicus as their new commander in chief, and some time later to resume the siege of Martyropolis which they had abandoned.[104] But Gregory's position was nevertheless not beyond challenge. On two occasions, in 580 and 588, Gregory was in serious difficulty, when a banker accused the bishop of having had sex with his (the banker's) sister, and of having taken part in pagan rites.[105] He survived the attack. But the incident shows that if Christianization provided new means of winning power, it also offered new weapons to be used against power-holders.[106]

The actual extent of any bishop's involvement in secular affairs, even at this late stage, depended very much on local circumstances, the cohesion of the secular administrative structures, and the personality of the bishop himself. The bishops of the East had still not become simply part of the civic or imperial executive. The Church had its own sense of priorities, and its own canons agreed in the ecumenical councils, and recognized by the emperor as having the force of law.[107] It also had its own growing

103 Evagrius *HE* VI.11–13. Did he also fix the price or the *adaeratio* of the army's *annona* (see above, n. 96)?

104 Allen 1981: 254–6.

105 Evagrius *HE* V.17, VI.7; John of Ephesus *HE* III.27–34, V.17. Allen 1981: 229–30, 250. That the alleged victim was the banker's, not the bishop's sister was seen by Festugière 1975: 451 n. 13.

106 See below, pp. 265–9.

107 Sancimus igitur vicem legum obtinere sanctas ecclesiasticas regulas quae a sanctis quattuor conciliis expositae sunt aut firmatae (Just. *Nov* 131.1).

financial resources, which were quite separate from those of the city, and from those of the Empire.[108] Some churches received imperial subsidies but that was always a special favour. It was understood that the Church would use subsidies and privileges for charitable purposes. This did not however mean that the state made the Church into a branch of administration to which it delegated 'welfare responsibilities'. Subsidies were a Christian government's gifts to the Church to help it in its work as understood and organized by bishops and clergy. The fact that the emperor considered himself responsible for the good functioning of both state and Church does not mean that he saw no essential difference between the two. Neither emperor nor clergy would have seen the relation of Church to state as one of subordination. The emperor legislated for the good order of the Church, but in matters of morality he was himself subject to its discipline. Church and state were distinct organizations with separate spheres. They were both gifts of God, and if each performed its proper role they would be the source of every kind of benefit to the human race.[109]

Even after Justinian's legislation, episcopal leadership in secular affairs of the city normally became conspicuous only in exceptional circumstances. Normally most bishops were kept fully occupied running their churches. Papyri provide us with a relatively detailed view of the administration of the towns of Egypt.[110] It is remarkable how rarely the documents mention the bishops in connection with secular affairs. In Egypt the bishop certainly does not seem to have become the virtual ruler of his city.[111]

It may be that Justinian's legislation assigning duties to bishops involved an element of wishful thinking. There evidently was a vacuum of leadership in the cities. The bishop was in many ways ideally placed to fill it—as indeed bishops eventually did in the much reduced cities of the West. But Eastern bishops did not take the road towards secular lordship. Perhaps Cyrus, patriarch of Alexandria and the last Byzantine governor of Egypt (631–40),[112] and Pope Gregory the Great (590–604)[113] and his successors in the Byzantine Italy, are the exceptions which prove the rule.

[108] Following Gaudemet 1958: 288–310 rather than Durliat 1984 and 1990*b*; see Appendix B, below, p. 168.

[109] Expressed in preface of Just. *Nov* 6: maxima quidem in hominibus sunt dona dei a superna collata clementia sacerdotium et imperium, illud quidem divinis ministrans, hoc autem humanis praesidens ac diligentiam exhibens. . . . Ideoque nihil sic erit studiosum imperatoribus, sicut sacerdotum honestas, cum utique et pro illis ipsis semper deo supplicent. Nam si hoc quidem inculpabile sit undique et apud deum fiducia plenum, imperium autem recte et competenter exornat traditam sibi rempublicam, erit consonantia quaedam bona, omne quidquid utile est humano conferens generi.

[110] The bishop of Alexandria is of course an exception.

[111] On the activities, charitable and otherwise of Egyptian bishops, see A. Martin 1998 and Wipszycka 1998, also cf. below, p. 198.

[112] *PLRE* IIIA.377–8 s.v. Cyrus 17.

[113] See below, p. 199, n. 185.

The case can be made that when Justinian promulgated his laws the influence of bishops had already passed its peak. As we have seen there is evidence that by the second half of the sixth century in large areas of central Anatolia the city was already in retreat, and power was passing to the countryside to be wielded by landowners, abbots, or hermits.[114] The great urban bishops were a feature of the fourth and fifth centuries.[115] Certainly when the structure of the Eastern Empire was rebuilt in Asia Minor after the Arab invasions, bishops—apart from the patriarch of Constantinople—played a far more marginal role than they did in contemporary Germanic states in the West.

4. *The Position of Bishops in the West: Fifth and Sixth Centuries*

In much of the West the influence of the bishop grew more slowly than in the East.[116] While Augustine was bishop of Hippo in Africa proconsularis (395–430) municipal power was still firmly in the hands of the *curia*, and the *curiales* were still largely pagan. In many areas of the West, for instance in large parts of Spain, in central Gaul, and in much of the Balkans, Christianity came comparatively late, and 'the rise of the bishop' was largely a fifth-century phenomenon. We are relatively well informed about Northern Italy in the late fourth and early fifth centuries.[117] Here paganism remained strong both among the *curiales* in the cities and among the villagers on the estates of the urban ruling group. Bishops urged landowners to convert their tenants to Christianity, and reinforced moral arguments with hints that failure to act made landowners liable to the penalties of imperial anti-pagan legislation. Ambrose of Milan and Chromatius, bishop of the wealthy city of Aquileia, realized large church-building programmes. But bishops in many of the smaller cities could not yet afford to do this. They were content to appeal for generous giving to assist the Church's charitable support of the poor and the sick. Sermons of the age of invasions in the first decade of the fifth century show the bishop in a position of crisis leadership.[118] Ecclesiastical charity was needed to look after the victims of war and to ransom prisoners,[119] and there must have been much scope for the bishop to exercise his natural role of conciliator in the areas recommended by Ambrose, between

[114] See above, pp. 68–70.

[115] Cf. remarks of Mitchell 1993: ii. 120–1.

[116] The slow growth of the bishop's secular power, esp. in Italy and North Africa, emerges clearly from the papers in Rebillard and Sotinel 1998. See also Mochi Onory 1933; Humphries 1999 and Pack 1998: 1159–1202.

[117] See the excellent analysis of Lizzi 1990: 156–73.

[118] Lizzi 1989. See also the perceptive Humphries 1999.

[119] Cf. a century later, Klingshirn 1985: 183–203.

quarrelling landowners, between landowners and workers on the land, and above all between hosts and billeted soldiers.

We have an informative account of the role of a civic bishop during the disturbed period towards the end of the fifth century in Ennodius' *Life of Bishop Epiphanius of Pavia*.[120] Epiphanius personally negotiated the entry of Theoderic and his Ostrogoths into Ticinum.[121] Subsequently, he used the resources of the Church, to which both Theoderic and his opponent and rival Odoacer had contributed, to relieve the food crisis after tens of thousands of Goths had crowded into the little city.[122] After Theoderic's victory Epiphanius together with his colleague Lawrence of Milan successfully interceded on behalf of the followers of the recently murdered Odoacer.[123] Later Epiphanius, acting for Theoderic, got leading citizens of ruined towns in the neighbourhood to move their residence to Pavia.[124] One of Epiphanius' last acts was to obtain from Theoderic one year's relief from taxation for the province of Liguria.[125] Presumably he had been asked to do this by the assembled notables of the province, who some years earlier had requested the overbearing commander in chief Ricimer to send Epiphanius to Rome to restore relations with the emperor Anthemius,[126] and subsequently induced Anthemius' successor Nepos to send Epiphanius on an embassy to the Visigothic king Euric.[127] That notables in their relations with the imperial government should act collectively at the provincial rather than at city level is a feature of this late period.[128]

As has been shown earlier, the *Variae* of Cassiodorus throw considerable light on municipal administration in Ostrogothic Italy. Contrary to what has sometimes been argued, bishops do not figure prominently in regular administration.[129] In AD 527 bishops are called to join *honorati* in action to deal with hoarding of corn in a time of famine.[130] Individual bishops are employed on special missions within their city but also elsewhere in the kingdom and, as we have seen in the case of Epiphanius, on

120 *Ennodio, Vita del beatissimo Epifanio*, edited with Italian translation and commentary by M. Cesa (Como, 1988) (abbreviated hereafter as *VE*).

121 *VE* 109.

122 *VE* 111–15.

123 *VE* 125 ff.

124 *VE* 120–1.

125 *VE* 185–7.

126 *VE* 53.

127 *VE* 81–2.

128 For discussions at a provincial council between *honorati* and Roman officials, see letter of Honorius setting up Council of Seven Provinces of Gaul in AD 418. *MGH Epistulae* III.13–15. Answers to petitions by provinces in Cassiodorus' *Variae*: III.13; IV.10 (Campania); IX.14 (Sicily); XII.16 (Venetians); addressed to Ligurians: XI.15, 16.

129 See above, pp. 125–7.

130 IX.5, cf. above, p. 152, for related laws in *CJ*.

diplomatic missions abroad. A bishop Aemilianus (probably of Vercellae) is ordered to complete an aqueduct which he had begun to build.[131] Bishop Datius of Milan is instructed to supervise the selling of corn from the public granaries at Ticinum (Pavia) and Dertona.[132] Bishops and *honorati* are to deal with problem of hoarding of corn by certain people in anticipation of a shortage.[133] Bishops are asked to distribute compensation for requisitioning by soldiers in transit.[134] On taking over the office of praetorian prefect, Cassiodorus asked the bishops to pray for him, and also to report on the conduct of his officials.[135] Most of these tasks are related to the duty of the bishop to feed the hungry and to promote justice. In the abundance of official correspondence assembled in the *Variae*, relatively very few letters concern the duties of bishops. Bishops are certainly much less prominent in the *Variae* than in the *Novels* of Justinian. There can be no question of bishops having been given a significant role in routine administration.

In the course of the sixth century, and above all during the terribly destructive war to 'liberate' Italy from the Goths, populations of cities shrank and the scope of whatever was left of civic self-government was reduced. In the confused situation of the Lombard invasions, the effectiveness of imperial administration shrank also. Subsequently, administrative arrangements varied from region to region, and according to whether an area was ruled by the Byzantines or the Lombards.[136]

Among Italian cities of this time Rome is by far the best known because of the correspondence of Gregory the Great.[137] Of course Rome was not a typical Italian city. Though certainly very much reduced compared with earlier times, the population of Rome was still very large by the modest standards of sixth-century Italy. Moreover the Roman church brought wealth to the city, since it still owned much landed estate in Sicily,[138] with smaller holdings in Italy, North Africa, the south of France, and elsewhere. The pope exercised supervision over many sees in central and southern Italy. Nevertheless Rome shared one important development with the less illustrious cities of Italy. That was the collapse of local secular self-government, which in Rome had of course been administered by the imperial senate. In the second half of the sixth century, mainly

[131] IV.31. He had started building *ex nostra* (i.e. *regis*) *auctoritate*, but evidently at his own expense.

[132] XI.21. Against view of Heinzelmann 1988: 23–82, this is not evidence of routine involvement by bishops in civic administration.

[133] IX.5, province not stated.

[134] II.8.

[135] XI.3.4.

[136] T. S. Brown 1984: 175–89 on Church in Byzantine Italy; D. Harrison 1993: 171–82.

[137] Richards 1980.

[138] Greg. *Ep.* II.38: 400 *conductores*. Value of estates confiscated by Leo III in AD 729 said to have been 250,000 solidi (Theophanes s.a. 6224).

perhaps as a result of Justinian's 'war of liberation', the senate had ceased to be of practical importance—just as small local senates elsewhere had ceased to be politically significant. The imperially appointed *praefectus urbi* disappeared from the scene.[139] The political vacuum was as elsewhere filled by the local bishop in this case, the pope. Gregory the Great (590–604) in particular, from the moment of his election by the people in the middle of a plague epidemic, showed himself a civic leader out of the ancient mould. Like the republican senate in similar situations, Gregory proclaimed a *supplicatio*, calling upon the whole population, clergy, monks, men, women, and children to march through the town in a series of processions to the principle shrines to pray for divine help.[140] Of course the shrines were now basilicas and the cult Christian. Subsequently, Gregory was repeatedly involved in peace negotiations between the city and the Lombards.[141] When the Lombards had to be bought off, it was the Church which provided the money.[142] The Church was self-sufficient as far as the feeding of its own staff was concerned. In addition it regularly fed 'the poor' and 3,000 widows.[143] But in time of famine, the Pope, relying on the Church's estates in Sicily, brought extra corn into the city.[144] The city's food supply still received some subsidy out of imperial taxation.[145] When that ceased, the feeding of the city's much reduced population was left to the Church. The Church responded by setting up some new farming communities in the neighbourhood of the city. It also established a number of diaconal monasteries whose duty it was to distribute food, significantly several of them on the site of a former distribution centre of the imperial *annona*.[146] Gregory himself was very conscious that involvement in secular matters of this kind had its dangers, in that it diverted clergy from their primary duty of looking after souls, including their own. He insists, that if at all possible, his clergy should delegate worldly tasks to subordinates. But they must nevertheless not be shirked altogether, 'for the word of instruction does not enter the mind of a man in want.'[147]

We have much less information about smaller cities, but it would seem

[139] On the last known prefect Ioannes (AD 597–99), see *PLRE* IIa.683 s.v. Ioannes 109.

[140] Greg. T. *HF* X.1 reports these events.

[141] *Regesta Pontificum Romanorum*, ed. P. Jaffé, revised F. Kaltenbrunner and others, 2 vols. (Leipzig, 1885, 1888), 1359, 1349, 1591.

[142] Greg. *Ep.* V.39.

[143] John the Deacon, *V. Greg. Magn.* II.24–8.

[144] *Ep.* I.70.

[145] *Ep.* I.2.

[146] O. Bertolini, 'Per la storia della diaconia Romane nell'alto medioevo alla fine del secolo VIII', *Archivio della Società Romana de Storia Patria*, 70 (1947), 1–145.

[147] *Reg. Past.* II.7. *PL* LXXVII.38–42; ibid. 41B: Egentis etenim mentem doctrinae sermo non penetrat.

that in the absence of an officer representing the Byzantine emperor or the Lombard king or duke, what was left of civic society rallied round the bishop. Cathedral[148] and related buildings, churches, monasteries, and other ecclesiastical institutions now often took up a considerable part of the walled area, and were the nuclei around which the houses of the much reduced lay population clustered. Of the urban population clergy formed a significant proportion. Suburbs grew up around extramural monasteries. The cult of the relics of saints and martyrs was available to all, but it was the bishop who administered the cult, and it was he who propagated evidence of the effectiveness of the local saint's help to those who had sought it.[149] The Church made provision for pilgrims, and these together with clerics travelling on Church business, maintained communications in a world which tended towards greater regional self-sufficiency.[150] As Italy slowly recovered from the upheaval of Justinian's wars and the Lombard invasion, the bishops emerged as civic leaders, particularly in the north,[151] though generally speaking, bishops were less involved in the secular administration of cities under the Lombards, who were still largely pagan when they came into Italy,[152] than in the Eastern Empire and in Byzantine Italy.[153] Civic identity came to be based on the cult and patronage of early bishops who were now believed (unhistorically) to have been martyrs. Ravenna showed the way with saints Vitalis and Apollinaris, and in the course of the sixth and seventh centuries other cities followed the example. Bishops were buried in churches in the middle of their city with epitaphs to commemorate their pious deeds.[154] Lists of bishops were kept as evidence of unbroken continuity between the contemporary Church and the Church of the martyrs. In the eighth century many of the earlier bishops received the cult of saints.[155]

Bishops became prominent in society all over the West, though their position differed from area to area. In North Africa bishoprics were small and extremely numerous. One reason for this was that new sees had been created to look after the more or less forcibly converted Donatists. African bishops might be of comparatively humble origins.[156] Letters of Augustine relate how he chose a promising young man of poor parentage to fill one such see, only to find him exploiting his new position to acquire an estate

[148] Testini, Wataghin, Pani Ermini 1989: 1–231, summarized Guyon 1991*b*: 431–41.

[149] P. Brown 1981: 8–9, 31–3, 93–6; Van Dam 1985: 167–72, 233–8.

[150] Mathisen 1992.

[151] Picard 1988. It is significant that bishops' lists have survived from 18 cities in the north and only 4 in the south.

[152] Christie 1995*a*: 183–8. D. Harrison 1993: 171–5.

[153] On Byzantine Italy: Wickham 1981: 77–8.

[154] Summary: Picard 1988: 387–92.

[155] Ibid. 571–2, 713–14.

[156] Eck 1983.

and build himself a fine town house.[157] The orthodox bishops of Vandal Africa were under intermittent pressure—certainly much exaggerated in our ecclesiastical sources—from the Arian government, while the Arian bishops, as in Ostrogothic Italy and under the Arian kings in Visigothic Spain, remain shadowy and in the main anonymous figures. They clearly lacked the social and political influence of their orthodox contemporaries.[158] After the Justinianic reconquest the orthodox bishops of North Africa refused to accept Justinian's Three Chapters, and later the Monothelite religious policy of the emperor Heraclius. On each occasion many bishops were exiled and replaced by imperial nominees.[159]

The orthodox bishops of Visigothic Spain seem to have lacked the social status and wealth of the aristocratic bishops of Gaul. But within their city they were men of authority. This is shown most strikingly by the career of Masona, bishop of Merida (571–605), who maintained his position successfully against an Arian rival supported by the formidable king Leovigild (568–86) during and after a civil war.[160] We hear very little about the activities of Arian bishops in Arian Spain. Evidently they nowhere achieved the status of a Masona. It was in Spain that bishops eventually became most closely integrated into secular administration. Leovigild the unifier, and his successors who established the Catholic monarchy, imitated the Byzantine system and went beyond it. Annual national synods of bishops were held on royal invitation, and under strict royal control. The king addressed the opening meeting and presented the bishops with a list of themes he wanted discussed, and also indicated the decisions he wanted them to reach. The canons of the council were given the force of law by a royal enactment. Much of the debate was concerned with ecclesiastical discipline, the rooting out of heresy, and the penalizing of Jews. But the national synods also provided a useful forum in which to condemn actual or potential rebels.[161] The involvement of bishops in secular administration is most striking in the field of taxation. Bishops of the provincial synod, or perhaps of a smaller fiscal area, had the right to accept or refuse the directors of taxation appointed by the *comes patrimonii* to supervise tax-collecting in the various towns. They were also authorized to fix the rate of *adaeratio* of the tax in kind, and to set limits to the labour services that could be demanded. Moreover it was the duty of these bishops to report abuses by the officials involved in tax-collecting and to

[157] *Ep.* 209; 20*.

[158] Thompson 1969: 40–1.

[159] Averil Cameron 1993*a*. But the episcopate remained overwhelmingly Latin: see lists of names of councils of 646 in Maier 1973: 80–4.

[160] Macias 1988: IV.2.1–8.19 (pp. 58–69) and the comments of Thompson 1969: 78–80 on a very one-sided text.

[161] Thompson 1969: 277–89.

ensure that they were punished.[162] The later Visigothic kings of Spain were more dependent on their bishops than the kings of the other successor kingdoms. Savage laws against the Jews were the obverse of this dependence.

We know far more about the role of the bishop in the cities of Gaul than we do about those in Spain or Italy. The written sources for Gaul in the fifth and sixth centuries are more abundant than those for any other region in the West, probably precisely because its bishops were regularly drawn from the old Roman senatorial aristocracy.[163] The end of the Empire and the opportunity of gaining imperial office gave the provincial aristocracy of Gaul an incentive for returning to public life and the service of their city as bishops.[164] In fact the history of Gaul in this period might easily be seen as a succession of lives of bishops: the life of Sidonius Apollinaris, bishop of Clermont (470–*c.*480), spans the years of the collapse of imperial power in Gaul, dramatic events in which Sidonius played a considerable part as a high aristocrat, and successively as an imperial office holder and as bishop.[165] Caesarius, bishop of Arles (502–42), experienced the victory of the Franks over the Visigoths, Ostrogothic rule of Provence, and finally the incorporation of Provence by the Franks.[166] Gregory, bishop of Tours (573–94), was not only an active bishop, but also an important figure in the wider world of Merovingian politics, and he became the historian of the Merovingian kingdom and church.

Like the Visigothic kingdom and the Eastern Roman Empire, the Frankish monarchy was based on alliance with the Church.[167] Synods of bishops in Merovingian Gaul, if not as closely integrated into the royal administration as the national synod in Spain, still played a considerable part in holding the kingdom or kingdoms together, if only by asserting the unity of the Church.[168] In the context of a book which is largely concerned with civic administration and politics, it would be easy to treat the Gallic bishops simply as administrators and politicians. But this impression is in many cases misleading. A bishop had to be a politician to maintain his position, but even in this wild age many a bishop regarded himself as a pastor rather than an administrator. This fact emerges clearly from the writings of Caesarius of Arles.

[162] *LV* XII.1.2; *De fisco Barcinonensi* in Mansi X.473 f.

[163] I. Wood 1994: 20–32.

[164] Prinz 1973; Kopecek 1974; Mathisen 1984.

[165] Harries 1994.

[166] Klingshirn 1994.

[167] Hilgarth 1986: 89–116: translated texts with introductions from each of the barbarian kingdoms.

[168] I. Wood 1994: 154–5.

Certainly Caesarius had to keep the support of whatever king happened to be exercising sovereignty over Arles. Without that, he could hardly maintain himself in the city, and certainly not exercise metropolitan authority over the other bishops of his province, much less as primate of Gaul. In any case his authority as a primate never extended beyond the sway of, as the case might be, the Visigothic, Gothic, or Frankish ruler of Arles. Caesarius was determined to uphold his episcopal authority in his city and province, and as far as he could also in the Gallic Church as a whole. Caesarius obtained immunity from taxes for Church lands in Arles.[169] In short he was, and had to be, both a diplomat and a politician. But his ultimate objectives and interests were very different from those of a secular politician.

Caesarius' life's work was to influence his flock, both cleric and lay. Caesarius—like Augustine—organized his cathedral clergy into an ascetic community.[170] This strengthened control by the bishop, and gave him an opportunity to train them in their duties, and to set an example of the perfect life for the laity. In AD 506 the Visigothic king called the bishops of his kingdom to the Council of Agde. Caesarius was senior bishop. The canons lay down principles of conduct for clergy. Their hair, clothes, and shoes must be suited to their profession. They are not to wed after ordination, and not to attend weddings and other parties where suggestive dancing would take place. Married priests and deacons are not to sleep with their wives. Bishops without descendants are to designate the Church as their heir. Gifts received by the bishop while in office are to be used for the Church's benefit. Only real property of 'little value' could be sold, exchanged, or given away without consultation. Valuable property including real estate must not be alienated. Any sale or gift of property on the part of the bishop needs to be validated by two or three other bishops. Only the bishop is allowed to bless the congregation, or the penitents, or to supervise public penance. On principal feasts, Easter, Christmas, Epiphany, Ascension, Pentecost, and St John the Baptist's, everybody must attend service in the cathedral or at least in another church under the control of the bishop, but not in a private chapel or estate church. Laymen engaged in feuds of long standing are to be censured by bishops for refusing reconciliation, and subsequently to suffer excommunication. Perjurers and murderers and those maliciously persecuting the Church or clerics are to be excommunicated.[171]

Caesarius' daily work centred on the people of Arles and the surrounding countryside. He strove to get his congregation to show deference during the service, not to talk, to remain standing, and not to lie down on the floor of the church as if in bed—evidently his cathedral had no

[169] *Vita* I.20. [170] Klingshirn 1994: 91. [171] Ibid. 97–104.

seating. He instructs his congregation to genuflect and bow in the appropriate places in the liturgy. Caesarius arranged for Terce, Sext, and Nones to be sung in public in the cathedral, rather than as previously privately in the bishop's house. He had the laity taught to sing hymns and psalms like clergy in antiphonal style.[172] He instructs members of his congregation to make themselves fit for mass before attending the celebration. They are to give alms to the poor, to settle disputes among themselves, to confess their sins. They are to remember to bring offerings of bread or wine to communion, and to offer tithes from their harvest. Secular pursuits are to be avoided on the day of mass. Both agricultural work and sexual relations are covered by this ban. Caesarius gives the warning that children conceived on Sundays or feast days would become lepers or epileptics or possessed by the devil. Caesarius condemns concubinage between the end of boyhood and legitimate marriage. The practice was too frequent to be punished by excommunication.[173] Caesarius points out as discreditable the double standard involved. He seems to assume that the concubines were normally female slaves. Caesarius refuses to give nuptial blessing to bridegrooms who were not virgins. He condemns abortion and infanticide. Caesarius spent much time and energy on persuading his flock to abandon numerous customs derived from the old pagan religion which still formed part of their way of life.[174] To be more easily understood Hilarius of Arles had adopted a simple speech when preaching to peasants but a more graceful style when educated persons came into the church. Caesarius used the same simple style always.[175]

Caesarius' community had enormous trust in him. People sought Caesarius' help when they were afraid, whether of illness, or natural threats, or demonic possession. Caesarius solved their problems by ritual means, praying, anointing with consecrated oil, blessing with holy water, laying on of hands, or by making the sign of the cross. Caesarius always acted in the presence of the public, whether of the household affected, or the congregation, or of other bishops. He always left after the ritual, and did not wait for visible success. He explained that he wished to avoid the

172 Ibid. 92–3.

173 Caesarius of Arles *Sermones* 42.5; 43.5.

174 Ibid. 33.4; 192.3; 193.3; no one should refuse to work on Thursday in honour of Jupiter (19.4); church attenders make vows at trees, pray at springs, practise diabolical divination (53.1); make sign of cross before eating sacrificial meat (54.6); acquire amulets from members of clergy (50.1). Some are unwilling to pull down pagan shrines, some even rebuild shrines that have been pulled down, or attack those who are trying to overturn idols (53.1). Some of those who do not work on Thursdays do the missed work on Sundays instead. People refuse to take home for fuel wood of sacred trees cut down (54.5). Feasts at sacred sites at which meat and drink offered in sacrifice was consumed (19.4; 54.6).

175 *Sermones* 86.1. He did however use figures of speech, rhetorical questions, exclamations, vivid metaphors, imagined dialogue, figures of parallelism, repetition, and sound. Consistent use of *clausulae* (Klingshirn 1994: 149–51).

appearance of arrogance. He clearly also avoided the embarrassment of failure. Finally he made a public announcement of success.[176] Relics of the bishop, pieces of clothing, in fact anything that had been in contact with him: his saddle cloth, oil he had blessed, water and linen used to prepare his body for burial, the bed he had slept in, were all used to assist individuals in distress. Different relics had specialized use: after Caesarius' death, water and linen used to wash his corpse were used to treat fevers; his clothing to stop uncontrolled bleeding. His relics were used like medicines, applied to the body, soaked in water which was drunk, or as a talisman, fastened to the wall of a building.[177]

This portrait of Caesarius of Arles, based on the bishop's edifying writings, is one-sided in its focus on pastoral concerns, but it is nevertheless significant and important. For it illustrates the fact that the power and influence of bishops, in the East as well as the West, even their power and influence in what we would call secular matters, was not of the same kind as that of secular magnates, and was not achieved and maintained by the same kind of actions. We have quite a different impression of Gregory, bishop of Tours (573–94). Gregory probably was a different kind of bishop from Caesarius of Arles, but we also get a very much wider view of him, since we have not only his edifying writings, but also his *History of the Franks*, the later books of which are in part autobiographical, and show the author in the context of the society and politics of Merovingian Gaul. Gregory was an important figure not only at Tours, but over a much wider area, and at the courts of Merovingian kings. The tomb of a saint like Martin of Tours provided an ever-present source of supernatural patronage and protection from which the whole city benefited.[178] The saint brought glory to the city and prestige to the bishop. The fact that Gregory was as it were the spokesman of St Martin gave almost irresistible force to his claim that Tours ought to remain immune from taxes.[179] It is clear that he and king's *comes civitatis* were the leaders of the town. Which of the two was superior depended on circumstances. On at least one occasion Gregory was allowed to appoint the *comes* himself. We find

176 Klingshirn 1994: 163–5.

177 Ibid. 166–8.

178 P. Brown 1981: 94–9; Van Dam 1985: 230–300; Harries 1992: 77–98, esp. 85–9.

179 *HF* IX.30 referring to events in AD 589. According to the literal meaning of the passage: 1. Immunity meant the right not to pay any taxes (not immunity from intervention by collectors from outside). 2. Immunity for all people of Tours (not just of the Church). 3. The text suggests that a king's grant of immunity would need to be accepted at least tacitly by his successor. When Gregory implies that Tours had not paid taxes for 14 years, he omits to say that in AD 580, when Tours was under count Eunomius (V.47), king Chilperic *did* collect taxes at Tours (VII.23). Chilperic evidently not only imposed heavier taxes but he also inflicted them on groups that had been allowed immunity by his predecessors and rivals (V.28). At Tours the count borrowed the money from a Jewish money lender, and no doubt subsequently collected it from the taxpayers through his agents in order to be able to repay the loan—which he nevertheless failed to do.

Gregory taking the lead when the town had to choose between rival Merovingians. The estates of the Church and its building schemes surely dominated the local economy.[180] The bishop's court played a part in settling disputes between the city's unruly and violent magnates, even if they did not necessarily accept his judgements.[181] The Church's right of asylum was more often than not respected.[182] At that time it clearly was an important institution, which could force a stay of execution when a powerful and violent individual had decided to have somebody murdered or executed. For the fact that the intended victim was in asylum in church, and so under the protection of so formidable a saint as Martin of Tours, could induce an angry king or magnate to think twice, and perhaps even to negotiate before resorting to murder.[183]

The bishop's authority was to a great extent moral. It is as if the bishop as God's representative was the only individual to whom an enraged king or magnate might yield without disgrace or dishonour, not that they invariably did. If the bishop's authority was challenged the actual coercive force at his disposal was very limited indeed. Gregory certainly could not prevent attacks on church property by a royal official in residence at Tours[184] nor could he stop bloodshed in church if a Frankish king or one of his magnates was determined to have blood.[185] After Eberulf and his murderer had both been slain in the church of St Martin, the remaining men who had violated the church were sought out and killed, but not by police—which do not seem to have existed—but by the beggars who regularly received food at the sanctuary.[186]

Gregory's influence was certainly greater than that of the average bishop. This was due to a combination of factors: Gregory's senatorial descent and the standing of his family,[187] a strong personality, courage, and outspokenness,[188] and also the fact that his private life was beyond reproach. Gregory was on close and trusted terms with several of the kings.[189] Once he was sent on a diplomatic mission to confirm a treaty between Guntram and Childebert II, feuding royal uncle and nephew.[190] Several times he was able to act as conciliator between the king and

[180] X.18.
[181] VII.47
[182] Men in sanctuary V.4, 14, 24; VI.16; VIII.18. Leudas takes and abuses sanctuary and is driven out: V.49.
[183] VIII.6, 30.
[184] VIII.40, cf. 21.
[185] Eberulf takes asylum: VII.21, is murdered in church: VII.29.
[186] *HF* VII.27.
[187] All but five bishops of the province of Tours were relatives of his: *HF* V.49.
[188] V.18; VIII.5–6.
[189] VIII.2–3; VIII.14.
[190] IX.20.

grandees in disgrace. Gregory was an influential figure able to offer conciliation to angry men in a wild and unforgiving age. But as we have seen, there were quite close limits to what he might achieve, whether at court or in his own city.

The power of Gregory was probably outstanding among the Gallic bishops of his time. But the evidence of his *History* suggests that it differed only in extent, but not in kind, from that of his episcopal colleagues. It is certainly the case that wherever secular administration, whether urban or imperial, broke down, or was for some reason unable to assert itself, we find bishops left in charge. In the chronic rivalry between the bishop and the count of the city, the bishop seems to have prevailed more often than not, in the long run. It was because they were administrative centres of a diocese that many cities survived the troubles of the age of migrations. It was in the guise of the ecclesiastical diocese that the basic unit of Roman political geography, the *civitas* combining urban centre and rural territory, survived longest, and in some places perhaps even until today. The territory of the *civitas Agrippinensium* long survived as the diocese of the bishop of Cologne.[191] City states surviving as ecclesiastical dioceses were particularly numerous in Italy.[192]

In the successor states bishops certainly occupied an important place in society, and not only because of their activities as bishops. The kings of all the successor states regularly employed bishops on political, juridical, or diplomatic tasks which in classical times would have been performed by lay men. One reason was of course the moral standing of bishops. Another the collapse of secular education meant that the Church gained a near monopoly of education.[193] The Church needed educated clergy who could read the bible and discuss theology. It also required administrators with knowledge of Roman law. So when secular schooling ceased to provide suitably literate candidates for the priesthood, the Church had to train them itself. Not all pupils of episcopal or monastic schools became ordained. Men often spent some years in the king's service before becoming bishops.[194] Presumably they had received the educational qualifications needed by a bishop before entering royal employment. So lay-literacy was more common at court than scholars formerly thought. Nevertheless in Merovingian Gaul and Visigothic Spain a high proportion of the men with more than a minimum degree of literacy were bishops, or at any rate clerics. It was therefore inevitable for kings to employ bishops in positions which in earlier times would have been filled

[191] Ennen 1975: 38–91.
[192] Dilcher 1964.
[193] On this, see below, pp. 333–5.
[194] I. Wood 1990: 63–81 and Collins 1990: 109–33.

by lay men. In a world in which the boundaries of the secular were retreating,[195] the Church controlled the technology of secular administration.

Appendix A

Did the state pay a general subsidy to every Church in the Empire or only individual grants separately awarded to a selected number of Churches?

A subsidy granted by Constantine to the churches of all cities, and since reduced is suggested by Sozomen *HE* V.5.2; Theodoret *HE* I.11. But it is likely that the ecclesiastical historians, mistakenly or rhetorically, generalized probably quite numerous specific grants. For when we meet subsidies to the Church in the sources, they are generally grants to specific cities or individuals. So in Eusebius *HE* X.6.1 Constantine sends 3,000 folles to the bishop of Carthage 'since it has been my pleasure that through all provinces, namely the African, the Numidian and the Mauretanian something should be provided for certain specified ministers of the Catholic religion'. Athanasius, *Apol. c. Ar.* 18 mentions corn 'which had been granted by the father of the emperors separately for Libya, and for some places in Egypt'. This implies separate grants. The *diaconiae* of the church of Naples received subsidies out of taxation in the sixth century, Greg. *Ep* X.18. Constantine, Anastasius, and Justinian enabled the church of Constantinople to run a free burial service by assigning to it the tax revenue of a large number of shops and workshops, Just. *Nov* 59. But apart from the workshops given immunity from taxes and other *munera* for the benefit of the *diaconia*, the remaining workshops, even though owned by the Church and charitable institutions, were liable to tax and all other obligations (*Nov* 43.1.1). So far from being generally subsidized, the Church was actually taxed. A similar arrangement at Alexandria required the *corporati* to provide individuals (*parabalani*) who would minister to the sick, and perhaps also provide burial, under the orders of the bishop, *CT* 16.2.42 (416), 43 (418).

CJ I.2 12 (451—very near the time of writing of the two ecclesiastical histories—'ut pauperibus alimenta non desint, salaria etiam quae sacrosanctis ecclesiis in diversis speciebus de publico hactenus ministrata sunt, iubemus nunc quoque inconcussa et a nullo prorsus imminuta praestari'), seen on its own seems to be compatible with a general grant, but looked at in context favours the interpretation that the *salaria* were separately awarded to favoured churches. For the sentence about *salaria* does not follow the sentence confirming general privileges, but that invalidating certain *pragmaticas sanctiones*. Pragmatic sanctions directed to feeding the poor are thereby excluded from invalidation.

[195] Markus 1990: 14–17 and *passim*.

Appendix B

Imperium and *Sacerdotium* are separate and distinct.

J. Durliat (1990*b*: 58 ff.) paraphrases *Nov* 7.2, as follows: 'La différence est faible entre le sacerdoce et l'empire . . . puisque les liberalités du pouvoir impérial fournissent . . . aux saintes églises la totalité de leurs resources et de leur prosperité': that is he takes it literally, as an assertion of the near identity of the imperial and the priestly office. But this is unconvincing. The relevant sentence: 'Utique cum nec multo differant ab alterutro saerdotium et imperium, et sacrae res a communibus et publicis, quando omnis sanctissimis ecclesiis abundantia et status ex imperialibus munificentiis perpetuo praebetur' can only be taken literally if one ignores the context in which it stands. Read in isolation the sentence does suggest that Justinian felt that there is no essential difference between priesthood and imperial office, and that he was therefore entitled to use ecclesiastical property as freely as property of the state. In fact *Nov* 7, taken as a whole, underlines the wholly exceptional status of ecclesiastical property, which is declared inalienable wherever in the empire it might be situated. The phrase 'cum nec multo differant ab alterutro sacerdotium et imperium' is a rhetorical exaggeration that has the limited purpose of justifying one exception to the general inalienability of ecclesiastical property: the emperor may take over pieces of ecclesiastical property for some public purpose, but only if he compensates the Church by a gift of similar or greater value ('recompensanda re eis ab eo qui percepit aequa aut etiam maiore quam data est'). The emperor can give away as much as he likes of the lands of the *res privata*, but he is not free to do what he likes with the lands of the Church.

5

Civic Finance in the late Late Roman Cities of the East, with Special Reference to Egypt

1. *Introduction*

The decline and disappearance of political institutions centred on the city council was quite independent of the development of cities as centres of population and of administration. In the previous chapter I have suggested that civic politics developed in similar ways over much of what had been the Roman Empire even though the physical character of the cities might vary greatly from area to area. But if post-curial government by notables sooner or later emerged everywhere, the nature of the administrative tasks which the notables had to supervise depended on the size of their particular city and the character of its population. Clearly the administration of a city of tens of thousands of inhabitants was a much more complex task than that of a city of a few thousand. It is likely that in the East there still were numerous towns with a population of between 15,000 to 25,000, and some with many more inhabitants.[1] The vital needs of populations of this order of magnitude could not be met without institutions of civic administration. At the same time imperial administration, above all the collection of taxes, continued to be based on cities. If city councils and their members were no longer in a position to carry out the duties they had for so long performed for the imperial government, alternative arrangements would have to be set up. What these arrangements were is still obscure in many respects. This chapter will however attempt to throw light on some aspects of post-curial financial administration of Eastern cities.

[1] Population sizes are notoriously difficult, estimates often little more than guesses. Bagnall 1993: 53, on the basis of the list of *oikia* houses—or households—(*SPP* V. 101), estimates the population of Hermopolis in Egypt between 25,000 and 50,000, and the average Egyptian metropolis at around 16,000; in Bagnall and Frier 1994: 55, the average population of a metropolis is estimated at 25,000, and the number of such cities at around 50. I. F. Fikhman estimated Oxyrhynchus at between 15,000 and 25,000: 'Die Bevölkerungszahl von Oxyrhynchus in byzantinischer Zeit', *Arch. f. Papyrusforschung*, 21 (1971), 111–20. Late Late Roman Scythopolis has been estimated, no doubt with a very wide margin of error, at 30,000 to 40,000 (Y. Tsafrir and G. Foerster, from Scythopolis to Baysân, in G. R. D. King and Averil Cameron (1994), 95–115, relevant 106).

Much of the evidence on which the chapter is based comes from Egypt. It is written on the assumption that at this period the administration of Egypt was based on essentially the same principles as administration elsewhere. No attempt is made to prove this proposition, but it does emerge that as far as municipal administration is concerned the evidence of the Laws and of the papyri is compatible. It is not argued that administration in Egypt was identical with administration elsewhere in every detail—increasing local diversity is a feature of the late Late Empire. But it is suggested that in broad outline the model of post-curial government of cities by notables that can be constructed for Egypt is also applicable to cities elsewhere in the Eastern provinces of the Empire.

2. *Civic Finance in the* Novels *of Justinian*

The legislation of Justinian certainly assumes that cities are still in a position to spend money on municipal activities. Items on which they spend include: aqueducts, baths, harbours, fortifications, towers, roads, and bridges.[2] The laws do not distinguish between expenditure on new building and on maintenance. As has been shown earlier, it is likely that money was spent on secular non-military building, even if it was much more often spent on maintenance than on new construction. Some cities also regularly spent money on the purchase of corn, though not every city did this.[3]

The laws envisage that each city had its own revenue, but not that the city authorities were free to distribute the city's income between different areas of expenditure as they thought fit. What the laws suggest is that a city received income from a range of distinct sources, each of which was more or less permanently assigned to a particular object of expenditure. Funds from a particular source continued to be spent on the same objects year after year, with only occasional readjustments to cope with changing needs.[4]

That this was so is confirmed by information about the finances of Alexandria in *Edict* 13 of AD 538/9, the law enacting Justinian's reorganization of the administration of Egypt. Issued together with the *Edict*, but unfortunately now lost, was a document listing the various activities and objects on which the city spent money, together with the sources of the revenue assigned to each.[5] It looks as if the arrangements laid down in the

[2] *CJ* I.4.26 (530).

[3] *CJ* X.27.12; Karayannopulos 1958: 217–19.

[4] Suggested by *Nov* 128.16; *CJ* X.30.4. Cities had revenues in spite of the undoubted confiscation of cities' lands to the *Res Privata*. For discussions of the effect of confiscation, see Liebeschuetz 1959 and Delmaire 1989: 276–82 (*vectigalia*), 641–58 (landed property).

[5] *Edict* 13.14–15.

document were intended to remain in force indefinitely. This does not of course mean that there could never be any change, but it does seem as if regular revision of the kind required for instance by an annual budget was not anticipated. The *Edict* does in fact illustrate circumstances in which change became unavoidable. In the reign of Anastasius, Potamon the financial officer (*vindex*) of Alexandria had drawn up regulations on how the proceeds of the export duty (*exagogion*) were to be divided between corn transport, baths, and the mysterious '*anticantharus*'.[6] Subsequently another 100 solidi were assigned to the decurions of Alexandria, and 320 to the Augustalis to pay for 36 racehorses which that official regularly provided for the chariot races at Alexandria. But later these arrangements broke down as a result of an abuse of a kind only too characteristic of late Roman bureaucracy: certain exporters of pottery and some others managed to get their goods exempted from the export duty with the result that its income was sharply reduced and no longer sufficient to meet all the expenses which drew on it. Eventually Justinian found a way to restore the revenue of the export duty, but instead of returning it to the expenses of the city, he used it to finance an increase in salary for the praefectus Augustalis. Baths, corn transport, and *anticantharus* were subsequently to be financed (or subsidized) from other revenues, which were detailed in the appendix to the *Edict*, which has unfortunately not come down to us.[7] Another municipal expense, the regular maintenance of the aqueducts, had once been a *munus* of organizations of workers, the *corporati*. Theodosius II relieved the guilds of that burden, and ordered that 400 solidi should be taken from the *dinummi* tax,[8] later to be repaid out of a tax on shipping (*ex titulo navium*). This arrangement was still in force under Justinian.[9]

Civic revenue to meet such expenses came from two sources: income which was civic in the strict sense, and finance assigned to civic expenses from imperial revenues.[10] The imperial contribution was raised through the imperial tax system, the civic revenues were collected by the cities themselves.[11] The imperial share of civic revenue was collected by officials

[6] On the *exagogion*, see A. C. Johnson and L. C. West 1949: 104–5, 301; also Karayannopulos 1958: 152–3. The *anticantharus* was most likely a contribution to the expenses of the baths, Theoph. II.562. More generally on the *Edict* 13, see A. Müller, 'Getreide für Konstantinopel. Überlegungen zu Justinians Edict 13 für Aussagen zur Einwohnerzahl Konstantinopels im 6. Jahrhundert', *JÖB* 43 (1993), 1 ff.

[7] *Edict* 13.15–16; cf. also *P Oxy* 3636.17: items of tax to be spent on 'donkeys and oxen and bakers' wages for the great city of Alexandria'.

[8] Perhaps originally the tax of two *denarii* imposed on Jews by Hadrian, see A. C. Johnson and L. C. West 1949: 306. That tax seems to have faded out after AD 115–117, following the destruction of most of the Jewish community.

[9] *CT* XIV.27.2 (436) = *CJ* XI.29.1, but not mentioned in *Edict* 13.

[10] *Nov* 149.2: taxes are spent either on cities or for the benefit of cities.

[11] *CJ* I.4.26 (530), cf. VIII.12 (485–6). So also according to *CJ* IV.61.13 (431) cities have control

known as *apaitetai* (ἀπαιτηταί),[12] who handed it over to the city, presumably directly to the men responsible for the administration of the various civic activities to which subsidies from tax revenue had been assigned.[13] Tax-collectors were customarily allowed to keep a fraction of the imperial revenue that they had collected, but they were expressly forbidden to keep any part of the city's share. Justinian insisted that once the imperial contribution had been paid over to the city, the money must be spent by civic functionaries without interference by either the provincial governor or representatives of the central finance departments.

The income of customs' duties was shared between civic and imperial expenses.[14] As we have seen the emperor felt free to divert a large part of the customs' revenue of Alexandria to pay the salary of one of his governors. But the tax was nevertheless treated as part of the revenue of the city, and as such included it in the *vindex*'s regulations for civic expenditure.

While imperial revenue helped to finance civic activities, the bulk of civic expenditure was surely financed from civic revenues. The laws list different civic resources: the revenues of civic estates, which included land willed or given to cities,[15] as well as land forfeited to the *curia* from the property of curial families whose members had freed themselves from curial obligations.[16] Occasionally an individual might still volunteer to meet some expenditure on his city's behalf. As in the case of the imperial contribution, it seems likely that definite revenues were permanently assigned to particular civic activities, whether public works or the purchase of corn or whatever.[17] The work and the actual spending of the money was administered by individuals appointed by bishop and notables.[18] Bishop and leading citizens chose the *patēr*, a functionary in overall charge of finance.[19] The men involved in spending of public money faced annual audits.[20] It should be noted that these men were not *liturgants* in the old

of leasing of their properties, or at least of those from which their 'third' is derived. *CJ* XI.70.13 (480): Nicaea has right to exact canon from estates returned to city by emperor.

12 B. Palme, *Das Amt des 'apaitētes' in Ägypten*, *MPER NS* 20 (Vienna, 1989).

13 Assignment of civic revenues: *Nov* 128.16; *CJ* X.30.4. Assignment of taxation revenue: *P Cair* 67057, summarized in A. C. Johnson and L. C. West 1949: 275–80, shows to what expenses taxes of Antaeopolis were assigned. *IGLS* XIII.9046 (*Edict of Anastasius*, edited by M. Sartre): part of the customs revenue of Suez (Clysma) was assigned to the salary of the *dux* of Palestine (1.15), and of the revenues of the *commerciarius* of Mesopotamia to the *dux* of that province (ls. 12–14).

14 *Nov* Val.13 in 445: customs of Numidia divided 2/5 to cities, 3/5 to sacra largitio. Harbour dues of Mylasa were in 428 shared between city and sacra largitio. Lifshitz 1957: 118–33: 5629 solidi from customs and other (confiscated?) revenues of Caesarea in Palestine returned to 'horse rearers' of the city. Generally: Antoniadis-Bibicou 1963.

15 *CJ* I.4.26 (530), XI.32.3 (469), X.30.4 (530), *Nov* 128.16 (545).

16 *Nov* 38 (535).

17 e.g. *Nov* 128.17; *CJ* X.30.4.

18 *CJ* I.4.26.1.

19 C. Roueché 1979.

20 *CJ* I.4.26.1.

sense, as they did not as a rule have to spend their own money. Civic expenditure was no longer competitive and political. The notables took their turn to perform a defined task using financial resources designated for specifically that particular purpose. A law does however encourage volunteers to undertake civic tasks at their own expense. Such men are obliged to complete whatever they have started, but they are not subjected to the audit; and they are assured that undertaking financial responsibility for one civic duty will put neither themselves nor their children under further obligations.[21] Thus, volunteers are encouraged to benefit their city, and are given the assurance that the performance of one civic duty will not have the consequence of turning them into decurions.

This late period has provided evidence of voluntary munificence by civic notables. One might, for example, mention building schemes at Aphrodisias and in some Palestinian cities,[22] or the generosity displayed by the patrons of the Factions. But the role of this kind of giving had become altogether marginal in the secular field. Voluntary giving now overwhelmingly benefited the church.

A central objective of the late Roman system of municipal finance seems to have been to achieve stability and predictability. The competitive munificence of the classical period produced dramatic results, as competitive systems are liable to do. But it could only work to good effect while there were was an adequate number of wealthy and willing individuals competing. In the absence of suitably qualified volunteers the system became difficult to operate and unpredictable. In our period the bulk of munificent spending had been institutionalized, with civil servants or the clergy spending respectively communal or ecclesiastical funds, taking the place of competing decurions. In civic finance the various objects on which public money had to be spent, and the precise resources of revenue from which each head would have to be met, were laid down once and for all. There was now no room for conflict over division of available resources, or the coercion of unwilling *liturgants*. There no longer was any opportunity for individuals to build up a position of power by conspicuous public expenditure. Most of civic expenditure had been depoliticized and institutionalized.

This parallels the development of imperial financial administration. The extreme flexibility and adaptability of the Diocletianic system had been modified. The overall rate of the land tax for a particular area, the *canon*,[23] was now fixed, though the proportion of different levies of which the canon was made up could be varied very considerably in response to

21 *CJ* VIII.12 (485–6), X.30.4.

22 di Segni 1995: 312–32.

23 L. Wenger, *Canon in den römischen Rechtsquellen und in den Papyri* (Vienna, 1942).

changing needs, especially military needs, of the government.[24] Imperial land was normally leased out in perpetuity on so-called *emphyteutic* leases.[25] Politically motivated voluntary munificence was very largely replaced by Christian charity.[26] This might well result in conspicuous expenditure on the building of churches and charitable institutions.[27] But the buildings did not as a rule—though there were notable exceptions—bear the name of lay benefactors. The credit went to the Church, and the political benefit to the bishop.

The politics of competitive giving had centred on the city council and its members the decurions. In the Justinianic regulations of civic expenditure which were discussed earlier the title 'decurion' scarcely occurs. These laws could be applied, and no doubt were, in cities that no longer had any decurions or only a few impoverished individuals.[28] But Alexandria,[29] and many other Egyptian cities too, still had decurions,[30] and the abundance of Justinian's legislation concerning decurions proves that in the view of the emperor they were still performing essential functions.[31] The question arises as to what these functions were. I have argued earlier that the council was no longer either the official voice or the responsible authority of its city. The remaining duties of the councillors will have been organizational and financial. The likelihood is that these duties had been depoliticized, so that the decurions, instead of competing with each other, were now assigned certain defined tasks, whether these involved an essentially bureaucratic function, like the collecting of a particular tax under the direction of a director of taxation, or whether they required the spending

[24] Gascou 1989: 279–313. Bagnall 1985: 289–308.

[25] A. H. M. Jones 1964: 417–19; Delmaire 1989: 659–68.

[26] Patlagean 1977: 181–96.

[27] Wipszycka 1972: 36–7, 64–5, 78–85.

[28] *Nov* 38, pr. (535): absence or poverty of decurions reason for institution of *vindices*.

[29] *Edict* 13.12, 13. Anastasius, patriarch 605–16, was a former member of the council, a cousin of Benjamin, patriarch 616–22, a former 'head' (*proedros*?) of the council according to B. Evetts translator of the Arabic *History of the Patriarchs of the Coptic Church of Alexandria*, *PO* I.2.478, 484. The same history reporting the election of the patriarch Theodosius I in 535 by 'bishops and priests and the chief men of the city', without separate mention of the council (ibid. 456). Peter Mogus, patriarch 477–90 was chosen by 'prefect, duke, chief men, clergy, monks and sisters' (Zacharias of Mytilene, *HE* V.7). But Evagrius, *HE* II.9, cites a letter to emperor Leo claiming the city's support for the patriarch Timothy Aelurus in 457, purportedly written by people, *axiomatikoi* = *honorati*, councillors, and *naukleroi* = *navicularii*. According to Zacharias of Mytilene, *Vie de Sevère*, ed. M. A. Kugener, *PO* II.33–6, bishop Peter Mogus around 480 interrogated a pagan priest before the prefect, his staff, the council, and the *megistanes* and *ktētores* (= i.e. *honorati et possessores*?). So it looks as if the council then still had a representative function.

[30] Geremek 1981: 231–47; 1990: 47–54. Gascou 1994: 61: the codex lists four *politeuomenoi* including one from Antinoopolis, it lists 50 civilian or military officials. An inscription of 516/17 mentions a decurion of Petra, and a Petra papyrus a Boulê of Augustopolis (ch. 20 of *Petra Church Project Publication* (forthcoming) of which the author Z. T. Fiema sent me a copy). See also n. 97 below.

[31] *CJ* X.35.3 (528); *Nov* 38 (539), 86 (539), 101 (539).

of a sum of money, that is responsibility for a particular item of civic expenditure.[32]

3. *Civic Estates and Other Revenues*

From the mid-fourth century—with only a short interval during the reign of Julian—the imperial government exercised ownership and the ultimate right to dispose of land and rents of civic estates and of the revenue of civic taxes. As the decisive laws have not been preserved we have to conjecture the reasons for this drastic act of centralizing confiscation.[33] Of course, ownership gave the imperial government absolute control over the ways in which cities spent their revenues, something which has been sought by many a central government since. Irresponsible civic expenditure, or perhaps simply expenditure not authorized by themselves, had worried Roman emperors since the second century, when they appointed the first *curatores*. Control of civic estates gave the imperial government extra resources for its own expenditure on cities, which in the case of major cities like Antioch or Alexandria or Ephesus was growing.[34] Control of the estates might also be used to finance expenditure which would benefit cities indirectly,[35] for instance by strengthening the imperial army. Expenditure by the government could involve considerable redistribution with the result that some cities were considerably worse off, but a few perhaps better. The most generally damaging effect was that the confiscated estates were now the emperor's to dispose off as he wished: to enlarge his reputation for generosity, to reward service, to win over opponents, or even to sell. The laws make it abundantly clear that the confiscated estates were being continually dispersed through imperial largesse.

Civic estates fell into a number of categories: shops and workshops, buildings, gardens and sites situated within the wall and just beyond them, rural estates, animal-grazing, agonothetic lands whose revenues helped to support public games, and estates of temples which had helped to finance cults and the maintenance of the temple-buildings. In addition the cities had enjoyed the revenue of local taxes and customs-duties. The laws suggest that the act of confiscation took place soon after the death of Julian.[36]

[32] Tax collection, e.g. *Nov* 163.2; decurion's receipt for *arcarica*: *P Oxy* 2040. On *arca* of praetorian prefect, see Karayannopulos 1958: 82–3. One of the duties of councillors in Arabia seems to have been the registration of land transactions—as in the very late councils in the West. See Z. T. Fiema, cited n. 30 above.

[33] The following is a development of Liebeschuetz 1959.

[34] The confiscated civic estates were administered separately from other imperial properties, and are described in the laws as *fundi publici*, or *fundi ex iure publico*, or *f. reipublicae*, or *f. civitatis*.

[35] *Nov. Just. II* (569) 149.2.

[36] *CT* V.13.3; X.1.8 (temple lands); *CT* X.3.2 (372) estates; VII.7.2 (365) *pascua*; *N. Marc.* 3.1 (451) agonothetic lands; IV.13.7 (374) *vectigalia* in West, IV.6.10 in East.

The laws also give the impression that the act of confiscation from the first applied to all civic properties everywhere. This is certainly misleading. While it was no doubt imperial policy that temple land should be confiscated from soon after AD 364, we know that the endowments of the public cults at Rome were confiscated by Gratian as late as AD 382. A parallel wave of confiscations took place in the East in AD 383.[37] Further confiscation of temple properties took place in Africa in AD 415.[38] The policy was Empire-wide, but there were differences in administration between East and West. In the East civic estates became a separate category of property administered by the *res privata*. In the West they were placed under the *sacrae largitiones*.

It looks as if the original policy of confiscation was very radical: the cities were deprived both of the administration and of the collection of revenue. This cannot mean that cities were at one stroke deprived of all income. We have seen that in fact not all estates were confiscated at the same time. Furthermore, confiscation surely did not mean that cities were deprived of all income from the estates that had been confiscated. It must however have meant that they henceforth would only receive a small proportion of their former revenue, and that for definite and approved purposes, especially the building of fortifications. Before it was modified confiscation meant that the extent to which a city could maintain its services became totally dependent on the good will of imperial officials.[39]

At the same time the imperial authorities attempted to enforce a rule of long standing, that decurions should not be allowed to be tenants of civic estates.[40] The rule had presumably been established to prevent decurions from treating city property as a perquisite. Now there was the additional considerations that decurions might abuse their new status as imperial tenants to claim exemption from the financial obligations they owed to their city. The emperors Valens and Valentinian evidently attempted to re-let the properties to tenants, who were not decurions, by competitive bidding. The attempt failed because the bidders could not be persuaded to accept the poorer land. So these had to be returned to decurions.[41] It is likely that the law once more simplifies what happened. A law of AD 400 shows that, in the West at any rate, urban and suburban sites were still normally leased to curial or collegiate tenants.[42]

The Ephesus inscription shows that the original form of imperializa-

37 *CT* X.3.4; *CJ* XI.66.4.

38 *CT* XVI.10.20.

39 This follows from Valens' letter to Ephesus, *IGSK* XI.1 no. 42 = A. S. Riccobono *FJRA* I.108.

40 *CT* X.3.2 (372W). Decurions may not contract to collect *vectigalia*: *Dig* L.2.6; not be tenants of public land.

41 *CT* X.3.4 (383 E).

42 *CT* X.3.5 (400).

tion quickly proved unsatisfactory. The city authorities wasted time applying for money from the imperial officials, and there was no public benefit from higher rents obtained by more efficient administration. So it was decided to return administration, that is leasing and rent collecting, to the cities, while keeping ownership with respectively the *res privata* and the *sacrae largitiones*. Income was shared with two parts of the rents going to the emperor and one-third to be kept by the city, to be spent at the discretion of the city authorities—preferably on fortifications. Since it is unlikely that precisely one-third of the income would have met the essential expenses of every city in the Empire, it is likely that the one-third to two-thirds division was notional, and that we have here another case of the laws in the *Code* simplifying the actual situation.[43]

Local taxes and customs duties (*vectigalia*) were included in the confiscation, and also subjected to the two to one division.[44] In this area the division was certainly notional. We know from some unfortunately very fragmentarily preserved customs regulations that *vectigalia* comprised a large number of different levies and duties, and that in some cases at least fixed sums taken from a particular levy were assigned to particular areas of expenditure.[45] So it is unlikely that the division of customs revenue between city and emperor was made on a strict one to two principle.

When administration of the estates was returned to the cities, the increasing of rental income by competitive bidding for tenancies was seen as a practical proposition, and the cities were expected to benefit from higher rents. At the same time the *res privata* and *sacrae largitiones* favoured perpetual and hereditary tenancies at fixed rents, which ran indefinitely as long as the rent was paid. This arrangement was attractive to tenants and provided the imperial treasuries with a predictable revenue. Subsequently the imperial administration encouraged tenancies of this kind on civic estates as well.[46] So it is likely that civic estates too came to be leased more often than not to perpetual tenants.[47] The resulting income, which—barring 'acts of God'—was unchanging and predictable, could be made the basis for the long-term assignment of designated revenues to particular objects of civic expenditure.

[43] Valens' ruling for Ephesus and other cities of Asia evidently allowed some redistribution of estates between cities *IGSK* II.1. no. 42 c. 17.

[44] *CT* IV.13.7 (374 West).

[45] Lifschitz 1957: 118–32 concerns *inter alia* customs of Caesarea. R. Mouterde, 'Un tarif d'impôt tardif sur les ventes dans le Béryte byzantine', *CRAI* (1945), 377–80 and J. L. Robert, 'Bulletin epigraphique', *REG* 59/60 (1946/7), 359 discuss a fragmentary inscription concerning customs at Berytus. J. Durliat, 'Taxe sur l'entrée de marchandises dans la cité de Caralis (Cagliari) à l'époque byzantine 582–602', *DOP* 36 (1982), 1–14. Dagron and Feissel 1987: no. 108 on customs at Anazarba. *Inschriften von Mylasa, IGSK* 34, nos. 611 and 612 (AD 427/9): customs' revenue of Passala assigned to Mylasa. Antoniadis-Bibicou 1963.

[46] *CT* X.3.3 (380 West); X.3.5 (400 West); *CJ* XI.71.3 (400–405).

[47] But not universally: *CJ* XI.71.4.

The most conspicuous disadvantage of imperial ownership from the city's point of view was the continual drain of properties as a result of imperial grants to individuals. Such grants were often obtained corruptly. The Emperors had to sign far more documents than they were able or perhaps willing to read. Emperors regularly tried to check or reverse the drain. It is impossible to assess how far they succeeded. The repetition of legislation suggests that the situation was out of control.[48] At the same time cities were still acquiring new properties in gifts or bequests. Decurions who had achieved exemption from curial duties were obliged to cede a proportion of their property to the city council. The same proportion had to be given to the council if property of curial families passed by will or donation to men who were not councillors. The proportion was one-quarter up to Justinian's law of AD 535 and three-quarters thereafter.[49] These lands may well have remained under civic ownership. In these ways cities might build up estates to compensate for land and revenues lost.[50] We are far from possessing the information to draw up a balance of gain and loss even in the case of a single city. The differences between cities are likely to have been very great indeed.

4. *Finance in Practice: The Evidence of Antaeopolis*

If we want to get behind the generalizations of the laws to observe what was actually happening at civic level, we largely depend on the papyrus documents of Egypt, above all the two accounts of the taxes collected and paid out by the tax department of the city of Antaeopolis,[51] and a series of similar accounts of the village of Aphrodito which enjoyed the privilege of 'autopract' status, that means it managed the administration of the imperial taxes of its territory itself, and was not subject to the taxation office of the city in whose territory (in this case that of Antaeopolis) it was situated.[52] These documents confirm the impression gained from the laws that taxes of cities and autopract villages were not paid globally to a central imperial treasury to be expended as and when the administration incurred expenditure. Instead the tax due to be collected by city or autopract village was divided in advance of collection into a large number of

[48] *CT* XV.1.41 (401), 42 (404), 43 (405); *Nov Theod* 17.2.5 (444); *Nov Marc* 3 = *CJ* XI.70.5.

[49] *Nov* 38.

[50] Aphrodisas in Caria received legacies in gold which it lent out in return for high interest which it spent on the baths and public works. There is no suggestion that the state took a share of this, Just. *Nov* 160.

[51] *P Cair* 67057, cf. A. C. Johnson and L. C. West 1949: 275–8. *P Freer* 0845c–d, edition and commentary: Gascou 1989: 279–313.

[52] *P Flor* 297 and *P Cair* 67056; *P Cair* 67058; 67287; 67210, 67212; cf. A. C. Johnson and L. C. West 1949: 280–6; Rémondon 1965: 401–30.

items, some small some great, each earmarked to contribute to a particular area of government expenditure. It then fell to the city or autopract village not only to collect the tax but also to pay the due amounts to the predetermined recipients of payments from the government.

5. *The Expenditure of Imperial Taxation*

Of the taxation collected in kind a large proportion contributed to the '*embolē*', the levy of Egyptian corn destined to feed the inhabitants of Constantinople. Part of the tax in kind was paid to the local garrison. Part might be paid to an expeditionary force on campaign. Some of the tax collected in gold was paid to the *arca*, perhaps the local tax office of the praetorian prefecture, some, described as *largitionalia*, was presumably owed to a treasury of the *sacra largitio*. Separate headings of tax were levied on behalf of respectively animal and human employees of the *cursus publicus*. The taxes of Antaeopolis and of Aphrodito contributed to the gratuities of a large number of imperial officials. For Antaeopolis this item amounted to 370 solidi. An amount of comparable size, namely 301 solidi, was paid to the functionaries administering taxation in the territory. This included 124 solidi for the clerks of the pagarchy, 12 for the *logographos* (λογογράφος), the chief accountant, 36 for the *hypodektēs* (ὑποδέκτης), the receiver of taxes, and 36 for *curiales*. It is not clear whether these payments are salaries or gratuities or a mixture of both. Functionaries who received a contribution to their gratuity from the taxes of the village of Aphrodito included the *defensor* and the *riparius* of Antaeopolis. Taxes also provided Antaeopolis with 25 solidi to pay a doctor, 122 modii of corn for use in a prison, and 183 modii for a martyrium, presumably to be given in charity by the clergy.[53]

The documents make no reference to revenue from taxation subsidizing public building, the price of corn, the baths, or the games at Antaeopolis. This could conceivably be because the city simply had no expenses at all in these fields. But this is unlikely. The real reason why these headings do not figure in our accounts is surely that these documents are accounts of the imperial taxes of Antaeopolis and Aphrodito, and not the budgets of the local expenditure of those two places.[54] So the documents do not list expenses which were met out of local revenue. As we have seen earlier, the laws suggest that the administration of imperial finance and municipal finance remained distinct.[55]

[53] For summary of expenditure of taxes of Antaeopolis, see Gascou 1989: 296; of Aphrodito: A. C. Johnson and L. C. West 1949: 281–2.

[54] Gascou's title 'La Table budgétaire d'Antaeopolis' is in that sense misleading.

[55] I cannot accept J. Durliat's: 'L'état qui confiait à la cité la levée de l'impôt, lui accordait, pour son budget propre, la disposition du tiers de tout ce qui était perçu' (Durliat 1990*b*: 43–4). This is based

6. *The Expenditure of Civic Revenues of Antaeopolis: A Problem*

We should certainly assume that Antaeopolis and Aphrodito had their own revenues, and financial departments to administer them. We certainly know that Egyptian cities had civic revenues[56] and civic finance departments[57] in the fourth century, when their finance was supervised first by the Council, later by the *logistēs*.[58] There is no obvious reason why this should have changed in the sixth century. The laws assume that cities are in a position to spend income derived from civic property. I have not seen any references to civic property income in the papyri of the period, but it is likely that at least some Egyptian cities, like some cities elsewhere, had such income. One law allows cities to raise levies from inhabitants for civic purposes.[59] The papyri provide examples of such levies,[60] but no detail of how they were assessed or assigned. It is therefore likely that besides the office or offices[61] directed by the pagarch (or pagarchs), with responsibility for the administration of imperial taxation, there also existed at Antaeopolis a bureaucratic organization, probably supervised—as elsewhere in the Empire—by a *patēr*,[62] to administer the income of the city, which was assigned to such items of civic expenditure as the upkeep of roads and public buildings and water supply, the payment of the police and other civic employees, the maintenance of the public baths,[63] and perhaps the provision of cheap corn in times of shortage.[64] One item that must have loomed very largely in the expenditure of cities and decurions in earlier periods altogether ceased to do so in our period: chariot races and theatricals continued to be a feature of city-life in the East. But they were now largely financed by the Empire out of taxation.[65]

Unfortunately, we do not have any accounts of the local finance of an Egyptian city to match the accounts of imperial revenue from Antaeopolis and Aphrodito.[66] We can therefore form only a very vague notion of the

on a total misunderstanding of *CT* IV.13.7 (374), as I have argued in Liebeschuetz 1997: 135–51, esp. 150–1. Durliat's response (ibid. 153–79) leaves me unconvinced.

56 Bowman 1971: 91–4.

57 Ibid. 87–8, 100.

58 J. D. Thomas, 'The office of the exactor in Egypt', *CE* 34 (1959), 124–40. Bagnall 1993: 60–2.

59 *CJ* I.4.26.15.

60 e.g. *P Oxy* 2040.

61 Gascou 1972.

62 Or perhaps by a *logistēs* or the tripartite office into which the *logisteia* had been merged. See below, p. 193.

63 Apions and baths of Oxyrhynchus: *P Oxy* 148, 915, 1921, 2015; *P Wisc* 66; *P Turner* 52.

64 *CJ* X.30.4 and *Nov* 128.16 list items on which cities might spend money in the 6th cent. The games no longer figure among them. We do not know whether the regular distribution of corn at Oxyrhynchus (*P Oxy*, vol. 40, ed. J. R. Rea (London, 1972); Carrié 1998*a*) continued into our period.

65 See Gascou 1976*b*: 185–212 and below, pp. 205–6.

66 The 'budget of Alexandria' of Justinian's *Edict* 13 is concerned mainly with imperial revenue and so corresponds to the accounts, or part of the accounts, of Antaeopolis. It was drawn up by the

nature and range of the civic expenses of a typical provincial town in Egypt. We know no more than we can deduce from stray references, and we are not very much better informed about the relatively humble full-time clerks and accountants who kept the administration going. We do however get some interesting glimpses of an organization which was markedly different from that of the fourth century.

7. *Financial Administration in the late Late Antique City and the Role of the 'Houses': A Discussion of the Views of Gascou (1985)*

It is evident that even in the sixth century many cities in the East had a considerable income out of which they maintained a significant range of 'services'.[67] Besides which they had duties for the imperial government, from whose point of view, the cities had no purpose more important than that of administering the collection of the taxes which paid for both army and administration, and without which the Empire could not function. So while the political responsibility for the government of the cities had become more informal and uncertain there remained the need to ensure the stable functioning of a considerable volume of administration. This was a real problem.

One might say that the administration of the Empire had depended on a bargain between Empire and decurions by which the decurions were guaranteed a privileged position in their city in return for their collecting the Empire's taxes and performing other essential administrative tasks for the Empire. This arrangement was fatally damaged by the progressive decline of the councils in the course of the later Empire. It is clear that from say AD 400 onwards the Empire would increasingly need to find new arrangements to supplement or replace the failing system. But it has not been at all clear what these new arrangements were or how they worked.

In one of a series of important articles, which have very greatly enlarged our understanding of 'post curial' municipal administration in Egypt, J. Gascou has put forward a most interesting 'model' of the administration of the late Late Roman cities of Egypt in which a central role is played by great 'houses', the *oikoi*.[68] The 'divine house' was the property of the emperor, 'the glorious house' that of the Apion family.[69] These were on a

vindex, who corresponded to the pagarch in provincial cities of Egypt, and not to the *patēr civitatis*. On the *vindex*: Chauvot 1987: 271–81.

[67] 'Civic Services' is a section heading in A. H. M. Jones 1940, pointing to an analogy with the municipal services of a modern city.

[68] Gascou 1985: 1–90.

[69] The property was subdivided into 'houses', e.g. separate blocks of administration at Oxyrhynchus, at Cynopolis, and at Heracleopolis: Hardy 1932.

very large scale, but there were others, evidently much smaller.[70] In Gascou's view complexes of property described as 'houses' came to form a collective group who between them assumed financial responsibility for the performance of civic duties and civic levies, as decurions had done in earlier times. But while the decurions had depended on their own resources to meet their public obligations, each of the houses—so Gascou argued—received contributions from a block of smaller property-owners attached to it. In fact the imperial government had allowed the 'houses' of Byzantine Egypt to come into existence,[71] and had even encouraged their growth precisely, in order that they might mediate between the authorities and the mass of the taxpayers and thus simplify administration.[72] Whether Gascou's theory is right or not, this arrangement would produce precisely the stability and predictability which was a principal objective of late Late Roman financial administration in the East.

Gascou has seen that the establishment by the imperial government of a new category of semi-public (or semi-private) ownership linked with an obligation to collect taxes and perform a wide range of civic *munera* would have necessitated the creation of a legal vocabulary to describe it. But his argument that there was indeed such a vocabulary is not convincing. Gascou maintains that the word *suntelestēs* (συντελεστής) (in Latin *collator*) is a technical term for a member of the consortium of landowners responsible for the taxes of a city or village.[73] This definition is ultimately derived from Preisigke and was accepted into the Greek dictionary of Lewis, Short, and Stuart Jones, and also by Johnson and West.[74] But it is nevertheless—I would suggest—mistaken. For it is not a meaning which one would deduce from the way the word is used in imperial legislation, where it regularly seems to have the simple meaning of 'taxpayer', or

[70] *P Oxy* 2039 'house' of Theon, of Leontius, of Philoxenus, of Mousaius; 2040: of the glorious comes; *P Warren* 3: of Timagenes.

[71] Already in the 4th cent. property was divided unevenly with a high proportion of a city's land in relatively few hands, but there is no evidence for vast holdings like those of the Apions in the 6th cent.: Bagnall 1993: 68–71. See also works cited n. 91.

[72] Gascou 1985: 48: 'Il semble donc que les propriétaires des cités égypto-byzantines formaient une sorte de collège se partageant les responsabilités fiscales et liturgiques, et représentant auprès des autorités municipales l'ensemble des contribuables du ressort. Ainsi, les hommes et produits versés par la patrice Sophie et les Apions, au titre de leurs parts, comprenaient non seulement leurs contributions propres, mais aussi, et nécessairement, celles d'autres redevables dont ils étaient, à mon avis, tenus pour responsables.'

[73] Ibid. 49–51.

[74] *WB* ii, s.v. συντελεστής: 'Mitglied der byzantinischen Grunbesitzergenossenschaft mit der Verpflichtung die fälligen Steuern gemeinsam aufzubringen.' So also *LSJ* s.v., though the texts referred to do not support this meaning, least of all *Nov* 163.1. Nevertheless A. C. Johnson and L. C. West 1949: 103 n. 20; 326 n. 37 accept that it describes a group with collective responsibility for tax. The references in Stephanus, *Thesaurus Graecae Linguae* (repr. Graz, 1954), VIII. 1465 s.v. suggest simply 'taxpayer'.

perhaps 'taxpaying landowner', that is a taxpayer registered in his own name and not on the estate of somebody else.[75]

Gascou at least implies that 'house', *oikos* (οἶκος), is used in these late papyri as a technical term for the kind of privileged estate postulated by his theory. Now *oikos* is certainly not a synonym of *suntelestēs*. In a list of *suntelestai* of Oxyrhynchus cited by Gascou some of the names are *oikoi*, but more are not. Furthermore, this list of *suntelestai* is not a list of intermediaries between the taxpayers and the state. Some of the names are stated to be making payments on behalf of somebody else, others have paid in their own name.[76]

In the context of a wider discussion of Late Roman taxation Durliat has put forward a related theory: he suggests that the term *possessor* is consistently used in the laws to describe not simply the man in physical control of a particular piece of land, but the man who has the right to collect the taxes due on the land. Durliat proceeds to argue that the technical term for a complex of land over which the *possessor* has acquired the right to collect taxes is *fundus*.[77] This theory too is unconvincing. For while both *possessor* and *fundus* occur extremely frequently in the laws they are never used unmistakably and unambiguously in the specialized sense proposed by Durliat. The word *possessor* when used in the *Novels* of Justinian still has the same meaning as it has in the rulings of the classical jurists assembled in the *Digest*, which was equally part of the Justinianic law.[78] The obvious translation of *possessor* is 'land-holder', i.e. the person in actual control of a piece of land,[79] while *fundus* normally just seems to mean 'estate', that is a complex of farms owned by a single owner. *Fundi* or fractions of a *fundus*, usually twelfths, were bequeathed, donated, or sold with as it seems full property rights.[80] The owners who had acquired one or more twelfths of a *fundus* by gift or purchase may well have continued to be registered together on the tax register, and thus remained jointly liable for the tax previously charged on the complete *fundus*. But that does not mean that they ceased to be owners, and became tax-collectors. To sum up, the way *fundus* and *possessor* are used in the laws

[75] *Nov* 163.1 συντελεσταῖς, ταυτὸν δέ ἐστιν εἰπεῖν τοῖς τῶν χωρίων κυρίοις; 128.15 συντελεσταί seems synonymous with ὑποτελεῖς, so also ibid. 1. The term is not very common either in the laws or in papyri, but where it is found the meaning 'landowning taxpayer' makes good sense, e.g. *Nov* 17.1, 9; *Nov* 128.4, 9; *CJ* I.4.18.

[76] *P Oxy* 2020.

[77] Durliat 1990*b*: 65–9.

[78] The point is conclusively made by Delmaire 1996: 59–70, esp. 66–70.

[79] Sometimes *possessores* is used in a narrower sense to describe the leading citizens, see above, pp. 110–15, but then too without any suggestion of a collective responsibility for taxes.

[80] A. H. M. Jones 1964: 785–6, esp. n. 37. In individual cases it is often hard to disprove that *fundus* could mean a block of tax rights, but so it would often be in literary contexts to prove that an author writing 'blue' does not mean 'red'. It is very difficult to believe that the Ravenna documents of gift or sale of *fundi* or fractions of *fundi* are anything other than transfers of full property rights.

does not support the theory that they are technical terms of a vocabulary describing a system of tenure based on the right to collect taxes, nor does the use of the term *suntelestēs/collator* prove the existence of an organized body of holders of this tenure jointly responsible for collecting a city's taxation.[81]

What the papyrus documents do show is that very many taxpayers had their taxes paid for them by somebody else. But the evidence of the tax registers does not fit the theory that the individuals or institutions 'through' whom taxes were paid belonged to a small group of 'houses' that performed this role as a public duty. The situation could arise in a variety of ways, almost certainly more than have so far been suggested.[82] For instance a landowner had since AD 371, at the latest, been responsible also for the taxes of those of his tenants, whose tenancies were entered on the tax register as part of the estate. So it became normal for the landlord to collect the tax owed by the tenants at the same time as the rent. Estate accounts do not normally distinguish money collected as rent from money collected as tax. But tenants who were also landowners in their own right, even if their holding was very small, were registered under their own name.[83] This remained the situation in the sixth century except that such tenants were allowed to choose whether they wished to be registered under their own name or that of the landlord.[84] It was therefore up to them whether they paid their tax themselves or had it paid for them.

It is likely that sometimes freeholders deliberately chose to have their taxes paid by somebody else. The arrangement would be equivalent to taking a loan on the security of the land,[85] and as in the case of a modern mortgage might easily result in the lender eventually taking possession of the debtor's land.[86] Another way in which tax payment through somebody other than the owner might arise was for a villager belonging to a *metrocomia* to sell his land illegally to an outsider. Subsequently the new but illegal owner—and his heirs after him—would pay tax on the land through the original owner—or his heirs—who remained the owners in

[81] The above discussion does not attempt to explain the precise role of a *suntelestēs* in all contexts in which the term might be found. For instance Dioscorus and several others in the village of Aphrodito are described as *suntelestai* (Gascou 1985: 49–50, nn. 287–8), mostly when they accept the tax burden of land they are leasing from another owner. There is no suggestion that any of them has a general responsibility for tax collection, or that *suntelestai* form a collective. See Mirkovic 1997.

[82] See Gascou 1994: 21–8 on 'titulaires ou *onomata*' and 'les intermédiaires' in the early 7th-cent. tax codex of Hermopolis. Gascou does not propose that any of these 'intermédiaires' were '*suntelestai*', in the sense of his earlier theory.

[83] *CT* XI.1.14 (371).

[84] *Nov* 128.14.

[85] e.g. *P Nessana*, 54, 59.

[86] J. G. Keenan, 'Aurelius Phoibammon, son of Triadelphus: A Byzantine Egyptian land entrepreneur', *BASP* 17 (1980), 145–54.

law, and this might go on for generations.[87] Gascou, in his edition of the text, suggests that the majority of the numerous intermediaries in the Hermopolis tax register were in fact paying tax on what was now their own land, though in the out-of-date register the land was still registered under the name of a former owner.[88] Again a patronage agreement might result in the tax being paid through a powerful or influential patron rather than directly by the registered owner, with the advantage to the peasant that he would avoid direct contact with the public tax-collectors. Such arrangements would tend to have the long-term effect of reducing the number of free peasants who paid themselves, and increasing the number who had their tax paid through the landowner—that is why such arrangements were illegal.[89] On the other hand, indirect payment of taxes meant fewer taxpayers, which simplified collection. In fact it had many of the advantages which collection by *suntelestai*, as suggested by Gascou, would have had. That may be a reason why the government tolerated such arrangements—or perhaps even tacitly encouraged them. In spite of this the tax registers show that many independent peasants still had their land registered under their own name, and paid their taxes directly to tax collectors, as they had always done.[90]

It used to be thought that by the sixth century Egypt was a country of large estates, which had grown up since the fourth century at the expense of independent peasants. On general grounds this view remains plausible, though evidence available today seems to be against it.[91] Certainly the Apions controlled a very large number of farms spread over several city territories, and they were not the only large landowners.[92] But we lack the evidence to assess the importance of very great estates in Egypt as a whole. In addition it is evident that in the sixth century a significant number of country-folk had their taxes paid for them by a great—or at any rate greater[93]—landowner. But this would seem to have been the result of a long-term trend, there is no evidence at all that the imperial government

[87] e.g. Maehler 1974: nos. 21765–6, 21768, and Maehler's commentary 64–8.

[88] Gascou 1994: 25–8.

[89] *CT* XI.24.6; *CJ* X.19.8; XI.54.1; XI.56 (all three 468). For payment of taxes of resident tenants and labourers by estate owners in 3rd cent., see Rathbone 1991: 117, 121–5, 404–6.

[90] See Gascou and MacCoull 1987: 104–58.

[91] There certainly were large estates. But it is still quite uncertain whether estates on the scale of those of the Apions were exceptional or not, and it is even debatable whether there had been a significant concentration of landownership. Bowman 1985: 137–63. M. Lewuillon-Blume, 'Enquête sur les registres fonciers (P. Landlisten): La Répartition de la propriété et les familles des propriétaires', *Proc. XVIII Int. Congr. Pap. 1988*, 279–86. Bagnall 1992: 128–40.

[92] See n. 121 below.

[93] The Aphrodito register shows that it was common for a taxpayer to pay taxes in the name of somebody else as well as their own, but this practice was by no means restricted to large landowners. It usually seems to have been a private arrangement between the individuals involved, not part of a general reform of taxation. See Gascou and MacCoull 1987: 128–40.

by a deliberate administrative act created in each city a limited group of tax-collecting 'houses' to mediate between government and peasant tax-payer.

There remains the question of how taxes were actually collected and by whom. As we have already seen, certain great landowners, of whom the Apions are by far the best known, collected the taxes of their tenants at the same time as they collected the rent, and probably also saw to the delivery of the tax in kind, especially the '*embolē*' of grain for shipment to Alexandria, or to wherever the government wanted it delivered.[94] But smaller landowners still paid to tax-collectors. Who they were, and how designated is not at all clear. The Apions made contracts with groups of peasants from their estates to collect the taxes of their fellow-villagers, in which the collectors pledged their own property to meet any deficit in the collection.[95] It is probable that in a limited number of cases collection was still performed by decurions for whom this was a hereditary duty.[96] While we rarely hear of the Council (*boulē*) acting as a body at this late period, there are a significant number of references to decurions (*politeuomenoi*).[97] It is moreover likely that some estates undertook—or were compelled to undertake—duties related to the collection of taxes of a particular area as a permanent duty. So the Alexandrian monastery of the Metanoia was regularly obliged to ship tax-corn, paid for instance by the Apions and count Ammonius, down the Nile to Alexandria.[98] Sometimes collection from the villages was undertaken by members of the staff of the pagarch.[99] It was certainly this office, the *dēmosion logistērion* (δημόσιον λογιστήριον), that issued tax receipts. These documents were signed by an official of that bureau, and they mention the intermediary 'through' whom the tax owed by a 'name' on the tax register had been paid, but the receipt does not mention any decurion or other collecting agent who had actually received the payment.[100] Presumably the officials of the *dēmosion logistērion* had collected it themselves.

[94] The conclusion that Gascou draws from the Apion accounts *P Oxy* XVI.1911, XVI.1912, XVIII.2195 that after delivering the government's tax in corn the estates were left with little profit for the owner (1985: 36–7) is vitiated by the fact that money income is ignored. There is also the problem that unless an item of expenditure is expressly stated to be for the '*embolē*' it is not clear whether it is a tax payment or a charitable gift (ibid., n. 216). There is also the difficulty that the Apions seem to have been allowed to make up the total of their quota of tax from the different estates as suited themselves (J. R. Rea on *P Oxy* LV. 3804, pp. 131–2). So they could pay their tax from some estates and make their profit from others.

[95] *P Oxy* I.36; VIII.1134; XVI.1894; LXXXII.4350–51.

[96] e.g. *P Oxy* 1921.2; 2020.1.

[97] Councillors Elias, Victor, Panolbius, Marcellinus on tax register of Aphrodito: Gascou and MacCoull 1987. Four councillors on tax register of Hermopolis: Gascou 1994: 62. *Politeuomenoi* under Arabs: *P Apoll* 75 (703/15); *P Edfou* III.479.

[98] Gascou 1976*c*: 157–84.

[99] Gascou 1994: 27 on *P Würzb* 19, and references, p. 287, to collection by *dēmosion logistērion*.

[100] Wipszycka 1971: 105–16. The documents discussed were issued by the office, not by the actual

8. *Duties of 'Houses' for the Empire in Sixth-Century Egypt*

It remains true that complexes of property described as *oikoi* of certain families are linked to certain public functions in late Late Antique Egypt in a way which seems to have no parallel in earlier centuries. In the field of imperial taxation, we have evidence of two 'houses' that were permanently obliged to provide staff for an 'exactorial' office at Oxyrhynchus, whose duties included the keeping up-to-date of the tax register.[101] The 'House of Timagenes of respected memory' is known to have provided men in AD 444, in *c.*500 and 538.[102] We do not of course know whether it performed this duty continuously or as part of a rota. The fact that the duty was assigned to an estate rather than to an individual suggests that it was a long-term arrangement to ensure the uninterrupted functioning of an essential organ of the tax-system. In AD 572 staff for a tax office was provided by the 'House of Theon of respected memory'.[103] It looks as if the men supplied to staff the tax office were in fact seconded from the service of the House that had to provide them.[104]

Paucity of evidence hinders us from assessing the full significance of this arrangement. But the epithet '*exaktorikē*' makes it likely that the office was related to what had formerly been the department of the *exactor civitatis*, about whom we have a considerable amount of evidence, mainly from the fourth century.[105] The *exactor* was the successor of the *stratēgos* of the Nome, the official responsible for taxation in the territory of the city,[106] and particularly for the collection of arrears of taxation.[107] His department maintained tax records and recorded changes of ownership.[108] The office itself was filled by decurions.[109] The *exactor* might be held

collector, so they do not totally exclude the possibility that in some cases the tax had been collected by a decurion and not by an *apaitētēs* or other official of the bureau.

[101] The taxation of Egypt as of other areas of the Empire was administered on the basis of city territories. But responsibility for the administration of taxation within the single city might be divided into several parts. So a city might have two (or more?) directors of taxation (pagarchs): Gascou 1972: 60–72, and as we see two, and probably more, offices to maintain the tax register.

[102] *P Oxy* 3583; *P Warren* 3; *P Oxy* 1887: τῇ ἐξακτορικῇ τάξει μερίδος καὶ οἴκου τοῦ τῆς περιβλέπτου μνήμης Τιμαγένους.

[103] *P Oxy* 126: τῇ ἐξακτορικῇ τάξει μερίδος καὶ οἴκου τοῦ τῆς περιβλέπτου μνήμης Θέωνος.

[104] This follows from the title of the office. Also the Cyros, of the '*exaktorikē taxis*' in *P Oxy* 126, seems to be the same man as the representative of the 'house of Theon' in *P Oxy* 2780.7–11.

[105] J. D. Thomas, 'The office of *exactor civitatis* in Egypt', *CE* 34 (1959), 124–40; P. J. Sijpesteijn, 'List of *exactores* and ex-*exactores*', *ZPE* 90 (1992), 247–50. The *exactor* is the official, only sometimes a *curialis*, who exacts arrears after the *curiales* have collected: Delmaire 1996: 59–70, esp. 62–6 (evidence from Codes).

[106] *P Thead* 13.321; *P Oxy* 2408.3 (397).

[107] *CT* XI.7.16.

[108] *P Michael* 33 (4th/5th); *P Amh* II.142.

[109] *CT* XII.6.20 (386); *PSI* VI.684 (4th/5th). Retired *exactor* in *curia*: *P Oxy* 2110.

personally liable for any arrears he failed to collect.[110] This could be the reason why in some cities at least the office sometimes came to be shared by several holders.[111] In the sixth century taxation received a new director in the pagarch, but there is no reason why the clerical offices of the *exactors* should not have continued to perform the essential task of keeping the land register up-to-date. If so, the houses of Timagenes and Theon would seem to have taken over permanent responsibility for the staffing of two of these offices. There may well have been others not taken over by a 'house'.[112] Certainly there are documents recording a transfer of land to a new owner which have no reference to the *exaktorikē taxis* of a 'house', but to a *dēmosion logistērion*.[113]

There is no reason to believe that when a 'house' provided staff for a taxation office, it also provided the director of the whole organization, the pagarch. The appointment of the pagarch was surely a quite separate operation. Formally pagarchs were appointed by the provincial governor or even the praetorian prefect at Constantinople.[114] In practice local political conditions are likely to have had a decisive influence. But there is no evidence that this powerful post was reserved for a member of a particular 'house' or that it was filled from a rota of 'houses'. At Antaeopolis the office was in AD 553 jointly held by Julianus[115] and a woman, the *gloriosissima* Patricia, whose duties were presumably performed by her administrator Menas 5, who is witnessed in office in AD 553[116] and 566–7.[117] The pagarchy of Arsinoe was repeatedly held by heads of the house of the Apions.[118] Since these individuals were grandees of the Empire with a residence at Constantinople, it is evident that the duties of the office, that is the supervision of taxation in city and territory of Arsinoe, were carried out by subordinates. The Apions are also known to

110 *P Lips* 64.22 ff. (368/9)—if this is addressed to an *exactor*, *BGU* IV.1027.

111 *BGU* IV.1027 (Hermopolis: 4th/5th); *P Princ* III.183 (345); *P Lond* V.1911 (Heracleopolis); *P Lips* 98 (4th).

112 Wipszycka 1971: 113–14 on *P Lips* 90 and *P Würzb* 19 shows that at Hermopolis the *dēmosion logistērion* was divided into several *merides* (μερίδες) each named after an individual. Perhaps the staffing of these sub-branches was a *munus* imposed on certain inhabitants of the district concerned, a duty which in the case of the 'houses' of Theon and Timagenes had been made hereditary—or had been permanently tied to the estates once owned by Theon and Timagenes.

113 Transfer of land without reference to 'house' or *exaktorikē taxis*: *P Cair* 67048, 67117–19, 67164—all from the village of Aphrodito. *P Michael* 33; *P Würzb* 19; *P Laur* II.26, III.77; *Excavations at Nessana*, ed. J. Kraemer (Princeton, 1958), iii. 77–80, no. 24. On *dēmosion logistērion*, see Wipszycka 1971: 105–16. R. Pintaudi, 'P. Herm. Rees 67', *ZPE* 25 (1975), 213–16 notes that requests for the transfer of taxation (*epistalmata sōmatismou* / ἐπιστάλματα σωματισμοῦ) were addressed to the *dēmosios logos* (τῷ δημοσίῳ λόγῳ) at Aphrodito and Hermopolis.

114 Justinian *Edict* 13.2.

115 *PLRE* IIIB.734 s.v. Julianus 13, on joint tenure, see Gascou 1972.

116 *P Lond* 1660.

117 *P Cair* 67002.I.10 and *PLRE* IIIB.875 s.v. Menas 5.

118 *PLRE* IIIB.1496–9 s.v. Apion 3 (556), Apion 4 (612); 1203–4 s.v. Strategius 10.

have held the pagarchate at Oxyrhynchus on several occasions.[119] The great majority of the individuals known to have been pagarchs cannot be proved to have been associated with any particular family, whether as kinsman or as dependent.[120] But then we know practically nothing more than the name and honorary title of most of these men. So we cannot tell whether they were dependents of a 'house' like that of the Apions, or not. There was a class of large landowners, and this included a considerable number of families of hereditary senatorial rank, a few perhaps approaching the position of the Apions;[121] though the Apions are still the only 'House' of which it is possible to write some kind of family history. The men appointed to be pagarchs presumably either belonged to this class, or were dependents of members of this class. But there is no evidence that tenure of the pagarchate was restricted to members of a limited number of families.

The pagarchate was an executive office. Its holder had at his disposal considerable coercive power to enforce the payment of taxes.[122] In addition he incurred personal financial liability for taxes that his department failed to collect. This is probably the reason why the office was sometimes held collegially by two individuals. The pagarch had an office staff of his own, seemingly separate from the *exaktorikē taxis*, which was paid at least partly out of taxation,[123] and these men are likely to have played an important part in the collection of taxes, especially from reluctant taxpayers.

In earlier times decurions had to provide the expensive and unpopular service for the Empire of running the *cursus publicus*. We have some evidence for its organization in the late Empire. Gascou has discussed two contracts of service between the House of the Apions and individuals performing the duties of a functionary whom Gascou convincingly argues to have been director of the imperial post at Oxyrhynchus.[124] If Gascou is right, this post was held continuously by a professional who was employed under a succession of short-term contracts with whatever 'house' was at the time responsible for paying his salary.[125] We have no evidence for 'houses' other than that of the Apions paying the *stablitēs* (σταβλίτης) at Oxyrhynchus. Payment of the salary of the accountant (*tabularius*) of the

[119] *P Oxy* 133 (550), 139 (612), 1981 (612), probably 1829 (577–9). Evidence (scanty) for other pagarchs at Oxyrhynchus being linked to Apions, see Gascou 1972: 70–1 n. 3.

[120] See list *PLRE* IIIB. 1498–9.

[121] *PLRE* IIIB.830 s.v. Fl Marianus—evidently a great family, ibid. 953 s.v. Olybrius 3 and A. C. Johnson and L. C. West 1949: 269; also Menas of Oxyrhynchus and Christodora of Cynopolis (ibid. 273).

[122] Liebeschuetz 1974; *PLRE* IIIB 875–6, s.v. Menas 5.

[123] *P Cair* 67057.25. The staff receives no less than 301 solidi 22 1/2 carats of gratuities, of which the *hypodektēs* receives 36 and the *logographos* (λογογράφος) 12.

[124] *P Oxy* 140 (550); 138 (610/11).

[125] See Gascou 1985: 55–7. The Apions are the only house known to have performed the duty.

cursus publicus was an obligation not of the Apions, nor of any other 'house' but of two guilds, who paid him through the *dēmosion logistērion* of Oxyrhynchus.[126] But part at least of the cost of draught animals and their drivers was probably met out of imperial taxes, as it was at Antaeopolis.[127]

Important administrative tasks were permanently delegated to owners of particular properties. So the transport of much tax-corn to Alexandria was paid for by the great monastery of the Metanoia,[128] and presumably also by other institutional or individual property-owners. The maintenance of a particular category of soldiers in readiness for active service on behalf of the Empire, the so-called *bucellarii*, was a duty performed by the Apions and other great landowners.[129] What all such arrangements have in common is that the imperial government found it convenient to delegate certain administrative functions to the administrators of certain great estates, secular or religious. Delegation of administrative tasks to particular individuals, 'houses', monasteries, and one might add guilds,[130] saved the imperial government the expense and trouble of having these tasks performed through its own bureaucracy,[131] and at the same time avoided the discontinuity and unpredictability involved in the old system of delegation to city councils. The assignment of duties to institutions and 'houses' rather than to individuals had the additional advantage that the arrangement was not terminated by death.

So 'houses' certainly played a role in financial administration in sixth-century Egypt. But it is by no means clear what qualifies an estate to be treated as an *oikos*. 'The glorious House' of the Apions and 'the divine House' of the emperor always have the epithet. We also hear of the 'House' of the glorious count.[132] Other references to 'houses' occur in the context of the long-term arrangements for the internal administration of the city which will be discussed later in this chapter. But there are many properties belonging to individuals or heirs of individuals, whose titles of rank clearly proclaim them to be among the notables of their town, which are not dignified by the title of *oikos*. The reality of post-curia municipal

126 *P Goth* 9, cf. A. C. Johnson and L. C. West 1949: 174–5 on *dēmosion logistērion*, which they think was the financial bureau of the pagarchy. Hermopolis: *P Lond* 1756; *P Cair* 67169; *Pkl Form* 118, 1035–6. Antaeopolis: *P Cair* 67054, 67057. Oxyrhynchus: *P Oxy* 125; *P Goth* 9.

127 A. C. Johnson and L. C. West 1949: 275; Gascou 1989: 296.

128 Rémondon 1971: 771–81. Gascou 1976*c*: 157–84.

129 J. Gascou, 'L'Institution des Bucellaires', *BIFAO* 72 (1976), 143–56; Rémondon 1961: 41–93; Liebeschuetz 1990*a*: 43–6. Carrié 1995: 27–60, esp. 52–9.

130 C. M. Roueché 1993: 124–6. R. Rémondon, 'Papyrologica', *CE* 41 (1966), 173–8, concerning *P Goth* 9. Rémondon 1965: 401–30; R. Rémondon, *Papyrus Grecs d'Apolōnus Anō* (Cairo, 1953), 163–5, no. 75 (*c.* AD 700); A. J. Hoogendijk and P. van Minnen (eds.), *Papyrologica Lugduno-Batava*, 25 (1991), 225–9 (mainly 4th cent.).

131 One might describe the procedure as privatization.

132 *P Oxy* 2020 and 2240.

organization was very much more untidy, and has many more obscure areas than Gascou's model would suggest.

As we have seen there is no evidence at all that 'houses', monasteries, etc. accepted any collective responsibility for the full performance of the services owed by their city to the imperial administration to match that which in earlier times had been born by the city councils. But our knowledge of delegation to 'houses' depends on a very small number of documents and these derived from less than a handful of towns. So we have no idea of the extent of delegation to 'houses'. It may well be that the involvement of 'houses' was an ad hoc response to breakdowns in limited areas of administration rather than the imposition of a comprehensive new system.

9. *'Houses' in the Internal Administration of the City*

We hear of 'houses' once more in connection with certain long-term arrangements for the administration of the city itself. So we have a rota of police officers (*riparii*) of Oxyrhynchus,[133] described as '*riparii* of the House of Theon', which covers no less than seven indictional cycles, 105 years in all, ending in AD 562/6.[134] According to Rémondon's interpretation this document shows that the house of Theon was formally obliged to provide *riparii* for 65 years of the cycle,[135] but that in fact 33/96 of these 65 years were covered by the House of the Apions. Other houses, those of Leontius, Philoxenus, and Mousaius, were responsible for shorter periods.[136] A duty assigned to estates rather than to individuals must have been essentially financial: each 'house' will have born the cost of policing for a period proportional to its wealth.[137] The tenure of the man who was actually responsible for efficient policing would not necessarily have come to an end at the same time as the term of duty of the financing 'house'.[138]

[133] Bibliography: *P Harr* II.218 introd.

[134] Rouillard (1928: 167) thought that these were officials of private estates, but a rota combining different estates for a common obligation is surely more likely to have been drawn up for a public purpose.

[135] In fact it is not down for *any* period on the surviving part of the list.

[136] Rémondon 1959: 91 ff.

[137] Cf. substitution of *riparius* under an earlier system acc. to *P Oxy* VI.904: 'Philoxenus . . . gave me his word of oath and promised that he would surely fulfil . . . every requirement for the office of *riparius*, providing for my support both servants and assistants [*summachoi*—cf. A. Jördens, 'Die ägyptischen Symmachoi', *ZPE* 66 (1986), 105–17)], and others whose duty it would be to undertake the guarding of the city; and . . . he promised that if anything extraordinary happened he would himself make up the loss to those who suffered injury. . . . But all this he has evaded. Accordingly I make entreaties to your highness [the governor] that I should be released from so grievous an office, and that the original holder should be compelled to finish it either himself or through some other person.'

[138] Rouillard 1928: 163–4, 167 n. 2. A *riparius* who was also a *cartularius* of the Apions is recorded as late as AD 606 (*P Oxy* 3942.7).

We are not told who drew up the list or on what criteria these particular 'houses' were chosen for this particular duty.

We are similarly short of evidence concerning an arrangement for filling what ought to be the principal civic office. This office combined what in earlier times had been three separate posts: the *proedria* (προεδρία), that is the office of the *prytanis*, the chairmanship of the council,[139] the *logisteia* (λογιστεία), which was the office of the *logistēs* (λογιστής) the curator,[140] and finally the *pateria* (πατερία), the office of the functionary in charge of civic finance and building.[141] Once again 'the House of Timagenes of respected memory' seems to have been responsible over a long period: at least its liability is witnessed in AD 458, 553, and 571.[142] We do not know what precisely the responsibility of 'the House of Timagenes' involved. For it seems that the actual duties of the triple office were not performed by a member of the 'House of Timagenes'. In fact responsibility was spread over three different levels. In some sense 'the House of Timagenes' remained ultimately responsible. However in each of the three years for which we have evidence, the title-holder of the office was not a member of the 'House', but an individual (or individuals) holding the office on the House's behalf. So in AD 458 the office was held by the counts Phoibammon and Samuelios and a third individual whose name has been lost,[143] in AD 553 by the patrician Gabrielia,[144] and in AD 571 by the head of the Apions.[145] We do not know what others took a turn in holding the title on behalf of the 'House of Timagenes'. But it may well be that there was a rota of office holders for the triple office 'of the House of Timagenes' of the same kind as for the *riparii* of the 'House of Theon'. We do not know whether the 'House of Timagenes' was ever required to provide the title-holder itself. But the actual work was probably not done by the high-ranking deputizing title-holder but by a trusted employee of his. On the analogy of the *riparii* of the 'House of Theon', it might be suggested that the triple office was assigned in turn to different houses or individuals for varying periods on the basis of their respective financial resources. Alternatively, the rota might have been drawn up many years ahead with individuals performing the duties perhaps for

139 Bowman 1971: 59–60; Drecoll 1997: 86–94.

140 Rees 1953–4: 83–105.

141 C. Roueché 1979: 173–85, 1989*a*: 78, 321–2; Dagron and Feissel 1987: no. 24 and Appendix 1. 215–20.

142 AD 458: Sijpesteijn 1986: 133–7; AD 553: *P Oxy* 2780; AD 571: *SB* XII.11079.

143 Sijpesteijn 1986: 133–7.

144 *P Oxy* 2780.7–11.

145 *SB* XII.11079.7–8.

a year at a time,[146] perhaps for three years, if that had been the normal length of office of the *logistēs* in earlier times.[147]

The documents give us only a very inadequate glimpse of the duties. Each of the three titles had formerly played an important role in the city. The combination of the three should signal the holder as the chief executive of the town. The *proedria* must originally have been the chairmanship of the Council. There is some evidence that councils, of which the *politeuomenoi* were members, still existed and met,[148] and owned property.[149] Presumably the holder of the triple office in his capacity of *proedros* (πρόεδρος)/*prytanis* (πρύτανις) presided over meetings of the council of Oxyrhynchus. In AD 567/8 the poet Dioscorus addressed an encomium to the pagarch Colluthos of Antaeopolis, who seems to have doubled that office with that of *proedros*/*prytanis* and who presumably also presided over the council of his city.[150]

The *logistēs* in the fourth century fixed prices and mediated between the city and the provincial administration.[151] The *logistēs* supervised the expenditure of civic revenues.[152] Besides the supervision of finance he had a wide range of functions.[153] He was normally a senior decurion who might already have performed other curial *munera*, and he was selected by his fellow councillors for appointment by the emperor. The *patēr* only made his appearance in the fifth century. As we have seen his responsibilities too were in the area of civic finance. It is not clear how his functions were demarcated from those of the *logistēs*. The duties of the triple office must have included duties which had formerly been performed by the holder of one or the other of the three offices.

But the fact that in the sixth century the three offices had been combined into one suggests that there had been significant change in the administration of Oxyrhynchus. We do not have the evidence to know to what extent the duties of the holder of the triple office still corresponded

146 *P Oxy* 2780 does not exclude the existence of a rota as for the 'riparius of the House of Theon': λαχούσῃ τὴν λογιστείαν καὶ προεδρίαν καὶ πατερίαν . . . ὑπὲρ οἴκου τοῦ τῆς περιβλέπτου μνήμης Τιμαγένους ἐπὶ τῆς εὐτυχοῦς λογιστείας δευτέρας ἰνδικτίωνος.

147 There is no certainty. Three years is possible. See discussion in Rees cited n. 140 above, pp. 95–6. For the *defensor* it was two years which could exceptionally be continued into a second term of two years by a *nem. con.* vote of all citizens: *Nov* 15, *epilog*: 'cuncta civitas reluctante nullo elegerit eum.'

148 *P Cair Masp.* 67004 council of Ombi in the Upper Thebaid accuses Colluthus (*PLRE* III.1.320 s.v. Colluthus 3) of paganism.

149 The council of Antinoopolis twice figures on the Hermopolis tax register as intermediary paying tax for the 'name' under whom a piece of land is registered (Gascou 1994 on 23.5 and 24.13).

150 See MacCoull 1988: 100–2 on H16.1–2. Differing from MacCoull, I now consider that *prytanis* and *boulē* are used in a literal sense. On Colluthus, see *PLRE* III.320 s.v. Colluthus 3.

151 See Rees 1953–4.

152 Bowman 1971: 91–8.

153 See now R. A. Coles in *P Oxy* LIV. 3727–76, esp. 3757–8: proceedings before the λογιστής, and pp. 222–9: the *curatores* of Oxyrhynchus AD 303–46.

to those that had formerly been performed by the three distinct office holders. Our evidence—as far as it goes—suggests that the scope of the office was now much more limited. The fact that the office could be held by a woman makes it likely that the responsibilities were financial rather than executive, that is the title-holder had to provide security for the conscientious performance of their duties by the men they nominated, and whose wages they will in some cases have been obliged to pay. The documents show that the individuals performing the duties of the office in the name of 'the House of Timagenes' supervised the nomination of individuals to humbler places in the local administration which were assigned as a compulsory public service. So the representative of the two counts acting for the 'House of Timagenes' received a nomination from the butchers' guild for an undefined liturgy. The patrician Gabrielia through a delegate[154] paid a salary of two solidi to some kind of bath-attendant.[155] Fl. Apion through a delegate received a pledge for the performance of unspecified duties by a humble underling.[156] When the House of Apion assumed the *logisteia* at Heracleopolis in AD 492 it had to provide an *apparitor* for the residence of the provincial governor.[157] Some years later we hear that a 'house' (perhaps the Apions) performing the *logisteia* at Heracleopolis received a guarantee and surety of continuing presence from a guild of shopkeepers 'in the interest of the provisioning of the city and of the governor's staff'.[158] Judging by this extremely meagre evidence the duty of the triple office was to supervise the appointment of the possibly quite large number of *liturgants* needed to perform subordinate roles in the administration.

The merging of traditional civic offices was not restricted to Oxyrhynchus. At Arsinoe in AD 584 the *pateria* and the *stratēlateia* (στρατηλατεία), on the face of it the command of the local garrison,[159] were held in combination. Moreover they were held by women, the patrician Theophania and her two daughters, who had inherited the duty from their father Strategius,[160] who judging by his name might have been

[154] Perhaps a senior administrator of the estate of the titular office holder, in the way Menas pagarch of Antaeopolis was the delegate of the *gloriosissima* Patricia (*P Lond* V.1660, cf. Gascou 1972: 70), and Theodorus pagarch of Oxyrhynchus seems to have been a colleague ('brother') of administrators of the Apions (*PLRE* 3. 1284, s.v. Theodorus 170.)

[155] *P Oxy* 2780.

[156] *SB* XII.11079.7–8.

[157] *SB* VI.9152.

[158] *Corpus Papyrorum Raineri* V.17.

[159] So Maspero 1912: 88–9. R. Rémondon, in *Akten des XIII internationalen Papyrologenkongresses* (Munich, 1974), 369, suggests an officer who would command troops of *bucellarii*. Durliat, 'Magister militum-stratēlatēs dans l'empire byzantin (VI–VIIe siècles)', *BZ* 72 (1979), 306–20, esp. 318, points out that in Egypt *stratēlatai* are normally members of the greatest families. That the office could be held by a woman together with her daughters, and that she held it jointly with that of *patēr* (*CPR* X. 127 of AD 584), suggests that it was a civilian office.

[160] *CPR* V.17.

an Apion. The document is a pledge of good behaviour—the circumstances are not explained—of a group of villagers imprisoned at Arsinoe, signed among others by the priest of the village. The duty performed by Theophania as holder of the double office at Arsinoe is therefore of the same kind as those performed by the Apions as holders of the *logisteia* at Heracleopolis in AD 492, and of the triple office on behalf of the House of Timagenes at Oxyrhynchus in AD 571. The fact that the *stratēlateia*, which sounds highly military, was held jointly with the *pateria*, which was a civilian office, and furthermore that the holders were women, shows that the *stratēlateia* cannot have been a military command. That the office could be divided between three persons, more between three women, and that it was sometimes combined with the pagarchate,[161] suggests that its principal function was to assume financial responsibility. It could not have involved command of troops, but it might have perhaps have been concerned with their pay and supplies. Administrative arrangements evidently differed from city to city. The separate existence of the pagarchate and the triple office at Oxyrhynchus suggests that civic finance remained separate there, while the linking of the offices of *patēr* and of στρατηλάτης,[162] and of στρατηλάτης and pagarch at Arsinoe,[163] makes it likely that in that city the civic and the imperial levels of administration had been largely unified.

The 'houses' had a position in some way comparable to that of the *curiales* of earlier times: they were required to organize sections of the administration and sometimes to provide and pay the functionaries involved from their own property. But as far as we can tell, there was no question in the case of the 'houses' of a *cursus honorum*, that is an obligation to perform a regular succession of duties, each for a period of a year or so. Instead 'houses' seem to have been attached to particular duties for an indefinite period covering many generations. It is significant that the heads of these 'houses' are never described as decurions, and that they and even their administrators regularly use titles of high senatorial rank.[164] These men were much higher up the social scale than the remaining decurions.

Unfortunately, we have little information about the circumstances in which these arrangements were set up. The rota of the *riparii* seems to go back to AD 456/7 at the latest.[165] It is likely that these arrangements were made as the need arose, presumably as a result of the breakdown of some aspect of the curial liturgical system. We know that as early as AD 432 an

[161] See list *CPR* X. pp. 153–6.
[162] *CPR* V.17
[163] *Stud. Pal.* XX.240.4–6.
[164] Hornickel 1930.
[165] Rémondon 1959: 91 argues that the latest duty on the roster cannot be later than 562/3 and that the start, 7 indictional cycles earlier, must therefore have been 457 or before.

individual called Timagenes, with the rank of *lamprotatos* (i.e. *clarissimus*), was responsible for registering the transfer of tax liability by the *exactorial* staff of part of the financial district of Oxyrhynchus.[166] It looks as if Timagenes in person was performing the same duty as the 'House of Timagenes' is first recorded to have performed in AD 444.[167] The House is first mentioned as holding the triple office in AD 458, but this arrangement too could go back to the lifetime of Timagenes himself. Perhaps Timagenes was an outstandingly rich notable of Oxyrhynchus who in the course of some civic crisis had agreed to take over responsibility for the staffing of a tax-office and the triple office. Certainly the *proedros* and the *logistēs,* like the *riparius,* had normally been decurions.[168] The arrangement could have been a response to a shortage of suitable, or at least willing decurions. It is possible that some 'houses' started as outstandingly wealthy curial families. This is likely in the case of the Apions.[169] Other families might have acquired the land of decurions, or perhaps perpetual tenancies of land belonging to the council. In these cases the duties would have been acquired together with the land. But by the middle of the fifth century much of the land around Oyrhynchus would have been owned by officials. The setting up of a 'house' must have required some arrangement to ensure that the property would remain together indefinitely, or at least to make sure that whoever would come into possession of any part of it would contribute his share to the obligations of the 'house'. So the imperial authorities must have been involved from the start, and they would have continued to take an interest in the survival and perhaps even in the enlargement of that block of properties.

But however these 'houses' had achieved their position,[170] such rights and duties as went for instance with administration of a tax-office and the maintaining of tax registers, or with the obligation to hold a combination of three of the four principal municipal offices,[171] involved the exercise of power, and surely resulted in a permanent expansion of a family's

[166] J. Andorlini, *Trenta testi greci da papiri litterari e documentari editi in occasione de XVII Cong. Int. di Papirol.* (Florence, 1983), no. 29.

[167] *P Oxy* L.3583.

[168] Bowman 1971: 144, 146, 147 (*logistēs*); 140, 142, 145, 147 (*riparius*).

[169] *P Flor* III. 325 as read by Hornickel 1930: 11.2; Gascou 1985: 63 n. 356; *PLRE* 2, s.v. Strategius 8. *P Oxy* 3584–6 refer to a decurion and imperial office holder who may have been the father of the earliest known member of the Apion dynasty.

[170] It was possible to make money by efficient farming: Rathbone 1991. But it is likely that the biggest fortunes were made by a combination of landed wealth and office holding in the imperial administration in Egypt and/or at Constantinople. That certainly was what made possible the rise of the Apions. See Gascou 1985: 60–75. On the economic and social rise of the Taurini, a much smaller family of landowners, aided by commissioned service in the army and in the *officium* of the duke of Thebaid, see H. Maehler, 'Papyri aus Hermupolis ', *BGU* 12 (1974), xxi–xxvi.

[171] The fourth is the *defensor*.

influence.[172] So too, for a family that could easily afford the expense, to assume financial responsibility for the running of the public baths was a means of gaining popularity rather than a disagreeable burden.[173] It is likely therefore that the most powerful 'houses' had volunteered to be placed in these positions of financial responsibility precisely in order to wield the power they conferred. Something of the kind seems to have been developing around AD 400 in Africa, for the emperor thought it necessary to prohibit slaves or freedmen from performing the duty of *tabularius* of a municipality.[174] Now these officials were the men who maintained the tax registers,[175] like the clerks serving in an *exactorikē taxis* in Egypt, and the government's objection to this duty being performed by slaves or freedmen was precisely that this involved a confusion of the public and private interests.

Gascou envisages an alternative model: that a strong imperial administration had forced the wealthiest municipal families into a system of compulsory public services different in detail, but comparable in substance, to the liturgical system to which decurions had been liable.[176] At the moment we lack the evidence to decide between the alternatives.[177]

But the general impression given by Byzantine Egypt is not one of strong government. For instance, inflation of titles was blatant in Egypt.[178] We find it in Byzantine Italy too, but there it was much less extreme.[179] The high rank was not simply assumed by individuals, or used as a polite form of address in social intercourse, but it was officially recognized. For the titles of elevated senatorial rank are recorded on an official document, the tax-register.[180] It looks as if the central authorities had lost control of the hierarchy of imperial rank. This is surely an indication of weakness.

Moreover the problems mentioned in Justinian's edict, and even more John of Niciu's account of the troubles in Egypt at the end of the sixth

172 *P Oxy* 133, 139, 1981 show villagers becoming indebted to the house (the Apions) exercising the pagarchy over them.

173 Apions and baths at Oxyrhynchus: *P Oxy* 1921, 2015, 148, 915; *P Wisc* 66.

174 *CT* VIII.2.5 (401), cf. VIII.2.1 (341).

175 *CT* XIII.10.1 (313).

176 Gascou 1985: 51–2.

177 There is much else we do not know. We lack the evidence to decide whether, or to what extent, the administration of civic and imperial expenditure was kept separate in the cities of Egypt. Was the pagarch involved in municipal finance as well as the collection of taxation? Was the *dēmosion logistērion* concerned with municipal accounts as well as the updating of the imperial tax register? Did cities like Oxyrhynchus have significant income from civic estates or urban properties? What precisely were the remaining functions of decurions?

178 Hornickel 1930.

179 T. S. Brown 1984: 131–3.

180 The inflation of rank is conspicuous on the Hermopolis tax-register, even though we have only a fragment of the document. It lists 40 *lamprotatoi* (*clarissimi*)—of both sexes, 20 *illustrioi* (*illustres*), and around 20 counts, some of whom are also *clarissimi*. These ranks serve as the only markers of rank of the individuals concerned, see Gascou 1994: 62.

century suggest a breakdown of administration. This is indeed what one would expect in view of the fact that the notables who occupied the principal positions in cities, whether they were representatives of 'houses' or not, now also filled a high proportion of key posts in the provincial administration.[181] So it is altogether more likely that the new role of the 'houses' reflects a shifting of power from the imperial administration to the local landowners than the opposite.

10. *The Problem of Civic Leadership*

Our picture of the financial administration of the cities of Byzantine Egypt, though detailed in some respects, is fragmentary in the extreme. So while we have evidence that the 'houses' took turns to provide and pay staff for some branches of the bureaucracy, we have no information about how the responsibilities were assigned. Who had drawn up the rota of the *riparii*? Who decided that the Apions should take over responsibility for the *cursus publicus* in a particular year? What precisely was the relation of the House of Theon to the administration of the police, or of the House of Timagenes to the triple office? When money had to be raised, for instance for paintings in the public baths,[182] or some other purpose,[183] who decided what estates would be required to pay, and how much would be required from each of the chosen contributors? In earlier times the making of appointments to civic office and the supervision of civic finance was the responsibility of the council. There is no evidence at all that the councils were still performing these tasks in sixth-century Egypt. So who provided leadership, coordination, and long-term supervision?

The pattern assumed in Justinian's legislation—which might well be the emperor's ideal model rather than an accurate description of how things were actually managed in the majority of cities—is that leadership was in the hands of the notables who of course included the heads of the 'houses' and of the bishop and clergy.[184] The effectiveness of such a system must have been hampered by the fact that the notables and the clergy were not fulfilling a long-established and precisely defined role, nor were they under the same constraint as the *curiales* had been. So the working of the system must have depended very much on the humble clerks and accountants who formed the permanent staff in the various offices.

[181] Though we do not know the country of origin of the great majority of civil and military or civil/military office holders in 6th-cent. Egypt (*PLRE* IIIB 1490–1, 1511–14), most of the individuals whose origins we do know are Egyptian. See also Banaji 1992 and below, p. 280.

[182] *P Oxy* 2040.

[183] *P Oxy* 1921.2.

[184] Fullest account in Claude 1969: 107–45. But on the limits to the bishop's secular activities, see Ch. 4 above.

But some continuous supervision was needed to make sure that the offices remained staffed, that 'houses', estates, and institutions continued to make the payments and to perform the services which they had undertaken to perform, to make sure that the various rotas of office holders were drawn up and adhered to, and to cope with inevitable unforeseen exigencies. The papyrus documents give us very little evidence of the working of leadership in the late Late Roman system of civic government.[185]

As we have seen the fourth century saw the creation of a new type of imperial/municipal official, notably the *curator/logistēs* and the *defensor/ekdikos*, who worked with the council but received their instructions from the provincial governor or the prefect of Egypt.[186] In the course of the fifth century they were joined by the pagarch,[187] and their selection transferred from the council to the notables, as it was elsewhere in the Empire. In cities with a garrison there was also the garrison commander. One of these must have acted as executive head of the city, unless, as sometimes happened, the provincial governor had appointed a deputy.[188] The pagarch, the governor's deputy, and above all the garrison commander had coercive power not at the disposal of *logistēs* or *defensor*. It probably depended on local circumstances which of these functionaries actually had control. But of course these functionaries held office for only relatively short spells of duty. The bishop was in office for life. But the papyri do not show bishops exercising a significant role in secular administration in Egypt.[189] So the functioning of the system must have depended to a considerable extent on supervision and coordination by the imperial administration.

John of Niciu's account of the Aykelāh revolt, and of the civil war between the supporters of Phocas and Heraclius for the control of Egypt, confirms that the cities of the Delta area normally had a recognized secular leader, who determined or at least greatly influenced the city's choice of allegiance. Unfortunately, descriptions like 'prefect', '*apūlon*', and sometimes 'lieutenant' or 'governor', which we read in our mutilated, and successively translated version of John's *Chronicle*, cannot be identified

[185] For a list of references to bishops, usually in other contexts than that of municipal administration: R. L. B. Morris, 'Bishops in the papyri', *Proceedings 20 Int. Congr. Papyr. Copenhagen 1992*, ed. A. Bülow-Jacobsen (Copenhagen, 1994), 582–7; Worp 1994: 283–318. Under the Muslims a pagarch demanded sureties from taxpayers in the presence of the *defensor* and bishop: Rémondon 1953: 114–17, no. 46.

[186] Bowman 1971: 49–50, 124–6. See *P Oxy* 3757.4 ff.; 3758.10 ff., 78 ff.

[187] Liebeschuetz 1973: 34–46. Under the Arabs he was given the unofficial title of 'count of the city'. Rémondon 1953: no. 37.14, 40.6, 41.13, 60.18.

[188] Something the emperor tries to prevent: *Nov* 17.10 (535), 28.4, 29.2 (535), 134 (556), more references A. H. M. Jones 1964: 759 n. 105.

[189] Steinwenter 1956: 75–99, who has been able to find remarkably few papyrus references to participation of bishops in the administration of their cities.

with particular offices with any degree of certainty. The most favoured interpretation is Maspero's, that the first two stand for pagarch and tribune, respectively.[190] In two cities for which there is abundant evidence, Oxyrhynchus and Arsinoe, a single 'House', the Apions, was overwhelmingly richer than the rest,[191] and while it lasted their combination of local wealth and high office at Constantinople must have made them irresistible. In any gathering of notables, such as that which Justinian envisaged appointing the *defensor*,[192] the representative of the Apions is likely to have had the last word.

It is significant that the heads of 'Houses', and indeed other notables exercising power in Byzantine Egypt, and even their principal administrators regularly used titles of high senatorial rank.[193] The extreme elevation of their titles of rank, whether they were assumed, bought, conferred, or earned, is an Egyptian phenomenon. In Byzantine Italy too, the notables had titles of senatorial rank, but they had to be content with the rank of *clarissimus*.[194] Earlier I have cited the inflation of rank as evidence of a weakening control of the central administration over what was happening in Egypt.[195] Another way of looking at the phenomenon is to interpret it as a pointer to an important political development, the coming into existence of a hierarchically graded provincial aristocracy, which overlapped the court-centred, imperial aristocracy, but which was in many ways more Egyptian than imperial.[196]

From the imperial point of view, the financial administration as reformed in the sixth century was nevertheless up to a point effective: the buildings and wars of Justinian are evidence of restored finance. But the Empire did not regain the degree of control which it had exercised through the decurions in the fourth century. The Apions, and presumably other great landowners, were able to obstruct the imperial administration just as senatorial houses were able to do in the West in the fifth century; but not to the extent that the feudal barons of the Middle Ages could resist medieval monarchs. For the grandees of the Empire, East and West, even though they maintained *bucellarii* on the government's behalf,[197] and were able to arm their messengers (*summachoi*/*σύμμαχοι*) with swords and

[190] Maspero (1912: 136) argues that *apūlon* = *tribunus*. The leadership of tribunes in a number of cities would imply an incipient militarization of civic government, as in post-Justinianic Italy, cf. T. S. Brown 1984: 56–8.

[191] *P Oxy* 1921: Apions pay 2/5 of tax of Oxyrhynchus and Kynopolis, see Gascou 1985: 45–6; 1992: 243–8.

[192] *Nov* 15 *epilogus*.

[193] Hornickel 1930.

[194] T. S. Brown 1984: 131–3.

[195] On inflation of rank, see above, p. 197 n. 180.

[196] See below, pp. 280–1.

[197] Gascou 1976*a*: 143–56.

shields,[198] lacked effective independent military power.[199] The old view of Gelzer concerning a state of 'Verwaltungsmisere' in 'Byzantine' Egypt was probably right,[200] and without a strong provincial administration, the late Late Roman cities of Egypt were politically unstable.

11. *Wider Significance of Egyptian Evidence*

The question arises how far the evidence from Egypt can be used to make generalizations about conditions elsewhere. In the first section of this chapter it has been argued that in terms of fundamental principles administration in Egypt was not very different from that in other regions of the East.[201] For instance laws of Empire-wide application share with papyrus documents the assumption that definite and distinct sources of revenue are assigned to particular areas of civic or imperial expenditure, and it is clear that in the East generally, as well as in Egypt, public expenditure was generally assigned for many years ahead. In the papyri the notables under their various names (*prōteuontes*, *ktētores*, etc.) are much less prominent than in the laws and the narrative sources for both East and West. But this is not because they were not important. It is rather a consequence of the fact that the papyri look at society from a different point of view. Law-givers and historians look at society from a distance and are concerned with the behaviour of groups. The papyri of our period are largely derived from private archives, and document the activities of single estates. But there can be no doubt that the owners of the estates, the heads of the 'houses', played the same role in Egyptian cities as the notables did elsewhere in the Empire. It is only when it comes to reconstructing the administrative organization in detail that it would be unwise to rely on the phrasing of the laws of the Code to reconstruct the administrative arrangements of a particular Egyptian city or province. It would be equally unwise to rely on papyrus evidence for a detailed reconstruction of administration in, say, Asia. Pagarchs are only known in Egypt, though an official with a different title, the *vindex* is likely to have performed roughly similar functions elsewhere in the East, as he did even at Alexandria.[202] The laws do not mention the assigning of administrative

198 *P Oxy* XVI.2045, list of 30 *summachoi spatharioi*, also ibid. 2057 and *P Oxy* 1839.4.

199 That may be the reason why, for all their wealth and influence, the Apions vanished from history early in the 7th cent.—well before the end of papyrus documentation.

200 M. Gelzer, 'Altes und Neues aus der byzantinisch-ägyptischen Verwaltungsmisere', *Archiv für Papyrusforschung*, 5 (1913), 346–77.

201 So also N. Lewis, 'The Romanity of Roman Egypt, a growing consensus', *Atti XVII Congr. Int. di Pap.* 1984, 1077–84 = *On Government and Law in Roman Egypt: Collected Papers of Naphtali Lewis* (Atlanta, 1995), 298–305.

202 At Gerasa an inscription of AD 578 is dated by exarch and *logeutēs* (λογευτής). Perhaps the latter was the local equivalent of pagarch or *vindex* (Zayadine 1986*b*: 17–18).

tasks over several generations to 'houses'. But it is likely—even if there is no direct evidence—that it was not only in Egypt that authorities and notables found it convenient for a number of 'houses' to take turns to perform a particular public service in rotation, or for a single 'house' to assume ultimate responsibility for a particular public duty over a long period. The disorder which afflicted Egypt around the end of the sixth century is also witnessed elsewhere in the East, and it is reasonable to use the more abundant Egyptian evidence to construct at least provisional explanations for the internecine strife elsewhere.[203]

In this book the account of financial administration of cities in the East will not be complemented by a comparable section on the West. The West has left less evidence. But the relative lack of evidence for urban administration from the West[204] is not an accident. As has been shown in Chapter 3 from the early fifth century the bulk of the cities of the West no longer had civic services that required a complex administrative organization, nor the population to demand services. Except in a few principal cities, notably Rome, Ravenna, and Carthage, and on rare and special occasions in residences of barbarian kings the public spectacles were abandoned. The support of the poor, in the widened sense to include all those who could not support themselves without the help of a patron, was taken on by the church.[205] Urban infrastructure was allowed to decay as urban populations shrank. So there certainly was very much less need for urban administration in the cities of, say, sixth-century Gaul, than in contemporary cities of Egypt.

This does not however mean that municipal administration in the West collapsed everywhere at the same time or to the same extent. The West covers a large area with marked regional differences. Its cities included Rome, Ravenna, Carthage, Merida, and Cordova, as well as fortress cities like Nicopolis ad Istrum, bishop's cities like Tours or Arles, and mere shells of cities as was Cologne around AD 500. Evidently the extent to which Roman administrative structures survived into and through the sixth century varied greatly from region to region, and between cities in the same region. No doubt too, such evidence as there is will in time be exploited more comprehensively than it has been here.

[203] See below, pp. 276–82.

[204] Western documentary evidence, that is of charters and wills, relates largely to rural estates, see I. Wood 1994: 203–7.

[205] P. Brown 1992: 97–9; Rouche 1974: i. 83–110.

6

Shows and Factions

1. *The Reorganization of the Shows*

The previous chapter has dealt with the financial administration of cities of late Late Antiquity, with the collection of imperial taxes as well as with the way cities financed their civic services. But the chapter has very little about the public spectacles which had for so long been an outstanding feature of life in a classical city. The shows were of course still going on, though there now were fewer of them, and there was less variety. The reason that they have not been treated alongside other civic activities is that responsibility for providing them had been taken away from the local administration, and handed over to an Empire-wide organization. One might say that they had been 'nationalized'.[1]

Traditionally the shows had been provided for their fellow citizens by members of the governing class, that is by the decurions. In one sense they were an appeasement offered by the rich and powerful to their less fortunate compatriots.[2] Seen from another point of view, they gave competing local politicians an opportunity to display civic patriotism and munificence. The presenter of the games did not normally have to bear the full expense, or even anything like it. The cities had endowments whose revenues subsidized civic festivals. The city also provided the permanent infrastructure of buildings and equipment needed by the decurions to produce their show. But the distinction and splendour of a particular spectacle depended on the munificence of the *agonothete*, and there is plenty of evidence that city magnates gave freely to make their games magnificent, and sought glory by entertaining their fellow citizen generously.

Money was not enough for a successful show. Expert performers were required: athletes, actors, dancers, musicians, hunters, and charioteers. There was also a need for specialists qualified to produce various kinds of spectacle. Under the High Empire, when games were numerous and cities wealthy, it is possible that the largest cities could offer a living to a full

[1] Against C. M. Roueché 1993: 46 and 50, I would maintain the analogy with 'nationalization'. The comparison is not so much with control by the imperial authority, as with the substitution of an Empire-wide organization for local initiative. Correspondingly the political ideology of the games shifts from local to imperial politics. The reform also amounted to 'Romanization'.

[2] See for instance A. H. M. Jones 1940: 227–35.

range of performing artists to compete in the contests at the local festivals. But even so, to be interesting a competition badly needed new and exciting competitors who had not yet appeared before the spectators. The wider the field, the higher the standard of performance, and the better the competition. So organizers in search of athletes or artists looked far afield. They were helped by the fact that performing artists were organized in synods or guilds through which the *agōnothetēs* could get the performers he wanted.[3] Already under the Early Empire there was a tendency for the guilds of different specialists to amalgamate, and eventually there came into existence two Empire-wide unions, one of athletes, the other of theatrical artists.[4] Merging of performers' guilds was clearly helpful to givers of games, as it meant that they would have fewer organizations to deal with. At Rome and later at Carthage, and perhaps one or two other cities in the West, charioteers and horses for chariot races were provided by contracting organizations, known as 'factions', distinguished by their team colours of blue and green.[5]

In consequences of the fading of the epigraphic habit, we know much less about the organization of the spectacles and performing artists in Late Antiquity. There now were far fewer games in provincial cities, though more than ever in the capitals. Athletic games and gladiatorial shows in general did not survive beyond the fourth century.[6] Wild beast hunts lasted somewhat longer but were only shown at a few great spectacles in honour of the emperor. Theatrical shows, that is mainly performances by mimes and pantomimes,[7] flourished in spite of being under continuous attack from Christian preachers. Chariot racing of the Roman type, that is races between professional charioteers seems to have become the principal entertainment in larger cities. Many provincial capitals and some ordinary cities now had a hippodrome.[8] Dancers, jugglers, musicians might amuse the spectators in the intervals between chariot races.[9] All the shows, even the theatrical performances, were competitive, and the partisans of the rival performers, whether charioteers or actors or dancers, were passionately involved.

[3] C. M. Roueché 1993: 46–7.

[4] Ibid. 50–5.

[5] On the history of the factions of the Blues and Greens at Rome, see Alan Cameron 1976: 6–13.

[6] *CJ* X.54.1 (325) omnino gladiatores esse prohibemus. But at Rome gladiator shows continued to the reign of Valentinian III (425–455), in the East they are not mentioned after the reign of Arcadius (383–408), see C. M. Roueché 1993: 76–9; G. Ville, 'Les Jeux de gladiateurs dans l'empire chrétien', *MEFR* 72 (1960), 273–335.

[7] Some detail in C. M. Roueché 1993: 25–8.

[8] Alan Cameron 1973: 228–32; J. H. Humphrey 1986. But at Scythopolis, Caesarea (one of two), Neapolis, and Gerasa a hippodrome was converted into an amphitheatre in Late Antiquity (Tsafrir and Foerster 1997: 134–5; Ostrasz 1989).

[9] *P Oxy* 2707.

Sometime in the fifth century there was a radical change in organization of the shows: the provision of performers of every kind—charioteers, actors, dancers, and even wild-beast hunters—became the responsibility of two Empire-wide contracting organizations modelled on the 'factions' that had from time immemorial furnished the chariot races at Rome and Carthage, and since the fourth century also at Constantinople and Alexandria.[10] These organizations supplied all the personnel, animals, and equipment needed for a show. It has been plausibly argued by C. Roueché that the old performers' guilds were merged into the new organizations.[11] As there were two factions, the Greens and the Blues—or four, if you count their respective subsidiaries, the Reds and the Whites separately[12]—they provided the competition too.[13] Eventually the Blues and the Greens came to operate in a large number of cities all over the East.[14]

It is probable that the factions received the bulk of their resources from the state.[15] Performers drew state salaries paid out of taxation[16] and chariot races were sometimes subsidized out of the revenue of customs duties.[17] In the fourth and early fifth century cities still had their own *agonothetic* endowments as well as equipment and performers which the emperor insisted must not be diverted to games elsewhere by the provincial governor.[18] At the reorganization the cities did not lose their endowments,[19] but the revenue now presumably went to the factions. Already in AD 426 Constantinople had an accountant for the theatre and race horses (*actuarius thymelae et equorum*).[20] Since we know that the factions were operating at Constantinople by this time, it is likely that the function of this officer was to issue pay, rations, and fodder to the staff of

[10] Factions at Constantinople: Greg. Nazianzen *Or* 37(31) *PG* 36.301, 304; at Alexandria in AD 315: *P. Cairo Isidore* 57–8.

[11] C. M. Roueché 1993: 57–60.

[12] On pairing of colours, see Alan Cameron 1976: 61–73.

[13] C. M. Roueché 1993: 57–60.

[14] Listed in Alan Cameron 1976: 315–17.

[15] Alan Cameron 1976: 218–21; C. M. Roueché 1993: 8–10. The most explicit evidence concerns Rome in the time of Theoderic: Cassiodorus *Variae* III.51 (105.9 ff., 107.3); IX.20; I.31: ideo tot expensarum onus subimus; I.33 ei . . . solitum menstruum partis prasini tribuatis. Procopius *HA* 26.6 confirms that at Constantinople the shows were financed by the state, but implies that elsewhere they were financed out of civic funds and largely closed down when Justinian seized civic revenues. This is certainly one-sided and oversimplified. There is nothing in Justinian's laws about a takeover of civic funds (cf. pp. 170–3 above). But it may be that in some cities some of the old civic revenues had been permanently assigned to the factions for expenditure on shows, as had been the case with some customs' revenues, and that Justinian diverted this revenue to other purposes.

[16] Procopius *HA* XXVI.6, 9 (Constantinople); Cassiodorus *Variae* I.32, 33 (Rome).

[17] See above, p. 171 (Alexandria); p. 172 (Caesarea).

[18] *CJ* XI.41.5 (409) nemo judicum ex quacunque civitate in aliud oppidum vel ex provinciae solo equos curules, aurigas, bestias, histriones cives temptet traducere.

[19] Procopius *HA* XXVI.6; *CJ* XI.42.1.

[20] *CT* VII.8.22 (426) Praef. Urb. Cpl.

the factions.[21] *Actuarii* and *cornicularii* with the same title were found in some cities other than Constantinople, and their appointment had to be confirmed by the emperor himself.[22] It is not clear what happened to the traditional munificence of decurions and other magnates. Henceforth we hear very little of it, except in the case of a few great traditional events like the consular games at Rome and Constantinople.[23] At Antioch the funds and the presidency of the Olympic games and the games of the Syriarch were in AD 465[24] transferred respectively to the consular of Syria and the *comes* Orientis. Decurions were henceforth prohibited from holding either office. If what happened at Antioch was typical, it would follow that under the new system the president at public spectacles in a provincial city was now generally the provincial governor.[25] But from the point of view of civic politics what is significant is that the fans acclaimed their faction rather than a civic magnate.

This does not mean that magnates had altogether stopped making financial contributions to the games. The accounts of the great Apion family show that it made payments in money or kind to benefit staff and horses of the factions, mainly to the Blues,[26] but sometimes also the Greens.[27] At Constantinople the Blues and Greens had official 'patrons', who were wealthy and powerful men, for instance Chrysaphius the principal minister of Theodosius II, and Plato prefect of Constantinople in AD 498, and the 'illustrious' Theodosius Zticca.[28] The title of 'patron' was surely given as a reward for material assistance to the faction concerned, whether it took the form of money, or of wine, or horses, or even of performers.[29] No doubt the Apions figured among the 'patrons' at Oxyrhynchus. The wealthy youths, who were prominent among the fans of each faction surely did not limit their support to applause, but also helped their chosen team with material contributions. There was however an important change: individuals who had contributed to the resources of

21 *Actuarius* was the title of the officer who issued pay and *annona* to a unit of the army, see A. H. M. Jones 1964: 706.

22 *CT* VIII.7.21 (426) P.P.Or., taken into *CJ* XII.59.6, where appointment is by the praetorian prefect.

23 Just. *Nov* 105 (538).

24 *CJ* I.36.1.

25 C. Roueché 1989*a*: 69–73, no. 40 (= Roueché 1993: 188). Governors might be assigned public funds to be able to make a regular contribution to games. So the Augustalis drew 320 solidi to give 36 horses to the chariot races of Alexandria (Just. *Ed* 13.15).

26 *P Oxy* 140 (AD 550), 152 (AD 618, 2480.28, 82, 83, 90, 99, 101, 106–7 *PSI* 953.42, 77.

27 *P Oxy* 145 (AD 552).

28 See *PLRE* II. s.v. Plato 3. He was appointed prefect of Constantinople, conceivably because as patron of the Greens he might be able to stop them from rioting, ibid. s.v. Theodosius 19, ibid. s.v. Chrysaphius qui et Ztumas; also Damianus, a decurion, patron of Blues at Tarsus (Proc. *HA* XXIX.25; two patrons at Rome chosen by Theoderic (Cass. *Var* I.20, cf. 33).

29 See below, n. 30.

a faction gained popularity as a supporter of the faction, and no longer as an individual benefactor of his fellow citizens. If these men had political ambitions they now furthered them by gaining support of a faction, not by direct generosity to a civic cause. As what we would now call 'charitable contributions' came to be mediated through the Church, so private contributions to public entertainment were mediated through the factions.[30]

We do not know exactly when or how this reform was introduced. Alan Cameron has convincingly argued that the decisive step towards the creation of the Greens and Blues of late Late Antiquity was the amalgamation of the organizations providing performers for the theatre with the Blues and Greens responsible for organizing races in the hippodrome.[31] A second essential preliminary to the reorganization was the setting up of branches of the Blues and Greens in a large number of provincial towns. The most likely period for the reform is the reign of Theodosius II (408–450). We are told that this emperor reorganized the seating in the hippodrome at Constantinople so that the Greens should sit to the left of the imperial box and the Blues opposite. He also gave to the Greens seats, stretching over six-column spaces, which had previously been occupied by members of the garrison. These seats were immediately opposite the kathisma, and thus enjoyed the privilege of being always within view of the emperor. According to Malalas, Theodosius ordered this seating to be observed in all cities of the Empire. Malalas reports these arrangements as an example of Theodosius' favouring the Greens. They could nevertheless also have been part of a far-reaching reorganization of the public shows, of which we have otherwise no evidence.[32] At any rate, the public disturbances, which have made the Late Roman factions notorious, began soon after. Theodosius' successor Marcian (450–457) prohibited any Greens from holding public office because the faction had started a riot.[33] The first of the big riots to enter our sources happened at Antioch in AD 489, the last year of Zeno.[34]

Did the reorganization happen everywhere at the same time? We do

[30] The private munificence in any case only supplemented the tax-derived contribution of the state. At Rome, where the factions had always operated in the circus, consuls, praetors, and *quaestors* still furnished horses and charioteers for their games around AD 400 (e.g. Symmachus *ep* IV.8, 59–60, VI.33, 41; and Alan Cameron 1976: 7–8).

[31] Alan Cameron 1976: 214 ff.

[32] Malalas 351–2. On this passage Michael Whitby 1999. Malalas admittedly implies that by this time factions were already involved in the races in the hippodrome in many cities. Yet at Antioch decurions organized the Olympic games and the games of the Syriarch until AD 465 (*CJ* I.36.1). This could mean that previously the factions had not yet taken over the organization of these games. The factions in small towns of Egypt are witnessed only from mid-6th cent., Alan Cameron 1976: 316–17.

[33] Malalas 368.

[34] See below, p. 254.

not know. The fact that at Antioch Syriarch and Alytarch were still giving their traditional games in AD 465 suggests that the reform had not yet happened there. In Egypt, apart from Alexandria, there is no evidence for the existence of Blues and Greens before the sixth century.[35] In any case the setting up of consolidated branches of Greens and Blues must have involved complicated administrative changes and much local negotiation. A lot depends on the precise reasons for the change. Was it brought about everywhere in response to a single decree from Constantinople, or did it happen more gradually as a result of piecemeal reform of a failing system? In many ways the setting up of branches of the factions in the provincial cities was the logical consequence of long-term trends: the decline of the liturgical system of financing civic activities,[36] the establishment of tight imperial control over civic finance, and the taking over by the Empire of the spending of two-thirds of civic revenues,[37] and finally the progressive amalgamation of the synods of performers.[38] In any case reform was inevitable wherever the local *curia* was no longer in a position to provide shows.

The emperors certainly could not afford to let the spectacles die. They were too popular for that, and in any case, at this late period it was the imperial administration rather than the *curia* or individual local magnates that gained popularity by providing shows for the people. The spectacles had become part of the structure holding the Empire together. The games had long provided an opportunity for venting popular grievances: the spectators assembled at public shows had in a real sense taken the place of the long extinct public assembly.[39] In theory any individual or group could use the games to bring grievances to the notice of the authorities, whether local or imperial. In practice it needed some organization if the demonstration of a group was to be taken up by the mass of spectators. At Antioch in the late fourth century, acclamations and associated complaints seem to have been led by the theatre claque.[40] But the most fully documented series of civic demonstrations took place at Edessa in Mesopotamia, where the acclamations were made the medium of an organized campaign by an ecclesiastical faction against their bishop Ibas.[41]

The games and their claques had been adapted to serve the Empire. Every show opened with acclamations of the emperor,[42] and the theatre or

35 Alan Cameron 1976: 316–17.

36 See above, pp. 172–3.

37 See above, pp. 175–8.

38 C. M. Roueché 1993: 54–60.

39 On popular demonstrations in connection with the nomination and honouring of magistrates, see Lewin 1995*a*: 108–12.

40 Liebeschuetz 1972: 211–16.

41 Flemming and Hoffmann 1917.

42 See below, pp. 209–10.

hippodrome provided a setting for close contact between emperor and his capital at Constantinople and between governor and governed in the provinces. In the theatre or hippodrome the governor could not avoid hearing expressions of public opinion, whether approving or critical.[43] The games were privileged occasions.[44] Since the time of Augustus, emperors had used the games as an occasion for their subjects to air grievances. In the Later Empire this applied not only to the games in the capitals but also to those in provincial cities. Reports of provincial acclamations were taken down in writing and sent to the capital so that the emperor might learn his subjects' feelings, and reward or punish his officials accordingly.[45] Surviving texts show that these demonstrations were an organized ceremony with acclamations made in a fixed order. They began with praise of God. This was followed by acclamations of the emperor, the principal officers of state, the local governor, and perhaps of the patriarch or the bishop. In addition these performances often included shouts of praise specific to that particular occasion, whether of a munificent private individual or an imperial official. Frequently the acclamations were interrupted by bursts of invective, rhythmical demands for the punishment of some individual who had incurred the anger of a large part of the population. The ceremony concluded with a final burst of phrases laudatory of the emperor.[46] Civic life offered many occasions for acclamations: the setting up of imperial statues, the arrival or departure of the provincial governor or visiting high official, the honouring of a civic benefactor, but most regularly the shows in the theatre or hippodrome.[47]

Over the years emperors issued numerous laws to ensure the continued functioning of the shows,[48] and at a local level governors regularly intervened in the games, not least in the hope of increasing the volume and frequency of their own acclamations.[49] It is significant for the imperial aspect of the games that it was the Roman form of chariot racing, that is the professional spectator sport, that came to be the core element in Late Antique programmes. The imperially directed amalgamation of all groups concerned with the production of games into two factions, modelled on the factions of Rome and Constantinople, was only the culmination of a long history of imperial intervention. Whatever the circumstances of the introduction of the reform, its effect can reasonably be summarized as

[43] See below, pp. 216–18.

[44] e.g. Cass. *Var* I.27; Alan Cameron 1976: 157–92.

[45] *CJ* I.40.3, cf. Malalas 443: texts of acclamations at Antioch kept at Constantinople.

[46] C. Roueché 1989*a*: 126–36, text and commentary on inscr.83.i.

[47] At Carthage when the governor announced the nomination to the office of *exactor*, the people were given a chance to protest, *CT* XI.7.20 (412).

[48] C. M. Roueché 1993: 6–7.

[49] Cf. Libanius *Or* XXXIII.11–12.

the 'imperialization' of public entertainment. Subsequently, it was the emperor who paid most of the regular expenses, and it was his representative, the provincial governor, or at Constantinople the emperor himself, who presided. What had been celebrations of the city-community became celebrations of the emperor.

As for the factions, the reorganization meant that they became politicized. For they not only took over the production of the games and theatricals, but also the duty of leading the spectators in the acclamations. In a society without television, wireless, or newspapers the acclamations performed the important function of reminding subjects spread over a vast area of the majesty and indeed even the identity of the emperor, his family, and his ministers.[50] So each of the factions organized a chorus which had the double duty of leading applause for the emperor, and of rousing the fans' enthusiasm on behalf of the competitors of its particular colour. The choruses were large and were made up not only of the unemployed or rootless, attracted by pay, but also of young men of good family with their own money to spend. Motives were presumably mixed: sheer colour-enthusiasm, the opportunity for licensed hooliganism, fashionable slumming, battle of generations.[51]

These choruses quickly became a key institution in what was left of civic politics. When the factions succeeded the theatre claque in the leadership of the acclamations, they also came to play a leading part in the voicing of complaints. Rhythmical phrases, whether of praise or of criticism, chanted by the chorus of one or both factions[52] could give a massive lead to the assembled spectators, and the fact that the factions operated not only in the theatre but also the hippodrome gave their demonstrations a much greater impact than could have been achieved by the theatre claque. So the factions were the obvious 'medium' to publicize demands of groups, or even of powerful individuals. A comparable capacity for leadership was only possessed by ecclesiastics, that is bishop, or parties of clergy or monks.[53] But ecclesiastics normally organized demonstrations only to further religious causes. Individuals or groups wishing to publicize a secular issue would have to use one or the other faction.

[50] The acclamations gained in importance as the imperial cult, which had performed a similar function, had to be dismantled, since it was incompatible with Christianity.

[51] Alan Cameron 1976: 77–9; C. Roueché, 'Acclamations in the later Roman Empire: New evidence from Aphrodisias', *JRS* 74 (1984), 181–99; also 1993: 135–40 suggests that the old organizations of young men had been absorbed into the factions.

[52] P. Maass, 'Metrische Akklamationen der Byzantiner', *BZ* 21 (1912), 28–51.

[53] Examples in P. Brown 1992: 147–50.

2. *The Factions and the Making of the Emperor*

At the root of the political power eventually gained by the factions was the fact that from the mid-fifth century the making of an emperor required that he should be acclaimed by the people. It is difficult to say whether this acclamation was simply a regular ceremony, or a constitutional requirement. It partook of elements of each, for without it an emperor was not fully legitimate. This ceremony originated at the time when it became normal for emperors to be 'made' at Constantinople, instead of some garrison town in the provinces. Acclamation by civilians first supplemented and later replaced acclamation by the army.[54] But the point to note here is that this ceremony gave an essential role to the factions. For the acclamation of the new emperor—like more ordinary ceremonies of acclamation—was initiated and led by at least one of the factions, and preferably by both, so that the people followed the lead given by the factions. It was not of course this ceremony which selected the individual who was to be emperor. That was done by the grandees of court and the officers of the guard,[55] or sometimes the army. If the succession was clear, and the notables of court and soldiers were unanimous, the acclamation in the hippodrome was a formality, even though a necessary formality. But the succession was scarcely ever clear: between Theodosius II (402–450) and Heraclius (610–641) scarcely one emperor was succeeded by his son: Leo II's reign of ten months in AD 474 hardly counts! In these circumstances the acclamations mattered and the factions exercised real power.

The most detailed account of the making of an emperor in our period is that of the accession of Justin I, following the death of Anastasius. In this case the Blues actually prevented the acclamation of a tribune called John, who was supported by the *excubitors* but evidently had influential opponents. There followed discussion among prominent courtiers with the outcome that Justin was chosen. Both Greens and Blues were present at the talks and presumably they agreed with the choice of the candidate, whom they subsequently acclaimed.[56]

The political role of the factions did not end with the acclamation of a new emperor. They became an important factor in the political situation whenever an emperor had become so unpopular that an attempt to replace him was thinkable. The events preceding the deposition of the emperor Maurice are the best documented example.[57] Maurice had become unpopular with the army in the Balkans. The soldiers refused to obey

[54] S. G. MacCormack, *Art and Ceremony in Late Antiquity* (Berkeley, 1981), 242 ff.

[55] Averil Cameron 1976: i. 202–366, with Cameron's commentary.

[56] Const. Porph. *De Caer. PG* 112.784–94.

[57] Theophylact Simocatta VIII.4.9–10.8; Michael and Mary Whitby 1986; Michael Whitby 1988. Chronology in *Chron. Pasch.*, 693 s.a. 602.

orders, and began to look for a new emperor. The most likely candidates were Germanus, the father in law of Maurice's eldest son Theodosius, and Phocas who was then only a centurion. Eventually Germanus approached Sergius, the leader of the Greens, and tried to negotiate terms on which the Greens would acclaim him emperor. But the Greens refused to help him on the grounds that he was a notorious supporter of the Blues. Incidentally they were to do this a second time after he had offered them money in AD 605–6.[58] In fact by the time Germanus approached them, the Greens had already had successful talks with Phocas and their negotiators were already on the way from Constantinople to Phocas' camp.[59] They acclaimed Phocas on the same day as they rebuffed Germanus. The Blues evidently had no objections. For Phocas at once approached the capital, and the two factions jointly led the people in the Hebdomon to proclaim him emperor. Two days later the factions quarrelled over a question of precedence. When Phocas came down on the side of the Greens, the Blues hinted that they might return to the allegiance of Maurice, who was still alive but had fled from the capital. Phocas took this so seriously that he immediately had Maurice killed, together with all five of his sons.[60]

Clearly any emperor had to take factions seriously and make sure that at least one could be relied upon to support him. John Malalas anachronistically maintains that this concern was as old as Rome itself.

When Romus (i.e. Romulus) saw members of any faction supporting the populace or senators who were disaffected and opposed him because of the death of his brother, or for any reason whatever, he would decide to support the other faction, and so he secured their favour, and their opposition to the aims of his enemies. From that time the emperors of Rome after him followed the same principle.

The story is clearly anachronistic, but the fact that Malalas tells it shows that he assumed it to be a fact that notable people or groups at variance with the emperor did seek the support of one of the factions, and that the emperor's normal response was to seek the support of the other.[61] In fact most emperors did not wait for opponents to win the favour of a faction, before he would make advances to its rival. As a rule an emperor would

58 Theophanes, s.a. 6098.

59 Theophylact, VIII.9.13.

60 Theophylact was certain that Theodosius was among the slain, and that the widespread belief that he survived caused much bloodshed was mistaken (VIII.15.8).

61 All references to Malalas are to the English translation of text and 'sub-text' in E. Jeffreys, M. Jeffreys, and R. Scott (eds.), *John Malalas*, Byzantina Australiensia 4 (Melbourne, 1986). The 'sub-text' provides evidence of what Malalas wrote other than that of the *Baroccianus Graecus*, 182 on which Dindorf's edition was based.

make sure of the firm support of at least one of the factions from the very beginning of his reign.[62]

Most emperors publicized their factional allegiance, and in this way ensured that when it came to the pinch one faction at least would support him through thick and thin.[63] An emperor disposed of a wide range of favours to demonstrate his partisanship: he could simply show enthusiasm at the victory of his colour, he could offer gifts in money or kind, posts in the administration, and, more sinisterly, positive discrimination in the law courts. Procopius insists that in the reign of Justinian the Blues got away with any amount of criminality, and given that emperor's need for the Blues' support this is only too likely.[64]

The factions could afford to be rude to the emperor in a way no other group could. So the Blues reminded Phocas just after his coronation that his predecessor was still alive,[65] and on a later occasion, when Phocas' cruelty and paranoia were manifest to all, the Greens dared to tell him that he was drunk and out of his mind.[66] In fact the factions enjoyed an independence which was shared by no other institution, except the Church and the army. One aspect of this was their extraordinary ability to recover from setbacks. All riots were eventually put down by force, and often the emperor or his officials exacted savage punishment. But what is significant is not that the factions lacked the strength to escape punishment for even the most destructive excesses, but that punishment never had more than a temporary effect on their behaviour.

3. *The Role of the Factions in Civic Politics*

The relationship of the fans to their faction was rather like that of modern football fans to the club they support. It is certainly not an accident that Cameron was able to make his considerable contribution to our understanding of this phenomenon in an age of football hooliganism. But faction behaviour must not be seen simply as an earlier version of

[62] On factions favoured by different emperors, see Alan Cameron 1976: 127–9. Theodosius II—Greens (Malalas 351); Marcian—Blues (Malalas 368); Zeno—Greens (Malalas 379); Anastasius—reds (Malalas 392); Justinian—Blues (Proc. *HA* IX.35–42); Maurice—Greens (Theophanes 287.13); Phocas—first Greens, then Blues (Alan Cameron 1976: 281–5); Heraclius—Greens (ibid. 284–5); Justin II—neutral (Theophanes 243.3–4); Leo, Tiberius—not known.

[63] Eg. when both factions had united in the Nika Riot and proclaimed Hypatius emperor, some of the Blues—the faction always favoured by Justinian—returned to their allegiance (*Chron. Pasch.* p. 626; Malalas XVIII.476.3–7).

[64] Justinian's unjust favours to the Blues is a recurring theme of the *Secret History*. In the ways they exploited their position the factions bear some resemblance to the Mafia or Camorra.

[65] Theophylact, VIII.10–11.6, with notes in English translation cited in n. 57 above.

[66] Theophanes, s.a. 6101, Phocas against ancient tradition punished them severely. In the following year the Greens helped to make Heraclius emperor.

contemporary Saturday night disturbances after a football match. The political role of the acclamations, led by the choruses and reinforced by the fans of the two factions, has no parallel in modern sport, and its existence meant that the activities of the factions could not avoid having a political aspect.

The circumstances of government by notables were bound to develop the political role of the factions. This created a very different situation from that obtaining in the fourth century, when cities were run by decurions, whose names were registered in the *album* of the *curia*, and who had either been born into the order, or had been formally enrolled. Decurions had always formed an oligarchy, but they had been an open one, operating in the public eye. The notables of the fifth century and after were an oligarchy too, but an oligarchy whose members could not be clearly identified, and which did its business not in public, but in the *triclinium* of a palace, whether that of the governor, or the bishop, or the *defensor* or whoever.[67]

This was bound to affect the way tensions within the city were resolved. The only means open to outsiders to bring their views to the attention of such a closed circle was through public demonstrations. The chance that a serious riot would result was evidently considerable. It is not, I would argue, a coincidence that the period which saw the consolidation of civic government by notables also became notorious for rioting. When Alexandria was governed without a council under the Early Empire, it suffered much civic unrest, disputes within the élite, bitter conflict between Jews and Greeks, and repeated clashes with the Roman authorities.[68] The city became notorious for the frequency and destructiveness of its riots. It is therefore unlikely to be a coincidence that in the later fifth century and subsequently riots became a recurring feature at Constantinople, Antioch, and Alexandria, and of the smaller cities of Egypt as described by John of Niciu. Moreover the fact that one of the factions was invariably courted by the emperor, together with the intense competition which existed between them, made it natural that the other faction would be supported by the opposition, or at least by rivals of those in power. So the partisanship of the factions brought the conflict between rivals for imperial power into every city where the factions were operating.

Scholars have looked for an explanation of the cohesion of the factions in terms of urban topography. Alan Cameron has provided strong arguments that the division between adherents of the Greens and adherents of the Blues was related to neither the administrative nor the geographical

[67] On post-curial city government, see Claude 1969: 114–39 and above, pp. 110–20.

[68] A. K. Bowman and D. Rathbone, 'Cities and administration in Roman Egypt', *JRS* 82 (1992), 107–27, esp. 114–19. N. Lewis, *Life in Egypt under Roman Rule* (Oxford, 1983), 198–202.

divisions of the city.[69] He has also shown that neither colour was consistently associated with particular issues or policies. We can however observe one area of consistency: xenophobia. In AD 512 the great religious riot at Constantinople had a definite anti-Syrian aspect,[70] and the Greens at Antioch were consistently anti-Jewish,[71] as the crowd of eighteenth-century London was regularly anti-Irish.[72] But, as Cameron has shown, neither of the factions had any consistent religious bias or allegiance, in spite of the fact that they operated in an environment fraught with religious controversy.[73] No doubt each faction as a rule simply proclaimed itself orthodox, leaving it to individuals to define for themselves what was orthodox and what heresy. The sources do not as a rule associate the factions with religious riots, which were often quite as serious as the riots of the hippodrome. Clergy and monks were after all the one section of society which could cause mayhem without outside help.[74]

Against the earlier scholars whose views he criticized, Alan Cameron was surely in the right. Since the publication of Cameron's book Charlotte Roueché has put forward a more subtle theory of the composition of at least part of the following of a faction, arguing that it was made up of the membership of certain organized groups that regularly occupied blocks of seats in the faction's sector of the auditorium. The seat-inscriptions in the stadium, and in the odeon at Aphrodisias—the city had no hippodrome—show that blocks of seats were occupied by respectively tanners, gardeners, gold-workers, Jews (and old Jews), and finally, and most significantly because of their prominence in faction-fighting, young men.[75] It could follow that the faction allegiance of these groups was determined by the position of their seats. Alternatively, and this is surely more likely, they had chosen to sit in a particular sector because they identified with the faction that sat there. It is moreover likely that a faction would draw fans from the district in which its headquarters were situated,[76] where it was certainly the largest employer, and where it probably performed administrative functions, like the collection of certain taxes.[77]

But on certain critical occasions the supporters of a faction were certainly not limited to those individuals who had chosen for whatever

[69] 1976: 24–44.
[70] Malalas 407.
[71] Malalas 389–90 (XV.15); 396 (XVI.6).
[72] Rudé 1964: 51–5.
[73] 1976: 126–53.
[74] P. Brown 1992: 148–50.
[75] C. M. Roueché 1993: 122–40, 153–6. On survival of youth organizations into 4th cent.: Lewin 1995*b*: 623–8.
[76] Alan Cameron 1976: 90–3.
[77] *P Lond* III.1028.

reason to have seats on their side of the theatre or hippodrome. In the riots that quite regularly resulted after one or the other factions had got into trouble with the authorities, huge crowds became involved on its side.[78] I suspect that what really rallied so many people on the factions' behalf was awareness that they had often publicized grievances in the past, and would be needed to do it again in the future. The riots themselves were not as a rule explicitly political. But the show-centred feuding of the factions could only achieve the scale and destructiveness it did, because the factions also had a political role, and could attract what was in effect political support, to achieve political ends.

One important long-term effect of the reform of the shows was to create a division in the cities which had not existed before, not between rich and poor, but between the fans of one faction and those of the other. Moreover Blues and Greens of one city felt solidarity with Blues and Greens all over the Empire. An emperor who supported one colour at Constantinople would support that colour everywhere.[79] A cause taken up by members of a faction in one city had a good chance of being taken up by members of the same faction in all the others, and riots in one city could easily spread to all the cities of the East.[80] Faction violence came in Empire-wide waves. Faction solidarity would tend to carry the divisions arising out of the politics of the capital into the politics of the provinces.

The factions had a political role. But Late Roman politics was not that of a modern political system. Late Antiquity was a world which lacked a forum where political issues could be formulated and discussed. There was no public debate in which the factions could have taken sides, even if they had been interested. That is why the political activities of the factions, such as they were, were less about issues than, for instance riots in eighteenth-century London or Paris.[81] The politics of the factions was principally concerned with praise or abuse of individuals. The Nika rioters did not complain about the level of taxation or issues of imperial policy, but they demanded, and obtained, the dismissal of the praetorian

[78] On the riots, see below, pp. 249–57.

[79] See above, p. 213.

[80] C. M. Roueché 1993: 155 points out that refugees arriving at Jerusalem AD 609/14 were designated not by their place of origin, but simply as Greens and Blues (Antiochus Strategius, tr. G. Garitte, *CSCO* Script. Arab. 29 (1974), 2); similarly Blue refugees at Rhodes (*Doctrina Jacobi nuper baptizati* V.20.15. Procopius *HA* XXIX.29–38), the case of Blues of Tarsus taken up by Blues at Constantinople. This Empire-wide solidarity was early enough for Justinian's encouragement of the Blues to produce troubles all over the Empire, *HA* VII.6–7. See also below, p. 254.

[81] The faction riots have most of the characteristics of riots in 18th-cent. London and Paris, as noted by Rudé 1964: 59–63, but there was nothing like the parliament of Paris which, according to Rudé, indoctrinated Parisians in the use of catchwords like 'citizen', 'nation', 'social contract' (ibid. 50).

prefect, the prefect of the city, and the *quaestor*.[82] It was a regular consequence of riots at Antioch that the count of the East was replaced, sometimes by a man who was an Antiochene by birth.[83] Our sources do not give us very much detail of the demands of the factions. That is surely because the sources focus on the riots and destruction. Routine acclamations, which represented the factions' staple activity, are scarcely recorded at all. But riots, which were reported, did not normally originate out of political protest, though they might acquire political objectives as they developed.[84]

If we want to learn what kinds of political demand were included in the factions' acclamations, we mainly depend on earlier evidence, especially the acclamations of the theatre claque at Antioch in the fourth century,[85] and of the demonstrators against bishop Ibas at Edessa.[86] These earlier demonstrations too had most often been directed at individuals. In times of food shortage there were protests against high prices, and attacks on the officials responsible for the market, or the bakers who charged too much for the staple food.[87]

Detailed evidence of demands voiced after the acclamations had been taken over by the factions is meagre, but not non-existent. In AD 515/16 at Alexandria faction fighting was interrupted, while the two factions joined forces to riot, in protest at a shortage of oil.[88] In AD 540 the Blues in Cilicia protested at requisitions ordered by the dux Marthanes.[89] Around the same time the Greens at Cyzicus murdered an unpopular bishop.[90] In AD 556 and 559 the factions at Constantinople were involved in protests over the price of bread.[91] Several faction riots started with attacks on a particular official, the prefect of the city at Constantinople,[92] or the count of the East at Antioch.[93] The factions might sometimes have had private reasons for their hostility to the official they attacked, but perhaps more often the man was widely unpopular because of his conduct in office. The factions often demanded that clemency should be shown to individuals sentenced in court. Mostly this was for the benefit of their own

82 Procopius I.24.7; *Chron. Pasch.* 621 (calling the *quaestor* mistakenly Rufinus); Malalas XVIII.475.

83 Malalas 389, 393, 396–8, 416–17.

84 So also in 18th-cent. London and Paris, see Rudé 1964: 61–2.

85 See Liebeschuetz 1972: 211–16.

86 See above, p. 106.

87 Liebeschuetz 1972: 278–80; cf. Alan Cameron 1976: 162–6.

88 Malalas 401, *De Insid.* 41 (169.1–7).

89 Proc. *HA* 28–38.

90 Proc. I.25.37–40.

91 Malalas 488 (XVIII.121).

92 Malalas 407 (XVI.19), 496 (XVIII.146).

93 Malalas 392–3 (AD 491); Malalas 476 (AD 522–3), all cities.

activists, but not always. The proconsul and *comes domesticorum* Phlegethius reminded the people of Ephesus that he had pardoned the people of Smyrna in response to their acclamations, we are not told what they had done wrong.[94]

So far I have stressed the formal aspect of the political activities of the factions which arose from their leadership of the regular ceremony of acclamation. But there is no sharp dividing line between a formal acclamation and spontaneous demonstration in the streets and indeed behaviour calculated to intimidate. There is no doubt that the factions practised intimidation and their victims ranged from governors and judges to private individuals. For though they might support the demands of others, they also ruthlessly pursued their own financial advantage. Paradoxically the factions were part of the established political system, but they also displayed many characteristics of gangsterism and organized crime (Procopius *HA* VII.30–42).

4. *The End of the Games*

The public spectacles were regularly attacked by the Church, chariot races because they attracted congregations away from church services,[95] theatricals because they aroused strong erotic emotions. They were criticized in innumerable sermons, again and again. So Chrysostom asks members of his congregation how they can hope to benefit by hearing the Gospel of St John in church, if they continue to visit the pageant of Satan that is the theatre to listen to harlots and effeminates (that is mimes who might be women and pantomimes who were men dancing both male and female roles) saying filthy things and doing worse.[96] People should think and talk about religion, and the state of their souls, not gossip about their neighbours' affairs, which are no concern of theirs. But gossip is much to be preferred to talk about players and dancers and charioteers, which defiles men's ears, and corrupts their souls. For as soon as someone utters the name of a dancer, immediately his soul pictures to itself his looks, his hair, his delicate clothing, and the person himself more effeminate than all. Somebody else introduces a harlot into the conversation, with her words, her attitudes and glances, her languishing looks . . . her painted eyelids . . . At that point the preacher turns on his hearers: 'Are you not aroused even by my description?'[97] Rather than attend the shows, members of Chrysostom's congregation are urged to visit the prison and

94 *Inscr. Eph.* 1352.
95 John Chrysostom, *C. ludos et theatra* 1–2 (*PG* 56.263–7).
96 John Chrysostom, *In Joh. Hom.1*, 6.
97 Ibid. 18 4, tr. P. Schaff in *Post Nicene Fathers*, 14.62.

the prisoners. He compares the effect on the soul of theatre-going and prison visiting. A man returning from the theatre is excited, burning with desire, one who has experienced the misery of the prisoners is calm and tranquil, filled with pity and compassion and aware of the inevitability of punishment for wrong-doing. Even the allure of a prostitute will leave such a man unmoved.[98] Chrysostom was only the most eloquent of innumerable preacher of the same message. But the shows continued,[99] perhaps not in all cities, and not in all cities to the same extent.[100] But where there was a large urban population there was also a need for mass entertainment, and besides there was really no alternative to the shows as a setting for ceremonies to bring home the reality, power, and benevolence of the emperor. Even so strongly Christian an emperor as Justinian had to legislate for the continuation of the games.[101] The shows only came to an end, together with large citizen populations, and many other features of classical city life, in the course of the seventh century.

The games ended much sooner in the West. Already by the end of the fourth century public entertainments in Italy had come to an end in all but a few towns.[102] The tradition of senatorial munificence was maintained above all at Rome and especially in the praetorian and consular games. Emperors occasionally gave games at Rome (where the factions continued to operate) or Ravenna, and the Ostrogothic king Theoderic continued the imperial tradition by supporting in one way or another the production of games at Rome,[103] at Milan and Pavia. But these games did not survive the Justinianic reconquest. In North Africa the tradition of the games continued more strongly and longer than in Italy.[104] The Vandal conquest did not put an end to it, certainly not at Carthage.[105] The priest Salvian writing his *De Gubernatione Dei* probably in Marseilles between AD 439 and 451 included a vigorous attack on the immorality of the games, but at the same time admitted that in most cities they were no longer held: to see a theatrical show a provincial would have to go to Rome or Ravenna.[106] Visigothic kings in Spain[107] and Frankish kings in

[98] Ibid. hom. 60, 4–5.

[99] Cf. Severus of Antioch (at Antioch as patriarch 512–18), *Cath. hom.* 26 (*PO* 36.541–57); C. A. Moss, 'Jacob of Serugh's homilies on the spectacles of the theatre', *Le Muséon*, 48 (1935), 87–112.

[100] Alan Cameron's list of places where there is evidence for factions in late Late Antiquity (1976: 314–17) does not mention many well-known cities. It is relatively abundant, including even small places, for Syria and Egypt, but much less so for Asia Minor and Greece. See also Humphrey 1986.

[101] Just. *Nov* 105.1 (AD 536).

[102] See Ward-Perkins 1984: 92–7.

[103] *Variae*, I.27; III.51.

[104] See Markus 1990: 107–23 on Augustine's attitude to the games.

[105] C. Courtois, *Les Vandales et l'Afrique* (Paris, 1955), 228 n. 5; Procopius, *Vandal Wars*, II.6.7. Stevens 1989: i. 152–78.

[106] *De Gub.* VI.8.39–44 (136–7); VI.9.42–50 (138–40); VII.1.6 (156) and Markus 1990: 171–3.

[107] e.g. s.a. 504 at Saragossa, *Chron Caes. Aug* in *Chron Min.* II.223: 'His consulibus Caesaraugustae

Gaul might occasionally organize chariot races or other spectacles, echoing the patronage of the hippodrome of the Roman emperors. But the games as a regular public entertainment did not survive in their kingdoms and theatres and arenas were demolished for building material, or adapted for new purposes. The West had neither the large urban populations that needed to be entertained nor the centralized monarchy which needed to impress distant populations with its reality and effectiveness. So the conditions, which preserved the games in the East far into the sixth century and beyond,[108] did not exist in the Western provinces which were in any case impoverished by the barbarian invasions. Needless to say the bishops who in so many respects took up the reins dropped by the derelict secular administration were not interested in reviving the games.

circus spectatus est'. King Sisebut (612–621) criticized bishop Eusebius of Tarraco for watching games (*PL* 80.370). Who organized these?; cf. also above, p. 91.

[108] Public theatricals ended after the 7th cent., private performances continued much longer, C. Mango, 'Daily life in Byzantium', *JÖB* 30/i (1981), 337–53.

PART II

A Society Transformed

7

Transformation of Greek Literary Culture under the Influence of Christianity

1. *Literary Culture in the Late Antique Cities of the East*

So far the book has been concerned with the transformation of the government of the classical city. This was a secular process, largely governed by worldly factors, above all the impact on cities of the Empire. But even so the process was not entirely secular: Christianization played a significant part. The office of bishop was as we have seen a quite unclassical phenomenon, and the rise of the bishop to pre-eminence in his city was part of the profound transformation not only in the administrative structure of the city, but in the way people looked upon their institutions and the duties to their fellow townsmen, that had been brought about by deepening Christianization. It is to exaggerate only a little to suggest that the Greco-Roman world abandoned the model of the citizen-state as presented in Aristotle's *Politics* or in Plato's *Laws*, to replace it by that of the people of Israel with its monarch and prophets and God-given laws.[1]

But the rise of the bishop was only one aspect of the radical cultural transformation brought about by the Christianization of society. A conspicuous feature of the Greco-Roman city was the high prestige of classical literary culture. The classical city was many things, but certainly not least among them, it was a centre of education. In it there were to be found teachers of various levels, from elementary teachers who taught the elements of literacy,[2] to grammarians,[3] who introduced boys to classical literature and the literary language based on it, and finally, though only in larger cities, sophists who taught the art of rhetoric. The traditional education dominated life. All public life, especially politics and law, was carried on in the literary language, learnt at school, which differed considerably from spoken Greek. Correspondence between the educated employed the literary language and gave them an opportunity to combine

[1] P. Brown 1992: 152–8.
[2] H. Harrauer and P. J. Sijpesteijn, *Neue Texte aus dem antiken Unterricht* (Vienna, 1985).
[3] Kaster 1988.

an artistic hobby with the exchange of information and social courtesy. Recitations of declamations by professional orators or gifted amateurs provided entertainment for social occasions comparable to recitals of classical music in our days. Higher literacy marked out the member of the upper class. Rhetorical schooling gave a common interest, a world of shared literary experience, and a treasury of generally understood examples and allusions to all who had undergone it. In this way it bound together not only the leading group of each city, but also the whole administrative class of the Empire. For the classical ideal and the education based on it were the same all over the Empire, even if its language was Greek in the East and Latin in the West.[4]

The depth of the higher literacy is difficult to quantify. It is clear that nearly all who played a part in public life whether as city councillors or advocates or members of the higher grades of the imperial civil service were likely to have received at least the full course of a grammarian, so too in all likelihood most bishops. Sons of leading curial families and of higher civil servants and senators will have had the full rhetorical education up to the age of 18. 'Higher education' beyond this, perhaps at a major centre of education such as Athens or Alexandria, was taken by young men hoping to become sophists themselves, or seeking a specialized qualification in Roman law to improve their prospects of advancement in the imperial administration. In the Late Roman world, as under the Earlier Empire, it was literary education more than origin that distinguished the gentleman, the person thought worthy of posts of distinction in city or Empire. It was the religion of rhetoric which united the ruling groups of the Empire. So a literary education was sought by everyone with ambition or ambitious parents. The number of the merely literate will certainly have been much greater than of those who had acquired higher literacy.[5] But the cultural values of the literary culture were to some extent shared also by those who had little education, and even the illiterate. For the annual round of festivals, which marked out the year and proclaimed the seasons, generally honoured the gods of mythology, while the spectacles in the theatre, the vastly popular performances of mimes and pantomimes, enacted pagan myths. The shows were often attacked on grounds of their supposed immorality, they could however be defended as cultural experiences.

[4] A book like Kaster's on late sophists would be useful. Liebeschuetz 1991: 858–911. On rhetoric as a guide to conduct, see the sensitive comments of P. Brown 1992: esp. 41–58. On the contents and purpose of rhetorical education, still see Marrou 1938 and 1955.

[5] Literacy is impossible to quantify: Harris 1989 argues that under the Later Empire the prevalence of literacy declined from an already low level. See also Humphrey 1991; Bowman and Woolf 1991: 126–215, essays by R. Lane Fox, S. P. Brock, C. M. Kelly, P. Heather, and Averil Cameron. Various definitions of literacy: Kaster 1988: 35–44.

The entire literary culture was of course based on texts which assumed the reality of the pagan gods, and took for granted that their worship was the foundation of all social life. The advance of Christianity, first to be the religion of the emperor, then that of the state, was incompatible with the 'religion of rhetoric'. But in fact the two coexisted quite happily for a long time. This is not really surprising. A whole complex of cultural values could not and did not change overnight when Constantine was converted to Christianity. The Church did not even attempt to replace the traditional education and the literary values it upheld. It excluded allusions to pagan mythology from religious writings, but it gave preferment to clerics who had received a literary education. The Fathers of the Church, among the Greeks Basil, Gregory of Nyssa, Gregory of Nazianzus, and John Chrysostom, and Augustine and Jerome among the Latins, had got all they possibly could out of the traditional schools, and were supreme masters of rhetorical style. But not only the great names. For instance an anonymous cleric of the little city of Seleucia in Isauria around AD 470 wrote *The Life and Miracles of St Thecla*, the mythical friend of St Paul, whose tomb made the town into a famous centre of pilgrimage. It was a saint's town and the book was to publicize the sanctity and effectiveness of the saint. But the pious author shows that he was quite conscious of writing in the tradition of Thucydides and Herodotus, and his portrait of Thecla shows her to be not only an uncompromising enemy of local pagan gods, but also a decided friend of traditional education, whose protagonists benefited from positive discrimination in the matter of miracles.[6] The Christianization of culture, if you like the triumph of the Bible over Homer, was a process drawn out over more than two centuries. In the East Hellenism, that is the traditions of secular culture based on classical and necessarily pagan literature, retained its high prestige and its function as a cement of society for something like two centuries. It was only in the course of the sixth century that what had been a pluralistic society became monolithically Christian.[7]

It is quite clear that in the first two centuries of the Christian Empire the homes of the well-to-do, pagan or Christian alike, might still contain many objects displaying[8] images from mythology, whether in the form of sculpture,[9] mosaic floors, or silverware.[10] It is not yet possible to say

[6] Dagron 1978; discussion of authorship, ibid. 13–19.

[7] Perceptively described by Markus 1990.

[8] Elsner 1998—though there seem to have been considerably fewer objects carrying such images than in the Early Empire.

[9] N. Hannestad, *Tradition in Late Antique Sculpture* (Aarhus, 1994). D. M. Brinkerhoff, *A Collection of Sculpture in Classical and Early Christian Antioch* (New York, 1970).

[10] e.g. M. M. Mango, 'Der Sevso-Schatzfund', *Antike Welt*, 21 (1990), 70–88; also *JRA* suppl. 12.1 (1994).

whether the relative popularity of different themes had changed significantly compared with pre-Christian times. Hunting pictures remained extremely popular. Other relatively common themes are Hippolytus and Phaedra,[11] Marsyas and Apollo,[12] and the birth and early life of Achilles.[13] It is usually very difficult to tell whether or not the owner of such objects was a pagan or a Christian. While a display of Christian imagery presumably identifies the owner of a house as a Christian, the presence of the representation of a god or goddess is certainly not enough to stamp the owner as a pagan. Something more is needed.

For instance a combination of themes may suggest that a definite statement is being made to one who can decode the message. The process is described in an essay of Procopius of Gaza, a description of certain paintings in a public building at Gaza painted between AD 495 and 535, which is followed by an exposition of the moral that can be drawn from them.[14] The main themes of the paintings are Phaedra falling in love with Hippolytus, Hippolytus rejecting the advances of Phaedra, Ariadne helping Theseus to kill the Minotaur, and Aphrodite saving Paris from being killed by Menelaus. The pictures have the erotic appeal of all love stories, but read at another level they constitute a warning of the danger of sexual passion. The stories illustrate the fatal power of love, which in each case had disastrous consequences for one or both the persons under its influence. The stories involve a pagan goddess, but there is nothing in the pictures that a Christian could possibly object to, and the moral is one which a Christian would have to applaud. Procopius the author of this description was indeed a Christian who wrote commentaries on the Old Testament.

The problem of how to interpret mythological imagery has arisen in a particularly intriguing form over some late Roman mosaics discovered during the last decades. One of the most striking of recent finds is a floor of the so-called house of Aion at Nea Paphos in Cyprus, dating perhaps from around AD 350. The floor is composed of six separate scenes. They represent in order: (1) Leda and the swan;[15] (2) preparations for the first bath of Dionysus;[16] (3 and 4) Cassiopeia is awarded the crown in a

[11] *LIGMC* VI.2.445–64, summarized 463 (de Bellefonds), cf. ill., p. 227.

[12] *LIGMC* VI.2.366–78 (A. Weiss).

[13] *LIGMC* I.58–65 (A. Kossatz-Deissmann), birth and first bath (nos. 1–4) only in Late Antiquity.

[14] Friedländer 1939.

[15] Could this be read allegorically? J. Lanzière, 'Le Mythe de Léda dans l'art copte', *Bulletin de la société d'archéologie copte*, 2 (1936), 36–46 points out a Coptic text explaining that Leda and the swan represent Anna the mother of the Virgin becoming pregnant through a dove settling in her lap. H. Torp, 'Leda Christiana', *Acta ad Archaeologiam et Artium Historiam Pertinentia*, 4 (1969), 101–13 argues that most of the quite abundant mythological sculpture found in 'Coptic' Egypt, i.e. dating from roughly our period, was associated with tombs.

[16] Cf. E. M. Meyers, E. Netzer, C. L. Meyers, 'Artistry in stone: The mosaics of ancient Sepphoris', *Biblical Archaeologist*, 50 (1987), 223–31 for a comparable image.

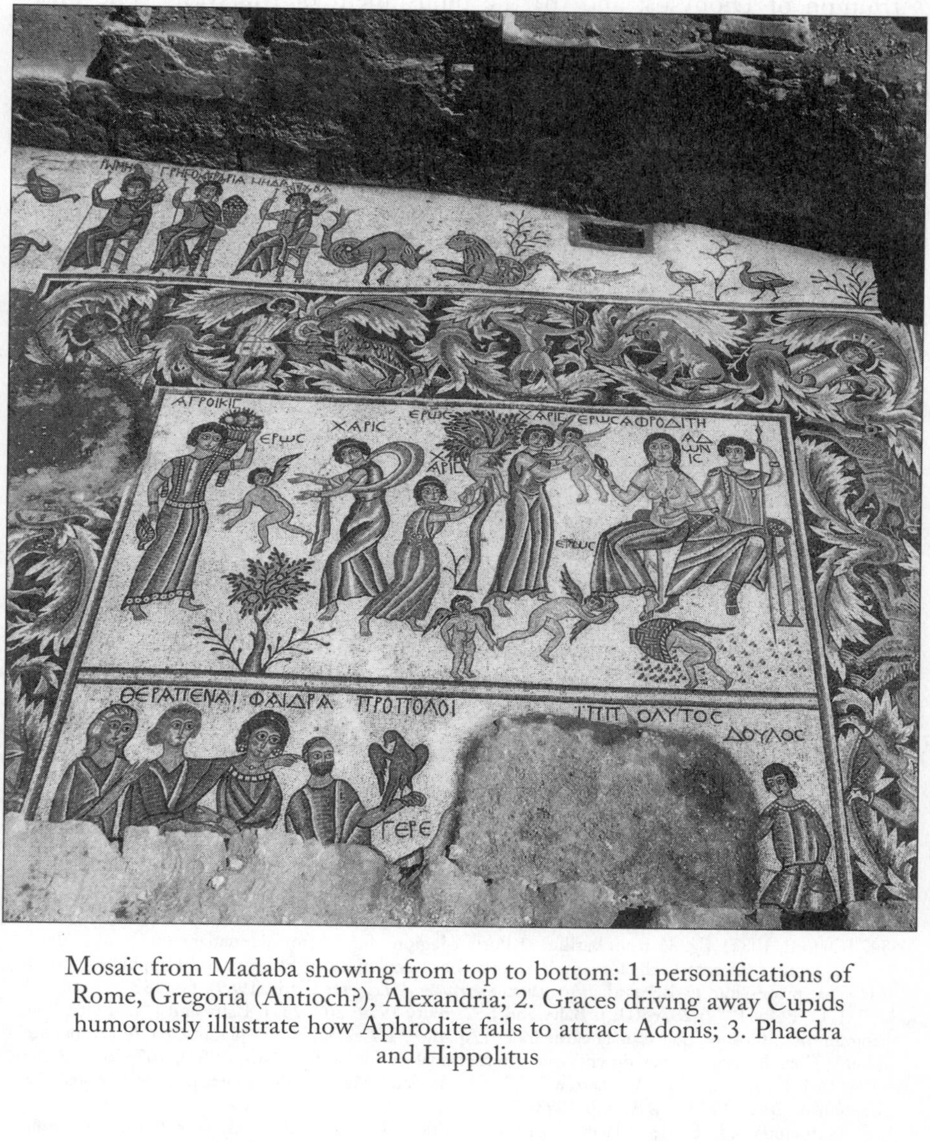

Mosaic from Madaba showing from top to bottom: 1. personifications of Rome, Gregoria (Antioch?), Alexandria; 2. Graces driving away Cupids humorously illustrate how Aphrodite fails to attract Adonis; 3. Phaedra and Hippolitus

beauty competition with the nymphs of the sea, the nereids; (5) the triumph of Dionysus; and (6) the punishment of Marsyas.[17] The first point is that the mosaics are self-sufficient. They do not need interpretation. Taken at face value they provide a satisfactory scheme of decoration.[18] No moral is forced on the viewer. There is nothing solemn about the presentation. Both the grouping and the subject-matter of the mosaics nevertheless encourages the viewer to search for deeper meanings. First, the middle register, whose two mosaics really form a single scene, is the most conspicuous, and therefore surely the key to the whole. What is represented is the myth of Cassiopeia, but it is represented provocatively with a reversal of the central role. Instead of being punished—because she had boasted that she was more beautiful than all the nereids (which is usual version of the story)—Cassiopeia is awarded a crown. This suggests that some philosophical reinterpretation is being suggested.

This is confirmed by the fact that the unusual feature of this version, that Cassiopeia is rewarded instead of punished, is also found in a sequence of mosaics at Apamea in Syria, in a sequence of mosaics that seem in some way related to philosophy. The group has been convincingly interpreted by the Baltys.[19] Most significantly, a mosaic of Socrates sitting among six sages of Greece looks like a pagan parallel to Jesus and his disciples. If this is so, it becomes possible that a mosaic in the same house showing Odysseus coming home to Penelope, is a philosophical allegory, representing—as the Baltys argue on the basis of literary parallels—Odysseus' achievement of philosophic calm after overcoming the physical and mental upheavals of his earthly existence, or at a more general level, the return of the soul to its true home.[20] The Baltys go on to argue that the mosaic of Cassiopeia throwing off her mantle parallels that of the homecoming of Odysseus, and represents allegorically the soul freeing itself from material entanglements.[21] They may be right. If so, perhaps Cassiopeia's triumph at Nea Paphos also represents the triumph of a soul

[17] Cf. P. B. Rawson, *The Myth of Marsyas in the Roman Visual Arts: An Iconographic Study*, BAR Int 347 (Oxford, 1987), fig. 33 from basilica at Porta Magiore, fig. 34 from Herculaneum.

[18] Epigram (4th cent.) calls for simple enjoyment of depictions of Phaedra and Hippolytus and of a Bacchic procession: E. Bernard, *Inscriptions métriques de l'Égypte* (Paris, 1969), no. 122.

[19] J. C. Balty 1972: 267–304; J. Balty and J. C. Balty 1974: 267–78. J. Balty and J. C. Balty, 'Un programme philosophique sous la cathédrale d'Apamée: L'Ensemble néo-platonicien de l'empereur Julien', *Texte et image*, Actes du colloque international de Chantilly (Paris, 1984), 167–76. J. Balty 1995: 291–7. See also W. A. Daszewski, 'Le Mystérieux Message des mosaïques de Paphos', *Le Monde de la Bible*, 112 (July/August 1998), 30–5.

[20] Numenius, ed. É. des Places (Paris: Coll. Budé, 1973), fr. 33: Odysseus figures the soul passing through successive generations on its way to home and peace, cited by Porphyry, *De Antr. Nymph.* 34–5: alluded to by Plotinus *Enn.* V.9.1; Porph. *V. Plot.* 22.11, 25–6. Proclus *In Parm.* p. 1025.32.

[21] Philosophical allegorization of stripping off of clothes: Plotinus *Enn.* I.6.7.5–7, cf. Proclus *In Alcib.* 63 (18); Porphyry *De Antr. Nymph.* 35; Proclus *In Cratylum*, 155.

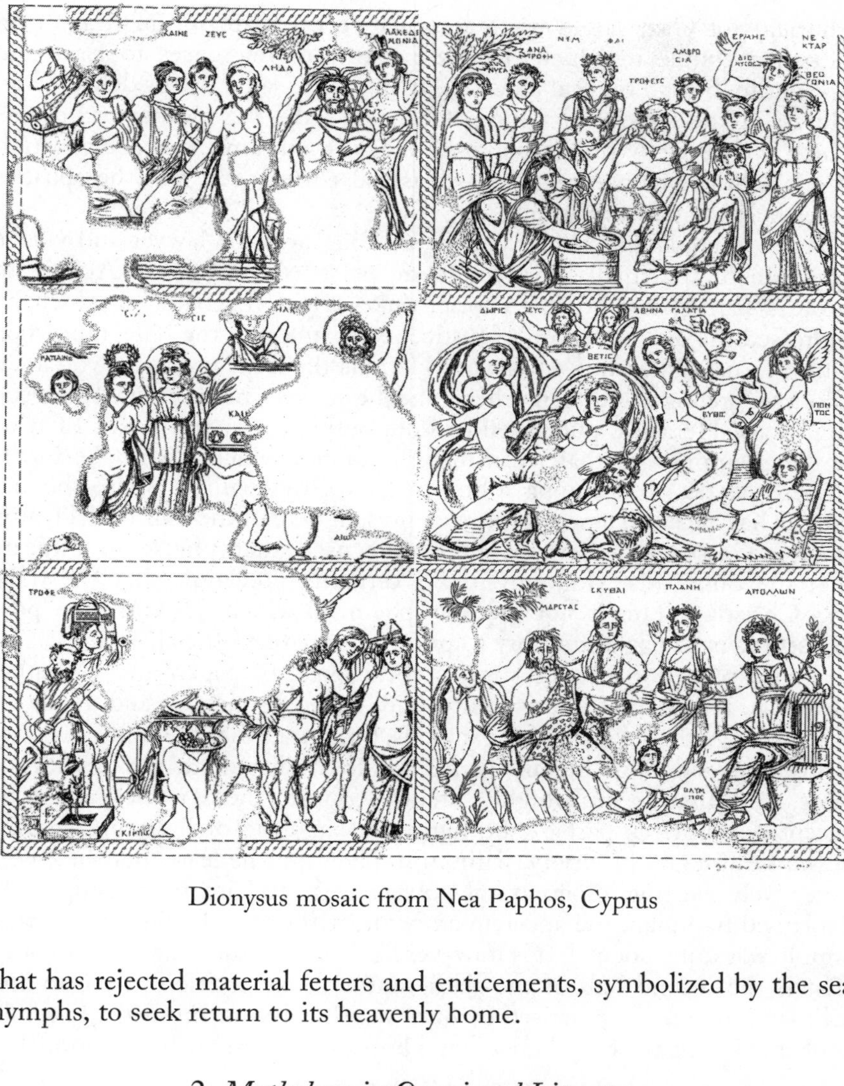

Dionysus mosaic from Nea Paphos, Cyprus

that has rejected material fetters and enticements, symbolized by the sea nymphs, to seek return to its heavenly home.

2. *Mythology in Occasional Literature*

It was not only in the visual arts that mythology continued to flourish under the Christian emperors. Formal orations and recitals of poetry still were essential components of ceremonies of every kind: at receptions of officials, at dedications of secular buildings, at birthdays, funerals, and especially weddings; and the imagery of these orations and poems long remained surprisingly pagan. Even in the first half of the sixth century

Choricius of Gaza could write a speech to celebrate the marriage of a Christian couple in which there are plenty of references to Eros and Aphrodite, but no biblical allusions at all.[22] The same orator delivered an address at the funeral of a pious Christian lady, the mother of bishops which is a perfectly traditional *consolatio*, without any explicit invocation of the Christian hope to mar its classical correctness. But the spirit is nevertheless totally Christian.

A few years later, around AD 573–6, Dioscorus the lawyer and village headman of the small Egyptian town, or strictly village, of Aphrodito wrote a panegyrical poem to John, duke of the Thebaid, in which he addressed the official as 'son of Justice . . . Ammon of the Nile, renowned John . . . new Phaethon of Egypt'. He tells the new governor: 'you are a Dionysus giving wine to revellers' and he makes the request: 'I beseech you, brave Heracles, put an end to our sufferings at the hands of tribe of the Blemmyes so that I can find the money which I will take to the emperor as tax.' But among John's praiseworthy qualities is also the fact that he has 'received as a gift the ever-present help of the unmixed Trinity, single in essence'.[23] Perhaps Dioscorus used that phrase to indicate that the duke was Monophysite. It certainly proclaims that the duke was Christian. This is not the only poem, in which the Christian poet Dioscorus used pagan imagery to praise a Christian official.[24]

The explanation of this curious coexistence of pagan and Christian elements is not that Christianity had become tolerant and ready to acknowledge the divinity of pagan gods, but rather that the traditional but living convention of literary genre required allusion to the traditional gods, and that in this highly literary context these names could be accepted simply as part of the figurative language of literature, a concession to literary propriety, without implying in the least that they were objectively existing supernatural powers with a claim to worship.[25] As explained by Julian, the apostate emperor, without such allusions a poem simply was not a poem.[26] It is however likely that at the time of Dioscorus, that is the second half of the sixth century, juxtaposition of pagan and Christian themes as practised by him was already anachronistic. It would probably have been found unacceptable even at Oxyrhynchus, around 120

[22] Choricius, *Opera*, ed. R. Foerster (Stuttgart, 1939), *Or.* VII, Epitaphius for Maria, mother of bishops; *Or.* V and VI, *Epithalamia*.

[23] MacCoull 1988: H3, pp. 137–46. Cf. also H6, pp. 63–6; H5, pp. 91–6. On these poems, see Kuehn 1995.

[24] MacCoull 1998: H2, pp. 134–6; H.19, p. 107.

[25] This applied even more to visual arts, e.g. F. Zayadine, 'Peintures et mosaïques mythologiques en Jordanie', in L. Kahil and C. Augé (eds.), *Iconographie Classique et Identités Régionales*, Bull. Corr. Hell. Suppl. 14 (Paris, 1986), 406–32, esp. 431 a bare-breasted Thetis represents the sea on a church floor.

[26] Julian, *Or.* VII, 'To the cynic Heracleios', 207B–C.

miles further south. In the capital of Constantinople the emperor was by now being praised in entirely Christian terms, even in writings governed by the traditional conventions of high literature.[27]

3. *The Late Epic: The* Dionysiaca *of Nonnus*

As classical literature began with the epic poems of Homer, so it continued with each period giving rise to its epics, which expressed the spirit of the age and displayed their authors' skill at handling of the Homeric genre. If any single literary form could be said to have embodied the essence of classical culture, the epic was it. Epic poems generally treated mythological themes and their plots almost by definition involved intervention by the Olympian gods. So the arrival of Christianity did produce a problem, but epic poetry nevertheless continued to be written. In fact the longest of all surviving epics the *Dionysiaca*, was composed by the Egyptian poet Nonnus at Alexandria around the middle of the fifth century, perhaps a generation after the composition of the *Life and Miracles of St Thecla*.[28]

This poem tells the story of the life and triumph of the god Dionysus, above all his military victories in India, and his subsequent triumphal progress through the territories of the cities of the Near East. He tells it in forty-eight books, quite explicitly the *Iliad* of Dionysus followed by his *Odyssey*. From beginning to end the poem proclaims the irresistible power of Dionysus. There is no hint—or at least no explicit indication—that the poet was writing in a Christian environment in which traditional pagan worship was illegal, and pagans, even pagans at Berytus, liable to suffer sudden bursts of persecution.[29] It is not surprising that the poem has been taken as evidence for the continued strength of paganism in the eastern provinces of the Roman Empire. Bowersock has argued that Nonnus has used the form of the Homeric epic to present an up-to-date version of paganism, which has been modified by the influence of Christianity. He describes Nonnus' Dionysus as a polytheist Christ.[30]

But does the glorification of Dionysus and his fellows really mean that the epic is a religious poem in the sense that the author is actually presenting Dionysus as an all powerful saviour god, and that his audience

[27] Mary Whitby 1985: 215–28; Macrides and Magdalino 1988: 47–82.

[28] Text, introductions, and notes of the edition supervised by F. Vian, *Nonnos de Panopolis: Les Dionysiaques* (Paris: Les Belles Lettres, in progress), represent a very important collective contribution to our understanding of Nonnus. Vol. i (1976), ed. F. Vian; vol. ii (1976), ed. P. Chuvin; vol. iv (1985), ed. G. Chrétien; vol. vi (1992), ed. J. Gerbeau and F. Vian; vol. vii (1994), ed. B. Gerlaud; vol. viii (1994), ed. N. Hopkinson; vol. ix (1990), ed. F. Vian. Discussion of date: vol. i, p. ix.

[29] Zacharias Scholasticus, *Vie de Sévère*, ed. and tr. M.-A. Kugener, *PO* 2.57–75.

[30] Bowersock 1990: 41–2.

would have recognized the poem as advocating the traditional religion with Dionysus as its supreme deity? The ambiguity of the genre means that there can never be a certain answer to that question. But the way Dionysus is presented makes it difficult to take the religion of the poem at face value. It was a fundamental development of Late Antiquity that religion had become moralized. Gods were thought of as moral beings, and they were believed to demand above all moral behaviour from their worshippers. The moralizing of divinity was as marked in late paganism as in Christianity.[31] Moreover Late Roman morality, whether Christian or pagan, placed great value on sexual restraint, on the need for man's soul to achieve the greatest possible degree of control over the body. Dionysus as represented by Nonnus is the opposite of this. His principal recreation is to seduce virgins who happen to take his fancy, without showing the slightest consideration for their feelings or future well-being. In fact the poem focuses on the kind of behaviour which had been exploited by Christian apologists to discredit the ancient worship by demonstrating that the recipients of the worship were not gods but devils. Nonnus must have been tiresomely familiar with this form of attack, for the formidable and fanatical abbot Shenute had been preaching it for decades from his headquarters in the White monastery on the opposite bank of the Nile from Nonnus' home-town Panopolis.[32]

The polemic of Shenute and his like was effective precisely because pagans agreed with its premiss: that the behaviour of gods in mythology was frequently disgraceful and incompatible with divinity. That is why serious pagans felt the need to allegorize such stories; but not Nonnus, who might well have been a Christian.[33]

In fact it is a mistake to interpret the *Dionysiaca* as primarily a religious poem. What it undoubtedly is, is a very learned poem. Nonnus certainly was an extraordinarily learned poet, who has woven into the fabric of his epic an enormous number of allusions to a very wide range of earlier writings. The structure and language of the epic are of course based on Homer.[34] Homeric episodes, including the theomachia, the shield of Achilles, the catalogues of Greeks and Trojans, the funeral games, the seduction of Zeus by Hera, Achilles battle with the river Scamander, and

[31] Aug. *Ep.* 91 *CSEL* XXXIV.2.430: Ita vero in templis populis congregatis recitari huiuscemodi salubres interpretationes heri et nudiustertius audivimus.

[32] See now the vivid account of van der Vliet 1993: 99–130. Perhaps significantly Dionysus seems not to have been one of the gods explicitly attacked by Shenute.

[33] Proof that Nonnus was, or became, a Christian has been seen in the paraphrase of St John's Gospel, written in his style, and attributed to him, though L. F. Sherry argues plausibly that its author was a later poet influenced by Nonnus (L. F. Sherry, 'The paraphrase of St John attributed to Nonnus', *Byzantion*, 66 (1996), 409–30).

[34] N. Hopkinson, 'Homeric episodes in Nonnus', in Hopkinson 1994: 9–42.

the death of Hector reappear transformed but obviously intended to be recognized in Nonnus' poem. There are allusions to Hesiodic situations too, and also to later poetry, notably Euripides' *Bacchae*. Numerous passages in Nonnus can be seen as variations on themes by Hellenistic poets such as Callimachus, Moschus, and Apollonius.[35] There are likely to be very many more allusions which we cannot recognize because the model has not survived. Nonnus also made use of epics of the imperial period: the lost *Bassarica* in 18 books of one Dionysios may well have been the source of much detailed incident. The '*Heroicae Theogamiae*', an encyclopaedic mythological poem in no less than 60 books which Pisander of Laranda wrote in the reign of Alexander Severus may have given Nonnus the idea of organizing a collection of myths into a history—or rather prehistory—of the world.[36] The account of Dionysus' campaign against the Indians around lake Nicaea and in the neighbourhood of Antioch seems to mirror that of the emperor Septimius Severus against the usurper Pescennius Niger, and may well go back to a passage in Pisander's poem, praising Septimius Severus in the guise of Dionysus.[37] Nonnus alludes not only to earlier writers, but also to commentators on the writers, including commentators who interpreted myths in terms of philosophy or natural phenomena. He also seems to have incorporated the myths of a great many localities in Asia Minor and Syria.[38]

The poet handles his material very much in the spirit of the ancient novel, and surely wanted it to be read very much like a novel.[39] There is a great variety of treatment, with much literary parody, and altogether a great deal of humour. There are pleasing descriptions of natural scenery and also a good deal of straightforward sexual titillation. The poem in many ways recalls Ovid's *Metamorphoses*. Attempts to prove that Nonnus has imitated particular passages of Ovid[40] have been far from conclusive, but the general kinship in spirit remains intriguing. One might compare the resemblance of Musaeus' *Hero and Leander* to Ovid's treatment of the same theme. It appears that prior to Musaeus the story of Hero and

[35] A. Hollis, 'Nonnus and Hellenistic poetry', in Hopkinson 1994: 43–62.

[36] Macrobius, *Sat.* V.24: Pisander . . . beginning with marriage of Jupiter and Juno, has brought within the compass of a single sequence of events all the history of the world down to its author's own day, . . . among other stories telling . . . the destruction of Troy. On this, see Vian's introduction to vol. i of his edition of Nonnus, p. xliv and R. Keydell, 'Die Dichter mit Namen Peisandros', *Hermes*, 70 (1935), 301–11; *RE* XIX.1 (1936) 145–6. Nonnus traces the history of the world but only to the end of the earthly presence of Dionysus. *Theogamiae* involving Dionysus are extremely prominent.

[37] P. Chuvin, 'Local traditions and classical mythology in the Dionysiaca', in Hopkinson 1994: 167–76, esp. 173.

[38] Chuvin 1991; Keydell 1961.

[39] Vian, vol. i, pp. xlviii–xlix.

[40] J. Braune, *Nonnus und Ovid*, Greifswälder Beiträge zur Literatur und Stilforschung 11 (Greifswald, 1935), reviewed by R. Keydell, *Gnomon*, 11 (1935), 597–605.

Leander has only come down to us in Latin authors.[41] This suggests that literary men of fifth- and sixth-century Egypt were more familiar with Latin literature than one might imagine.[42]

Nonnus is surely as far from being a religious writer as Ovid. When he composed his *Dionysiaca* he clearly set out to display his close familiarity with classical literature, and his skill in writing in different modes. He was writing for readers who had the education and sophistication to appreciate his particular skills. A principal aim of Nonnus, as of the authors of ancient novels, was surely to give readers the pleasure of recognizing as many as possible of the vast number of literary allusions—even occasionally to Christian writings[43]—embodied in the text. If the poet has a message, it is to celebrate the ancient literature which he has gathered together in his own way into a kind of encyclopaedia. His text is not committed to any doctrine, religious or otherwise. The poem illustrates the long survival in the East of the traditional autonomy of secular literature.

Nonnus' writing celebrates a venerable tradition, but his point of view inevitably reflects the concerns of his own time. Chuvin has shown that a great deal of Nonnus' mythological and topographical material must ultimately be derived from civic traditions. An interest in local cultural antiquities was characteristic of the age. In the East the writing of *patria*, seems to have been particularly popular in the fifth and sixth centuries, and to have shaped a literary convention which can be traced deep into the Byzantine middle ages. Of most of these writings we know little more than that they existed. For instance Christodorus of Coptos wrote *patria* of Nacle, Miletus, Tralles, and Aphrodisias, and at great length of Constantinople. He also wrote *Lydiaca*. A certain Claudian, who is probably not identical with the famous Latin poet, wrote *patria* of Nicaea, Tarsus, Anazarbus, and Berytus.[44] None of these poems has survived. But it has been plausibly argued that the development of the genre can be reconstructed from the extensive sections of the Chronicle of John Malalas dealing with the history of Antioch and its monuments,[45] from

41 Musaeus, *Hero and Leander*, ed. Th. Gelzer, Loeb library (London, 1975). See Gelzer's discussion of different versions of the story (ibid. 304).

42 Cf. Krüger 1990: 227–45, a survey of survival of classical literature per century. Note the relative frequency of Latin texts from 6th cent. See also I. Martlew, 'The reading of Paul the Silentiary', in P. Allen and E. Jeffreys (eds.), *The Sixth Century End or Beginning?* (Brisbane, 1996), 105–111, esp. 108–10.

43 J. Golega, *Studien über die Evangeliendichtung des Nonnus* (Breslau, 1930), 68–74. III.425 ff., VII.366–8, VIII.27 ff., IX.72 allude to the salutations of Mary or Elisabeth (*Luc.* I.28, 42), unmistakeably pointing to a parallel between the birth of Jesus and Dionysus.

44 *PLRE* II s.v. Chrystodorus, Claudianus 4; Bowersock 1990: 68; Dagron 1984*a*: 11 and *passim*, about the patriographic traditions of Constantinople. More names in A. Moffatt, 'A record of buildings and monuments', in Jeffreys *et al.* 1990: 87–109, on p. 97 n. 3.

45 E. Jeffreys, M. Jeffreys, R. Scott, A. Moffatt *et al.*, *The Chronicle of John Malalas: A Translation*, Byzantina Australiensia 4 (1986). On sources of Malalas, see E. Jeffreys, 'Malalas' sources', in Jeffreys

fragments of the sixth-century *patria* of Constantinople of Hesychius Illustris, and from Constantinopolitan 'patriographies' of the eighth century and later.[46] This literature was as far as we can see quite unpolitical. Its emphasis was on foundation legends and on the origins of customs, prominent buildings, and monuments. Its scope did not extend to the accurate reconstruction of civic history and politics. Much of Nonnus' antiquarian material must derive directly or indirectly from this literature. In any case the epic reflects the same antiquarian but not strictly historical interest.[47]

For Nonnus' interest in cities is entirely cultural and bookish. Cities are of interest to him as part of traditional lore. Tyre and Berytus apart, he ignores the actual situation and appearance of cities. He is not at all interested in cities as political communities, or indeed as institutions without which the traditional culture, which is the covert theme of his poem, could not have come into existence, much less been transmitted from generation to generation.

There is an abundance of city-names in the catalogue of Dionysus' army, as there must be since it is modelled on the catalogue of Greeks.[48] But in the main narrative of the campaign there are few names of cities. That many legends alluded to by Nonnus were in fact associated with particular cities is something that Chuvin has had to deduce from topographical details, mythological characters, and gods mentioned in the narrative. It is true that the periphrastic avoidance of proper names is a regular feature of later Greek literature, but with Nonnus it is not the case that he merely obscures the identity of cities by using periphrases: as a rule Nonnus gives no hint that anything like a city existed in the locality which he happened to be describing—or indeed that a city would arise in that place in the future.[49] It was certainly not part of his poetic design to foreshadow the future of the great cities of Asia Minor and Syria.

There are two exceptions to this: Tyre and Berytus, the only cities whose sites are described and which are individualized.[50] Nonnus gives a

et al. 1990: 167–216. On monuments, Ann Moffatt, 'A record of buildings and monuments', in Jeffreys *et al.* 1990: 87–109.

[46] Dagron 1984*a*: 23–6 on Hesychius, also *PLRE* II, s.v. Hesychius 'Illustris' 14, p. 555. Averil Cameron and Herrin 1984.

[47] On the differences between antiquarian and historical interest in antiquity and in more recent times, see A. Momigliano, *The Classical Foundations of Modern Historiography* (Berkeley, 1990), 54–79. But the antiquarian tradition represented by the *patria* was not concerned to separate legend from historical fact.

[48] *Iliad* II.484 ff.

[49] Of course Nonnus' epic is set in 'prehistory', antedating the historical foundation of the actual cities, but this difficulty did not stop other classical writers, and it did not stop Nonnus when he came to write about Berytus and Tyre.

[50] P. Chuvin, 'Local tradition and classical mythology', in Hopkinson 1994: 167–76, p. 171 suggests that Tyre and Berytus were given special treatment because they kept faith to a much greater

description of the site of Tyre which might be based on eyewitness. He goes on to tell a fantastic tale of how the site of the city was revealed to the founders by two floating rocks: an olive tree grew on one of the rocks and an eagle perched on the tree. The tree was on fire, but like the burning bush in Exodus the fire did not consume it. The story reads like an extraordinary invention, but the evidence of Tyrian coin and of a relief proves beyond doubt that Nonnus has related a genuine legend about the origin of the principal cult of Tyre.[51] The reason why Tyre was given this special treatment was surely the fact that Dionysus was the grandson of Cadmus king of Tyre.

The account of the origins of Berytus is much longer and more elaborate than that of Tyre. One reason for this is that it has given Nonnus the opportunity to write a long humorous account of the contest between Dionysus and Poseidon for the hand of its eponymous founder, the nymph Beroe, daughter of Aphrodite, and subsequently consort of the victorious Poseidon.[52] But the real claim to fame of Berytus is its law school, by virtue of which the city 'exercises jurisdiction over land and sea and fortifies the towns of the world with an unshakeable wall of law'.[53] But these two cities are the exception which prove the rule. In the case of other cities of Asia Minor, though Nonnus may allude to their myths, he shows no interest whatsoever in the cities themselves. The material he used happened to be grouped around cities, but Nonnus separates it from the cities, and uses it for its value as narrative, not out of consideration for local patriotism.[54] His attitude is very different from that of Greek literary men of earlier periods, for whom life in a city community was the essential precondition for the Greek way of life, and the Roman Empire no more than a confederation of city states, whose duty it was to ensure the well-being of the individual cities.[55] Nonnus' lack of interest in cities as cities reflects the weakening of political life of the cities, and a fading of the sense of citizenship, the consciousness of being members of a political community, which was a strong feature of later Late Antiquity.

extent with their local cults. This cannot be disproved. But the aspect of Berytus that Nonnus has underlined is its law school, the only contemporary secular institution to be mentioned in the immensely long poem. Perhaps Nonnus had studied there, and wished to express gratitude to his alma mater. Tyre was the home of the family of Dionysus' mother. Athens and Aphrodisias were at least as loyal to the traditional religion. Yet Nonnus has not included their foundation myths.

[51] *Dionysiaca* XL.466–500; G. F. Hill, *Catalogue of Greek Coins of Phoenicia* (London, 1910), 281, nr 429–30; E. Will, 'Au sanctuaire d'Héraclès à Tyr', *Berytus*, 10 (1952/3), 1–12, pl. 1. W. Fauth, *Helios Megistos, zur synkretistischen Theologie der Spätantike* (Leiden, 1995), 167–9.

[52] Nonnus XLII.521, XLIII.384.

[53] Ibid. XLI.395 ff.

[54] Otherwise Chuvin 1991: 320: '. . . complaisance pour un patriotisme local alimenté par les traditions païennes'.

[55] See esp. 'Libanius' oration in praise of Antioch (*Or.*XI), translated with introduction and commentary by Glanville Downey, *Proceedings American Philosophical Society*, 103.5 (1959), 652–86.

Nonnus was culturally a Greek, and his poem is a glorification of Greek culture. But it is significant that Nonnus was not concerned to trace its origin to geographical Greece. Of the Greek cities Thebes,[56] Argos, Athens, and Sparta are named and some fairly long mythological narratives are associated with them. This was unavoidable since important episodes of the myth of Dionysus happened there. But none of these cities is praised for itself, nor is a glorious future forecast for any of them. I cannot see that Athens is singled out as the mother of civilization.[57] None of the cities of Greece is praised in the way Tyre and Berytus are praised. Indeed since the bulk of the epic is concerned with Dionysus' campaigning through Asia Minor and all the way to India, Greece has rather a marginal role in Nonnus' epic. At any rate it is certainly not treated, as Libanius treated it, as the unique source of everything worthwhile. Dionysus' own background, as far as it was human, was Phoenician not Greek, and in Nonnus' epic the focus is on Dionysus' activities in the Near East, as well as on the origins of Cadmus, his maternal grandfather, at Tyre.[58]

Apart from Dionysus' own contribution of wine, the one achievement of civilization that is privileged to have a separate encomium in the *Dionysiaca* is a gift of the Phoenician city of Berytus: the law taught at the law school of that city. This will bring justice to land and sea and 'fortify cities with an unshakeable wall'.[59] This law was of course not Greek but Roman, and Berytus was not geographically a Greek city but a Phoenician city which had been colonized by the Romans in the reign of Augustus. For Nonnus the contribution of the Near East to civilization was at least as important as that of Greece, and the contribution of Rome was important too. The perspective is quite different from that of a 'Hellene' of an earlier generation, Libanius for instance. In this respects Nonnus shows himself not simply a 'Hellene', but a 'Hellene' of the Roman Empire of the East.

Nonnus' handling of legendary material in several respects anticipates that of the *Chronicle* of John Malalas (*c*.490–*c*.565 AD). Like Nonnus, Malalas has assembled something of a compendium of myth from a great variety of sources to fill five books with mythical prehistory treated as

[56] Cadmus' Thebes, with 7 gates named after 7 planets, symbolizes heaven-Olympus (V.63–87). One might compare the much more complicated symbolism embodied in Paul the Silentiary's *Ekphrasis* of S. Sophia, Macrides and Magdalino 1988: 47–82, esp. 59–60, and the plainer symbolism of a Syriac inauguration hymn, Palmer and Rodney 1988: 117–67, esp. 131–3.

[57] 'How Solon will invent inviolable laws and, and Cecrops the union of two linked together under the indissoluble yoke of marriage legalised by the Attic torch' (XL.383–4), hardly amounts to 'admiration pour la civilisation représentée par Athènes' (Chuvin 1991: 320).

[58] Cadmus learnt the art of writing which he brought to Greece in Egypt (IV.264 ff.).

[59] XLI.389–98.

history.[60] According to Malalas not Zeus but a mortal man seduced Semele, who bore Dionysus in a thunderstorm. Dionysus is said to have eventually died in exile and to have been buried at Delphi.[61] Malalas covers historical events from Italy to Persia, a wide geographical range, if not as wide as that of Nonnus' poem whose action moves from Italy to India. In both authors the point of view is Near-Eastern. Malalas, like Nonnus, has reduced the importance of Greece relative to the Near East. Most notably he reports practically nothing about events in Greece between the Trojan war and the rise of Macedonia under Philip.[62] Like Nonnus, Malalas includes Roman traditions, only much more extensively. He records the adventures of Aeneas, and the history of Rome under its kings. There is very little information about the Roman republic, but the origins of the institutions of the imperial system of Malalas' own times are traced back to the kings.[63] Malalas, like Nonnus, was very far from focusing attention on the city as the basic social unit of the Empire. He shows a consistent interest in only a very few cities, notably Antioch and in the later sections Constantinople, in other words the two principal administrative centres of the Eastern Empire. Malalas was almost certainly a citizen of Antioch, but his *Chronicle* has very little information about Antiochene politics or what the Antiochenes felt and did for their city.[64] Most of his notices are about what was done for the city by emperors. Malalas relates the foundation legends of only Antioch and Constantinople. He does however report the setting up of quite a number of Roman provinces, among them Syria, Egypt, and Phoenicia, and he reports the subdivision of a great many others.[65] For him the Empire evidently was a conglomerate of provinces rather than of cities.

Malalas' work is a chronicle tracing the history from the creation to the reign of Justinian. The *Dionysiaca* is an epic describing the life on earth of Dionysus. But it too has elements of a chronicle in that it sets its events in a chronological scheme which spans the period from the beginning of the world to the reign of Augustus.[66] Malalas' *Chronicle* is of course an eminently Christian work. But it follows a pattern of chronicle writing invented by Julius Africanus and perfected by Eusebius in which the events of biblical history and the history of the Church are placed within the chronological context of secular history, in a way that would show to

[60] E. Jeffreys, 'Malalas' sources', in Jeffreys *et al.* 1990: 167–216.

[61] II.39–45. G. Bowersock, 'Dionysus as an epic hero', in Hopkinson 1994: 155–66 argues that Malalas provides a Christian refutation of precisely Nonnus.

[62] Cf. R. Scott, 'Malalas and his contemporaries', in Jeffreys *et al.* 1990: 67–85, esp. 76–7.

[63] R. Scott 1990: 146–64.

[64] E. Jeffreys, 'Malalas' world view', in Jeffreys *et al.* 1990: 55–66, esp. 55–6.

[65] M. Jeffreys, 'Formulaic phraseology', in Jeffreys *et al.* 1990: 225–31, relevant 227–8.

[66] V. Stegemann, *Astrologie und Universalgeschichte*, Studien zu dem Dionysiaka den Nounos von Panopolis, Leipzig/Berlin 1930.

Christians and non-Christians alike the progress of God's scheme for the administration of the world and the salvation of man from the creation to the time of writing.[67] One assumption underlying this scheme is that the Christian history of salvation is essentially compatible with the accepted secular traditions about the history of the world, and that the biblical narrative from the beginning of the world can be integrated into the account of creation and prehistory given by classical mythology and history.

So Malalas' *Chronicle* includes five books of pagan myth-history, the kind of material out of which Nonnus built his epic, but he has completely depaganized it. In his version the so-called gods had in fact been benevolent human rulers,[68] who propagated a remarkably Christian morality, and whose line of descent is traced back to Adam by way of Shem son of Noah. Later generations addressed these men as gods, thinking them immortal because of their good deeds. 'Men did this because they were full of ignorance.'[69] The facts as related by Malalas were that Kronos of the tribe of Shem became king of Assyria and the East. Kronos had a son Picus, whom his parents also called Zeus, who became ruler in the West.[70] Aphrodite was a granddaughter of Zeus Picus. She became a philosopher and married Adonis, the Athenian, himself a philosopher.[71] Heracles is said to have been a philosopher victorious in an earthly struggle with base desires.[72] Hephaestos invented agricultural implements—and issued a law that women were to be monogamous and live chastely.[73] Helios succeeded Hephaestos on the throne of Egypt and punished adultery with death.[74] Nonnus' Dionysus in his prime role as the originator of viticulture falls into the same category of benefactors of mankind.

4. *The End of the Tradition*[75]

Malalas wrote in the reign of Justinian and his work is a synthesis of Christian and Greco-Roman traditions. The autonomy of the literary tradition was ending. In fact the reign of Justinian marks the cultural turning point. In the second half of the sixth century the composition of

[67] A. Momigliano, 'Pagan and Christian historiography in the 4th century AD', in Momigliano (ed.), *The Conflict between Paganism and Christianity* (Oxford, 1963), 79–99 = A. Momigliano, *Studies in Ancient and Modern Historiography* (Oxford, 1977), 107–26, esp. 110–11. Croke 1990: 27–54, esp. 30–4.

[68] Cf. the gods Pan, Hermes, Apollo as inventors among human inventors, *Dionysiaca* XLI.373 ff.

[69] II.54 = p. 27.

[70] I.12–13 = p. 8, foreshadowing the Eastern and Western Empires.

[71] I.9 = p. 6.

[72] I.18 = p. 9.

[73] I.19 = p. 10.

[74] II.1 = p. 11.

[75] This owes much to Averil Cameron 1991: 190–200.

mythological poems and the uninhibited use of mythology came to an end, as ever wider areas of life came to be governed by positively Christian values. This was largely a consequence of deeper Christianization as a result of successive generations having been brought up in a Christian household. Public ceremony became Christianized, and with it ceremonial oratory and occasional poetry. This can be observed very nicely in a sequence of three imperial panegyrics: the oration Procopius of Gaza delivered in AD 502 in honour of Anastasius, the Latin poem in praise of the same emperor recited by Priscian in AD 512/13,[76] and finally Corippus' *In laudem Iustini minoris*[77] of AD 566/7. Procopius, though himself a Christian, recalls the emperor's descent from gods. He praises him conventionally by comparing him favourably with heroes of classical Greece. He repeatedly stresses the emperor's duty to look after the cities. Priscian speaking at Constantinople avoids mentioning the gods of mythology. He has few historical comparisons, and does not treat of the emperor's guardianship of cities. On the other hand, he repeatedly stresses Anastasius' dependence on divine help. His comparisons are with characters from the Bible, and the poem has numerous allusions to the biblical text. Corippus departs furthest from the traditional imperial panegyric. Instead of praising the great feats in war and peace of the ruler, he describes the ceremonies of his accession, emphatically the accession of a Christian emperor, in accordance with the will of God. The emperor's virtues, prayed for and promised, are Christian virtues. Though the language is that of the classical Latin epic, there is no place for pagan gods or mythology, and the 'literary' allusions are neither to Homer nor to Virgil but to the Bible.

Public ceremony had become Christianized. The most significant evidence is the remarkable poem which Paul the Silentiary wrote for the formal reopening in AD 562/3 of the new S. Sophia after the repair of earthquake damage. It goes without saying that there could be no mention of the old gods on this occasion. Paul the Silentiary wrote his poem in the language of high literature: a detailed description of the great building, composed according to the rules of 'ekphrasis', combined with a panegyric of the emperor Justinian. But the encomium of the emperor is accompanied by one of the bishop, and the whole poem is packed with Christian symbolism. Moreover the poet emphasizes that the joint achievement of emperor and bishop was only possible with the aid of God. In a memorable passage he evokes a vision of the church at night, when the dome lit up by innumerable lamps inside will serve as a light-

[76] Chauvot 1986.

[77] *Flavius Cresconius Corippus, in laudem Iustini Augusti minoris*, libri IV, edited with translation and commentary by Averil Cameron (London, 1976).

house to guide ships into the harbour of Constantinople, while at the same time reminding the sailors of God's many gifts to man through the Church.[78]

At this time there arose the *kontakion*, a new genre of non-classical but highly sophisticated poetry for liturgical use. The great poet Romanos wrote a *kontakion* to celebrate the rebuilding of S. Sophia after its destruction in the Nika riot.[79] This poem, or rather hymn, includes verses in praise of the emperor: Justinian at prayer for his people is successively compared to Moses and David, and his reconstruction of the cathedral is compared favourably with Solomon's building of the temple at Jerusalem, and Constantine's of the first S. Sophia. But it is essentially a sermon in verse, which explains that the disasters which Constantinople had recently suffered, notably a severe earthquake, and the terrible violence and bloodshed of the Riot, followed by a conflagration which destroyed a large part of the town, ought nevertheless be accepted as signs of the benevolence of God, who punishes men only to save them from far worse and never-ending evils, which are inevitable if they persist in sinning. The congregation must realize that God has sent the recent suffering because he wants to give them eternal life, which he can only do if they repent.[80] The *kontakia* of Romanos show that Christian writing was ready to take over public and private ceremonial.

Throughout his reign the emperor Justinian was determined to bring about religious uniformity in his realm, and made every effort to get sectarian Christians, Manichaeans, Jews, and of course pagans to conform.[81] Right at the beginning of his reign Justinian increased pressure on pagans dramatically.[82] For the first time officials and bishops were encouraged actively to seek out pagans and to punish them.[83] Bequests to temples were made illegal.[84] A second law ordered pagans to report at a church with their families.[85] There they were taught Christianity, and eventually baptized. If they refused at any stage, their property would be confiscated and they would lose the rights of citizens. Baptized Christians who were found to have taken part in pagan practices were to be put to

78 Mary Whitby 1985: 215–28; Macrides and Magdalino 1988: 47–82.

79 A translation of a *kontakion* celebrating the opening of the rebuilt cathedral by probably a pupil of Romanos is given in Palmer and Rodley 1988: 117–67, esp. 137–49.

80 *Romanos le Melode, Hymnes*, v, ed. J. G. de Matons, Sources Chrétiennes 283 (Paris, 1981), 455–99: text, Fr. tr. and commentary on no. LV 'Sur le tremblement de terre'. E. C. Topping, 'On earthquake and fires', *BZ* 71 (1978), 22–35.

81 Michael Whitby 1991: 111–31. F. R. Trombley, 'Paganism in the Greek world at the end of antiquity: The case of rural Anatolia and Greece', *HTR* 78 (1985), 329–36.

82 Trombley 1993–4: i. 81–2 attributes the undated laws *CJ* I.11.9–10 to Zeno, after pagans had supported the rebel Illus, cf. p. 260 below. I prefer the traditional attribution to Justinian.

83 *CJ* I.11.9 *praef.*

84 *CJ* I.11.9.1.

85 *CJ* I.11.10.1.

death.[86] Holders of pagan beliefs were excluded from state office, as they had been several times before.[87] Pagans were forbidden to teach, and if they were in receipt of a public salary this was to be withdrawn.[88] A few years later the right to teach was restricted to orthodox Christians.[89] It is not to be supposed that these ferocious laws were systematically enforced all over the Empire. That would have been quite beyond the power of the administration. Like much other legislation they represented a response to a particular situation which remains obscure to us. So it is likely that pagans or paganizing Christians, who were not teaching in state employment, and who lived in the provinces, were more often than not left alone. But the existence of these laws must have made all pagans feel insecure. For even if they were not consistently enforced, they could always be activated, whether from motives of fanaticism or of greed. Moreover Justinian was in earnest. The Academy at Athens was closed in AD 529, and in all probability never reopened.[90] There was an investigation followed by punishment of alleged pagans in high places at Constantinople and elsewhere. Their property was confiscated. Some of them were executed.[91]

But the prosecution of particular individuals may well have been launched by political antagonists. Phocas, one of those accused in AD 529, was a leading man at court, who was rehabilitated and made Praetorian prefect in 532, during the critical period following the Nika Riot. It is likely that the accusations against him were instigated by political enemies.[92] There was a second wave of persecution of pagans in AD 545/6. This was a real witch hunt. Most of the victims were prominent intellectuals, sophists, lawyers, and doctors. Phocas was accused once more, and died in the course of the investigation. His opponents claimed that his death was suicide and therefore an admission of guilt. John of Ephesus, later known as the Monophysite bishop of Ephesus, and author of an ecclesiastical history from the Monophysite point of view, who was at this time in the confidence of both Justinian and the empress Theodora, and

86 *CJ* I.11.10 *praef.*

87 Malalas XVIII.449 = p. 263, AD 529.

88 *CJ* I.11.10.2–3.

89 *CJ* I.11.10 (529); I.5.18.4.

90 Malalas 451.16–18, AD 529, cf. Agath. II.29–31. In spite of arguments of Alan Cameron, 'The last days of the academy at Athens', *PCPS* 15 (1969), 7–29, there is no definite evidence that teaching was ever resumed at Athens. See Liebeschuetz 1991: 889–90 for literature on end of the Academy. See also G. af Hällström, 'The closing of the Neoplatonic School in AD 529', in P. Castrén (ed.), *Post-Herulian Athens* (Helsinki, 1994), 141–60.

91 *CJ* I.11.9; Malalas XVIII.449; Theophanes 6022 (AD 528).

92 *PLRE* II.882, s.v. Phocas 5. Phocas was alleged to have been a pagan, but John Lydus praises his piety and his charity, including the giving of an income to a church at Pessinus, in terms which suggest Christian charity, though Lydus does not use the word Christian. But then Lydus was a classicizing purist, who like Procopius avoided, where possible, the use of non-classical technical terms (*Mag.* III.73–6).

had been entrusted with an intensive missionary campaign in western Asia Minor, boasts that he himself had instigated the persecution of AD 545/6.[93] But it is significant that this persecution took place at a time of food shortage and earthquakes, and not very long after the plague had killed thousands at Constantinople and in the provinces.[94] In AD 562 pagans were arrested and paraded, and books, statues, and pictures of gods publicly destroyed in the arena at Constantinople. This too was a difficult year with several riots, and a conspiracy at the end of it.[95] Episodes of persecution were not limited to Constantinople. Sometime after AD 539, the 'gloriosus referendarius and sacred [i.e. imperial] judge' Hyperechius conducted a trial of pagans at Sardis condemning one of them to ten years of penal social work in a hospital.[96] A similar series of trials took place at Antioch between AD 554 and 559. Some pagans were condemned to work in hospitals, others interned in monasteries, or even put to death.[97] Unfortunately, we know nothing about the context of these trials.

Persecution under Justinian certainly hit protagonists of classical literary culture, but it was not directed at the high literary tradition as such. After all Lydus wrote his treatises on the pagan calendar (*De mensibus*), and on pagan divination (*De ostentis*), at Constantinople in the middle of the reign of Justinian. Paul the Silentiary, the author of the poem about S. Sophia, also wrote some very effective erotic epigrams in the high classical tradition.[98] Agathias published an anthology, which included recently composed poems addressed to pagan gods,[99] at Constantinople in the 560s, early in the reign of Justinian's successor.[100] It was not simply censorship that banished pagan mythology from literature.

But the intellectual atmosphere was changing. Educated people became tolerant of writings whose language did not meet the traditional criteria for high literature. Malalas' *Chronicle* is one example of this. Ecclesiastical writers, even the highly sophisticated Romanos, from time to time

[93] Pseudo-Dionysus of Tel-Mahrē, tr. W. Witakowski 77–8 (pp. 71–2).

[94] On plague, see above, p. 53 and below on p. 410; Theophanes 225.4–5.

[95] Malalas XVIII.491 = pp. 300–1. Procopius' *HA* XIX.11 suggestion that prosecution of rich pagans was motivated by Justinian's wish to confiscate their property, is a commonplace of rhetorical abuse.

[96] *CIG* 8645 = *Sardis VII*, ed. W. H. Buckler and D. M. Robinson (Leiden, 1932), no. 19, cf. Trombley 1994: 180.

[97] *Vita Symeonis iunioris*, ed. Van den Ven, 2 vols. (Brussels, 1962–70), 146; and Trombley 1994: 181.

[98] *AP* V. 239: 'The raging flame is extinct, I suffer no longer of Cypris, but I am dying of cold. For after having devoured my flesh, this bitter love, panting hard in his greed creeps through my bones and vitals. So the altar fire when it has lapped up the sacrifice, cools down of its own accord for lack of fuel to feed it' (tr. W. R. Paton); cf. the sensual 252 and 272 and the homoerotic 232.

[99] *AP* IV.3.113–16: 'I will first select for you, competing with men of old time, all that the parents of new song wrote as an offering to the old gods, for it was meet to adhere to the wise model of the ancient writers' (tr. W. R. Paton in Loeb edition).

[100] Averil Cameron 1970: 12–29.

ventured rhetorical criticism of traditional literature,[101] though the Church still did not set up Christian schools, and education continued to be provided by secular grammarians and sophists. But the object of schooling gradually changed from the transmission of traditional literary values to the acquisition of background knowledge and reading skills needed to interpret the Bible and to discuss and proclaim theology. But secular schooling was still needed. Administration continued to be based on written documents and the Codification of Justinian remained the law of the Empire. So there was need for civil servants able to understand and apply the law. But it is significant that academic training of lawyers at law schools seems to have come to an end soon after the death of Justinian.[102] Subsequently, the law was administered by men who had received only a rhetorical education and who acquired their legal expertise 'on the job', and by reading epitomes of the older legal literature, a number of which have survived.[103]

The process by which education was transformed is still very obscure. Already in the reign of Valens (364–378) a Syrian elementary teacher called Protogenes taught boys shorthand together with the Bible, especially the Psalms.[104] A Coptic text tells of a legal expert, perhaps a notary (*nomikos*), supposedly at the time of the Diocletianic persecution (AD 302–5), who taught boys elementary mathematics, the Old Testament, and writing in both uncial and cursive scripts, presumably training his pupils to become clerks or notaries.[105] These relatively humble educators, who gave their pupils an elementary education with a professional slant, which was designed to fit them for a clerical career and at the same time made them familiar with the scriptures, could well have been pioneers in the transformation of education.[106] In ninth-century Constantinople there was a guild of *paidididaskaloi nomikoi* whose members trained boys to be notaries.[107] It is likely that over the years a humbler schooling, focused on practical training, and including the scriptures in its

[101] See Jeffreys *et al.* 1990: 77–9.

[102] Even if law teachers returned to Berytus sometime after the earthquake of 551 (Agath. *Hist.* 2.15.3), the law school does not seem to have survived much longer (Ant. Placent. *Itinerarium*, 1 = *CCL* 175, 129–30). Incidentally recent archaeology has shown that the sources exaggerate the earthquake destruction at Berytus: there is practically no evidence of earthquake damage on the 'souks site', Butcher and Thorpe, 'A note on excavation in central Beirut 1994–96', *JRA* 10 (1997), 299–306. We have no evidence for the continued existence of the law school at Constantinople in the later 6th cent., but none for its closure either.

[103] H. Hunger, *Die hochsprachliche profane Literatur der Byzantiner* (Munich, 1978), ii. 429–44.

[104] Theoderet *HE* IV.18.7–9. On psalms in education, see B. Boyaval, 'Le Cahier scolaire d'Aurélios Paphnoutios', *ZPE* 17 (1975), 225–35.

[105] T. Orlandi, *Il dossier copto del martire Psote* (Milan, 1978), 98.

[106] A. Steinwenter, 'Studien zu den koptischen Rechtsurkunden aus Oberägypten', *St Pal*, 19 (1920), 66; a list of *tabelliones didaskaloi* in Egypt: *CPR* XIII, pp. 65–8.

[107] *The Book of the Prefect*, ed I. Dujĉev (London, 1970), I.13–14; cf. Lemerle 1971: 262–3.

syllabus, gained ground at the expense of the academic education of the grammarian and rhetor.[108] What changed was the perceived object of education. Schooling narrowed from the transmission of traditional literary values to the acquisition of background knowledge and reading skills needed to understand basic administrative or theological texts, above all to interpret the Bible and to discuss and proclaim theology. While the people involved did not of course know Augustine's work, and were probably not even fully aware of the cultural trend they were living through, something like the programme of Augustine's *De Doctrina Christiana* came to be accepted as the goal of education.

The transformation of literary culture did not happen over night. The succession of early Byzantine historians only ended with Theophylact Simocatta, and secular poetry with George of Pisidia, both writing in the reign of Heraclius (610–641).[109] Nevertheless the change was dramatic enough. First mythological poetry and the uses of pagan imagery in secular writing disappeared, then secular writing itself. By, say, the second quarter of the seventh century new writing had become almost exclusively theological, and for a time there was not very much of that.[110] Books became difficult to obtain and there was little circulation of new writing between the provinces and Constantinople.[111] The *Parastaseis Syntomoi Chronikai* reveal a deep cultural divide.[112] This compilation of the early eighth century is a description of historical monuments, especially statues, visible in Constantinople at the time of writing. It is the heir of the writings on local antiquities which provided so much material for Nonnus and Malalas. But the compilers had no direct access to those writings. As far as they are derived from earlier histories, the comments of this guide book seem to be based on florilegia.[113] It is clear that the compilers were quite unable to untangle myth and fact. The result is a confused mixture of legend and history. The quality of the book's historical information about emperors only begins to improve with the reign of Justin II (565–578).[114] How precisely this extraordinary 'epistemological excision'[115] came about is still very unclear. But the crucial period was certainly the second half of the sixth century.[116]

Excision leaves a gap, a gap which would need to be filled. The cultural

[108] The references are from Gascou 1994: 63.

[109] Michael Whitby 1988: esp. on the sources, 92–137, 222–49; Mary Whitby, 'Defender of the cross, George of Pisidia on the emperor Heraclius and his deputies', in Mary Whitby 1998: 247–73.

[110] See survey in Lemerle 1986.

[111] Mango 1975: 29–46.

[112] Averil Cameron and Herrin 1984.

[113] Dagron 1984*a*: 53–60.

[114] Averil Cameron and Herrin 1984: 34–8.

[115] The expression is Robert Markus's in Markus 1990: 224–5.

[116] For an account stressing the positive, see Averil Cameron 1991: 189–222.

gap left by the demotion of activities centring on classical literature was filled by Christian activities centred on the Bible. But Christian culture was no more bounded by the Bible than classical culture had been bounded by Homer or Virgil. What was Christian was defined in the works of the Church Fathers,[117] taught by example through the hagiography of martyrs and saints, exemplified in living holy men, and confirmed by supernatural signs such as the miracles experienced at the tombs of saints or mediated through venerated icons. It is surely not a coincidence that it was in the post-Justinianic period, which saw the sharp decline in the production of secular literature, that the sources began to mention the existence, veneration, and power of icons more and more frequently.[118] Icons taught through pictures, and in that way communicated much more widely than either secular or even theological writings, in the words of Gregory the Great: 'What writing presents to readers the picture presents to the unlearned . . . in it the unlearned read.'[119] Icons taught in that they publicized the gospel narrative and the deeds and virtues of the various holy person represented. The decline of secular literature and the rise of icons are complementary developments. But this does not mean that icons caused the retreat from literature, but rather that both developments are aspects of the same cultural shift as a result of the general acceptance of an all-embracing Christian view of the world.

Icons did more than publicize. For it was thought not only that they portrayed, as the case might be, Christ or the Virgin or a saint, but also that they radiated some of the power of the sacred person represented. When in AD 626 Constantinople was besieged by the Avars the patriarch Sergius set up the Virgin's picture on the Golden Gate.[120] In AD 544 the Mandylion, a portrait of Christ not made by human hands, saved Edessa from capture when it helped to ignite a siege mound built against the walls by the Persians.[121]

[117] P. Gray, '*The Select fathers*: Canonizing the patristic past', *Studia Patristica*, 23 (1989), 21–36; Averil Cameron, 'Models of the past in the late 6th century: The life of the patriarch Eutychius', in G. Clarke (ed.), *Reading the Past in Late Antiquity* (Canberra, 1990), 205–33 = Averil Cameron 1996: ch. 2.

[118] Haldon 1990: 405; A. Grabar, *Martyrium*, ii (Paris, 1946), 343 ff.; E. Kitzinger, 'The cult of images before iconoclasm', *DOP* 8 (1954), 84–150, esp. 95–115.

[119] *PL* 57.1128C.

[120] N. H. Baynes, 'The supernatural defenders of Constantinople', *Analecta Bollandiana*, 67 (1949), 165–77 = *Byzantine and Other Studies* (London, 1955), 248–60; Averil Cameron, 'The Theotokos in the sixth century', *Journal of Theological Studies*, NS 29 (1978), 79–108 = Averil Cameron 1981: ch. 16.

[121] The Mandylion: Evagrius *HE* IV.27. On this, see Averil Cameron, 'The language of images: The rise of icons and Christian representation', in D. Wood (ed.), *The Church and the Arts*, Studies in Church History 28 (Oxford, 1992), 1–42 = Averil Cameron 1996: ch. 12 and ch. 11, 'History of the image of Edessa'. See also E. v. Dobschütz, *Christus Bilder* (Leipzig, 1909), 102–96; G. Dagron, 'Le Culte des images dans le monde byzantin', in J. Delumeau (ed.), *Histoire vécue du peuple chrétien*, i (Toulouse, 1979), 133–60 = Dagron 1984*b*: ch. 11.

Icons were not the only medium through which heavenly power was thought to enter the human world. Holy men, and their relics, and even material objects that had only been touched by them, all seemed available to those who needed divine help or divine comfort. And they were available not only to individuals, but also to communities and indeed cities. So Constantinople was defended by its saints as well as its icons, not least those of the Virgin whose robe and girdle were housed in her church at Blachernae and Chalkoprateia.[122]

All these phenomena helped to confirm the truth of Christian teaching about God, and the ways of God to man. They helped to inculcate a view of the world that allowed for frequent interventions by the divine in human affairs, and which assumed as a matter of fact that natural causation could be set aside, so that the wicked would be punished or the good rewarded. Communication with the divine, and present divine help, were available to those whose life made them worthy, and what kind of behaviour qualified a man for divine aid was clearly laid down in the Bible and in the Lives of saints and holy men.

In the long run, the Christian view of the world would provide a powerful basis for communal action within the Christian state. Defence of the Empire, particularly against pagans or Muslims, came to be identified with the defence of the Christian religion, and thus as fighting for God. The emperor was seen as God's representative on earth, whose God-given task it was to rule his people like the 'good' kings of the Old Testament, and both to safeguard the Church, and to ensure that it was governed in accordance with God's will as expressed in the scriptures, and in ecclesiastical canons and traditions. Increasingly elaborate court ceremonial, closely bound up with ecclesiastical ritual, demonstrated the God-given role of the emperor, and so helped to provide a religious basis for his claim to allegiance.[123] But before Christianization could bring cohesion, it increased division. By introducing the distinction between orthodox and heretics, it was responsible for discriminatory laws and increasingly frequently for persecution of otherwise irreproachable citizens.

Christianity had no doctrine of secular citizenship. It induced the state—needlessly as we would see it—to oppress and to antagonize fellow townsmen who happened to be sectarian Christians, or Jews, or continued to adhere to the ancestral religion. Icons and relics strengthened people's attachment to their locality: they focused the worshippers attention on

[122] Averil Cameron, 'The virgin's robe, an episode in the history of seventh century Constantinople', *Byzantion*, 49 (1979), 42–56.

[123] On the growing use of 'Christian resources' in war, see Michael Whitby 1998*a* and Averil Cameron, 'Images of authority: Elites and icons in late sixth century Byzantium', *Past and Present*, 84 (1979), 3–35 = Averil Cameron 1981: ch. 18.

local images, local saints, local sanctuaries, and local practices and beliefs.[124] But the loyalty fostered in this way was unpolitical. It was in no way a substitute for the old concept of city as the common interest of its citizen. It provided no motive for communal political activity. It did not even necessarily strengthen the authority of the bishop. For the faithful did not need an intermediary to approach an icon—or to consult a holy man for that matter. There is here a contrast between East and West. For in the West the cult of saints, and to a considerable extent the foundation of monasteries, were under the control of bishops.

This book is about the disintegration of the ideal and reality of the classical city. The adoption of the Christian world picture was part of this process. That the new world view had triumphed was manifest by the second half of the seventh century, but it is a mistake, I think, to explain this profound transformation as a result of any single change, as for instance the emergence of a new meritocratic 'social and political élite' at precisely this time.[125] What happened was the culmination of a long and complex development over centuries going back to the conversion of Constantine and beyond, the background to which has been discussed in this book.

[124] Haldon 1990: 403–35, esp. 406.
[125] Against Haldon 1990: 428 in a context from which I have otherwise learnt much.

8

Conflict and Disorder in the East

1. *Preface: The Problem*

Did the collapse of a view of the world that had united city communities for centuries and its replacement by another, embodying a different system of values, and one not centring on the city and its political community have a detrimental effect on the functioning of that community? In other words, did Christianization make cities less stable? This is a very difficult question to answer. For even if it can be shown that the East was more disorderly in AD 600 than it had been say in AD 400, Christianization was not the only development that made for greater instability.

We have quite a lot of information about urban disturbances in late Late Antiquity. Most of it concerns rioting that involved the factions. But that was not the only kind. Often disturbances were caused by religion, above all by conflict between clerics and laymen who accepted the Council of Chalcedon and those who did not (generally known as Monophysites). There were also a number of episodes of popular demonstrations leading to violent suppression of paganism, or at least of alleged pagans. The frequency of rioting increased in the last quarter of the sixth century, and reached a peak in the reign of the usurper Phocas (602–610) in the years leading up to the Persian invasion and occupation.[1] In this chapter I will discuss the different kinds of disturbance in turn, starting with faction riots, and then go on to seek an explanation for what seems to be a pattern of increasing disorder.

2. *Sources for Disorders Involving the Factions*

The number of references to factions and their riots is impressive. The evidence is nevertheless less informative than would appear at first sight. The consistent expression of indignation at the irrationality of the

[1] Miracles of S. Demetrius *PG* CXVI.1262 (miracle 10) mentions strife in Thessalonica, Anatolia, Asia, Cilicia, and Palestine. The 'demes', surely the factions, were responsible; being no longer content to be violent in public places, they attacked private houses.

factions' rioting and other illegalities is not an objective assessment.[2] A similar emphasis dominates newspaper reports of football-hooliganism and the crime wave today. Not that irrationality and motiveless violence are lacking today, but there is nevertheless a link with deeper social developments. So it is likely to have been with the factions.

Then, the bulk of the evidence comes from chronicles. But it is a feature of chronicles that they do not provide background information. Chronicles, as a rule, are composed of a succession of brief notices of striking events, assembled in chronological order. They do not explain the events.[3] The only riot of which we have abundant historical documentation is the Nika Riot of AD 532, for which we have exceptionally full notices in several chronicles, reinforced by a detailed narrative of Procopius.[4] Comparison with the account of Malalas and the other chronicles shows that Procopius has simplified and stylized the story.[5] No doubt he was moved by political caution to understate the public discontent which evidently played a part in the development of what would prove to have been the worst riot of the century, culminating, as it did, in the proclamation of a rival emperor, that is in full revolt; and whose suppression involved the massacre of tens of thousands assembled in the hippodrome, the execution of two leading senators, and the exiling of eighteen patricians, *illustres*, and consulars. The accounts of the Nika riot enable the historian to glimpse wider discontents underlying the mindless violence in the street or hippodrome.

The majority of faction riots are known only from a single source: John Malalas. This means that we have a very restricted view of the phenomenon. For Malalas was concerned above all with Antioch, and in 'the Extension', the later part of Book XVIII,[6] with Constantinople. He has little about events in other cities. So we cannot follow the development of faction activities in the provinces generally, and are unable to tell how far Empire-wide solidarity, or 'copy-cat rioting', was a feature of faction behaviour from the beginning. The widespread character of faction disturbances in the early seventh century therefore may come as a

[2] e.g. Proc. I.24.1–6; Menander Protector fr. 1; Malalas 418; Agathias V.14.4.

[3] Croke 1983: 116–31. Jeffreys *et al.* 1990. On Western chronicles: S. Muhlberger, *The Fifth Century Chronicles: Prosper, Hydatius and the Gallic Chronicler of 452, A.R.C.A. 27* (Leeds, 1970).

[4] Proc. I.24.7–58; Malalas, 473–7; *Chron. Pasch.* 620–9; Theoph. 6024. See Greatrex 1997: 60–86; Michael Whitby 1999.

[5] Malalas 473–7 (XVIII.71–7 = pp. 275–81). Subsection and page references to Malalas are to the English translation of text and 'sub-text' in E. Jeffreys, M. Jeffreys, and R. Scott 1986. The 'sub-text' provides evidence of what Malalas wrote other than that in the *Baroccianus Graecus* 182, on which Dindorf's edition was based. Also on the Nika Riot: Theophanes 181.24–186.2; and *Chron. Pasch.* 620–9. On the latter, see Michael Whitby and Mary Whitby (eds.), *Chronicon Paschale 284–628 AD*, translation with notes and introduction, Translated Texts for Historians 7 (Liverpool, 1989), 620–9.

[6] See Croke in E. Jeffreys *et al.* 1990: 18–25.

surprise.[7] It was nevertheless not altogether new. As early as the reign of Justin I (AD 518–27), the rioting of the Blues was already Empire-wide.[8]

That we depend so largely on Malalas means that our regular gazette of faction activities comes to an end with the extended version of Malalas around AD 565. In the following decades, up to the overthrow of Maurice by Phocas in AD 602, we hear very little about factions. We might conclude that the factions had abandoned their internecine fighting, perhaps because they saw that it was doing them no good. It is however more likely that the factions continued to behave as before, and that the absence of information after AD 563 is simply due to the changed character of the sources. For some reason, which we do not know, the compiler of the *Chronicon Paschale* has copied practically no information about urban events at Constantinople or elsewhere, other than the consular *fasti*, for the decades after the death of Justinian. Theophanes has longer annual notices, containing mainly information about campaigns, and certainly nothing like the abundance of urban information available for the years covered by Malalas.[9]

Notices of faction riots resume after AD 600. The reason for the resumption of information is twofold. The first is that the factions played a significant role in the overthrow of both Maurice and Phocas, the second that by pure chance there have survived two texts which throw light on politics in the provinces. These are the *Chronicle* of John bishop of Niciu, and Strategius the Monk's *Capture of Jerusalem by the Persians in 614*. These works describe the troubled times from the respective points of view of the bishop of a small town in the Nile delta, and of the patriarch of Jerusalem,[10] and like Malalas they record the activities of the factions in provincial cities, which the *Paschal Chronicle* and Theophanes, our principal sources for the period do not. By this time the factions were

[7] See Alan Cameron 1976: 198–201, 314–17, for evidence about factions in Eastern provincial cities; ibid. 201–14, on spreading of Roman type chariot racing in the East.

[8] Disturbances by Greens early in reign of Anastasius at Antioch and Constantinople: Malalas 393–4 (XVI.2–4 = pp. 220–2) (AD 494/5). Widespread rioting from 1st to 6th year of Justin: Malalas 416–17 (XVII.12 = pp. 235–6) (AD 550), Blues of Constantinople take up case of Blues of Tarsus: Procop. *HA* 29.29–38.

[9] For an explanation, see the discussion in Michael and Mary Whitby 1989: xxi–xxii. Theophanes 6061, AD 568/69 records a message of Justin II that he would treat both factions with equal severity, but subsequently has only slightly more urban information than *Chron. Pasch.* Coming to the reign of Phocas, the annual notices of the *Chron. Pasch.* are still very short and include only one reference to the factions (p. 695 for AD 603). In the longer notices of Theophanes the factions are now much more prominent. Note that in the *Chronicle* of Pseudo-Dionysius of Tel Mahrē there also is an absence of urban information after AD 568, see tr. of W. Witakowski (1996), 127 ff.

[10] *The Chronicle of John Bishop of Niciu*, translated from Zotenberg's Ethiopic Text by R. H. Charles (London, 1916). Strategius Monachus, *La Prise de Jérusalem par les Perses en 614*, ed. and tr. from Georgian by G. Garitte, CSCO 202, Scriptores Iberici 11 (Louvain, 1960); English tr. by F. C. Conybeare, *EHR* 25 (1910), 502–17.

operating even in small towns in the Delta of Egypt. We cannot tell how long they had existed there. Papyrus evidence for the presence of factions in Egypt is not found before the mid-sixth century.[11]

3. *The Anatomy of the Faction Riot*

A faction riot often started over a relatively trivial incident, typically fighting between fans of the two factions,[12] or the refusal of the authorities to release activists of one of the factions under arrest for some misdemeanour, as happened in AD 490, 495, 532, and 563.[13] But attempts by the authorities to check the disturbance and to punish breakers of the peace regularly produced escalation, until great crowds were roaming the streets and setting fire to buildings, and the situation completely out of control.[14] The solidarity shown by a very large part of the population with one or the other of the factions when these bodies were under pressure from the government, notwithstanding the fact that misbehaviour by the factions was—to put it mildly—a terrible public nuisance, strongly suggests that the factions were widely felt to be champions of the people.

The popular sense of solidarity emerges very clearly from the more detailed accounts of riots. The Nika Riot, the biggest and best documented of all these disturbances, arose because the city prefect refused to pardon two convicted murderers, one from each faction, who had survived hanging as the gallows collapsed.[15] The factions united, and proceeded to set fire to the prefect's headquarters. The fire quickly spread through the city centre. At this stage the crowd began to chant slogans attacking not only the prefect of the city, but also John the Cappadocian the praetorian prefect, and Tribonius the *quaestor*. Next, the army was called in against the rioters, and numbers of them killed. The result was further escalation, so that even the sacking of the unpopular officials did not restore order. Finally the crowd proclaimed a new emperor. This act of open revolt had the support of an important group of senators, and the passive support, at

[11] Gascou 1976*b*: 185–211.

[12] Fighting between rival fans either during, or more often after, a meeting was probably the most common start of rioting, e.g. Malalas in E. Jeffreys, M. Jeffreys, and R. Scott 1986: 389–90 (XV.15 = p. 218 sub-text); 394–5 (XVI.4 = p. 222 sub-text); 483 (XVIII.99 = p. 288); 484 (XVIII.105 = p. 289); 490 (XVIII.132 = p. 299); 491 (XVIII.135 = p. 300).

[13] e.g. Malalas 389 (XV.15 = p. 218 sub-text); 394 (XVI.4 = p. 221); 473 (XVIII.71 = p. 275) (the Nika Riot); 496 (XVIII.146 = p. 304); 496 (XVIII.150 = p. 305). The misdemeanours were generally related to inter-faction fighting, but allegations of simple gangsterism are too many to be discounted. The factions had power and they misused it.

[14] e.g. Malalas 389 (XV.15 = p. 218); Malalas 394–5 (XVI.4 = p. 222); 396–7 (XVI.6–7 = pp. 222–3); 484 (XVIII.105 = p. 289); 491 (XVIII.135 = p. 300); *Chron. Pasch.* 695.

[15] Proc. I.24.7–8; Malalas 473 (XVIII.71 = p. 275).

least, of part of the imperial guard.[16] It is difficult to avoid the conclusion that at a time of extreme unpopularity of Justinian, and of John the Cappadocian, his principal minister,[17] a lot of the discontented, and by no means only members of the lower classes, were prepared to identify with the factions, and to see government action against the factions as a threat to themselves.[18] They regarded the factions, in spite of the abundance of trouble they caused, as in some sense their bulwark against misgovernment.

We are not nearly as well informed about the causes of any other riot. It is clear that many simply originated from fighting between Greens and Blues after a race meeting, perhaps after the losers had insulted the winners. Sometimes Blues and Greens joined forces.[19] During one Green riot, the Blues remained neutral.[20] A very serious riot at Antioch was provoked by the killing of Green rioters who had taken refuge in a church.[21] But on this occasion too, the scale of the ensuing disturbance, and the helplessness of the authorities, suggest a snowballing of the rioting masses similar to that which occurred during the Nika Riot. So it would seem that a large number of people who did not take part in the street-battles of the fans were prepared to go into the street when they saw the activists being disciplined. It was evidently a situation, familiar enough in our own times, where a limited number of violent activists had the passive support of a large part of the population.

4. *The Temporal Distribution of Faction Riots*

The vast majority of the public appearances of the Greens and Blues at dozens of shows every year, year after year, have not been recorded by our sources. The large and enormously destructive riots which we read about were exceptional events, which were unequally distributed in time. For very many years no riot at all is recorded, either at Antioch or at Constantinople, and it was rare for either city to experience more than one major riot in a year. The riot-disturbed years do however come in blocks.

The reorganization of entertainment which inaugurated the age of faction notoriety may go back to Theodosius II, who reorganized the seating at Constantinople.[22] His successor Marcian (AD 450–7) prohibited

[16] *Chron. Pasch.* 626, including some *excubitors* and *scholarii*, cf. Proc. I.24.39.

[17] J. Lydus *De mag.* III.70: provincials flock to Constantinople to complain against John the Cappadocian.

[18] On the Nika Riot as a demonstration that got out of hand because it was badly handled, see Greatrex 1997: 60–86.

[19] So in Nika Riot; also 496 (XVIII.150 = p. 305) Blues rescue a Green.

[20] Malalas 496 (XVIII.151 = pp. 305–6).

[21] Malalas 396–7 (XVI.6 = pp. 223–4).

[22] Malalas 351 (XIV.2 = p. 191), apparently an Empire-wide regulation, implying that by this time

Greens from holding public office because their faction had started a riot.[23] The first of the big riots recorded in our sources happened at Antioch in AD 489, the penultimate year of Zeno. It is said to have started with fighting between Greens and Blues, but anti-Semitism was evidently an issue too. It may not be a coincidence that the usurper Leontius, who four years earlier had been defeated by a general of Zeno's, had his headquarters at Antioch, and had recently been executed. Certainly it was the Greens who were the aggressors in this riot, and the Greens were the colour favoured by Zeno. Just conceivably the Greens were paying back old scores from the time of the usurpation. In any case, the late 480s, and the early 490s which saw the death of Zeno and the troubled accession of Anastasius, were a period of political instability, which is likely to have been a factor in this outburst of factional and other violence.[24] It is not the case that all the big riots coincide with uncertainty about the position of the emperor, but the serious and widespread rioting in AD 522–3 is blamed by Procopius on the fact that the young Justinian, the emperor Justin's nephew and partner, protected the Blues and so encouraged lawlessness on their part.[25] It is likely enough that he was building up support to make sure that he would succeed his uncle. This phase of unrest culminated in the catastrophe of the Nika Riot, following which the city was free of major disturbances for some years. Serious riots at Constantinople are again recorded after AD 547, and particularly between 559 and 563.[26] Justinian was nearing 80, and a change of ruler was obviously imminent.

There follow decades without reports of faction riots. This could be misleading. As we have seen the *Chronicles* have very little information of any kind for these years. We cannot safely conclude that there were no faction riots. The years AD 579–80 saw a large-scale anti-pagan witch-hunt.[27] The political background will be discussed more fully later in this

factions were already organizing games in many cities. But at Antioch decurions organized the Olympic games and the games of the Syriarch until AD 465 (*CJ* I.36.1). The factions in small towns of Egypt are witnessed only from mid-6th cent.

23 Malalas 368 (XIV.34 = p. 202).

24 For references, see above, p. 251.

25 Malalas 416 (XVII.12 = p. 236), Procop. *HA* IX.35–42, *Histor.* I.24.1–6.

26 Riots in later part of reign of Justinian: AD 547 Malalas 483 (XVIII.99 = p. 288); 484 (XVIII.105 = p. 289); AD 550 Malalas 484 (XVIII.108 = p. 290); AD 553 Malalas 486 (XVIII.117 = p. 293) debasement of coinage (factions not mentioned); AD 556 Malalas 488 (XVIII.121 = p. 295) bread shortage; AD 559 Malalas 490 (XVIII.131 = p. 298) bread shortage, rumour of death of emperor (factions not mentioned); AD 560 Malalas 490 (XVIII.132 = Theophanes 235.26–237.1 = p. 299); AD 561 Malalas 491 (XVIII.135 = p. 300); AD 561 Malalas 491 (XVIII.136 = p. 300) at Cyzicus; AD 562 Malalas 491 (XVIII.138 = p. 308) drought, conspiracy; AD 563 Malalas 496 (XVIII.146 = p. 304, ibid. 496 (150–1) = p. 305) a difficult period with recurring plague, earthquakes, famine, invasion, and conspiracies.

27 Rochow 1976: 120–30.

chapter. Now it will suffice to note that it was accompanied by violent street demonstrations at Antioch and Constantinople, and that it was to the spectators in the hippodrome, at Antioch[28] as well as at Constantinople,[29] that the authorities, lay and ecclesiastical, promised favours in order to restore order. The colours are not mentioned, but it is difficult to believe that they had not been involved. The reason for their not being mentioned could be that in this episode they were on the same side—as they were in a subsequent wave of demonstrations against the bishop Gregory of Antioch in AD 588–9.[30]

In the violent local conflict within and between some of the cities of the Nile delta known as the Aykelāh revolt, the factions were active participants, though their allegiance was not consistent.[31] This was in the 590s, and significantly before the very disturbed period ushered in by the usurpation of Phocas and the deposition and murder of Maurice (AD 602). The factions played an important role in the overthrow of Maurice,[32] and they are prominent right through the reign of Phocas (602–10). Phocas came to be extremely unpopular and provoked the rebellion of Heraclius. He incurred the hostility of the Greens and was generally supported by the Blues. There was faction fighting in many cities all over the Empire. When the Persians besieged Jerusalem in AD 614, the factions were united in pressing for resistance, opposing the patriarch who advocated surrendering the city.[33] When the Roman generals Menas (41) and Domentianus quarrelled in Alexandria at the time of the Arab invasion (AD 641), one was supported by the Greens and the other by the Blues, and in this case Monophysitism was an issue.[34]

What explanation can there be for the pattern of faction rioting? Rioting by pre-industrial crowds in Western Europe occurred most commonly in times of famine and high food prices.[35] It is likely that this was also to some extent true of the riots in Late Antiquity.[36] The fact that the headquarters of the city prefect were repeatedly a target of rioters at

[28] Demonstrations, without mention of factions: Evagrius *HE* V.18, John of Ephesus *HE* III.29. To restore order bishop Gregory promised to build a hippodrome and to import a troop of pantomimes (John of Ephesus *HE* III.29). This suggests that the factions had been involved. At Constantinople there was an escalating riot (not begun in the hippodrome (John of Ephesus *HE* III.31)), followed by a meeting of emperor and the people at an extraordinary race meeting in the hippodrome (*HE* III.32).

[29] John of Ephesus *HE* III.29.

[30] Evagrius *HE* VI.7. This time the demonstrations were instigated by the *comes* Orientis Asterius.

[31] See below, pp. 269–72.

[32] See above, p. 212.

[33] Strategius Monachus, *La Prise de Jérusalem*, V.10.

[34] John of Niciu 119.

[35] Rudé 1952: 18, 55–7.

[36] Malalas 488 (XVIII.121 = p. 295 in AD 556); 490 (XVIII.131 = p. 298 in AD 561); 492 (XVIII.139 = p. 301 in AD 562).

Constantinople might suggest that the rioters were motivated by resentment at judicial decisions generally, not only those pronounced against fans of the factions themselves.[37] At Antioch tension between Christians and Jews was evidently one of the causes of rioting.[38] This does not mean that economic or judicial or religious grievances were explicitly formulated by the rioters. Our sources do not give the impression that these riots had any formulated objectives at all—other than that of inflicting damage on the opposite colour. But in this respect too[39] the faction riots resemble many of the urban riots of the eighteenth century studied by Rudé: starting 'from relatively small beginnings (say a meeting of housewives outside a baker's shop)' the disturbance is transformed 'into a wholesale rebellion and attack on property'.[40] The faction riots were not of course started by housewives outside a baker's shop, but by fans excited by a day at the races. But the escalation was the same, and all sorts of grievances could be vented in the subsequent destruction. This is clearly what happened in the Nika Riot, but there are hints of the same process in some of the very brief notices we have of other disturbances. The riots were not started deliberately by individuals with clear political objectives, but in times of political tension the normal behaviour of the factions was more likely to lead to an explosion. For discontented groups were liable to join in disturbances started by the factions for reasons of their own. This is what happened in the Nika Riot and in the riot of AD 515/16 at Alexandria.[41]

But the pattern of faction rioting of later Late Antiquity is not adequately explained by reference to famine, popular hardships, injustice, or even boredom, though each of these factors is likely to have contributed to individual outbreaks. The history of these disturbances can be linked with other developments in the Empire. As we have seen the basis of the phenomenon was laid by the reform of the public games in the later part of the reign of Theodosius II (402–450). But the first wave of serious rioting is only recorded in AD 489 and subsequent years,[42] more than thirty years later, in the days of failing curial government, a decade or two before Anastasius established government by notables. Faction riots are a phenomenon of the age of civic government by notables.

[37] e.g. AD 561: 491 (XVIII.135 = p. 300) burn house of prefect; AD 563: (XVIII.146 = p. 304) prefect attacked, crowd breaks into prison; AD 563: 496 (XVIII.151 = p. 305): riot to prevent arrest.

[38] On Jews and Greens at Antioch, see above, p. 215. In AD 529 a Samaritan rebel symbolically executes a victorious Christian charioteer in hippodrome at Scythopolis: Malalas 446 (XVIII.35 = p. 260) factions not mentioned; AD 556 at Caesarea Jews and Samaritans unite (as a Green/Blue faction?) against orthodox, Malalas 487 (XVIII.119 = p. 294).

[39] Note also that like the riots of the 18th cent. (Rudé 1952: 27–8), faction riots were clearly directed against property rather than persons.

[40] Rudé 1952: 19.

[41] See above, nn. 15, 19; p. 217, n. 88.

[42] Malalas 389–90 (XV.15 = p. 218 sub-text), on riots at Antioch late in reign of Zeno.

The temporal distribution of the riots also suggests some correlation with crises involving the position of the emperor. This would not be surprising in view of the factions' role in the making of the emperor.[43] It is clearly not a coincidence that the very serious and widespread faction fighting in the first decade of the seventh century occurred in a period of imperial instability.

But apart from imperial politics, it looks as if by this time the factions had begun to act something like political parties using their strength in the struggle for local power at the city level. This at any rate is the impression given by the evidence of John of Niciu.[44] Moreover the development can already be observed in the Aykelāh troubles, that is before the fall of Maurice, and the subsequent uncertainty about who was the legitimate emperor. It would seem that by the 590s, at least, the factions were taking an active part in the political conflicts dividing the cities of Egypt.

5. *Violence in Doctrinal Conflicts*

The sources have many accounts of street violence which are not associated with the factions. The majority of these are linked to doctrinal controversies, above all the conflict between 'Orthodox' and Monophysites, that is the supporters and the opponents of the doctrinal decisions of the Council of Chalcedon (AD 451). In many ways the competition between the supporters and opponents of Chalcedon in cities where both groups were represented in significant numbers resembled the competition of political parties. The competition centred on the election of a bishop with the right doctrinal attitude. Each side tried to build up the support for its candidate by offering patronage and straightforward gifts to potential supporters. This process might have resulted in the more or less peaceful victory for one side or the other, according to the strength of the parties in a particular city, if it had not been for intervention by the emperor to impose a bishop of his choice in the interest of his particular policy in the area of doctrinal unity. When a candidate had been imposed by the emperor, the rival party would probably use the next suitable moment, for instance a prospect of a change of ruler, to launch a campaign of violence.

The use of violence for or against the Council of Chalcedon is a very big story which cannot be told here in full. One example will have to

[43] This does not mean that riots held at such time were either 'for' or 'against' the reigning emperor. Riots would be more likely at times of imperial uncertainty because both the reigning emperor and hopeful contenders would encourage one or other of the factions, in whatever way was available, and the emperor would be less likely to enforce discipline.

[44] See below, p. 277.

suffice.[45] At Alexandria violent protest was triggered by the implementation of the decision of the Council to depose the patriarch Dioscorus.[46] The consecration of his successor Proterius by four Chalcedonian bishops immediately produced a popular uprising which caused many casualties, and was only suppressed after troops had been sent from Constantinople to reinforce the local garrison. In spite of much opposition Proterius remained bishop until the death of the emperor Marcian in AD 457. Then the succession of a new emperor was exploited by a strong faction claiming to represent people, *honorati*, councillors, and shipowners,[47] to have Timothy Aelurus an opponent of Chalcedon consecrated as bishop. Rioting broke out and Proterius was murdered. Timothy Aelurus was left as sole bishop, but in AD 459 he was deposed by the emperor Leo, only to be restored once more in 475 by the usurper Basiliscus. Zeno overcame the usurper but did not dare to replace Timothy by a Chalcedonian. But in the long run, street violence of Monophysite monks and laymen could not prevail against imperial policy backed by soldiers. From *c.* AD 538 to the capture of the city by the Arabs in AD 641 the bishops residing in Alexandria were 'orthodox', or according to the Monophysites 'imperial' (melkite).[48] There was a rival succession of Monophysite bishops of Alexandria. But these resided in a monastery outside the city.[49]

Violence in the service of religion was up to a point distinct from other kinds of urban violence. Doctrinal partisanship had objectives and opponents which were not directly linked to any secular grievances. Moreover the demonstrations and rioting of doctrinal parties did not need the assistance of one of the factions to make a powerful impact. At Alexandria—and elsewhere—demonstrations and strong-arm tactics on behalf of the opponents of Chalcedon were dominated by monks from the monasteries situated in the neighbourhood of the city. In Palestine and Syria II it was largely the monks that won these regions for Chalcedon.[50] Doctrinal conflicts certainly were not simply secular conflicts in disguise.

This does not however mean that religious controversy was carried on in a world of its own. For instance it would be extremely surprising if ecclesiastical parties had renounced all attempts to enrol one or the other faction on their side. Indeed we hear that at Apamea in Syria, around AD

45 For parallel violence at Antioch, see Downey 1961: 485–90.

46 Haas 1997: 87–8, 317–20; Frend 1972: 148–55, 160–2.

47 Evagrius *HE* II.9.

48 *DHGE* II s.v. Alexandrie, 328–35.

49 *History of the Patriarchs of the Coptic Church of Alexandria*, Arabic text translated, edited, and annotated by B. Evetts in *PO* I (Paris, 1907).

50 A lot of evidence for violence by monks on behalf of one or the other religious party is cited by H. A. Bacht, 'Die Rolle des orientalischen Mönchtums in den kirchenpolitischen Auseinandersetzungen um Chalcedon', in A. J. Grillmeier and H. A. Bacht, *Das Konzil von Chalkedon*, ii (Würzburg, 1953), 193–314.

515, the Blues incited the people to attack a Monophysite monastery.[51] Furthermore it must be assumed that such unpleasant secular phenomena as famine, disease, earthquake, war, taxation, and also social class and individual ambition, did have some effect on the way people took sides in doctrinal conflicts. The trouble is that we rarely have enough information to place a particular outbreak of religious conflict in its secular context.[52]

Two secular factors can however be seen to have regularly influenced the behaviour of religious groupings. One I have already mentioned, the policy and position of the emperor. Another regularly recurring factor, though not necessarily one of which the people involved were fully conscious, was the division between city and country. The anti-Chalcedonians in Syria and Egypt derived much—but far from all—of their support from villages and rural monasteries. They devised liturgies in Syriac and Coptic. They nurtured the growth of new lingo-religious forms of self-consciousness. This did not make the two religious groupings opposed to Chalcedon into national movements under another name.[53] But they certainly did have some of the political impact of a national movement in that they helped to break up the unity of the Greco-Roman world. It may well be true that the Monophysites were not dogmatically hostile to the Empire. We are indeed told that Monophysite monks defended the Tur Abdin in Mespotamia against the Persians when the army had abandoned it.[54] Nevertheless, when the Persians occupied large parts of the Roman East they expelled Chalcedonian bishops and installed Monophysites everywhere. This meant consecrating new bishops. We are told that villages in the patriarchate of Antioch refused to accept the new bishop because he had not been consecrated canonically by the Patriarch of Antioch, but by a bishop in the territory of the Persian king.[55] Clearly the Persian king would not have gone to such trouble unless he had good reason to believe that Monophysite bishops would be more supportive of Persian rule.

Leaving aside their attitude respectively to the Empire and its invaders, the sense of solidarity of Syriac Monophysitism would tend to consolidate

[51] *Act. Conc. Oec.* (ed. E. Schwartz) III.96.19–24.

[52] Ecclesiastical historians and ecclesiastical controversial writings consistently ignore the secular context.

[53] The resemblances as well as the differences between nationalist movements of more recent times and the anti-Chalcedonians in Egypt and Syria are brought out very well in W. H. C. Frend 1972.

[54] Michael the Syrian X.25; Theophylact II.1.1–2; 3.9; 18.7 on campaign in Tur Abdin 587 is evidence that there was some local support for the imperial army, but not for the extent of that support e.g. II.18.7: country dwellers near Beïudaes (Fafi) encouraged the imperial officer to attack the town, but among the defenders too there were 'natives' (18.9).

[55] Michael the Syrian X.25. Persian occupation of Egypt (*c.*617–29) was less markedly pro-Monophysite, though no Chalcedonian bishop was consecrated after the death of John the Almsgiver of Alexandria, see Frend 1972: 342–3, 349.

a Mesopotamian–Syrian regional block, while Coptic Monophysitism would tend to widen the distance between Egypt and the rest of the Empire, including their fellow Monophysites in Syriac-speaking Syria.[56] Both religious and secular factors contributed to the growth of Syriac and Coptic self-consciousness, which was to a considerable extent a reaction against imperial religious policies.

6. *Persecution of Pagans*

Compared with the resistance aroused by the imperial government's attempts to enforce religious uniformity among Christians, the episodic persecution of pagans produced surprisingly little violent protest from the victims. Violence, or demonstrations demanding violence, usually came from Christians, above all Christian urban crowds. There are two such episodes for which the sources are more detailed than for any of the incidents of popular violence discussed so far, with the exception of the Nika Riot. Both episodes throw light on the sources of tension in the cities of the East and at the same time reveal the interplay of phenomena that are generally observed in isolation from each other: the civic role of the bishop, urban rioting, the conflict between Chalcedonians and Monophysites, the suppression of paganism and uncertainty about the succession to the Empire.

The first episode took place at Alexandria between AD 483/4 and 489. The principal sources are Zacharias of Mytilene's *Life of Severus*, the Monophysite patriarch of Antioch, and Damascius' *Life of Isidore*. The neoplatonist philosopher is our source for the first phase of the persecution, Zacharias for the second.[57] The series of events began with an investigation involving torture, followed by the imprisonment of certain pagan philosophers teaching at Alexandria. This action was a response of the emperor Zeno to the rebellion of the Isaurian general Illus. He had learnt that pagan philosophers at Aphrodisias and elsewhere had encouraged the rebels with prophecies of success, which would in due course produce a revival of the cult of the gods. The pagan grammarian Pamprepius, a leading supporter of Illus, had visited the philosophers at Alexandria.[58] No doubt a suspicious emperor feared that these pagan academics were trying to spread the rebellion to Egypt. It has been argued that legislation intensifying the suppression of paganism which is generally attributed to Justinian was in fact issued by Zeno at this time,

[56] Frend 1972: 341–2.
[57] Zacharias of Mytilene, *Vita Severi*, ed. M. A. Kugener, *PO* II.1; Damascius, *Vita Isidori*, ed. C. Zintzen (Hildesheim, 1967).
[58] Athanassiadi 1993: 1–29, esp. 18–22.

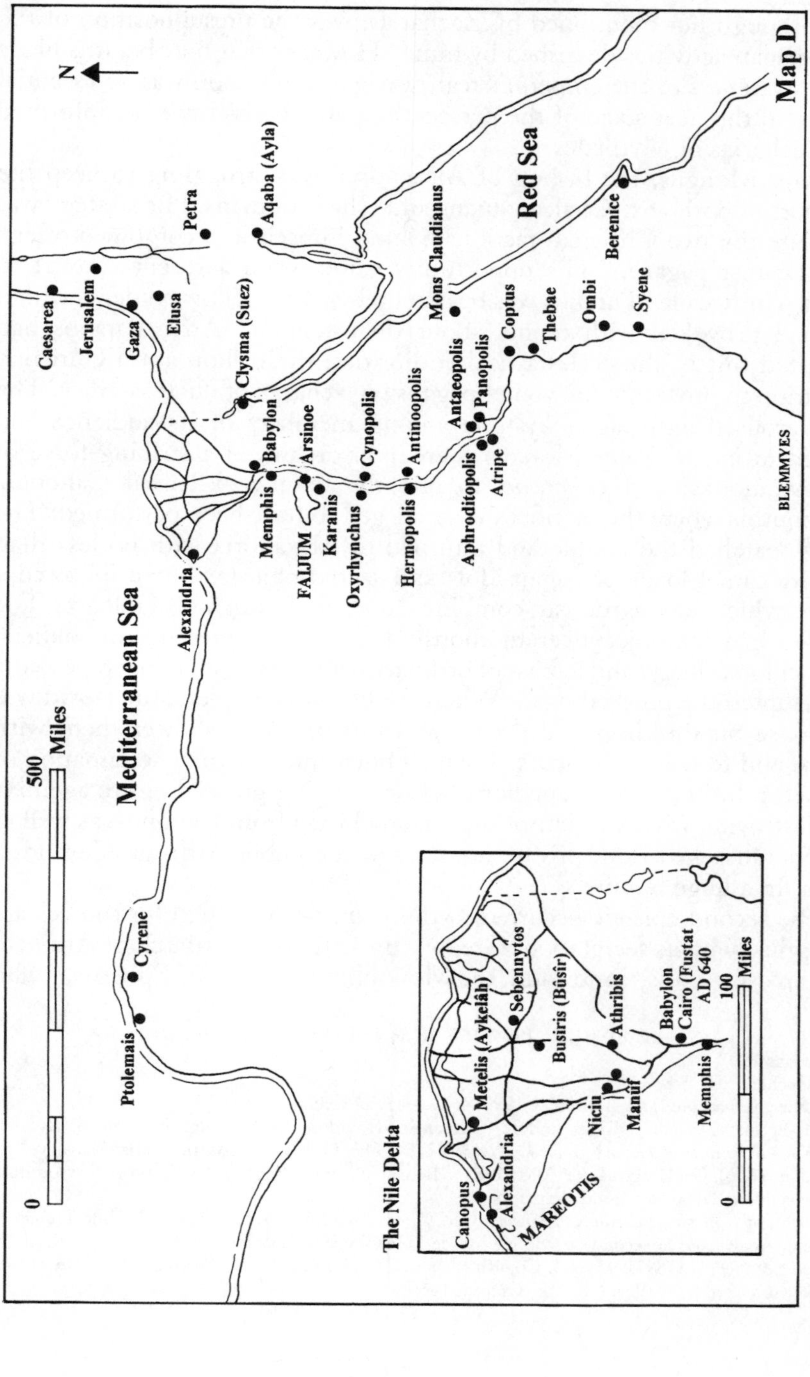
Map D
N
0
500 Miles
Mediterranean Sea
Red Sea
Ptolemais
Cyrene
Alexandria
Caesarea
Jerusalem
Gaza
Elusa
Petra
Aqaba (Ayla)
Clysma (Suez)
Memphis
Babylon
Arsinoe
FAIUUM
Karanis
Oxyrhynchus
Cynopolis
Hermopolis
Antinoopolis
Aphroditopolis
Antaeopolis
Atripe
Panopolis
Mons Claudianus
Coptus
Thebae
Ombi
Syene
Berenice
BLEMMYES
The Nile Delta
Canopus
Alexandria
MAREOTIS
Metelis (Aykelah)
Sebennytos
Busiris (Būsīr)
Niciu
Manūf
Athribis
Babylon
Cairo (Fustat)
AD 640
Memphis
0
100 Miles

16. Cities in Egypt

and, though not mentioned by Zacharias, was the presupposition of the anti-pagan activities described by him.[59] However that may be, it is likely that awareness of the emperor's fear of pagan subversion was an essential factor in the next stage of the persecution, about which we are informed by Zacharias of Mytilene.

Peter Mongus, the bishop of Alexandria, was struggling to keep the support of both anti-Chalcedonians and Chalcedonians. His strategy was to unite the two Christian factions behind himself in a combined offensive against pagans.[60] His opportunity came when a recent convert to Christianity called Paralios was beaten up by pagan fellow students whom he had provoked with taunts about their religion. After Paralios had reported this to the ecclesiastical authorities, the bishop got a Christian decurion to prosecute the young pagans on a charge of illicit sacrifice. The trial aroused anti-pagan hysteria among members of its audience and ended in chaos. Peter Mongus thereupon organized a striking-force of clergy, monks, and *philoponoi* to raid the temple of Isis at Canopus/Menouthis where the sacrifices were alleged to have been performed. The band searched the temple and returned to Alexandria with no less than twenty camel loads of pagan idols and sacred objects. There followed a scene which incongruously combined formality and mob violence. The bishop had the objects ceremoniously listed in the presence of soldiers, councillors, clergy, and a mass of ordinary people, whose shouts repeatedly interrupted the proceedings.[61] When the list was complete, the crowd was let loose on the disgraced deities and proceeded to shower them with abuse and to tear them apart. Then all burst into a formal acclamation of emperor, bishop, and councillors, before bringing proceedings to a climax by destroying what was left of the pagan objects from Canopus, as well as others ransacked from private houses and the public baths at Alexandria itself, in a huge bonfire.[62]

The second episode occurred in the years AD 578–88. Our sources are Evagrius, who as secretary of Gregory the orthodox patriarch of Antioch, was an eyewitness,[63] and John, the Monophysite bishop of Ephesus,[64] who

[59] Trombley 1993–4: i. 81–94; *id.* 1994: 167–82 on *CJ* I.11.9–10, cf. p. 241 above.

[60] Haas 1997: 323–30.

[61] Zacharias, *V. Severi* 34 f.

[62] For a full account, see Trombley 1993–4: ii. 4–15, 219–25.

[63] Evagrius *HE*, ed. J. Bidez and L. Parmentier (London, 1898); English tr. by S. Bagster, *Evagrius' Ecclesiastical History from 431 to 594 AD*, The Greek Ecclesiastical Historians, vol. vi (London, 1866). On Evagrius, see Allen 1981. Michael Whitby (1998*b*: 321–44) shows that a central theme is divine favour for 'good' emperors.

[64] John of Ephesus, *Ecclesiastical History*, CSCO, Scr. Syri 55 (Louvain, 1936). Tr. into French in F. Nau, 'Analyse de la seconde partie inédite de l'Histoire Écclésiastique de Jean d'Asie', *Revue de l'Orient Chrétien*, II (1897), 455–93. English version: *The Third Part of the Ecclesiastical History of John Bishop of Ephesus*, tr. R. Payne Smith (Oxford, 1860).

also was very well informed. His life had been a queer alternation of imperial favour and persecution.[65] Each author was strongly partisan. The last two books of Evagrius' *History* are an apology for the controversial episcopacy of Gregory. John of Ephesus wrote as a spokesman for the persecuted Monophysites. Both men wrote ecclesiastical history, and observed the conventions of the genre, which means that they did not delve into the secular background of the events described by them.

The persecution began in AD 578, when the authorities at Constantinople were informed that the pagans of Baalbec in what is now Lebanon, were planning a violent assault on Christians in that city. The report was taken extremely seriously. Theophilus an official who had just crushed a rebellion of Jews and Samaritans in Palestine was sent to Baalbec, where he began what can only be described as a witch-hunt. The accused were put to torture and duly produced names, mentioning 'numerous persons in every district and city in their land, and in almost every town in the East, and especially at Antioch the Great. Of most of these Theophilus was contented with sending the names to the magistrates of the place where they resided, with orders that they should be arrested immediately and sent to him.'[66] As a result many prominent citizens were crucified or otherwise executed. His investigation then took Theophilus to Edessa in Mesopotamia, where he interrupted, or at least claimed to have interrupted, a sacrifice to Zeus. Theophilus' official backing was evidently very strong, for he was in a position to accuse no less a man than Anatolius, the provincial governor of Osroene, who also held the rank of deputy praetorian prefect.[67] Anatolius gave bail, but was nevertheless arrested and taken under guard to Antioch. There he and his assistant Theodore were put on trial. Under torture Theodore implicated others, among them Gregory the bishop, and Eulogius a cleric who later became Chalcedonian bishop of Alexandria. They were alleged to have taken attended the nocturnal sacrifice of a boy at Daphne.[68] The confessions caused enormous excitement. There were riots in the streets and in the theatre. The cathedral was closed. The imperial government responded as it usually did when faced with an urban riot: it replaced the official responsible for the town, the Count of the East. Anatolius and Theodore were sent for trial to Constantinople. Here too the accusations

[65] *HE* III.2: 'When the king Tiberius was but a youth . . . we both of us together with the rest of the court were constantly in each other's company in attendance upon his late majesty Justin'.

[66] John of Ephesus *HE* III.27; Trombley 1994: 170–9.

[67] Cf. persecution of pagans by bishop Stephen on instructions of the emperor Maurice at Harran in Osroene (*c.*589), where Acindynus a high official was crucified as a crypto-pagan on the accusation of a subordinate who succeeded him, Michael the Syrian X.24.

[68] John of Ephesus *HE* III.29. That Gregory was accused of having committed incest with a married woman (Evagrius VI.7) belongs to the episode of 587.

and alleged confessions caused enormous excitement. When the specially convoked court delayed sentence—or perhaps passed only a sentence of banishment when death sentences were demanded—large-scale rioting broke out.

The course of the riot was very much like that of a faction riot, though the factions are not mentioned: the court building was attacked and two of the accused lynched. The crowd ransacked the headquarters of the praetor of the plebs and took away documents bearing on cases of Christian prisoners, i.e. presumably opponents of Chalcedon. They then broke into the prison and released the prisoners.[69] The rioters next invaded the headquarters of the urban prefect and were only with difficulty prevented from seizing the official and burning the building. The government made its standard response: it sacked the urban prefect: a man called Sebastian was replaced by one Julian. The emperor brought up units of the army, but he also offered concessions. He ordered a day of races in the hippodrome and had an edict read to the assembled spectators,[70] promising that 'every man shall be recompensed according to his deeds'. A new court was set up and Anatolius promptly condemned to the beasts. There followed a long succession of arrests and trials of men, mostly it would seem outwardly Christians, who were alleged to have taken part in pagan rites.[71] Condemnation and sentences followed. The number of victims was very great. Accused were brought in from Syria and Asia. These must have been men of standing, as were many of those accused at Constantinople. But a large numbers of humble people were also among the accused.[72] Whatever its original cause, the persecution gained a momentum of its own.[73] The events demonstrate vividly the degree of Christianization of the populations of Antioch and Constantinople, and the way in which large masses could be roused to indignation and violence by religious issues. This was of course an essential background to the 'rise of the bishop' discussed in an earlier chapter.

The episode raises interesting questions. Why did the government choose that particular moment to launch a violent attack on men who

[69] John of Ephesus *HE* III.31. On duties of prefect of plebs, see Just. *Nov* XIII. Eventually the trials were transferred from the urban prefect to the praetor of plebs (John of Ephesus *HE* III.34).

[70] John of Ephesus *HE* III.32.

[71] John of Ephesus *HE* III.34.

[72] *HE* III.33–4; V.15 translated only J. M. Schönfelder, *Die Kirchengeschichte des Johannes von Ephesus aus dem Syrischen übersetzt* (Munich, 1866): 'Die mehrzahl der Senatoren wurde unter jenen angeklagt. So dass der Kaiser (Maurice) in Bestürzung gerieht, dass sich dies gleich beim Anfang seiner Regierung ereignete, (fürchtend) es möchte einer von seinen *principes* abgesandt werden, und seinen ganzen Senat tödten und vernichten.'

[73] The narrative: John of Ephesus *HE* III. 28–34. Discussion: Trombley 1994; Michael Whitby, 'John of Ephesus and the pagans: Pagan survivals in the sixth century', in M. Salamon (ed.), *Paganism in the Late Roman Empire and Byzantium*, Byzantina et Slavica Cracoviensia I (Cracow, 1991), 111–31; Rochow 1991: 133–56; also Rochow 1976.

professed to be Christians, on the alleged grounds that they had taken part in pagan rites? And why did it go to the trouble of seeking out victims over so wide an area?[74] It is true that the legal basis for such a mission as that of Theophilus existed since early in the reign of Justinian,[75] but enforcement had been extremely spasmodic, even in the reign of Justinian with his passionate interest in religious affairs.[76] One factor can be recognized: Monophysites exploited an opportunity to discredit Chalcedonians. Whether or not Monophysites originated the accusations, they certainly joined in the public demonstrations. At Antioch demonstrators took up the call for the punishment of the Chalcedonian patriarch Gregory, and at Constantinople the crowd unsuccessfully assaulted the palace of Eutychius, the Chalcedonian patriarch. The released prisoners included Monophysites arrested in a recent persecution.[77]

That Monophysites should have exploited an unusually favourable situation to have a go at their enemies is not surprising. The imperial government had been intermittently hostile, sometimes more, sometimes less actively, ever since the death of Anastasius in AD 518. Monophysite churches and monasteries were liable to be confiscated, and their clergy and bishops to be exiled or imprisoned. Since the failure of negotiations for unity in AD 569–70 there had been repeated episodes of active persecution both at Constantinople and in the provinces.[78] The Monophysites were numerically strong. They probably formed a majority in eastern Syria and in Mesopotamia, though not in Antioch itself. In Constantinople they represented a significant minority. They never challenged the imperial government directly; they were after all a religious not a political movement. But resentment must have been very strong. So an opportunity to counter-attack their oppressors by charging them with covert paganism, a capital offence, was too good to miss.[79]

Moreover in AD 579 circumstances were particularly opportune. For the powerful Arab chieftain, Alamundarus of the Ghassanite family, had not long before 578 reached an important agreement with the emperor Tiberius, and Alamundarus was a Monophysite. It was agreed that

[74] While the persecution was sustained by public opinion in the two cities, it had been launched by the imperial government when Theophilus was sent to Baalbec to carry out an extraordinary investigation with wide powers.

[75] *CJ* I.11.9–10.

[76] See above, p. 242.

[77] III.31: 'And thence they ran into the praetor's government-house, and broke open the doors, and having entered . . . the record offices in which all processes against Christians [i.e. Monophysites?] are deposited, they abstracted the papers and cut them up . . . and set those who were imprisoned there free' (tr. Payne Smith).

[78] Frend 1972: 321–3.

[79] Rochow 1991: esp. 133–46 ff. gives examples of Monophysite use of the charge of paganism against Chalcedonians. But for the charge to have been taken at face value and produced so massive a response as that of the emperor Tiberius in the late 570s additional factors must have been involved.

Alamundarus and his tribesmen should undertake an essential role in the defence of the eastern frontier against the Persians and their Arab allies. In return he received the title of patricius; and when he personally came to Constantinople in 580 he was given an assurance that persecution of Monophysites would stop, and he was allowed to make a public proclamation to this effect when he passed through Antioch on his way home.[80]

The antagonism between the upholders of Chalcedon and those who were persecuted for rejecting it was certainly a contributory factor in the long drawn out persecution of pagans under Tiberius II and Maurice. It does not however account for the fact that the accusations against the pagans of Baalbec were immediately taken so seriously by the government that an official was sent with power to make investigations in three different provinces (Syria Phoenicensis, Coele Syria, and Osroene), and to arrest and take away for trial, without delay or any appeal, the governor of Osroene who also held the high rank of deputy praetorian prefect. At Baalbec itself the persecution took the form of an attack on the civic establishment, which had long remained loyal to the ancestral religion.[81] At Antioch and Constantinople, where many of the accused were at least ostensibly Christians, there was mass involvement in the persecution, and popular anger that the accused might get themselves acquitted by using wealth and influence. As we have seen, John of Ephesus reports that at Constantinople many members of the senate were accused. So it is likely that the individuals who provided the information, without which no prosecution could have been launched, had political as well as religious grievances: the affair had elements of an attack on the establishment. Moreover it is likely that the informers came not from Baalbec alone but from the whole area which was to be covered by Theophilus' investigation, in other words the persecution was probably instigated by a regional group, and not only by individuals from one city. The later stages of the witch-hunt were presumably driven forward not only by the crowd, but also by men of standing, whether motivated by greed, religion, or political ambition, or a combination of all three.

At this time there was much discontent in Syria quite apart from the disaffection of the Monophysites. Year after year there had been serious fighting against the Persians in Mesopotamia or Armenia, with the needs of the army as always resulting in heavy demands on the Syrian taxpayer. In AD 573 the Persians had invaded Syria and sacked Apamea. Antioch was not defended 'because the greater part of its walls were in ruins, and the populace had made resurrection in the hope of gaining ascendancy, a

[80] John of Ephesus *HE* IV.39–42, *PLRE* IIIA s.v. Alamundarus.
[81] Trombley 1993–4: ii. 154–6.

thing of frequent occurrence and especially in situations like this'.[82] Consequently a large part of the population had temporarily abandoned the city, among them Gregory the bishop, taking with him the treasures of the Church. In AD 577 there was a severe earthquake. Damage was done at Antioch but the neighbouring resort of Daphne was almost destroyed.[83] For many years there had been severe unrest among the Samaritans in Palestine, which the Roman commander Photius[84] and his successor Theophilus had put down with great difficulty and cruelty. It surely was no coincidence that precisely Theophilus was sent to investigate and bring to trial the alleged pagans at Baalbec and elsewhere.[85] None of these events would have made the government popular. The administration might well have feared an outbreak in Syria/Mesopotamia similar to that just suppressed in Palestine.

Meanwhile the Empire was under heavy pressure. There was war not only in the East but also in the Balkans.[86] Yet another factor made for instability: from AD 574 the emperor Justin II was mentally ill, and government was carried on by the Caesar Tiberius Constantine. Tiberius was on bad terms with Justin's formidable wife, the empress Sophia, who after her husband's death is said to have frequently plotted against Tiberius.[87] In the circumstances leading dignitaries are likely to have fancied their chances of becoming emperor, whether by intrigue or by usurpation. One grandee who is likely to have had such hopes was Justinian 3, a close kinsman of Justin, who was commander in chief (AD 575–7) of the army fighting on the eastern frontier.[88] In earlier times,[89] large-scale investigations followed by trials were usually motivated by fear of a conspiracy against the emperor. On this occasion we do not hear of charges of treason. It is however likely enough that a situation which in earlier centuries would have produced magic and treason trials, in the late sixth century gave rise to a major witch-hunt for alleged pagans.[90]

[82] Evagrius *HE* V.9.

[83] Evagrius *HE* V.17, for date Downey 1961: 525 n. 11.

[84] John of Ephesus *HE* I.32.

[85] John of Ephesus *HE* III.27.

[86] John of Ephesus *HE* III.21.

[87] John of Ephesus *HE* III.10.

[88] According to Gregory of Tours *HF* V.30 and Paul the Deacon *HL* III.12 he actually made an attempt with the help of the Justin's widow Sophia, but according to John of Ephesus *HE* VI.27 he died before Justin. His brother Justin 4 had been murdered in AD 571 at Alexandria at the instigation of his namesake the emperor (Evagrius *HE* V.2).

[89] e.g. in AD 359, Ammianus XIX.12.6 (Constantius); AD 371, Ammianus XXIX.1.4 ff. (Valens).

[90] Cf. the trial and execution for alleged sorcery on the insistence of John patriarch of Constantinople of the highly educated Paulinus in AD 583, Theophylact I.11.3–21, and with some differences: John of Niciu 93.

Religious persecutions were often initiated by bishops (e.g. John Ephesus *HE* III. 35), but greed for a share of the condemned person's property (ibid. V.15, 21) is said to have motivated large

According to John of Ephesus the affair of AD 578/9 really only ended in AD 587/8 when Gregory of Antioch came to Constantinople to answer the charges brought against him before a court of bishops and lay dignitaries, and was successful in doing so, much to the historian's disgust.[91] Evagrius gives rather a different and very interesting account.[92] In fact he provides us with an analysis of the opposition to Gregory. The bishop had quarrelled with the principal imperial official at Antioch, the count of the East Asterius. We are not told what they quarrelled about. All the city, that is the three principal divisions of the population, the leaders, the populace, and the shopkeeper-craftsmen, are said to have taken the count's side. Each group declared that they had been injured by Gregory. There followed demonstrations in the streets and in the theatre in which even the actors took part. The factions are not named, but Evagrius' use of the dual, and the participation of the actors shows that the factions were involved, and in this case on the same side. As often in such situations the government replaced the official responsible for the city, the Count of the East. It also assembled a special tribunal composed of metropolitan bishops or their deputies, and of senators, to try Gregory.

One charge, made by a banker/money changer, was that Gregory had had an affair with his (i.e. the banker's) sister, who to make things worse was a married woman. Other individuals of similar status accused him of having repeatedly disturbed the peace of the city. Evagrius does not mention any resumption of the accusation of covert paganism which had been made ten years earlier.[93]

In fact the earlier and the later accusations are likely to have been linked in some way. Gregory had many enemies in his city. We can identify two groups that he certainly antagonized. First, the local Monophysites who did not recognize him as bishop but had a bishop of their own. Monophysites were probably a minority in the city of Antioch.[94] But among the Chalcedonians too Gregory is likely to have had enemies, since he had been appointed to replace Anastasius who had been deposed by Justin II.[95] Anastasius retained enough support to be reinstated after Gregory's death. But if Gregory had enemies, he also had a high reputation, and was in fact a very powerful figure in Syria. In AD 579 the charges were not taken up, in 589 the court at Constantinople acquitted him and punished his

numbers of accusers. So it remains likely that political tensions were exploited by prosecutors in religious trials, as they had been by informers in treason trials.

91 John of Ephesus *HE* V.17.

92 Evagrius *HE* VI.7.

93 Evagrius *HE* V.18.

94 Relative weakness of Monophysitism in Antioch itself: Frend 1972: 294, 344. Michael the Syrian X.17: Gregory has imperial edict for tolerance of Monophysites revoked in *c*.580.

95 Evagrius *HE* V.5–6; John of Ephesus *HE* I.41.

accusers.[96] It was after his acquittal that Gregory persuaded the mutinous army to accept as its commander the general Philippicus whom they had previously rejected. He addressed a mass meeting of officers and men, urging them to accept Philippicus. He offered to release the mutineers from an oath they had sworn never to accept Philippicus, and when the soldiers had at last yielded to his pleading, he gave communion to all 2,000 of them, and followed this up with a feast on benches hastily constructed from turf.[97]

It is evident that the basic cause of the hostility aroused by Gregory was not the suspicion that he might be a covert pagan. That the bishop had so many enemies was a consequence of political conflict, ecclesiastical and secular, at Antioch: the charge of paganism was merely a handy weapon to use against a very powerful opponent.

7. *John of Niciu and the Aykelāh 'Revolt' in the Reign of Maurice*

John of Niciu's *Chronicle* is an unusual, and potentially exceptionally useful source for the student of the troubled politics of the late sixth and early seventh centuries. For it is a chronological account of political history as seen by the bishop of a small city in the Nile delta. Histories written from a provincial point of view are rare in any case, but as a history written from a provincial Egyptian point of view John's *Chronicle* is unique. Of course Egypt has left us a lot of documentary evidence, but without the framework provided by a chronological narrative it is difficult to fit the documents into a wider picture. This difficulty is illustrated by the earlier, largely document-based, chapter on civic administration and finance in Egypt which leaves many basic questions unanswered.[98] John of Niciu provides information of a kind the papyrus documents do not. Unfortunately, however, the text we have has been translated at least three times, from Greek into Arabic, from Arabic into Ethiopic, and from Ethiopic into French or English. Besides the original version would seem to have been shortened.[99] It is very difficult, or even impossible, to penetrate through the layers of translation to the original Greek technical terms of administration, and so to achieve a clear understanding of John's narrative in terms of the administrative structure of Byzantine Egypt as we know it

[96] Evagrius *HE* VI.7. He was even given money to build, or perhaps to repair a hippodrome at Antioch, as well as a troop of pantomimes (John of Ephesus *HE* V.17).

[97] Evagrius *HE* VI.13.

[98] See above, pp. 198–9.

[99] Situations and individuals appear without explanation where an explanation would be expected, e.g. 105.1–2, the story of Theophilus of Meradā is unfinished, being telescoped into the beginning of the revolt against Phocas (105.3 ff.).

from the papyri. Nevertheless a general impression of political conditions emerges.

The relevant part of the *Chronicle* deals with three principal events. First the so-called Aykelāh revolt, next the rising of Heraclius against Phocas, and finally the Arab conquest of Egypt. John of Niciu's account of the Aykelāh 'revolt' late in the reign of Maurice (582–602), some ten years earlier than the revolt of Heraclius, is very obscure but in some ways it reads like a small-scale rehearsal of the war which would be waged between the partisans of Heraclius and Phocas. Abaskīrōn, his brothers Menas and Jacob and his son Isaac evidently dominated the little town of Aykelāh (Metelis) not far from Alexandria. The Augustalis John appointed these men 'governors' over 'many' cities of Egypt.[100] What this means is not at all clear. It is usually taken to mean that he appointed them pagarchs or perhaps 'deputies'[101] to a number of cities. The difficulty with this view is that the 'revolt' centres on one or at most two cities,[102] while a revolt of three or four pagarchs (or 'deputies') should involve three or four cities. What is clear is that these men constituted a great 'house', probably not as wealthy as the Apions and lacking the Apion's influence at Constantinople, but sufficiently powerful to pose a real military threat to the imperial administration in the Delta region of Egypt. Whatever the official status of these four men may have been, and whatever public business they claimed to be engaged in, the outcome was that they attacked the Blue faction and sacked the two cities of Benā and Būsīr, and they did this, as we are told, without the permission of the governor of the province (Aegyptus II?). The 'governor' of Būsīr thereupon fled to Constantinople.[103] The fact that he did not flee to Alexandria suggests that he thought that the men of Aykelāh were acting under orders of the praefectus Augustalis. When the news got round that the emperor had ordered the Augustalis to depose the four men from their posts, they rebelled, or at least they mustered an armed band and ships, and proceeded to harass the food supply of Alexandria.[104] At this point opinion at Alexandria about John the Augustalis was evidently sharply divided. A letter was sent in the name of the citizens asking the emperor to remove John from office. At the same time he did have some support, particularly among Monophysites ('the faithful'), who we are told 'fought on his

[100] John of Niciu 97.1–3.

[101] Perhaps 'deputies' (*topotērētai*) is more likely because pagarchs had to be confirmed by the emperor.

[102] Aykelāh and perhaps Abūsān. Could the passage mean that all the men had been governors of provinces in the past, i.e. that they were *honorati*? But they definitely held an office at the start of the episode, which could be taken away from them (John of Niciu 97.7).

[103] Obviously not the same as the 'governor' of the province. Was he the illustrious Zechariah described as 'lieutenant' of John at Būsīr in 97.16?

[104] Ibid. 97.7.

behalf because of his justice', and gave him an escort of honour out of the city when he was recalled to Constantinople. The eventual outcome was that John justified his conduct to the emperor and was given back his office with special authority to deal with Aykelāh.[105] Now a group made up of three notables and the two factions at Aykelāh and the 'orthodox' bishop of Būsīr[106] became worried, not perhaps because they were opposed on principle to the aggressive four, but because they feared—with good reason—that the city as a whole would be punished for the misdeeds of its leaders. So they secretly began negotiations with Eulogius the 'orthodox' patriarch of Alexandria, with Mīnās the 'assistant', and with Ptolemy the commander of the barbarians (*foederati*?). The aim of the negotiations is not clear. There are two possibilities according to whether we follow the translation of Zotenberg or that of Charles. According to Charles's version they tried to prevent the reappointment of John, fearing that he would punish the leaders of the city of Aykelāh too severely. The implication is that they cooperated with the opponents of John the deposed Augustalis at Alexandria.[107]

Whatever the correct interpretation of the sentence, one thing is clear: a group of notables of Aykelāh negotiated with a similar group at Alexandria,[108] with a view to petitioning the emperor about the appointment of the Augustalis. The eventual outcome was that John did come back, gathered an army, and defeated the inhabitants of Aykelāh. The three brothers were executed, the son Isaac was transported to an island for life. The cities of Aykelāh and Abūsān were destroyed by fire. That was the end of 'the Aykelāh revolt'.

In this episode the factions played a political role. The four notables of Aykelāh attacked the Blues. We are not told whether at Aykelāh, or at Benā and Būsīr, or at all three. There is no suggestion of a link with public spectacles. The Blues were attacked simply because they were opponents of this particular family group. It could be that the powerful 'house' was supported by the Greens. But this is not said. When some notables of Aykelāh became worried about what the three brothers were doing, and

[105] Ibid. 97.7–9.

[106] That they approached orthodox bishops need not mean that they were orthodox themselves: after all the orthodox had the ear of the imperial government.

[107] According to Zotenberg, they wished to bring about precisely his reinstatement. Ch. 97, fo. 120: 'Plusieurs personnes . . . se réuniren en secret à Aykalâ, à l'insu des habitants, et délibérèrent avec Euloge, patriarche d'Alexandrie, Aylas, diacre, Ménas, assesseur, et Ptolémée préfet des barbares. Ils désiraient rétablir le préfet Jean qui, disaient-ils, n'avait point égard au rang des personnes, haïssait l'injustice, et ferait ce qu'ils voudraient.' According to Charles, they 'wanted to appoint a prefect in the room of John, for they said: "This John has no respect for persons, he hates injustice and he will ⟨not⟩ treat us as we wish"' (97.12). The original account must have related the result of this initiative, the version we have does not.

[108] There evidently had been severe fighting, which is not described by John, in Alexandria itself (97.7, 17).

started secret negotiations with leading men at Alexandria with a view to preventing the return of John the Augustalis, they had the support of both factions (if Charles's translation is correct). Finally, when John the Augustalis was at last in a position to confront the men of Aykelāh with units of the army, a decisive part was played by one Cosmas son of Samuel who was released from prison for that purpose:[109] for it was he who persuaded a large number of the rebels to desert. But this Cosmas son of Samuel was a leader of the Blues, who later fought prominently in Bonosus' army for Phocas,[110] and later still, now surely a very old man, led a force of Blues who joined with a force of Greens under their leader Menas 'to besiege the city of Misr (Babylon, Old Cairo) and harass the Romans in the days of the Moslem'.[111] So it looks as if the Aykelāh revolt began with an attack on the Blues, perhaps even an officially authorized attack on the Blues, at a time when leading Blues were in prison, and ended with a return of the Blues to the support of the imperial administration. This incidentally is the reverse of what happened in the Heraclius campaign in which the forces of the emperor supported by the Blues were defeated by those of the usurper Heraclius supported by the Greens.

The Aykelāh 'revolt' throws interesting light on late Late Roman politics and administration. It reveals the power and range of influence of a family group.[112] It shows the factions playing an active part in the political conflicts of the Delta region. Finally, it is a striking feature of the Aykelāh 'revolt' that provincial governors played a very small part. Provincials are seen to have had influence over the replacement or retention of governors and important decisions and, as is shown even more clearly in the rising of Heraclius against Phocas, the decisions as to which side a city was to support was generally made at the city level.[113]

8. *Risings in Syria and Palestine in the Reign of Phocas (602–10)*

Political instability in the first decade of the seventh century was not restricted to Egypt. There is clear evidence that conditions were just as disturbed elsewhere in the East. The evidence is however extremely bitty. The general political background to the items of information we have remains obscure in the extreme, but some of the factors making for instability are clear enough. An important factor, perhaps the most important, was opposition to Phocas as a usurper. In late AD 603

[109] Ibid. 97.15–17, 20–2.

[110] Ibid. 107.37, 109.15.

[111] Ibid. 118.3.

[112] Not only could they seize grain ships sailing from Alexandria to Constantinople (97.13), but they evidently also caused serious damage in Alexandria itself (97.17).

[113] See below, pp. 274–5.

Narses,[114] a very distinguished magister militum per Orientem, rebelled at Antioch, perhaps in the name of a man claiming to be Maurice's surviving son Theodosius.[115] He received help from Chosroes king of Persia, and judging by the fact that he had the Chalcedonian bishop of Edessa executed,[116] he also sought the support of the Monophysites of Syria and Mesopotamia. This was clearly a very serious rebellion which was suppressed within two years, but not without deceit.[117] In AD 608 or early 609 there were further serious disturbances in Syria and Palestine.[118] The sources differ as to who was responsible. According to Theophanes, it was the Jews of Antioch who murdered the orthodox patriarch and many landowners, and went on to defeat the Count of the East, Bonosus, and the general Kottanas, who had been sent against them with a specially gathered force.[119] John of Niciu mentions a rising of Monophysites at Antioch which spread to Palestine and Egypt.[120] When Bonosus restored order at a second attempt,[121] he deposed Isacius, the orthodox bishop of Jerusalem.[122] So it would appear that the revolt involved not only Jews and Monophysites, but some 'orthodox' Christians as well. The Factions too were prominently involved both at Antioch[123] and in Jerusalem,[124] with the Blues supporting Bonosus and Phocas, and the Greens being savagely punished by Bonosus for having supported the other side.

The events in Syria and Palestine illustrate how the imperial structure had been weakened by the antagonizing of Jews and Monophysites.[125] The fact that the Persians were systematically conquering Mesopotamia

114 *PLRE* III B. 933–5 s.v. Narses 10.

115 *PLRE* III B. 1293–4 s.v. Theodosius 13; for various traditions about his fate, see Stratos 1968: i. 55–6. Proclaimed emperor at Edessa by Narses: Sebeos, *Histoire de Héraclius*, tr. F. Macler (Paris, 1940), 56–7 = Sebeos, *History*, tr. R. Bedrosian (New York, 1985), 82; his presence, or that of a pretender, persuades the commander of Erzerum (then Theodosiopolis) to surrender the city: Sebeos (tr. Macler), 62; (tr. Bedrosian), 89.

116 Dionysius of Tel Mahrē 13 (220) in Palmer 1993: 120–1.

117 Theophanes 6097 (AD 605). Important: Whittow 1996: 73–4.

118 Downey 1961: 571–4; Stratos 1968: i. 76–7. What precisely happened and when is very unclear.

119 Theophanes 6101. The *Chronicon Paschale* 699 states very precisely that the killing of the Patriarch Anastasius by soldiers was announced at Constantinople 'at the end of the month September in the 14 indiction', i.e. in September 610. If this is right the bishop was killed in a further and distinct outbreak at Antioch, encouraged perhaps by the defeat of Bonosus in Egypt. If Anastasius was indeed killed by soldiers, this would cast serious doubt on the central role given to the Jews in the rising of 608/9.

120 104–5, p. 166 (tr. Charles).

121 Theophanes *s.a.* 6101; Michael the Syrian X.25; Sébéos 55.

122 *Chron. Pasch.* 699 (AD 609).

123 *Doctrina Iacobi nuper baptizati*, ed. Dagron and Deroche 1991: 40 (p. 39.7–9).

124 Strategius Monachus 4.7 = tr. Conybeare: 502–10.

125 In 599/600 bishop Domitius allegedly on orders of Maurice had expelled the Monophysite bishops of Mesopotamia from their churches (Michael the Syrian X.23; Dionysus of Tel Mahrē reconstituted in Palmer 1993: 117–18, 125, 126 n.

had no doubt encouraged the rising.[126] Invasions always tended to instigate usurpers in the areas behind a frontier which the ruling emperor had failed to defend. It certainly did not help that the government of Phocas was resented as both illegitimate and cruel. Strangely enough we are not told the objective of the revolt.[127] The impression left by the sources is that the troubles were a case of mindless perversity on the part of Jews and others involved. Chronologically it is possible that the rising in Syria and Palestine was already linked with the revolt of Heraclius in Africa.[128] In many ways the situation recalls the crisis suffered by the Empire in the mid-third century. What was different, and aggravated the situation, was the existence of division and conflict among the inhabitants of so many cities of the Empire.

9. *The Rebellion against Phocas in Egypt (609–610)*

When Heraclius rose against Phocas, the decision whether to remain loyal to Phocas or to transfer allegiance to Heraclius appears to have been made more often than not at city level. When Bōnākīs a general of Heraclius entered Egypt, he first gained the support of the tribune of Mareotis.[129] Then after taking control of a divided Alexandria, he was joined by the cities of Niciu and of Manūf (Onouphis), and subsequently by many others.[130] But Athrībis and Samnūd (Sebennytos) remained loyal to Phocas. Moreover the cities of Egypt were deeply divided.[131] At Alexandria three principal officers, John, the 'governor of the city, prefect of the palace and military commander of Alexandria',[132] Theodore (153), the prefect of the *annona*, and Theodore the orthodox patriarch remained loyal to Phocas.[133] But a lot of clergy,[134] perhaps particularly Monophysite clerics, and many citizens,[135] including the Green faction,[136] and also the popular Menas, the 'coadjutor', favoured Heraclius, and recognized

126 Summarized in Stratos 1968: i. 59–66.

127 Conceivably the rebels believed that Theodosius son of Maurice was still alive, as some conspirators did at Constantinople in 606/7 (Theophanes 6099). Theophylact thought that the belief was mistaken and the cause of great evil, VIII.15.8.

128 Solidi were struck for the exarch Heraclius, father of the future emperor, as early as AD 607/8, see Michael and Mary Whitby 1989: 149 n. 416. Unfortunately, the sources are too scrappy to allow us to describe the interaction of the various factors that could have motivated revolt and civic unrest.

129 Maspero 1912: 125, 138.

130 John of Niciu 107.26.

131 Ibid. 107.26–33.

132 = *dux et Augustalis*? See *PLRE* III A s.v. Ioannes 235.

133 John of Niciu 107.6.

134 Ibid. 107.19.

135 Ibid.

136 Ibid. 107.46.

him after the first victory of his force.[137] At Niciu the bishop Theodore together with the 'scribe' Menas brought the city over to Heraclius. At Manūf where the *apūlōn* together with the blue faction had kept the city loyal to Phocas, one senatorial family, the descendants of Aristomachus,[138] and three other notables, Isidore, John, and Julian,[139] and perhaps the Greens, evidently favoured the other side. At any rate the Blues confiscated their property as soon as the city had declared for Phocas.[140] At Samnūd the 'prefect' Paul had been appointed by Phocas and was personally popular and so managed to keep the city loyal to Phocas. At Athrībis a grandee called Aisāilīlūn had been assassinated, presumably by opponents in the town, and the lady Christodora, the sister of the murdered man, was strongly on the side of Phocas. The 'prefect' was a friend of the family and together they kept the town on Phocas' side. The murder is said to have divided all Egypt,[141] an indication that deeper and locally based antagonisms and partisanship, which we lack the evidence to assess, influenced allegiance in this civil war.

In the course of the civil war the Blues and the Greens behaved as political groupings with their own armed resources, the Greens favouring Heraclius and the Blues Phocas. Eventually the Blues too joined Heraclius, but only after it was evident that his general Nicetius had won the war in Egypt.[142] There is no evidence that in this episode the faction fighting arose out of the chariot races or the theatre. The antagonism of the factions did however outlast the civil war. After Nicetius' victory the Greens attacked the Blues[143]—just as the Blues had attacked their opponents when the supporters of Phocas had gained the ascendancy at Manūf.[144] Nicetas proceeded to punish some Greens and make peace between the factions.

Events at Constantinople explain why the Greens opposed Phocas. Given the Empire-wide solidarity of the factions—which is easier to observe than to explain—it is not surprising that the Greens also opposed Phocas in Egypt. What is still quite obscure is why individual Egyptians chose to favour one faction, or one side in the civil war, rather than the

137 Led by *apūlōn* of Alexandria.

138 *PLRE* 2 A s.v. Aristomachus 2, a former citizen of Niciu and a high official whose career was based on a private army. Like the Apions, this family evidently was powerful in more than one city.

139 John of Niciu 107.42.

140 Ibid. 107.25. The Greens are not mentioned here, but the fact that the Blues were on the offensive immediately after the city had sided with Phocas, suggest that here, as at Constantinople, and probably at Alexandria, the Greens opposed Phocas, while the Blues supported him.

141 Ibid. 107.29.

142 Ibid. 108.14, Alan Cameron 1976: 284 is wrong to take this as evidence that the Blues (and the Greens) were basically not concerned with the political issue.

143 John of Niciu 108.16–17. For the argument that the Ethiopic nonsensical word *elwanutes* corresponds to *prasinoi*, Greens, in the Greek original, see Alan Cameron 1976: 82.

144 John of Niciu 107.25.

other. In Egypt the division between Monophysites and Chalcedonians certainly created deep antagonisms, which are plainly visible in the narrative of the Monophysite John of Niciu. For instance what I have taken to be the Chalcedonian bishop is described as 'the enemy of God from Būsīr',[145] while people described as 'pious' or 'god-fearing' are usually Monophysites. But John of Niciu identified with neither the Greens nor the Blues. In the Aykelāh affair he is against the disturbers of the peace, and therefore if anything for the Blues who helped to suppress them. But he describes the revolt against Phocas with sympathy for the Heraclians, the side supported by the Greens. So he did not think that either faction was unambiguously for or against Chalcedon.[146] But at the very end of his Chronicle he describes a deadly quarrel between two Roman officers at the time when the Arabs were occupying Egypt, and he reports that the Monophysite Menas mustered a large force of Greens, while the Chalcedonian Domentianus mustered one of Blues.[147] So it may well be that Monophysites tended to be drawn to the Greens and Chalcedonians to the Blues, even if neither faction was primarily concerned with religion. In fact in a society where the religious division was as deep as it evidently was in Egypt it would be surprising if religion had been totally irrelevant to faction allegiance.[148]

10. *The Growth of Disorder?*

This chapter has been concerned with a number of rather disparate episodes. Did they have any features in common? Above all, do they provide evidence for a steady increase of disorder in the cities of the East? The answer to the last question is probably yes. The almost universal troubles of the reign of Phocas were not simply a consequence of the special circumstances of his reign. The Aykelāh 'revolt' shows that order broke down in Egypt before the usurpation of Phocas. Unfortunately we lack sources which can throw light on the history of that breakdown. The episodes of disorder discussed earlier in this chapter are too discontinuous to serve as evidence for a long-term trend. They do however reveal certain developments which must have made it more difficult to maintain the traditional order.

[145] John of Niciu 97.11.

[146] Alan Cameron (1976: 126–56) is quite right to point this out. In fact overt partisanship in the ecclesiastical conflict would have been incompatible with the factions' regular duties. For the acclamations would certainly include phrases praising whatever bishop was recognized by the emperor.

[147] John of Niciu 119.9.

[148] Everton and Liverpool football clubs at Liverpool, and Celtic and Rangers at Glasgow, are anything but religious organizations. Nevertheless in each city the fans of one club are predominantly Protestant and the other Catholic, their respective membership reflecting the religious division of their city.

At the city level there was an important development in the role of the faction. The factions had always been, and would continue to be, a cause of urban rioting. This, given the nature of these organizations, was inevitable. Even without any political involvement, the fans of the two factions were liable to fight and to wreak widespread havoc after, with the supporters of the losing charioteer generally being the aggressors. Among a large and impoverished urban population, riotous behaviour even by a relatively few—and the registered choruses of supporters at Constantinople in AD 602 numbered as many as 2,400[149]—was likely to be seen as an opportunity for looting by others.

But by the beginning of the seventh century the partisans of the colours were not simply hooligans, if they had ever been that. Moreover their role was no longer simply that of a medium through which conflicting groups might get their slogans publicized. In the events described by John of Niciu the factions behave like armed political parties, participating in a political initiative at Aykelāh, and firmly committed to particular sides in the civil conflict, as they do not appear to have been in earlier times. Unfortunately, we lack the evidence to trace the history of this development. So we do not know how recent it was.[150] But that the factions should have acquired a role of this kind is not surprising. The factions could not really help becoming a power in late Late Antique cities. After the army, the imperial administration, and the Church, they were easily the largest organizations in the Empire. Both factions had branches in every major city. Wherever they operated they needed a large staff to organize the chariot races and whatever other shows might be given. They had close links to wealthy patrons and large numbers of supporters in all ranks of society. Next to the Church, they were in the best position to influence a mass public. Although the rioting fans caused a lot of trouble, the administration found these two large organizations indispensable, and not only because of their primary functions of organizing games and leading acclamations. The government had long made use of the guilds and colleges of craftsmen and shopkeepers for public services such as raising levies, fighting fires, cleaning sewers.[151] The factions were by far the largest of the trades associations, and the government used them to organize the building of city walls, and for raising citizen militias to man them.[152] The

[149] Theophylact VIII.7.10.

[150] But Alan Cameron (1976: 281–5) has argued that the 'political' partisanship displayed by the factions in the deposition first of Maurice, and then of Phocas, merely represents the exploitation of chaos and disorder for their own ends.

[151] Craft associations collect from their members: C. M. Roueché 1993: 125–6; see also *Papyyrologica Lugduno-Batava* XXV, ed. F. A. J. Hoogendijk and P. van Minnen (Leiden, 1991), 225–9, no. 62. Rémondon 1965: 401–30. *P Oxy* 3987: nomination of *prōtodēmotēs* by butchers.

[152] Alan Cameron (1976: 105–25) assembles the evidence for the military role of the factions, but

factions often abused their power. From time to time the government put adherents of one or both factions to death or inflicted severe and brutal punishments on them. The effect was never more than temporary. The factions could not be tamed. In a period of weakening civic and imperial patriotism,[153] it is not surprising that a kind of political loyalty should crystallize around the factions. But they remained a threat to law and order.

The structure of politics of which the factions were a part did not however have a future because all its presuppositions were swept away by the Arab conquest.[154] The factions survived at Constantinople to perform a conspicuous role in the complex ceremonial of the Byzantine emperor. But while titles and appearance of the performances may have remained similar, the context in which they performed had surely become totally different.[155]

Another development making for instability was that the imperial administration found it more difficult to exercise control over the provinces. It is a striking feature of the Aykelāh 'revolt' that provincial governors played a very small part either in the 'revolt' or its suppression. In the civil wars between the forces of Heraclius and Phocas, the decisions as to which side a city was to support was generally made at city level.[156] On the question as to who made the important decisions on behalf of the city, a question which has been raised earlier in this book,[157] John of Niciu must have offered clear evidence in the original Greek version of the *Chronicle*. In the Aethiopian version that has come down to us the evidence is far from clear, all titles have been hopelessly distorted by repeated translation. One does however get the impression that there was no uniform system. In three of the cities the decisive voice in deciding whether the city was to support Phocas or Heraclius seems to have been that of a functionary whose title has come down to us as the 'prefect'.[158] This official is most likely to be equated with the pagarch of the papyrus documents, though he could be the *defensor*. At Manūf the role seems to

to my mind he is wrong to minimize the significance of this wall-manning role. An indispensable role in defence was the surest basis for political power in antiquity. *P Lond* III 1028: use of Greens to collect a levy?

153 See below, pp. 347–50.

154 Most fundamentally, the games sponsored by the Empire and publicizing the ruler ceased. Thus there was no place for factions. But the Islamic futuwwa organizations may well have become the heirs of the political side of the factions' activities, as argued by Sp.Vryonis, 'Byzantine circus factions and the Islamic Futuwwa organizations', *BZ* 58 (1965), 46–59, notwithstanding the rejection of this argument by Alan Cameron 1976: 341–3.

155 Alan Cameron 1976: 297–308.

156 See above pp. 274–5.

157 See above, pp. 198–201.

158 John of Niciu 107.13, 26, 29.

have been played by the so-called *apūlōn*, while Athrībis seems to have had both a prefect (Marcian) and an *apūlōn*,[159] perhaps the tribune commanding the garrison. The prefect Augustalis sometimes appointed 'governors' (deputies?) over cities.[160] But clearly individual notables like Cosmas' son Samuel, leader of the Blues, and Theodore bishop of Nikiu also had great influence. We are told that 'all the province of Egypt was divided on the ground of the murder of Aisāililūn', a notable of Athrībis.[161] His sister Christodora was a leading supporter of Phocas,[162] and together with the 'prefect' Marcian she kept the city of Athrībis loyal to the emperor.

It is another sign of imperial weakness that the imperial authorities were unable to concentrate the garrisons of the cities of Egypt into an effective striking force to meet the crisis, either in the case of the Aykelāh 'revolt' or of the rising against Phocas. The Aykelāh revolt was only suppressed when the Blues came to the aid of the authorities. Bonakis, the commander of the Heraclian forces, needed only to defeat the troops of the *apūlōn* of Alexandria to become master of Egypt[163]—until he encountered Phocas' general Bonosus who arrived in Egypt with an army from Syria. The army of Egypt had become effectively garrison-bound. The military weakness in Egypt suggests that the continued failure of Roman armies against the Persians at this time was due to Roman weakness as much as Persian strength.

There had been an important change in the relationship between provincials and imperial officials. We know from the Laws that provincial notables now had a direct say in the appointments of governors.[164] John of Niciu illustrates this process, describing how a group of notables of Aykelāh discussed with certain notables of Alexandria how to prevent the reappointment of a certain praefectus Augustalis.[165] This is probably why the law that no man may become governor of the province of his birth[166] had become dead letter. Governors now often were natives of the area they governed.

159 Ibid. 107.9.

160 Ibid. 97.16: Zechariah, lieutenant of the Augustalis at Būsīr, presumably he was the same as the 'governor' of 97.5. The four troublemakers of Aykelāh were appointed by the Augustalis 'governors of many cities of Egypt'. We are also told of one Theophilus of Meradā (Thmuis) who was 'governor' of five 'cities'. The 'officers of the city and a large body of men revolted against him' and attacked and captured the five cities (105.1). Maspero takes him to have been an officer commanding several garrisons, perhaps a *praepositus limitis* (J. Maspero, *Organisation militaire de l'Égypte byzantine* (Paris, 1912), 135–6), but that is uncertain.

161 John of Niciu 107.29.

162 Ibid. 107.3–34.

163 Ibid. 97.15, 24.

164 See above, p. 123, n. 121.

165 Ibid. 97.11.

166 *CJ* I.41.

The development was not restricted to the level of governor. The distinction between imperial administration and local ruling groups was breaking down at all levels of administration. Banaji has very convincingly demonstrated this for Egypt.[167] Earlier, say in the fourth century, the men sent to govern provinces might originate from any part of the Empire other than the province they were about to rule. Their administration was carried on with the help of civil servants of the provincial *officium*, who were certainly local men, but comparatively humble both in property and esteem. They certainly ranked far below the city councillors whom they supervised. By the later sixth century the situation was totally changed. In Egypt a large proportion of the high officials, civil as well as military, whose origin is known were natives of Egypt.[168] The provincial *officiales* now formed a large part of the propertied class in the average Egyptian town. In fact they will have constituted the greater part of the *ktētores*, if perhaps not of the *prōteuontes*. So the imperial administration, or at least many of its bureaucrats, now had a profound personal interest in the province from which they were supposed to extract the government's levies. Not surprisingly the administrative machine became less effective. Justinian tried to counter this effect in Egypt and in a number of other provinces by putting soldiers and civilian administrators under the same head.

From another point of view, the Egyptianization of the administration can be seen as one aspect of the coming into existence of a provincial version of the imperial senatorial hierarchy. The leading landowners of Egypt came to hold the highest titles of senatorial rank, titles such as *illustris* and *gloriosus*, which had in earlier times been the insignia of the most elevated positions in the imperial service, distinguishing the likes of praetorian prefects, masters of soldiers, and heads of the principal departments of the central administration from lower, if still elevated functionaries. Epithets that had in earlier times been attached to lower ranks of the senatorial order were now used by many landowners of the second rank. Even administrators of great estates were addressed by titles that had formerly been monopolized by senators. It is not at all clear on what principle these titles of rank were awarded, if indeed they were awarded and not simply assumed. Banaji has argued that they were earned grade by grade by local magnates as they held successive posts of a provincial cursus of imperial offices: stratelates, pagarch, dux of one of the provinces. This may indeed sometimes have been the case. But in the majority of cases we simply do not know how a landowner became a count, or an

[167] Banaji 1992.
[168] e.g. John of Niciu 95, on career of Aristomachus of Niciu; also 105, on Theophilus of Meradā (*PLRE* III B 1309 s.v. Theophilus 4).

illustris, or a patrician. It is likely that in very many cases the titles were not gained by actual office-holding, but that they had been awarded, bought, inherited, or simply assumed. But however these titles were obtained and transmitted, the important result of their prevalence was that Egypt now had an aristocracy in which rank in many cases reflected not service to emperor and Empire, but status in Egyptian society.[169] We lack the evidence to assess whether this development happened outside Egypt, but it is difficult to think of a reason why it should not have done.

Moreover the provincial aristocracies tended to split into even smaller regional groups. The Aykelāh affair illustrates regional politics in the Delta. Under the leadership of a single family, a small number of cities of the Delta were able to achieve a military potential strong enough to defy the imperial authorities. Not only did they seize grain ships sailing to Constantinople,[170] but they also caused damaging conflict in Alexandria itself,[171] and stirred up civil strife in many parts of Egypt.[172] We have here an example of regionalized politics of the kind that, in my opinion, instigated the campaign against the pagans in Syria and Mesopotamia in AD 579. If that persecution of pagans was indeed instigated by a pressure group operating in both Syria and Mesopotamia, the group extended over a remarkably wide area. A possible explanation springs to mind. The Persian war strengthened links between Syria and Mesopotamia. It was from Syria that the troops fighting in Mesopotamia got their supplies and reinforcements. Antioch was the headquarters of the magister militum per Orientem and it was from him that the soldiers got their orders. At the same time Northern Syria and Mesopotamia were linked by religion in that both were predominately Monophysite. The persecution of the pagans, as we have, involved an element of paying back of old scores on the part of the Monophysites. The influence bishop Gregory of Antioch exercised over the Mesopotamian army was facilitated by the close relationship between the neighbouring provinces just as the campaign against him. The political unit that was coming into existence in the last years of imperial rule was to have a place in the Arab organization, in which the Jund of Hims (Emesa) included both Syria and Euphratensis.[173]

Regional solidarity must have been strengthened by the increasingly rigid character of the financial system: that taxes were no longer sent to the centre of the Empire to be redistributed, but were to a large extent expended, year after year, on public services, in the region were they had been collected, must have created a strong sense of shared interest

169 Banaji 1992: 134–63.
170 John of Niciu 97.13.
171 Ibid. 97.17.
172 Ibid. 97.9.
173 J. Haldon 1995: 379–423, relevant 394–9 and map II.

between the soldiers and officials who received state pay and the authorities who procured it for them. Such solidarity would be strengthened further if, as often was the case, officers and officials were native to the area. It is worth noting that the decentralization of the financial administration was a long-term development, which was to be continued by the Arabs, who adopted or rather adapted the Roman organization.[174] It is equally significant that this procedure has been thought 'an important, perhaps the most important, cause of unrest in the Caliphate'.[175]

Trade too tended to create new units. So it seems that the Red Sea became a principal trade route with increasing trade with the Hejaz and East Africa and with India and Arabia passing through Suez or Berenice into Egypt, or via Aqaba to Palestine, rather than entering the Empire via the Persian Gulf, Mesopotamia, and Syria.[176] Arabia and Egypt, and indeed Nubia, coalesced into an economic block, further strengthened by Monophysite Christianity. Monophysitism itself felt the strain of regionalization: for thirty years AD 586/7–616 there was no communion between the Monophysite patriarchates of Antioch and Alexandria over the question of Tritheism.[177]

The distribution of pottery seems to reflect increasing regionalization. Under the Empire, Syria, Egypt, and Asia Minor formed part of a single Empire-wide economic system which was reflected in an Empire-wide distribution of fine pottery and types of amphorae. Say, from the second half of the seventh century, that is after the Arab conquest of Syria, Egypt, and North Africa, the long-distance trade in pottery came to an end in what remained of the Eastern Empire. The economy of the Arab world remained much stronger, but even there the distribution of pottery suggests that trade had become regionalized. One can distinguish different groups of pottery that were traded in Southern Iraq and the Gulf, in Syria and Western Iraq, in Palestine and the Hejaz, and linked to the latter an Egyptian group.[178]

Among factors tending to disrupt the unity of the Empire, religious division must surely be included. Monophysites, Jews, and Samaritans had good reason to be disaffected. The Monophysites were numerically the

[174] H. Kennedy, 'The financing of the military', in Averil Cameron (1995), 361–78.

[175] Ibid. 369.

[176] D. Whitcomb, 'The commercial crescent: Trade and the port of Ayla (Aqaba)', in G. Bisheh (ed.), *The Archaeology of Jordan* (Amman, 1997).

[177] Frend 1972: 341–2.

[178] Based on C. Wickham's unpublished paper to the Fifth Workshop on Late Antiquity and Early Islam, citing: D. Whitcomb, 'Mahesh ware', *Annual of the Department of Antiquities of Jordan*, 33 (1989), 269–85; 'Glazed ceramics of the Abbasid period from the Aqaba excavations', *Transactions of the Oriental Ceramics Society* (1990–1), 43–66; A. Melkawi, K. Amr, D. Whitcomb, 'The excavation of two seventh century pottery kilns at Aqaba', *Annual of the Department of Antiquities of Jordan*, 38 (1994), 447–68.

most important. Scholars have stressed that Monophysitism was not a national movement, and that its adherents were dogmatically hostile to neither classical civilization nor the Roman Empire. On the other hand, Monophysites would not have been human if they had not resented the repeated spells of sharp persecution. Their launching of charges of paganism against 'orthodox' Christians surely expressed bitterness, and the Persians when they replaced the 'orthodox' bishops of Syria, and later of Egypt also, by Monophysites clearly expected their support. The establishment of separate Churches with respectively Syriac and Coptic liturgies was not motivated by hostility to Greek language and culture, but it was a response to persecution by the imperial government, and it was an act of separation. In the circumstances the creation of a separate hierarchy was a challenge to the imperial government. Moreover the existence of country-based bishops further widened the already widening gap between city and territory, and in times of emergency when the bishop was potentially the most effective civic leader, the fact that an 'orthodox' bishop in the city might have a Monophysite rival residing in a rural monastery must have caused serious difficulties.[179]

It should also be born in mind that from around AD 540 the eastern provinces, or at least Syria and Mesopotamia, were under heavy pressure. The balance of military power was now more favourable to the Persians than it had been since the third century.[180] The Syrian taxpayer had to pay for the maintenance of the imperial armies. Syria was invaded twice. Antioch was sacked and burnt and large numbers of its inhabitants deported in AD 540. Apamea suffered the same fate in 573.[181] The area suffered several visitations of plague and repeated earthquakes. This was the background to the disorders discussed earlier, and to the collapse under Phocas.

It may be that in less testing times the late Late Roman institutions would have delivered order and stability. As it was they were not given the chance, and the whole system was swept away by the Arabs. Then Islam—at least for a time—provided the unity which neither Roman administration, nor at this stage Christianity, had been able to provide.

[179] Well documented in case of Cyrus, patriarch of Alexandria and governor of Egypt at the time of the Muslim conquest (Frend 1972: 349–53).

[180] J. Howard-Johnston, 'The two great powers in Late Antiquity: A comparison', in Averil Cameron (1995), 156–226.

[181] J. C. Balty 1989: 79–96, esp. 91–2.

9

Decline and the Beginnings of Renewal in the East

The strength of its cities was a conspicuous feature distinguishing the provinces of the Eastern Empire from those of the West. Of course conditions in the East were not uniform. The fortress cities along the Danube were certainly more like the cities of Gaul than those of Anatolia. The urban system of Syria, Palestine, and Arabia was stronger than that of Anatolia—at least so I have argued. But in the seventh century the whole area was in crisis which left few institutions unchanged. The impact on cities was not uniform, it was rather to greatly increase existing regional differences. The acceleration of regional divergence will be the subject of this chapter.

1. *The Balkans and Greece*

In the Balkans large areas were practically deurbanized. The end of many cities, particularly of the fortress towns along the Danube and of many cities in western and central Greece, was linked with the settlement of Slavonic peoples, with Avar backing, after AD 580.[1] The first wave of invasions occurred in 579–87. The Avars and Sclavenes captured many of the Danube fortresses. Thessalonica was besieged unsuccessfully by a huge force for eight days.[2] There followed a brief period of imperial recovery. Then a second major wave of invasions was launched in AD 614, while the Empire was fully engaged in war with Persia. Almost all the cities on the Danube were captured and sacked once more. The same fate was suffered by many inland cities, among them Naissa and Sardica.[3] Large numbers

[1] On the military history of the events that led to de-romanization of large parts of the Balkans, see Michael Whitby 1988: 138–83. H. Ditten, 'Zur Bedeutung der Einwanderung der Slaven', in F. Winkelmann, H. Köpstein, H. Ditten, and I. Rochow (eds.), *Byzanz im 7. Jahrhundert* (Berlin, 1978), 73–160. For detail, see Pohl 1988: 85; V. Popovic, 'Byzantines, slaves et autochtones', in *Villes et peuplement dans l'Illyricum protobyzantin*, Collection de L'école française de Rome 77 (Paris, 1984): 181–243; B. Fejancic, 'Invasions et installation des slaves dans les Balkans', ibid. 85–109.

[2] Theophylact I.8.10: Avars capture Aquis, Bononia, Ratiaria, Durostorum, Zaldapa, Pannasa, Marcianopolis, Tropaeum Traiani. On events at Thessalonica: Lemerle 1979–81: i, *Miracles* I.13–14 (117–58); on date, see ii. 46–65.

[3] *Miracles* II.1 (179).

of inhabitants were deported by the Avars from the Pannonias, Dacias, Moesia, Dardania, and elsewhere in eastern Illyricum.[4]

Refugees poured into Thessalonica from the Danube area,[5] and the city itself was attacked from the sea in AD 615,[6] and was besieged for thirty-three days in 618. The refugees did not stop at Thessalonica.[7] Many fled to Monemvasia,[8] to the islands and beyond. The bishop of Corinth came to reside on Aegina.[9] The inhabitants of Patras together with their bishop migrated to Sicily.[10] The migration of Greeks to Sicily and southern Italy was clearly on a considerable scale. Sicily which was a Latin-speaking territory in Late Antiquity, had been re-Hellenized by the mid-seventh century.[11] Even relics were evacuated. Pope John IV (640–642) extended the baptistery of St John's cathedral in the Lateran with a chapel to house the relics of eight martyrs which he had transferred to Rome from Salona and other cities of Dalmatia and Istria.[12] With a few exceptions along the Dalmatian coast,[13] this period saw the end of Roman urbanism in the Balkans.[14] Practically none of the cities of central and western Greece, of the Danube provinces, and of Illyricum (with the exception of Dyrrhachium) are recorded to have been represented by bishops at the Councils of Constantinople of AD 680 and 692.[15] It would seem that the Balkans had become largely deurbanized.

[4] *Miracles* II.5 (284).

[5] *Miracles* II.1 (181).

[6] *Miracles* II.2 195–215.

[7] *Chronica di Monemvasia*, ed. I. Dujĉev (Palermo, 1976), 9.

[8] *Chronica di Monemvasia* 9 ff. The reliability of the chronicle has been disputed, a positive judgement: Charanis 1950: 136–66. Lemerle 1963: 5–49, argues convincingly that the chronicle was written soon after the rebuilding of Patras and the re-establishment of its metropolitan see. That its author did not invent history is suggested by the fact that it has no information about Greece for 208 years, from the 6th year of Maurice to the 4th year of Nicephorus. Lemerle supposes that the few sentences about the expulsion (or emigration) following the Avar invasions represent traditions learnt by the chronicler from descendants of the exiles on their return to Greece.

[9] *Chronicle of Monemvasia* 9 ff.

[10] *Chronicle of Monemvasia* 9, but *DAI* c.48 (pp. 228–32) records that in AD 807 inhabitants of Patras, inspired by St Andrew, sallied out against besieging Slavs.

[11] *Chronicle of Monemvasia* 9 ff.; Lilie 1976: 229–30; Charanis 1950; P. Charanis, 'On the question of the hellenization of Sicily and Southern Italy during the Middle Ages', *AHR* 52 (1946), 74–86. See also H. Ditten, *Ethnische Verschiebungen zwischen Balkanhalbinsel und Kleinasien vom Ende des 6. bis zur zweiten Hälfte des 9. Jahrhunderts*, BBA 59 (Berlin, 1993).

[12] *Liber Pontificalis*, 74. On transfer of martyrs from Illyricum, see R. Egger, 'Der heilige Hermagoras', *Carinthia*, 136/8 (1948), 208 ff.

[13] Constantine Porphyrogenitus, *De administrando imperio*, ed. G. Moravcsik and J. J. H. Jenkins (Budapest, 1949), 30.130–140, on Dalmatian cities which paid tribute to the emperors up to Basil I (867–86), and then to Slavs.

[14] See also V. Popovic, 'Les Témoins archéologiques des invasions avaro-slaves dans l'Illyricum byzantin', *MEFR* 87 (1975), 445–504.

[15] G. Ostrogorsky, 'Byzantine cities in the early Middle Ages', *DOP* 13 (1959), 45–66, relevant 56–7. This is in sharp contrast to presence of bishops of very many cities of Anatolia even though these were under heavy pressure from Arab raids. For comparison: Chrysos 1966. This does not mean that all the cities were totally depopulated or even completely without Christian population. See

It is not necessary to suppose that all cities were totally depopulated, that the Roman population disappeared entirely, and that for a time there were no Christians at all left in these areas. Some Latin place-names have survived, for instance Naissus as Nis.[16] The cathedral of Serdica (Sophia) has stood outside the walls of its city intact to the present day.[17] Whether you describe what survived as cities is to some extent arbitrary, but not altogether. The cities and their bishops disappear from the historical record for more than two hundred years. There are very few, if any, local traditions of continuity. The Bulgar Kingdom was not based on the Roman cities but on a new city of a new type.[18] In this respect the history of the cities in the inland regions of the Balkans—and of western and central Greece too—is unlike that of the cities of eastern Greece and Dalmatia, not to mention that of the cities of Anatolia or Italy or even the Rhineland. The fate of the Balkan cities was in fact more like that of the cities of Roman Britain.

In Late Antiquity much of Greece had enjoyed the combination of a flourishing countryside with flourishing cities which prevailed over most of the East.[19] That condition was not quite universal. A continued shrinking of settlement has been observed in the country around Patras,[20] and there was only a 'modest recovery' from the depression of the third century on Northern Keos, on Crete, and in central Laconia.[21] But field surveys in Boeotia and Arcadia, and on the Methana peninsula, have found evidence of a strong recovery of site density, and presumably of population, from

Whittow 1996: 268, on continuity at Serdica (Sophia), Philippopolis (Plovdiv), and Patras, largely based on material in J. D. Howard-Johnston, 'Urban continuity in the Balkans in the early Middle Ages', in A. G. Poulter (ed.), *Ancient Bulgaria*, ii (Nottingham, 1983), 245–54. Howard-Johnston to my mind greatly overestimates the extent of continuity established by his evidence.

16 M. Vasmer, *Die Slaven in Griechenland*, Abhandlungen der preussischen Akademie der Wissenschaften, Phil. Hist. Kl. 12 (Berlin, 1941; Leipzig, 1970). M. W. Weithmann, *Die slawische Bevölkerung auf der griechischen Halbinsel* (Munich, 1978). P. Lemerle, 'Invasions et migrations dans les Balkans depuis la fin de l'époque romaine jusqu'au VIIIe siècle', *RH* 211 (1954), 265–301. For survival of place-names, see fold-in map in Pohl 1988.

17 V. Velkov, 'Zur Geschichte der Stadt Serdica/Sofia im 4.–9. Jahrhundert', *Études Historiques*, 3 (1965), 33–6; M. Stanceva, 'Sofia au moyen age à la lumière de nouvelles études archéologiques', *Byzantino bulgarica*, 5 (1978), 211–28. P. Schreiner, 'Städte und Wegenetz in Moesien, Dakien und Thrakien nach dem Zeugnis des Theophylactos', in his *Studia byzantino-bulgarica*, Miscellanea Bulgarica 2 (Vienna, 1986), 59–69.

18 Rashev 1983: ii. 255–69.

19 J. L. Bintliff and A. M. Snodgrass, 'The end of the Roman countryside: A view from the East', in J. Jones *et al.* (eds.), *First Millennium Papers: Western Europe in the First Millennium AD*, BAR S401 (Oxford, 1988), 175–217. Castrén 1994.

20 M. Petropoulos and A. D. Rizakis, 'Settlement patterns and landscape in the coastal area of Patras', *JRA* 7 (1994), 183–207.

21 See M. Rautman, 'Field survey in Northern Keos', *JRA* 7 (1994), 421–5; C. Nixon, S. Price, J. Moody, and O. Rackham, 'Rural settlement in Sphacteria, Crete', in P. N. Doukellis and L. G. Menoni (eds.), *Structures rurales et sociétés antiques*, Actes du colloque de Corfu 1992 (Paris, 1994), 255–64. Cavanagh *et al.* 1996: 123 (summary of pottery survey).

the fourth century lasting well into the sixth.[22] In the Argolid, settlement recovers from a low around 300 with an increase in the number of sites up to the end of the sixth century. But then a rapid decline ensued, culminating in nearly total abandonment.[23]

There is still very little archaeological evidence for living conditions in the countryside in the time of the Slavonic raids and settlement. A rural site in the neighbourhood of Corinth, dated AD 550–650 gives an impression of simplified living conditions. The site lies over a levelled early Byzantine fort. Finds include coarse Slavonic pottery, rotary mill stones, hearths of tiles set in mud mortar. The houses are built of re-used stone and apsed. These houses are more substantial than the still very few Slavonic houses excavated elsewhere, which are either round or nearly square and completely or partially subterranean.[24]

As for the cities, Athens flourished into the early sixth century.[25] The same was true of the little towns of Ascra and Thespiae in Boeotia.[26] But in the later sixth century rapid decline began.[27] At Corinth, the circuit of walls had already been greatly shortened in the fifth century. Much of the forum area was abandoned, and parts of it were used for burials, though traces of a large fifth-century building have been found near the South Basilica. It may be that at Corinth the centre of population shifted to a part of the site which has not yet been excavated.

The seventh century brought about great changes everywhere, unfortunately also an almost complete drying up of written evidence.[28] The great city of Nicopolis on the west coast which had flourished in the sixth century was abandoned. A number of cities along or near the coast in eastern and southern Greece survived the Dark Age, but they emerged

[22] J. Bintliff, 'The Roman countryside in central Greece: Observations and theories from the Boeotia survey', in Barker and Lloyd (1991), 122–32. C. Mee, D. Gill, H. Forbes, and L. Foxall, 'Rural settlement in the Methana peninsula Greece', in Barker and Lloyd (1991), 223–32. J. Roy, J. Lloyd, and E. J. Owens, 'Megalopolis under the Roman empire', in S. Walker and A. Cameron (eds.), *The Greek Renaissance under the Roman Empire*, Bulletin London Institute of Classical Studies Suppl. 55 (London, 1989), 146–51.

[23] C. N. Runnels and T. H. van Andel, 'The evolution of settlement in southern Argolid Greece', *Hesperia*, 61 (1987), 303–34. M. H. James, C. N. Runnels, T. H. van Andel, *A Greek Countryside: The Southern Argolid from Pre-history to the Present Day* (Stanford, Calif., 1994), 113–14, 554, see also 241–2, figs. 4.26–4.28.

[24] T. E. Gregory, 'The Corinthia in the Roman period', *JRA Suppl* 8 (Ann Arbor, 1993), 149–60; houses of slavs: Lemerle 1979–81: ii. 235–41.

[25] Castrén 1994.

[26] J. L. Bintliff and A. M. Snodgrass, 'Mediterranean survey and city', *Antiquity*, 62 (1988), 57–71, but decline after 600.

[27] Sharp contraction of inhabited area at Athens around 600, K. M. Setton, 'The archaeology of medieval Athens', in *Essays in Medieval Life and Thought Presented to Austin Patterson Evans* (New York, 1955), 227–58. T. L. Shear, 'The Athenian Agora Excavations of 1972', *Hesperia*, 42 (1973), 395–8.

[28] Pohl 1988: 99–112, 240–3.

transformed. At Corinth, by the eighth or ninth century the whole forum area appears to have been abandoned, and now not only for housing but even for burials. The city as rebuilt after destruction was very different from classical, and indeed Late Antique Corinth.[29] The regular street plan had disappeared. There were no public buildings and no public spaces. Churches were much smaller than they had been in late Antiquity. The houses were small and irregularly spaced. There was little continuity with the classical city.[30] Thebes contracted to the Cadmeia. At Patras inhabitants moved from the site of the port to a fortified hill.[31] Olympia was abandoned from the seventh century.[32] So was Sparta.[33] Butrotum (Butrint) in Epirus had flourished well in to the sixth century. Late in the sixth and early in the seventh century dry stone walling appeared in all parts of the city, particularly in the shape of party-walls, dividing up large old stone houses. In the middle of the seventh century the lower city was abandoned and the population contracted into a fortified upper city.[34]

It is conceivable that the evacuation of cities in the Balkans and eastern and central Greece was at least in part organized by the Imperial government. We know that this happened at Sirmium in AD 582.[35] But we do not know whether Sirmium was at all typical. Such a strategy would have had clear military advantages. At this time the imperial government had to wage war on two fronts, in the Balkans against the Slavs and Avars,[36] and in the East against the Persians. The Empire was unable to maintain adequate armies in both theatres,[37] and when the war against the Persians had to be given priority, the army facing Slavs and Avars in the West was quite inadequate.[38] So there was no alternative to abandoning the inland cities to the enemy, and to concentrate on the defence of a few fortified

[29] E. A. Ivison, 'Burial and urbanism at Late Antique and Early Byzantine Corinth (c.400–700)', in Christie and Loseby (1996), 99–125.

[30] Bouras 1981: 611–53. See also chapters in *Villes et peuplement dans l'Illyricum protobyzantin*, Collection de l'école française de Rome LXXVII (Rome, 1984): G. Dagron, 'Les Villes dans l'Illyricum Protobyzantin', 1–20; B. Bavand, 'La Ville dans le nord de l'Illyricum', 245–87 (Sirmium, Gamzigrad, Caricingrad); J. R. Wiseman, 'The city in Macedonia Secunda', 289–313 (Stobi abandoned soon after 570, and destroyed some time after abandonment); J. M. Spieser, 'La Ville en Grèce du IIIe au VIIe siècle', 315–40.

[31] H. Saradi-Mendelovici, 'A propos de la ville de Patras au 13e–15e siècles', *Revue des Études Byzantines*, 38 (1980), 219–32.

[32] A. Harvey 1989: 28–9.

[33] Bouras 1981: 622.

[34] Hodges, G. Saraçi, *et al.* 1997.

[35] See below, p. 379.

[36] These were formidable enemies, as nomad peoples were liable to be, but in addition they had armoured cavalry (*Miracles de S. Demetrius*, 199) and catapults capable of breaching city walls (*Miracles*, 200).

[37] It was evidently very difficult to get units stationed in cities to fight as part of a field army, as is illustrated by refusal of garrison of Asemus, supported by citizens, to join the field army of Peter in 594 (Theophylact VII.2.3.1–10).

[38] Menander the Protector (ed. R. Blockley), fr. 21 and 26.45 ff.

coastal cities, which could be supplied by sea. In that situation it would have been logical to withdraw the inhabitants from indefensible inland towns in order to strengthen the defence of cities that could be defended successfully. The imperial government certainly founded a few new fortress-cities on coastal sites. Monemvasia was one of these. Others are Split, Dubrovnik, Arkadia, Kalamata, and Korone. Clearly these must have drawn their population from elsewhere. Their greater safety will have made them attractive. It is likely enough that the authorities used compulsion to people these new fortresses, if there were not enough volunteers. Deliberate evacuation of the cities of a territory would have had other advantages. It would deprive invading armies of logistic support.[39] The evacuation of cities would also make it impossible for the invader to take over the Roman city-based administration, and to base their own power on it, which is what the Goths and Vandals had done in the West, and the Arabs were to do in the East. A strategy of evacuation would have enabled the Empire to retain the technical skills of the inhabitants of lost cities, while depriving the enemy of this advantage.[40] When the Arabs captured the cities of Syria, many of their skilled inhabitants fled, so that the Arabs found it necessary to make up the loss by settling craftsmen from Mesopotamia.[41] Avars and Slavs would not have been able to replace the evacuated population with individuals of similar skills.

An imperial strategy of evacuation would provide a neat explanation for the dramatic deurbanization of the Balkans in the seventh century. Unfortunately, there is no conclusive evidence that the imperial government pursued such a strategy. *The Miracles of St Demetrius*, the principal, and almost only contemporary source for these events, does not mention a single case of organized evacuation.[42] There is however some archaeological evidence that buildings at Nicopolis ad Istrum were dismantled and abandoned before being destroyed by fire.[43] Similarly at Stobi in

[39] Lilie (1976: 345) cites William of Tyre, *Historia rerum in partibus transmarinis gestarum*, *PL* 201.245 f. explaining the use of this strategy by the Byzantines in the Balkans in the 11th cent.

[40] The Persians, who had no intention to permanently occupy the cities of Syria, deported their inhabitants; see R. N. Frye, *The History of Ancient Iran* (Munich, 1984), 371 ff., which has a translation of Sapor's inscription. They used the captives to populate newly founded cities, in fact to further urbanization; see. S. Lieu, 'Captives, refugees and exiles: A study of cross-border civilian movements between Rome and Persia from Valerian to Jovian', in P. Freeman and D. Kennedy (eds.), *The Defence of the Roman and Byzantine East*, ii, BAR Int. 297 (Oxford, 1986), 475–507. Pusai (whose martyrdom is recorded in the Syriac *Acta martyrum et sanctorum*, ed. P. Bedjan (Paris, 1890), ii. 209–10, translated in S. Lieu, *The Roman Eastern Frontier and the Persian Wars: A Documentary History* (London, 1991), 163, no. 6.4.4) a weaver and embroiderer and 'chief craftsmen of the shah' was the son of deportees.

[41] Lilie 1976: 233, citing Baladhuri 1966: 180 ff.

[42] J. Ferluga, 'Untersuchungen zur byzantinischen Ansiedlungspolitik auf dem Balkan von der Mitte des 7. bis zur Mitte des 9. Jahrhunderts', *Zbornik Radova*, 23 (1984): 49–61.

[43] Poulter 1995: 44–5.

Macedonia, archaeologists have found some indications that buildings had been abandoned some time before they were destroyed. The latest coin on the site dates from AD 569/70.[44] We know that some seventy years later the Empire did adopt a strategy of deliberate evacuation of cities in the face of the Islamic invasion of its eastern provinces. This was the period after the Arab victory in the battle of the Yarmuk, in AD 636, when Heraclius ordered the evacuation of the flourishing cities of late Late Roman Cilicia in order to create an empty buffer zone between imperial lands and those occupied by the Arabs.[45] Subsequently these lands were repeatedly reoccupied, captured, and devastated, and the area became a deserted zone between the combatants. But that is still no proof that a comparable strategy was adopted in the Balkans.

In retrospect the Byzantines liked to think that the resettlement of the Balkans—what is now seen as their deurbanization and indeed de-Romanization—was actually carried out with permission of the imperial government, and under its direction. So we read that the inhabitants of Salona obtained permission from the emperor to settle in Spalatum (Split).[46] According to Constantine Porphyrogennetus' *De Administratione Imperii* the Croats were given permission by Heraclius to settle in Avar territory.[47] So were the Serbs.[48] The resettlement of Diocleia too is attributed to Heraclius.[49] These notices may well represent wishful thinking on the part of Constantine Porphyrogennetus (913–57), or of his ninth-century sources. However these alleged measures of Heraclius would have represented a continuation of the long-established imperial policy of supporting the 'hungry' barbarians against well established ones.[50]

[44] Wiseman 1984: 310. See also K. Hattersley Smith, *Byzantine Public Architecture between the Fourth and Early Eleventh Centuries AD with Special Reference to the Towns of Macedonia* (Thessaloniki: Society for Macedonian Studies, 1996).

[45] See Lilie 1976: 186–95. Baladhuri 1966: 253, Heraclius leaves devastated Cilicia between Empire and the Arabs, cf. Michael the Syrian XI.7 (419).

[46] On the end of Salona: Thomas Archidiaconus, *Historia Salonitana*, ed. Racki, Monumenta spectantia historiam Slavorum meridionalium XXVI (Zagreb, 1894), 25–33: AD 638–9. See Michael Whitby 1988: 188–90; Pohl 1988: 243–5. It was assumed that coins end 614/15, but a recent find of copper coins includes one minted 625–30: F. Oreb, 'Archaeological excavations in the Eastern part of Ancient Salona', *Vjesnik za Arheologiju i Historiju Dalmatinsku*, 70 (1984), 24–36. Excavation shows that transfer of its population, presumably to Spalato, was only complete by the mid-7th cent. There are two versions of the capture, respectively chs. 29 and 30 of Const.P. *DAI*. The former version which Pohl prefers has Salona captured by unarmed slavs called Avars settled across a river (the Cetina acc. to Pohl). In other words a similar attack to that on Thessalonica in 604. But Michael Whitby emphasizes that in the 9th cent. it was in the interest of both the emperor and of tribal groups to maintain that the settlement had been in accordance with imperial wishes. What actually happened must remain uncertain.

[47] Const. P. *DAI* 31.19–20.

[48] Ibid. 32.10–11; 32.20.

[49] *DA* 35.6–9.

[50] Pohl 1988: 52–3. J. Koder,'Zur Frage des Siedlungsgebietes im mittelalterlichen Griechenland', *BZ* 71 (1978): 315–31.

Whatever was the precise course of events in the Balkans and western Greece in the seventh century, it is evident that cities fared very much less well in territories settled or controlled by Avars and Slavs than in lands ruled by Goths or Vandals, or indeed by Lombards or Franks. The essential difference between Avar/Slavs and the Germanic peoples was that they neither settled in cities, nor gave cities an essential role in their administration.[51] The Avar economy was for a long time based on plunder and enforced tribute, and therefore had no need for towns. Their material culture was simple and did not depend on commerce. The Avars were not Christians, and they did not try to rule with help of bishops. So cities had no role. By this time most of the cities in territories about to be occupied by the Avars can only have had small populations. Flight when capture by Avars or Slavs was imminent, whether it was organized or simply motivated by panic, certainly reduced populations further. Once the cities were under Avar/Slav, and later Bulgarian, rule, there was no motive for refugees to return to them, or for any remaining inhabitants to stay. The fact that most of the cities captured and occupied temporarily by Avars during their first great invasion in AD 581–2, did not disappear, but still figure in accounts of campaigns around 600, proves that the Avars did not deliberately and systematically destroy cities. It was after the Empire had in fact abandoned interest in the Balkans under Heraclius that cities and bishops disappear from history.[52] The cities that remained under imperial government survived.[53]

2. *Asia Minor*

As for Byzantine Asia Minor, the mid-seventh century marks the beginning of a century or so which has left very little evidence. To a large extent developments have to be deduced from conditions in the better known eighth and ninth centuries.[54] In many respects the social evolution of Late Antiquity had already foreshadowed the society of the Byzantine Empire after the 'Dark Age': villages were gaining in social importance. Monks and monasteries were increasing their power and influence at the expense of the episcopal church. Culture had become thoroughly Christianized,

[51] Perhaps characteristic Theophylact VII.10.1: Avars pull down walls of Sigidunum, resettle population. This does not mean that individual Avars or Slavs might not sometimes appreciate the amenities of city life, e.g. the hot baths at Anchialus (Theophylact I.4.5), or the comforts of Thessalonica (*Miracles S. Demetrius* 235 on Perbundus), or the fact that tribute could be raised from cities (Michael the Syrian X.21 (379)).

[52] Whittow 1996: 48–51, 74–5, 262–75. Pohl 1988: 242.

[53] Pohl 1988: 423 n. 33, cities kept by Empire: Philippopolis (name survives as Plovdiv), Adrianopolis (name survives as Edirne), Develtos, Mesembria, and Sozopolis.

[54] A. Harvey 1989.

and secular literature all but ceased to be written. All these phenomena are conspicuous when our information resumes. But it is nevertheless very difficult to trace continuity between actual institutions of late Late Antiquity and of the Byzantine period.

Conciliar lists of Asia Minor suggest that most of the sees of the late Roman period survived,[55] but archaeology shows that all, or nearly all, had been reduced to the condition of villages, or of fortresses.[56] Ephesus split into two fortified centres, one by the harbour and another around the church of St John.[57] Sardis became a cluster of small settlements around a fortification.[58] Ancyra (Ankara) was reduced to a fortress.[59] So was Pergamum.[60] Perhaps the settlements whose character remained closest to that of cities in the old sense were Ephesus, Nicaea, and Trapezont. There is some evidence that at Armorium the wide circuit of walls enclosing the lower city *was* maintained intact, and presumably inhabited, until the destruction of the city in AD 838.[61] But in a very real sense Constantinople was now *the* city of Asia Minor.

That the period saw a very considerable fall in population is perhaps a safe deduction from the shrinking area of circuit walls.[62] That the countryside had suffered depopulation must be the principal reason why the Byzantine emperors adopted a policy of resettlement. Starting with Constans II in AD 658, the emperors repeatedly made efforts to replenish the population of Asia Minor, and to gain manpower for their armies by settling large numbers of Slavonic prisoners.[63] In AD 685 Justinian II (685–95, 705–11) made an agreement with the Arabs, by whose terms he was required to withdraw the Mardites from Syria, and to settle them within the Empire.[64] When Justinian II was forced to evacuate Germanicia he settled its inhabitants in Thrace.[65] On another occasion he settled many captured Slavs in the theme of Opsikion.[66] In 691–2 a large number of Cypriots were settled together with their archbishop in Nova

55 Chrysos 1966.

56 A. Harvey 1989: 23.

57 Foss 1979: 111–13.

58 Foss 1976: 55f.

59 Foss 1977*c*: 27–87; A. Harvey 1989: 28–9. Most of Harvey's generalizations are based on C. Foss.

60 Brandes 1989: 110 f.; Rheidt 1991.

61 See R. M. Harrison, 'Amorium Excavation: The Preliminary Reports', *Anatolian Studies*, 38 (1988), 175–84 and 42 (1992), 207–22; C. S. Lightfoot, ibid. 43 (1993), 147–62; C. S. Lightfoot and E. A. Ivison, ibid. 45 (1995), 105–38 and ibid. 46 (1946), 91–110. 30,000 are said to have been killed when Armorium was captured by the Arabs, according to the Arab al-Mas'ūdī, translated by A. A. Vasiliev, *Byzance et les Arabes*, i, French edn. by H. Grégoire and M. Canard (Brussels, 1959), 332, discussed sceptically by Brandes 1999: 36–41.

62 A corresponding growth of population in suburbs or villages must not be assumed.

63 Theophanes 347.

64 Theophanes 363.15.

65 Theophanes 391.

66 Theophanes 365.

Justinianopolis, a new city situated near the then derelict Cyzicus.[67] This was a fully planned transfer of population, which is likely to have been part of the agreement, sharing the revenues of Cyprus between the Arab and the Roman empires, which Justinian had made in AD 688.[68] The settlement of captives first in Asia Minor and later in Thrace became regular Byzantine policy.[69]

When economic revival eventually occurred there was a shortage of workers on the land in spite of the policy of resettlement. In Greece, and especially on Athos from the tenth century, monasteries made efforts to settle more *paroikoi* on their lands; and there is evidence from some monastic estates that the number of settled *paroikoi* was indeed increased.[70] Since it was the function of *paroikoi* to bring, and keep, more land under cultivation, we can conclude that in the Dark Ages there had been a reduction in the area of land cultivated which was now being reversed. The manpower that made this possible can only have become available through a resumed growth in population.[71]

Late Antiquity had seen the establishment of numerous substantial and well-built villages, whose dead were commemorated with inscribed tombstones in the uplands of Phrygia and Pisidia in central Anatolia. We do not know what happened to them. Few or none have been excavated, but visible remains show little evidence of activity from the later fifth century. The Life of S. Theodore of Sykeon shows that the villages of Bithynia and Galatia were still very much alive in the late sixth century. But then came the Persian invasions, and the centuries of Arab raids. When peace returned, the economic exploitation of the Anatolian plateau had changed from arable farming to grazing,[72] in other words the region was again farmed as it had been before the Roman occupation, and as it has continued to be farmed until very recent times.[73]

The evidence of the Farmer's Law of the late seventh or eighth century[74] suggests that far-reaching changes in the condition of the

[67] *DAI* 47.6 ff.; 47.11 ff.

[68] The suggestion of Lilie 1976: 103 is plausible because according to *DAI* 47 seven years later the Cypriots (or some of them) were to return to Cyprus at the same time as some others who had been deported by the Arabs to Syria. Against Lilie's suggestion is the statement of Theophanes that the deportation of the Cypriots to Asia was treated by the Arabs as a breach of treaty (ed. de Boor, 365.9). For agreement to share revenues, see ibid. 363.11.

[69] See Lilie 1976: 227–54; movement of populations made it possible to resettle deserted lands and to acquire new sources of recruits. Also P. Charanis, 'The transfer of population as a policy of Byzantine emperors', *Comparative Studies in Society and History*, 3 (1961), 140–54; also 'Ethnic change in the Byzantine empire in the seventh century', *DOP* 13 (1959), 25–44.

[70] A. Harvey 1989: 48–50.

[71] Ibid. 47–60.

[72] Ibid. 30–1.

[73] Mitchell 1993: i. 245–55.

[74] W. Ashburner, 'The Farmer's Law', *JHS* 30 (1910), 85–108; 32 (1912), 68–95. The question is

peasantry had taken place: the Roman colonate had disappeared. The typical cultivator, whether he enjoyed full ownership or only the rights of 'possession', now had become entitled to freely dispose of the land he was working.[75] An increased proportion of peasant proprietors, and a greater independence of tenants, implies a reduction in the pressure by landowners to increase the production of corn for the market. This would be a likely response if there had been a reduction in the demand for corn to feed the cities, or to pay the taxes.

In all areas that remained under the government of Constantinople the quantity of money in circulation was greatly reduced.[76] At Corinth and Athens for example very few coins have been found from the years between the government of Constantine IV (AD 668–85) and the mid-ninth century. The same is true of Pergamum, Priene, Ephesus, and Sardis.[77] There is no self-evident explanation of this. The absence of coins suggests that the government put much less money into circulation, presumably because it needed less to pay its army and officials. Conceivably the armies of the themes now received a great part of their sustenance in kind.[78] Lacking readily available coin, the population must have carried out most transactions by exchange or barter.[79] Trade was reduced to a minimum. Along the coast the long-distance amphora trade came to an end and inland distribution of pottery became extremely localized.[80]

To sum up, the seventh century undoubtedly saw very great changes in Anatolia. There can be no doubt that the raids by Arab armies which year

whether the 'Farmers' Law' was a substitute, or perhaps rather a supplement of the Justinianic laws, in the same way as the *Code of Euric* in my view was a supplement rather than a replacement of the Theodosian *Code* and Alaric's *Breviarium*. Haldon suggests that many elements of the Farmers' Law go back to Justinian, and deal with rural matters too trivial to be of concern to *CJ*. The *Basilica* are essentially (99%) a reissue of the *CJ* with the Latin technical terms now translated into Greek. A few texts of penal law date to 9th. The 113 *Novels of Leo* VI (886–912) supplement the *Basilica*, as the *Novellae* had supplemented *CJ*.

75 A. Harvey 1989: 1–19; Lemerle 1979: 90 ff.

76 Metcalfe 1967: 270–310. Grierson 1960: 411–53.

77 A. Harvey 1989: 20–1; Sodini 1993: 139–84, fig. 29. C. Morrisson, 'Monnaie et finances dans l'empire byzantin Xe–XVe siècle', in V. Kravari and J. Lefort (eds.), *Hommes et richesses dans l'empire byzantin*, ii (Paris, 1991), 291–315, figs. 2a and 2b (pp. 302–3). But note that at Antioch the early Arab period has produced an increase in coin finds. A subsequent fall results in very few finds of coins from around 1000; see F. O.Waagé (ed.), *Antioch on the Orontes*, 4/i. *Ceramics and Islamic Coins* (Princeton, 1948); Dorothy B. Waage (ed.), *Antioch on the Orontes*, 4/ii. *Greek, Roman, Byzantine and Crusader Coins* (Princeton, 1952).

78 W. Brandes and J. Haldon, 'Town, tax and transformation: State, cities and their hinterlands in the East Roman world *c.*500–800', in Christie, Gauthier, Brogiolo (forthcoming).

79 Examples from a later period: Saradi 1995.

80 Long-distance exchange: C. Panella, 'Merci e scambi nel Mediterraneo in età tardoantica', *Storia di Roma*, iii/2 (Turin, 1993), 657–73. Example of localization of pottery: L. Brown, in R. M. Harrison, 'Amorion 1989', *Anatolian Studies*, 40 (1990), 213–15; 41 (1991), 212–16. Dramatic decline in production of both fine pottery and amphora: J. Hayes, 'Problèmes de la céramique des VII–IX siècles à Salamine de Chypre', in *Histoire et archéologie, état des recherches* (Paris, 1980), 375–80.

after year, with very few interruptions, penetrated deep into the remaining imperial territories contributed very considerably to the drastic transformation.[81] The Arabs were not the only factor. As we have seen urban decline in Anatolia had begun well before the end of the sixth century. It is doubtful whether scholars will ever be in a position to assess the relative importance of long-term trends, and the disorganization produced by many decades of Arab raiding.

3. *Syria, Palestine, and Arabia*

Change was very much less conspicuous in the areas conquered by the Arabs. The long-term effect of the Arab conquest was to impose an Arab tribal culture where previously a late Hellenistic urban culture had been dominant. The structure of existing cities, and the agricultural exploitation of the countryside, were not immediately affected, though a reduction in the number of rural sites in marginal areas on the desert fringe, in fact in precisely the areas which had been developed so dramatically in the early Byzantine period, seems to have set in under the Abbasids and Fatimids, i.e. after *c.*750.[82]

As we have seen the economies of the cities of northern Syria and of the villages of the massif were linked. In this area the prosperity of the cities ended before that of the villages: the cities flourished as long as the villages expanded, that is until around AD 550. Then while the villages stagnated, Antioch and other cities went into sharp decline. Plague, earthquakes, and Persian raids, often involving deportation of large parts of the urban population provide a perfectly adequate explanation of that decline. A field survey has noted a drastic decline in the number of settlements on the left bank of the Euphrates opposite Birecik in Mesopotamia after AD 600. This could well be a consequence of the same calamities as the regression further south. It has however been suggested that economic decline in northern Mesopotamia happened considerably later than was concluded by the Birecik survey. The alternative explanation proposed is overcultivation in the Umayyad and Abbasid periods.[83]

[81] Haldon 1990: 105–13.

[82] G. R. D. King and Averil Cameron 1994; to be supplemented by J. H. Humphrey (ed.), *The Roman and Byzantine East*, JRA Suppl. XIV (Ann Arbor, 1995), and esp. C. Foss, 'The Near Eastern countryside in Late Antiquity, a review article', in ibid. 213–34. See also E. M. Meyers and others (eds.), *The Oxford Encyclopedia of Archaeology in the Near East* (New York/Oxford, 1997).

[83] On northern Syria: H. Kennedy 1985*b*: 141–83; 1985*a*: 3–27; 1992: 181–98. On cumulative effect of Persian deportations: Trombley 1997. The Birecik survey: Wilkinson 1990: summarized i. 117–29. See also the discussion in 'Land use and settlement patterns in Late Sassanian and Early Islamic Iraq', in G. R. D. King and Averil Cameron 1994: 221–9. For possible late dating of rural decline in northern Mesopotamia on analogy of decline linked to overproduction evidenced in lower Mesopotamia, see Morony 1984, 1987.

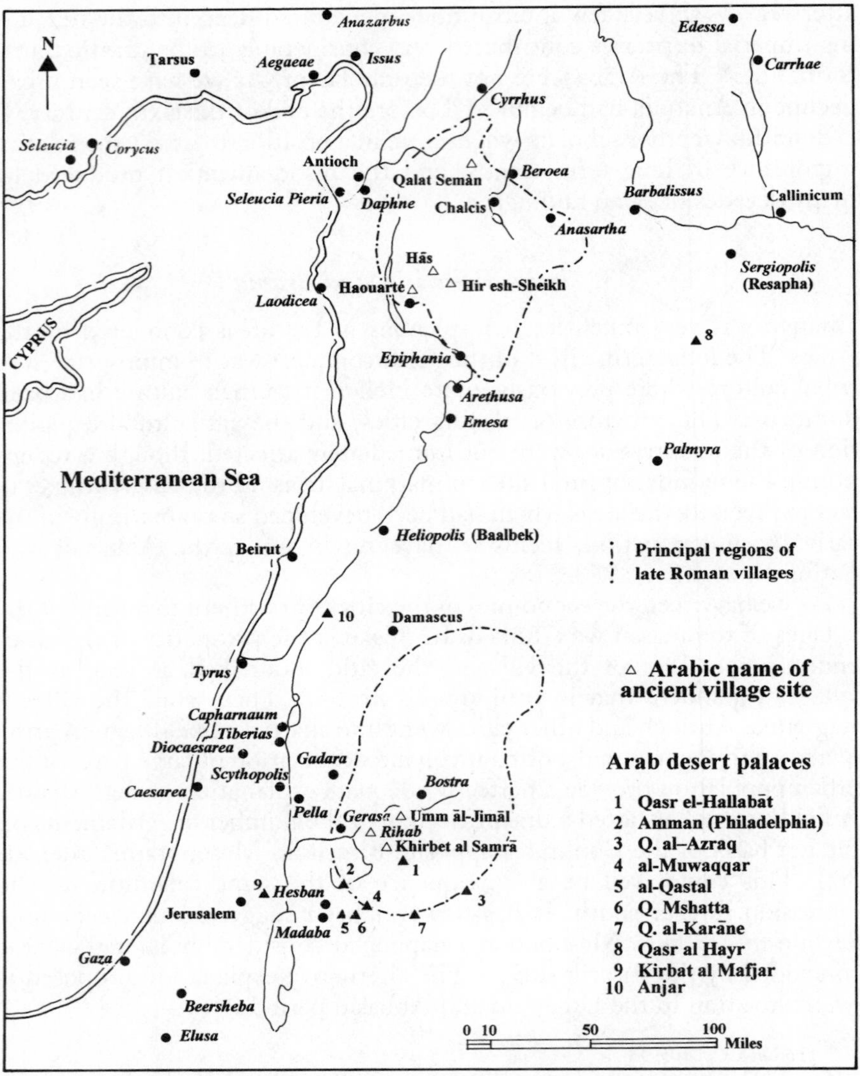
N
Anazarbus
Edessa
Tarsus
Aegaeae
Issus
Carrhae
Cyrrhus
Seleucia
Corycus
Antioch
Qalat Semàn
Beroea
Seleucia Pieria
Daphne
Chalcis
Barbalissus
Callinicum
Anasartha
Hās
Sergiopolis
(Resapha)
Haouarté
Hir esh-Sheikh
Laodicea
CYPRUS
8
Epiphania
Arethusa
Emesa
Palmyra
Mediterranean Sea
Heliopolis (Baalbek)
Beirut
Principal regions of
late Roman villages
10
Damascus
Tyrus
Arabic name of
ancient village site
Capharnaum
Tiberias
Diocaesarea
Gadara
Scythopolis
Arab desert palaces
Bostra
Caesarea
Pella
Gerasa
Umm āl-Jimāl
Rihab
Khirbet al Samrā
1 Qasr el-Hallabāt
2 Amman (Philadelphia)
3 Q. al–Azraq
4 al-Muwaqqar
5 al-Qastal
6 Q. Mshatta
7 Q. al-Karāne
8 Qasr al Hayr
9 Kirbat al Mafjar
10 Anjar
9
Hesban
Jerusalem
Madaba
Gaza
Beersheba
Elusa
0 10 50 100
Miles

17. Cities and villages in Syria, Palestine, and Arabia

In Northern Jordan too the countryside came to be extremely densely settled in the Byzantine period. Mittmannn found 208 Byzantine sites against 103 Roman sites, and only 95 modern sites.[84] Most, but not all, villages in the southern Hauran provide evidence of continued habitation from 550 to 750. Umm al-Jimal displayed explosive growth from the fifth to the seventh century. Fourteen churches and two monasteries have been found in what was constitutionally not a city but a village. The collapse of buildings in the southern part of the settlement has been dated to the end of the Umayyad period. They were not rebuilt.[85]

Among the cities of the decapolis, Pella,[86] Gadara,[87] Abila,[88] Capitolias,[89] provide evidence of prosperity up to the Arab conquest, and the sites continued to be busily occupied for many decades after that. Most of the cities were eventually struck by disaster and, as has been thought, at more or less the same time. The destruction is generally attributed to the earthquake of 747/8. None of the towns is at present believed to have fully recovered from this calamity, but occupation of many sites continued. It may well be that the impact of the earthquake, as also that of the near contemporary Abbasid revolution have been exaggerated. The reduction of these quite spectacular Late Roman cities to a more much more modest and village-like condition was probably a much more gradual process. For instance at Pella the decline of the three churches and of the 'civic complex' appears to have begun well before AD 750.[90] Subsequently, if the earthquake put an end to the splendour of the city, it did not end its existence.[91]

The city of Gerasa itself was changing. As we have seen earlier,[92] change began long before the arrival of the Arabs. The city had gradually become more utilitarian in appearance, and it continued to evolve in the same direction. Potters' furnaces were built in the former sanctuary of Artemis.[93] Shops and public buildings came to be used as stables. Gerasa

[84] S. Mittmann, *Beiträge zur Siedlungs und Territorial-Geschichte des nördlichen Ostjordanlandes* (Wiesbaden, 1970).

[85] MacAdam 1994: 57–8. For a fuller account, see De Vries 1998; D. L. Kennedy 1998*b*. But Umm al Jimal, and other sites mentioned later, may well have had a history under the Abbasids and Fatimids, which has been overlooked by archaeologists as a result of insufficient knowledge of Islamic pottery sequences. See Whitcomb 1992; Walmsley 1992*a*.

[86] McNicoll, Smith, *et al.* 1982; McNicoll, Edwards, *et al.* 1992. R. H. Smith, Day, *et al.* 1989. A. Walmsley, 'Pella/Fihl after the Islamic conquest', *Mediterranean Archaeology*, 1 (1988), 143–53.

[87] Mershen and Knauf 1988: 128–32.

[88] MacAdam 1994: 76–7.

[89] E. A. Knauf, 'Beit Ras/Capitolias: A preliminary evaluation of the archaeological and textual evidence', *Syria*, 64 (1987), 21–46.

[90] McNicoll, Edwards, *et al.* 1992: 144–98.

[91] Walmsley 1992*a, b*.

[92] See above, p. 62.

[93] Crowfoot's notes *Syria*, 66 (1989), 37–9.

had become a major centre for the production of pottery. Under Umayyad rule a small mosque (10 × 13 metres), was built, and around AD 660 a residential area was totally rebuilt in the southern part of the city.[94] Eight ceramic kilns were set up in the North Theatre, which had been disused since the fifth century.[95] The city now produced its own coins. Most of the structures that have been excavated were destroyed, and not rebuilt, at a date or dates usually assigned to the eighth century. There is at present little or no evidence for occupation beyond the eighth century. However references in Arab geographers, and the survival of the name in an Arabized form, prove that the site was not deserted.

Around Gerasa some remarkable late Roman villages have been found.[96] Among them are Rihab and Khirbat al Samra,[97] each with eight churches constructed between AD 533 and 635. Jordan's central plateau, like the regions to the north of it, was more densely populated in Byzantine times than before or since.[98] The same incidentally seems to have been true of the very much more thinly populated territory of South Jordan.[99] Amman/Philadelphia itself seems to have passed the peak of its prosperity in the fourth century.[100] Although six churches are known from the city they were poorly built.[101] Under the Umayyads Amman once more gained in political importance, since it became the capital of an Arabic military district, or *jund*.[102] A palace and a mosque were built on the acropolis. The approximate area of the lower city in the Umayyad period, judging by the extent of surface debris, was 15.3 hectares. The citadel covered an additional 9 hectares, of which only 3.5 hectares were covered by buildings.[103] The palace dates from around AD 720, and was rebuilt after *c*.750. Some time later, under Abbasids, the governor was withdrawn, and Amman became once more a small country town. This is what it was at the time of the Crusades.

The villages of central Jordan have many remains of sixth-century churches. At Quwaysma (Quweismeh), on the edge of modern Greater

[94] Zayadine 1986*a*: 120.

[95] Gawlikowski 1992: 357–61.

[96] MacAdam 1994: 73–5.

[97] Plans: N. Duval 1994: 153–4.

[98] R. Ibach, 'Expanded archaeological survey of the Hesban Region', in R. S. Boraas and L. T. Gerarty (eds.), *Heshbon 1976* (Berrien Springs, 1978), 201–13. Other references to fieldwork in Northedge 1992: 40, 50, and notes.

[99] R. Schick, 'The settlement pattern of southern Jordan: The nature of the evidence', in G. R. D. King and Averil Cameron 1994: 133–54, essentially a survey of dated tombstones. The earliest is from AD 375. The stones become more abundant through the 5th cent., and are most frequent in the second half of the 6th. Their use fades out after the Arab conquest.

[100] Northedge 1992: 39–45.

[101] Ibid. 59–60.

[102] Ibid. 71–104. On the *jund*, plural *ajnâd*, see J. Haldon 1995: 381–3 and fig. 2.

[103] Northedge 1992: 61.

Amman, there are two Byzantine churches, one with sumptuous mosaics and an inscription commemorating Stephanus, a tribune, who had evidently paid for the church.[104] Other village churches in the neighbourhood of Amman are evidence that building continued through the sixth century and later still.[105] South-west of Amman and in the Madaba plain there is an abundance of village remains.[106] At the heart of this area was the pilgrimage centre on Mount Nebo, the site of the tomb of Moses, with a monastery and several churches. At the city of Madaba no fewer than eleven churches have been found, dating from the sixth and seventh centuries.[107] At Umm el Rassas there are remains of churches and fine mosaics.[108] One mosaic has eighteen views of Jordanian cities.[109] It was here in the church of St Stephen that a mosaic dated to AD 785 has been found, the latest in the whole area. The mosaics in this church were disfigured by iconoclasts, later repaired, and even the repairs show traces of wear. Eventually the building was abandoned, but it is still uncertain when.[110]

In Israel, the Roman Palestine, villages and towns flourished in the late Late Roman period. Numerous mosaic floors witness to the building of churches in villages, especially in the area between Caesarea and Beyruth, and in the neighbourhood of Jerusalem.[111] Impressive remains of late Roman villages have been found in the Negev,[112] in Galilee and on the Golan heights.[113] Rural occupation in Palestine in the fifth and sixth centuries was much denser than in the third and fourth, but perhaps not denser than under the Early Empire.[114] The houses on the circumference of large villages were built one against the other to form a continuous wall around the settlement. In this and other respects they conform to the rules

104 *IJ* II.54b.

105 Northedge 1992: 42.

106 MacAdam 1994: 80–4.

107 P.-L. Gatier, *Inscriptions de la Jordanie II* = *IGLS* XXI (Paris, 1986), 87–9, 93–4, 101–5, 109–11, 125–6, 127–38, 141–6, 179, 186, 189.

108 M. Piccirillo, 'Les Églises paléochrétiennes d'Umm el-Rassas: Cinq campagnes de fouilles', *CRAI* (1991), 273–94.

109 M. Piccirillo, 'Il complesso di Santo Stefano à Umm el-Rassas-Kastron Mefaa in Giordania', *Liber Annuus* (Jerusalem, Studium Biblicum Franciscanum) 41 (1991), 327–64.

110 On latest building and eventual abandonment, see N. Duval 1994: 205–8; M. Piccirillo, 'Les Problèmes resolus et les questions posées par les trois premières campagnes de fouilles à Umm er-Rassas-Kastron Mefaa: La Fin de la civilisation urbaine en Jordanie', *SHAJ* 4 (1992), 343–6. The site was eventually abandoned, but the date of abandonment is still obscure.

111 Donceel Voûte 1988: esp. 14. Remarkably few have been found north of Beyruth.

112 J. Shereshevski, *Byzantine Urban Settlements in the Negev Desert* (Beer Sheva, 1991), and C. Foss, 'The Near Eastern countryside in Late Antiquity, a review article', *JRA Suppl* 14 (1995), 223–34.

113 Dauphin 1987: 257–67.

114 See ibid.: figs. 1–6. But a recent survey along roads from the coast to Jerusalem suggests that late Late Roman settlement was denser than ever before or since: see M. Fischer and Isaac 1996.

laid down in rabbinic texts.[115] Occupation continues after the Arab conquest, but at least in some areas decline set in. At Nessana in the Negev papyrological evidence ends abruptly in AD 700, and no archaeological data can be placed later than AD 750.[116] In the East Jordan valley a survey found 19 sites for the Umayyad period against 55 from the Byzantine, in the Hisban survey 29 against 133.[117] Northedge suggests that this rapid decline in occupation could be explained by soil exhaustion. It may however be that archaeologists are not yet sufficiency familiar with the chronology of Islamic material, and that it is this, here and elsewhere, that has led them to overlook evidence of Abbasid and Fatimid occupation.[118]

The development of cities in Palestine is well illustrated by the archaeology of Scythopolis.[119] The temples were allowed to fall into ruin. The amphitheatre was abandoned in the fourth century, the theatre only in the course of the sixth. The odeon was pulled down in the sixth century to make way for a commercial piazza. Statues were removed and mutilated. Churches and monasteries and two synagogues were built on the fringes of the city. But Hellenism was not dead. Mosaic floors in shops of the sixth century could still display mythological themes, for instance an image of Tyche, the goddess of fortune, and a picture of the sirens tempting Odysseus. As late as the first half of the sixth century, the city was the scene of major urban developments. At about the same period the city acquired new suburbs, while the centre became more densely occupied. The population of Late Antique Scythopolis has been estimated at 30,000–40,000.[120]

Scythopolis was capital of Palaestina Secunda, and inscriptions on new buildings generally name the governor. But once, at the request of an embassy of two Samaritan citizens, each bearing the title of *scholasticus*, the Emperor Anastasius donated money for a great scheme of 'urban renewal' in the area of the so-called Silvanus street. The street was extended to the south-west, providing communications between the new developing area and the old city centre. A large basilica was built, occupying the whole space between the now disused eastern bath-house and the street. It incorporated what had been the colonnade of the Roman street, and covered the site of a reflecting pool. Subsequently the whole length of

[115] *Tosephta*, Makot 3.8 cited by C. Dauphin.

[116] Kraemer 1958: 35.

[117] Northedge 1992: 50.

[118] C. Foss ('The Near Eastern countryside in Late Antiquity', *JRA Suppl* 14 (1995), 222) points out that also in Cilicia and Lycia numerous villages prospered in the 6th cent. and subsequently disappeared.

[119] Y. Tsafrir and G. Foerster, 'From Scythopolis to Baysan, changing concepts of urbanism', in G. R. D. King and Averil Cameron (1994), 95–122.

[120] Mazor 1987–8: 19; Tsafrir and Foerster 1987–8: 38–42.

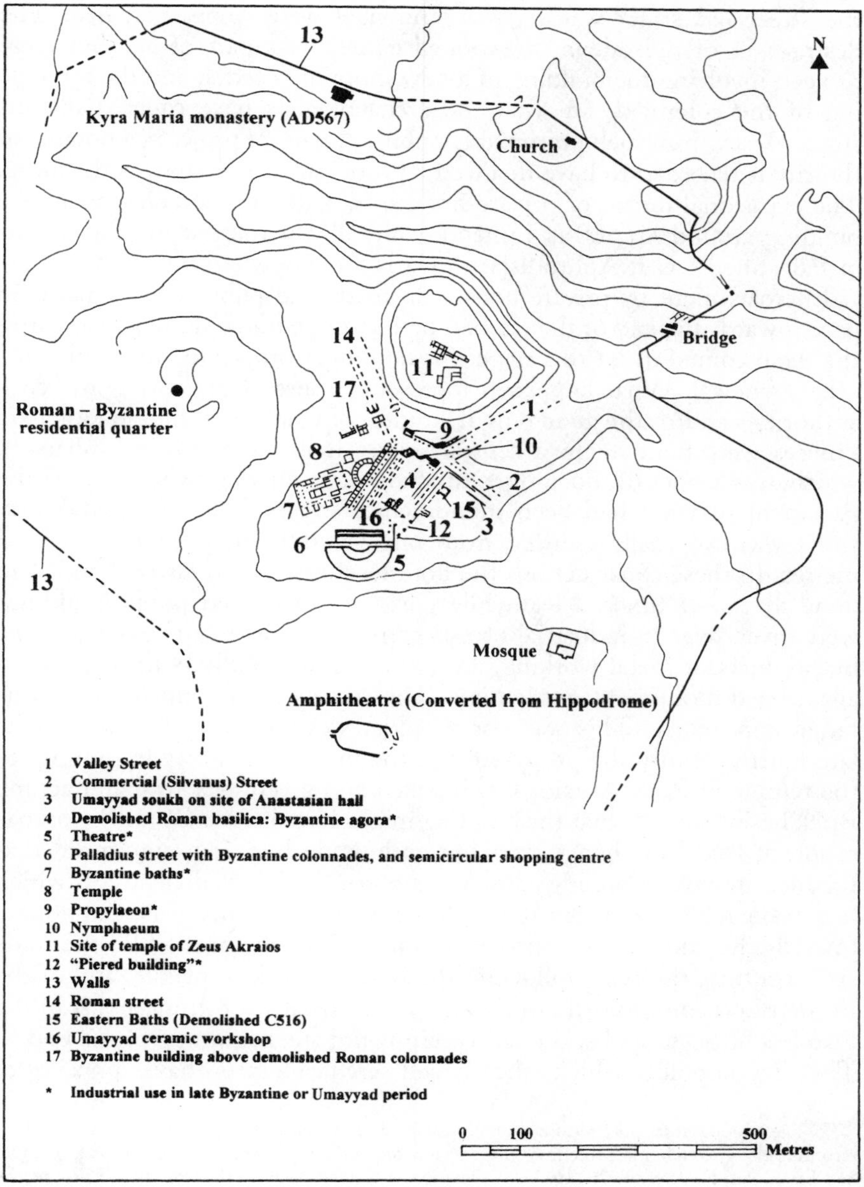
13
N
Kyra Maria monastery (AD567)
Church
Bridge
14
11
17
1
Roman – Byzantine
residential quarter
9
8
10
4
2
7
15
16
3
12
6
5
13
Mosque
Amphitheatre (Converted from Hippodrome)
1 Valley Street
2 Commercial (Silvanus) Street
3 Umayyad soukh on site of Anastasian hall
4 Demolished Roman basilica: Byzantine agora*
5 Theatre*
6 Palladius street with Byzantine colonnades, and semicircular shopping centre
7 Byzantine baths*
8 Temple
9 Propylaeon*
10 Nymphaeum
11 Site of temple of Zeus Akraios
12 "Piered building"*
13 Walls
14 Roman street
15 Eastern Baths (Demolished C516)
16 Umayyad ceramic workshop
17 Byzantine building above demolished Roman colonnades
* Industrial use in late Byzantine or Umayyad period
0 100 500 Metres

18. Scythopolis (Bet Shean)

the street old street was repaved and new water pipes installed. The destruction of the odeon, mentioned earlier, was part of another large project, involving the building of a new shopping exedra, and the rebuilding of the colonnade in what the archaeologists have called Palladius street. Apart from such presumably publicly financed projects, a notable of the city is recorded to have financed a portico in the western bath-house. The occasional return of private finance (donated by notables) to public building around AD 500 is a phenomenon also witnessed in other towns of Palestine,[121] as at Aphrodisias in Caria and elsewhere.

Encroachment by private houses on roads and public spaces gathered pace towards the end of the Roman period and became quite general after the Arab conquest. At this stage it is no longer proper to talk of planned urban renewal. What happened represents a loss of control by the civic authorities and/or the giving up of an ideal of what a city should look like. Houses were built on to a central square in front of the nymphaeum, which was evidently no longer functioning, and everywhere on to the pavement of what had been monumental streets. The so-called Valley street was eventually reduced from uncovered 12 metres of street to 3 metres. In these constructions the floor level rose much faster than it had done in earlier times. Meanwhile parts of abandoned public buildings were given over to industrial use. Potters' kilns, or fullers' basins, or the by-products of metal working, are found in the solidly built interiors of abandoned monumental structures. The city took on a much more utilitarian appearance. This was not a sudden development. As early as the late fourth century the propylaeon of the processional way leading up to the temple of Zeus Akraios was blocked and given over to manufacture. Brick basins suggest that the building might have been used for the preparation of flax. But change does not exclude decline. It is significant that the monumental shopping complex, the so-called 'Palladian street', which had been rebuilt as recently as the early sixth century was abandoned, towards the end of that century, or not far into the next.[122] So the mid-sixth century, the years following the first outbreak of plague, and of the Persian invasion of northern Syria, was apparantly a turning point in the fortunes of Scythopolis, though certainly not the beginning of the end.[123] The Scythopolis, which the Israeli archaeologists have uncovered,

[121] The building inscriptions at Scythopolis usually do not mention a donor, but date the work by recording the governor and sometimes the *prōtos* of the city under whom the work was carried out. See Tsafrir and Foerster 1997: 116–17. A donation by a notable ibid. 119. Donors in Palestine: Di Segni 1995: 312–32.

[122] G. R. D. King and Averil Cameron (1994: figs. 20–5) illustrate the encroachment. Tsafrir and Foerster 1997: figs. 47–50 and pp. 135–40.

[123] The Samaritan revolts of 529, 556, and the reign of Justin II (A. D. Crown, *The Samaritans* (Tübingen, 1989)) may well have damaged Scythopolis.

remained essentially intact until it was destroyed by the earthquake of AD 749. That disaster was not the end of the city, but it was only partly rebuilt, and without regard for the old street plan. But even then, some of the buildings were large, and built around a court paved with basalt blocks. Small curving lanes now surrounded the irregular *insulae*. Scythopolis may well have lost its classical character more quickly than other cities in the neighbourhood. The city had resisted the Arabs and was punished for its resistance. It was heavily fined and half its houses transferred to the victors, to be given to settlers. The provincial capital was moved to Tiberias. Nevertheless, an Arab governor in the 720s–730s built a new monumental line of colonnaded shops on the site of the Anastasian basilica in 'Silvanus street', which had been derelict for many years following an earthquake.[124]

The development of Scythopolis /Bet Shean can be paralleled at cities all over Palestine. There was active public building early in the sixth century notably at Caesarea, Sepphoris, and Jerusalem.[125] There was a noticeable reduction in the amount of new building in the second half of the century and in the early seventh century, but archaeologists have not so far found evidence that either town or country in Jordan or Palestine suffered a major setback.[126]

4. *The Arab Conquest and after*

It will have been observed that the immediate impact of the Arab conquest on the archaeology of the provinces of Palestine and Arabia was far from dramatic. In fact this momentous event is scarcely visible archaeologically. Plenty of pottery, coins, and artefacts bear witness to abundant urban activity under the Umayyads.[127] At Gerasa and Pella there is evidence of new residential building. Essentially cities continued to evolve under the Arabs in the same direction as they had done during the previous hundred years under the Empire. A small mosque has been found at Gerasa, a large one on the citadel at Amman.[128] At Damascus the Muslims built a mihrab into what had been the colonnade of the *temenos* of the principal temple, whose cella had been converted into the cathedral

[124] On the Umayyad shops, formerly and mistakenly dated to the Byzantine period, see Tsafrir and Foerster 1997: 138–9.

[125] R. L. Vann, 'Byzantine street construction at Caesarea Maritima', in Hohlfelder 1982: 165–77. Doren Chen, 'The dating of the *cardo maximus* excavated at Jerusalem', *PEQ* 114 (1982), 43–5. E. Netzer and Z.Weiss, 'New evidence for Late Roman and Byzantine Sepphoris', *JRA Suppl.* 14 (1995), 164–76.

[126] H. Kennedy 1985*b*: 141–83.

[127] A. Zeyadeh, 'Settlement patterns, an archaeological perspective: Case studies from northern Palestine and Jordan', in G. R. D. King and Averil Cameron (1994), 117–31.

[128] Northedge 1992: 63–9.

of St John. The cathedral itself was replaced by the great mosque seventy years later.[129] But there are far fewer remains of mosques in the ruins of towns and villages of this area than one would expect. The continuing decline of monumentality and encroachment on public spaces and streets points to population pressure rather than urban decline; though there has scarcely anywhere been enough excavation to assess whether, or to what extent, infilling in the town centre coincided with abandonment of peripheral districts. On the other hand, encroachment on the scale seen at Scythopolis surely reflects a weakening of civic administration, and by implication the fading of the classical concept of the city as the property of its citizens,[130] and of its corollary the conviction that the community has a duty to maintain its rights against the claims of individuals. But this was a long-term development. The dominating impression is one of continuity extending at least to the end of the Umayyad period, and the subsequent transfer of capital of the caliphate from Damascus to Baghdad.

There was something like a consensus among scholars that this changed after AD 750, the time of the Abbasid revolution, when the whole area was thought to have gone into a steep recession.[131] This conclusion, based largely on surface surveys, may however be distorted by the fact, mentioned earlier, that archaeologists had difficulty in recognizing Abbasid and Fatimid pottery. As this difficulty is being overcome Abbasid and Fatimid pottery is being found on sites which earlier to archaeologists had seemed abandoned.[132] It looks as if the consensus view will have to be revised. On the other hand, most of the structures excavated at Gerasa were eventually destroyed without being replaced, and there is little or no positive evidence that they survived long into the Abbasid period and the same is true of many of the village churches in the area. Even if there is a question mark over the chronology of the process, there is little doubt that the extraordinary economic development undergone by the lands on the fringe of the desert in Late Antiquity went into reverse in the eighth and subsequent centuries.

It is also beginning to look as if there were indications of declining prosperity even before AD 750. Excavations of the last twenty years have found areas where signs of early decline could be registered in Arabia at Petra[133] and Gerasa,[134] and in Palestine at Pella, Scythopolis, and

[129] Sack 1989: 20.

[130] e.g. Cicero, *de Rep.* 1.35: Est igitur . . . res publica res populí.

[131] Northedge 1992: 54–5.

[132] Walmsley 1992*a*; Whitcomb 1992.

[133] Z. T. Fiema, 'The Petra Project', *ACOR Newsletter*, 5.1 (1993), 1–3; *id.*, ch. 20 in *Final Petra Church Publication*, forthcoming.

[134] Zayadine 1986*a*: 12 (North Decumanus and north theatre), 59 (shops along eastern façade of sanctuary of Zeus complex).

Caesarea. It may be that the decline which is so conspicuous in northern Syria in the second half of the sixth century, began further south too, though it set in later, and was less severe. The south did not experience the deportation of large number of its inhabitants and the destruction of its principal cities by the Persians, but it did suffer the calamities of recurring plague.[135]

The decline of the great city of Alexandria in Egypt appears to have begun well before the mid-eighth century. The lively and prosperous district excavated by the Polish team at Kom el Dikka, with its baths, lecture-rooms, houses, and workshops, was in ruins and covered with debris from the seventh century.[136] While excavating the later layers the archaeologists found progressively less imported pottery from North Africa, Asia Minor, and Cyprus, and a relative increase of pottery from Upper and Middle Egypt. Mediterranean trade was giving way to regionalized exchanges.[137] Under the Arabs Alexandria suffered two further blows: after AD 868 Cairo became the capital of an independent Muslim Egypt, and first the canals linking Alexandria to the Canopic branch of the Nile, and then the Canopic branch itself silted up. The Roman walls of Alexandria probably enclosed something like 1,000 hectares, the ninth-century wall no more than 300. By Western standards Alexandria was still a large city, but it was no longer the super-city of Late Antiquity and classical times.[138]

The sources have plenty of evidence that the Arab conquest was followed by large-scale flight of Christian inhabitants of Jordan[139] and Syria.[140] But it is possible that the extent of the flight of the former owners is exaggerated in the Arab sources.[141] Certainly some families, in at least some cities, preserved their wealth and influence.[142] In the case of the great majority of cities we have no prosopographical information at all. But chronicles have survived at Edessa in Mesopotamia, and they suggest

[135] On Caesarea, see above, p. 58; on cumulative devastation and depopulation by the Persians in the north, see Trombley 1997; on plague, see above, pp. 53–4 and on possible links with an eruption in 536 and/or climatic change, see below, pp. 409–10.

[136] Haas 1997: 342.

[137] Ibid. 343–4, citing G. Majcherek, 'The late Roman ceramics from sector G-Alexandria (1986–87)', *Études et travaux*, 16 (1992), 81–117. See also P. Arthur and E. D. Orer, 'The North Sinai Survey and the evidence of transport amphorae for Roman and Byzantine trading patterns', *JRA* 11 (1998), 193–112, evidence for trade between Tunisia, Egypt, and Palestine up to 680.

[138] Haas 1997: 339–51.

[139] Baladhuri 1966: 180.

[140] References in Lilie 1976: 232–4. Principal source Baladhuri 1966: 189 ff., e.g. Damascus 196, coastal towns 198, Baalbek 201, Emesa 204, Antioch 230, Cyrrhus 231. At Apamea the great mansions were now converted to farm houses. So the leading families either fled or became impoverished (J. C. Balty 1984: 497–501). S. Borsari, 'Le migrazioni dall'Oriente in Italia nel VII secolo', *Parola del Passato*, 17 (1957), 133–8.

[141] Averil Cameron and Conrad 1992.

[142] Palmer 1990: 166–7.

that at least some of the families that were most powerful in Byzantine times, continued to be wealthy and influential under Islam, even though they had not abandoned their Monophysite Christianity. When, in the year AD 628, the emperor Heraclius recovered Edessa from the Persians, Isaiah the Monophysite patriarch, refused him communion unless he anathematized the Council of Chalcedon. Angered by this unnecessary rebuff, which even the Monophysite chronicler Sergius considered idiotic, Heraclius expelled the bishop, and together with him five of the leading families of Edessa who were supporting the Monophysite cause. It may well be that Heraclius was not sorry to have been provoked: for the Monophysite bishops at Edessa and elsewhere owed their possession of the churches to the Persian king, who had evidently assumed that Monophysites would prefer his rule to that of the orthodox emperor.[143] The families were the Rospaye (Rusafōyō), the Tel-Mahrē (Tel-Mahrōyō), the family of Cosma son of Araby, and the family of Nōlar. These families had endowed the Great Church of Edessa with gold, silver, shops, mills, gardens, and public baths. They had evidently been rich and powerful for some time. Certainly already in AD 590, the later Persian king Chosroes II, then a refugee in the Roman Empire, had stayed in the palace of Ioannes Rospaya.[144] When Chosroes captured Edessa in 606 he deported Ioannes' son and heir Sergius 38, but invited him to eat at the royal table, even though he was prisoner. After some time Sergius was allowed to return to Edessa, and got much of his property back.[145] The Arab conquest in AD 640 evidently did not deprive the family of its position: in the late seventh century a woman of the Rospaye married into the Tel-Mahrē family. A descendant of this marriage was the historian Dionysius of Tel-Mahrē. He was metropolitan of Edessa 818–45, and his brother Theodosius was to hold the same office. The Tel-Mahrē were evidently still one of the leading families of Edessa. Towards the end of the seventh century the heiress of the Rospaye married a member of another, probably less ancient Monophysite family, the Gummaye (Gumōyō), who had gained enormous wealth first as tutor to the brother of the Caliph Abd el Malik (684/5–705), and then as the brother's assistant and chief minister in the government of Egypt.[146] In AD 803/4 the Caliph Harun al Rashid forced the family to surrender a large part of its wealth, though he allowed them to keep some.[147]

143 Segal 1970: 126; Palmer 1993: 140–1 = Text no. 13: *Dionysius Reconstituted*, 41–3 (pp. 140–2).

144 *Dionysius Reconstituted*, 15–19 (pp. 122–4), cf. *PLRE* III s.v. Ioannes 102.

145 *Dionysius Reconstituted*, 18–19 in Palmer 1993: 124.

146 Segal 1970: 202; Palmer 1993, *Dionysius Reconstituted*, 132–3 (pp. 202–4): 4,000 slaves, villages, estates, gardens, 300 shops in Edessa. He built two churches in Fustat in Egypt, and renovated the Church of the Mother of God at Edessa.

147 Segal 1970: 203.

We know about the Rospaye–Tel-Mahrē–Gummaye cousinage because they wrote the history. Dionysus of the Tel-Mahrē obtained his information about earlier periods from the chronicle of his grandfather, David son of Samuel of Tur Abdin, and from writings of an earlier kinsman, Sergius 38, son of Ioannes of the Rospaye (fl. 627). There were other notable families at Edessa. When Chosroes in exile lived at Edessa he first stayed in the palace of Marinus which was in the same street as the mansion of Ioannes Rospaye. This was evidently one the largest houses in Edessa, for in AD 604 the general Narses chose it as his headquarters when he rebelled against Phocas. But we do not hear any more about Marinus, perhaps because he and his descendants were Chalcedonians.[148] But if the Rospaye and related families were typical, interesting conclusions follow. The Arab conquest did not cause a social revolution in Edessa. The city's patriciate, at least the Monophysite part of it, retained its position. From time to time they suffered arbitrary and tyrannous exactions, rather like wealthy Jews in the medieval West. On one occasion in AD 770, the Gummaye were prosecuted at Harran for alleged paganism.[149] Three were executed, but the family survived. We get a glimpse of the comparable survival of a great family into Arab times at Damascus, where one Sergounas (Sergius) was appointed to collect taxes by Maurice. His son Mansur appears to have held a similar position in AD 635 when he betrayed the city to the Arabs.[150] Later in the seventh century a Sergius son of Mansur, a Chalcedonian, was secretary of the calif Abd al Malik (685–705) at Damascus. In AD 691 he dissuaded the calif from removing pillars from the church at Gethsemane for building at Mecca.[151] His son, John of Damascus (675–749), also served the Umayyads, but ended his life as a monk in the monastery of St Sabas in Arab-held Palestine. He was a Chalcedonian theologian and a consistent opponent of iconoclasm.[152]

It is significant that orthodox Christian communities flourished in ninth-century Palestine. Unlike Monophysite ritual and theology, the liturgy of the orthodox (Melkites) was now in Arabic, and orthodox theologians, writing in Arabic, addressed Muslim criticism of Christian theology, for instance of icon worship. At this stage the gap between Islam and Christianity was not as wide as it later became. Muslims did not on

148 Palmer 1993, *Dionysius Reconstituted*, 15 (pp. 122–3).

149 Segal 1970: 206.

150 Eutychius, *Annales*, col. 1089, cf. *PLRE B* 1137, s.v. Sergounas (?Sergius), ibid. 810 s.v. Mansur. Was the financial office held by father and son that of *vindex*? Or was it that of *logeutēs* documented at Gerasa in 578, see Zayadine 1986*b*: 17–18.

151 Palmer 1993, *Dionysius Reconstituted*, 134 (p. 204); Theophanes 6183.

152 I. P. Sheldon Williams, *Cambridge History of Later Greek Philosophy* (Cambridge, 1967), 509–11.

principle object to holding their worship in churches, providing they contained no objectionable symbols such as representations of living beings.[153]

No doubt one reason why Christian families of Edessa and Damascus could maintain their wealth and influence under the Muslim government was that the Umayyads took over much of the Roman administrative machinery, and therefore found it convenient to employ men who were used to running it. Moreover the Muslims did make full use of cities. In Syria and Palestine Muslim commanders assigned houses or plots for houses (*qatâ'i*) to their soldiers mainly in existing cities, particularly in cities along the coast. Elsewhere along their line of advance they set up large permanent camps (*amsâr*), each with its mosque and palace. Outstanding among the early *amsâr* were Fustat in Egypt, Kufa, Wasit and Basra in Iraq, and Cairouan in what is now Tunisia. The camp-settlements might be small or large; and though they might be in close proximity to an existing city, they ensured a certain segregation of Muslims from the non-Muslim inhabitants. Some of the settlements had urban dimensions and population from the start. Some developed some did not. So Ramla in Palestine,[154] and a settlement near Qinnasrin (Grk. Chalcis) in Syria did not grow into major cities. But others did, and many have continued as great urban centres to this day, among them Bagdad, Basra, and Cairo.

Because they founded numerous new cities, the Arabs differed fundamentally from the barbarians who settled in the western provinces of the Empire. As the Muslim cities originated as settlements for tribal armies, separate areas were assigned to the different tribal units. So Arab cities were composed of distinct, self-administering quarters and lacked the corporate unity of the classical city.

In Syria and Palestine, as the majority of the Umayyad soldiers were accommodated in or near existing cities and villages, new settlements were generally small. A few have been found.[155] In area they range from 2 to 11 hectares. That on the citadel of Amman covered 9.3 hectares, of which the palace occupied 16.7 per cent. Anjar extended over 11.47 hectares with the palace filling 3.5 per cent of the site.[156] It was probably left to the leader of a particular military detachment to lay out the settlement, to build a mosque, and to construct a palace for himself. This regularly occupied a disproportionately large part of the built-up area. The followers then built their own houses. The extent of the complex would depend on

[153] Schick 1995; J. L. Bodjamra, 'Christianity in Greater Syria', *Byzantion*, 77 (1997), 148–78.

[154] D. Sourdel, 'La Fondation umayyade de Ramla', in H. R. Römer and A. Noth (eds.), *Studien zur Geschichte und Kultur des vorderen Orients: Festschrift b. D. Spuler* (Leiden, 1981), 385–97.

[155] Northedge 1994: 231–65 and figs. 43–57. On Syria, ibid. 233–44. Hillenbrand 1999; C.-P. Haase, *Untersuchungen zur Landschaftsgeschichte Nordsyriens in der Umayyadenzeit* (Kiel, 1975).

[156] Northedge 1992: 151–65.

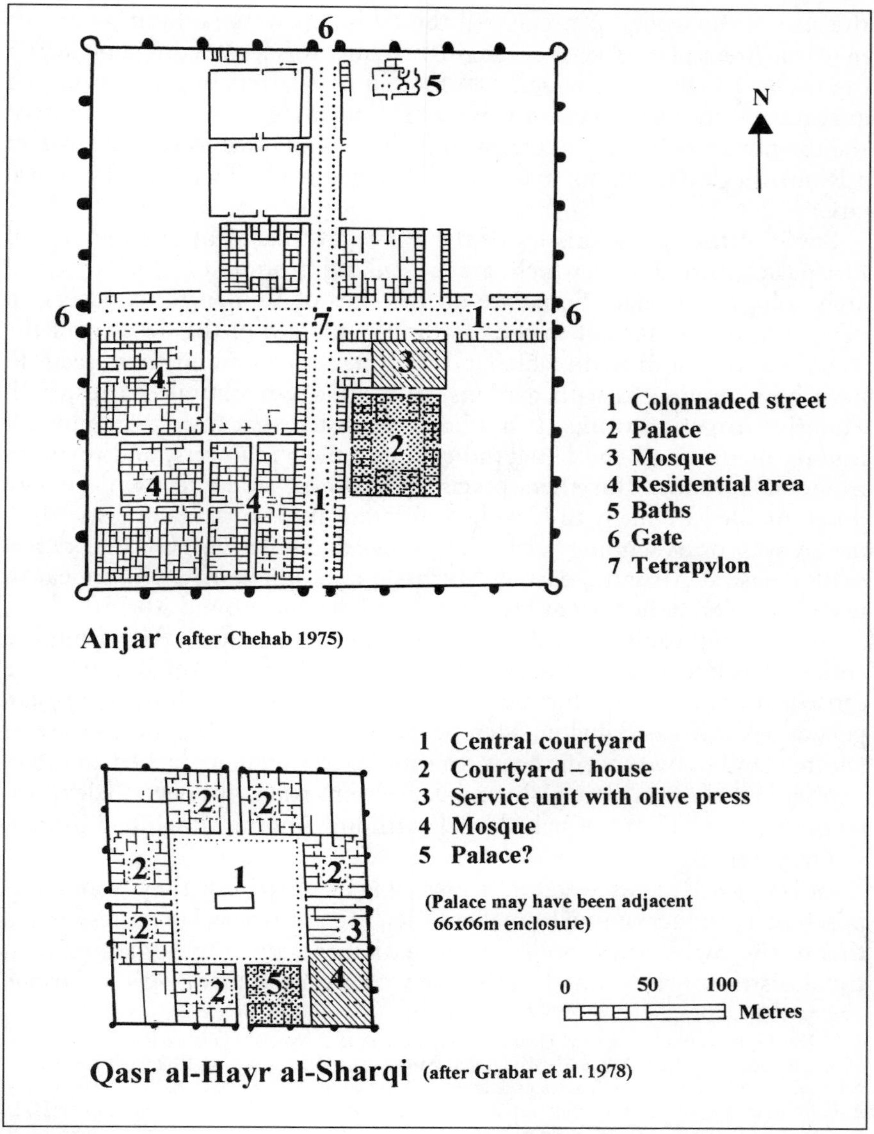

19. Anjar, an Umayyad settlement
Qasr al-Hayr, Umayyad settlement described as madîna

the size of the leader's retinue. All the buildings were laid out on a geometrical street plan. Ayla, the original Aqaba, was a walled rectangle 165 metres by 140 metres, divided into four equal quarters by streets running at rectangles from the four city gates. The meeting point in the centre of the town was marked by a tetrapylon. There is an obvious resemblance to a Roman legionary camp, and indeed to a geometrically planned classical city.[157]

Some of the characteristics of the *amsâr* are shared by the remains of fort/palace complexes, which are a striking feature of the Umayyad archaeology of Jordan. Some are on the sites of Roman forts, others on new sites, mostly far out in the east on the margin of the desert and the sown (i.e. the cultivated arable land).[158] These, or some of these seem to have been residences with gardens, as well as agricultural centres, with extensive irrigation works. It has been suggested that they were built for leading members of the Umayyad clan and their followers, and financed from tax revenue. But their precise purpose is still uncertain. In fact different sites are likely to have had different functions. In any case their prime was brief, ending with the Abbasid revolution. Of the 'desert castles' qasr al-Mshattā, qasr al-Mushāsh, and qasr al-Kharāna appear to have been abandoned, or at least gone into decline around AD 750.[159]

In the camp capital of Islamic Egypt, the settlement at Al-Fustat, the core of modern Cairo, it appears that the soldiers of Amr's army were settled around a small fortified centre which was the Roman fortress, generally known as Babylon. Members of each of the different tribes were allotted land in two specific areas. In time the settlement reached an urban density. The houses were plain and densely crowded, but nevertheless two stories high, and built of baked brick with lime mortar. Each had its own sanitary unit.[160]

In Iraq settlements were on a vastly bigger scale, but they were composed of a number of much smaller units, each of whose layout resembled that of the Syrian sites. Some of the settlements grew by agglomeration, tribal districts being added successively to a central area, with a mosque

[157] Whitcomb 1994: 155–70.

[158] Palaces in southern Hauran: Dayr al-Kahf, Burqu', al Azraq, al-Hallabat (MacAdam 1994: 65–8); in central Jordan: Qastal, al-Mshattā, al-Muwaqqar, al-Mushāsh, al-Kharāna (86–91). See Northedge 1992: 169, table 4 (names of palaces and geological environment), fig. 13 (distribution). A palace near Jericho: R. W. Hamilton, *Khirbat al Mafjar* (Oxford, 1959). Aerial exploration: D. L. Kennedy, 'La Jordanie antique vue du ciel', *Archéologia*, 346 (June 1998), 56–65, photographs, 61–3. Full discussion of possible purposes of Anjar (town? village? market? fortress? palatial residence?) in Hillenbrand 1999.

[159] MacAdam 1994: 86–9; G. R. D. King, 'Settlement patterns in Islamic Jordan', *SHAJ* 4 (1992), 369–95. Anjar was left unfinished and perhaps even abandoned around 715 (Hillenbrand 1999: 64–5). On 'abandonment', see warning of n. 85 above.

[160] G. T. Scanlon, 'Al-Fustat: The riddle of the earliest settlement', in G. R. D. King and Averil Cameron (1994), 171–9 and figs. 28, 33–40.

and palace and perhaps a prison and a registry at the centre. Samarra founded in AD 836, on a site of 378 hectares, eventually covered an area of 57 square kilometres and stretched for nearly 50 kilometres along the Tigris.[161] Bagdad, founded in AD 762–7 by the Caliph al Mansur on a circular plan, had a built-up area of around 285 hectares. Thirteen kilometres south of Samarra was the octagonal city at al-Qadisiya of circa 185 hectares.

These cities might acquire irregular shapes, but they were originally laid out on a strictly geometrical street plan. The irregular street plan which has been considered characteristic of the 'Islamic city', and which we find in the large villages of the Late Roman Near East, and whose beginnings we can also observe in some of the Late Roman cities, was not at all characteristic of the Islamic foundations in their original state.[162] That Arab foundations, whether large or small, always have a very prominent palace, reflects the fact that their origins were generally closely associated with a particular ruler and his followers. Unlike the classical cities, they were not given collective civic institutions. In a sense they continued the Greco-Roman urban tradition, but they also have features of a great Roman villa complex with a large and elegant residence for the owner and housing for his dependents and workers.

Not all Arab settlements survived. Rapid rise and equally rapid decline were sometimes closely linked to the rise and fall of a particular dynasty, or even of the founding ruler.[163] In some cases the competition of the Muslim town squeezed out a neighbouring older city. So in Mesopotamia Kufa replaced al-Hira, Basra Ubulla,[164] and Bagdad Ktesiphon. In Egypt Cairo took the place of Memphis, in Tunisia Cairouan that of Carthage. But it is obvious that Arab rule was anything but hostile to city life as such. In fact classical cities that became centres of Muslim government benefited exceedingly. Damascus had been a minor city. Under the Umayyads it was the centre of an empire. Cordova became the site of a great mosque and the capital of Muslim Spain and a very large city.[165] A huge palace complex was built a few miles outside the old Roman city, but if this was ever intended to become a Muslim city, it evidently did not survive the end of the Spanish Umayyad caliphate, being destroyed in civil war in 1013.[166]

[161] C. F. Robinson 1998.

[162] Northedge 1994: 244–65, figs. 48–57. According to R. Hillenbrand (1999: 83 n. 95), the *muhtasib* of an Arab town had a legal duty to ensure traffic could flow unhindered along a road, but not to intervene to prevent changes in its width or alignment.

[163] Ibid. 231–65, a late example is Abd al-Rahman III's Madīnat al-Zahrā near Cordova, see n. 166 below.

[164] Whitcomb 1994: 155–70, relevant 161–3.

[165] E. Lévi-Provençal, *Histoire de l'Espagne Musulmane*, iii (Paris, 1953), 356–95.

[166] *Cuadernos de Madīnat al-Zahrā*, 3 vols. (Cordova, 1987–91).

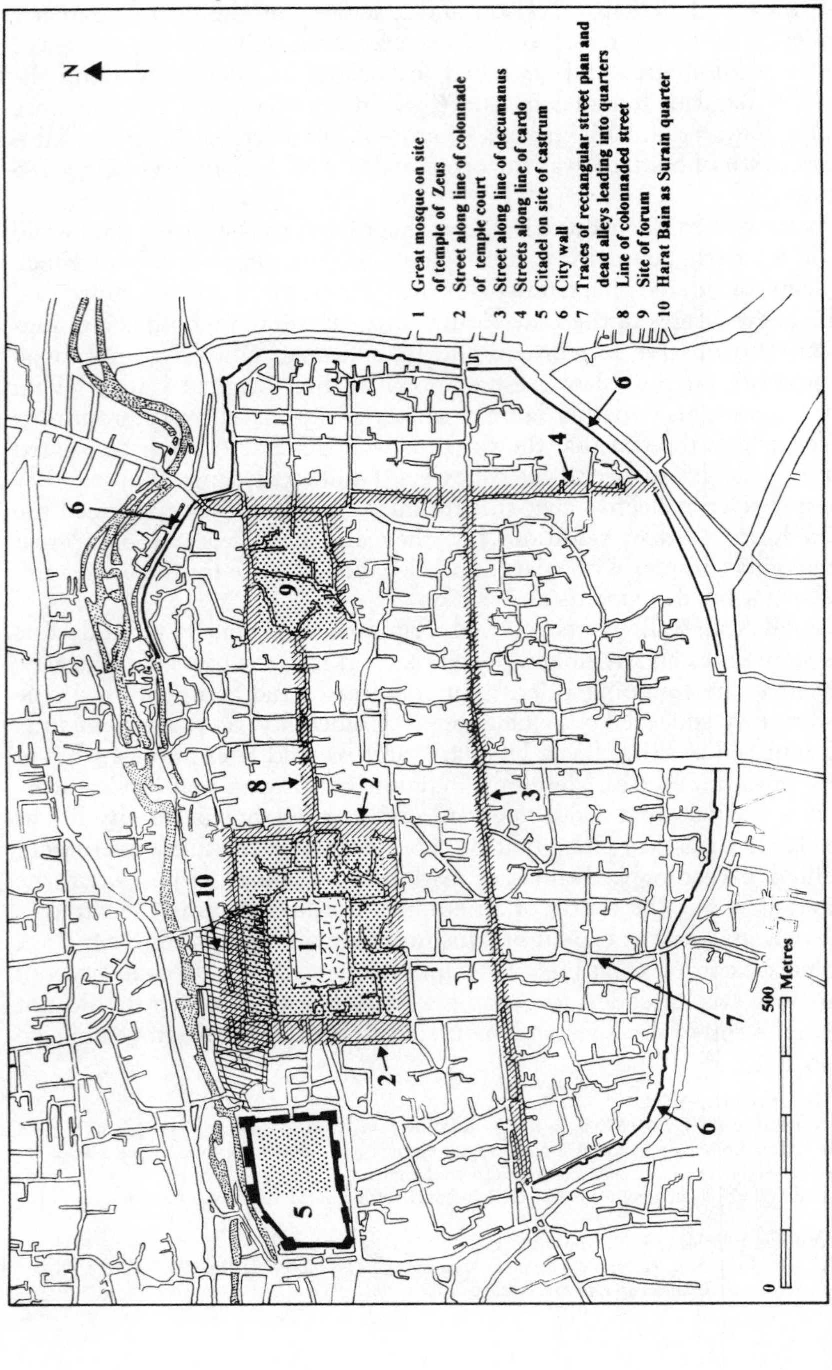
N
1 Great mosque on site of temple of Zeus
2 Street along line of colonnade of temple court
3 Street along line of decumanus
4 Streets along line of cardo
5 Citadel on site of castrum
6 City wall
7 Traces of rectangular street plan and dead alleys leading into quarters
8 Line of colonnaded street
9 Site of forum
10 Harat Bain as Surain quarter
0
500 Metres

20. Damascus: classical into Arab city

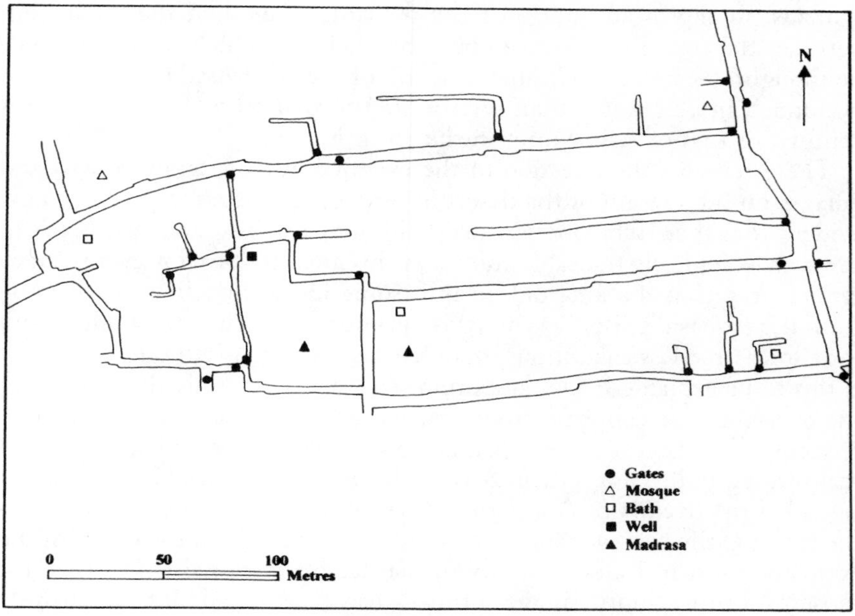

21. Harat Bain: a quarter of Damascus

The history of urban sites from the Roman to the Arab period sometimes turns out to have been less continuous than it appears at first sight. It has been observed particularly in Andalusia that Roman cities fade away to the point of extinction in the early Arab period only to re-emerge on a nearby site, sometimes with a new name, around an Arab settlement. This appears to have happened to the cities that were surrendered to Arab rule by the pact of Theodemir.[167] Even though it made little immediate impact on the archaeology, the Arab conquest did make a difference. The former Roman territories in the Near East no longer had their principal political and economic links with the lands around the Mediterranean, but with Arabia, Mesopotamia, and Iran. This inevitably changed the relative importance of old centres. The coastal cities of Palestine and Phoenicia declined. Damascus became for a time the capital of an empire. Beroea/Aleppo, previously a minor city, became an important economic centre, and a regional centre of government.[168] The Arab conquest brought with it a significant shift in the relative political influence of peasants and

[167] Lloret 1993: i. 13–35, esp. 22–6. M. Acién, 'Poblamiento y fortificación en el sur de al-Andalus. La formación de un país de husūn', *III Congreso de arqueología medieval española* I (Oviedo, 1989), 135–50.

[168] Sauvaget 1941.

nomads, to the disadvantage of the peasants—but then the distinction between the two is now seen to be very much more blurred than used to be thought. Certainly the transformation of society caused by Islamic rule was much more gradual than say the transformation of Italy in the fifth century, or that of Asia Minor in the seventh.

There remains the question of the eventual fate of the old towns and villages on the margin of the desert in Jordan and eastern Syria. It is now evident that the Arab conquest itself did not cause any dramatic break in the archaeologically traceable culture of this area. It does however seem to remain true that the area did go into some kind of decline, particularly from the Abbasid period, even if this decline was much more gradual, and for a long time less calamitous, than has been previously thought.[169] How is this to be explained? One important factor was certainly the transfer of the capital of the caliphate from Damascus to Mesopotamia and a consequent redirection of state expenditure. The Abbasid caliphate marked a real turning point, not only in Syria-Palestine, but also in Egypt where it signalled the decline of Alexandria.[170] Another factor to be considered is the fact that the conspicuous development of the lands on the fringe of the Arabian desert in Late Antiquity took place on marginal land which for most of history, until modern times, has been much less intensively exploited, and has supported a much smaller population than in Late Antiquity. What looks like prosperity to us can only have been achieved by a never-ending struggle against adverse natural conditions. It may well not have been sustainable. Soil exhaustion is an explanation of the decline that should not be rejected out of hand.[171] Perhaps migration to an Islamic settlement, and service in the Islamic armies gave some of the peasants a chance to get themselves settled in an easier environment.

Looking at the Islamic world as a whole, the contrast between the shrinking urban structures in the western provinces of the Empire, and indeed in Byzantine Anatolia, and the revived urbanism in the lands occupied by the Arabs is very striking. Neither the West nor Byzantine Anatolia had spectacular new settlements like the Arab camp-cities, nor did they have anything to compare with the desert palaces, with their gardens and irrigated agriculture, where previously there had been nothing, or at most a Roman fort.[172] The condition of the early Islamic

[169] H. Kennedy (1992: esp. 196) cites Gerasa/Jerash and Philadelphia/Amman in Jordan and Chalcis and Apamea in northern Syria as inland cities which survived the first 150 years of Islamic rule, but declined to vanishing point in the 9th and 10th cent. Pentz 1992: 58–9, for agricultural expansion in the Negev highlands in the early Islamic period.

[170] Haas 1997: 346–51, cf. above, p. 305.

[171] Though the very careful Libyan Valleys Survey has produced no evidence that loss of fertility was a cause of the abandonment of land on a significant scale. See below, p. 410.

[172] But the systems for collecting rain water could have been for watering herds.

Near East is extraordinarily different from that of, say, Italy in the late sixth to mid-eighth centuries, where much of the population seems to have become archaeologically invisible, and money disappeared except in garrison towns.[173] Clearly the Arabs attitude to cities was much closer to that of the classical Greco-Romans than that of the northern barbarians. In fact it would seem that from very early times a city furnished the ideal setting for the setting up of a Muslim society, and that it was precisely in the rapidly growing city or city-like settlements that you were likely to find large numbers of Muslims in the first century or so after the Arab conquest.

The Arab conquest was not followed by a hiatus in the arts of the kind that was experienced in the West in the seventh century. The Dome of the Rock, and the Damascus mosque exemplify both continuity of traditional skills, and their use in a characteristic new way. Money continued to circulate and merchants to travel from one end of the Arab world to the other. There was definite progress in agriculture:[174] many new crops—cotton, citrus fruits, bananas, watermelons, spinach, artichokes, aubergines—were cultivated more widely in the Near East or North Africa during the Umayyad and Abbasid periods than ever before.[175] Summer cropping and new rotations seem to have been introduced at this time. These advances had a parallel in the West. One might cite the widespread adoption of the use of the horse shoe and stirrup, the invention of the horse collar, and the invention of the windmill which provided a basis for the leap forward in the late eighth century.[176]

The role of the Arabs in the East to some extent corresponds to that of the Germanic tribes in the West. The character of the Arabs before they took over the eastern provinces of the Roman Empire is as obscure as that of the ancient Germans, in some ways more so. Scholars are only beginning to assess the pre-Islamic condition of Arabia and its inhabitants—for instance the question of whether or not the inhabitants of the peninsula had a sense of common Arabhood before Islam.[177] A survey of recent archaeological work in Arabia[178] shows that conditions there were con-

[173] Part of the trouble in the West is that archaeologists are still insufficiently familiar with post-classical material. In the East there is clearly much more continuity at least until around 750, but after that similar difficulties arise, and the picture is still very obscure.

[174] A. Watson 1983; Glick 1996. Public works to improve the agricultural infrastructure: Hillenbrand 1999: 69 n. 41. Land grants with relief from taxation to bring land under cultivation—with eventual soil exhaustion?: Morony 1984, 1987.

[175] For the view that wheeled transport was to a significant extent replaced by camels and mules, see Bulliet 1975, qualified by Graf 1997: 43–9.

[176] L. T. White, *Medieval Technology and Social Change* (Oxford, 1962).

[177] Millar 1993: 512–14.

[178] 'Settlement in Western and Central Arabia and the gulf in the sixth–eighth centuries AD', in G. R. D. King and Averil Cameron (1994), 181–212; M. B. Piotrovsky, 'Late Ancient and early Medieval Yemen: Settlement traditions and innovations', ibid. 213–20.

siderably more varied and complex than was once assumed. There were sedentary farmers, towns, and town-based traders. But research is still at a very early stage, and we are evidently still a long way from being able to explain the Arabs' conquests, and their cultural achievements, in terms of the conditions of pre-Islamic Arabia.

A phenomenon that can be observed on many frontiers of the Roman Empire and in East and West alike is the consolidation of small frontier tribes into larger confederations. Franks and Allemans were only the largest of such groupings. The development was no doubt partly a defensive reaction to Roman imperialism. But it was also from time to time encouraged by the Roman authorities who found it convenient to make frontier arrangements with larger units. The same process was happening on the Eastern frontier. The Lakhmids operated on the Persian side of the frontier, the Ghassanids on the Roman side.[179] But of course infinitely the most important factor in the 'ethnogenesis' of the Arabs was the Islamic religion. The new religion not only brought about the unification of the tribes inhabiting Arabia but subsequently also the assimilation of large numbers of the inhabitants of adjoining lands. The role of Islam in the 'making' of the Arabs might be compared to that of Arian Christianity in the ethnic development in the West of Goths and Vandals. Islam did indeed incorporate some features of Christianity and Judaism, but it proved to be something new and different from either, and became a vastly more powerful and more durable bond of unity than the Arianism of the Germanic peoples.

Even if it was populated to its natural limit, the Arabian peninsula, which is largely desert, can have supported only a small population. Whatever the total, it is not likely to have been adequate to provide the manpower needed by the Islamic armies for their far-flung campaigns of conquest. It would seem more probable that the succession of conquests followed by widespread settlement was made possible by the speedy assimilation, and integration into the Islamic armies, of at least some of the conquered. We know that Berbers played a big part in the Islamic conquest of Spain.[180] The enrolment of the population of occupied territories presumably began almost immediately after the first advances.

It certainly is a question where and how the early converts were gained. In what circumstances in fact did the inhabitants of the Near East make contact with followers of the new religion? It is likely that enslaved prisoners of war frequently turned to Islam and joined the armies.[181] In other cases conversion is likely to have followed more peaceful encounters

179 Shahid 1984, 1989.
180 H. Kennedy 1996: 5–6, 18.
181 Bulliet 1994: 37–43; examples: 44, 47 (Dinar, grandfather of Abu Taiba), 53 (Abu Taiba).

with members of the advancing armies. Above all the new Arab settlements seem to have attracted immigrants from the non-Muslim population on a very large scale, with conversion to Islam following soon after settlement.[182] The Muslim settlements thus seem to have been the growing points of the new religion and no doubt also the principal source of recruits for the ever-growing manpower needs of the early Islamic armies.

Hope of booty and eventually of land will have encouraged conversion. The Arab system depended on regular campaigning as much as the Roman Republic had once done,[183] or even more so. The Arab conquests established an imperial concentration of power, but did not create an accepted system of legitimizing power and handing it on. War for the sake of Islam and above all war against potential or actual enemies of the faithful justified the possession of power. But the soldiers who campaigned for them needed to be rewarded. The war offered legitimacy to the ruler, but also plunder and resettlement to the follower.[184] Did this situation encourage a remilitarization of some of the long settled and demilitarized inhabitants of the Near East?[185] Is this the explanation of the almost annual raiding of Byzantine Anatolia?

The occupation of much of the Near East by the Muslim Arabs was altogether unexpected. Yet when we look at the history of this area in later Late Antiquity with hindsight we can see that the Arab conquest was the culmination of a long-term trend, the emancipation of the Near East from the Greco-Roman culture and government.[186] Settlers with Arab names had been moving into eastern Syria and what is now Jordan for centuries.[187] Syriac Christianity had taken root in Syria and Mesopotamia and Coptic Christianity in Egypt. Large territories were practically controlled by the Ghassanid Arabs who were entrusted with the defence of the Frontier.[188] These facts are not sufficient to explain the collapse of the Empire in the Near East, but they help to explain why there never was any possibility of recovering the lost provinces.

[182] Ibid. 67–79, although the detailed evidence is from Iran.

[183] W. V. Harris, *War and Imperialism in Republican Rome 327–70 BC* (Oxford, 1979).

[184] On the problem of rewarding Arab armies and of retaining their loyalty, see H. Kennedy 1996: 6; and 'The financing of the military in the early Islamic state', in Averil Cameron (1995), 361–78, which reports on works in progress.

[185] But in Spain the population remained pacific. Fighting against Christians and in civil war was performed by imported troops and mercenaries: H. Kennedy 1996: 20, 23, 25, 49.

[186] See the survey (from a different point of view) in Averil Cameron 1993*b*: 182–6.

[187] See books of Shahid cited in n. 179 above.

[188] B. Isaac, *The Limits of Empire* (Oxford, 1990), 239–45. D. Graf, 'The Saracens and the defence of the Arabian frontier', *BASOR* 229 (1979), 1–26.

10

The Transformation of Literary Culture in the West under the Influence of Christianity

1. *Change in Education*

From the end of the fourth century the histories of East and West were very different. The West experienced barbarian settlement and the establishment of barbarian kingdoms while the Empire carried on much as before in the East. One consequence was that the decline of the traditional secular education based on classical and pagan authors began in the West long before it did in the East, so that the full range of instruction, elementary,[1] grammatical, and rhetorical was offered in fewer and fewer places. The decline of civic institutions brought with it the end of publicly financed schools;[2] and as the cities shrank they could no longer provide a living for private teachers, at least not for the more advanced training given by grammarians and sophists. At the same time the attitude to the traditional education was changed by the fact that in the Germanic successor kingdoms the leading Germans, whether Ostrogoths, Visigoths, Franks, or Lombards, were a warrior aristocracy, membership of which did not require, even if it did not exclude, literacy. So rhetorical education ceased to have the enormous prestige which it had enjoyed in the classical world.[3] The shrinking of educational opportunity cannot be traced in detail. It was sometime in the course of the fifth century that rhetorical education ceased to be provided north of the Loire.[4] But information is scanty. It is likely that quite a few teachers whether keeping a school for local pupils, or employed in a senatorial household have gone unrecorded.

Traditional education survived longer in Provence and Aquitaine than

1 Liebeschuetz 1991: 858–911, esp. 907–9. On the difference between humble teachers of letters and the much fewer but much more highly respected grammarians, see Kaster 1988: 44–7, 119, 163.

2 Riché 1957: 421–36.

3 P. Heather, 'Literacy and power in the migration period', in A. K. Bowman and G. Woolf (eds.), *Literacy and Power in the Ancient World* (Cambridge, 1994), 177–97; R. W. Mathisen, 'The theme of literary decline in late Roman Gaul', *Classical Philology*, 83 (1988), 45–52.

4 See the writings of P. Riché, esp. 1957, 1962, 1965.

in the north.[5] The grammarian Pomerius[6] taught Caesarius, the later bishop, at Arles around AD 500. At Vienne funeral memorials with verse inscriptions were put up until 580. The practice certainly implies that individuals who could appreciate classical verse continued to be around until that time, and it is significant that by no means all men commemorated in verse were clerics.[7] In Italy the poet Venantius Fortunatus and Gregory, later to become famous as pope Gregory the Great, each received a full classical education around the middle of the sixth century, the former at Ravenna, the latter at Rome. In Vandal Africa the traditional Latin education was on offer at least until the Justinianic reconquest (AD 533). It is not clear what happened in Spain. Spain produced very little writing, whether secular or ecclesiastical between the early fifth and the first half of the sixth century,[8] but the strength of the literary revival following the conversion of the Goths to Catholicism (AD 587) would suggest that it was founded on a living tradition.[9] Taking an Empire-wide view, it is significant that the number of Western teachers known from our period is much smaller than the corresponding figure from the East.[10] It seems that already by the fifth century traditional liberal education was provided in relatively few places in the West, while it continued to be available in many, if not most, cities in the East.

The decline and disappearance of secular schools was to some extent compensated by the Church progressively taking over responsibility for education. The ability to read the Bible and theological texts, to engage in theological argument and to preach to congregations of different social levels remained of vital importance to the Church. In addition, the Church continued to be governed by Roman law so that the tradition of Roman legal expertise had to be kept up and transmitted by the clergy.[11]

[5] Nodes (1993) discusses biblical epics in classical style, written by Christian authors, of whom Victorius wrote at Marseilles in mid-5th cent. (Gennadius *Vir. Illustr.* 61), and Avitus was bishop of Vienne 490–*c.*518. Cyprianus and Ps. Hilarius may also have written in Gaul.

[6] Klingshirn 1994: 73–82 on this teacher of rhetoric, who also in his *De vita contemplativa*, *PL* 59.411–520 advocated a reform of the lives of clergy and bishops on ascetic lines.

[7] Descombes 1985: 187–201 (discussion); no. 11 (*c.* AD 500), 81 (517), 85 (524), 87 (*c.*530), 101 (580), for the mother of a *patricius* Celsus—the latest verse inscription.

[8] Of course it is the case that altogether very little Latin literature survives from any period of Roman Spain.

[9] But Martin of Braga's career (a monk from Pannonia, bishop at Dumium in Gallaecia in 556, by 572 bishop of Bracara (Braga), died 579) took place before 587. His writings: C. W. Barlow, *Martini episcopi Bracarensis opera omnia*, Papers and Monographs of the American Academy in Rome 12 (New Haven, 1950).

[10] See the geographical and chronological list of teachers in Kaster 1988: 463–78.

[11] I. Wood 1993: 161–77, esp. 167–9, on Praeiectus of Clermont, Bonitus of Clermont, Desiderius of Cahors, and Leodegar of Autun, who is said to have revised the laws of the Frankish kings. But Andarchius learnt Virgil and the *Theodosian Code* from his senatorial master Felix (Greg.T. *HF* IV.46; *PLRE* III.74 s.v. Andarchius; ibid. 481 s.v. Felix 3). Byzantine Italy had significant numbers of educated lay officials and jurists but they were educated by clerics, A. Guillou, 'L'École dans l'Italie

In Gaul the earliest monastic schools were founded by Martin of Tours at Marmoutier, by Honoratus at Lérins, and by John Cassian at Marseille.[12] In the course of the sixth and seventh centuries many episcopal schools were established: twenty are known from Gaul alone.[13] By the seventh century the Church had a monopoly of education and the great majority of the educated were clerics, who had been taught by clerics, whether attached to the household of a bishop or to a monastery.

Secular literacy was not dead. It is now thought to have been more common at the Merovingian courts than earlier scholars believed. The clerical teachers accepted not only boys already destined for the monastic life or a career in the Church, but also children who were simply to be educated.[14] Not all children taught at ecclesiastical schools became members of the clergy immediately. Some were only ordained after years of serving the king in secular posts.[15]

There is not nearly enough evidence to assess either the numbers of the literate or of the extent of literacy through society, or indeed the proportion of clergy and laymen among the literate. But the administration, private as well as royal, continued to make use of written documents. Accounts were kept in writing, gifts, wills, sales, manumissions, legal judgments were drawn up in writing using standardized formulae, going back to the Roman administration. The royal authority used writing to issue its orders, make appointments, and to grant protection to individuals. The staff that handled the written business did not consist exclusively of trained slaves and clerics, though both of these played their part. It included laymen, and it is evident that these too were capable of handling written documents. Paradoxically we know about some of these lay officials precisely because after their secular service they were ordained and ended their lives as bishops.[16] Nevertheless the proportion of clerics among the men with more than a minimum degree of literacy was certainly high. It was therefore inevitable that Germanic kings often employed clerics for duties which in earlier times would have been performed by laymen.

byzantine', *Settimane di studio del centro italiano di studi sull'alto medioevo,* xix (Spoleto, 1972), 291–311.

[12] J. Bardy, 'Les Origines des écoles monastiques en occident', *Sacr. Erud.* 5 (1953), 86–104. Riché 1962: 336–50. On Lérins as a source of sound teaching, see Markus 1990: 194–5.

[13] H. Leclercq, s.v. Écoles, *DACL* iv.2: 1831–83.

[14] Riché 1962, 1965: 1–21.

[15] Heinzelmann 1990: 105–36.

[16] I. Wood 1990: 63–81; Collins 1990: 109–33.

2. *Claudian, Macrobius, Martianus, and Dracontius*

Meanwhile literary culture was changing under the influence of Christianity, though changing slowly. As in the East, the Church was long content to coexist with a literary culture based on pagan writers. In the early fifth century the classical conventions of poetry were still accepted as firmly at the Western court as in the East. The old gods continued to provide images for secular writers, whether they happened to be Christians,[17] or adherents of the old religion. Of this fact the poetry of Claudian,[18] who wrote poems in various genres on behalf of members of the Western court, and above all on behalf of Stilicho in the decades around AD 400, provides ample evidence. Claudian wrote an epic on the rape of Persephone, and he started another on the war between Jupiter and the giants. Neither has any obvious trace of a Christian sub-text, though it has been plausibly argued that when Claudian represented the praetorian prefect Rufinus as an instrument of the powers of the pagan underworld, he was assuming that Christians would interpret his language as referring to the devils and hell. Claudian composed a lot of occasional poetry to be recited at great public occasions. The persons honoured, the emperor Honorius, Stilicho himself, Serena wife of Stilicho and niece of the emperor Theodosius, the two young Anician consuls of AD 395, were all Christians, some strongly so. The poems honouring them have no trace of Christian doctrine, no allusions to the Bible, and scarcely even such ambiguity as would leave references to the supernatural open to either a Christian or a pagan interpretation. The pagan imagery is used above all for hyperbolic comparisons. For instance: of the long line of Roman heroes Stilicho alone is beyond envy. People would no more think being jealous of him than they would envy Jupiter's rule in heaven, or Apollo's omniscience.[19] Jupiter once upon a time fought for Marcus Aurelius and shattered his barbarian foes with a thunderbolt, he would have helped Stilicho's army fighting Alaric in the same way, but he knew that Stilicho could win without the aid of miracles.[20] While his heroes generally succeed through their own merits, Claudian from time to time

[17] e.g. Ausonius (*c.* AD 320–393) and Sidonius Apollinaris (431–*c.*485), the latter even finally a bishop, see Harries 1994. In his panegyrical poems, Sidonius uses mythological imagery more frequently than Claudian, but he refused to use it when writing as a bishop, Carm. XVI.ff.; IX.20–120 a humorous compendium of topoi, mythological and other, which Sidonius is not going to use.

[18] Claudian wrote a Christian poem 'de salvatore' (XXXII [XCV]), but Augustine thought him a pagan and he surely knew (Aug. *Civ. Dei* V.26). Claud. L (LXXVII) 'In Iacobum magistrum equitum' makes fun of the cult of saints.

[19] Claudian invites a Christian reinterpretation of the pagan underworld: Paula James, 'Living legends in Claudian's, *In Rufinum*', in Mary Whitby (1998), 151–75. Pagan gods named for flattering comparisons: *De Cons. Stil.* III.39.

[20] VI Con. Hon. 331 ff.

reminds the readers that the ancestral gods are still watching over Rome. He lists the gods who have aided Rome in the past, and with whose help Stilicho will defend Rome now.[21] He prays that Jupiter will never allow barbarian eyes to desecrate the temple of Numa and the residence of Quirinus.[22]

Occasionally Claudian addresses Christian prejudice. After describing the frightening portents which preceded Alaric's invasion of Italy, he compares Stilicho, who ignored them and won, with Alaric, who trusted them, was deceived and lost the battle. Claudian draws a moral which would not be out of place in a Christian apologist: 'O oracles always spiteful and grudging with your uninformative circumlocutions, whose true meaning is hidden even to your priests, and is revealed only when it is too late—after the event.'[23] In another poem, Claudian describes how Serena and her sister sailed from Spain to join their uncle, the emperor Theodosius, at Constantinople. He compares the sea voyage of the young princesses to one undertaken by the virgin goddesses Minerva and Diana to visit their uncle Neptune: 'The waves grow smooth, to honour the coming of the chaste goddesses; Galatea interrupts her shameless frolics, dissipated Triton keeps his hands off Cymothoë, all over the ocean modesty rules, and Proteus even restrains Neptune's flocks (the seals) from their disgraceful coupling'. This curious combination of mythology and Christian prudishness (not without humour) was evidently perfectly acceptable in the Christian household of Serena and Stilicho.[24]

Claudian wrote before Alaric's second invasion of Italy, and before the Vandals and their allies had broken the Rhine frontier. The Gothic invasion and settlement put an end to the Gallic school of secular writing which had flourished at Bordeaux and elsewhere in the fourth century. This left the senatorial aristocracy at Rome, the Western imperial court, and subsequently in the fifth century the courts of the Vandal and Ostrogothic kings to provide patronage for secular writers.

A feature of the late secular literary culture shared by East and West was an interest in handbooks summing up a greater or a smaller part of the cultural heritage as transmitted in older writings.[25] We have seen that in the East John Lydus wrote antiquarian monographs, and Nonnus a

[21] *De Cons. Stil.* III.165–74.

[22] *Bell. Get.* 101–2.

[23] *Bell. Get.* 553–5.

[24] XXX.122–9. Serena had read both Homer and Virgil. She finds fault with Helen and cannot approve Dido. Her mind fastens on nobler examples: Laodamia following Protesilaus as he returned to the shades (XXX.147–50).

[25] Note also the use of illuminated handbooks as prestige gifts: e.g. the calendar of Filocalus, the *Notitia Dignitatum*, the anonymous *De Rebus Bellicis*, the herbal of Dioscurides, and the *Corpus Agrimensorum*. See K. Weitzmann, *Studies in Classical and Byzantine Illumination*, ed. H. L. Kessler (Chicago, 1971).

huge epic stuffed with literary reminiscences. In the West Vegetius wrote a little manual of the art of war which contains so much material about the Roman army of the great old days that it is easy to overlook its contemporary relevance. Palladius wrote a manual on agriculture. In his *Saturnalia* Macrobius used the dialogue form[26] to compile a readable manual of Roman antiquities. The *Saturnalia* reports what purports to be the table talk of some well-known Senators, a generation or two before the time of writing,[27] at the traditional banquet celebrating the December festival of the Saturnalia. Learnedly, yet urbanely, they discuss a variety of Roman topics, the ancient calendar and its feast-days, the gods, witty sayings of famous men, food and wine, and above all the writings of Virgil, his extraordinary knowledge of philosophy, astronomy, and of pontifical law, and the subtleties of his rhetorical technique. Martianus Capella wrote a textbook of the seven liberal arts. To make it more palatable he gave it a fantastic and humorous mythological introduction in the genre of Menippean Satire, varying narrative prose with short pieces of verse.[28] At the very end of this tradition there stands a work which has the form as well as the substance of an encyclopaedia, the *Etymologiae* of Isidore of Seville. It is composed of twenty books, each devoted to a different branch of secular or theological knowledge. The books consist of a succession of articles, each of which starts with the etymology of a technical term and goes on to explain the significance of the word.[29]

The purpose of this kind of writing emerges clearly from the introduction to the *Saturnalia*. Macrobus wants to put his own very wide reading at the disposal of his son: 'if ever you have occasion to call to mind some historical fact, buried in a mass of books and generally unknown, or some memorable word or deed, it will be easy for you to find it and produce it as it were from a literary storehouse.' The book is written to be useful, useful above all for improving the reader's style, both in conversation and in oratory: 'everything in it is calculated to quicken your understanding, to strengthen your memory, to give more dexterity to your discourse and to make your speech more correct.' The aim is of course not simply to make eloquence more persuasive, but above all to ensure that it is the speech of a cultured Roman, on the tacit assumption that style reveals the man. The work is made up of a very large number of extracts from earlier works, some cited verbatim, others paraphrased. It is essentially an anthology, a florilegium. But Macrobius explains that he intends it to be more than that. When bees gather nectar from a large number of

[26] R. Hirzel, *Der Dialog* (1895, repr. 1963).

[27] Alan Cameron, 'The date and identity of Macrobius', *JRS* 56 (1965), 25–38. M. Kahlos, *Saeculum Praetextati* (Helsinki, 1998).

[28] Shanzer 1986: 29–44.

[29] Fontaine 1959.

different flowers and store it in an orderly way in the hive, they transform the different juices to a single flavour by 'mixing with them a proportion of their own being'. So also Macrobius has arranged the material of his anthology not only to help the memory but also to blend the single extracts to produce a single flavour. Macrobius sees himself not only as a compiler but also as a creative writer. He takes for granted that the extracts of older writers which he is going to bring together are in fact compatible, and formed as it were fragments of a great cultural whole, so that the book containing examples drawn from many ages is nevertheless 'informed by a single spirit'. In fact they would all serve to instil in the reader the *mos maiorum*, the traditional ways of thought and behaviour which had made and kept Rome great.[30]

With hindsight we are tempted to imagine that Macrobius, writing as he did in an increasingly Christian environment, under a strongly Christian emperor, at a time when the Visigoths and Vandals had broken into the Empire, and had defeated all attempts to remove them, must have been motivated by fear that the Roman heritage was in danger. But if Macrobius feared for the future, the calm and Ciceronian tone of his writings shows no trace of it. As we have seen, he argues that there is need for an anthology because in the mass of old writings it is difficult to find what you are looking for. In other words the Roman heritage has become so unwieldy as to be in need of some condensation.

It has been argued that the *Saturnalia* is a defence of paganism, and some features of the book support that view. The men whose discussion Macrobius has reconstructed were undoubtedly pagan, and Macrobius himself surely identifies with their pagan views.[31] Moreover most of the first book[32] is about pagan religious themes, the Roman calendar, the annual round of festivals, and it culminates in Praetextatus' speech about the gods. The third book, which is only fragmentarily preserved, includes discussions of Virgil's knowledge of pontifical law and augural law. So while Macrobius has assembled also a lot of non-religious material, his book demonstrates that religious lore occupied a central place in the Roman cultural tradition. On the other hand, the *Saturnalia* are quite unpolemical. There is not a hint of criticism of Christianity, nor any

[30] Macrobius' assumption that the great Romans of the past shared the same outlook is comparable to that of philosophers who thought that the philosophies of Plato and Aristotle must be compatible, and of the compilers of Christian florilegia who assumed the Church Fathers taught identical theologies.

[31] In neither the *Saturnalia* nor in the *Commentary on Cicero's Dream of Scipio* does Macrobius hint at biblical teaching or Christian doctrine in his exposition of traditional lore and philosophical doctrine.

[32] In the senators' dinner talk, as in the senate itself, the agenda was headed with business concerning the gods.

suggestion at all that Rome and its citizens would fare better if they returned to the worship of the gods of their fathers.[33]

At the centre of all discussion of religion in the *Saturnalia* is the speech in which Praetextatus, the outstanding pagan senator of the late fourth century, argues that all the traditional gods are really personifications of some aspect of the sun, or that they are at least in some way related to the sun. Contrary to what has sometimes been maintained Praetextatus' argument is not philosophical in a Neo-Platonic sense. He does not attempt to demonstrate that the polytheistic deities represent different processes in the coming into being and regular functioning of the universe. This is what the emperor Julian did in the two hymns he addressed respectively to King Helios and to the Mother of the Gods, which he wrote quite explicitly as a Neo-Platonist and follower of Iamblichus.[34] Praetextatus' argument is not based on Neo-Platonism or indeed any other systematic philosophy, but on detailed knowledge of ritual. His procedure is that of an antiquarian closely examining the nomenclature, ritual, and iconography of the various gods, and pointing out features that seem to support his thesis. He systematically surveys details of ritual practice which suggests that whoever started it was somehow aware that the deity being honoured ultimately stood for some aspect of the sun, or was at least endowed with solar qualities.

The speech nevertheless shares an important complex of ideas with, many but not all,[35] Neo-Platonic writers: the doctrine that the sun was the supreme deity and that a number of[36] other polytheistic deities, above all Apollo, Dionysus, the Tyrian Heracles, and some of the Egyptian gods, although worshipped under their own names, all represented the sun. Praetextatus repeatedly tells us that the parts of the speech referring to this theology are derived from Orphic writings,[37] and the history of this doctrine can indeed be traced to the so-called Orphic hymns of the second or third century AD. It was incorporated into Neo-Platonic philosophy by

[33] Paganism could be safely defended in writing in the Christian Empire: the Histories of Eunapius (*c.*410) and Zosimus (*c.*500) are open pagan polemic. The Histories of Ammianus (*c.*395) and Olympiodorus (*c.*430) contain a significant number of passages which are critical of Christianity or positive in their attitude to paganism. (On Olympiodorus' paganism, J. Matthews, 'Olympiodorus of Thebes and the history of the West (AD 407–25)', *JRS* 60 (1970), 95–6). What might be punished was performance of pagan rites, esp. sacrifice or divination, F. R. Trombley 1993–4: i.1–97 on the legal status of sacrifice.

[34] J. Fontaine, C. Prato, and A. Marcone, *Giuliano Imperatore alla madre degli dei e altri discorsi* (Vicenza, 1987).

[35] It is not necessary that the Neo-Platonic Good or First Cause and its successive hypostases are identified with first, second, and third hypostases of the sun: they are not for instance in Sallustius' pamphlet 'The Gods and the World'. See my 'The Speech of Praetextatus', in P. Anastassiadi and M. Frede, *Pagan Monotheism in Late Antiquity* (1999), 185–205.

[36] Not all the gods included in Praetextatus' speech seem to have figured in this particular syncretism.

[37] Macr. *Sat.* I.18.12–13, 17–18, 22; 23.21 (theologians).

Iamblichus and Julian, providing a link between the logical constructions of their abstract thought and the anthropomorphic deities of practical religion. In the fourth century this theology also seems to have been taken up by some of the mystery cults popular among the Roman aristocracy, for it was attacked by Firmicus Maternus in a pamphlet directed against these cults.[38] In the fifth century the solar theology was expounded in a hymn in *The Marriage of Mercury and Philology* of the North African poet Martianus Capella,[39] in the *Dionysiaca* of Nonnus,[40] and, as part of a Neo-Platonic system, in the philosophy of Proclus. Praetextatus' list of Greco-Roman deities included in the solar syncretism is more comprehensive than that of any other of the authors, including as it does even abstractions like Echo, and the twelve signs of the Zodiac. It is as if the speaker was out to astonish his fellow-diners by showing how far he could take his argument.

The speech has been interpreted as the exposition of a monotheistic pagan theology, representing the views of philosophical pagans designed to challenge the philosophical appeal of Christian monotheism, while continuing to uphold the ancestral polytheistic worship. But is Praetextatus' speech really a sermon putting forward a pagan theology with polemical intentions? It is worthwhile to look more closely at the context of the speech, starting with the way in which it was received by Praetextatus' fellow-diners: everybody was astonished by so much learning, not to say ingenuity. They had clearly witnessed a tour de force.

> As Praetextatus ended his discourse, the company regarded him in wide-eyed wonder and amazement. Then one of the guests began to praise his memory, another his learning, and all his knowledge of the observances of religion; for he alone, they declared knew the secrets of the nature of the godhead, he alone had the intelligence to apprehend the divine and the ability to expound it.[41]

What had struck them was Praetextatus' learning, his intellectual grasp of a great mass of detail, one might almost say his encyclopaedic memory. I think one can also safely deduce that what Praetextatus had just expounded was not a generally shared theology, but something which the fellow-diners had heard for the first time. One can also say that they did not see this new perspective on their old religion as a discovery which would in any way change their lives.[42] They received the speech rather as

[38] Firmicus Maternus, *De Errore Profanarum Religionum*, VII.7, Sol expresses indignation at being drowned in the Nile as Osiris, castrated as Attis, killed, dismembered, and cooked as Dionysus.

[39] See below, pp. 327–30.

[40] See above, pp. 231–8.

[41] Macr. *Sat.* I.24.1.

[42] The only criticism raised is that Virgil should not be treated as an authority in philosophy (I.24.2–3). The point is methodological and academic. This is in no sense a discussion of practical religion.

an academic audience might receive a stimulating and original lecture on Roman religion today.[43]

Modern scholarship has picked on this speech as the key to the understanding of the *Saturnalia*. In fact it only occupies a very small part of this long work. Certainly the fact that Macrobius honours and values the Roman past in its entirety means that he honours and values Roman religious antiquities, but it does not follow that he must be calling on his contemporaries to return to the traditional worship. Since the Renaissance many generations of European academics have honoured and valued Greco-Roman antiquities, including religious antiquities, without urging their pupils to abandon Christianity. The purpose of Praetextatus' speech is something else.

The Roman gods were of course by far the most objectionable part of the Roman tradition from the Christian point of view. Praetextatus' argument that the whole of ancestral religion was fundamentally monotheist suggests that the incompatibility of the old religion and the new was not as complete as people might think. This argument would not of course have been accepted by most of the Christian authors whose writings have come down to us. It would however have made it easier for Macrobius' senatorial contemporaries to reconcile their fairly recent Christian religion with continued veneration of the pagan past. It supported a cultural compromise which had already been tacitly adopted in Roman high society.

Martianus Capella's *Marriage of Philology and Mercury*, written in Africa about the same time, or more likely a generation or so later than the *Saturnalia*,[44] is very much a handbook, though its subject matter is specialized. It is essentially a learned[45] exposition of each of the Seven Liberal Arts, a detailed and systematic compendium of the knowledge that ideally made up a traditional education. But Martianus has given literary interest to the utilitarian treatise by setting it in a mythological frame, a narrative of the marriage of Mercury and Philology, composed in the genre of Menippean satire. The two themes are linked through the device that Mercury presents the Seven Arts as a marriage dowry to Philology. Subsequently each Art in turn is called upon to expound her science for the entertainment of the wedding-guests.

The marriage tale is necessarily about the gods, and in the course of the narrative the pagan pantheon is fairly exhaustively described. The story combines quite different ways of thinking about the gods. They figure as the anthropomorphic, all too human deities of Greek mythology, but also

[43] Or as his contemporaries in Roman priesthoods might have read Cicero's *De Natura Deorum* or *De Divinatione*.

[44] Shanzer 1986: 17–21.

[45] Though perhaps compiled from a very limited number of sources: Stahl 1971: i. 41–54.

as planets. There are allusions to Orphic theology and Neo-Platonic philosophy, but no single conception dominates. Philology, a human maiden, receives the gift of immortality, before travelling to heaven for her wedding. The journey gives the author an opportunity to describe the universe of the astronomers, and to set each divinity in his or her place among the heavenly spheres, or above them. The fable of the marriage allegorizes a successful education in the Liberal Arts: learning combined with eloquence. The ascent to heaven enables Philology to see with her own eyes the structure of the universe about which she had so far only read in books.

The gods of the allegorical fable are of course part of the body of learning represented by the Liberal Arts. But are they intended to be more? Does the allegory have also a positively religious message? Is Martianus preaching paganism? Is the apotheosis of Philology also an allegory of salvation through some Orphic or Neo-Platonic mystery cult? The questions are similar to those raised by the *Saturnalia*, but they are more insistent because the gods are given an even more prominent place in Martianus' book, and because that fable does seem to contain elements of a myth of the return of the soul.[46] Scholarly opinion has been divided. Some see in the divine fable nothing but literary machinery, others have argued that it conveys a religious message to those ready and willing to receive it. There can never be a final answer. We cannot look into the mind of the long dead author.

We can however compare the space he has given to different themes developed in his work. So there can be no question in the case of the *Marriage of Philology and Mercury* that by far the greatest part of the book is a given to the exposition of the Liberal Arts. The book is in fact more than anything else a textbook, and its high quality as a textbook—or perhaps rather as a reference book—was to bring about its success over many centuries. The allegorical tale of the marriage with its picturesque cast of gods, goddesses, and abstractions has a subsidiary function. It provides a witty introduction and frame to what would otherwise be a dry as dust compilation. It sums up the book's educational programme which seeks to 'marry' learning with eloquence. It offers a journey through the heavens and its revolving spheres which is all part of the syllabus. Finally its numerous allusions to classical writers pay a tribute to the cultural tradition which the didactic chapters of the book will help to perpetuate.

But what about the religious aspect of the fable? The first thing to note

[46] Martianus combines in one work learned material which Macrobius has treated separately in the *Saturnalia* and the *Commentary* on Cicero's *Somnium Scipionis*. But the tone of the description of Philology's sight-seeing ascent to heaven is quite different from Macrobius account of the descent of the soul (*Somn. Scip.* 12).

is that Martianus has distanced himself from the gods by making fun of them from beginning to end of his work. Here are some examples: Mercury decides to marry. 'His nervous mother had pushed him to this decision when he greeted her among the Pleiades in his annual journey through the Zodiac.' What had made her nervous was that her 'young son's body, exercised in the palaestra, and by the frequent errands he had to run for Jupiter, glistened in masculine development . . . With his downy cheeks he could no longer walk around half naked, draped in a short chlamys covering only the tops of his shoulders, and leaving everything else exposed, without great laughter on the part of Venus.'[47] Besides presenting the god as a sexually maturing adolescent, Martianus here and elsewhere uses for humorous effect the paradox that the same god can be treated at the same time as a star and as an anthropomorphic being.[48] Another example of humour is Martianus' description of the gods assembled under the presidency of Jupiter following the procedure of the Roman senate.[49] At the end of the work Martianus is quite explicit: the whole fable is intended as entertaining nonsense.[50]

Nevertheless it is not only that. For one thing it has a lot of cultural information. Elaborate descriptions of gods and abstractions, detailing much symbolic ornament, would be in place in a manual of iconography. Martianus guides the reader through the sixteen regions of heaven and introduces him to the deities residing in each.[51] The goddess Juno lectures Philology on the daemons and spirits to be found in lower regions.[52] This is again quite appropriate for the handbook of cultural information. But there is one feature pointed out by Shanzer that deserves special note: Philology is of course a personification of all book learning[53]—she has to vomit out a vast library before she may embark on the vehicle that will take her to heaven (II.136–9). This learning quite definitely includes magic which enables her to call up gods even against their will;[54] and she also practices theurgy: at the highest point of her voyage she performs a magical rite to gain a vision of the supreme ultimate supercosmic deity.[55]

Shanzer bases her interpretation of the whole work on the abundance

47 Mart. Cap. I.5, tr. based on Shanzer.

48 Ibid. I.8 Mercury god/planet; I.12–13: Apollo/sun.

49 e.g. ibid. I.41, 90–6; II.208–18.

50 Ibid. IX.997–1000.

51 Ibid. I.45–62.

52 Ibid. II.150–68.

53 These include theurgy, but Shanzer (1986: 22–4) exaggerates the place of theurgy and magic in the activities described: Philology worked day and night at *all* the Arts.

54 Ibid. I.37, see also II.101–5, divination from numbers; II.109–110 magical prophylaxis against dangers of travel among the stars.

55 Ibid. II.203–4, P. Courcelle, *Les Lettres grecques en occident* (Paris, 1948), 204–5; H. D. Betz, *The Greek Magical Papyri in Translation*, 51–2 (*PGM* IV.655–730).

of religious pagan material, and especially the references to magic and theurgy, to conclude tentatively that the work is a crypto-pagan mystagogic compendium. The parody and the depreciation of the fable by the author are precautions because the subject-matter was dangerous to mention in Martianus' time.[56] This is going too far. Certainly the fact that he includes theurgy and magic among the arts which are properly part of his subject-matter—even if he only alludes to them in the humorous mythological frame—is significant. Macrobius did not mention them at all. On the other hand, he does no more than allude. The divinatory arts have disappeared from the earth. Oracular office-waste now litters what once were oracles of Apollo.[57] And in the last book the gods decide that there is no time for each of the Seven Divinatory Arts to expound her science to the divine assembly. So Martianus' compendium includes neither the traditional arts of Roman divination, nor astrology, magic, or theurgy, even though we are given to understand that strictly speaking these ought to have been included.[58] But apart from the expression of sympathy for the divinatory arts—undercut by being put in the mouth of gods—there is nothing in the *Marriage of Philology and Mercury* that would have rendered Martianus liable to persecution.[59] His book is no more than a compendium of the learned knowledge which an educated man might ideally be expected to know, or at least might want to look up.

Dracontius was a contemporary of Martianus in Carthage and his poems are further evidence of the continuing strength of the classical literary tradition at the Vandal court, though passages in which the classical form covers Christian ideas are more frequent than in Claudian.[60] For instance, Dracontius wrote a poem to celebrate the joint wedding of two brothers of a powerful family of Carthage who had helped to free him from prison.[61] The poem is a classical epithalamium. Dracontius calls on the gods, one after the other, to attend the wedding, and requests each divinity to bring his or her special gift to the young couples. The gods duly come, among them lascivious Cupid, who is followed by Liber, Pan, Silanus, and Venus herself, all appropriate patrons for a traditional, though not one would have thought for a Christian, wedding. But Cupid is also escorted by three personifications, namely Seemly Lust (*Justa Libido*), Controlled Pleasure (*Moderata Voluptas*), and Sobriety (*Sobrietas*),

[56] Shanzer 1986: 43.

[57] Mart. Cap. I.9–10.

[58] Ibid. IX.892–96. They probably were included in one of Martianus' sources.

[59] Prosecution was usually for alleged *performance* of illegal acts, sometimes for possession of a *manual* of illegal knowledge. Martianus was open to neither charge.

[60] B. Weber, *Der Hylas des Dracontius* (Romulea 2) Kommentar und Untersuchungen (Leipzig, 1995).

[61] *MGH AA* XIV, *Romulea* VI.36 ff.

whose attendance at a wedding might have been thought appropriate by Christians, but not by traditional pagans.[62] The house which the gods are visiting is praised for its charitable gifts to the poor, especially the clothing of naked girls. This the poet notes is 'in accordance with our laws', evidently the laws of Christian charity.[63] While actually in prison Dracontius wrote another epithalamium for a wedding at which a bride from Sitifis in North Africa was marrying a bridegroom from Sardis in Asia Minor. But although both young people seem to have been descended from bishops,[64] Dracontius ends his poem with a request to Venus, to intercede with Aeolus, the wind-god, so that the young couple might have a calm sea-crossing to their new home in Asia.[65] In another and very charming poem Dracontius tells how Venus while fleeing the embraces of Mars cut her foot on a thorn-bush. The blood of Venus spurted all over the bush, which ever since has flowered with red roses. Dracontius comments: 'just so it was fitting for a goddess, fitting for the divinity of love to bear pain: by avenging her wounds with presents of beauty.'[66] To repay injuries with presents is Christian, it is emphatically not the traditional behaviour of the goddess of love, or of any other of the old deities.

The poems discussed so far were written for ceremonies or entertainment. But two poems were written in graver circumstances. While languishing in prison, the poet addressed a plea for pardon to the Vandal king Gunthamund: the *Satisfactio*.[67] This poem too is composed in elegiac couplets, and the heightened language of traditional Latin poetry. But an argument for clemency addressed to a Christian—if Arian—king had to be explicitly Christian. In this context the poet allows himself to refer directly to the Bible. He reminds his king that 'in the flood the guilty perished, without calamity to the pious', and that Loth, 'that good and just

[62]
Iusta Libido coit, venit et moderata Voluptas,
candida legitimas accendens Gratia taedas
accurrit, venit alma Fides, Petulantia simplex,
casta Pudicitia procedit mente quieta,
Sobrietas per cuncta vigil devota cucurrit,
et quidquid iustos solite comitatur amores. *Romulea* VI.61–6.

[63] Legibus et nostris nudas vestire puellas. *Ibid.* 88–9.

[64]
Pontifices sacri Statulenius Optatianus
moribus inocuis, sancta quietate modesti,
religione pii, castis altaribus apti
quorum cana fides, per sacra palatia pollens,
floruit, unus erat Latialis mysticus aulae,
alter apud Danaos sacrata mente dicatus. *Romulea* VII.109–14.

[65] *Romulea* VII.140 ff.

[66]
Sic decuit doluisse deam, sic numen amorum
vindicet ut blandis vulnera muneribus.
(*De origine rosarum* 13–14; *MGH AA* XIV (p. 228))

[67] *MGH AA* XIV.114–21.

man was rescued from Sodom'. Dracontius goes on to call the king's attention to the Lord's Prayer, 'forgive us our trespasses as we forgive them that trespass against us'; and points out its relevance to the king's treatment of himself: 'whoever in accordance with that rule prays to God to free him from his sins, ought himself in all circumstances forgive the man who has offended against himself'.[68]

But the king kept Dracontius in prison notwithstanding, and there he wrote a long poem, still in classical style, but more personal, and religious, and on a biblical theme: praising God for the seven days of creation. The *Laudes Dei* were to be given a second edition by Eugenius archbishop of Toledo (646–57), who dedicated his version of the poem to the Visigothic king of Spain.[69] Dracontius and Eugenius of Toledo are evidence that the tradition of high literature survived the fall of the Western Empire to be maintained at the court of not only the Vandal, but also of the Visigothic kings.[70] But it is also significant that Dracontius was a layman, while in Spain Eugenius and the other leading writers were bishops. Literacy was more secular in Vandal Africa than in Visigothic Spain. But the fact that king Sisebut (612–21) wrote both poetry and prose[71] is evidence that at the Visigothic court too lay-literacy was not insignificant.

The poems of Dracontius show that literary culture in Vandal Africa was influenced by Christianity, and that Christian ideas can be found if you look for them. The poems of the so-called Latin Anthology confirm the impression that in Vandal Africa, the classical cult of high literature still had numerous followers. So it comes as a surprise that the whole tradition came to an end with the Byzantine reconquest in AD 534. The expulsion of the Vandals and the imposition of Byzantine rule meant not only the end of writing by laymen on secular themes, that is the replacement of literature by theology—which was something that was also happening at Constantinople—but the end of Latin writing altogether. Subsequently, theological controversy in North Africa was carried out by Greek bishops appointed by the imperial government in Greek. From the late seventh century when Roman North Africa had been conquered by the Arabs, evidence of Christian activities almost comes to an end. This is in the sharpest contrast to the continuing vitality of Christian theology in Arab-ruled Syria and Palestine. The rapid disappearance of the tradi-

[68] Diluvio periere rei, sine clade piorum,
Loth bonus et iustus tollitur ex Sodomis . . .
. . . quisquis poscit hac lege deum ut peccata relaxet
debet et ipse suo parcere ubique reo (*Satisfactio*. 285–6 and ibid. 305–6)

Cf. Nodes 1993: 108–18.

[69] *MGH AA* XIX.114–21.

[70] See below, pp. 337–40.

[71] See below, p. 338.

tion which had produced Tertullian, Cyprian, Lactantius, and Augustine is an extraordinary story, which is not yet fully understood. In terms of the breakdown of classical culture in the Latin West Roman North Africa ranks with Britain and the Balkan provinces.[72]

3. *Italy, Gaul, and Spain*

In Italy the tradition of secular literature was still very much alive in the early sixth century. Among works in this tradition to have survived are the *Letters* of Ennodius (died AD 521) and the official correspondence, the *Variae*, of Cassiodorus (AD 537). Boethius' *Consolation of Philosophy* (AD 525/6) has been taken for a work of pagan philosophy, and it is not a Christian work, although its philosophy is in no way incompatible with Christianity.[73] After the Justinianic reconquest of Italy Cassiodorus in high old age wrote the *Institutes* (*c.*560). This is a scheme of education for monks which gives the study of secular liberal arts, and the copying of secular manuscripts, a place in the education of inmates of Cassiodorus's monastery.[74] The role of the liberal arts is however ancillary, being altogether subordinate to the ultimate aim of this education: the fullest possible understanding of the Bible. Cassiodorus, highly educated himself, felt that only an educated individual could do full justice to the Bible, and he was still too much of a classical intellectual to think of anybody as educated who did not have some training in the Liberal Arts. So his *Institutes* are in the tradition of the Late Roman handbook, like the *Saturnalia* of Macrobius and the *Marriage of Mercury and Philology* of Martianus Capella. But his priorities are different. For him the Liberal Arts are no longer valuable for their own sake, no longer the ultimate goal of education, but only a means to an end. Accordingly the time to be given to secular studies is greatly reduced to make room for the Bible and theology. It is significant that Cassiodorus produced his educational programme for a monastery. Monasteries now came to perform a whole range of functions that had been performed by cities in the classical world. They became centres of local administration, and of agricultural production and marketing. They also established workshops for artisans.[75] It has been plausibly suggested, that urban or suburban monasteries possessing as they did large rural estates, provided the principal link between town and country, and played an essential role in the urban renewal from the later

[72] See Averil Cameron 1989 and 1993*a*.

[73] H. Chadwick, *Boethius: The Consolations of Music, Logic, Theology and Philosophy* (Oxford, 1981), 251 ff.; H. Liebeschuetz 1967: 535–639, relevant 550 ff. G. O'Daly, *The Poetry of Boethius* (London, 1971).

[74] J. J. O'Donnell, *Cassiodorus* (Berkeley, 1979).

[75] Hodges, Gibson, and Mitchell 1997.

seventh century.[76] That monasteries took on the responsibility for the preservation of literary culture, and for its transmission from generation to generation is thus only another example of monasteries taking on a role formerly performed by cities.

In Italy writing on secular themes came to an end in the second half of the sixth century. New writing was theological and concerned with disputes over dogma, or exegesis of the Bible, or moral or ascetic teaching. Practically all writing produced in this period in Italy was composed by clerics. The most important author by far was Pope Gregory the Great (AD 540–604). Gregory the Great showed that he could write quite elaborate classical prose, especially when addressing men of similar education to his own. For sermons and writings addressed to a wider public he preferred an idiom much closer to popular speech. But even in his lifetime the tradition of secular writing was not quite dead. This is shown by the career of Venantius Fortunatus (*c.*535–*c.*600), who had evidently received a very good traditional education at Ravenna around AD 555, even if we do not know who his teacher was. Lay teachers were dying out in Italy as elsewhere. By AD 600 the Church had attained a monopoly of education which it retained through the ninth and even into the tenth century.[77]

In AD 565 Venantius moved to Gaul. There he wrote poems in honour of secular nobles and churchmen, and occasional poems of various kinds. Evidently there were still quite a few people in Merovingian Gaul—at least in Merovingian court society—capable of appreciating his very classical poetry, on secular, and even on frivolous themes. But Venantius also wrote hymns, and Lives of saints, including two thousand lines of hexameters in honour of St Martin.[78] Eventually he took orders and ended his life as bishop of Poitiers. But significantly bishop Gregory of Tours (*c.*540–*c.*593), the scion of a great senatorial family, and writing at more or less the same time, and moving in the same circles as Venantius Fortunatus, used a very unclassical vocabulary and grammar in his extensive writings. It looks as if he had not had the kind of rhetorical training which a generation or two earlier would have been given to any young men of his class. But he was aware that some contemporaries remained eager to uphold the traditional rules of literary decorum, and felt it necessary to warn future bishops of Tours not to rewrite his *History of the Francs* in accordance with the rules of 'our Martianus'.[79] In Gaul the custom of

[76] R. Balzaretti 1997.

[77] D. Bullough, 'Le scuole cattedrali e la cultura dell'Italia settentrionale prima dei Comuni', *Italia Sacra*, 5 (1964), 111–43.

[78] Van Dam 1985: 221–9.

[79] *HF* VII.10. The wildest grammar is probably the fault of copyists of the 7th cent.: see K. Zeller, 'Zur Sprache Gregor von Tours', *Studia Patristica*, 18: 4 (1990), 207–11.

exchanging letters, composed in accordance with the strict rules of the genre, was maintained by some members of high society, laymen as well as clerics, and including even a few women, well into the seventh century.[80]

Much of the religious writing of the sixth century was composed in a simplified Latin style. The Gallic Church was increasingly prepared to sacrifice the archaizing and school-taught literary language for the sake of getting its message understood by a wider range of the people.[81] Hilary, bishop of Arles (AD 428–*c.*450), preached in the higher literary idiom if there were persons in the congregation who could appreciate his schooled eloquence, but used a 'humble' style to his normal hearers.[82] Caesarius of Arles (AD 502–42) always preached in the humble idiom on principle, as in Italy did Pope Gregory the Great.[83] So language closer to the spoken language, and without the structural elaboration of classical literary prose became standard in church use. But this too required a considerable educational effort: even the simplified Latin had to be taught and learnt, for it was a written language which preserved—more or less well as the case might be—distinctions of spelling and grammar which had long ceased to be audible in the spoken language. While the pronunciation was well on the way to that of the Romance languages, the writing even of simple Latin was still quite close to classical Latin.[84]

But the ever-widening gap between the syntax and grammar of the written and those of the spoken language could not be ignored for ever. Gregory of Tours surely knew this. The writer's modest apology for writing a form of Latin which some might despise, also reveals his satisfaction at being able to reach a much wider public than a more 'correct' writer could have done. He doubtlessly realized too that his popular idiom allowed him to create new effects, not achievable in the traditional language of high literacy. The *History of the Franks* is a work which has no precedent either in Latin secular historiography or in ecclesiastical histories. It is a mixture of the two genres, and in tone and language something altogether original. The Latin idiom of Gregory of Tours however only marked a stage in the emancipation of the spoken language. This was finally achieved only when Latin and French began to be treated as separate languages, perhaps from the reign of Charlemagne.

[80] I. Wood 1990: 63–81, esp. 68–71.

[81] Cf. the reforming advice of Pomerius *De vita contemplativa* I.23, also *Statuta ecclesiae antiqua*, ed. C. Munier (Paris, 1960), can. 79.

[82] *Vita Hilarii* 14.

[83] On 'humble language' of Christian discourse, see the classic treatment of E. Auerbach, *Literary Language and its Public in Late Antiquity and the Middle Ages* (London, 1965), 27–66; On Caesarius of Arles, see Klingshirn 1994: 73–4, 146–51.

[84] Wright 1982.

In Spain a very remarkable flourishing of literary culture took place, beginning around the middle of the sixth century but reaching a climax after the third council of Toledo of AD 589, and the conversion of the Goths to Catholicism.[85] It is likely that this revival was assisted by the survival in some cities of Baetica and Lusitania,[86] and on the east coast,[87] of traditional education, involving the teaching of the literary language, the reading of Christian and classical authors, and other elements of the traditional education in rhetoric. A key development however was innovative: the establishment of schools in the residences of bishops by the Church.[88] After unification, an effort was made by Church and monarchy to promote education as part of a policy to organize and make more coherent a society that had been divided by civil war and heresy.[89]

Teaching was provided principally by clerics and by monks. The relative importance of monastic and of episcopal schools is impossible to assess. It could be that even at episcopal schools most of the teaching was eventually done by monks. But monasticism came to Spain remarkably late, and only a handful of monasteries are recorded to have played a significant role in the educational revival.[90] The most important was Agali near Toledo, where four later archbishops of Toledo, Helladius, Justus, Eugenius, and Ildefons, are known to have been monks.[91] Another famous monastery was Servitanum, founded *c.*570, perhaps at Valentia.[92] Ildefons of Toledo suggests that it was Donatus the founder of Servitanum who introduced monasticism to Spain. That is certainly an exaggeration. The fact is that Spanish authors of the sixth century were

[85] Fontaine 1972: 142–202; J. Fontaine, 'Conversio et culture chez les Wisigoths d'Espagne', *Settimane di studio sull'alto medioevo* XIV (Spoleto, 1966), 87–147.

[86] Cf. Sid. Apol. IX.230: Cordova potens alumnis; see also the verse inscriptions in Vives 1969: 363 (Merida AD 483), 278 (Merida 549), 291 (Ebora 543), 276 (Arcavica 550). Episcopal schools were created by Council of Toledo II (527), canon 1, p. 42 (Vives). The tradition of fine late Roman epigraphic lettering lasted into the 6th and 7th cent. and beyond, though it is sometimes difficult to distinguish continuity from revival.

[87] Leander, bishop of Seville *c.*576, the considerably older brother of Isidore, presumably acquired his fine Latin style at his native Cartagena, before his family was exiled by the Justinianic 'liberation'. See also verse inscription, Vives 1969: no. 356 (Valencia AD 529–34).

[88] Conc. Tol. II, canon 1, Vives 1969: 42 (AD 527) = *PL* 84.335B.

[89] Canon 2 of fourth council of Toledo in 633 under presidency of Isidore himself ordering unification of the liturgy expresses the spirit: Unus igitur ordo orandi atque psallendi a nobis per omnem Spaniam atque Galliam conseruetur, unus modo in missarum sollemnitatibus, unus in matutinis vespertinisque officiis (Vives 1969: 188).

[90] The great founder of monasteries in Spain was Fructuosus who was consecrated bishop of Braga in 656. His foundations were therefore a generation or more later than those of Columbanus in Gaul. He was related to king Sisenand (631–6). See *Lives of Visigothic Fathers*, trans. and ed. by A. T. Fear, Translated Texts for Historians (Liverpool, 1997), ch. 2, p. 124 and n. 8.

[91] First certain reference AD 615, see *DHGE* I.872, s.v. Agali (L Serrano).

[92] Ildefonsus *De vir. illustr.* 4 (*PL* 96.200); Jo. Bicl. s.a. 571 (II.212). Donatus, fearing the Moors in Byzantine Africa, sailed with 70 monks and many books to Spain to found the monastery. Eutropius, bishop of Valencia , an important figure at Toledo III, had been abbot of Servitanum.

very badly informed about even recent events in their country. As a result we are even more so. At any rate it is certain that the intellectual life of sixth-century Spain received a strong stimulus from Augustine and other authors of Christian North Africa, and it is likely enough that North African monks fleeing persecution in the Three Chapters controversy were among the principal intermediaries.[93] But the Spanish literary revival of the sixth century is more likely to have received its decisive impulse from bishops than from monks.

At this time there were close links between Spain and Constantinople. John of Biclara, author of the chronicle which is our principal source for political events of the period, and later bishop of Gerona, spent many years in exile at the eastern capital. There he met his compatriot, Leander, who was to become bishop of Seville, and who was a brother of Isidore, the famous scholar, who eventually succeeded him at Seville.[94] Paul, bishop of Merida, was a Greek doctor, and his nephew and successor Fidelis a Greek who had come to Merida on a Greek merchant-ship.[95] The Visigothic *Code* was surely inspired by the *Code* of Justinian, and the characteristic decorative patterns of Visigothic architecture seem to come from the East. But the literary revival was nevertheless Latin-based, and the texts quoted, summarized, and taught, were those of Latin authors. Isidore the most learned of the Spaniards knew little or no Greek, even though he—like his brother—bore a Greek name. The Greek world was a catalyst and inspiration, rather than a direct source of texts and ideas.[96]

It is a notable feature of this Spanish revival that an unusually high proportion of its literary production, at least that part of it which has survived, consists of official records: laws, records of Church councils, and liturgical texts.[97] It would seem that in the official business of the recently unified Church and state of Spain more use was made of written documents than in the other Germanic kingdoms.[98] The state received a new legal code which was to be revised in several editions. The Church was

[93] Fontaine 1959: ii. 854–7.

[94] Isidore seems to have known little Greek, and probably received his knowledge of Greek writings through Latin florilegia written in Africa, see Fontaine 1959: ii. 852–4.

[95] *Vitas Patrum Emeritensium* IV.1.1; 3.1–12.

[96] Fontaine 1972: 158.

[97] R. Collins, 'Julian of Toledo and the education of kings in late 7th century Spain', in *Law Culture and Regionalism in Early Medieval Spain* (Aldershot, 1992), ch. 3.

[98] P. Classen, 'Fortleben und Wandel des spätrömischen Urkundenwesens im frühen Mittelalter', in P. Classen (ed.), *Recht und Schrift im Mittelalter* (Sigmaringen, 1977), 13–54, esp. 21–2 with ref. to the title *Lex Visig.* II.5, De scripturis valituris et informandis ac defunctorum voluntatibus conscribendis, with no less than 18 laws. It is not an accident that an exceptional large number of documents from the 10th and even the 9th cent. survive in Catalonia: P. Bonnassie, 'Sur les origines de la Catalogne: quelques remarques et orientations de recherche', *Memorias de la Real Academia de Buenas Letras de Barcelona*, 23 (1991), 437–45; J. Alturo i Perucho, 'Manuscrits i documents llatins d'origen català del segle IX', ibid. 273–80.

given an elaborate and rhetorical new liturgy.[99] While most of the writers were clerics, they were not exclusively so. King Sisebut (AD 612–21) wrote letters in elaborate rhetorical style as well as a life of the sainted bishop Desiderius of Vienne,[100] and a poem on the eclipses of the sun and the moon.[101] The correspondence of bishop Braulio of Saragossa includes letters addressed to laymen, who were not only literate but literary.[102]

In human terms, and in terms of geography the Visigothic revival was rather narrowly based. At the centre of it there was a single teacher–pupil line of descent, which started with Leander and Isidore, successive bishops of Seville, and was continued by Braulio, bishop of Saragossa, and then carried on by Eugenius (647–57), Ildefons (657–67), and Julian, who were all archbishops of Toledo, the royal residence.[103] But if the basis of the revival was narrow, its effects reached widely. After the Arab conquest the Visigothic cultural tradition continued—if at a lower level—at Cordova under the Arabs, in Catalonia, in Asturias, and in the Rioya.[104] The poetry, including some lively secular poems, and the theological writings of Theodulf of Orleans at the court of Charlemagne, bear witness to the continued vigour of this Visigothic 'renaissance'.[105] The writing of all these authors was of course mainly theological, and their object not to express original ideas, but above all to provide material for the training of clergy: that is to make written Latin intelligible, to explain doctrines of the Fathers of the Church, especially of St Augustine and of pope Gregory the Great, to compose prayers, and in fact to create a whole liturgy. These men wrote as pastors and teachers rather than as philosophers.

The voluminous writings of Isidore provide, as it were, an index for the Spanish revival. Most of them are course theological. In *Quaestiones in Vetus Testamentum* he draws on earlier expositors to explain certain books of the Old Testament. In the *Sententiae* he expounds the nature of the Trinity and the angels. In *De ecclesiasticis officiis* and *Regula monachorum* he describes the duties and way of life of respectively clerics and monks. But his most influential work, known alternatively as the *Etymologiae* or as the *Origines*, is a cultural encyclopaedia, which takes the form of a dictionary

99 M. C. Díaz y Díaz, 'Literary aspects of the Visigothic liturgy', in E. James (ed.), *Visigothic Spain: New Approaches* (Oxford, 1980), 61–76.

100 J. Fontaine, 'King Sisebut's *Vita Desiderii* and the political function of Visigothic hagiography', in E. James (ed.), *Visigothic Spain: New Approaches* (Oxford, 1980), 93–129.

101 Fontaine 1960: 328–35.

102 *Ep* 19, 28–30.

103 The *Vitas Patrum Emeretensium* were presumably written at Merida (around 630 acc. to A. Macia, *Ed* 29–30). But these lives of sanctified bishops of Merida are exceptional. The genre which is so common in contemporary Gaul is very rare in Visigothic Spain. This probably reflects the greater concentration of ecclesiastical and secular power in Spain.

104 R. Wright 1982: 145–95 (Spain 711–1050).

105 Ann Freeman, 'Theodulfus of Orleans a Visigoth at Charlemagne's court', in *L'Europe héritière de l'Espagne wisigothique*, Collection de la Casa de Velázquez (Madrid, 1992), 185–94.

of technical terms of Roman life and civilization, divided into twenty parts each devoted to one, or sometime two, subject areas. The book is therefore in a sense in the same tradition of the Late Roman compendium as the *Saturnalia* of Macrobius[106] and the *Marriage of Mercury and Philology* of Martianus, but it is much less self-consciously literary and much more utilitarian than either. Of course the Christian religion is at the heart of the work. Chapters are devoted to the Old and New Testaments, to God, angels and the *ordines* of the faithful, to the Church, and to diverse sects. Much of the material that is not overtly religious nevertheless has pastoral relevance. There is a great deal about grammar and rhetoric, that is the art of educated communication. There is a lot about the structure of the heavens, and that of the earth, including key concepts of different philosophies set side by side without their validity being discussed. This 'scientific' information also has a theological relevance. Knowledge of astrology helps to refute the claims of astrologers. Perhaps more importantly, ever since Plato, cosmology had been part of theological discussions. Isidore interprets the structure of the heavens as a symbolic demonstration of Christian doctrine. So the *Origines* are an epitome of Classical culture shrunk to what was relevant to Christian education, along the lines laid down by Augustine in *De doctrina Christiana* and in the *Institutes* of Cassiodorus.

But if for Isidorus transmission of traditional culture was ancillary to the teaching of Christianity, his selection of cultural material to be transmitted was very wide.[107] The *Origines* include chapters on the technical terms of law—especially of the making of wills, of medicine, and of military affairs. It explains the technical vocabulary of public games, agriculture, domestic equipment, stones and metals, architecture, and much besides. In short the book in some ways resembles the specialized word lists found in guidebooks for travellers. The *Origines* were of course not literally designed to make a traveller feel at home in a foreign land,[108] but its word lists provide a guide to the more specialized vocabularies of classical Latin authors, and so help the unsophisticated reader to feel at home in the classical culture which at the court of Toledo had not yet lost all validity.[109] It is a reference book which would be found useful by men

[106] Each article starts with an etymology of the term concerned. The name of a concept is taken as the key to its essence. This was one of the procedures used by Macrobius' Praetextatus to argue the essential identity of the polytheistic gods and the sun.

[107] Fontaine's great book (Fontaine 1959) makes the subject-matter of the *Origines* seem narrower and also altogether more metaphysical and 'high-brow' than much of it actually is.

[108] The metaphor (devised by Cicero for Varro) was used by Braulio of Saragossa to describe the role of Isidore: Nos in nostra urbe perigrinantes errantesque tamquam hospites tui libri quasi domum reduxerunt ut possimus aliquando qui et ubi essemus agnoscere (*PL* 81.17; Cic. *Acad.* I.3).

[109] See for instance the frequent use of metrical inscriptions on tombstones of prominent ecclesiastics: Vives 1969: 272, 273, 275–9, 285–6; also 287 of a lay warrior; 338–41, 357 on churches,

training for ordination, but also for future administrators, whether clerics[110] or laymen,[111] or indeed for would-be gentlemen who wanted to find their way through literary Latin, or at least to be able to use some of its old-fashioned words correctly. Many of the etymologies and explanations seem rather simple-minded. This should not be taken as an indication of low education and critical intelligence on the part of the author, who was clearly a man of outstanding ability and learning, but as a concession to the standards of the people for whom Isidore wrote the book. He wrote for native speakers of Latin, and this included many people of Gothic descent, for it is likely that the Goths too had long been Latin-speaking. But the conventions of written Latin, and the vocabulary and background knowledge necessary for understanding not only classical authors, but even patristic writings and the liturgy, will often have had to be taught from scratch.

4. *East and West Compared*

When one compares cultural developments in East and West, it is the differences that spring to mind first. There was more writing in the East, and it was more original. The East was the source of doctrinal thought and controversy. But there are similarities too, which are perhaps quite surprising bearing in mind the quite different historical experiences of the two halves of the Empire. In both regions the early sixth century, that is the years following the reigns of Theoderic in the West and of Justinian in the East, saw a sharp decline in the production of secular literature. Both regions experienced an Indian summer in late sixth and early seventh century which was represented by Gregory of Tours and Venantius Fortunatus in Gaul,[112] by Isidore and his successors in Spain, and by Theophylact and George of Pisidia in the East. The seventh and early eighth centuries were unproductive in East and West alike as far as writing was concerned, but what was produced was in many ways similar: homilies, lives of saints, sayings of the Desert Fathers, commentaries on books of the Bible, florilegia of extracts of the Church Fathers. The East produced a lot of anti-Jewish writings. In Visigothic Spain there were

361 on walls of Toledo. That the art of writing in classical metres was part of the culture of court clerics is shown by the secular poems of Eugenius of Toledo, *Carmina*, ed. F.Vollmer, *MGH* 14 (Berlin, 1905), 229–82.

[110] Bishop of Saragossa asked to thoroughly revise the Gothic law: Braulio, *ep.* 10 *PL* 80.633, cf. *eps.* 39–41. Bishops of Conc.VIII Tol. asked to check Recessuinth's new *Code*: *LV* Zeumer (*supplementa*) 474.3–12. The assumption is that legislation requires expertise in theology as much as in jurisprudence.

[111] Collins 1990: 109–33, esp. 115–16, 120–2; cf. I. Wood 1990: 63–81.

[112] J. George, *Venantius Fortunatus: Personal and Political Poems*, translation with notes and introduction, Liverpool Translated Texts for Historians 23 (Liverpool, 1995).

repeated waves of anti-Jewish legislation.[113] In spite of invasions and barbarian settlements, and despite the worsening of communications and the reduction in travel, cultural developments in East and West were still moving in roughly the same direction. After the Arab conquest of North Africa and Spain, the rise of the papacy and the establishment of the Carolingian Empire in Italy, and iconoclasm and the Macedonian revival in the East, would bring about increasing separation and divergence.

[113] Averil Cameron, 'Disputations, polemical literature and the formation of opinion in the early Byzantine period', *Orientalia Lovaniensia Analecta* 42 (Leuven, 1991), 91–108 = Averil Cameron (1996), ch. 3; also the same author, 'The eastern provinces and Hellenism in the 7th century: Hellenism and the emergence of Islam', in S. Said (ed.), *Hellenismos*, Actes du Colloque de Strasbourg 25–27 Octobre 1989 (Leiden, 1991), 287–313 = Averil Cameron (1996), ch. 4.

11

The Decline of Classical Citizenship and the Rise of Ethnic Solidarity in the West

1. *Roman Citizenship in the Early Empire*

This chapter has as its subject the breakdown of imperial cohesion, and the creation of new collective identities in the West. Inasmuch as it is concerned with division and increased diversity, it corresponds to Chapter 8 dealing with the growth of disorder in the East. The Eastern chapter was to a considerable extent concerned with urban disturbances, not least riots involving the factions. Urban disorder was not a major problem in the West in later Late Antiquity, since most cities had ceased to have large urban populations. In the West the scene was from the early fifth century dominated by the disintegration of the Empire and the establishment of barbarian kingdoms in its provinces. This was in the first place a military and political development, but the military and political events occurred against a background of changing attitudes to the Roman Empire, and to the duties and loyalties associated with being a Roman citizen. Something like this change of mentality happened in the East too, even though in this book it is only discussed with Western examples.

It is difficult to describe the complex of feelings and loyalties which the citizen of the classical city felt towards his city without using the anachronistic vocabulary of the nation-states of modern Europe, that is words such as patriotism, national pride, nationalism. These word are to some extent misleading when applied to the ancient world, but not totally so. The classical city did engender emotions related to modern patriotism and nationalism.[1] It did so most strongly while the cities were independent and self-sufficient political units, but civic patriotism survived to some extent when cities had been incorporated into larger territorial units such as the Roman Empire. In fact it was the survival of civic spirit and of a civic sense of solidarity that made the city organization so useful to the Romans. Incorporation into the Empire did however have the effect of

[1] 'Sense of identity' is often used to replace the anachronistic vocabulary of patriotism and sense of nationality, but has the disadvantage of being a term of individual psychology not a collective emotion.

progressively weakening civic loyalties, including that to the most powerful city of them all, Rome itself. Of all city state loyalties of Antiquity, those centred on Rome, that is the complex of rights, duties, and privileges associated with Roman citizenship, are by far the most fully documented, as well as being the ones which made the biggest impact on history.[2] The story of the decline of Roman citizenship is a theme of first-rate importance in itself. It is also important as an example of a process that was happening at local level to the local citizenship of every city of the Empire, and contributed greatly to the decline of the classical city.

The Romans were great conquerors, but Romanization, the adoption by provincials of a Roman way of life, had been to a considerable extent voluntary: the manners and customs of the ruling people were worth imitating, just as it was a most desirable thing to become a Roman citizen. For until the year AD 212 when the *Constitutio Antoniniana* made all inhabitants of the Empire—except perhaps the *dediticii*—Roman citizens, the Roman Empire represented the rule of the Roman people over foreigners (*peregrini*),[3] and to be a Roman citizen was to be a very superior person. The essence, if not the full legal implications, of Roman citizenship is brought out vividly in a famous episode in Acts:

> And as they bound him with thongs Paul said unto the centurion that stood by, is it lawful for you to scourge a man that is a Roman and uncondemned? When the centurion heard that he went and told the chief captain, saying: 'Take heed what thou doest; for this man is a Roman'. Then the chief captain came and said unto him: 'Tell me art thou a Roman?' He said, 'Yea.' And the chief captain answered, 'With a great sum obtained I this freedom.' And Paul said: 'But I was Roman born.' Then straightaway they departed which should have examined him: and the chief captain was afraid after he knew that he was a Roman and because he had bound him.[4]

Already on an earlier occasion at Philippi Paul had used the revelation that he was a Roman with similar dramatic effect.[5]

In the provinces Roman citizens were marked out as members of the ruling people by the possession of three names. In the courts they clearly enjoyed considerable advantages, which were rhetorically summarized by the sophist Aristides: 'To be safe it is sufficient to be a Roman.'[6] Even if the legal implications of the narrative of Acts are not quite correct, and provincial Romans did not in fact have an absolute right of appeal to the

[2] The citizenship of Athens in the 5th and 4th cent. BC is the second.

[3] A. H. M. Jones, 'The dediticii and the Constitutio Antoniniana', in *Studies in Roman Government and Law* (Oxford, 1960), 129–40 on *P. Giessen* 40.

[4] Acts 22: 25.9.

[5] Acts 26: 19–39.

[6] 'On Rome', *Or* 26.100.

emperor,[7] the general impression that possession of Roman citizenship carried enormous prestige must be right. Roman citizens, or strictly speaking upper-class Roman citizens, had a monopoly of leading posts in the administration of the Empire; governors, governor's staff, imperial procurators, officers in the army were Roman citizens. The legions, the army's crack regiments, were recruited entirely from Roman citizens. The public spaces of Provincial communities of Roman citizen (*coloniae* and *municipia*) were crowded with numerous monuments commemorating the distinguished careers of fellow citizens in army and administration. In the Greek East such monuments continued to be in Latin well into the third century.

A formidable legal barrier separated Roman citizens from foreigners. For Roman law recognized marriage only between citizens. There could be no marriage between the ruling people and its subjects—except those privileged by a special grant of the *ius connubii*. Thus, children born of a union of a Roman and foreigner were illegitimate, and not entitled to inherit through the will of their father. On the other hand, when an individual was granted Roman citizenship he ceased to be legally part of his family of birth.[8]

The institution of citizenship provided powerful motivation to work for the Empire for citizens and non-citizens alike. Citizens felt a sense of obligation to the Roman state very much like that inspired by patriotism of the European nations of modern times. In any case citizens had every reason to sustain an Empire which boosted their self-esteem and offered them tangible privileges. Non-citizens, *peregrini*, could look forward to the prospect of being rewarded with a grant of citizenship in return for loyal support of the Roman state, for on the whole the Romans were generous with grants of citizenship to individuals or to communities who had proved their worth to the Empire.[9]

One would imagine that the living together in the same community of citizens and non-citizens might have proved seriously inconvenient in the business of everyday life. In fact this seems not to have been the case. While the legal principles governing the separation of citizens from non-citizens were strictly maintained, devices were found to minimize their inconvenience on the life of individuals living in the same community, while subject to different systems of law. For instance *peregrini* were excluded from full legal ownership of all *res mancipii*, i.e. objects whose ownership was transferred by the legal procedure of *mancipatio*.[10] These

[7] Garnsey 1970: 70–6.

[8] F. Millar, *The Emperor in the Roman World* (London, 1977), 483–5: modification of disadvantages through liberality of emperor.

[9] Sherwin White 1973.

[10] Gaius I.119.

included Italian land, farm animals, and slaves. But for practical purposes *peregrini* were able to obtain adequate rights of ownership of these things by an alternative process, *in iure cessio*.[11]

In at least some chartered cities (*municipia*), whose citizens were of mixed Roman and Latin status, and whose inhabitants included *incolae* who might be neither Latins nor Romans, the resulting legal problems were catered for to a considerable extent.[12] Together with its charter the municipium of Irni received part of a new legal system, and for situations not covered in the charter it was laid down that 'for everything else not explicitly covered in the law concerning the *ius* according to which the citizens of Irni are to deal with each other, they are to deal with each other in all these matters by the civil law, under which Roman citizens deal or will deal with each other.'[13] That meant that the *municipes* of Irni, whether Roman citizens or not, were treated as if they were Roman citizens as long as they remained within the territory of Irni.[14] The *incolae* were less favourably treated, but they received some concessions too.[15]

Of course difficulties would arise for citizens of Irni if they had legal needs outside their municipium. But even then they might be lucky in that nobody might notice if they assumed the rights of Roman citizens away from their municipium too.[16] This is exemplified by the case of certain Alpine tribes, the Annauni, Tuliasses, and Sinduni, who had been attached for administration to the municipium of Tridentum and not only behaved like Romans within the territory of Tridentum, but in some cases managed to be commissioned in the army, and even to be enrolled on the panel of equestrian jurors at Rome. Eventually they were challenged, but the emperor Claudius allowed them to keep the privileges of citizenship which they had wrongfully assumed.[17]

Auxiliary units, which made up nearly half the Roman army, were recruited from non-citizens. But on retirement from the army the veterans were given citizenship together with their children and the women with whom they were living at the time they received citizenship.[18] Only citizens were allowed to serve in legions. However in provinces with few or no citizen inhabitants, it looks as if the legionary garrison was kept up to strength with non-citizen recruits—who must have been given citizen-

[11] Gaius II.22–4.

[12] González 1986: 147–243; cf. H. Galsterer, 'Municipium Flavium Irnitanum: A Latin town in Spain', *JRS* 78 (1988), 78–90.

[13] *Lex Irnitana* ch. 93.

[14] Gardner 1993: 188–90.

[15] *Lex Irnitana* ch. 94 and commentary in González 1986: 237.

[16] Gardner 1986: 1–14.

[17] *ILS* 206.

[18] M. Roxan, *Roman Military Diplomas 1954–74*, University of London Inst. of Arch. Occasional Publications 2 (London, 1978).

ship on enrolment.[19] Roman citizenship was a valuable and much desired commodity, and the Roman emperors were generally concerned not to cheapen it by excessive prodigality in its award. Nevertheless it spread quite rapidly, no doubt partly from the sheer impossibility in many cases of checking the status of an individual who had moved away from his birthplace, where he and his family were known.[20]

2. *The Unimportance of Roman Citizenship in the Later Empire*

After Caracalla had conferred citizenship on all inhabitants of the Empire, except the *dediticii*, through the *Constitutio Antoniniana*,[21] the distinction between citizens and non-citizens ceased to be of practical importance. People no longer remembered what it had once meant to be a Roman citizen. John Chrysostom preaching on Acts at Constantinople around AD 400 had to explain that in the days of the apostles people having the right to be called Roman citizens were shown great consideration.[22] In the fourth century, status, wealth, birth, public office, imperial favour were the principal sources of privilege. Not that these advantages had been insignificant in earlier times. Quite the reverse. At Rome, as far as we can look back, wealth and birth had been privileged in court even among citizens, and in the provinces Roman officials dealing with *peregrini* were certainly more considerate of the rights and feelings of the leading men of the province than of those of ordinary provincials, or even of humbler Roman citizens.[23] In the course of the second century this discrimination became formalized in that imperial edicts began to prescribe alternative penalties, more severe, painful and humiliating for so-called *humiliores*, and the opposite for *honestiores*. Neither status was ever defined precisely, but roughly speaking the section of the population on which the government of the Empire depended, that is senators, equestrians, soldiers, veterans, and decurions, were treated as *honestiores*. To be an *honestior* it was not necessary to be a Roman citizen. Already in the later second century in many situations it was more advantageous to be an *honestior* than to be a Roman. After AD 212 the distinction between citizen and non-citizen ceased to be of importance within the Empire, and the *honestior/humilior* distinction was left as the basic class division among free inhabitants of the Empire.

19 Mann 1983: 41–4.

20 Gardner 1986: 1–14.

21 Sherwin White 1973: 279–87, 380–93.

22 *PG* 60.333, cf. E. Chrysos, 'The late Roman political identity in Late Antiquity and Byzantium', in K. Fledelius (ed.), *Byzantium Identity, Image, Influence*, XIX International Congress of Byzantine Studies (Copenhagen, 1996), 7–17, relevant 9 n.12.

23 Garnsey 1970: a large subject with abundant evidence.

In the fourth century and subsequently, the concept of Roman citizenship was given a very low profile. The use of three names (*praenomen*, *nomen*, and *cognomen*) which had served to show that their holder was a Roman citizen fell into disuse when everyone was a citizen. Instead of a *nomen* many individuals now used the imperial family names Aurelius or Flavius. Flavius was the name of the Constantinian family and it came to be conferred on all office holders. Aurelius commemorated Caracalla to whom so many owed their citizenship. The two status nomina therefore roughly correspond to the *honestior/humilior* distinction and can be taken to symbolize the overshadowing of citizen status by elevation or lack of it in the social hierarchy.[24]

It is significant also that the legal term for a non-Roman, *peregrinus*, occurs only very rarely in the imperial constitutions of the fourth century and after. When it is used, the word *peregrinus* now means an individual living in a city or province other than that of his registered *origo*.[25] In a similar way '*politeia*' the Greek word which had regularly been used to express the concept of citizenship seems to have extended its meaning to include groups of non-naturalized barbarians who had acquired the right to live within the Empire, well expressed by the German *Reichsangehörigkeit*.[26] The fading out of the importance of citizen status contrasts sharply with the continued importance of the distinction between slave and free, and of the legal procedures for transferring an individual from one status to the other. Numerous constitutions were still being issued to regulate these procedures, not only by Roman emperors, but also by the kings of the successor states.

At the same time Late Roman laws reveal the existence of a large and growing number of status groups, each subject to privileges or restrictions which profoundly affected the way its members could live. The *honestiores* split into a growing number of grades of imperial rank, each with its own title and privileges. Soldiers became a hereditary class subject to the jurisdiction of their officers.[27] Many groups in the imperial service enjoyed the privilege of *praescriptio fori*, that is they were under the jurisdiction not of the public courts but of their own head of department.[28] Large numbers of tenants were hereditarily tied to the land which they worked, and had both rents and taxes collected by their landowners.[29] Christian clergy

[24] Salway 1994: 124–45.

[25] B. Kübler, *RE* XIX.639–55 s.v. *peregrinus*, e.g. *CT* I.34.1; VI.37.1; IX.1.10; XVI.2.37. In IV.6.3 *peregrinos* is used in the sense of *alienos*.

[26] Synesius, *De Regno* 25C (Visigoths); Procopius I.11.3 ff. (Vandals), see M. Cesa, 'Überlegungen zur Föderatenfrage', *MÖG* 92 (1984), 307–16.

[27] By far the best account of this is still in the relevant chapters of A. H. M. Jones 1964.

[28] Ibid. 484–94 nn. 31–52.

[29] Ibid. 796–8.

formed a separate class, with its own privileges and generally its own courts.[30]

We have very little evidence about the attitude to the Roman state of the peasantry and of the urban plebs. We know that the peasantry, once the citizen soldiers, had long ago ceased to be called up to defend their country, and had more or less at the same time lost all share in the political process.[31] In the fourth century the landowner to whom they paid both rent and taxes must have loomed much more prominently than the state in the lives of most of them. To the average *colonus* the fact that he was a Roman citizen is not likely to have meant very much. For the upper classes what distinguished Romans from barbarians was literary culture, Latin in the West, Greek in the East. For the nobility the state was the source of honour and distinction conferred by imperial appointments; for humbler functionaries the provider of more or less profitable jobs. These people were broadly speaking in favour of the Roman state but their attitude could not be described as active patriotism. When faced with the question of whether to cooperate with foreign invaders or to risk life and fortune for the preservation of the Empire, their choice was determined by immediate advantage not by an overriding claim of loyalty to 'king and country'.[32]

The multitude of status distinctions of the Later Empire differed from citizenship in that they served not unity but fragmentation, emphasizing the vertical layering or the segmentation of society rather than its cohesion. Status still implied duties, but the duties associated with the status groups of the Late Empire were specialized and professional: to sit in the senate, to serve in the army, to work in an office, to transport corn to the capital, to work in the fields, etc. They did not, like the old citizenship, involve a sense of obligation to the community, the *res publica*. What could conceivably have united the various groups was loyalty and gratitude to the emperor, the ultimate source of honour as of justice. But the emperor was also the source of tax demands and of prohibitions of various kinds; and for many provincials beset by local troubles, say in Britain, Gaul, or Spain, he was also very far away. The development can be summarized as the transformation of a state which was the property of all its citizens (*res publica*) into one which belonged to an all-powerful monarch, or, seen from a different point of view, as the change

[30] Gaudemet 1958: 240–71.

[31] De Ste Croix 1981: loss of political rights, 300–26; turning against the state: 474–88. But the theory of steadily worsening condition of the peasantry does not fit the evidence of Syria or Egypt.

[32] Harries 1992*a*: 298–308; H. C. Teitler, 'Un-roman activities in late antique Gaul: The cases of Arvandus and Seronatus', in J. Drinkwater and H. Elton (eds.), *Fifth Century Gaul: A Crisis of Identity* (Cambridge, 1992), 309–17.

from a classical to a biblical view of power.[33] One symptom of the changed relationship between the people and their government is the increased use of the term 'subject' in legal literature.[34]

Christianity contributed to the new view of society. Christianity attached no religious value to social distinctions. Among the baptized in the words of St Paul 'there is neither Jew nor Greek, there is neither slave nor free, there is neither male nor female', for all are one in Christ.[35] It followed that in a Christian society the distinction between Christians and non-Christians—or indeed between those Christians recognized as orthodox and heretics—was more important than that between citizen and non-citizen. The Church emphasized the common humanity of all children of God and their mutual responsibility for each other. But within this mass of common humanity Christian teaching isolates for special attention those in need, the hungry, the sick, the beggars, the prisoners, the orphans, in short the poor.[36] In sermon after sermon Christian preachers called upon the more fortunate members of their congregation to give to the poor, or to make donations to enable the Church to look after the poor. Unlike the traditional civic munificence Christian giving did not expect a return, whether political or economic. The poor were entitled to charity simply by virtue of their being Christians in need. As for the rich, the existence of the poor offered them a chance to atone for the sins they were likely to have committed in the arrogance of wealth. Christian charity did of course have political implications.[37] Inasmuch as it alleviated suffering and hardship it furthered social cohesion. Since it was directed by the Church it certainly increased the Church's influence, wealth, and power. As we have seen, it was a significant factor in the 'rise of the bishop'. But it did not require any political activity from the poor themselves, and it did nothing to strengthen the involvement of the recipients of charity with the secular institutions of the Roman Empire.

As the concepts of the citizen and citizenship lost their meaning, a sense of Roman identity survived in a non-political form. This is strikingly shown by the fact that the emancipated Greek-speaking Empire of the East was known to the very end as the Roman Empire. But the concept was now a cultural, and increasingly a religious one, which

33 See P. Brown 1992: 152–8.

34 W. S. Thurman, 'The application of *subiecti* to Roman citizens in the imperial laws of the Late Roman Empire', *Klio*, 52 (1970), 453–63; Cl. Dupont, 'Sujets et citoyens sous le Bas-empire romain de 312 à 565 après Jésus Christ', *Rev. Int. des droits de l'antiquité*, 3e série, 20 (1973), 325–39.

35 Galatians 3: 28.

36 Patlagean 1977: 25–35.

37 P. Brown 1992: 152–8 on 'condescension' as characteristic of Late Roman society: of God to the emperor and indeed all men, of the emperor to his subjects, of the wealthy to the poor.

involved no consciousness of an obligation to maintain the Roman Empire against its enemies.[38] In short the population of the Late Empire lacked a strong sense of common obligations and shared interest. In the long run no amount of centralized administration could compensate for this.

This was strikingly demonstrated in the war which the armies of Justinian fought to 'liberate' Italy from the Goths (AD 536 ff.). The very detailed account of Procopius leaves no doubt at all that throughout the twenty years and more of that campaign the numerical strength of the imperial field army depended entirely on reinforcements brought in from outside Italy. Evidently Belisarius and his successors made no attempt—or otherwise proved quite unable—to build up their armies with Italian recruits. This is all the more remarkable in that Italians regularly took part in the defence of their own city,[39] and were even on occasion ready to take part in a sally against the besiegers.[40] But Belisarius was quite determined that these auxiliaries must not fight in the ranks of his field army.[41] He rejected their help because without training or discipline they would do more harm than good in battle. That was reasonable enough. But it is also clear that, for whatever reason, neither Belisarius nor the other Roman generals gave to significant numbers of Italian civilians the weapon-training, discipline, and drill which would have turned them into soldiers. Perhaps Italians were unwilling to face the prospect of becoming part of an expeditionary force, which would have taken them away from their homes for an indefinite duration. Certainly they felt no duty to fight for the Roman Empire. When the imperial army arrived outside a city the population sometimes welcomed it and opened the gates, sometimes not. In general the Italian population did not feel that the imperial army was their army, and that it had come to liberate them from foreign tyranny. Italians seem to have been motivated principally by anxiety for the safety of their city and their family.[42] In terms of civilian suffering it did not make much difference whether a city was captured by the imperial forces or the Goths. It was well worth fighting to prevent this. But it was quite

[38] See below, p. 365.

[39] V.18.34; 5.20; 25.11–12 (all at Rome); VI.12.41 (Milan); VII.10.19–20 (Tibur).

[40] V.28.18.

[41] V.29.25 disorder of civilian auxiliaries throws regulars into confusion; VI.3.23–9 Belisarius rejects help of the untrained.

[42] In this paper examples will have to take the place of analysis of the full evidence: V.8–10 (Naples), V.14.4, 18.40, 24.14 (Rome); V.15.3 (Apulia, Calabria); V.16.1–4 (Tuscans) VI.17.1–7 (Picenum); Agathias I.12 ff. (Lucca). It is a feature of the war that provincial areas that had favourably received the imperial forces later just as quickly submitted to Totilla and paid their taxes to him: VII.6.4 (Bruttii, Lucani, Calabria, Apulia). One wonders whether an organization of the notables made the decision. VII.18.20 suggest that one notable, Tullianus could determine the allegiance of the Lucani and Bruttii. But VII.22.20: senatorial landowners, under pressure from Totilla, persuade Tullianus' peasant auxiliaries to abandon the imperial cause and return to farm work.

another thing to enrol as a soldier, and to leave city and family in order to re-establish the emperor's rule in Italy. There could be no greater contrast than that between the almost unlimited access to Italian manpower enjoyed by the senate in the Hannibalic war, and the seemingly complete absence of Italians from the armies that eventually defeated Totilla.[43]

3. *Citizens and Federates in the Late Empire*

When the distinction between citizens and non-citizens ceased to be of practical importance within the Empire, it continued to distinguish the legal status of inhabitants of the Empire from that of people beyond the frontiers, that is between Romans and barbarians. But the barbarians did not stay behind the frontiers. In the course of the fourth century large numbers of them were recruited into the Roman army,[44] either from captured barbarians settled in the provinces,[45] or from outside the Empire altogether. What gave this trend high visibility was the fact that it resulted in men of barbarian origin rising to the highest positions in the army, and achieving very great power and influence in the Roman state.

Modern analogy would suggest that this situation would arouse hostility among the native Romans against the newcomers. This did indeed happen, but not to the extent of becoming a chronic problem. We know of only two really violent outbursts of hostility, the Gainas affair in AD 399–400 at Constantinople,[46] and the fall of Stilicho in AD 408 in Italy,[47] and on both occasions anti-Germanism was only one among a number of political motives. Above all it is notable that such antagonism as there was did not focus on the legal issue of citizenship. There was no demand that the benefits enjoyed by inhabitants of the Empire should be reserved for Roman citizens. Nor do we hear of any political movement to make it as difficult as possible for barbarians who had been admitted into the Empire to become citizens. In fact the issue of citizenship is scarcely mentioned, either in the historical narratives or in the laws. As far as we can tell the presence of large numbers of foreigners in garrison towns and in the capitals did not cause legal problems. Moreover when bands of barbarians inside the Empire became sufficiently powerful to make demands, their leaders demanded money or corn or land for the rank and file, and high military commands for themselves. We are never told, as far

[43] This is fully argued in my 'The Romans demilitarised: The evidence of Procopius', *Scripta Classica Israelica* 1996 (dedicated to the memory of Addi Wasserstein), 230–9.

[44] Liebeschuetz 1990*a*: 7–47; a different view: Elton 1996: 128–54.

[45] De Ste Croix 1981: 500–18.

[46] Liebeschuetz 1990*a*: 96–125; Alan D. Cameron and J. Long, *Barbarians and Politics at the Court of Arcadius* (Berkeley, 1993), 301–36.

[47] Matthews 1975: 253–83. S. Mazzarino, *Stilicone*, 2nd edn. (Rome, 1990), 201–16.

as I know, that they demanded to receive the rights of Roman citizens.[48] In the fifth century German war bands were in a position to demand and receive land to settle on and to farm, not however as Roman citizens, but as practically independent allies.

A probable reason for the unimportance of the issue of citizenship in the context of the accommodation of barbarians is that the assimilation of immigrants no longer was a matter of turning them into citizens, but rather of fitting them into one or another of the hierarchy of status groups, whether as *laeti*,[49] or as *gentiles*, or as a particular class of *colonus*,[50] or as soldiers, or as guardsmen (*scholares*), or as officers,[51] or, with more insecurity, as allies (*foederati*).[52] Presumably some of these occupations were in law open only to citizens. If so, it would seem that barbarians who needed citizenship to qualify say for a commission in a regular unit, or for a conspicuous marriage,[53] were given citizenship as a mere formality—in the same way as non-citizen recruits for the legions stationed in the East had received citizenship on entry even in the Early Empire. Since only the highest aristocrats, and they only on very formal occasions, now used the 'three names' (these aristocrats often used many more than three[54]) lack of citizenship would not have been conspicuous, particularly as all imperial officers whether civilian or military now used the name of Flavius as a title.[55] Moreover those who did not get citizenship probably did not suffer significant legal disadvantage compared with citizens of the same status group. For most purposes there will have been legal arrangements to facilitate the everyday business of the immigrants of the same kind as we now know to have existed for the *municipes* and *incolae* at Irni in the reign of Domitian.

But to this there would seem to have been one outstanding exception:

No provincial of whatever rank or status is to enter into marriage with a barbarian woman, nor is a provincial woman to be joined to any individual of the *gentiles*. But if any alliances between provincials and *gentiles* have arisen out of marriages of this kind any suspect or harmful behaviour uncovered in connection with them is to be liable to capital punishment.[56]

48 e.g. Heather 1991: 215–17, 222–3.

49 Liebeschuetz 1990*a*: 12–13.

50 e.g. *Pan. Lat.* Iv (VIII) 8.4, 9.1–4.

51 M. Waas, *Germanen im römischen Dienst im 4. Jahrhundert* (Bonn, 1965).

52 e.g. Cesa 1993: 21–9, also 1994*a*.

53 The later *magister militum* Fravitta is the only case we know of a barbarian receiving special permission to marry a Roman woman (Eunapius fr. 60 Müller = 59 Bockley), discussed in Demandt 1989: 75–86, esp. 78–9.

54 Alan Cameron 1985: 164–82; Salway 1994: 124–45.

55 Alan D. Cameron, R. S. Bagnall, and K. A. Worp, *Consuls of the Later Empire* (Atlanta, 1987), 36–9; Keenan 1973: 33–63, 1974: 283–304, 1983: 245–50.

56 *CT* III.14.1 of 373 to Theodosius (father of later emperor) mag. mil. in West: nulli pro-

This law seems to prohibit categorically intermarriage between Roman citizens and barbarians. But it also raises problems, for marriages between barbarian officers and Roman women did undoubtedly occur quite frequently.[57]

It is likely therefore that the law has a more limited scope than appears at first sight.[58] *Gentiles* in the Theodosian Code are either pagans (which is not relevant here), or tribesmen, who might be settled in frontier provinces for purpose of defence,[59] or live across the frontier under the rule of 'kinglets' (*reguli*).[60] It may well have been thought that marriage links between *gentiles* understood in the latter sense and Romans were undesirable. The second sentence of the law seems to confirm this interpretation: what was punished was not the marriage itself, but the fact that harmful consequences of the marriage link have come to light.[61] In other words marriage between a Roman and a barbarian became punishable if it seemed to have been the starting point of some kind of conspiratorial activity between Romans and their barbarian kinsmen.[62] That the marriage law was viewed by the Roman government as of limited, or at least only passing importance, is suggested by the fact that it was not included in the Code of Justinian.

As we have seen the Roman Empire tended to undermine first local loyalties but eventually also the claims of its own citizenship. At the same time by its very existence the Empire encouraged the growth of new groups each with a new sense of identity and new claims to the loyalty of its members both within and outside its frontiers. One very important body of that kind was the Christian Church. Others sprang up among the barbarians across the borders of the Empire through the amalgamation of small tribal units into much larger ones. So German peoples mentioned in the *Germania* of Tacitus vanished from history and in their place we find

vincialium, cuiusque ordinis aut loci fuerit, cum barbara sit uxore coniugium, nec ulli gentilium provincialis femina copuletur. Quod si quae inter provinciales atque gentiles affinitates ex huiusmodi nuptiis exstiterunt, quod in iis susceptum (suspectum?) vel noxium detegitur capitaliter expietur. H. S. Sivan, 'Why not marry a barbarian: marital frontiers in Late Antiquity', in R. W. Mathisen and H. S. Sivan, *Shifting Frontiers in Late Antiquity* (London, 1996), 136–45 argues convincingly that this law was a response to particular problems that had arisen in the course of Theodosius' campaign against Mauretanian rebels. Roman law recognized only marriage between citizens, this edict goes much further.

57 Demandt 1989: 75–86. Demandt's evidence relates almost exclusively to marriages involving members of the imperial family and the very highest ranking barbarian officers.

58 E. Demougeot, 'Le Conubium dans les lois barbares du VIe siècle', *Recueil de mémoires et travaux publiés par la société d'histoire du droit et des institutions des anciens pays de droit écrit*, 12 (1983), 69–82.

59 *CT* VII.1, 2, 4; XI.30.62.3, and *ND Oc* XLII.46–70.

60 *CT* XII.12.5.

61 'quod in iis susceptum (suspectum?) vel noxium detegitur capitaliter expietur'.

62 e.g. espionage? *barbara conspiratio*? armed support for usurpation or more local strong-arm tactics?

the Franks, Alamanni, and Goths of Late Antiquity. The precise process is not clear. One could imagine that neighbouring tribes realized that it was only as part of some kind of federation that they would be able to make an impression when confronted with overwhelming Roman power. It may be that Roman diplomacy and Roman subsidies to trusted barbarian rulers provided nuclei for the crystallization of large tribal units. The last and largest of these developments was the consolidation of the Arabs under the influence of Islam.

The process of tribe formation did not cease when these peoples entered the Roman Empire. Life in utterly changed conditions called for the radical cultural change involving the adoption of important elements of the civilization of the Empire: the Christian religion, elements of Roman Law, the Latin or Greek language, as well as the expansion of membership of the ethnic group. At the same time they had to maintain the cohesion and group loyalty without which they would not be able to maintain, much less to expand their recently won position. What is significant is that the process of adaptation did not in the case of the *gentes* lead to complete assimilation and the extinction of their sense of ethnic identity. Quite the reverse: it was the Roman neighbours who eventually took on the identity of the barbarians and became Goths or Franks.

4. *Constructing and Maintaining a Sense of Gothic Identity*

The process of ethnogenesis and continuing adaptation to the conditions of the Roman world is particularly well documented in the case of the Visigoths.[63] By the time they had conquered Spain, the Goths had built a remarkable number of Roman elements into their political and religious institutions, but they had done this without becoming Romans. This is a remarkable transformation. The development that made it possible is a long story which is worth telling even though it will take us away from the central theme of this study, the evolution of the Late Roman city. The most important institution they adopted from the Roman world was certainly Christianity. But by a chance, which proved fortunate for their continued existence as a separate people, they adopted Christianity in its Arian form.[64] That they subsequently remained loyal to Arianism when it was rejected and persecuted in the Roman world, was surely deliberate. The hostility of the powerful Catholic bishops must have made their control of Spain—as earlier of Gaul—more difficult. But this they were prepared to accept, with the consequence that their Arianism built a fence

[63] Liebeschuetz 1990*a*: 48–85 and a more conservative view: Heather 1991.

[64] P. Heather, 'The crossing of the Danube and the Gothic conversion', *GRBS* 27 (1986), 289–318.

around the Gothic people, an artificial fortification like the Berlin wall, that would help to preserve the ethnic consciousness and cohesion of a group threatened with disappearance through assimilation.[65] This is not to say that the Goths remained loyal to Arianism simply in order to remain separate. Their motives were certainly much more complex. But Gothic leaders will have been aware that Arianism strengthened ethnic cohesion, while Catholicism would have undermined it. By the time Reccared in AD 587 abandoned Arianism at the Third Council of Toledo, Gothic ethnic consciousness had been firmly established in Spain.

One consequence of the Goths being Arians was that they had their own liturgy based on the Bible in Ulfila's Gothic translation.[66] In this way Arianism helped to preserve knowledge of the Gothic language, which would otherwise have died out very much more quickly than it actually did. At the time of Reccared, and probably long before, a great many Goths had acquired knowledge of Latin.[67] After their conversion to Catholicism, Latin quickly became *the* language of the Goths, who did not however thereby lose their sense of Gothic identity.

The Gothic identity was based not only on religion and language, but also on common descent—or perhaps more correctly, a myth of common descent.[68] It was surely for the purpose of fortifying their ethnic separateness, that the Goths adopted the Roman law of AD 373 forbidding marriage between barbarians and Romans. The law was included in the *Breviarium of Alaric*, the *Lex Romana Visigotorum*, issued in AD 506,[69] together with a commentary (*interpretatio*) stating that the prohibition was now to be applied without any qualifications: it was strictly the fact of the intermarriage, and not any criminal act resulting from the marriage, that was punishable with death.[70] That the Goths actually took a stricter view of intermarriage than the Romans had done is an indication of how important they considered the maintenance of tribal cohesion.[71] It was that which had enabled them to retain their military potential during many years of campaigning within the Empire, and eventually to establish a state of their own first in Gaul, and then in Spain.

[65] Ripoll and Velázquez 1995: 86–92.

[66] P. Heather and J. Matthews, *The Goths in the Fourth Century* (Liverpool, 1991), 155–97.

[67] Though they kept Germanic names, already Euric's *Code* was in Latin.

[68] As Wenskus and Wolfram showed, the story of the Goths was a continuous 'ethnogenesis', in which the absorption of members of the surrounding population played an essential part. See also Liebeschuetz 1990*a*: 76–8.

[69] *CT* III.14.1.

[70] Nullus Romanorum barbaram cuiuslibet gentis uxorem habere praesumat, neque barbarorum coniugiis mulieres Romanae in matrimonio coniungantur. Quod si fecerint, noverint se capitali sententiae subiacere.

[71] Far from only 'not excluding' that the marriage ban was intended to keep Gothic and Roman elites apart, as is misleadingly suggested by Pohl in Pohl, with Reimitz 1998: 12, I would insist that precisely this was the purpose of the law. The interpretation of Sivan 1988 that the law was specifically directed against Frankish influence in 507 cannot conceivably be right.

The separate identity cannot have been easy to maintain at any stage of their progress. In Spain the Visigoths formed only a small minority of the population on any estimate, and they were ruling over a very large territory. It is now established that the cemeteries in the Meseta, which have long been suspected of being Gothic, were indeed Gothic places of burial, and mark the principal area of Gothic settlement.[72] Even here[73] the Goths lived in close proximity to Romans whose estates they shared.[74] Place-names suggest considerable settlement in Gallaecia and northern Lusitania.[75] Outside the central area there must have been smaller settlements. Presumably the leaders lived in cities, for instance in Seville, Merida, or Toledo, or in villas not far away from these cities.[76] But there must have been settlements of rank and file too. Were they settled in *pagi* of some strategically situated *civitates*?[77] We do not know, but wherever, and however, they were accommodated, they can only have represented small islands of Goths living in a sea of Romans. So it is perhaps not surprising that they emphasized the difference between themselves and their near neighbours by prohibiting intermarriage.

That the Goths described themselves as an ethnic entity, a *gens*,[78] should not be taken to imply that the apartheid between Goths and Romans was so strictly observed that breaches of the law never occurred.[79] It is true that the law remained in force until it was abolished by the great king Leovigild (568–86). But by then, we are told, it had often been honoured in the breach.[80] To what extent it was observed earlier we simply do not have the prosopographical information to do more than

[72] See the important work of Ripoll 1991*a*; 1993: 187–250. See also Ripoll 1989, 1991*b*; and with Katherine Reynolds Brown 1993. A concise discussion: Heather 1996: 202–10.

[73] See below, fig. 22; Heather 1996: 204, fig. 7.2.

[74] The system of Gothic *sortes* and the associated sharing of estates between Goths and Romans survived into the 7th cent.: *LV* X.1.8; X.1.9; X.1.16; X.2.1; X.3.5.

[75] José Mattoso, 'Les Wisigoths dans le Portugal médiéval', in *L'Europe héritière de l'Espagne wisigothique*, Collection de la Casa Velázquez (Madrid, 1992), 325–39. J. Piel and D. Kremer, *Hispano-gotisches Namenbuch: Der Niederschlag des Westgotischen in den alten und heutigen Personen und Ortsnamen der iberischen Halbinsel* (Heidelberg, 1976). It used to be thought that the settlement in modern Portugal only occurred after the reconquest from the Arabs. It is now linked with the conquest of the Suebi.

[76] Ripoll 1998*b*.

[77] Cf. Ewig 1958: 644 on Frankish settlement in Gaul: 'Die *civitas* war ein regionaler Verband in den auch Barbaren eintreten konnten . . . Lebenszelle der Barbaren war der *pagus*.'

[78] Of course they were still a *gens* after the marriage bar was abolished, as were the Franks who never had a marriage bar.

[79] The strictly biological view of kinship is post-Darwinian. For the Romans an adopted son was no less a member of the *gens* into which he had been adopted than a biological son.

[80] *LV* III.1 cum fractas vires habuerit prisce legis abolita sententia. The gradual mixing of the two populations well before the law of Leovigild is suggested by the mingling of Roman and Visigothic names on slate documents, and by the juxtaposition of Visigothic and Roman graves in at least some Visigothic cemeteries. Ripoll and Velázquez 1995: 76–80; Ripoll 1993: 187–250. I. Velázquez Soriano, *Las pizarras visigodas, edición crítica y estudio*, Antigüedad y Cristianismo VI (Murcia, 1989).

speculate.[81] As has been noted, there is reason to believe that intermingling of the two peoples began very early.[82] Perhaps the institution of *commendatio*, which allowed a man to introduce himself to a patron with a view to be accepted by him as an armed follower, was open to outsiders who wished to enter the Gothic people.[83] Gothic laws do not define what constituted a Goth. Perhaps the right to decide whether an individual was to be given the status of a Goth or not was something the kings reserved for themselves. But a small group governing a huge territory, in which they were a small minority, will scarcely have been able to avoid intermarriage.[84] When the marriage bar was abandoned by Leovigild some years before the conversion to Catholicism the ethnic identity of the Goths was secure. They remained a *gens* without legal fortification of their ethnicity.

It has been thought that Gothic ethnic separateness and sense of identity was strengthened by the maintenance of a Gothic system of law separate from the Roman one. This view is based on the coexistence of the *Breviarium* of Alaric, the *Lex Romana Visigotorum*, and two Codes issued by Gothic kings, the *Code of Euric* (466–84) and the *Leges Visigothorum* of which the first version was published by king Leovigild (568–86). On the assumption that the creation of a law code must be seen as an affirmation of national or ethnic identity,[85] it is argued that the Codes produced by the Visigothic kings were intended for their Gothic subjects only, and that they were compiled precisely in order to proclaim and preserve the sense of Gothic identity. But this does not necessarily follow. The Law was certainly the principal symbol of Jewish identity, and Roman law and Roman citizenship were indissolubly linked, but it is not necessary that the Germans kings took the same view of the Codes which they issued for their kingdoms. I have argued elsewhere that the Codes of the Visigothic kings were from the first intended for all their subjects.[86] Their motives

[81] Thompson 1969: 19 n. 1 refers to two possible cases of intermarriage in addition to that of king Theudis (531–48), who was an Ostrogoth.

[82] See above, n. 80.

[83] *LV* V.3.1 = *L. Eur.* 310; *LV* V.3.2 = *L. Eur.* 311; *LV* V.3.3–4.

[84] Calculations of the total number of Visigoths have to be based on extremely shaky foundations such as the number of known burials, and perhaps analogy with the almost equally elusive total of the Ostrogoths in Italy (see below, p. 365). Estimates range from 100,000–200,000, with the majority nearer the lower estimate. They certainly formed a very small part of the population, cf. Ripoll and Velázquez 1995: 84–6. The most comprehensive calculation, which necessarily still involves important arbitrary assumptions is that of Ripoll 1989: 389–418, esp. 392–6. Her total is 130,000 persons or 13,000 families.

[85] A. J. Sirks, 'Shifting frontiers in Roman law, Romans, provincials, barbarians', in Mathisen and Sivan (1996), 146–57.

[86] See my 'Citizens, status and law in the Roman Empire and the Visigothic Kingdom', in W. Pohl with H. Reimitz (eds.), *Strategies of Distinction: The Construction of Ethnic Communities, 300–800* (Leiden, 1998), 131–52, esp. 141–6.

were practical. The Germanic settlement created new conditions which required new laws. The issue of laws was an act of assimilation and adaptation. It was also an assertion of royal power, showing the Germanic king performing one of the functions of a Roman emperor. The Visigothic laws certainly had a symbolic function. What they symbolized however was not Visigothic ethnicity but the power of a strong and centralized monarchy—a monarchy which was almost certainly stronger and more centralized in intention than in fact. The Gothic laws probably do include some traditional Germanic elements. But not even the *Code of Euric* is simply a codification of primaeval folk-custom. A Code written in Latin, showing very considerable influence of Roman Law, embodying scarcely any Gothic technical terms, and very rarely even using the words Goth or Gothic,[87] would not seem well suited to be a symbol of Gothicity.[88]

The *Leges Visigothorum* are in fact the laws of a developing new community blending Goths and Romans. By the end of the sixth century there will have been very little to separate Goths from Romans. The Goths were no longer kept apart and defined by the marriage bar. They no longer practised a form of Christianity which the Romans condemned as heretical. They had probably long been Latin-speaking. Certainly when they converted to Catholicism, nobody seems to have seen an obstacle in the fact that they would henceforth no longer be able to worship in the Gothic language. Gothic custom could well have survived a long time in dealings between Goths, in local courts, in areas of Gothic settlement, but we have no evidence of this.[89] Perhaps tribal custom of Germans in the successor kingdoms survived rather like Jewish law among orthodox Jews, but the practical significance of the survival is difficult to assess. In Frankish Gaul as late as the ninth century individuals belonging to various peoples each had their own law, but this was the law of a particular

[87] Treason is against the *gens* and *patria Gothorum* (Zeumer 1902: 483.10; 473.30; 54.16, 19. The king's advisers are the *seniores Gothorum* (485.25; 127.4). Almost all other references to Goths are in the context of the division of property between Goths and Romans (389.2; 386.1–5; 385.25; 19.22; 4.20; 5.7); or in laws applying to both Goths and Romans: 37.5; 301.1. Law XII.2.4 allows marriage between Goths and Romans. Only IX.2.2 seems to apply to Goths alone: servi dominici quando Gothos in hostem exire compellunt.

[88] It is significant that the Visigothic law does not lay down differential penalties for injuries done to or by Goths and Romans respectively, as the Frankish law does, e.g. *L. Sal* 41.8–10.

[89] Skavilla a Goth lived according to Gothic law at Brescia in N. Italy in 679: Th. Mommsen, 'Ostgotische Studien', *Gesammelte Schriften*, vi (Berlin, 1910), 475 cites *Cod. dipl. Langob.* no. 38, col. 72. In Spain the earliest reference to trial by combat between two Goths dates from 820. The so-called *fueros* sometimes recall Germanic custom. But the earliest in Castille were granted by local lords in the 10th cent., while the oldest surviving texts date from the 12th: R. Collins, 'Visigothic law and regional custom in early medieval Spain', in W. Davies and P. Fouracre (eds.), *The Settlement of Disputes in Early Medieval Europe* (Cambridge, 1986), 85–105 = *Law, Culture and Regionalism in Early Medieval Spain* (Aldershot, 1992), ch. 6.

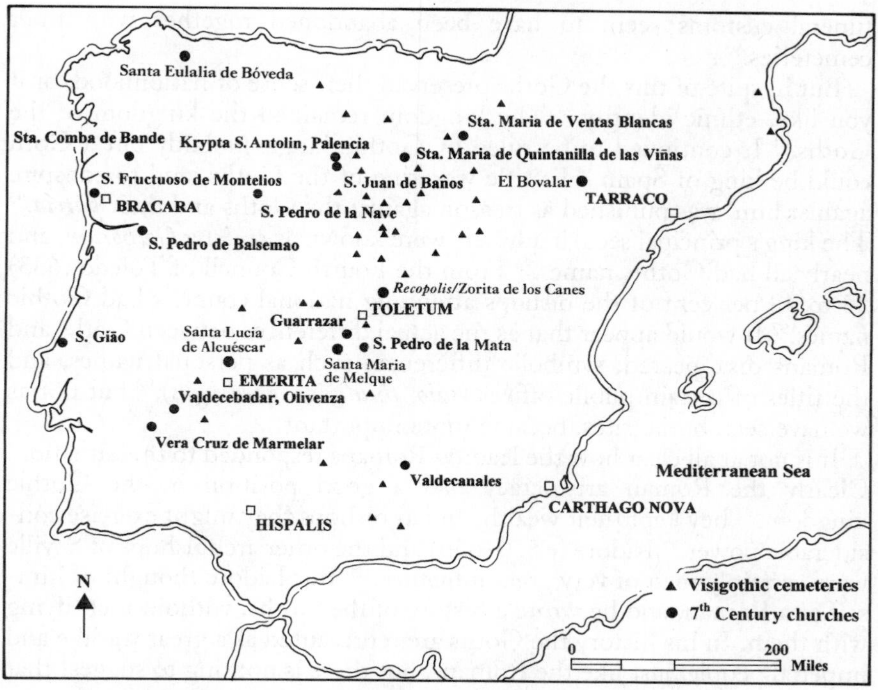

22. Visigothic cemeteries in Hispania and 'seventh'-century churches

territory, i.e. of Francia or of Burgundy or of Aquitaine or of Lombardy. This seems to have been a Carolingian development.[90]

Archaeologically Romans and Goths are very hard to distinguish. A considerable number of large cemeteries on the Meseta starting from the end of the fifth century show distinct burial customs with characteristic grave goods in about 20 per cent of the graves. Comparable objects have been found in late fifth-century graves on the Danube and in Ostrogothic Italy. These cemeteries have been recognized as the places of burial of the Goths in their main area of settlement. Corresponding cemeteries have not yet been found in what had been Gothic Aquitaine. It looks almost as if the Goths migrating from Gaul, and settling in Spain, after suffering defeat at the hands of the Franks, began to feel a need to make themselves more distinct, by emphasizing their Gothic roots. The *fibulae* and buckles found in these graves evidently reflect conspicuously Gothic clothing worn by the living. By the early seventh century however the Goths no longer felt the need to emphasize their separateness.[91] For their specific

[90] See below, p. 363.

[91] Ripoll 1991*b*: 111–32, pls. IX–XIV. Ripoll and Brown 1993: 41–69.

funeral customs seem to have been abandoned together with their cemeteries.[92]

But in spite of this the Goths preserved their sense of nationhood, or if you like, ethnic identity.[93] The kingdom remained the kingdom of the Goths.[94] It continued to be ruled by Gothic kings. Nobody but a Goth could be king of Spain. His title was king of the Goths, and to conspire against him, was punished as treason against the Goths and their *patria*.[95] The king's principal secular advisers were known as *seniores Gothorum*, and nearly all had Gothic names.[96] From the Fourth Council of Toledo (633) 33 to 42 per cent of the bishops attending national councils had Gothic names.[97] It would appear that as the actual differences between Goths and Romans disappeared, symbolic differences such as personal names, and the titles of certain public offices (*saio*, *thiufadus*, *gardingus*),[98] but not as we have seen burial rites, became more important.

It is not at all clear how the leading Romans responded to this situation. Clearly the Roman aristocracy had a good position in the Gothic kingdom. They kept their wealth, and as bishops they might exercise considerable power.[99] Isidore (*c*.570–636) and the other archbishops of Seville were certainly men of very great influence.[100] But Isidore thought of himself as a Roman, and he wrote a history of the Goths, without identifying with them. In his history the Goths are represented as a great warlike and imperial people, just like the Romans, but there is nothing to suggest that

[92] P. Périn, 'L'Armée de Vidimer et la question des dépôts funéraires', *L'Armée romaine et les barbares du IIIe au VIIe siècle*, in F. Vallet and M. Kazanski (Paris, 1993), 411–23. M. Kazanski, 'Contribution à l'étude des migrations des Goths', in *Gallo-Romains, Wisigoths et Francs en Aquitaine, Septimanie, et Espagne: Le Témoinage de l'archéologie* (Rouen, 1981), 11–25.

[93] *LV* IX.2.9 quisquis ille est . . . seu sit Gotus sive Romanus . . . (Ervig's army law). The *Vitas Sanctorum Patrum Emeritensium* (*El Libro de las vidas de los santos padres de Mérida*, ed. A. C. Macías (Mérida, 1988)) mentions the Roman or Gothic origin of important individuals, e.g. II.1 sanctus Masona . . . genere quidem Gothus; X.6–7 Claudius nobili genere ortus Romanis fuit parentibus; XIV.4 Renovatus . . . vir denique natione Gothus, generoso stigmate procreatus. Cf. also Isidor. *De Vir. Ill.* 31 Joannes gerundensis ecclesiae episcopus natione Gothus.

[94] *Conc. Tol.* IV.75; Tol. VII.1. Note they were Goths not Visigoths: J. L. Abadía, 'Godos, hispanos y hostolenses en la órbita del rey de los Francos', *Memorias de la Real Academia de Buenas Letras de Barcelona*, 24 (1991), 35–74, esp. 37–41.

[95] *LV* II.1.8, cf. extract from *Act. Conc. Tol. VIII* of 653 (Zeumer 1902: 473.30) and from *Act. Conc. Tol. XVI* of 693 (ibid. 488.10).

[96] See *subscriptiones virorum illustrium* in Zeumer 1902: 485–6.

[97] Thompson 1969: 289–96.The great majority of 'Roman' names of clergy are names of saints or otherwise Christian.

[98] *Saio* as law enforcement officer (as opposed to retainer) appears in 7th-cent. laws. In the *Lex Theudi* the same officer still figures as *compulsor* or *executor*, see Thompson 1969: 142–3. The *iudex loci* is replaced by *thiufadus* in Recessuinth's code, ibid. 213; P. D. King 1972: 82. The *gardingi* are mentioned only in documents of Wamba (672–80) and Erwig (680–7), see Thompson 1969: 252–3; P. D. King 1972: 57–61.

[99] Thompson 1969: 291: Goths were rarely appointed to Metropolitan sees.

[100] Fontaine 1959.

the difference between ruling people and ruled was being eliminated in the Gothic kingdom, as it had been long ago in the Roman Empire.[101] Nevertheless one cannot help wondering. Does the fact that in the seventh century almost the entire known secular leadership of Visigothic Spain bore Gothic names[102] really mean that they were all of Gothic descent?[103] In sixth- and seventh-century Gaul, which has left us far more prosopographic information, Frankish names were fashionable with the result that the fact that an individual has a Frankish name does not at all exclude the possibility that he is descended from a Roman family.[104] I would suggest that it is likely that the same is true of Spain and that in the kingdom of the Goths, just as in the kingdom of the Franks, the Roman and the Germanic aristocracies were becoming one.

It may seem surprising that a culturally more advanced majority population should take on the 'national' identity of a ruling minority that had already accepted its language and religion. But this is what certainly happened in Frankish Gaul and Lombard Italy.[105] Clearly the sense of identity of a ruling minority, if it is powerfully entrenched, particularly if it is in alliance with the Church, becomes very attractive to the governed people. It is also relevant that 'Romanity' as sensed by the Late Roman aristocracy consisted largely of loyalty to the Roman Emperor as a source of honour, and of pride in belonging to the fellowship of classical literary culture. In Visigothic Spain the Gothic king was the source of honour,

[101] See Isidorus *HG praef.* Gregory of Tours (539–594) did not identify with the Franks: *HF* V. *praef.*

[102] Apart from the *seniores Gothorum* (n. 96 above) the names of leading followers of the usurper Paulus captured by Wamba in Spain and Gaul: *Iudicium in tyrannorum perfidia promulgatum*, 4; 6 = *PL* 96.804, 806.

[103] Thompson 1969: 289: 'while Goths sometimes took on Roman names, Romans are not known to have ever called themselves by Gothic names'. But our knowledge of families and even of the descent of known individuals in Visigothic Spain is so poor that a fashion among Romans for giving Gothic names to their children could easily have escaped our notice. See L. A. García Moreno, *Prospografía del reino visigodo de Toledo*, Acta Salmaticensia, Filosofía y letras 77 (Salamanca, 1974). There must have been considerable intermarriage. If Leovigild could refer to the marriage-bar as having lost its force while intermarriage was still a capital offence, it is exceedingly unlikely that intermarriage ceased after it had become legal.

[104] G. Kurth, 'De la nationalité des comtes Franques', in that author's *Études Franques*, i (Paris/Brussels, 1919), 169–81 discusses origins of 50 counts from Auvergne and Touraine; H. Wieruszowski, 'Die Zusammensetzung des gallischen und fränkischen Episkopats bis zum Vertrag von Verdun 843', *Bonner Jahrbücher*, 127 (1922), 1–83. For names of Frankish officials, see J. R. Martindale, *The Prosopography of the Later Roman Empire* (*PLRE*) (Cambridge, 1992), IIIB, 1524–32. The names of *Maiores domus*, *comites palatii*, *comites stabuli*, *cubicularii*, *duces*, are overwhelmingly Frankish; *comites* are more mixed. On the de-romanization of the bishops in Provence, see J.-P. Poly, '*Agricola et eiusmodi similes*, la nobless romane et la fin des temps mérovingiens', in C. Lepelley *et al.*, *Haut moyen age, culture, éducation et société*, Études offertes à P. Riché, Centre de recherches sur l'antiquité tardive de L'Université Paris-X-Nanterre (1990), 197–228.

[105] In the Arab-ruled East the majority took on not only the sense of national identity, but also the religion and language of the ruling minority.

and the upper-class culture had undergone profound change. High literary culture had lost its place as a central value of society. There still were some highly educated laymen, but surely fewer than in Roman times, and also presumably many men of high social standing who had little education or even were illiterate.[106] Moreover literacy had become Christianized and that too must have helped to unite the two peoples, because the Bible could bring Goths and Romans together in a way secular literature could not have done. So these cultural changes tended to make Roman and Gothic aristocrats undistinguishable.

At the same time the way of life of the Roman ruling groups was becoming more like that of leading Goths. They ceased to have their main residence in a city, and came to be live mainly on estates in the country. The great villas were not all suddenly abandoned, but it is likely that in time the way of life of the Roman aristocrats became simplified in many ways. They became poorer[107] and the Christian ascetic ideal discouraged conspicuous consumption.[108] They were all liable to call-up, and their ethos became more military, while that of the Goths seems to have become more civilian.[109] So the considerations which had once led a Roman aristocrat like Sidonius Apollinaris to despise barbarians had lost much of their force. In fact there will not have been very much difference between well-to-do, or well-born, Romans and their Visigothic equivalents, and consequently little reason why a Roman should not wish to identify with the *gens et patria Gothorum*.[110]

But the process of amalgamation must have taken time, and was probably not complete by the time of the Arab conquests. It was complete by the beginning of the reconquest. For Spain we lack the evidence to observe the development in detail, but our information is much better for Gaul where the coexistence of Franks, Burgundians, and Romans was quite parallel to that of Romans and Goths in Spain. It is evident that for most of the seventh century, and even beyond the end of the century, Romans and Franks and Burgundians remained quite distinct, that is among the leading families in Gaul—and these are of course the only people we know about—there was no uncertainty who belonged to which ethnic group. Indeed besides the three principal peoples small bodies of

[106] See above, p. 318.

[107] Difficult to prove, but likely because: (1) they no longer had a monopoly of administrative posts; (2) the country as a whole was impoverished, cf. below, p. 398.

[108] Also giving to the church would reduce hereditary fortunes.

[109] Isidore *HG* II.294 stresses their skill with javelin and lance on horseback, but some of them received a literary education (see above, p. 338) and some presumably lived comfortably in villas.

[110] The dilemma of Gallic nobles faced in earlier times with the problem of whether to enter the service of the Visigothic king is reflected in the correspondence of Sidonius Apollinaris. See Jill Harries, 'Sidonius Apollinaris and the frontier of Romanitas', in R. W. Mathisen and H. S. Sivan (eds.), *Shifting Frontiers in Late Antiquity* (Aldershot, 1996), 31–44; also Harries 1992*b*: 298–308.

other *gentes*, for instance Thaifales, Saxons, Suevi, Goths, Alamanni, who had long ago been settled by the Roman government in the territory of one or another of the *civitates*, still retained their tribal identity. It was only in the later eighth century, that ethnicity and territory came to coincide in different parts of the Frankish kingdom, so that roughly speaking everybody in the north took on the identity of a Frank, in the east of a Burgundian, and in the west of a Roman, and later of an Aquitanian.[111] Agobard of Lyon mentions the laws of Franks, Burgundians, Alamanni, Lombards, and Aquitanians. The disadvantage of this situation—in Burgundian Lyon at any rate—was that men were not allowed to give evidence against individuals living under a different law, so that right and wrong in many cases could only be decided by the unsatisfactory method of trial by combat. There is no suggestion that individuals living in the same city but belonging to different nationalities were tried in different courts. That surely would have been quite impractical.[112]

By this time in the corner of north-eastern Spain which had not been conquered by the Muslims everybody was Gothic.[113] Germanic names are abundant on documents produced in the Christian kingdoms of the north in the ninth and tenth centuries.[114] The reconquest was begun in the name of a Gothic kingdom. In the days of the Republic and Early Empire the Romans had been masters at fusing peoples of different background, and imbuing them with a common sense of Roman pride and Roman patriotism. The Romans had long lost this capacity. The Visigoths had it—though as we will see not to the same extent as the Romans of old. The Visigoths were not alone in this: all the successful Germanic bands had the ability to instigate and inspire a process of ethnogenesis, resulting in the formation of large ethnic groups. The history of the 'migration period' is full of examples of this.[115]

One particularly well-documented case is the ability of the Ostrogoths to rally Italians against the imperial armies of the generals of Justinian.[116] While—as has been shown earlier—the imperial forces depended on reinforcements from outside, the Goths had to rely on resources in Italy.

[111] The evidence is fully set out in Ewig 1958: 587–648, reprinted with some revision in *Spätantikes Gallien*, i (Munich, 1976), 231–73.

[112] Agobard, *Lib. adv. legem Gundobadi*, *PL* 104.114–26. Even then individual Franks might live in Burgundia, or Aquitain; and Burgundians or Aquitanians (Romans) in Francia. Of course Jews were the odd men out everywhere.

[113] C. Duhamel-Amado, 'Poids de l'aristocratie d'origine wisigothique et genèse de la noblesse septimanienne', in *L'Europe héritière de l'espagne wisigothique* (Madrid, 1992), 81–99.

[114] R. d'Abadal de Vinyals, 'A propos du legs Wisigothique en Espagne', *Settimane di studio del centro italiano di studi sull'Alto Medioevo* V (Spoleto, 1958), 541–85, esp. 551–4, 557–8.

[115] It will suffice to note *honoris causa* the two authors who have drawn this phenomenon to the attention of other scholars: Wenskus 1961; Wolfram 1987.

[116] For full documentation, see my 'The Romans demilitarised', *Scripta Classica Israelica*, 15 (1996), 230–9.

The course of the war showed that these were remarkably abundant, and what is more resilient, so that the Gothic army in the field at the end of the war seems to have been scarcely smaller than at the beginning. This would be surprising if the Gothic armies consisted only of descendants of the 10,000–25,000 warriors who had entered Italy with Theoderic two generations ago in AD 489.[117] One would expect a closed tribal group of that kind to have been greatly reduced by the casualties of twenty years of war fought with varying fortune, and great destruction and loss of life among the population.[118] But this does not seem to have happened, at least not until the very end of the war.[119] In his last battle Totilla opposed Narses' army of 20,000–25,000[120] with a Gothic army that was significantly smaller, though we are not given numbers.[121] In their defeat the Goths lost 6,000 dead and many prisoners.[122] Nevertheless they were able to recover, to rebuild their army, and to meet Narses in a second, and very hard-fought two-day battle later in the year.[123] The battle ended with the imperial forces victorious, but even then it was not a victory of annihilation. An agreement was reached, and the Goths were allowed to return to their areas of settlement in Tuscany, Liguria, and Venetia, much as they had been allowed by Belisarius at the surrender of Ravenna in AD 540.[124] After the agreement of 552 there were still Gothic garrisons resisting in fortresses in Campania, Tuscany, and northern Italy.[125] Within a short time the Goths resumed war in alliance with Franks, who invaded Italy with a massive army. The war did not even end in spring 555, when the fortress of Campsa surrendered to Narses together with a garrison of no fewer than 7,000 Goths. Verona and Brixia were only recovered in 562.[126] The resilience of Gothic manpower through more than twenty years of war, and at times facing the Franks[127] as well as the Empire, is remarkable.

I would suggest that the Goths would not have been able to wage war,

[117] T. S. Burns, 'Calculating Ostrogothic population', *Acta Antiqua*, 26 (1978), 457–63: 35,000–40,000 immigrants which would mean *c.*10,000 warriors; W. Ensslin, *Theoderich der Grosse* (Munich, 1947), 66: 20,000–25,000 warriors; Wolfram 1987: 279: 100,000 individuals, 20,000 warriors.

[118] VI.20.15–33 on famine in Picenum, Aemilia, and Tuscany—only the first was an area of Gothic settlement.

[119] See the—ex eventu?—prophecy I.9.4–5.

[120] VIII.26.8–13.

[121] VIII.30.17, 36.

[122] VIII.32.20.

[123] VIII.35.31–3.

[124] Agathias I.1.6, cf. Proc. VI.29.35–7 on surrender of Ravenna in AD 540. Procopius VIII.35.36 stating that in AD 552 the Goths agreed to leave Italy is clearly wrong. Evidently Procopius exaggerated the decisiveness of the imperial victory at Mons Lactarius.

[125] Cumae (Agathias I.8–11), Lucca (ibid. 12), Campsa (ibid. II.13–14).

[126] Agathias II.13.1–14.7. Malalas XVIII.492.

[127] The Franks played an important and ambiguous role throughout these events. Around 549 the Franks took control of large parts of Venetia (VII.33.7–8), and subsequently made parts of Liguria and the Cottian Alps and most of Venetia tributary (VIII.24.6), and came to some kind of agreement

on this scale, and for so long, if the armies of Vittigis and Totilla had been made up exclusively of descendants of the original 10,000–25,000 warriors. The number of potential soldiers available at the beginning of the war, and the smaller but still very considerable forces at the disposal of Totilla right up to the battle of Busta Gallorum imply a reservoir of military manpower greater than could have been produced simply by natural increase of Theoderic's followers.[128] The implication is that the Goths could do what the imperial government could not, that is draw on the population of Italy to man and replenish their field armies and garrisons. Elsewhere I have suggested that the Gothic institution of *commendatio* provided a means by which outsiders could come into the Gothic ethnic community.[129] Unfortunately, Procopius did not think it part of his duty as a historian of the Gothic War to explain the social organization of the Goths. He does however mention one Velas, a Gepid, who served in the following of Ildibadus, uncle of Totilla and briefly king of the Goths.[130] He also relates that under Theoderic the Rugi and certain other tribes were singled out and brought into the people of the Goths.[131] The phrase does not really tell us very much about the status of these close allies of the Goths, but Procopius does tell us that Goths and Rugi did not intermarry. It is also clear that close relationship with Goths was not restricted to people of Germanic descent. Totilla regularly offered captured imperial soldiers the option of fighting in the Gothic army 'on equal terms'.[132] He does not explain the precise legal connotation of 'equal terms', but his narrative shows that the offer was evidently extremely attractive and often taken up.[133] Procopius' wording also strongly suggests that the Goths enrolled Italian civilians, at least in the lands north of the river Po. In 540

with the Goths to remain at peace as long as the Goths were at war with the Romans (ibid. 9–10). Hannestad argues that these happenings strengthened the Goths by enabling them to withdraw their fortress troops from the north and to engage them against the imperial forces (K. Hannestad, 'Les Forces militaires d'après la guerre Gothique de Procope', *Classica et Mediaevalia*, 21 (1960), 136–83, relevant: 172). I think it more likely that the Goths will have kept significant numbers of warriors in their settlement areas to protect their families from the unpredictable and primarily self-seeking allies. The Franks in Venetia and Liguria are likely to have been a further handicap for the Goths.

128 Possible rates of increase: E. Lo Cascio, 'The size of the Roman population, Beloch and the Roman census figures', *JRS* 84 (1994), 23–40, esp. 34 nn. 73 and 38.

129 Liebeschuetz 1990*a*: 17. It could be argued that at this time for the rural population geography and social situation mattered more than ethnic status. But then why did this not work in favour of the Romans?

130 VII.1.43.

131 VII.2.1–3.

132 VII.30.21; 36.28: according to Belisarius a majority of the imperial army in Italy had deserted to the Goths (VII.12.8–9).

133 Romans in Gothic army: VII.11.11: neither Goths nor Romans answer appeal to desert Goths. VII.8.26; VII.30.8: Romans threaten to join Goths unless paid. VIII.26.6: Narses has money to attract deserters back from Goths. VIII.32.20: Narses executes Romans fighting with Goths. Such treatment of military prisoners was exceptional.

the Goth Uraias led a force of 4,000 Ligurians who would seem to have been recruited from both Goths and non-Goths.[134] Later in that year Ildibadus began the revival of Gothic fortunes by winning over little by little all the inhabitants of Liguria and Venetia to the Gothic side.[135] Liguria and Venetia included the two most important areas of Gothic settlement. It may well be that in this part of Italy a new Italo-Gothic 'nation' was already coming into existence.

The Italo-Gothic nation was destroyed before it could reach the maturity eventually to be achieved by the Visigothic nation in Spain. But it is worth noting that even the Visigothic ethnogenesis did not achieve anything like the cohesion of the old Roman citizenship. In the Visigothic state everybody regardless of origin was liable to the call up. One might therefore expect that the military values of the Goths would spread to the Roman population. In fact the opposite seems to have been the case. The unmilitary, totally civilian, outlook of the late Romans spread to the Goths. That at least is the impression given by the rapid success of the Islamic invasion. One battle in which a not very large Berber army defeated the army of the last Visigothic king was enough to bring down the Visigothic kingdom. Subsequently, a few cities continued to resist, but no further army appeared in the field. In the next hundred or two hundred years the most serious wars in Spain were fought between different parts of the invading army and subsequent reinforcements from outside Spain.

If it is the ultimate test of successful ethnogenesis that the assimilated groups become ready to fight for their new ethnic organization, the process was not equally successful in every case. The tendency to assimilate members into an enlarged ethnic group was probably strongest while the group was on the move or engaged in the process of settling. Once settled the tribal groups seem to have had some difficulty in converting the people among whom they had been settled to their military ethos, and even in preserving it among themselves.

Of the successful invaders of the Roman Empire, Vandals and Visigoths seem to have eventually adopted the unmilitary outlook of the population on whose land they settled. The Vandals were quickly defeated by the armies of Justinian and the Visigoths by the Arabs. Neither was able to replace a defeated army, or to inspire subsequent revolts by the people of North Africa or Spain to restore the Vandal or the Visigothic Kingdom. The Ostrogoths in Italy who had been settled for only forty years put up much longer and more determined resistance to the imperial armies as a result of finding ways of enlisting part of the Italian population on their own side. Only the Franks and the Arabs[136] succeeded

[134] VI.28.31, 34–5. [135] VII.1.25, 27.

in maintaining their own military qualities, and in incorporating the Roman provincial population into their military organization. Why nation-building was so much more successful in some cases than in others is an interesting question. In the case of the Arabs their success must have been largely due to Islam. But why were the Franks so much more successful than the Vandals and Visigoths?

One factor was surely that the ethnic consciousness of the successor kingdoms was a much weaker ideology than that of Roman citizenship, not to mention that of European nations until quite recently. Once the *gens* had settled, ethnic identity became much less important than it had been during the period of migration. It did not disappear. In Spain Gothic ethnicity played an important role at the start of the reconquest. There continued to be Goths in Italy long after the disappearance of the kingdom of the Ostrogoths.[137] The land once governed by the Franks is still called France, and its people the French. But the loyalties and obligations on which the everyday functioning of society depended were now largely personal: the bonds of loyalty and duty between magnate and followers, and between the monarch and his leading followers. Personal allegiance was not ultimately dependent on the ethnic identity of the lord or monarch, or even on his religion. When the Arabs came, Visigothic magnates could come to terms with an Arab ruler—even though he was a Muslim—in much the same way as the Roman aristocracy of Gaul had come to terms first with Visigothic and then with Frankish rulers.[138] The Arabs are said to have won their decisive victory with the help of the sons of Witzia, the previous king of the Goths.[139] There has survived a treaty in accordance with which the Gothic magnate Theodemir handed over a number of towns to the Arabs and was allowed to go on ruling them.[140] It is likely that Theodemir was not the only Gothic magnate to come to terms in this way. The Banu Qasi and the family of Ibn al-Qutiya were descendants of Gothic families who converted to Islam and continued to wield great local power under the Arabs.[141] It is significant that in Spain and elsewhere in this period political creativity manifested itself

[136] See above p. 317.

[137] L. Schmidt, *Die letzten Ostgoten*, Abhandlungen der preussischen Akademie der Wissenschaften, phil.-hist. Klasse 10 (Berlin, 1943).

[138] See above, n. 000.

[139] *Chron. Alfonso III*, 7; cf. *Chron. 754*, 54.

[140] C. Melville and A. Ubaydli, *Christians and Moors in Spain*, iii, Arabic Sources (Warminster, 1992), 10–13 text and translation of treaty of Theodemir; see also *The Chronicle of 754*, 87. More generally, see E. Manzano Moreno, 'Árabes, bereberes y indígenas: al-Andalus en su primer período de formación', in *Incastellamento*, Actes des rencontres de Gérone (26–27 Novembre 1992) et de Rome (5–7 Mai 1994), ed. M. Barceló and P. Toubert, Collection de L'école française de Rome 241 (Rome, 1998), 157–77.

[141] H. Kennedy 1996: 68; R.d'Abadal, *Els primers comtes catalans* (Barcelona, 1958), 192–7.

above all in the invention of ritual that would give strength and sanctity to personal bonds of loyalty and obedience.[142]

This chapter on the development of new kinds of ethnic solidarity within the Roman world has taken us a long way from cities. But this itself is significant. The cultures of the new societies that were being established in the territory of what had been the Roman Empire in the West were not city-based. Cities of one kind or another did play a greater or a lesser part in the organization of the new societies, but the political institutions of cities, the rights and obligations of citizens, and the festivals and spectacles of the civic calendar no longer provided the motivation for collective action. Instead this was governed by personal obligations to powerful individuals. But the most powerful secular individuals in Gaul and Spain,[143] and to a lesser extent in Italy, now resided in the country.

[142] J. L. Nelson, *Politics and Ritual in Early Medieval Europe* (London, 1986).

[143] Díaz 1994*a*: 457–76, esp. 471–5. The king at Toledo had difficulty in controlling the great landowners.

12

Decline and the Beginnings of Renewal in the West

By the end of our period, say around AD 650, the appearance of Western Europe had been transformed. Material aspects of life had been enormously simplified. Over the whole West, from Britain to Thrace, building in stone was replaced by building in wood, or wattle and clay, for all buildings other than churches. After *c.*600, the age of Gregory of Tours, there were not very many churches being built either. Of Lombard Italy it has been noted that domestic material culture 600–800 is barely legible archaeologically.[1] The problem is that there is very little material that can be dated, but that in turn is a consequence of a reduction in long-distance trade: the widely traded African pottery, which is used to date archaeological levels in earlier periods, is no longer found. The pottery of this period is crude, more often than not locally produced, and not as yet sorted out into chronological series. Coins are very rare. In domestic building, solid mortared stone walls, tiled roofs, and solid floors are the exception. Bricks are mostly reused. Something like this had been the case in Britain since the early fifth century, but from the late sixth century it becomes true of the Balkans, of Greece, and North Africa as for instance evidenced by Cherchel,[2] and even in the seventh-century in Asia Minor.

1. *The Late Late Roman Cities as Seen through Archaeology*

Urban archaeology of this period is still in its beginnings. Nevertheless a pattern is emerging. The first phase of the transformation of the classical city, a phase which as we have seen, was well on the way in most areas of the West in the fourth century, was the running down and even the abandonment of the forum and other monumental structures in the old civic centre.[3] A striking development of later Late Antiquity is a simplification of well-to-do private life. A symptom of this which can be observed everywhere, though not everywhere at the same time, is reduction in domestic living space. In the East[4] as well as in the West,[5] large peristyle

[1] Christie 1995*a*: 155.

[2] Potter 1995: 60–1.

[3] See above, Chapter 2, esp. sections 2 and 5.

[4] J. C. Balty 1984.

[5] Thébert 1987: 313–409.

houses were subdivided for multi-occupation by the insertion of poorly constructed party-walls. Something like this has been the fate of large older properties at all times. What is however significant in this period is that no large new houses appear to have been built to replace outmoded ones, though a few of the old mansions were updated to the needs of notable politics by the addition of an apsed reception hall, and sometimes an addition of a dining room (*triclinium*) with several apses.[6] The latest peristyle house known to have been built anywhere within the Empire was built at Argos around AD 530. The subdivision of older houses was however generally only a stage in the decay of these buildings, leading either to abandonment or to the construction of very much more basic accommodation in their ruins.

Archaeology is beginning to reveal the running down of the urban fabric in several cities of Italy. For instance excavations at Brescia have clearly revealed the running down of the structure of the Roman city in the fifth century.[7] In the course of that century the forum fell into ruin, and the districts surrounding it were abandoned. While the circuit of walls remained intact, the built-up area appears to have been reduced to around 25 hectares, perhaps one-third of its former extent.[8]

The S. Giulia excavation uncovered a very large Roman domus which declined into multi-occupation in the fifth century and was destroyed in the sixth. Then it was levelled and the site occupied by a scattered group of twelve houses of timber, or of timber with stone footings or of walls of clay or wattle and clay. Some of the huts are sited along the road, others not. Spaces between the houses served as rubbish dumps and even for burials. The bones show signs of malnutrition and suggest a short life-span.[9] A large area in the south-east of the city was eventually covered with black soil and cultivated. Excavation in the via Alberto Mario has given an idea of the history of this quarter. As in the S. Giulia area the fourth and fifth century saw the subdivision and degradation of a large town house. But in this case, the decrepit structure was replaced by a smaller, and more basic, but still large house, towards the end of the century, that is during the Ostrogothic period. This in turn suffered sub-division, degradation, and eventually destruction by fire. Around the beginning of the seventh century the site was covered with black earth,[10]

[6] Ellis 1988; partitioning which was not related to multi-occupation: Thébert 1987: 313–409, esp. 389–92.

[7] Brogiolo 1993. More briefly: Brogiolo 1989: 156–65; and 'La città longobarda nel periodo della conquista (569-VII)', in Francovich and Noyé (1994), 555–66; also his 'A proposito dell'organizzazione urbana nell'alto medioevo', *Archeologia Medievale*, 14 (1987), 27–46.

[8] Brogiolo 1993: 85–6. The sewers were blocked (ibid. 79).

[9] Ibid. 90–6.

[10] Ibid. 74–83.

and in all likelihood used for agriculture or grazing. The whole S. Giulia area was in all likelihood owned by the Lombard kings who eventually gave it to the great monastery of S. Salvator which they founded on the site. The huts probably belonged to fairly humble dependents of the king engaged among other things in metal work. The housing of this class may well give an excessively sordid impression of the overall condition of life at Brescia in Lombard times. There is reason to believe that in the area of the old cathedral there was housing of a better quality. This is suggested by slower rise in the ground level. The foundations of the eleventh-century cathedral are only 50 centimetres above the Roman level. In this part of the town there is evidence on some, but not all, sites of continuous occupation to the twelfth century.[11] But knowledge of this quarter is still based on soundings rather than excavation.

At Verona the Cortile del Tribunale excavation has shown classical Roman building being replaced by houses of better quality than the huts of the S. Giulia excavation at Brescia. They face along a street encroaching on the old carriage way. On some sites along the Via Dante, there is continuity of housing from the fifth to the twelfth century. Most of the houses have stone foundations and stone façade elevations,[12] making use of reused Roman material bonded with clay.[13] It is however likely that the superstructure in the sides and in the rear was generally built of wood. The soil level rose rapidly as one series of lightly built houses was replaced by another. The forum appears to have been covered by a layer of around 70 centimetres of soil.[14]

At Luni excavators have found remains of irregularly sited timber houses built on some 30 centimetres of silt over the remains of the Roman forum. These seem to date from between AD 550 and 640.[15] They are therefore more or less contemporary with the irregularly shaped and sited stone houses, built of reused materials on the forum of Cherchel in Algeria.[16]

By late Roman standards Milan was certainly a great city. A poem of *c.*740 expresses pride not only in the city's saints and fortifications but also in its paved street and the aqueduct which supplies water to the baths.[17] Yet at Milan too, in the very centre of the city archaeologists have found

[11] Ibid. 89–90.

[12] Photograph showing rough masonry, reused material, and the successive door thresholds indicating rising ground level in Ward-Perkins 1988: 25, fig. 13. La Rocca Hudson 1986: 31–78.

[13] Christie 1995*a*: 155–9.

[14] La Rocca Hudson 1986; also G. Cavalieri Manasse, 'Il foro di Verona: recenti indagini', in *La città nell'Italia settentrionale in età romana*, Coll. de l'école française de Rome 130 (Rome, 1990), 579–616.

[15] Ward-Perkins 1978; 'Two Byzantine houses in Luni', *PBSR* 49 (1981), 91–8.

[16] Potter 1995: 48–61.

[17] *Versum de Mediolano civitate*, ed. G. B. Pighi (Bologna, 1960).

wooden buildings, and in the sixth century much of the city area that had once been built up was lying waste.[18] There is evidence also of the abandonment of villas in the hinterland of Milan and in the Po valley generally from the fifth century.[19]

Systematic excavation of late Late Roman levels in Italy is still at an early stage. But as far as the available evidence goes impoverishment, simplification of building techniques, and the emptying out of the urban space, was general.[20] The process seems to have been almost universal by the early fifth century.[21] In some cities of Tuscany monumental town centres appear to have begun to decay in the course of the fourth century or even earlier.[22] At Florence S. Reparata was built in the early sixth century, in the age of Theoderic, on what had earlier been a built-up part of town, but was now a cemetery. The medieval—and modern—Piazza della Signoria covers the area of Roman baths, but is separated from the classical remains by no less than 2 metres of dark soil, which contains some finds of the sixth century, but which was not built on before the eleventh/twelfth century.[23] Simplification of building techniques meant such private buildings as still took place made use of wood and daub, and of course the remains of older buildings. Stones and tiles were reserved for public buildings, mainly for churches, and even of these the materials were often spolia.[24] In the countryside caves were re-occupied.[25]

The findings of archaeologists can to some extent be supplemented by descriptions in literary sources and papyrus contracts from Ravenna.[26] The latter give details of houses owned by such people as a deputy commander of a *numerus*, a banker, and the daughters of a tribune. These must have

[18] G. P. Brogiolo, 'Milano', in Francovich and Noyé (1994), 561–3, with survey of emergency excavation linked to building of underground line 3.

[19] G. P. Brogiolo and G. Cantino Wataghin, 'Tardo antico e alto medioevo nel territorio padano', in Francovich and Noyé (1994), 141–50.

[20] D. Andrews and D. Perring, 'Milano gli scavi in Piazza Duomo 1982', *Notizario-Soprintendenza Archaeologica della Lombardia* (1982), 63–5; ibid. (1983), 91–2. A. Ceresa Mori, 'Milano vicolo di S. Maria alla Porta', ibid. (1983), 93–4. *Cremona*: L. Passi Pitcher, 'Cremona Piazza Marconi', ibid. (1983), 81–3. *Mantua*: C. Cazorzi and E. Roffia, 'Mantova Piazza Sordello', ibid. (1983), 86–7. *Pescara*: A. Staffa, 'Scavi nel centro storico di Pescara', *Archeologia Medievale*, 18 (1991), 201–36.

[21] V. Bierbrauer, 'Die Kontinuität städtischen Lebens in Oberitalien aus archäologischer Sicht, 5–7/8 Jahrhundert', in W. Eck and H. Galsterer, *Die Stadt in Oberitalien und in den nordwestlichen Provinzen des römischen Reiches* (Mainz, 1991), 263–86.

[22] Ciampoltrini 1994: 615–33: on Lucca, Fiesole, and Florence. Ada Gunella, 'Il coplesso cimiteriale di S. Felicit', in A. Benevenuti, F. Cardini, and E. Giannarelli (eds.), *Le Radici Cristiane di Firenze* (Florence, 1994), 13–32. Valenti 1996: 81–106, esp. 93–5.

[23] Francovich 1989: 166–71; also Ciampoltrini 1994: 615–33, on Lucca, Fiesole and Florence, and Chiusi.

[24] Francovich 1989: 167.

[25] Ibid. 168.

[26] B. Bavard, 'Cadre de vie et habitat urbain en Italie centrale byzantine', *Mélanges de l'école française de Rome*, Moyen Age 101–102 (1989), 465–532.

been relatively well-off people. Their houses were two-storied, but by classical standards relatively small. The largest belonging to a *magister militum* had a triclinium and five rooms. It was entirely built of stone and the roof was tiled. This was evidently exceptional. The house of the deputy commander was of stone only up to the level of the main floor, but it too was roofed with tiles. Another house was partly tiled and partly shingled. None of the houses were built on the traditional peristyle plan. Instead the owner's residence and auxiliary structures were situated around a courtyard which might be paved. One of the houses is stated to have a bath with pipes—it is not clear whether for water or drainage.

The typical picture of the late Late Roman town in Italy is one of a fortified enclosure, with a system of roads[27] on to which shops open. Houses are grouped in clusters surrounded by a lot of open space, some of which is cultivated. The ground level of the towns rises rapidly as one generation of short-lived housing is replaced by another. Civic buildings there are few or none. Silt and rubbish accumulates in abandoned monumental structures of the classical town. In the course of time some are adapted to new uses,[28] for instance to provide residences for Lombard kings, dukes, or gestalds. The remains of amphitheatres and baths must have stood out from the humble contemporary structures like the buildings of another race.[29]

Burials take place within the old urban area between the clusters of housing, perhaps marking off islands of building. The population tended to move from the old civic centre to the neighbourhood of the cathedral or other churches, or also out of the walled city altogether into the neighbourhood of extramural monasteries or cemetery churches. 'Island' occupation was particularly conspicuous inside the huge circuit of the imperial fortifications of Rome,[30] but as far as we can tell it became a characteristic feature of the old Roman towns everywhere. Abandoned sites no doubt sometimes reflect movement of population rather than depopulation. This fact makes it difficult to quantify the loss of population, which is suggested by the evidence of urban decay, and of

[27] Ward-Perkins 1984: 17: 23 Italian cities retain substantial elements of the Roman grid street plan. The number which had a demonstrably continuous history since Roman times is of course much longer.

[28] La Rocca 1992: 161–80; J. Vaes, 'Christliche Verwendung antiker Bauten', *Ancient Society*, 15–17 (1984), 305–443; *idem*, 'Nova construere sed amplius vetusta servare: La Réutilisation chrétienne d'édifices antiques (en Italie)', *Actes du XI Congrès International d'Archéologie Chrétienne*, i (Rome, 1989), 299–319; J.-P. Caillet, 'La Transformation en église d'édifices publics et de temples à la fin de l'antiquité', in C. Lepelley (1996), 191–211; Ward-Perkins 1999.

[29] See the *Iconographia Rateriana*, a copy of a 10th-cent. drawing of Verona, Ward-Perkins 1984: fig. 4.

[30] R. Meneghini and R. Santagelli Valenziani, 'Sepolture intramuranee e paesaggio urbano a Roma, Ve–VIIe secolo', in Paroli and Delogu (1993), 89–100; Cantino Wataghin 1999.

large spaces left waste or cultivated, in what had formerly been built-up areas.[31]

In the midst of so much squalor and decay it does however look as if churches continued to be maintained. There had been much church-building in the late fourth and early fifth centuries, and even more in the later fifth to early sixth centuries.[32] These churches were not as a rule allowed to fall into ruin, but were from time to time restored and even embellished.[33] A few new churches were built even in the late sixth and seventh centuries, notably at Rome.[34] These were much smaller and plainer than those put up while the Empire was still intact.[35] Presumably it was mainly work on churches, and perhaps on royal residences, that provided a living for the members of the builders' guild whose prices for certain items of skilled and specialist work were fixed by royal regulations.[36] It follows that while much contemporary housing makes an extremely primitive impression, sophisticated building-skills were not totally lost, to provide the foundations for a technological and artistic recovery. At Brescia this showed itself in the construction of the first church of S. Salvator in the second half of the seventh century, and achieved an impressive level of skill in the second church and the buildings of the monastery founded by king Desiderius in AD 753.[37]

[31] Potter 1995: 90–6 on the two views. See also the enormous range of estimates of the population of Rome. R. Hodges: a maximum of 5,000 (assuming that the whole population worked for ecclesiastical institutions) in 'The riddle of St Peter's Republic', in Paroli and Delogu (1993), 353–66. Krautheimer 1980: 165: 30,000–40,000. Delogu, in Paroli and Delogu 1993, argues that in the time of Gregory the great bulk of the population was fed by local produce. The estates of the Church in Sicily helped to feed the clergy and dependents of the Church and to provide general help in emergencies. The scale of the Church's resources can be estimated from Greg *Ep.* V.30. Gregory provides 30 lbs of gold, 2,160 solidi which would perhaps have fed 1,700 poor people for a year. On cost of living: A. H. M. Jones 1964, 447. *Ep.* VII.23, Gregory gives 80 lbs of gold for 3,000 nuns.

[32] Testini, Cantino Wataghin, and Pani Ermini 1989.

[33] Potter 1995: 93–5; Christie 1995*a*: 196–8 on foundations of monasteries, some in 7th cent.; Ward-Perkins 1984: 236–47 on church-building at Rome, Ravenna, Pavia, and Lucca from 4th to 9th cent. P. Delogu, 'The rebirth of Rome', in Hodges and Hobley (1988), 32–42: building and giving of gold and silver by the popes recovered earlier in the 7th cent. than building did elsewhere.

[34] Coates-Stephens 1997: 177–232.

[35] See Ward-Perkins 1988: 20, fig. 8.

[36] Law of Rothar (636–52), 144–5.

[37] Brogiolo 1993: 99–101. Lombard kings did occasionally construct relatively major buildings: the basilica of Queen Theodolinda at Monza (593–603), see Paul the Deacon (*HL* IV.22); S. Maria alla Pertica at Pavia (677), ibid V.34. Palatium of Luitprand at Corteolona, C. Calderini, 'Il palazzo di Liutprando a Corteolona', *Contributi dell'Istituto di Archeologia*, 5 (1975), 174–203. None has been excavated. But at Brescia on S. Giulia site *c.*750 the site of two *insulae* was cleared preparatory to building of a monastery, 120 metres × 60 (Brogiolo 1989: 162–3; 1993: 96–107). There was a striking revival of arts from the second decade of 8th cent. which requires survival of basic skills, see Christie 1995*a*: 190–203.

2. *Shrinking and Destruction of Cities*[38]

The long-term fate of the Roman cities leaves many questions. For instance the survival rate of cities in Lombardy was much higher than in Liguria. Why was this? Some factors can be isolated. The cities of Lombardy are surrounded by excellent farmland. They are also situated on the routes by which Mediterranean trade must pass to reach Gaul and the Rhineland. By the year 1000 and for centuries after they were the most highly developed cities of Europe.[39] But why was survival rate among cities of the north so much higher than in the south? It may be that smallness of territory and poor soil was an important factor in the demise of many of these hill-towns. It may be that the fate of many of these was already sealed by the destruction of Justinian's Gothic wars.[40] Middle-Byzantine organization was not particularly favourable to cities and their institutions,[41] except for principal centres of administration like Thessalonica, and in Italy, Ravenna and Naples. The urban revival instigated by the needs of Lombard administration began at Benevento, in what in spite of its classical past was practically a new foundation, and later resulted in the rapid development of Gaeta, Amalfi, and Salerno.[42]

As we have seen, Arab rule was generally favourable to cities. This also proved to be the case in Spain. Cordova grew to be a very large city, probably the largest in Europe. The new rulers built the great mosque which has dominated the city ever since, and a huge palace complex five miles outside the Roman city. Seville too was a great city under the Arabs. In both Cordova and Seville there must have been a great deal of continuity from Roman times, but that does not necessarily mean that they were still fully built up with large populations when the Arabs came. Neither city has retained its Roman street plan. As late as the early ninth century, the bishop Hostegesis of Cordova collected poll-tax from the Christians of his city for the Arabs.[43] Very little evidence bearing on early Arab administration has survived, the case of Hostegesis does however show that Arabs at first made use of the powerful position bishops had acquired in Visigothic Spain for their own administrative purposes. In the longer run progressive Islamization must have reduced the importance of the bishops. In view of the fact that many a city in the West managed to

[38] Schmiedt 1974.

[39] Ward-Perkins 1988. For a fuller discussion of the varied fates of cities in different parts of Italy see Brogiolo 1999, esp. 108–20.

[40] L. Duchesne, 'Les Évêchés d'Italie et l'invasion lombarde', *Mélanges d'archéologie et d'histoire*, 23 (1903), 83–116; 25 (1905), 365–99.

[41] Wickham 1981: 157–8.

[42] Ibid. 149.

[43] H. Kennedy 1996: 51.

survive only because it had a bishop, the downgrading of bishops must have had a detrimental effect on cities in Islamic Spain. Archaeological evidence does indeed suggest that the cities that surrendered to the Arabs under the famous *pactum* of Teodomir went into a decline culminating in virtual abandonment. Valencia, Orihuela, and Lorca eventually recovered. Others disappeared, or rather were replaced by new foundations on neighbouring sites. Cartagena had already shrunk to the condition of a fortified citadel in Byzantine times, though it had several suburbs outside its fortifications. Murcia, the new regional centre, was an Arab foundation.[44] Generalizing from what happened in this region of south-eastern Spain one might speculate that the flourishing condition of many cities in Islamic Spain was not so much a result of urban continuity, as of cities being given a new start on the same, or a neighbouring, site.

Not all cities survived. Italica was unable to compete with the neighbouring Seville. In the valley of the Guadalquivir too some of the smaller towns disappeared or shrank to the condition of villages. It has been suggested that exhaustion of the soil was a causative factor in this area.[45] In Lusitania, Merida was partly destroyed after a rebellion, and lost its administrative functions and much of its population to Badajoz. Its archbishopric was transferred to Santiago de Compostela. Conimbriga had been destroyed by the Suebi as long ago as AD 465–8 but nevertheless continued as a bishopric.[46] Along the middle course of the Ebro a number of towns disappeared.[47] The development of hill-top settlements had begun in many parts of Spain in the fifth century. This trend continued under the Visigoths and was consolidated under the Arabs. Very similar developments have been noted in the Balkans and in Italy.[48]

Among Roman cities that fell under Islamic rule those of North Africa fared worst. The story of the decline of urban civilization of Roman North Africa is remarkable, and far from clear.[49] Proconsular Africa, modern Tunisia, had certainly been one of the most intensely urbanized regions in the Empire, and the city, in its classical form, flourished there longer than anywhere else in the West. Its decline was slow but inexorable. It would be interesting to establish how far urban decline in Africa was in step with decline in Italy, or indeed in Anatolia. Unfortunately, both the geo-

[44] Lloret 1993: 13–35, summed up 25–7 with maps.

[45] C. Choclán and M. Castro, 'La campiña del Alto Guadalquivir en los siglos I–II d.C.', *Arqueología Espacial*, 12 (1988), 205–21.

[46] R. Etienne (ed.), *Fouilles de Conimbriga*, vii (Paris, 1979), 254–5, 264.

[47] J. L. Corral, 'Las ciudades de la Marca Superior de al-Andalus', *Symposium Internacional sobre la ciudad islámica* (Saragossa, 1991), 253–87.

[48] Cuenca 1997: 270–1.

[49] On Libya, see J. A. Lloyd, 'Urban archaeology in Cyrenaica 1969–89: The Hellenistic, Roman and Byzantine periods', *Libyan Studies*, 20 (1989), 77–90; G. R. D. King, 'Islamic archaeology in Libya', ibid. 193–208.

graphical pattern and the chronology of the decline of cities in North Africa is still quite uncertain owing to the inadequacy of literary and, to date, also of the archaeological evidence. The eventual outcome was that Carthage, one of the super-cities of the ancient world, was abandoned. It was in fact replaced by the Arab foundations of Qayrawan (AD 670), and later of Tunis. The final phase at Carthage is still quite obscure. It has been suggested that in the ninth century there was a mosque on the site of the church of St Cyprian. The earliest Islamic pottery found on the site dates from the tenth century. The extent of the occupation at this time, and the degree of continuity with Roman Carthage, remain to be discovered.[50] Very many of the Roman cities of the region ceased to be inhabited, without our having any evidence to suggest when, or why this happened. At Cherchel the earliest islamic pottery found so far dates to the thirteenth century.[51] At Sétif there is evidence that the baths were used until the beginning of the seventh century and later demolished. The earliest known Islamic building, as at Carthage dates to the tenth century. One suspects that there was occupation in the interval that is still illegible to archaeologists; but it was presumably of rather a modest kind.[52] There is likely to have been more continuity of occupation and use on the coast than inland.[53] But evidence of post-Roman occupation has been found for instance at Haïdra,[54] and at Tebessa,[55] and no doubt more will turn up in the future.

Christianity certainly did not collapse immediately following the Islamic conquest, but it has left only scanty evidence of its continued existence.[56] One can only speculate about the combination of unfavourable factors that destroyed the Christian and Latin urban civilization of North Africa. One factor was presumably the conflict between the North African episcopate and the government at Constantinople, which resulted in the imposition of Greek bishops. Another perhaps even more important factor was the consolidation of Berber tribes into larger units, and their advance from the desert fringe towards the coast. The Berbers were nomads, and some of them still pagans, and not urbanized. They were

[50] G. Vitelli, *Islamic Carthage: The Archaeological and Ceramic Evidence* (Tunis, 1981). D. Whitehouse, 'An early mosque at Carthage?', *Annali dell'Istituto Universitario Orientale*, 43 (1983), 161–5.

[51] Potter 1995: 61.

[52] A. Mohammedi, A. Benmansour, A. Amamra, and E. Fentress, *Fouilles de Sétif 1977–84*, 5e Supplement au Bulletin d'Archéologie Algérienne (Algiers, 1991), 29, 93.

[53] Y. Thébert and J.-L. Biget, 'L'Afrique après la disparition de la cité classique', in *L'Afrique dans l'occident romain 1er siècle avant J.C.–4e siècle après J.C.*, Collection de l'école française de Rome 134 (Rome, 1990), 575–602.

[54] A mosque at Haïdra: F. Baratte, 'La Citadelle byzantine d'Ammaedara Haïdra', *CRAI* (1996), 125–54.

[55] D. Pringle, *The Defences of Byzantine Africa*, BAR Int. 99 (Oxford, 1981), 424 n. 101.

[56] N. Duval 1982: ii. 760.

strongly militarized. It was the Berbers more than the Byzantines, or the African Romans, that resisted the Arab armies. In the end they made treaties with the Arabs to become *mawali*, and as such played an important role in the Islamic armies that conquered and settled Spain.[57] Their gaining control of an area was probably more damaging to city life and everything that went with it, than conquest by armies from Arabia and Syria.

Looking at the Roman West as a whole we note that survival of cities, normally in a reduced and transformed state, was much more common than destruction and abandonment. Mortality among towns was as a rule a regional phenomenon. It is true that sometimes a city went into decline to the point of depopulation as a result of the growth of a neighbouring locality which enjoyed some considerable advantage in changed conditions. More often terminal decline resulted in all or very many of the cities of an area becoming depopulated together, as they had done in Britain in the fifth century, and were to do in North Africa, perhaps from the eighth. In much of northern Italy the old Roman cities had a great future, but in Liguria and in the Marche many cities were abandoned. In southern Gaul by the seventh century the expansion of the Basques had brought about the disappearance of twelve cities between the Pyrenees and the Garonne,[58] and about the same time much of the Balkan area was being deurbanized. After AD 620 there is very little archaeological evidence for urban activity outside the territories that remained Byzantine.[59] The process of deurbanization is hardly ever well documented.

Among the factors that might have produced deurbanization in the East, I discussed the deliberate evacuation of urban populations by the imperial authorities for strategic reasons. The flourishing cities of late Late Roman Cilicia were evacuated by Heraclius to create an empty zone between the imperial lands and those occupied by the Arabs. Subsequently they were repeatedly reoccupied, captured, and destroyed and the area became an empty zone between the combatants.[60] A few examples of this occurred in the West. The deliberate evacuation of cities on the northern border of Noricum around AD 480 is described in the *Life* of St Severinus, who ordered the abandonment of cities that could not be defended and the concentration of their inhabitants in the cities that

[57] M. Brett, *Cambridge History of Africa* (Cambridge, 1978), ii. 510–13.

[58] Rouche 1979: 271–7.

[59] S. Michailov, 'Die Erforschung des frühfeudalen Städtewesens in Bulgarien', in Jankuhn, Schlesinger, and Steuer (1973–74), ii. 289–304. Some place-name continuity suggests that the localities were not completely depopulated. The residences of Pliska and Preslav represent a new start.

[60] See above, p. 290, n. 45.

could.[61] Later these too were evacuated by Odoacer.[62] In AD 546–7 the emperor Justinian gave the Lombards the towns of Noricum and the fortresses of Pannonia.[63] In AD 568 the Lombards were invited into Italy by the Byzantine commander Narses and their king Alboin evacuated Pannonia, both the land and the remaining cities,[64] in order to assemble the maximum army for invasion of Italy, and also perhaps to prevent the imperial government from restoring the imperial structure in the lands he was leaving.[65] The territory was subsequently occupied by the nomad Avars, who proceeded to besiege what had once been the great city of Sirmium. In AD 582 after a long siege the Eastern government evacuated the population.[66]

3. *The Reduction in the Number of Rural Sites in Italy and Elsewhere*

Change in cities did not occur in isolation from developments in the surrounding country. Archaeological surveys of many areas have revealed a steady reduction in the number of rural settlements starting around the end of the second century.[67] The phenomenon has been observed not only in Italy but all over the Western provinces. Roman occupation almost invariably was followed by a more or less gradual concentration of property into fewer hands, and the amalgamation of landholdings into larger units.[68] So the reduction in the number of sites can—and no doubt often does—reflect the existence of a smaller number of still prosperous estates or farms, and is compatible with a still sizeable population living in fewer but larger settlements. It does not necessarily mean impoverishment and depopulation. But it certainly sometimes did. Whether concentration resulted in a reduction of the rural population or not, depended on the kind of reorganization involved, and in the longer term on the sustainability of the new form of organization. In fact the extent of the loss of sites

[61] Eugippius, *V. Severini* 31. F. Lotter, *Severinus von Noricum Legende und historische Wirklichkeit* (Stuttgart, 1976) argues that Severinus, whom he controversially identifies with Severinus 5 the consul of 461 (*PLRE* II.1001), had a position of sub-Roman ruler like Marcellinus in Dalmatia, and Aegidius (*PLRE* II.11–13), and Syagrius 2 (*PLRE* II.1041–2) in N. Gaul, by virtue of his previous high Roman office. Even if the identification is wrong, it is significant that comparable positions of power could be built up on a basis of religious authority.

[62] *V. Severini* 42, the inhabitants were distributed through different districts of Italy (ibid. 44).

[63] Procopius *Goth. War* III.33.

[64] Paul the Deacon *Hist. Lomb.* II.5 ff.

[65] Of course it remains a question how complete the evacuation was. Is the impression of total uprooting given by Marius of Avenches, *Chron.* II.24. s.a. 569, with its account of the burning of the old homes, exaggerated?

[66] Menander prot. *Frgs.* 12.3–8; 25; 27; Pohl 1988: 75.

[67] Green 1986: 98–123; Barker and Lloyd 1991.

[68] Barker and Lloyd 1991: practically every landscape surveyed shows this process of concentration.

varies a great deal from region to region, and so no doubt did the social consequences of the process. By and large the greatest reduction occurred where the structure of landholding had been most deeply affected by the Empire, that is the areas where the wealthiest Romans, that is the senators and knights preferred to invest the gains of Empire, by buying up very large amounts of land to set up farms worked by slaves, concentrating on a single cash crop, especially wine or olive oil.

Field surveys have thrown extremely interesting light on changing land use on the west coast of Italy, from Etruria to Naples and beyond. Eighty-seven miles north-west of Rome was the Roman colony of Cosa, which has been carefully excavated, and its agricultural hinterland subjected to archaeological survey.[69] Between AD 50–600 there was a catastrophic fall in the number of sites from around 245 at the end of the first century to 115 by the end of the third, 84 by the end of the fourth, and 53 by the end of the fifth. The reduction in small sites is especially noteworthy. There evidently was a continuous process of concentration of ownership throughout the period.[70] Amalgamation of smaller farms first resulted in the growth of large slave worked estates. Later the villas were abandoned—presumably because the wine which was their only crop had become unprofitable—and the countryside became derelict also. The city of Cosa decayed from the late second century AD in spite of some imperial attempts to reverse the decline. By the fourth century the economy of the countryside must have been largely independent of the city. When the countryside lost its population the town lost its purpose.[71] One might compare the 'rust-belts' of derelict industry in contemporary Europe and the USA. Significantly this breakdown of the agricultural economy did not happen in the territory of Saturnia, in the more hilly area further away from the coast, where smaller villas produced a wider range of crops, and might also engage in pig-rearing for the Roman market.[72]

The British School at Rome has surveyed a large area in southern Etruria north-east of Rome. This is an area whose economy must have been enormously affected by its closeness to the capital. Here decline began in the third century AD. By 500, between 50 and 80 per cent of sites in the area surveyed had been deserted, and the cultivation of marginal

[69] Cambi and Fentress 1989: 74–85.

[70] Ibid. 74, fig. 1.

[71] S. L. Dyson, 'Settlements patterns in the Ager Cosanus: The Wesleyan University Survey 1974–76', *J. Field Archaeology*, 5 (1978), 251–68; 'Settlement reconstruction in the *ager cosanus* and the Albegna valley', in Barker and Hodges (1981), 269–74. Fentress 1994: 208–22. On the revival of Cosa as a Byzantine fortress, with a *mansio*, a church, a cemetery, and a few huts, see M. G. Celuzza and E. Fentress, 'La Toscana centro-meridionale: i casi di Cosa-Ansedonia e Roselle', in Francovich and Noyé (1994), 601–13.

[72] Attolini *et al.* 1991: 142–52.

land abandoned—as it has remained until the present century.[73] The Vicus Augustanus to the east of Ostia, like other vici in the same area, was abandoned by the fifth century and only reoccupied in the twelfth.[74] Once more an area which experienced rapid development in the early years of the Empire proved extremely vulnerable to changing economic conditions. Again it is significant that nothing like that decline happened in the Biferno valley on about the same latitude in the much more remote north-western Samnium on the other side of the Appenines.[75]

Another case of dramatic development followed by equally dramatic regression happened further down the coast in Northern Campania where the rich and densely populated lands with their rich volcanic soils entered into gradual but inexorable decline from the mid-imperial period. By the fourth to fifth centuries 45 per cent of sites that had survived into the mid-Empire had gone. Roads, harbours, aqueducts, drains, and field systems had fallen into disrepair. With the later fifth/sixth centuries rural settlement—as far as perceptible to field surveys—seems to have all but ceased. Of the cities, Sessa Aurunca survived the Dark Ages. Minturnae and Sinuessa were gradually deserted. By possibly the sixth century the sites were completely abandoned.[76] But the development along the inland valley of the river Liri was quite different. Here too Roman rule produced a dense network of villas, but these did not replace all farms of more modest size. This mixed system survived from the republic into the sixth century.[77]

Regions that had not undergone a marked boom in the Early Empire did not suffer a comparable reduction in the number of occupied sites. A survey of late Roman settlement in western Apulia and Basilicata shows that in this area sites were if anything more numerous in Late Antiquity than earlier, and that they continued to be occupied as long as there is datable pottery, that is into the sixth century.[78] A comparable state of

[73] Potter 1979; *id.*, 'Population hiatus and continuity: The case of the south Etrurian survey', in H. M. Blake, T. W. Potter, D. B. Whitehouse (eds.), *Papers in Italian Archaeology* 1, BAR S141 (Oxford, 1978), 99–116. Barker and Hodges 1981. But see V. F. Nicolai, 'Considerazioni sull'archeologia del territorio laziale nell'altomedioevo', in Francovich and Noyé (1994), 403–6. The implications of the field surveys are contradicted to some extent (but to what extent?) by the archaeology of churches and their cemeteries in continued use during the relevant period.

[74] A. Claridge, 'A date for the medieval settlement at the vicus Augustanus Laurentius (Castelporziano)', in L. Paroli and P. Delogu (eds.), *La storia economica di Roma nell'alto medioevo alla luce dei recenti scavi archeologici*, Biblioteca di Archeologia Medievale (Florence, 1993), 287–93.

[75] J. Lloyd and G. Barker, 'Rural settlement in Roman Molise', in Barker and Hodges (1981), 289–304; Barker 1995.

[76] These are the conclusions of Arthur 1991: 101–4; see also Barker and Lloyd 1991: 153–79.

[77] S. L. Dyson, *The Roman Villas of Buccinino*, BAR Int. 187 (Oxford, 1983).

[78] A. M. Small, 'Late Roman settlement in western Apulia and Basilicata (San Giovanni, Venosa, Gravina and Fossa Bradanica)', in Barker and Lloyd (1991), 204–22; Small and Buck 1994: illustration 297, fig. 14: more sites around the villa of San Giovanni di Ruoti in 400–550 than 350–400. The

affairs has been found in the Mingardo/Bussento area of western Lucania.[79] Farming in these 'uplands and margins' had certainly been Romanized too, but its economy proved far more resilient than that in areas which attracted heavy investment by the senatorial aristocracy of Rome itself. It is surely not a coincidence that at least some cities of Lucania and Bruttium remained relatively prosperous well into the sixth century.[80] In the Marche on the north-east coast there was a considerable loss of cities, but paradoxically the survival of place-names derived from the names of Roman landowners on the Farfa documents before 1000 suggests that the basic structure of landowning survived. This is quite unlike the situation found along the west coast.[81]

While change was most dramatic in areas where agriculture had been most radically transformed in the classical period, reduction in the number of settlements and simplification of living conditions in a way to make them less accessible to archaeology appear to have happened to a greater or lesser extent all over Italy. In Tuscany caves were reoccupied.[82] Woodland and marshes expanded at the expense of cultivated land in the Po region[83] and in the coastal areas of Tuscany.[84] In the Cornia valley the majority of Roman sites lasted only until the fifth century.[85] If we look at these changes in the Italian landscape with hindsight, that is if we relate them to the pattern of landholding dominant in the Middle Ages, we can see that what was happening was nothing less than a complete transformation of land settlement. The Roman pattern of landholding had almost disappeared by the late sixth century. *Incastallamento*, the new pattern, is only formally attested from the tenth century, but the term appears to define the consolidation of new forms of settlement that began to take shape in our period. It is significant that the new system that came

villa was abandoned before 550 and the surrounding sites about the same time (ibid. 22). A. M. Small and Joan Freed, 'S. Giovanni di Ruoti (Basilicata): Il contesto della villa tardo-romana', in Giardina (1986), 97–138.

79 M. Gualtieri and F. De Polignac, 'A rural landscape in western Lucania', in Barker and Lloyd (1991), 194–203.

80 G. Noyé, 'Villes, économie et société dans la province de Bruttium-Lucanie du IVe au VIIe siècle', in Francovich and Noyé (1994), 693–733.

81 U. Moscatelli, 'The evolution of rural settlement in *regiones* V–VI from Roman to early medieval period', in Christie (1995*b*), 303–9.

82 M. Valenti, in Brogiolo (1996), 83.

83 P. Tozzi and M. Harari, 'Air survey of the Valli Grandi Veronesi 1984–88', in E. Herring, Ruth Whitehouse, and John Wilkes (eds.), *Papers of the 4th Conference of Italian Archaeology* (London, 1992), 123–7: centuriation, villas, and roads of Roman period replaced by marshland as a result of disrupted drainage.

84 Francovich 1989: 168. F. Cambi, C. Citter, S. Guideri, M. Valenti, 'Etruria, Tuscia, Toscana: La formazione de paesaggi alto medievali', Francovich and Noyé (1994): 183–215, extensive decline into marshland a medieval phenomenon?

85 Francovich 1989: 168 cites M. Montanari, *Campagne medievali* (Turin, 1984); V. Fumagalli, *Terra e società nell'Italia padana* (Turin, 1976).

into existence between the fifth and the eleventh centuries was no longer centred on the cities, but largely independent of them.[86]

A pattern similar to the Italian one has been observed in Baetica, for many years the wealthiest and most densely urbanized area of Spain; one might call it the Spanish Campania. The surveys of M. Ponsich have shown a dramatic fall in settlements in Baetica from the third century.[87] On the evidence available to Karen Carr, when she wrote her thesis in 1992, there were 71 per cent fewer sites in the Visigothic than in the Roman period.[88] It must be said that the effect on the economy as a whole cannot have been anything like as disastrous as in Campania. In Late Antiquity Baetica certainly had fewer cities than under the Early Empire, but even in the sixth and seventh centuries under the Visigoths Cordova, Seville, and perhaps Italica, were probably still among the most classically urban cities not only in Spain but in the West. Under Arab rule, around AD 1000, Seville and Cordova, together with Palermo in Sicily were the largest cities in Europe.[89] The territory of Tarraco which had enjoyed a significant boom under the Early Empire also shows a reduction in the number of sites in Late Antiquity, though the reduction was smaller than in Baetica. A recent estimate is that the territory contained around 2,000 sites in Late Antiquity against *c.*3,300 under the Early Empire.[90] In Tarraconensis as in Italy the reduction in the number of archaeologically visible sites seems to reflect the breakdown of a settlement pattern. The Roman system of land use appears to have been replaced by one involving widespread grazing. The existence of the new settlement pattern, which was to prevail through the medieval and subsequent periods, can however only be demonstrated from the tenth or even eleventh centuries.[91]

The pattern of continuing rural decline starting in the third, or even late

[86] Francovich 1989: 166–71. Christie 1991. On the new fortified village settlements in Italy, Hispania, and elsewhere around the Mediterranean, see *L'Incastellamento*, L'école française de Rome (1998).

[87] M. Ponsich, *Implantation rurale antique sur le Bas-Guadalquivir*, t. 1 (Paris, 1974–in progress), vols. 3 (1987) and 4 (1991) reviewed by S. Keay in *JRS* 83 (1993), 236. See the discussion in K. E. Carr, 'Did Roman Government Matter? The Standard of Living in the Guadalquivir Valley AD 300–700', Ph.D. thesis (Univ. of Michigan, 1992; UMI Dissertation Services), esp. 163–200. Carr calculates that there were 71% fewer sites in the Visigothic than in the peak of the Roman period.

[88] Ibid. 198. See also A. R. Rodríguez, M. Molinos, and M. Castro López, 'Settlement and continuity in the territory of the Guadalquivir valley (6th century BC–1st century AD)', in Barker and Lloyd (1991), 29–36, relevant settlement development, p. 33, fig. 3.

[89] Bairoch 1991: 158.

[90] Carreté, Keay, and Millett 1995: 277–8.

[91] Ibid. 281; J. M. Recassens, *La ciutat de Tarragona*, ii (Barcelona, 1975), 69–85. S. Riera Mora and J. M. Palet Martinez, 'Landscape dynamics from Iberian-Roman (2nd–1st centuries BC) to early medieval times (12th century) in the Montjuïc-El Port sector (Plain of Barcelona)', *Archeologia Medievale*, 21 (1994), 517–38. See also Palet 1997.

second century has been observed in many areas of the West.[92] For instance the region around the Somme in the north-east of France was covered with a dense network of Roman type farm-villas in the Early Empire. The decline of this system began even before the third century and was succeeded by a pattern of occupation less dense, and certainly much less conspicuous.[93] But the number of rural sites did not fall dramatically everywhere. In Provence a survey in the environment of Béziers and another of land around the Étang de Berre to the north-west of Marseille show dense villa occupation continuing well into the fifth century.[94] It may well not be a coincidence that Marseille too is known to have been remarkably prosperous right through to the sixth century. This prosperity was evidently related to its continued function as a harbour, particularly for shipping from Africa well into the seventh century. Not only did it keep its old circuit of walls, but the enclosed area seems to have remained built up, and suburbs sprang up beyond it. Other cities of Provence, Orange, Fréjus, Riez, Aix en Provence show contraction of their inhabited areas. By the end of the fifth century the built-up area of Narbonne had split into islands around two principal churches. By the late sixth century at Marseille too areas within the city had been abandoned by their inhabitants. From the mid-seventh to the tenth century archaeology has found very few traces of urban activity in the cities of Provence.[95]

4. *The Breakdown of the Distribution of Pottery in Italy*

Ceramic evidence gives the impression that in the fifth century the whole system of distribution and exchange was breaking down.[96] Until the mid-fifth century the pattern of ceramic consumption in urban and rural sites in southern and cental Italy was essentially the same.[97] Imported pottery,

[92] Randsborg 1991.

[93] Greene 1986: 116–20 and the discussion in Wightman 1985: 243–66. Was the Romanization of landholding in N. Gaul a result of the need to supply corn to the legions on the Rhine, and can the decline of the villa system be linked to the development of corn farming in the Rhineland, together with a reduction of the military importance of the Rhine relative to the Danube frontier?

[94] Greene 1986: 120–1; P. Leven, 'Villas and Roman settlement in Basse Provence', in Barker and Lloyd (1991), 169–75.

[95] S. T. Loseby, 'Marseille, a Late Antique success story?' *JRS* 82 (1992), 165–85, esp. 184–5 analysis of pottery finds. The economy of Provence must have been helped by the fact that the praetorian prefecture of Gaul was moved to Arles early in the 5th cent. Wealth will have produced a demand for goods, which would in turn have attracted ships to the ports of Arles and Marseilles, which was the more convenient port. Later the breakdown of trade in Northern Italy as a result of the Lombard settlement (see below, p. 385) may have helped Marseille. The urban history of Provence is perhaps more like that of Northern Italy than that of the cities of the rest of Gaul. But the cities of Provence did not share the North Italian towns' strong revival after AD 800.

[96] Arthur and Patterson 1994: 409–41.

[97] Ibid. 424.

above all the African red slip-ware, reached everywhere and pottery produced in a number of Italian centres was traded at great distances from its place of production. From the mid-fifth century imported pottery becomes very much rarer on rural sites while continuing reasonably abundantly in towns. African red slip-ware practically ceased to be found in inland areas of Southern Italy (it had always been rare in Northern Italy) and was replaced by local ceramics, some imitating African ware. Even the rich villa of S. Giovanni di Ruoti in Basilicata was without African red slip-ware. But the African fine pottery continued to reach Naples, and Canosa on the Adriatic. In the course of the last decades of the fifth century, many of the Italian centres producing fine pottery closed down in turn.[98] It looks as if the rural demand for superior tableware had come to an end, and that as a result production and distribution of quality ware ended also.

By the middle of the sixth century, finds of pottery in the country are almost exclusively from cemeteries. The pots have been produced locally or even domestically, and can be dated only with the aid of coins and metalwork found in the same burial.[99] The import of the African ware has now practically ceased, but in a few cities, above all Naples and Rome, good quality and professionally produced painted cooking ware was still being used. This is never found in rural sites. Interestingly it also does not appear to have reached the cities of the north, which were now under Lombard ruler. The relative strength of urbanism in Northern Italy at this time was evidently not trade-based. Even the cities of Lombardy, in spite of their strategic situation on the routes between the Mediterranean and the passes of the Alps which was to make them great centres of trade from the Carolingian age onwards, had been reduced to units in cellular local economies in the later sixth century. Far from playing a role in interregional exchanges, they rarely interacted with each other.[100]

Wickham has put forward a plausible explanation of the dramatic shrinking of trade. The subsidized transport of tax-corn, the *annona*, from Africa to Rome, had enabled shippers to transport very large amounts of other goods cheaply and to sell them for profit, especially in Italy. When the *annona* stopped the African exports became more expensive and the markets shrank. The market in Italy was especially badly affected, because the Italian economy was greatly impoverished by the ending of the inflow of African taxes. This model is very convincing. But the commercial consequences ensued more slowly than one would expect. Evidently the

[98] The disappearance of African pottery from inland sites and its substitution by local products in Italy after *c.* 450: Wickham 1994: 94–5; Marazzi 1998: 136–41. The disappearance of the substitution wares: Arthur and Patterson 1994: 422.

[99] Ibid. 427.

[100] Balzaretti 1996: 213–34.

shippers, who were no longer subsidized to sail to Italian ports, did not simply give up trading, but developed new types both of amphorae and of tableware, and for some decades at least, kept most of their Italian markets, and expanded their trade elsewhere. A lot of oil-amphorae from the period of the Vandal occupation of North Africa have been found in Catalonia. The fifth century did however see a great reduction in the export of African red slip pottery to the East—whether in consequence of the Vandal occupation or for some other reason. The export of amphorae to the East continued, but as in the fourth century, on a fairly small scale. During the same period paradoxically, Eastern exports to North Africa increased significantly, bringing more Eastern pottery to Carthage. This trade continued well into the sixth century. By then significant quantities of African fine table pottery were again exported to the East, though on a smaller scale than in the fourth century.[101] The trade between North Africa and the East peaked in the mid-sixth century. The eventual cessation of the production of African ware, in the late sixth century and after, seems to have been linked with the collapse of trade between North Africa and Constantinople.[102] The urban decline of Carthage followed. Large-scale pottery production came to an end all round the Mediterranean. It lasted longest in the immediate neighbourhood of Constantinople, and in the Umayyad heartland of Syria, and in Egypt.

If, as is posited in Wickham's model, long-distance trade in the Roman world had been greatly assisted by the transfer of purchasing power and subsidizing of shipping resulting from imperial taxation and the Roman *annona*, it is worth noting that private trade had sufficient flexibility to adapt to a significant extent to the collapse of this system.[103] For it would appear that the end of the *annona*, drastic as its immediate effects are likely to have been for many people in Italy, had little immediate impact on the commercial exchanges in Italy—at least that is the impression conveyed by the evidence available at the time of writing. The long-term effect is of course another matter. But the delay between the effect and its suggested cause presents an intriguing puzzle.

[101] C. Abadie-Reynal, 'Céramique et commerce dans le bassin égén du IVe au VIIe siècle', in *Hommes et Richesses* (1989), i. 143–62. Note that the growth of eastern trade with N. Africa precedes the Justinianic reconquest and that it in fact developed during the period of Vandal occupation. Judging by evidence known today, Vandal Africa had a negative trade balance with the East. On African trade elsewhere, see C. Panella, 'Gli scambi nel mediterraneo occidentale dal IV al VII secolo dal punto di visto di alcuene merci', in *Hommes et richesses* (1989), i. 131–41; A. Carignani, 'La distribuzione delle anfore africane tra III e VII secolo', in Giardina (1986), 272–7.

[102] M. G. Fulford, 'Long distance trade', in Fulford and Peacock (1984), 255–75.

[103] Wickham 1989: 140–51.

5. *Shrinking Technology*

In Italy archaeological exploration of this period is still in its beginnings, but such as they are the findings of archaeologists give an impression of simplified housing, a reduced standard of living, and of more basic technology. It may well be that little technological knowledge had been altogether lost. It is clear however that many skills which had been very widespread, and had been applied to many types of building in Italy in the classical period, were now only found in a few localities, and employed almost exclusively in the service of the Church.[104]

Houses whether urban or rural were generally built of wood, with their roofs supported on posts and/or low dry stone foundations. Houses of this kind, if built by craftsmen, can be as functional and comfortable as those of stone, but they certainly require a narrower range of building skills. It has been suggested that stone quarries and quarrying techniques did not continue in use in Italy beyond the sixth century, presumably if building-stone was needed it could be taken from the building of earlier times. Medieval quarrymen had to start from scratch. They used simpler techniques than those of classical times, and seem not to have rediscovered the technique of stone-cutting by horizontal trench. Bricks with Roman dimensions are found in use until the Lombard period, that is until around the end of the sixth century.[105] Medieval bricks have different measurements (1 ft × 1/2 ft) and appear in the ninth century. They seem to mark a new start in brick building.[106]

As we have seen fine pottery disappeared from many parts of Italy.[107] In the North this was not replaced by new locally manufactured ware. Regional pottery used pre-Roman techniques. The quantity of pottery in use was reduced very substantially, and so has the number of functional forms. Sometimes bowls and plates of pottery were replaced by 'testi', large flat pottery plates made at home, also by wooden tableware. Elsewhere in the North soapstone vessels reappeared and their manufacture developed into a fine craft. In many regions such skills as making of slips and glazes seem to have been lost. Early medieval documents refer to manorially manufactured pottery. Specialist centres of metal production disappeared, together with the distinction between miners and smiths. In the tenth century, metal-working was a craft performed by

[104] See P. Galetti, 'Le tecniche costruttive fra VI e X secolo', in Francovich and Noyé (1994), 467–77; Parenti 1994: 479–96.

[105] Is the explanation that ancient brick manufacture was carried out, not as a cottage industry, but by large units of production whose viability ultimately depended on the orders of great imperial building schemes?

[106] Parenti 1994: 487–9; Mannoni 1989: 152–5.

[107] See Arthur and Patterson 1994: 409–40.

peasants on estates.[108] There appears to have been a breakdown and dispersal of glass-making, bronze-working, and iron-working industries. All became small-scale quasi-domestic activities.[109]

Vessels in glass, wood, and soapstone, were not necessarily functionally worse than their ceramic predecessors. But as the plants producing them were small and family run, the advantages of large-scale specialized production had been lost. Blowing of glass, working of iron, bronze, or gold on a domestic scale were widespread. Water power came to be used to work a lathe to hollow out soapstone ware. This was an important technological innovation. Perhaps the outstanding change was not so much the loss of technology, as the end of its application to specialized production for the market. What was lost, at least for the time being, was the possibility of distributing the production of specialized craftsmen for sale over a wider area.[110] Few techniques were actually lost altogether. But for various reasons, cultural and economic,[111] there was very much less demand for them, with the result that very much fewer craftsmen were able to make a living. In fact they ceased to be available in most parts of Italy, for most kinds of employers and customers.

6. *The Credibility of Field Survey Evidence*

The pattern of declining rural settlement, decline of trade, and decline of population outlined in this chapter is largely based on the findings of field surveys rather than of excavation. This introduces a significant amount of uncertainty, because the dating of Late Roman sites is to a very large extent dependent on finds of African fine red ware and therefore distorted by variations in the volume of imports of African fine slip-ware which is used to date sites. This can be vividly illlustrated from the Albenga Valley-Ager Cosanus survey. This investigation found what appeared to be a marked decline in occupied sites in the course of the third century, a decline which was however almost completely reversed in the course of the fourth. But they also found that many of the 'new' fourth-century sites not only contained fourth-century pottery, but second-century pottery as well. In other words they were not new at all. Their continued existence through the third century had merely not been picked up by the survey. The archaeologists attribute the absence of evidence of third-century occupation of these sites to the fact that altogether relatively little African

[108] V. Fumagalli, 'Strutture materiali e funzioni dell'azienda curtense. Italia del nord: sec VIII–XII', *Archeologia Medievale*, 7 (1980), 21–30.

[109] Francovich 1989: 157–71, esp. 70–1.

[110] Mannoni 1989: 153.

[111] See the discussion with the school of Carandini in Wickham 1994: 89–97.

red slip-ware of the mid-third century reached the area. This they think would have been a natural consequence of certain known problems affecting production in Africa. In other words, imports of pottery had declined for a few decades because during this time few pots were being produced, and not because there had been a sharp decline in demand, as a result of a reduction in the number of potential customers.[112]

If a temporary crisis in the production and trading of African pottery could result in a field survey producing misleading results in the third century, the fifth and sixth centuries offer plenty of scope for the same kind of error. For just as the number of sites identified in field surveys declines throughout the fifth and sixth centuries, so does the volume of imported pottery from around AD 450. From that point, the continuing reduction in the quantity of datable material must mean that, increasingly, occupied sites escape identification, and this necessarily exaggerates our estimates of abandoned sites. Our perception of decline is further distorted by the fact that African red slip-ware was increasingly limited to coastal areas. Locally produced substitutes for the lost imports appear in some regions. For instance a globular bodied, strap-handled jug, of a coarse, pale grey ware, on some sites takes the place of African red slip-ware for dating purposes in the fifth and sixth centuries. But for the following century many regions of Italy have produced practically no material at all that archaeologists can date—at least at the time of writing. Occupation which produced pottery that cannot be dated, simply does not register. In these conditions if archaeology has produced no data, this is presumably often due not to a total lack of people, but to the absence of datable pots.[113]

So it is evident that the results of field surveys not supported by excavation are to a significant degree misleading.[114] Are they therefore worthless, and to be discounted? The answer is 'no', and for the following reasons. First of all, the falling number of sites was a long-term trend, a consequence of the progressive concentration of landownership, and it can

[112] Chronological pattern of supply of African red slip-ware to various sites around western Mediterranean: L. Fentress and P. Perkins, 'Counting African Red Slip Ware', *L'Africa Romana* 5, Atti del V Convegno di Studio (Sassari, 1987), 205–14. Quantity of pottery found in Albenga valley traced chronologically against number of sites registered: F. Cambi and E. Fentress, 'Villas to castles: First millennium demography in the Albenga valley', in Randsborg (1989), 74–86, relevant p. 74, fig.1. See also M. Millet, 'Pottery: Population or supply patterns, the *agger tarraconensis* approach', in Barker and Lloyd (1991), 18–26.

[113] For the history of pottery imports, esp. into Italy, see C. Panella, 'Le merci: Produzioni, itinerari e destini', in Giardiana (1986), 431–59. On the substitute pottery, see Cambi and Fentress 1989: 80; Arthur 1994: 412–14. Increase of painted ware at San Giovanni di Ruoti during 5th cent.: Small and Buck 1994: 120, table 5.

[114] A classical case is Mattingly and Hayes 1992: 408–18: Leveau's field survey had suggested 5th-cent. decline, subsequent excavation proved remodelling of oil production for large-scale exports.

be shown to have begun many years before the large-scale import of African pottery. It was one of the consequences of the Empire. After the cessation of pottery import from Africa the distribution of the substitute wares confirms, in at least some regions, the reduced rural settlement suggested by the surveys. When evidence resumes, the pattern of settlement had been transformed, and in many parts of Italy the whole rural environment also. So it is certain that during the years in which field surveys register a reduction in the number of rural sites a radical upheaval was indeed going on in the countryside.

Moreover when mapped chronologically, the disappearance of rural sites revealed by field surveys can be shown to be a recognizable process. Successive maps tell a story that makes sense in terms of local topography, and one that is different from region to region. The surveys reveal something that was really happening, the scale of which however depended on local conditions.[115] Then, the 'model' of the emptying countryside is not entirely dependent on African pottery. The chronology of excavated villas, and even of visible remains, have made a contribution to the general picture.

It must also be remembered that first the shrinking, and later the ending of pottery-imports, are themselves indicators of profound economic change. Not only did imports from overseas come to an end, trade links broke down inside Italy itself.[116] Furthermore the appearance, at whatever date, of large empty spaces in what had been built-up areas points to economic or demographic decline or to both. Again the fact that building largely reverted from stone and brick to wood and wattle and clay suggests that living conditions had changed quite fundamentally.

7. *Fall in Population*

If we look at the changes in town and country together it is clear that they have one thing in common: the appearance of large areas of empty space. In cities, centres tended to decay and inhabitants preferred to live on the periphery, so that houses now tended to cluster around churches or near the gates, with large empty spaces, sometimes covered with black earth and farmed, occupying the old centre. In the countryside there was a dramatic reduction in the number of inhabited sites. It is hard to avoid the conclusion that Late Antiquity from the third century onwards witnessed

[115] See the maps produced by the Albegna survey in Attolini *et al.* 1991: 142–52, figs. 1–7; and for later developments Cambi and Fentress 1989: figs. 2–6. The Tarraconensis survey made allowance for variations in pottery supply, and still registered a decline in settlements. See Millett 1991; Carreté, Keay, and Millett 1995: 273–82.

[116] Balzaretti 1996: 213–34; Wickham 1994: 105 n.13.

a long and continuous fall of population in large parts of Italy and probably also in many of the provinces of the West.[117]

This itself needs an explanation. Jones's theory of excessive taxation making it impossible for the peasants to feed their children will not do. It cannot account for the fact that in the East, where taxes were surely collected more efficiently, the population actually continued to rise from the third to the middle of the sixth century. The fact that in the course of the fifth century Italy ceased to benefit from the taxes of Africa and other areas of the Empire certainly resulted in severe impoverishment—and must have greatly reduced the number of heads that could be fed in Italy. But the decline in population began more than a century before the collapse of the overseas revenue. It is likely that disease played a part even though we have no evidence that the inhabitants of Italy were aware of any deterioration in health compared with earlier times.

It has now been shown that the Plague in the reign of Marcus Aurelius *c.*AD 166–175 had a calamitous effect on the economy of many parts of the Empire, which lasted long after the end of the epidemic. In Egypt some villages show a great reduction in the number of taxpayers. Over the whole of the country there seems to have been a trough in money rents for land. In Rome itself there was a gap in inscriptions AD 166–181, and in the whole of Italy far fewer inscriptions were put up in these years than in previous decades. Public building declined steadily from AD 160–210. The years of the plague seem to have produced a fall in the production of dated bricks. A feature of the phenomenon is that disruption was regional, leaving some areas little affected. For instance none of the indications of regression can be documented in Africa.[118]

It has been argued that in more recent and better documented times, the effect of even calamitous outbreaks of plague has not had long-term consequences of the kind we are trying to explain in the Late Roman world. But in the case of the Black Death of 1348–50 rapid recovery was checked and reversed by repeated recurrences of the disease. In some areas the population was reduced to something like half of what it had previously been, and it was not before *c.*1460 that we have evidence of persistent recovery. Moreover the effects of later outbreaks of plague in Western Europe appear to have lasted much longer in the country than in towns, as heavy urban mortality was very soon compensated by heavy immigration from the countryside, leaving the countryside under-populated.[119] After the Black Death the survivors adapted to the reduced

[117] Wickham 1989: 145–6 is unconvincing. After all, the contrast between the abundance of finds around AD 200 and the extreme scarcity around AD 600 is massive and established all over Italy.

[118] Duncan Jones 1996: 108–36.

[119] J. Bolton, 'The world upside down: Plague as an agent of social change', in Ormrod and Lindley

population and benefited from the fact that the agricultural resources now had to feed fewer mouths.[120] But there is no evidence at present that the peasants or anybody else benefited from the reduction in the number of mouths to feed as a result of the plague in the second half of the sixth century in Italy, or even in Anatolia. There was nothing like the 'perpendicular' building boom.

So analogies from the history of the Black Death need not deter us from constructing a disease-based model to account for what available evidence suggests was a large reduction in the population of Italy. The Antonine plague, followed as it was in the second quarter of the third century by the prolonged crisis of the Empire, set up a chain reaction resulting in a long-term decline of population. Conceivably the recovery of the fourth century was not of sufficiently long duration to repair the damage of the third. Subsequently, barbarian invasions and the end of the *annona* in the first half of the fifth century hit many parts of the Empire very hard indeed. Then from the mid-sixth century bubonic plague returned and became endemic, and significantly reduced the population in many lands around the Mediterranean. The extent of its effect is still controversial even for the East, and very much more so for the West. The disease was—and is—undoubtedly both deadly and extremely infectious, though its spread is limited by the fact that it is carried by lice who are in turn parasitic on rats.

The balance of evidence that there was a fall in population is to my mind at present overwhelming. That the disease was among the causal factors is likely. But it is unlikely to have been the only factor. After all this was a period of fundamental change. An empire fell. The whole way of life and thought were transformed. The explanation of the demographic decline must take into account a whole range of factors interacting contemporaneously or in succession.

8. *Possible Explanations*

The developments discussed in this chapter must have complex causes. The transformation of the countryside clearly had its roots in the high imperial period. A plausible model, designed to explain what happened in the area around Cosa,[121] has a much wider application. A villa economy had been built up in this area specializing in large-scale viticulture with a view to producing wine for export. As the market for wine weakened, less

(1996), 17–78, esp. 29–33. J. De Vries 1984: 218: London lost 35,000 in 1625, the loss was made good by 1627. In 1630 Venice lost 40,000, within twenty years the city had returned to its normal level.

120 Bridbury 1973: 573–92, esp. 590–1.

121 E. Fentress, 'Cosa in the Empire: The unmaking of a Roman town', *JRA* 7 (1994), 208–22.

intensive forms of land use were introduced, with a consequent reduction of the farming population. Landownership came to be concentrated among the owners of a few extensive estates, with large areas probably given to pasture. The disappearance of small sites suggests that the working population was now concentrated in the estate centres. From the end of the third century, little African pottery came to Cosa. The port was and remained derelict. The Lombard period produced no distinctive pottery. The red painted ware of the south and the forum ware of late eighth- and ninth-century Rome did not come here. Eventually a number of *castella* appear in the area. Their establishment cannot be dated, but seems to be older than first documentary mention. It is suggested that the *castella* represent the remaining villas but moved to more convenient and defensible, and more evenly distributed sites.[122] One might generalize from the Cosa model to suggest that the establishment of a villa system, with enlarged farm units, worked by dependent labour whether slaves or tenants for absentee landlords, was a common consequence of Roman rule. This in itself would reduce the rural population, though the extent of any reduction would depend on circumstances. The Romans themselves worried about the effect of replacing free peasants by slaves. The villa system had the greatest potential for damage to the ecology if it employed slaves on the production of a single cash crop, as a rule wine or olive oil. For if this crop for some reason lost its market, the absentee owner might abandon the villa altogether, or replace cultivation by grazing. Either procedure would tend to empty the countryside of population and be destructive of the whole neighbourhood, town and country alike. If there were tenant farmers on the land, or the slaves achieved a tenant-like position, the effect would not be so bad: there would still be people on the land with an interest in working it for their own subsistence, and to pay their rent.

If the owner was not a member of the imperial nobility but a local grandee—or indeed if he was an imperial noble who lived in the city in whose territory the estate was situated—another development could occur: the owner might choose to transfer his principal residence from the city to his estate and to develop his lands into an economically self-sufficient unit. Where that happened, and there is evidence for it in the hinterland of Tarraco,[123] and probably also in other areas of Spain, and in the Gaul of Sidonius Apollinaris,[124] villas might continue to flourish, but they would do so at the expense of the cities.

[122] Cambi and Fentress 1989.

[123] Carreté, Keay, and Millett 1995: 16–18, table 1.1. nos. 40, 41, 76, 82–3, 84. S. Keay, 'The *ager tarraconensis* in the Late Empire: A model for the economic relationship of town and country in eastern Spain', in Barker and Lloyd (1991), 79–87, esp. 85.

[124] Harries 1994: 34–5: the fact that senatorial landowners had relatives and estates in several cities weakened their link with any particular one.

One might say that these self-sufficient villas were in some respects an alternative to the city. Large rural monasteries were in a similar position. Unlike the city of Tarraco in earlier times, the late villas of Tarraconensis do not appear to have served as market centres for long-distance trade: at any rate for most of the sixth century imported African amphorae and fine ware only reached villa sites in the neighbourhood of Tarraco itself. They no longer appear to have penetrated deeper into the country.[125]

If as seems to have been the case in Tarraconensis in the sixth century—and earlier in the territory of Cosa—the villa economy was based largely on pasturage, it would reduce the population of the surrounding countryside. This in turn damaged neighbouring cities. For it was difficult for a city to remain populated in a depopulating rural environment. As dense population favours disease, urban mortality particularly child mortality tended to be extremely high until very recent times, and urban populations everywhere had difficulty in reproducing themselves.[126] At any rate there is evidence that medieval cities could only keep up population by continued immigration from the country.[127]

The economic developments described in the previous paragraphs might be seen as a self-destructive mechanism built into the imperial Roman economy. They were long-term trends, working themselves out over centuries. But the slow trends were greatly accelerated by catastrophic events. First, the occupation of North Africa by the Vandals from AD 430 onwards deprived the senatorial nobility of the income from its African estates, and the city of Rome of its *annona*.[128] Subsequently, Italy as a whole would have been much poorer. In the course of the century life in Italy became steadily less secure. After Theoderic had for a while briefly reversed the trend, the war which Justinian waged to 'liberate' Italy from

[125] Carreté, Keay, and Millett 1995: 280.

[126] F. Röring, *The Medieval Town*, tr. D. Bryant (London, 1967), 113–15. In the Ancient World it is certain that Rome and Alexandria depended on sustained and heavy immigration from the country to keep up their population, see R. Sallares, *The Ecology of the Greek World* (London, 1991), 88–9. King Ptolemais tried to stop the country-folk from moving into Alexandria because the outflow was damaging agriculture, *Letter of Aristeas* 108–11. Of course smaller towns would have been healthier, but for an example of the superior health of the country: C. Matessi and P. Menozzi, 'Environment, population, size and vital statistics: An analysis of demographic data from 18th century villages in the province of Reggio Emilia (Italy)', *Ecology*, 60 (1979), 486–93.

[127] Bairoch 1991: 157: in pre-modern Europe the proportion of population living in the towns changed comparatively little. Urban and rural population tended to rise and fall together. On migration and urban mortality, see J. De Vries 1984: 179–97, discussing 'the law of urban natural decrease and its critics' from early modern evidence, concluding that mortality was after all the chief determinant of urban natural decrease.

[128] The imperial government's practice of moving huge amounts of tax-derived corn to feed Rome, and later Rome and Constantinople, as well as its armies, certainly had an enormous impact on the economy. So in Sicily the transporting of corn to Italy, esp. in the later Republic and under the Late Empire, favoured the expansion of the coastal at the expense of the inland cities. See M. Bell's review of R. J. A. Wilson's *Roman Sicily* in *JRA* 7 (1994), 371–82.

the Goths was long drawn out, and extremely damaging to both the cities and countryside. There were recurrent outbreaks of plague. Italy was not given a chance to recover. Before the physical damage caused by the war of liberation could heal came the destructive Lombard invasion, the division of Italy into Byzantine and Lombard zones. If the Lombards collected taxes, this has left no record in the sources. But possible benefits of freedom from taxation were negated by chronic war. The Byzantine zone was under military government, and taxes continued to be exacted.[129] But Byzantine Italy too suffered economic regression similar to that which took place in the regions occupied by the Lombards. In these circumstances a fall in the population was likely to occur. Mortality was surely high. People may even have found ways of limiting families.[130]

The model proposed in the previous paragraph cannot of course prove that by AD 600 the population of Italy had shrunk to a fraction of what it had been under the Early Empire. But it does mean that when the evidence for occupation, or rather the apparent fading out of such evidence, suggests that there were fewer people around, the proposition that a very considerable degree of depopulation had taken place should not be rejected out of hand.

9. *The Effect on the People of Italy*

The present author is unable to avoid the conclusion that Italy as a whole was very much poorer in AD 600 than it had been in, say, AD 400. The fact that housing becomes much more inaccessible to archaeology in both town and country suggests prima facie that there was less of it. The general turning from stone and brick to wood as principal building material suggests impoverishment, and the reduction in the size of houses and the prevalence of earthen floors confirms the impression. Rural buildings in Tuscany that can be dated to around this period seem to have been wooden huts resembling the humble dwellings of the S. Giulia excavation at Brescia. The last villas were abandoned around the end of the sixth century.[131] This certainly did not mean that there no longer was a class of great landowners: history is full of evidence of their

[129] T. S. Brown 1984: 113–16.

[130] M. G. Maioli, 'Strutture economico-commerciali e impianti produttivi nella Ravenna byzantina', in *Storia di Ravenna*, cura di A. Carile, II.1 (Ravenna, 1991), 233–47. M. G. Maioli and M. L. Stopioni, *Classe e Ravenna fra terra e mare: Città-necropoli, monumenti* (Ravenna 1987), argue from archaeological evidence that the 'economy' of Ravenna collapsed after AD 600 and that after AD 650 trade was virtually non-existent. On family planning in Antiquity: Eyben 1980–1; that methods employed were more effective than has been assumed by ancient historians: Riddle 1991.

[131] Huts: M. Valenti in Brogiolo 1996: 83–91 and figs. 1–9. End of villas summarized by Brogiolo 1995: 107–9.

continued existence and power.[132] What the abandonment or transformation of villas—not only in Italy but also in Spain and Gaul—shows is that the landowners no longer could afford to live on the scale to which they had been accustomed. But that applied to everybody else too. This is a pessimistic view of the Italian development.

It is not universally held. La Rocca has argued that the phenomena which have been taken to be symptoms of deurbanization do not in fact have that significance. Burials within the wall indicate that areas of public land for which there now was no longer any other public use were assigned to burials. Areas of dark soil covering what had formerly been built upon represents a deliberate decision by some civic authority to give over land within the walls to food production. The reuse of material from older buildings indicates a shortage of building materials and can be taken as evidence that a significant amount of building was going on. She can of course also point to plenty of evidence that cities continued to function as secular and/or centres of administration.[133] To some extent this discussion about continuity or lack of continuity in the history of cities of Italy—and elsewhere—in the migration period turns on how one chooses to define a city. If in order to be considered a city an inhabited locality must have a population of at least, say, 8,000, or even only half as many, a significant number of inhabitants involved in trade and/or manufacture, and some monumental public buildings, most of the Roman cities of Italy ceased to be cities. On the other hand, if it is born in mind that many of these places remained centres of ecclesiastical and secular government, and that as fortresses they continued to dominate warfare, and that from the later eighth century the old Roman sites, especially in the north of Italy, witnessed a striking urban revival, it would seem more useful to stress continuity than discontinuity.[134]

Wickham argues that the actual changes to the economy were not as drastic as the archaeology would suggest.[135] The results of field surveys are vitiated by the inability at present of archaeologists to date Dark Age material. The cessation of spectacular building has cultural rather than economic causes.[136] Building was no longer used as a rhetoric of power. When it ceased to be so used by kings, private individuals ceased to display their power through architecture also. Such display as there con-

[132] At most there was an anarchic interlude in the later 6th and early 7th cent. before a rural hierarchy was re-established, see M. Valenti in Brogiolo 1996: 97–9.

[133] La Rocca Hudson 1986: 31–78, 1989: 721–8.

[134] On motivation of scholars of different nationalities taking part in this controversy, see B. Ward-Perkins, 'Urban continuity?', in Christie and Loseby (1996), 4–17.

[135] Wickham 1994: 99–118 relevant 113–15. The chapter is an updated version of Wickham 1989, which also appeared as 'L'Italia e l'alto medioevo', *Arqueologia Medievale*, 15 (1988), 105–24.

[136] Cf. Carver 1993.

tinued to be was expressed not in the external expressiveness of architecture, but in the richness of internal furnishings of churches, in mosaics and hangings. Fine cloths were coming to be more important for kings than good bricks. Kings when they built again after AD 650 built on much smaller scale than they could have done. Pope Hadrian I built the relatively small S. Maria in Cosmedin (still very reasonably sized), but he also re-roofed S. Peters, a huge task. That there was much poor building and decoration was not due to disappearance of skills, but to a very much reduced number of skilled craftsmen.[137] He concludes that neither kings nor their subjects were as poor as the remains of their buildings might suggest, and that town and country had more people than archaeologists have been able to find evidence for. Finally he argues that the collapse of the Roman system, the humbling of the imperial governing class and the breakdown of taxation benefited the peasants, who were now significantly better off than before.

These propositions leave much room for debate. As we have seen the evidence for the depopulation of the countryside is indeed overwhelmingly built on field surveys, and there is no doubt that the evidence of field surveys alone, without confirmation by excavation, is to a significant degree misleading.[138] But as I have argued they must nevertheless reflect changes of fundamental importance in the social organization and economy of the Roman world. When more abundant evidence again becomes available rural settlement in many parts of Italy has been transformed. There had been a tremendous upheaval.

Of course these changes cannot be quantified. As for population, it is certain that there were far more people in Italy in the seventh century than have so far been found by archaeologists. Nevertheless it is difficult to believe that there had not been a very considerable reduction in population. A great fall in population need not mean that the population had become poorer. On the contrary the fact that fewer individuals shared the resources of the same territory might mean that they would enjoy greater resources per head than their predecessors. As we have seen, the Black Death of the fourteenth century, that reduced the population of Western Europe by perhaps as much as one-third or even one-half, left the survivors significantly wealthier than before, and numerous churches built or rebuilt in the fifteenth century witness to the prosperity of their donors.[139] But nothing of that kind is observable in later sixth- and seventh-century Italy. Quite the reverse. Moreover it is not very plausible to explain the radical simplification of life as a result of cultural change, as a deliberate change to a plain lifestyle. It is true that Christianity

[137] Wickham 1994: 102–4.
[138] See above, pp. 388–90.
[139] See above, pp. 391–2.

advocated contempt of material comfort, and also that Germanic traditions, including traditions of royal display and royal reward, had originated in a much poorer environment than that of the cities of the classic world. Christian asceticism and Germanic warrior ideology would certainly have helped people to come to terms with simplified conditions of life, if these were unavoidable. But I doubt whether they would induce people to choose such a radical simplification in the first place.[140]

It can be argued that to inhabit buildings of wood and wattle and clay instead of stone or brick, and to use vessels made of wood or stone or leather in place of pottery, and the replacement of a market economy by barter and self-sufficiency can be just as comfortable as the traditional Roman way of life; so that the transformation need not be seen as evidence of impoverishment. But it is only in terms of the Stoic concept of wealth, according to which a beggar is as rich as a king, provided he has the right sense of what is truly important, that Dark Age Italy can fail to be judged impoverished compared with classical Italy. In terms of standard of living as generally assessed today, that is in abundance of material possessions, Italy in the Dark Age was surely enormously poorer than it had been even in Late Antiquity. A time-travelling journalist voyaging from classical to late Late Roman Verona could have had no doubt that he was entering an impoverished society. A comparable but less extreme contrast would have been observed by a journalist travelling from West Germany to the communist East.

And this impoverishment was not simply a matter of the rich having to do without luxuries, while the mass of the population was as poor as ever, or perhaps even better off than before, because the powerful were no longer able to extort so high a proportion of production. This would only have been so, if the Roman economy had been totally inflexible, if the Roman cities had been *only* parasitic, and the Empire *simply* an instrument of exploitation. If that had been the case, the consequence would have been that if one section of society enlarged its share, the rest got just so much less, and it would be possible to argue that the destruction of the Empire, and the reduction of the cities, merely removed a burden.

This view was argued from different starting points by A. H. M. Jones and M. Finley. It was an important advance in its time. It drew attention to aspects of the ancient 'consumer cities' which had not been given sufficient attention, and which indeed differentiate them from 'the medieval city', and cities of more modern times. But the Jones–Finley

[140] Cf. G. Halsall, 'Towns societies and ideas: The not so strange case of Late Roman and Early Merovingian Metz', in Christie and Loseby (1996), 235–61, summed up 256: Forms of towns illustrate particular ideas, but these ideas can only be made manifest in certain social circumstances. Towns and settlement patterns generally are 'reflections in stone' of particular social hierarchies.

view is not the complete answer. It is clear that the Empire actually increased the distributable wealth, so that for instance both taxpaying Africa and tax-receiving Italy became more prosperous through being part of the Roman system. The growth of the Empire extended urbanization and it is likely, though difficult to prove, that the creation of a network of cities led to an increase in wealth. 'Merchant's Houses' are not nearly as conspicuous in Classical as in medieval towns, but the large mansions of Pompeii offered space also to traders and craftsmen, in the shops on the street front. Moreover a close examination of the painted decoration of the houses shows not only steadily growing prosperity but also the spreading of painted wall decorations from the houses of the rich to those of the relatively poor.[141] Painted wall decorations are not edible, but they nevertheless raise the quality of life. The same is true of stone walls, paved floors, public drains, and also the possibility of moving food products over large distances. But if the imperial economy in this way raised the standard of living of very large numbers of people, it is inevitable that the collapse of the whole system had the opposite effect and proved a disaster for very many. The decline of the Roman system in Italy was more gradual and from a higher level than in say northern Gaul; but what happened in Italy in the second half of the sixth century, and in Anatolia in the seventh, was not so very different from what happened at and around Metz, in what is now Lorraine, between AD 388 and 450.[142]

[141] Wallace-Hadrill 1994: 149–74, the downward diffusion of wall decoration (ibid. 169).

[142] G. Halsall, 'The Merovingian period in north east Gaul, transition or change?', in J. Bintliff and H. Hameron, *Europe between Antiquity and the Middle Ages*, BAR Int 617 (Oxford, 1995), 348–57, esp. figs. 2–3; also Halsall 1995. It is significant that at Metz rapid decline seems to have set in after AD 388, that is the defeat of the usurper Maximus and the subsequent running down of the Roman administration in that area.

13

Summary and Conclusions

The city is an aspect of Greco-Roman civilization about which we have an abundance of information. But the nature of the evidence changes over the years in step with the transformation of the cities, and the changing character of the evidence itself throws light on the changing character and ethos of the cities. This is particularly true of the epigraphic evidence since the evolution of the epigraphic habit closely reflects both the depoliticization and the Christianization of the city. This is the subject of the first chapter.

The book is structured around the antithesis of East and West, that is roughly speaking of the Greek- and Latin-speaking regions of the Empire, or what is more or less the same, the territories governed by the Western emperor as long as there was a Western emperor, and the territories governed from Constantinople. This might seem an arbitrary division in a study that is concerned with cities and not primarily with literature or imperial administration, but I think that the developments themselves justify the procedure. Cities in the East did develop differently from cities in the West, even though in important respects the difference was a matter of timing. East and West still formed part of a single cultural zone, but they did not evolve at the same pace.

Cities take their character from their physical appearance, above all the architecture, and the arrangement, variety, and numbers of their buildings. This is obviously true of the classical cities, whose ruins have inspired architects for century after century. In the East cities retained large populations and monumental civic centres for much longer than in the West. But even in the East urban development was not monolithic. In Anatolia urban decline began in the middle of the sixth century, perhaps even earlier. In Syria, Palestine, and Jordan cities flourished demographically as well as monumentally longer than in Anatolia; and in Palestine and Jordan urban prosperity continued beyond the Arab conquest, and at least until the end of the Umayyad dynasty around AD 750. From around AD 750 developments in the urban system, which had begun earlier, become unmistakable, and cities are seen to decline in Jordan and Syria, and to grow in Mesopotamia. But even so the Near East as a whole remained urbanized in a way Anatolia did not.[1]

[1] Chapter 2, sections 2–3.

In the West the classical city in its full glory did not survive beyond the third century. After that cities in the Western provinces shrank—to a greater or lesser degree—in area and population. Generally speaking there was little attempt to conserve classical secular monumentality. The general appearance of the cities became very much more utilitarian, while the prominence of the cathedral and other churches among humble houses and ruins asserted the power of the Church and Christianity. Of course there was variation from region to region. As a general rule cities nearer to the Mediterranean remained larger, and more classical, longer than those inland.[2]

Common to East and West was the running down of curial government, and its replacement by a much less tangible and less clearly defined form of oligarchy. Following A. H. M. Jones I have described the new oligarchs as notables. In the East rule of notables was formally recognized in legislation of the emperors Anastasius and Justinian. In the West formal responsibility of the decurions for the administration of their city lasted longer; but eventually there too notables came to be in charge, or at least to represent the secular aspect of urban authority, operating together with the count who represented the king, and with the bishop who in times of crisis often proved himself the real leader of his city.[3] The bishop's role in civic government was something quite new and unclassical. The position which he eventually achieved had not been sought by either Church or state; it had evolved as secular government in the city weakened, leaving a vacuum. The bishop became an influential figure in civic administration in the East earlier than in the West, but it was in the West that episcopal power was of longer duration, and of much greater historical significance.[4]

Voluntary financing of public building, baths, games, and other civic services had been a characteristic of the competitive politics of the classical city. This tradition ended, or came near to ending, in the late Late Roman city. In the East almost all civic expenses were now met out of specifically assigned revenues. In the much smaller cities of the West there was much less need for civic expenditure. Municipal welfare facilities were replaced by charitable giving, which was administered by the Church, whose preachers week in and week out proclaimed the Christian duty of helping the poor.[5] Public shows, that is theatrical performances and chariot races, continued in very many cities in the East. They were now organized, financed, and staffed by the so-called factions, Empire-wide contracting organizations which drew most of their income from taxation. The factions operated in the West too, but there games were regularly held in only a small number of cities, at Rome, in the imperial

[2] Chapter 2, section 5. [3] Chapter 3. [4] Chapter 4. [5] Chapter 5.

residence of Ravenna, at Carthage, and perhaps at Milan. Public shows might be produced elsewhere too, but only occasionally, and at the special request of the ruler.[6]

The classical city represented a way of life which had been transmitted from generation to generation among the better-off by a lengthy and largely standardized,[7] literature-based course of education. The majority, who did not go to school, were initiated into the common culture by the festivities of the religious calendar, and by the public entertainments which were more often than not linked to religion. In the course of Late Antiquity both education and religion were transformed. Two factors were involved: the decline of civic educational institutions and Christianization. The decline of educational institutions started in the West earlier than in the East. From the fifth century,[8] Christianization advanced in both halves of the Empire at the same rate. The Church gradually introduced its calendar of Christian festivals, which in due course replaced the pagan calendar. The educational system was not so directly affected, because the Church was very slow to establish schools of its own. Christianization was a gradual process, but in the long term its consequences were enormous.

In the cities of the East the classical authors retained their prestige and exemplary function, in spite of its pagan character, until well into the reign of Justinian, that is the middle of the sixth century. Then subordination of traditional educational values to those of Christianity came very rapidly—certainly well before the collapse of urbanism in Anatolia.[9] Secular training in the higher literacy for sons of the leading families, and a more modest education for those lower in the social scale, continued up to the crisis of the seventh century, and in some places, above all at Constantinople, beyond that.

In the West the weakening of traditional institutions of the shrinking and impoverished cities, and the imposition of a new ruling class of Germanic warriors, which had no traditions of reading or writing, led to a decline in educational opportunities from the early fifth century. Eventually the range of literacy in society was greatly reduced. It became a specialist skill, whose propagation was left to the professional group for whom it remained an essential qualification, the clergy. The secular traditions transmitted through classical authors, history, and mythology ceased to provide the ideological bonds of society.[10] Their place was taken by the

[6] Chapter 6.
[7] Standardized by cultural conformity, not by public authority.
[8] For most of the 4th cent. the East was more strongly Christianized than the West.
[9] Chapter 7.
[10] Chapter 10.

Bible and the Lives of martyrs and saints. The crucial period in the West as in the East was the mid-sixth century, 'the age of Justinian'.

The downgrading of secular traditions, we can be sure, helped to undermine the political foundations of the Empire. It was not the only change in the realms of 'mentality' to contribute to that effect. From very early times, when the original classical cities had existed as independent states, each Greco-Roman city generated its own civic patriotism, and closely related to this the concept of citizenship, which could be defined as the complex of privileges, rights, and duties possessed by any inhabitant who enjoyed full membership of his civic community. This concept, and the sentiments associated with it, were gradually undermined by the incorporation of the cities into the larger units of the Hellenistic kingdoms, and ultimately into the Roman Empire. By Late Antiquity city patriotism had become a very weak emotion, and no sense of active loyalty to the Roman state, of which most inhabitants of the Empire were now citizens, had developed to replace it. Roman citizenship came to mean very little when almost everybody was a Roman citizen. The relative unimportance of Roman citizenship no doubt helped the barbarian military federates and settlers in cities and countryside to coexist peacefully with the Roman population. On the other hand, the weakness of citizenship, or if you like its shrinking to a cultural preference, was an important aspect of the profound demilitarization of the inhabitants of the Empire. This does not of course mean that the inhabitants of the Empire would never defend house and home when these were under attack. But what was important was that they could no longer be easily mobilized to fight on behalf of emperor and Empire. It was that which in the last resort made it impossible to keep invaders even from their homes and houses.

At the same time the fact that the mass of the population of the provinces, and even its social leaders, felt very little obligation to the Roman state, its institutions and its emperor, assisted growth of alternative loyalties, most significantly the 'ethnogenesis' of barbarians groups manoeuvring or settling within the borders of the Empire in the West.[11]

[11] See Chapter 11 above, more fully Wolfram 1987; Heather 1991and 1996; and my own view on the ethnogenesis of Alaric's Goths, Liebeschuetz 1990*a*: 75–8. On 'demilitarization', Michael Whitby 1995: 61–124 argues that the Eastern Empire had no significant recruiting problem. To my mind the military history, especially of the exceptionally fully reported campaigns of Justinian in Italy, and later the Eastern Empire's inability to defend its eastern and Balkan territories at the same time, and its inability to recover from defeat in battle, show that it was unable to mobilize its resources of manpower adequately. In AD 586 Maurice found it extremely difficult to recruit troops to defend the Balkans (Michael Syr. X.21, p. 362). In AD 589 recruiting for the Balkans caused a rebellion in Armenia (Sebeos, *Histoire de Héraclius*, tr. F. Macler, ch. 10, Theophylact III.8.5–8), cf. Michael Whitby 1988: 147. At the time of his fall Maurice was preparing to settle Armenian families in the Balkans in the hope that *they* would defend their land (Sebeos, ch. 20). The contrast with Hannibalic war could not be greater. The contrast demonstrates demilitarization.

In the East the framework of imperial administration survived much longer than in the West, though it is clear that ideological support for emperor and Empire was very weak. Neither the Persian war, nor the Arab invasion of the Eastern provinces produced lengthy sieges. With a few exceptions cities quickly came to terms with the invader.[12] Subsequently the provincials soon became reconciled to Muslim rule. Apparently they did not yet feel, as the inhabitants of Anatolia were to feel not so many years later, that they were defending Christian cities against the enemies of God, and that resistance was a religious duty, which would be rewarded in heaven.[13] In many ways the response to invaders of the provinces of the East after AD 600 was similar to that of the inhabitants of Gaul or Spain after AD 400.

When the Empire collapsed outside Anatolia, the factors which had favoured ethnogenesis in the West encouraged Arabization. The settlement of large numbers of outsiders on former territories of the Empire, and the absorption of the Romans into the fellowship of their conquerors only happened from the seventh century onwards,[14] but the disintegration of traditional unities had begun earlier. Urban populations came to be split between followers of the Blues and those of the Greens.

The schism between adherents and opponents of the decisions of the Council of Chalcedon created (or perhaps only reflected) tension between the imperial authorities at Constantinople and the inhabitants of the oriental provinces. That the opponents of Chalcedon were themselves split between Monophysites in Egypt who had services in Coptic, and in Syria/Mesopotamia whose liturgy was Aramaic, was a further symptom of the breaking up of the unity that had been maintained in the Orient by the Empire. Religious group-building, and the antagonisms aroused by it, were not political in origin and intention, but they had far-reaching political consequences. On the eve of the great Persian invasion of AD 603 the East was in a very disturbed condition. Whether the origin of the instability was recent, and directly caused by the usurpation of Phocas, or whether it was structural, and had developed in the course of the previous century, is still the object of scholarly debate.[15]

The question is important because our understanding of the catastrophes inflicted on the Eastern Empire successively by Persians and

[12] e.g. Palmer 1990: 158–9 on surrender of cities in Mesopotamia.

[13] On the development of the idea, which was not yet as powerful as later, see Michael Whitby 1998*a*.

[14] There was earlier immigration from the Arab world across a fluid frontier, see for example B. Isaac, *The Limits of the Empire* (Oxford, 1990), 245–8.

[15] See Chapter 8. It is fashionable to play down the depth of the divisions caused by Chalcedon. To my mind the fact that first the Persians and then the Arabs strongly favoured the opponents of Chalcedon against the 'Melkites' strongly suggests that the division was politically important.

Arabs depends on the way it is answered. Explanations of the disaster in the East after AD 600—as of comparable disasters in the West after 400—fall into two categories: those involving 'assassination', that is explanations which stress barbarian invasions, and those which look for 'natural causes', that is signs of decay in basic institutions.[16] As far as the Roman Empire in the Near East is concerned, the case for 'assassination' has recently been restated extremely ably by M. Whittow.[17]

Essentially the argument is this. In AD 600 the Eastern Empire was economically and politically in as strong a position as it had been since the fourth century, though it did face a very difficult military problem whenever it had to fight simultaneously a now very powerful Persian Empire in the East and a formidable combination of Avars and Slavs in the West. Then disaster struck. The Empire found itself at war with Persia at a time when Phocas had recently deposed and murdered Maurice the legitimate emperor, and there was powerful and widespread opposition to his rule. In its divided state the Empire could not withstand Persian offensives, resumed year after year with quite unprecedented perseverance. The Near East was lost, Asia Minor devastated. Eventually the Empire did turn the tables on the Persians, but then it had to face the Arabs before it had recovered from the destruction and disorganization of the Persian war. So there could be no recovery. The cities of Asia Minor remained destroyed. The cities in Syria and Palestine survived to continue a process of evolution which had already transformed them into something very different from the classical city. In this view a decisive role is given to the almost accidental political constellation of the year AD 602.

This is not the position I have taken in this book, which is focused on a long-term trend, the change from government by decurions to government by notables. It is a principal thesis of the book that this change did make significant difference, both to the functioning of cities themselves, and to their ability to perform the administrative tasks on which the Empire depended. It is true that under the notables, the cities were governed by landed oligarchs, as they had been under decurions, but this element of continuity is not what was important. What made a difference was the radical transformation of the conditions in which the oligarchs now carried on the government. Instead of responsibility for the city being born by an assembly of formally appointed councillors, meeting and voting in public, it now rested with a vaguely defined, self-appointed group of magnates, making decisions and nominating officials in the privacy of the audience hall of one of the great houses. A transformation of the political atmosphere of the city is unmistakable. The magnates were

[16] Piganiol 1947: 422, with application to the West. [17] Whittow 1996.

no longer restrained from displaying their wealth and power by consideration for the feeling of their fellow citizens. They lived in great houses. They displayed titles of high imperial rank. They were addressed in language of self-abasement. Their social obligations were no longer seen in political terms, but as acts of Christian charity.[18] Individual notables had no formal responsibility for anything, neither for the conservation of the physical structure of their city, nor even for the well-being of its inhabitants. This surely was one factor—though not the only one—which made for radical change in the physical appearance of cities.

It has been noted that the late Late Roman cities in the East were evolving towards the model of the Islamic city which was characterized by the looseness of its structure, and the absence of corporate municipal institutions.[19] In the Arab city the coherent social unit was the quarter rather than the city as a whole. The various quarters were separated by walls and gates and had their own bazaar and baths, and the inhabitants of a quarter predominantly belonged to the same religion or religious sect, or had a common ethnic origin.[20] Although the coming into existence of self-sufficient quarters seems to have happened in Islamic times, it was a logical consequence of the disintegration of the city as a corporative body in later Late antiquity.

The great Arab historian and political theorist Ibn Khaldun (1332–1406) noted that in the Arab world civic self-government was the exception. Normally cities were governed by representatives of the ruler. When the ruling dynasty failed there ensued conflict between factions of magnates for leadership. The winner would then rule autocratically until the return of strong government at the centre put an end to local self-determination.[21] Something like this appears to have happened in the cities of the East in the later sixth century. In the absence of open politics the disputes of the civic grandees were more likely to result in riots and civic violence, as likely as not under cover of religious or factional rivalry. I have argued that it was in these circumstances, and because of them, that the inhabitants gave their allegiance to the Blues or to the Greens, and

[18] See P. Brown 1992: 152–6 which is focused on imperial power, but the change from politically motivated giving to Christian charity applied at every level of society.

[19] Stern 1970: 25–36; J. Aubin, 'Élements pour l'étude des agglomérations urbaines dans l'Iran mediéval', in A. H. Hourani and S. M. Stern (eds.), *The Islamic City*, Papers in Islamic History 1 (Oxford, 1970), 65–75. M. O. H. Carver, 'Transitions to Islam', in Christie and Loseby 1996: 184–211, on p. 188 cites G. von Grunebaum 1976: 144: 'The Muslim is a citizen of the umma, the people of Mohammed, but mere resident of his town'. It would follow that his loyalty was first to his family, second to his ethnic group/tribe, and then to Islam. The town itself, as a municipality, was not a significant concept.

[20] Sack 1989: 62.

[21] Ibn Khaldûn, *The Muqaddimah*, an Introduction to World History, I.21 read in translation of F. Rosenthal, edited and abridged by N. J. Dawood (London, 1967), 292–4. Fabián Estapé, *Ibn Jaldûn o el precursor*, Real Academia de Buenas Letras de Barcelone (Barcelona, 1993).

took sides for or against the Council of Chalcedon, or instigated witch-hunts of alleged pagans, or of Jews.

The imperial governors certainly could not bully notables as they had bullied decurions. For one thing they were never made collectively responsible for particular administrative tasks as decurions had been. Furthermore, the distinction between imperial officials and civic notables was blurred. The notables of different cities with their epithets of senatorial rank, however acquired and transmitted, had now coalesced into hierarchically graded provincial or regional aristocracies. Their highest ranking members—the Apions of Oxyrhynchus are by far the best known example—exercised power both in their home city and at Constantinople. The imperial authorities responded to this situation when it gave provincials the right to nominate individuals for the post of governor of their province. One might see in this innovation a positive step, in that it involved decentralization and provincial self-government. But in fact it delegated power to the new provincial aristocracies, and incidentally involved abandonment of a very old rule that no one was permitted to become governor of his native province. The change surely made it much more difficult for the authorities at Constantinople to enforce decisions that were disliked by leading provincials.[22]

I am not suggesting that the government had lost the capacity to collect taxes. There is plenty of evidence, especially from Egypt, that taxes continued to be collected, and even for the rate to be raised several times in the course of the sixth century.[23] I suspect that the administration's real problem will have been how to assert control of the revenue after it had been collected. Justinian complained that pagarchs, curiales, collectors of taxes, and above all governors were managing the business of tax collection in a way that was obscure to everybody else, but profitable to themselves.[24] Apart from its vulnerability to peculation, the late Late Roman financial organization was extremely inflexible. The tax revenue was assigned more or less permanently to particular areas of expenditure.[25] When the government faced a military emergency it must have been difficult to switch the revenue from its normal recipients to new military expenses.

The units of the army were now dispersed in garrisons over many cities. No doubt they were well entrenched there, and could count on support from influential people in the provincial administration or the Church to obstruct attempts to move them.[26] We have seen that it was evidently very

22 Chapter 3, section 3.

23 Rémondon 1965 is the key discussion. It seems that the Arabs were able to raise taxes very considerably.

24 *Ed* 13, *praef.*

25 Chapter 5, section 2.

26 Theophylact VII.3.1–10. I am suggesting that what happened at Asemus was not uncommon.

difficult to concentrate the various garrisons of Egypt into a single striking force.[27]

As cities became less useful to the imperial government for the purpose of collecting taxes and generally for mobilizing the resources of the provinces, the government ceased to use civic institutions for that purpose.[28] It has been argued that it was precisely the fact that the government ceased to rely on cities to raise revenue that caused their decline. I maintain that it was the other way round: it was the way that civic government had evolved that made cities less capable of providing the services the government needed. That was why the government had to find other instruments.

The changes so far discussed have been political. The nature of our evidence makes it much more difficult to observe changes in other areas. Whether or not Eastern cities began to decline in a demographic or economic sense well before AD 600 is still controversial. The view taken here is that a significant number of cities began to lose population around the middle of the sixth century or even earlier.[29] To the question how far—if at all—demographic and economic regression contributed to the disasters suffered by the Empire after AD 600, the evidence available now does not allow a definite answer.[30]

The question of the evolution of the economy is difficult. It is by no means certain that it makes sense to talk of the 'economy', rather than of a number of economic activities, each influenced by social factors specific to itself. It is difficult enough to make statements about the economic role of even prominent cities on the basis of available evidence. To establish trends in their economy is almost impossible. But arguments put forward to show that economic activity over the whole area was maintained at a peak level right up to the disasters of the early seventh century are not convincing. The precise implications of coin evidence are difficult to draw. Above all there are still far too few coin lists from far too few sites. The evidence of a small number of places from which we have a significant number of coins—and of the Egyptian papyri—is that the money

[27] See Chapter 8, sections 6 and 8. Note that Heraclius' desperate offensive against the Persians in AD 620–1 was preceded by the assembly of troops 'scattered over many parts of the earth', Theophanes, AM 6113(303), in *The Chronicle of Theophanes Confessor*, ed. C. Mango and R. Scott with assistance of G. Greatrex (Oxford, 1997), 436, derived from Geo. Pisid. *Exp. Pers.* II.55–6.

[28] See Chapter 3, section 3 and Chapter 5, section 6, and for the later arrangement: Haldon 1990: esp. 240 on the *kommerkiarioi*; also W. Brandes and J. Haldon, 'Town, tax and transformation: State, cities and their hinterlands in the East Roman world c. AD 500–800', in N. Christie, N. Gauthier, and G.-P. Brogiolo, *Towns and their Hinterlands between Late Antiquity and the Early Middle Ages* (Leiden, forthcoming).

[29] Chapter 2, section 2.

[30] Though plague is likely to have contributed to Justinian's difficulties in raising adequate armies in the later part of his reign.

economy was not in retreat in the sixth century, if anything the reverse was true. But there are places where the evidence of coins, such as it is, suggests that regression had set in. There are also vast areas from which we have no evidence at all. So it is likely enough that in some regions there was abundance of currency, both in copper and in gold, while in others the money-economy, and in fact all economic and social activity was in retreat.[31]

If there was some reduction in economic activity in the course of the sixth century, this should not necessarily be seen as a universal depression on the analogy of the economic depressions of modern times. Nor should we look for a common cause for each symptom of economic downturn. Local or regional depressions could be produced by a variety of factors: movement of troops, reduction in the pay of certain categories of troops, changes in the distribution of imperial expenditure, transfer by grandees of their principal residence to the countryside, the development of some cities at the expense of others, the impact of Constantinople on cities in surrounding areas of Asia Minor, and in Syria the deportation of very large numbers of inhabitants by the Persians. I have argued that generally speaking villages and cities flourished and declined together,[32] so that when catastrophe came it hit both alike. This does not preclude the possibility that in the course of later Late Antiquity large villages, or indeed monasteries situated in the territory of a city, did draw wealth and power from town to country.

Natural causes too are likely to have affected the development of cities, and indeed of the Empire. The plague certainly did.[33] The desert fringe was, as it still is, a difficult environment. In Late and in late Late Antiquity there had been an extraordinary development of agricultural and architectural activity on the desert fringe all over the Near East. This must have been vulnerable to climatic change. In these marginal lands even slight or temporary changes of climate could lead to failure of crops, famine, and disease. Now continuous tree-ring chronologies show exceptionally low tree-ring growth in widely separate regions of the world between AD 530 and 550, and perhaps even as late as 560.[34] It follows that this period was exceptionally unfavourable for plant-growth, and is likely to have produced a succession of poor harvests and famine.[35] It has

31 Against Whittow 1996: 60–1, I would insist that it is not enough to point out the undoubted continuity of copper coin finds without looking at the quantitative trend. On the alternative to use of money in a much later period, see Saradi 1995: 405–18.

32 Chapter 2, section 4.

33 See above, pp. 53, 391–2.

34 Baillie 1995: 91–107.

35 J. Koder, 'Climatic change in the fifth and sixth centuries?', in P. Allen and E. Jeffreys (eds.), *The Sixth Century End or Beginning*, Byzantina Australiensia 10 (Brisbane, 1996), 270–85; P. Farquharson, 'Byzantium, planet earth and the solar system', ibid. 263–9, esp. 266–7.

indeed been argued that deteriorating climatic conditions—supposedly a result of an enormous volcanic eruption on Krakatoa—were an important causal factor in the emergence of bubonic plague.[36] Whether this is right or not, there is no doubt that in the 540s the Empire suffered simultaneously both famine and plague, and the important province of Syria large-scale deportation of population as well. Plague and famine visited different parts of the Empire with different degrees of severity, and for different lengths of time. When the three scourges coincided in northern Syria the effect must have been cataclysmic. But elsewhere too, years of chronic famine followed by recurring episodes of plague are likely to have left lasting consequences.[37] The 540s do in fact mark a turning point in the reign of Justinian. His run of easy victories ended to be followed by defeat and many years of military deadlock. Large-scale building operations, whether secular or ecclesiastical, seem to have come to an end in many cities of Asia Minor, and to have been noticeably reduced in cities of Syria and Palestine, even in regions not devastated by the Persians. The years saw the systematic suppression of paganism, and a striking Christianization of culture. The coincidence of these developments with a seemingly endless succession of calamities is unlikely to be an accident.

It would however be wrong to try to explain social and economic change in the Near East entirely in terms of changing physical conditions. For instance, the Unesco Libyan Valley Archaeological Survey strongly suggests that the rise and fall of cultivation in the valleys in the Tripolitanian pre-desert—which of course largely preceded the sixth century—was not dependent on such factors. There is no evidence of significant long-term change in climate in this region, and the farmers of the desert fringe appear to have been able to cope with climatic contingencies quite successfully over centuries.[38] Many more local investigations like the Libyan Valley Survey are needed before economic decline in the East in the sixth century can be fully assessed and understood.

Late Antiquity and later Late Antiquity saw the Roman world transformed. This was a complex process involving many factors. But the most important single factor was surely the running down of the Empire. This is not surprising. The classical city as such was not a creation of the Roman Empire—though many of the provincial cities were. The Empire did however exploit the institutions of the classical city state for its own purposes; and it introduced cities of the classical type to areas that had not known them before. Furthermore, there is plenty of evidence that the

[36] Keys 1999: 7–23, the book of a television programme. The author argues for causal links between the eruption and practically every important event that happened in the 6th cent. But when allowances have been made, enough of his case is left to be important.

[37] The disasters will have both reduced the population and changed 'mentalities' and behaviour.

[38] Barker *et al.* 1996.

prosperity and visual magnificence of cities of the Empire owed very much to the imperial policy. Subsequently, the decline of the Empire greatly affected the cities. Britain was the first major territory to be separated from the Empire, and it was also the first to be deurbanized. The end of the *annona* possibly did more than any other factor to impoverish and diminish the cities of Italy.

Contemporary scholarship assigns greater importance to the commercial and manufacturing functions of ancient cities than has been assigned to them in the writings of Weber, Jones, and Finley.[39] But the economic activities of the inhabitants of cities were also to a very considerable extent dictated by the needs of the Empire, or impelled by the gradients of supply and demand created when taxes were collected in one region and expended in another. Developments, which to the modern observer may look like evidence of general economic recession, may well have been the result of the redirection of government activity. As we have seen, the decline of cities of Anatolia in the sixth century could have been produced by a variety of causes, but most of them are directly related to imperial policy.[40]

It was an essential characteristic of the Greco-Roman city that it comprised both a built-up urban centre and a rural territory which was administered and controlled from the centre. This was something which the Roman imperial authorities had found particularly useful, since it gave them administrative machinery to collect taxes in the countryside. The transformation of the classical city in many regions involved the breaking up of this unity. A number of factors were involved. In the West the territory might be settled by barbarians, or the leaders of society might move their principal residence into the country.[41] But a development which loosened the ties between city and territory all over the West was the breakdown of the imperial city-based system of taxation. In the East imperial taxation did not break down, but the government ceased to rely on cities for its collection.

The effect of imperial policy might be indirect and far from the intentions of the imperial government. So the decline and fall of curial government was a consequence of the increased pressure on decurions by the imperial administration of the Late Empire, as well as of the new opportunities for social advancement offered by the enlarged civil service. Even more striking was the long-term effect of the conversion of Constantine. When Constantine became a Christian he was not thinking about the effect his action would have on the cities of the Empire. The eventual

[39] e.g. Parkins 1997.
[40] See above, p. 409.
[41] But in Italy the territorial leaders remained town-dwellers.

effect was nevertheless very great. In fact Christianity became an important independent factor for change. Christian institutions, teachings, and ideals developed independently of imperial policy, and their evolution followed a logic of its own. The Christian religion created the cult of martyrs, hermits, monasteries, and parishes with village priests. It also provided the individual believer with a vision of the good life made up of personal asceticism, charitable giving to the poor, and Bible-based education, which cumulatively was quite non-political and yet at the same time revolutionary in effect. Christianity transformed the appearance of cities and villages, as well as the relations between them, and the way in which their inhabitants lived. But the Church could not have attained the overwhelming position it eventually achieved, if it had not been in close alliance with emperors since Constantine, and later with the rulers of the successor kingdoms in the West.

Empire continued to have an impact on cities when it ceased to be Roman. After the Arabs had conquered Syria, the most flourishing cities were found inland, notably Aleppo, Damascus, and Homs (Emesa). All the cities on or near the coast, Antioch, Seleucia, Laodicea, Tyre, Berytus, Caesarea lost in importance. In other words there was a change of direction in the political and economic life of Syria and Palestine: instead of facing towards the Mediterranean, the inhabitants of the region had to build up relationships with the inland territories to the east and north-east. The region had ceased to be part of a Mediterranean empire, and had become part of an imperial complex stretching far into the East. Later when the Arab capital was moved to Baghdad, the transfer of government produced a widespread recession in town and country in inland Syria and Palestine also.

The argument that the Empire was the most powerful factor affecting the transformation of cities has an element of circularity, because the so-called cities of the Roman world were precisely the settlements recognized and defined as cities by the imperial government and used by the imperial administration for its own purposes. So whatever happened to the Empire was bound to have a powerful impact on the settlements promoted by it to perform much of its business of administration. On the other hand, it is a priori likely, and on the whole confirmed by such evidence as we have, that the places recognized as cities by the Empire were natural regional centres. Subsequently, the consequences of having been chosen by the Empire for good or ill overshadowed the factors which had originally caused these particular places to be regionally outstanding.

It will nevertheless not do to treat the vicissitudes of the Empire as the only factor that made for change in cities. For one thing the influence was not all one way. The inhabitants of cities, and of villages too, tried to manipulate the Empire to their advantage. Inhabitants of ordinary provincial cities saw the wealth that was drawn to provincial capitals, and it is likely that pressure from cities was one of the reasons for the multiplication of provincial capitals by the repeated subdivision of provinces. Similar motives led villages to press for city status which in late Late Antiquity was increasingly signalled by the presence of a bishop. So we have the paradox that the decline of the classical city was in many regions paralleled by an increase in the number of cities. A. Dunn has put forward a theory of 'disaggregation' of urban functions to account for the appearance of new fortified centres, and the shrinking or disappearance of classical cities in Thrace and Macedonia. He argues that the functions that had been performed by the classical cities came to be shared out between a larger number of smaller settlements.[42] This model may be of wider application. The developments in Thrace and Macedonia have parallels in the foundation of fortified settlements on hill tops elsewhere in the Balkans, in northern Italy, and in Spain. But all were surely to a considerable degree a response to growing insecurity resulting from the breakdown of the Empire.

The development of cities was influenced in important ways by factors, whose detailed working is obscure to us, though their overall effect is clear enough. Classical cities looked remarkably similar wherever in the Empire they were situated. But the classical pattern had in many places been superimposed, whether by compulsion or voluntarily, on an older regional organization, which it did not totally supersede, and which continued to make its influence felt. So it is evident that the 'third century' and the Diocletianic reorganization changed the cities in the West far more profoundly than those in the East. In the West the classical model had a stronger hold on cities around the Mediterranean than on cities situated away from the Mediterranean to the north or west. These differences can surely only be explained in terms of the interaction of the cities in different regions with their respective regional environments. Similar issues are raised by a comparison of the development of cities in the north and the south of Italy. The cities of the south were older. But in our period the cities of the north proved themselves stronger than all but a small number of southern cities. Why was that?

In the East too the decline of the classical city was not proceeding at the same pace everywhere. Regression in Tripolitania began much earlier than in Anatolia, and in Anatolia before it did in Syria, Palestine, and Arabia. The putting up of public inscriptions, the embellishment of the cities with secular buildings and with monumental colonnades, even the

[42] The very interesting Dunn 1993, 1994, 1997 and elsewhere forthcoming.

building of churches, continued longer in Syria, Palestine, and Arabia than it did in Anatolia.[43] It is true that Northern Syria suffered terrible damage at the hands of the Persians, but the rebuilding of Antioch and Apamea after destruction, and the repeated resumption of building activity on the northern plateau shows that Syrian society had considerable resilience, at least up to AD 600.[44]

The conclusion that in Syria, Palestine, and Arabia town and country were more vigorous than in Anatolia might be thought an illusion, resulting from the accidental fact that the desert fringe of Syria and Palestine happens to have more, and better preserved, archaeological remains than the Anatolian plateau, and the coastal plain of western Asia Minor. But it is more likely that the impression is correct: after all in the ensuing centuries city organization did prove considerably more robust in Syria/Palestine than in Anatolia, where the classical city network did collapse remarkably quickly in the seventh century. I have argued that the cities of Anatolia began to decline while those in Syria Palestine and Arabia were still flourishing. How are we to account for this? Could it be that social and economic trends which were to become evident after the Arab conquest had begun in a quiet way before the establishment of the Arab Empire, and that an economic region encompassing Arabia, Syria, and Mesopotamia had been developing well before the Arab conquest created the political one?[45]

The story of the city in late Late Antiquity, as I have told it, is a story of decline. Some choose to see only transformation,[46] but that is not the point of view taken in this book. Of course it is nature's way to use the material of dead organisms to fashion new life, and this can be observed in human history as much as in any other natural process. But the historian loses much if he insists on concentrating his attention exclusively on 'recycling'. The late Late Roman cities certainly were different. It is part of the function of the historian to assess the effects of the change. Plato and Aristotle wrote of the city as an institution that educated its citizens. The Christian late Late Roman city certainly produced a different kind of person from the classical city. The change can be summarized as an expansion of the sphere of religion at the expense of the

[43] Possible explanations spring to mind: the Holy Land attracted finance. Emperors and well-to-do individuals built churches and endowed monasteries. Pilgrims spent money and made donations. Wealthy men and women chose to spend the last years of their lives in the neighbourhood of the holy places. Subsidies were paid to the Ghassanids and their tribesmen to defend the settled land from raids from the desert.

[44] See the index of dated inscriptions in volumes I–IV of *IGLS,* the number of inscriptions from the second half of the 6th cent. from villages of northern Syria in *IGLS* IV (1955): 376–8. As one might expect those from the territory of Apamea are more numerous than from that of Antioch.

[45] For the emergence of regional trading networks, see Wickham, forthcoming.

[46] See the common sense of Ward-Perkins 1997: 157–76.

secular.[47] Whether we assess this as an improvement, or the reverse, is a value judgement, and therefore perhaps outside the remit of the historian. But it is one which a writer interested in both history and contemporary society can hardly avoid making. The story of the city in Late Antiquity involves the end of a political tradition, the end of a pattern of urban design related to the political tradition, the end of a particular ideal of what makes for the good life, the end of a secular ideal of education, and in many cases a shrinkage of population. All this happened within a context of the collapsing structures of an empire and of the associated economic system. It abundantly merits to be described as decline.

But of course the decline involved not only the end of one kind of city, but also the beginning of another, and indeed of several other kinds of city. The new developments did not advance at an even pace, but advanced irregularly, with peaks and troughs of progress. It is however interesting to note that for a long time peaks and troughs over much of the area of the old Empire kept more or less in step. The first thirty years of the sixth century were a period of high activity in the East and also, if at a lower level, in Italy. In the Moselle and Rhineland also, the episcopacies of Nicetius at Trier and Sidonius at Mainz are evidence of recovery in the age of Justinian. The corresponding peak came a bit later in Aquitaine, and towards the end of the century in Spain. Disaster struck the cities of Anatolia in the second half of the seventh century. The already much weakened cities of Italy suffered a corresponding further downturn from around AD 600. In the seventh century there was very little building in most cities of central France, the exceptions being Bourges, Poitiers, and Clermont-Ferrand; and even these cities ceased to build in the eighth century.[48] Recovery began in the north of Italy between AD 650 and 700, though in this region, and over most of northern Gaul, manifest urban recovery, as evidenced by widespread building, only came in the eighth century.[49] At this time urban development was linked with a rise of North Sea trade associated with the new settlements of craftsmen and traders at Quentovic and Dorestad and Hamwic and Ribe, and the growth of an extensive network of North European trade which produced settlements of craftsmen and traders, in many other places, including old Roman cities like London and York and Cologne and Mainz.[50] In the

[47] Markus 1990: 226: 'Corresponding to the epistemological excision of the secular from Christian discourse a desecularisation of its society took place on a variety of levels.'

[48] Rouche 1979: table p. 295. See also ibid. 299: in the 7th cent. building of rural monasteries partly compensated for the decline of urban building.

[49] B. Päffgen and S. Ristow, 'Christentum, Kirchenbau und Sakralkunst', in *Franken: Wegbereiter Europas*, 2 vols. (Mainz, 1996), i. 407–15, p. 409 map of Merovingian churches in NE Gaul.

[50] S. Lebecq, 'Routes of exchange: Production and distribution in the West (5th to 8th century)', in L. Webster and M. Brown (eds.), *The Transformation of the Roman World AD 400–900* (Berkeley,

Byzantine East recovery came last of all, after AD 800. In the lands conquered by the Arabs late Late Roman conditions continued with less change than in the Christian world. There late Late Antiquity might be said to have ended with the Umayyad dynasty after AD 750. Subsequently development of Islamic cities followed a rhythm of its own, as did that of cities in the Byzantine world after, say, AD 800.

1997), 67–78 and fig. 30. R. Hodges, 'Emporia and the end of the Dark Ages', in Christie and Loseby (1996), 289–305.

BIBLIOGRAPHY

Alfieri, N. (1977), 'L'insediamento urbano sul litorale delle Marche', in P.-M. Duval and E. Frézouls (1977), 87–98.

Alföldy, G. (1975), *Die römischen Inschriften von Tarraco*, 2 vols. (Berlin).

——(1987), 'Römisches Städtewesen auf der neukastilianischen Hochebene', *Abhandlungen der Heidelberger Akad. Phil. Hist. Klass.* (Heidelberg).

Allen, Pauline (1981), *Evagrius Scholasticus: The Church Historian* (Louvain).

Alston, R. (1997), 'Ritual and power in the Romano-Egyptian city', in Parkins (1997), 142–72.

Anton, H. H. (1986), 'Verfassungsgeschichtliche Kontinuität und Wandlung von der Spätantike zum hohen Mittelalter: Das Beispiel Triers', *Francia*, 14: 1–25.

Antoniadis-Bibicou, H. (1963), *Recherches sur les douanes à Byzance* (Paris).

Arce, J. (1982), *El último siglo de la España romana (284–409)*, 2nd edn. (Madrid).

——(1997*a*), 'Emperadores, palacios, y villae', *Antiquité tardive*, 5: 293–302.

——(1997*b*), '*Otium et negotium*: The great estates, 4th–7th century', in Webster and Brown (1997), 19–32.

——(1999*a*), 'The city of Merida (Emerita) in the *Vitas Patrum Emeritensium* (6th century AD)', in E. Chrysos and I. Wood (eds.), *East and West: Modes of Communication*, Proceedings of the First Plenary Conference at Merida (Leiden/Boston/Cologne), 1–14.

——(1999*b*), 'El inventario de Roma: *Curiosum y Notitia*', in W. V. Harris (ed.), *The Transformation of the 'Urbs Roma' in Late Antiquity* (Portsmouth, RI), 15–22.

Arthur, P. (1991), *The Romans in Northern Campania*, Archeological Monographs of the British School at Rome, 1 (London).

——and Oren, E. D. (1998), 'The north Sinai Survey and the evidence of transport amphorae for Roman and Byzantine trading patterns', *JRA* 11, 193–212.

——and Patterson, H. (1994), 'Ceramics and early medieval Central and Southern Italy: "A potted history"', in Francovich and Noyé (1994), 409–41.

Athanassiadi, P. (1993), 'Persecution and response in late paganism: The evidence of Damascus', *JHS* 113: 1–29.

Attolini, I., Cambi, F., Castagne, M., Celuzza, M., Fentress, E., Perkins, P., and Regoli, E. (1991), 'Political geography and productive geography between the valleys of the Albegna and the Fiora in N. Etruria', in Barker and Lloyd (1991), 142–52.

Ausbüttel, F. M. (1987), 'Die Curialen und Stadtmagistrate Ravennas im spätantiken Italien', *ZPE* 67: 207–14.

——(1988), *Die Verwaltung der Städte und Provinzen im spätantiken Italien* (Frankfurt).

Avigdad, N. (1984), *Discovering Jerusalem* (Oxford).

Avi-Yonah, M. (1954), *The Madaba Mosaic Map* (Jerusalem).

Avramea, A. (1989), 'Les Constructions profanes de l'évêque dans l'épigraphie grecque', *Actes XI Congr. Int. d'Arch. Chrét.* (Rome), i. 829–35.

Bachrach, B. S. (1971), *Merovingian Military Organisation 481–751* (Minneapolis).

Bagnall, R. S. (1985), 'Agricultural productivity and taxation in later Roman Egypt', *TAPA* 115: 289–310.

——(1992), 'Landholding in Late Roman Egypt: The distribution of wealth', *JRS* 82: 128–40.

——(1993), *Egypt in Late Antiquity* (Princeton).

——and Frier, B. W. (1994), *The Demography of Roman Egypt* (Cambridge).

——and Worp, K. A. (1980), 'Papyrus documentation in Egypt from Constantine to Justinian', in R. Pintaudi (ed.), *Miscellanea Papyrologia* (Florence), 13–23.

Baillie, M. G. L. (1995), *A Slice through Time: Dendrochronology and Precision Dating* (London).

Bairoch, P. (1991), *Cities and Economic Development*, tr. C. Braider (Chicago).

Baladhuri, Ahmad b. Yahyà (1966), *Kitāb Futūh al-Buldān*, tr. in P. K. Hitti, *The Origin of the Islamic State* (London/New York, 1916; repr. Beirut, 1966).

Balbás, L. T. (1998), 'Cities founded by the Muslims in al-Andalus', in Marín (1998), 265–89.

Balty, J. (1984*a*), *Apamée de Syrie: Bilan de recherches archéologiques 1973–79*, Actes du colloque à Bruxelles, Mai 1980 (Brussels).

——(1984*b*), 'La Maison aux consoles', in J. Balty (1984*a*), 19–78.

——(1995), *Mosaïques Antiques du Proche Orient* (Paris).

——and Balty, J. C. (eds.) (1972), *Apamée de Syrie, bilan des recherches 1969–71* (Brussels).

———— (1974), 'Julien et Apamée', *Dialogues d'histoire ancienne*, 1: 267–78.

———— (1981), 'L'Apamène et les limites de la Syria Secunda', in *La Géographie administrative et politique d'Alexandre à Mahomet*, Actes du colloque de Strasbourg, 14–16 juin 1979: Travaux du Centre de Recherche sur le Proche-Orient et la Grèce Antiques 6 (Leiden), 41–75.

Balty, J. C. (1972), 'Nouvelles mosaïques païennes et groupe épiscopal dit "cathédrale de l'est" à Apamée de Syrie', *CRAI*: 267–304.

——(1984), 'Notes sur l'habitat Romain, Byzantin et Arabe d'Apamée: Rapport de synthèse', in J. Balty (1984*a*), 471–501.

——(1989), 'Apamée au IVe siècle', in C. Morrisson and J. Lefort (eds.), *Hommes et richesse* (Brussels), 79–96.

——(1991), *Curia Ordinis: Recherches d'architecture et d'urbanisme antique sur les curies provinciales du monde romain* (Brussels).

Balzaretti, R. (1996), 'Cities, emporia and monasteries: Local economies in the Po Valley', in Christie and Loseby (1996), 213–34.

——(1997), 'Cities and markets in the early Middle Ages', in G. Ausenda (ed.), *Towards an Ethnology of Europe's Barbarians* (Woodbridge), 113–34.

Bammer, A. (1988), *Ephesos: Stadt und Fluss und Meer* (Graz).

Banaji, J. (1992), 'Rural Communities in the Late Empire 300–700: Monetary and Economic Aspects', D.Phil. thesis (Oxford).

——(1998), 'Discounts, weight standards, and the exchange-rate between gold and copper: Insights into the monetary process in the sixth century', in G. Crifò and S. Giglio (eds.), *Atti dell'Accademia Romanistica Constantiniana*, xii; Convegno Internazionale in Onore di Manlio Sargenti (Perugia), 183–202.

Banks, P. (1984), 'The Roman inheritance and topographical transition in early medieval Barcelona before a.d. 1200', in T. F. C. Blagg, R. F. J. Jones, S. Keay (eds.), *Papers in Iberian Archaeology*, i, BAR Int. 193 (Oxford), 600–62.

Barceló, M., and Toubert, P. (eds.) (1998), *L'Incastellamento*, Actes des rencontres de Gérone 1992 et de Rome 1994, Collection de l'école française de Rome 241 (Rome).

Barker, G. (1995), *Landscape Archaeology and 'Annales' History in the Biferno Valley* (Leicester).

——and Hodges, R. (1981), *Archaeology and Italian Society*, BAR S102 (Oxford).

——and Lloyd, J. (1991), *Roman Landscapes: Archaeological Survey in the Mediterranean Region*, Archaeological Monographs of the British School at Rome 2 (London).

——*et al.* (1985), *Cyrenaica in Antiquity*, BAR (IS) 236 (Oxford).

——(ed.), Gilbertson, D., Barri Jones, D., Mattingly, D. (1996), *Farming in the Desert*, i, UNESCO Libyan Valley Archaeological Survey (Paris/Tripoli/London).

Barnish, S. (1989), 'The transformation of classical cities and the Pirenne debate', *JRA* 2: 385–400.

Barral I Altet, X. (1982), 'Transformacions de la topografia urbana a la Hispània cristiana durant l'antiguitat tardana', in *II Reunió d'Arqueologia Paleocristiana Hispànica (Barcelona-Montserrat, 1978)* (Barcelona), 105–30.

Bates, G. E. (1971), *Byzantine Coins*, Archaeological Exploration of Sardis, Monograph 1 (Cambridge, Mass.).

Bavant, B. (1984), 'La Ville dans le nord de l'Illyricum', in *Villes et Peuplement dans l'Illyricum Protobyzantin*, Collection de l'école française de Rome 77 (Paris), 245–88.

——(1989), 'Cadre de vie et habitat urbain en Italie centrale byzantine', *MEFR* (MA) 101–2: 465–532.

Belke, K. (1994), *Galatien in der Spätantike*, Asia Minor Studien 12 (Bonn).

Bermejo, J. V. (1998), ' "The Zalmedina" of Córdoba', in Marín (1998), 289–429.

Bertelli, C. (1999), 'Visual images of the town in Late Antiquity and the Early Middle Ages', in Brogiolo and Ward-Perkins (1999), 127–46.

Bertolini, O. (1947), 'Per la storia della diaconia Romane nell'alto medioevo alla fine del secolo VIII', *ASR* 70: 1–145.

Beschaouch, A., Hanoune, R., and Thébert, Y. (1977), *Les Ruines de Bulla Regia*, Collection de l'école française de Rome 28 (Rome).

——————Khanoussi, R., and Olivier, A. (1980–3), *Recherches archéologiques franco-tunisienne à Bulla Regia*, 1–4, Collection de l'école française de Rome 28/1–4 (Rome).

Bingen, J. (1954), 'Inscriptions d'Achaïe', *BCH* 78: 74–88, 395–404.

Binns, J. (1994), *Ascetics and Ambassadors of Christ: The Monasteries of Palestine 314–631* (Oxford).

Biscop, J.-L. (1997), *Deir Déhès, Monastère d'Antioche: Étude architecturale*, Bibliothèque Archéologique et Historique 148 (Beirut).

Blake, H. M., Potter, T. W., and Whitehouse, D. B. (eds.) (1978), *Papers in Italian Archaeology*, i (London).

Blakely, J. A. (1996), 'Towards the study of the economy of Caesarea Maritima', in Raban and Holum (1996), 327–45.

Boll, P. C., Hoffmann, A., and Weber, T. (1990), 'Gadara in der Dekapolis: deutsche Ausgrabungen: Vorbericht', *Archäologischer Anzeiger*, 193–266.

Bouras, C. B. (1981), 'City and village: Urban design and architecture', *Jahrbuch der österreichischen Byzantinistik*, 31: 611–53.

Bowersock, G. W. (1990), *Hellenism in Late Antiquity* (Cambridge).

——*et al.* (1997), 'Peter Brown: The world of Late Antiquity revisited', *Symbolae Osloenses*, 72: 5–90.

Bowman, A. K. (1971), *The Town Councils of Roman Egypt* (Toronto).

——(1985), 'Landholding in the Hermopolite Nome in the fourth century', *JRS* 75: 137–63.

——and Woolf, G. (eds.) (1991), *Literacy and Power in the Ancient World* (Cambridge).

Brandes, W. (1989), *Die Städte Kleinasiens im 7. und 8. Jahrhundert* (Amsterdam).

——(1999), 'Byzantine cities in the seventh and eighth centuries—different sources different histories', in Brogiolo and Ward-Perkins (1999), 25–57.

——and Haldon, J. (forthcoming), 'Tax and transformation: State, cities and their hinterlands in the East Roman world, circa 500–800', in Christie, Gauthier, and Brogiolo (forthcoming).

Brandt, H. (1992), *Gesellschaft und Wirtschaft Pamphyliens und Pisidiens im Altertum*, Asia Minor Studien 7 (Bonn).

Brenk, B. (1993), 'La cristianizzazione della città tardoantica', *Actas del XIV Congreso Internacional de Arqueología Clásica* (Tarragona), 129–35.

——(1995), 'Die Christianisierung des jüdischen Stadtzentrums von Kapernaum', in C. Moss and K. Kiefer (eds.), *Byzantine East, Latin West: Studies in Honor of Kurt Weitzmann* (Princeton), 15–26.

——and Jäggi, C., and Meier, H.-R. (1995), 'The buildings under the cathedral of Gerasa: The second interim report of the Jarasch Cathedral Project', *Annual of the Department of Antiquities of Jordan*, 39: 211–20.

————— *et al* (1997), see under Jäggi, C., Brenk, B., and Meier, H.-R. (1997).

Bridbury, A. R. (1973), 'The Black Death', *EcHR*, 2nd series, 26: 573–92.

Brogiolo, G.-P. (1987), 'A proposito dell'organizzazione urbana nell'alto medioevo', *Archeologia Medievale*, 14: 27–46.

——(1989), 'Brescia: Building transformations in a Lombard city', in Randsborg (1989), 156–65.

——(1993), *Brescia Altomedievale: Urbanistica ed Edilizia dal IV al IX Secolo* (Mantua).

——(1996), *La fine delle Ville Romane: Trasformazioni nelle Campagne tra Tarda Antichità e Alto Medioevo* (Mantua).
——(1999), 'Ideas of the town in Italy during the transition from Antiquity to the Early Middle Ages', in Brogiolo and Ward-Perkins (1999), 99–126.
——and Gelichi, S. (1996), *Nuove Ricerche sui Castelli Altomedievali in Italia Settentrionale* (Florence).
——and Ward-Perkins, P. (1999), *The Idea and Ideal of the Town between Latin Antiquity and the Early Middle Ages*, The Transformation of the Roman World 4 (Leiden/Boston/Cologne).
Brooks, A. D. (1986), 'A review of evidence of continuity in British towns in 5th and 6th centuries', *Oxf. J. Arch.* 5 (1): 77–102.
Broshi, M. (1979), 'The population of Western Palestine in the Roman–Byzantine period', *BASOR* 136: 1–10.
Brown, P. (1971), 'The rise and function of the holy man in late antiquity', *JRS* 61: 80–101; repr. in P. Brown (1982), 103–52.
——(1978), *The Making of Late Antiquity* (Cambridge, Mass.)
——(1981), *The Cult of the Saints* (London).
——(1982), *Society and the Holy in Late Antiquity* (Berkeley and Los Angeles).
——(1992), *Power and Persuasion in Late Antiquity: Towards a Christian Empire* (Madison).
Brown, T. S. (1984), *Gentlemen and Officers: Imperial Administration and Aristocratic Power in Byzantine Italy AD 554–800* (Rome).
Browning, R. (1952), 'The riot of 387 AD in Antioch', *JRS* 42: 13–21.
Brühl, C.-R. (1975), *Palatium und Civitas: Studien zur Profantopographie spätantiker Civitates*, i. *Gallien*; ii. *Germanien* (Cologne and Vienna).
Bujard, J., with Trillen, W. (1997), 'Um al-Walid et Khan Az-Zabîb, cinq qsûrs omeyyades et leurs mosquées révisitées', *Annual of the Department of Antiquities of Jordan*, 41: 351–73.
Bulliet, R. W. (1975), *The Camel and the Wheel* (New York).
——(1994), *Islam: The View from the Edge* (New York).
Burgess, R. W. (1993), *The Chronicle of Hydatius and the Consularia Constantinopolitana* (Oxford).
Burnham, B. C., and Wacher, J. (1990), *The Small Towns of Roman Britain* (London).
Butcher, K. (1997–8), 'Coinage in sixth century Beirut', *Berytus*, 43: 173–80.
Butler, R. M. (1959), 'Late Roman town walls in Gaul', *Archaeological Journal*, 116: 25–50.
Buttray, T. V., Johnson, Ann, Mackenzie, K. M., and Bates, M. L. (1981), *Greek, Roman and Islamic Coins from Sardis* (Cambridge, Mass.).
Caesarius of Arles (1953), *Sermones*, ed. G. Morin, Corpus Christianorum Series Latina 103–4 (Brepols).
Caillet, J.-P. (1993), *L'Évergétisme monumental chrétien en Italie et à ses marges*, Collection de l'école française de Rome 175 (Rome).
——(1996), 'La Transformation en église d'édifices publics et de temples à la fin de l'Antiquité', in C. Lepelley (1996), 191–211.

Cambi, F., and Fentress, E. (1989), 'Villas to castles: First millennium A.D. demography in the Albegna Valley', in Randsborg (1989), 74–85.
Cameron, Alan (1973), *Porphyrius the Charioteer* (Oxford).
——(1976), *Circus Factions* (Oxford).
——(1985), 'Polyonomy in the late Roman aristocracy: The case of Petronius Probus', *JRS* 75: 164–82.
Cameron, Averil (1970), *Agathias* (Oxford).
——(1976), *Corippus, in Laudem Iustini Augusti Minoris* (London).
——(1981), *Continuity and Change in the Sixth Century Byzantium* (London).
——(1982), 'Byzantine Africa, the literary evidence', *Excavations at Carthage 1978 conducted by the University of Michigan*, vii (Ann Arbor), 26–92.
——(1985), *Procopius and the Sixth Century* (London).
——(1989), 'Gelimer's laughter: The case of Byzantine Africa', in F. M. Clover and R. S. Humphreys (eds.), *Tradition and Innovation in Late Antiquity* (Madison), 171–90 = Averil Cameron (1996), ch. 8.
——(1991), *Christianity and the Rhetoric of Empire* (Berkeley).
——(1993*a*), 'The Byzantine reconquest of North Africa and the impact of Greek culture', *Graeco-Arabica*, 5 (Athens), 153–65 = Averil Cameron (1996), ch. 10.
——(1993*b*), *The Mediterranean World in Late Antiquity* (London).
——(ed.) (1995), *The Byzantine and Early Islamic Near East*, iii. *States, Resources and Armies* (Princeton).
——(1996), *Changing Cultures in Early Byzantium* (Aldershot).
——and Conrad, Lawrence I. (eds.) (1992), *The Byzantine and Early Islamic Near East: Problems in the Literary Source Material* (Princeton).
——and Garnsey, P. (eds.) (1998), *The Cambridge Ancient History*, xiii. *The Late Empire AD 337–425* (Cambridge).
——and Herrin, Judith (1984), *Constantinople in the Early Eighth Century: The Parastaseis Syntomoi Chronikai*, Introduction, Translation, and Commentary, Colombia Studies in the Classical Tradition 10 (Leiden).
——and King, G. R. D. (eds.) (1994), *The Byzantine and Early Islamic Near East*, ii, see under King, G. R. D.
Campbell, S. (1996), 'Signs of prosperity in the decorations of some 4th–5th century buildings at Aphrodisias', in C. Roueché and R. R. R. Smith (1996), 187–200.
Canivet, P., and Rey-Coquais, J.-P. (eds.) (1992), *La Syrie de Byzance à l'Islam, VIIe et VIIIe siècles*, Inst. Franç. de Damas. (Damascus).
Carreté, J.-M., Keay, S., and Millett, M. (1995), *A Roman Provincial Capital and its Hinterland: The Survey of the Territory of Tarragona, Spain (1985–1990)*, JRA Suppl. 15 (Ann Arbor).
Carrié, J.-M. (1994), 'Les Échanges commerciaux et l'état antique tardif', in *État antique, les échanges dans l'antiquité: Le Rôle de l'état*, Entretiens d'archéologie et histoire Saint-Bertrand-de-Comminges (Toulouse), 175–211.
——(1995), 'Modes de financement des armées', in Averil Cameron (1995), 27–60.

——(1998*a*), 'Archives municipales et distributions alimentaires dans l'Égypte romaine', in *La Mémoire perdue: Recherches sur l'administration romaine*, Collection de l'école française de Rome 243 (Rome), 271–302.
——(1998*b*), 'Les Metiers de la banque entre public et privé (IVe–VIIe siècle)', in G. Crifò and S. Giglio (eds.), *Atti dell'Accademia Romanistica Constantiniana*, xii; Convegno Internazionale in Onore di Manlio Sargenti (Perugia), 65–93.
Carver, M. O. H. (1993), *Arguments in Stone: Archaeological Research and the European Town in the First Millennium* (Oxford).
Castrén, P. (1994), *Post Herulian Athens: Aspects of Life and Culture in Athens AD 267–529* (Helsinki).
Cavanagh, W., Crouwel, J., Catling, R. W. V., and Shipley, G. (1996), *Laconia Survey* 2, ABSA Suppl. 27 (London).
Cecconi, G. A. (1994), *Governo imperiale e élites dirigenti nell'Italia tardoantica, problemi di storia politico-amministrativa 270–476 AD*, Biblioteca di Athenaeum 24 (Como).
Cesa, M. (1988), *Ennodio: Vita del beatissimo Epifanio vescovo della chiesa pavese*, Biblioteca di Athenaeum 6 (Como).
——(1992–3), 'Il matrimonio di Placidia ed Ataulfo', *Romanobarbarica*, 11: 23–53.
——(1993), 'Römisches Heer und barbarische Foederaten: Bemerkungen zur weströmischen Politk in den Jahren 402–12', in F. Vallet and M. Kazanski (eds.), *L'Armée romaine et les barbares du IIIe au VIIe siècle* (Paris).
——(1994*a*), *Impero Tardoantico e Barbari: La Crisi Militare da Adrianople al 418*, Biblioteca di Athenaeum 23 (Como).
——(1994*b*), 'Il regno di Odoacre: La prima dominazione germanica in Italia', in B. and P. Scardigli (eds.), *Germani in Italia* (Rome), 307–20.
Chadwick, H. (1985), 'Augustine and Pagans and Christians', in D. Beales and G. Best (eds.), *History, Society and Churches: Essays in Honour of Owen Chadwick* (Cambridge), 9–26.
Charanis, P. (1950), 'The Chronicle of Monemvasia and the question of Slavonic settlement in Greece', *DOP* 5: 139–66.
——(1955), 'The significance of coins as evidence for the history of Athens and Corinth in the seventh and eighth centuries', *Historia*, 4: 163–7.
Charles, R. H. (1916), *The Chronicle of John Bishop of Niciu*, translated from Zotenberg's Ethiopic Text (London).
Chastagnol, A. (1978), *L'Album municipal de Timgad* (Bonn).
——(1996), 'La Fin du sénat de Rome', in Lepelley (1996), 345–54.
Chauvot, A. (1986), *Procope de Gaza, Priscien de Caesarée, panégyriques de l'empereur Anastase I* (Bonn).
——(1987), 'Curiales et paysans en orient à la fin du Ve et au debut du VIe siècle: Note sur l'institution du *vindex*', in E. Frézouls (ed.), *Sociétés urbaines, sociétés rurales dans l'Asie mineure et la Syrie hellénistique et romaine* (Strasbourg), 271–87.
Chavarría Arnau, A. (1996), 'Transformaciones arquitectónicas de los estab-

lecimientos rurales en el nordeste de la Tarraconensis durante la antigüedad', *Butlletí de la Reial Acadèmia Catalana de Belles Arts de Sant Jordi*, 10: 165–202.
Chavarría Arnau, A. (1997), 'Las transformaciones termales en las *villae* de la antigüedad tardía hispánica: La *villa* de els Atmetllers en Tossa de Mar (Girona)', in M. J. Peréx (ed.), *Termalismo Antiguo*, I Congreso Peninsular. Actas (Madrid), 511–18.
——(1999), 'Novedades bibliográficas sobre *villae* romanas en Hispania durante la Antigüedad tardía (1990–1999)', *Bulletin, Association pour l'Antiquité tardive*, 8: 57–67.
Chehab, H. (1975), 'Les Palais Omeyyades d'Anjar', *Archéologie*, 87 (Oct.): 18–24.
Christensen, A. P., Thomsen, R., and Ploug, G. (1931–8), *Hama*, Fouilles et Recherches, vol. iii/3 (Copenhagen).
Christie, N. (1991), 'The Alps as a frontier AD 168–774', *JRA* 4: 410–30.
——(1995*a*), *The Lombards* (Oxford).
——(ed.) (1995*b*), *Settlement and Economy in Italy 1500 BC–AD 1500*, Oxbow Monograph 41 (Oxford).
——(1996), 'Towns and peoples on the Middle Danube in Late Antiquity and the early Middle Ages', in Christie and Loseby (1996), 70–98.
——and Loseby, S. T. (eds.) (1996), *Towns in Transition: Urban Evolution in Late Antiquity and the Early Middle Ages* (Aldershot and Brookfield, Vt.).
——and Gauthier, N., Brogiolo, G.-P. (eds.) (forthcoming), *Towns and their Hinterlands and Territories between Late Antiquity and the Early Middle Ages*, ESF Transformation of the Roman World Series (Leiden/Boston/Cologne).
Chrysos, E. (1966), *Die Bischofslisten des V. Ökumenischen Konzils* (Bonn).
——(1971), 'Die angebliche Abschaffung der städtischen Kurien durch Kaiser Anastasius', *Byzantina*, 3: 93–102.
——and Schwarcz, A. (eds.) (1989), *Das Reich und die Barbaren*, Veröffentlichungen des Instituts für österreichische Geschichtsforschung 29 (Vienna).
Chuvin, P. (1991), *Mythologie et géographie dionysiaque: Recherches sur l'oeuvre de Nonnos de Panopolis* (Clermont-Ferrand).
Ciampoltrini, G. (1994), 'Città frammentate e città-fortezza: storie urbane della Toscana Centro-Settentrionale fra Teodosio e Carlo Magno', in Francovich and Noyé (1994), 615–33.
Clark, V. A. (1986), 'The Church of bishop Isaiah at Jerash', in Zayadine (1986*a*), 303–42.
Claude, D. (1960), *Topographie und Verfassung der Städte Bourges und Poitiers bis in das 11 Jahrhundert*, Historische Studien 380 (Lübeck).
——(1964), 'Untersuchungen zum frühfränkischen Comitat', *ZRG GA* 81: 1–79.
——(1969), *Die byzantinische Stadt im 6. Jahrhundert* (Munich).
——(1997), 'Haus und Hof im Merowingerreich nach den erzählenden und urkundlichen Quellen', in *Haus und Hof in ur- und frühgeschichtlicher Zeit*, Gedenkschrift für Herbert Jankuhn (Göttingen), 321–34.
——(1998), 'Remarks about the relations between Visigoths and Hispano-Romans in the seventh century', in W. Pohl and H. Reimitz (1998), 117–30.

Clover, F. M. (1982), 'Carthage and the Vandals', in J. H. Humphrey (ed.), *Excavations at Carthage 1978 conducted by the University of Michigan*, VII.1–22 (Ann Arbor).

Coates-Stephens, R. (1997), 'Dark Age architecture in Rome', *PBSR* 65: 177–232.

Coleman Norton, P. R. (1966), *Roman State and Christian Church*, a collection of legal documents to AD 535, 3 vols. (London).

Collins, R. (1980), 'Merida and Toledo 550–585', in E. James (ed.), *Visigothic Spain* (Oxford).

——(1983), *Early Medieval Spain 400–1000* (London).

——(1990), 'Literacy and the laity in early medieval Spain', in R. McKitterick (ed.), *The Uses of Literacy in Early Mediaeval Europe* (Cambridge), 109–33.

Congrès d'història de Barcelona III, 1993, Institut Municipal de Història (Barcelona, 1994).

Conrad, L. (1986), 'The plague in Bilad al-Sham in pre-Islamic times', in M. A. Bakhit and M. Asfour (eds.), *Proceedings of the Symposium on Bilad al-Sham* (Amman), ii. 143–63.

Conrad, L. I. (1994), 'Epidemic disease in central Syria in the late sixth century: Some new insights from the verse of Hanân ibn Thâbit', *BMGS* 18: 12–58.

Conrat, M. (1903), *Breviarium Alarici* (Leipzig).

Corbier, M. (1991), 'City territory and taxation', in Rich and Wallace-Hadrill (1991), 211–40.

Cormack, R. (1990), 'Byzantine Aphrodisias: Changing the symbolic map of a city', *PCPhS* NS 36: 26–41.

Cornell, T. J., and Lomas, K. (eds.) (1995), *Urban Society in Roman Italy* (London).

Cracco Ruggini, L. (1961), *Economia e società nell'Italia annonaria* (Milan).

——(1971), 'Le associazoni professionali nel mondo romano bizantino', in *Settimane di studio del Centro Italiano di Studi sull'Alto Medioevo* (Spoleto), 18: 59–193.

Crawford, J. S. (1990), *Byzantine Shops at Sardis* (Cambridge, Mass.).

Croke, B. (1983), 'The origins of the Christian World Chronicle; in B. Croke and A. M. Emmett (eds.), *History and Historians in Late Antiquity* (Sidney), 116–31.

——(1990), 'The early development of Byzantine chronicles', in Jeffreys *et al.* (1990), 27–54.

Crowfoot, J. W. (1931), *Churches at Jerash* (London).

——(1938), 'Christian churches', in Kraeling (1938), 171–262.

Cuenca, V. S. (1997), 'The origins of Al-Andalus', in Keay and Díaz-Andreu (1997), 265–78.

Cüppers, H. (1977), 'Die Stadt Trier und verschiedene Phasen ihres Ausbaues', in P.-M. Duval and E. Frézouls (1977), 223–8.

Dagron, G. (1970), 'Les Moines et la ville: Le Monachisme à Constantinople jusqu'au concile de Chalcédoine (451)', *Travaux et Mémoires*, 4: 229–76 = *idem.*, *La Romanité chrétienne en Orient* (London: Variorum, 1984), no. VIII.

Dagron, G. (1971), 'Le Christianisme dans la ville byzantine', *DOP* 31: 3–25 = Dagron (1984*a)*, ch. 9.
——(1978), *Vie et miracles de saint Thécla*, texte grec, traduction et commentaire (Brussels).
——(1979), 'Entre village et cité: La Bourgade rurale des IVe–VIIe siècles en Orient', *Koinonia*, 3: 29–52 = Dagron (1984*a)*, ch. 8.
——(1980), 'Two documents concerning mid-sixth century Mopsuestia', in A. E. Laiou-Thomadakis (ed.), *Charanis Studies* (New Brunswick), 19–30 = Dagron (1984*a)*, ch. 6.
——(1984*a*), *Constantinople imaginaire, étude sur le recueil des 'Patria'* (Paris).
——(1984*b*), *La Romanité chrétienne en Orient* (London).
——(1984*c*), 'Les Villes dans l'Illyricum protobyzantin', in *Villes et peuplement dans l'Illyricum protobyzantin*, Collection de l'école française de Rome 77 (Paris), 1–19.
——(1989), 'L'Organisation de la vie religieuse à Constantinople', *Actes du XIe Congrés International d'Archéologie Chrétienne 1986*, ii (Rome), 1069–85.
——(1991), 'Ainsi rien n'échappe à la réglementation: état, église, corporations, confréries; à propos des inhumations à Constantinople IVe–Xe siècle', *Hommes et richesses dans l'empire byzantin*, ii. 155–82.
——(1996), *Empereur et prêtre: Étude sur le césaropapisme byzantin* (Paris).
——and Deroche V. (1991), 'Juifs et chrétiens dans l'Orient VIIe siècle', *Travaux et Mémoires*, 11, 17–273, text French, translation and commentary of *Doctrina Iacobi nuper baptizati*.
——and Feissel, D. (1987), *Inscriptions de Cilicie*, Trav. et Mém. Monographies, 4 (Paris).
Dauphin, C. (1987), 'Les Kômai de Palestine', *Proche Orient Chrétien*, 3: 251–67.
——(1998), *La Palestine byzantine: Peuplement et populations*, i–iii, BAR Int 726 (Oxford).
Dauphin, C. M., and Schonfield, J. J. (1983), 'Settlements of the Roman and Byzantine periods on the Golan Heights: Preliminary report on survey 1979–81', *Israel Exploration Journal*, 33: 189–206.
Declareuil, J. (1910), 'Les Comtes de la cité', *Rev. Hist. du Droit Français et Étranger*, 34: 794-836.
Deichmann, F. W. (1989), *Ravenna, Hauptstadt des spätantiken Abendlandes*, ii/3 (Stuttgart).
Dekkers, J. G. (1989), 'Darstellungen der christlichen Stadt', *Actes du XIe Congrès International d'Archéologie Chrétienne 1986*, ii (Rome), 1283–1304.
Delmaire, R. (1989), *Largesse sacrée et res privata, l'aerarium impérial et son administration du IVe et Ve siècle* (Rome).
——(1996), 'Cités et fiscalité au Bas-Empire: A propos du rôle des curiales dans la levée des impôts', in Lepelley (1996), 59–70.
Demandt, A. (1989), 'The osmosis of late Roman and Germanic aristocracies', in E. K. Chrysos and A. Schwarcz (eds.), *Reich und die Barbaren* (Vienna), 75–86.
Dentzer, J.-M. (1985), *Le Hauran*, i–ii (Paris).

Descombes, F. (1985), *Recueil des inscription chrétiennes de la Gaule*, xv. *Viennoise du Nord* (Paris).
De Ste Croix, G. E. M. (1981), *The Class Struggle in the Ancient Greek World* (London).
Deubner, O. (1977–8), 'Das Heiligtum der alexandrinischen Gottheiten in Pergamum', *Ist Mitt.* 27–8: 227–50.
Dévréesse, R. (1945), *Le Patriarcat d'Antioche depuis le paix de l'église jusqu'à la conquête Arabe* (Paris).
Devreker, J., and Waelkens, M. (1984), *Les Fouilles de Pessinonte 1967–73*, i (Bruges).
De Vries, B. (1998), *Umm El-Jimal: A Frontier Town and its Landscape in Northern Jordan*, i. *Fieldwork 1972–81*, JRA Suppl. 26 (Ann Arbor).
De Vries, J. (1984), *European Urbanization 1500–1800* (London).
Dhondt, J. (1957), 'L'Essor urbain entre Meuse et mer du Nord à l'époque merovingienne', *Studi in onore di A. Sapori* (Milan), i. 55–78.
Diacre, Marc le (1930), *Vie de Porphyre, évêque de Gaza*, ed. and tr. H. Grégoire and M.-A. Kugener (Paris).
Díaz, Pablo, C. (1994*a*), 'La ocupación germánica del Valle del Duero: Un ensayo interpretativo', *Hispania Antiqua*, 18: 457–76.
——(1994*b*), 'Propiedad y explotación de la tierra en la Lusitania tardoantigua', in J.-G. Gorges and M. Salinas de Frías (eds.), *Les Campagnes de Lusitanie romaine: Occupation du sol et habitats* (Madrid), 297–309.
——(1997), 'La Rue au Merida au VIe siècle: Usage sacré et usage profane', in A. Leménorel (ed.), *La Rue, lieu de sociabilité*, Publications de l'Université de Rouen 214 (Rouen), 331–40.
Diehl, E. (1924–31), *Inscriptiones Latinae Christiane Veteres*, 3 vols. (Berlin).
Dilcher, G. (1964), 'Bischof und Stadtverfassung in Oberitalien', *ZRG GA* 81: 225–66.
Dillon, S. (1997), 'Figured pilaster capitals from Aphrodisias', *AJA* 101: 731–44.
Di Segni, L. (1995), 'The involvement of local municipal and provincial authorities in urban building in Late Antique Palestine and Arabia', *JRA Suppl.* 14: 312–32.
Divjak, J. (ed.) (1987), *Lettres 1*–29**, Œuvres de Saint Augustin 46B, Bibliothèque Augustinienne (Paris).
Dixon, P. (1992), 'The cities are not populated as once they were', in Rich (1992), 145–60.
Dölger, F. J. (1959), 'Die frühbyzantinische und byzantinisch beeinflusste Stadt', *Atti del 3 congresso internazionale di studi sull'Alto Medioevo, Benevento, Montevergine, Amalfi 1956* (Spoleto), 65–100.
Donceel-Voûte, P. (1988), *Les Pavements des églises byzantines de Syrie et du Liban* (Louvain).
Donner, F. (1981), *Early Islamic Conquest* (Princeton).
Downey, G. (1959), 'Libanius' oration in praise of Antioch (Or. XI)', translated with introduction, *Proceedings American Philosophical Society* 103.5 (Philadelphia), 652–86.

Downey, G. (1961), *A History of Antioch in Syria* (Princeton).

Drecoll, C. (1997), *Die Liturgien im römischen Kaiserreich des 3. und 4. Jh. n. Chr.*, Historia Einzelschrift 116 (Stuttgart).

Drinkwater, J. F., and Elton, H. (eds.) (1992), *Fifth Century Gaul: A Crisis of Identity* (Cambridge).

Duchesne, L. (1907), *Fastes épiscopaux de l'ancienne Gaule* (Paris).

Dufay, B. (1989), 'Baptistères de campagne dans l'Antiochène', *Actes du XIe Congrés International d'Archéologie Chrétienne 1986*, i (Rome), 637–50.

Duncan, G. L. (1993), *Coin Circulation in the Danube and Balkan Provinces of the Roman Empire AD 294–578* (London).

Duncan Jones, R. (1994), *Money and Government in the Roman Empire* (Cambridge).

——(1996), 'The impact of the Antonine plague', *JRA* 9: 108–36.

Duneau, J. F. (1971), *Les Écoles dans les provinces de l'empire byzantin jusqu'à la conquête arabe*, thèse dactylographiée (Paris).

Dunn, A. (1993), 'The *kommerkiarios*, the *apotheke*, the *dromos*, the *vardarios* and the West', *BMGS* 17: 3–24.

——(1994), 'The transition from *polis* to *kastron* in the Balkans (III–VII cc.)', *BMGS* 18: 60–80.

——(1997), 'Stages in the transition from the Late Antique to the Middle Byzantine urban centre in S. Macedonia and S. Thrace', in *ΑΦΙΕΡΩΜΑΣΤΟΝ N. G. L. Hammond* (Thessaloniki), 137–50.

Dupont, C. (1967), 'Les Privilèges des clercs sous Constantin', *Revue d'Histoire Ecclésiastique*, 62: 729–52.

Dupré, X., Massó, M. J., Palanques, M. L., Brunori, P. A.V. (1988), *El Circ romà de Tarragona*, i. *Les Voltes de Sant Ermenegild* (Barcelona).

Durliat, J. (1982), 'Les Attributions civiles des évêques byzantines: L'Exemple du diocèse d'Afrique 533–709', *Jahrbuch der Österreichischen Byzantinistik*, 32.2: 73–84.

——(1984), 'L'Administration civile du diocèse byzantin d'Afrique (533–703)', *Rivista di Studi Byzantinei e Slavi*, 4: 149–78.

——(1989), 'La Peste du 6e siècle', in *Hommes et richesses dans l'empire byzantin*, tome i. *IVe–VIIe siècles* (Paris), 107–25.

——(1990*a*), *De la ville antique à la ville byzantine* (Paris).

——(1990*b*), *Les Finances publiques de Dioclétien aux Carolingiens 284–889* (Sigmaringen).

Duval, N. (1972), 'Les Maisons d'Apamée et l'architecture palatiale de l'antiquité tardive', in J. Balty and J. C. Balty (1972), 447–70.

——(1982), *Loca Sanctorum Africae: Le Culte des martyrs en Afrique du IVe au VIIe siècle*, 2 vols. (Paris).

——(1984), 'L'Architecture religieuse de Tcharitchin Grad', in *Villes et Peuplement dans l'Illyricum Protobyzantin* (Paris), 397–482.

——(1987), 'L'Épigraphie chrétienne de Sbeitla, et son apport historique', in A. Mastino (ed.), *L'Africa romana, Atti del convegno di studio Sassari* (Sassari), 385–414.

——(1989), 'L'Évêque et la cathédrale en Afrique du Nord', *Actes du XI Congrès International d'Archéologie Chrétienne* (Rome), 354–43.

——(1990), 'Quinze ans de recherches archéologiques sur l'antiquité tardive en Afrique du Nord 1975–1990', *REA* 92: 349–87.

——(1993), 'Vingt ans du recherches archéologique sur l'antiquité tardive en Afrique du Nord 1975–94', *REA* 95: 583–637.

——(1994), 'L'Architecture chrétienne en Jordanie', in K. Painter (ed.), *Churches Built in Ancient Times* (London), 149–212.

——and Ben Abed, A. (2000), 'Carthage la capitale du royaume et les villes de la Tunisie à l'époque vandale', in Gurt and Ripoll (2000), 164–218.

——and Prévot, F. (1975), *Inscriptions Chrétiennes d'Haidra*, Recherches archéologiques à Haidra, l'école française de Rome 18 (Rome).

——Caillet, J.-P., and Gui, I. (1992), *Basiliques chrétiennes de l'Algerie* (Paris) = I. Gui (ed.), *Basiliques chrétiennes d'Afrique du Nord*, vol. i.

Duval, P.-M. (1959), 'Une enquête sur les enceintes gauloises', *Gallia*, 17: 37–62.

——and Frézouls, E. (eds.) (1977), *Thèmes de recherches sur les villes antiques d'occident* (Paris).

Dzielska, M. (1995), *Hypatia of Alexandria*, tr. F. Lyra (Cambridge, Mass.).

Eck, W. (1978), 'Der Einfluss der konstantinischen Wende auf die Auswahl der Bischöfe im 4 und 5 Jahrhundert', *Chiron*, 8: 561–85.

——(1983), 'Der Episkopat im spätantiken Africa', *Historische Zeitschrift*, 236: 265–95.

——(1989), *Religion und Gesellschaft in der römischen Kaiserzeit* (Cologne/Vienna).

——and Galsterer, H. (1991), *Die Stadt in Oberitalien und in den nordwestlichen Provinzen des römischen Reiches* (Mainz).

Ellis, S. P. (1988), 'The end of the Roman house', *AJA* 92: 565–76.

Elsner, J. (1998), 'Art and architecture 337–425', in Averil Cameron and Garnsey (1998), 742–61.

Elton, H. (1996), *Warfare in Roman Europe AD 350–425* (Oxford).

Ennabli, L. (1997), *Carthage, une métropole chrétienne du IVe à la fin du VIIe siècle*, Études d'antiquités africaines (Paris).

Ennen, E. (1975), *Die europäische Stadt des Mittelalters* (Göttingen).

Ensslin, W. (1961), 'Vindex', *RE* IX.A1: 25–7.

Evenari, M. (1971), *The Negev* (Cambridge, Mass.).

Ewig, E. (1958), 'Volkstum und Volksbewusstsein im Frankenreich', *Settimane di Studio del Centro Italiano di Studi sull'Alto Medioevo* V, 587–648 (Spoleto), reprinted with some revision in *Spätantikes Gallien* I, 231–73 (1976) (Munich).

——(1976), *Spätantikes und fränkisches Gallien*, 2 vols. (Munich).

Eyben, E. (1980/1), 'Family planning in Antiquity', *Ancient Society*, 11/12: 5–82.

Fabre, G., Mayer, M., and Rod, I. (1984–91), *Inscriptions romaines de Catalogne*, 3 vols. (Paris).

Fasoli, G. (1969), *Dalla civitas al commune nell'Italia Settentrionale* (Bologna).

Fear, A. T. (1997), *Lives of the Visigothic Fathers*, Translated Texts for Historians 26 (Liverpool).

Feissel, D. (1983), *Recueil des inscriptions chrétiennes de Macédoine du IIIe au VI siècle*, BCH Suppl. 8 (Paris).
——(1985), 'Inscriptions du Péloponèse', *Travaux et Mémoires*, 9: 267–383.
——(1989), 'L'Évêque, titres et fonctions d'après les inscriptions jusqu'au VIIe siècle', *Actes du XIe Congrès International d'Archéologie Chrétienne* (Rome), 801–28.
——and Kaygusuz, I. (1985), 'Un mandement impérial du VIe siècle', *Travaux et Mémoires*, 9: 397–419.
——and Worp, K. A. (1988), 'La Requête d'Appion, évêque de Syène à Théodose II', *Oudheidkundige Medelingen uit het Rijksmuseum van Oudheiden te Leiden*, 68: 98 ff.
Fentress, E. (1988), 'Sétif, les thermes du Ve siècle', in A. Mastino (ed.), *L'Africa Romana* (Sassari), 320–37.
——(1994), 'Cosa in the Empire: The unmaking of a Roman town', *JRA* 7: 208–22.
Festugière, A.-J. (1959), *Antioche païenne et chrétienne: Libanius, Chrysostome et les moines de Syrie* (Paris).
——(ed. and tr.) (1970), *La Vie de Théodore de Sykéon*, i–ii, Subsidia Hagiographica 48 (Brussels).
——(1975), 'Évagre, "Histoire Ecclésiastique" traduction', *Byzantion*, 45: 187–471.
Février, A. (1982), 'Archéologie et société: L'Exemple hispanique', in *Il Reunió d'Arqueologia Paleocristiana Hispànica (Barcelona–Montserrat, 1978)* (Barcelona).
Février, P.-A. (1974), 'Permanence et héritage de l'antiquité dans la topographie des villes de l'occident durant le haut moyen âge', *Settimane di Studi* 21 (Spoleto), i. 41–138.
——(1980), '*Velera et nova*. IIIe–VIe siècle', in Février *et al.* (1980), 399–493.
——and Fixot, M., Goudineau, C., and Krusa, V. (eds.) (1980), *La Ville antique des origines au IXe siècle*, Histoire de la France urbaine, ed. G. Duby, vol. 1 (Paris).
Fiema, Z. T. (1994), 'Jordanie, une église byzantine à Petra', *Archaeologia*, 302: 26–35.
——(1995), 'Culture history of the Byzantine ecclesiastical complex at Petra', *ACOR Newsletter*, 7.2: 1–3.
——(forthcoming), 'Byzantine Petra: A reassessment', in J. Eadie (ed.), *Shifting Frontiers in Late Antiquity*, iii. *Urban and Rural in Late Antiquity* (East Lansing, Mich.).
——(forthcoming), 'Historical conclusions', in *The Petra Church Project*, Archaeological Monographs of the American Center of Oriental Research (Amman).
Fischer, F. J. (1971), 'London as an engine for growth', in J. S. Bromley and E. H. Kossman (eds.), *Britain and the Netherlands*, iv (The Hague), 3–16.
Fischer, H. T., and Rieckhoff-Pauli, S. (1982), *Von den Römern zu den Bajuvaren* (Munich).

Fischer, M., and Isaac, B. (1996), *Roman Roads in Judaea*, ii. *The Jaffa–Jerusalem Road*, BAR Int. 628 (Oxford).
Fitzgerald, G. M. (1931), *Beth-Shean Excavations 1921–23: The Arab and Byzantine Levels* (Philadelphia).
Fixot, M. (1980), 'Les Villes du VIIe au IXe siècle', in Février, *et al.* (1980), 497–562.
Flemming, J., and Hoffmann, G. (1917), *Akten der ephesinischen Synode vom Jahre 449*, Abhandlungen der königlichen Gesellschaft der Wissenschaften Göttingen, Phil. Hist. Klass. 15.1.
Fleury, M. (1961), *Paris du Bas-Empire au début du XIIIe siècle* (Paris).
Fontaine, J. (1959), *Isidore de Seville et la culture classique dans l'Espagne wisigothique*, 2 vols. (Paris).
——(1960), *Isidore de Seville: Traité de la nature* (Bordeaux).
——(1972), 'Fins et moyens de l'enseignement ecclésiastique dans l'Espagne wisigothique', *Settimane di Studio sull'alto medioevo*, xix (Spoleto), 142–202.
Foss, C. (1975), 'The Persians in Asia Minor and the end of Antiquity', *Eng. Hist. Rev.* 90: 721–47 = Foss (1990), ch. 1.
——(1976), *Byzantine and Turkish Sardis* (Cambridge, Mass.).
——(1977*a*), 'Archaeology and the "twenty cities of Asia"', *Amer. Journ. Arch.* 81: 469–86 = Foss (1990), ch. 5.
——(1977*b*), 'Attius Philippus and the Walls of Side', *Zeitschr. Pap. Epig.* 26: 172–80 = Foss (1990), ch. 8.
——(1977*c*), 'Late antique and Byzantine Ankara', *DOP* 31: 27–87 = Foss (1990), ch. 6.
——(1979), *Ephesus after Antiquity: A Late Antique, Byzantine and Turkish City* (Cambridge).
——(1980), *Byzantine and Turkish Sardis* (Cambridge).
——(1983), 'Stephanus, proconsul of Asia, and related statues', in *Oceanus: Essays Presented to Ihor Sevcenko* (Cambridge, Mass.), 196–219 = Foss (1990), ch. 3.
——(1990), *History and Archaeology of Byzantine Asia Minor* (Aldershot).
——(1996), *Cities, Fortresses and Villages in Byzantine Asia Minor* (Aldershot), ch. 1, 'Lycia in history' = *The Fort at Dereagzi*, ed. J. Morganstern (Tübingen, 1993), 5–25; ch. 2 = 'The Lycian coast in the Byzantine Age', *DOP* 48 (1994), 1–52; ch. 3 = 'Cities and villages of Lycia in the Life of St Nicolas of Holy Zion', *Greek Orthodox Theological Review*, 36 (1991), 303–39.
Francovich, R. (1989), 'The making of medieval Tuscany', in Randsborg (1989), 157–71.
——and Noyé, G. (eds.) (1994), *La storia dell'alto mediovo italiano (VI–X secolo) alla luce dell archeologia* (Florence).
Frantz, A. (1975), 'Pagan philosophers in Christian Athens', *Proc. Am. Phil. Soc.* 119.1: 31–6.
French, D. H. (1992), 'Roads in Pisidia', in E. Schwertheim (ed.), *Forschungen in Pisidia*, Asia Minor Studien 6 (Bonn), 167–75.
Frend, W. H. C. (1972), *The Rise of the Monophysite Movement* (Cambridge).

Frere, S. S. (1977), 'Verulamium and Canterbury', in P. M. Duval and E. Frézouls (1977), 189–95.
Frézouls, E. (1988), *Les Villes antiques de la France*, ii (Strasbourg).
Frezza, P. (1974), 'L'influsso del diritto giustinianeo nelle formule e nella prassi in Italia', *Ius Romanum Medii Aevi* I.2.c.ee (Milan).
Friedländer, P. (1939), *Spätantiker Gemäldezyklus des Procopius von Gaza* (Rome).
Fulford, M. G., and Peacock, D. P. S. (1984), *Excavations at Carthage: The British Mission*, i/2, *The Avenue du président Habib-Bourguiba: Pottery and Ceramic Objects* (Sheffield).
——and Peacock, D. P. S. (1994), *Excavations at Carthage: The British Mission*, ii/2, *The Circular Harbour* (Oxford).
Gallinié, H. (1988), 'Reflections on medieval Tours', in R. Hodges and B. Hobley (eds.), CBA Research Report 68 (Oxford), 57–62.
Galvao-Sobrinho, C. R. (1995), 'Funerary epigraphy and the spread of Christianity in the West', *Athenaeum*, NS 83: 431–62.
García Moreno, L. A. (1977–8), 'La cristianización de la topografía de las ciudades de la península ibérica durante la Antigüedad tardía', *Archivo Español de Arqueología Tardía*, 50–1: 311–21.
Gardner, J. F. (1986), 'Proof of status in the Roman World', *BICS* 33: 1–14.
——(1993), *Being a Roman Citizen* (London).
Garitte, G. (1960), Strategius Monachus, *La Prise de Jérusalem par les Perses en 614*, ed. and tr. from Georgian, CSCO 202, Scriptores Iberici 11 (Louvain).
Garnsey, P. (1970), *Social Status and Legal Privilege in the Roman Empire* (Oxford).
Gascou, J. (1972), 'La Détention collégiale de l'autorité pagarchique dans l'Égypte byzantine', *Byzantion*, 43: 60–72.
——(1976*a*), 'L'Institution des bucellaires', *BIFAO* 72: 143–56.
——(1976*b*), 'Les Institutions de l'hippodrome en Égypte byzantin', *BIFAO* 76: 185–212.
——(1976*c*), 'Les Monastères pachômiens et l'état byzantin', *BIFAO* 76: 157–84.
——(1985), 'Les Grands domaines, la cité et l'état en Égypte byzantine', *Travaux et Mémoires*, 9: 1–90.
——(1987), 'Le Cadastre d'Aphrodito', *Travaux et Mémoires*, 10: 103–48.
——(1989), 'La Table budgétaire d'Antaeopolis', in Morrisson and Lefort (1989), 279–313.
——(1990), 'Remarques critiques sur la table budgétaire d'Antaeopolis', *ZPE* 82: 97–101.
——(1992), 'Les Revenus en espèces de la maison des Apions', *CE* 93: 243–8.
——(1994), *Un Codex Fiscal Hermopolite (P. Sorb II69)*, Am. Studies in Papyrology 32 (Atlanta).
——and MacCoull, L. S. B. (1987), 'Le Cadastre d'Aphrodito', *Travaux et Mémoires*, 10: 104–58.
Gatier, P.-L. (1985), 'Nouvelles inscriptions de Gerasa', *Syria*, 62: 298–307.
——(1994), 'Villages du proche-orient protobyzantin (4ème–7ème): Étude régionale', in G. R. D. King and Averil Cameron (1994), 17–48.

Gaudemet, J. (1958), *L'Église dans l'empire romain, IVe–Ve siècles* (Paris).
Gauthier, N. (1975), *Recueil des inscriptions chrétiennes de la Gaule antérieure à la Renaissance carolingienne*, i (Paris).
——(1999), 'La Topographie chrétienne entre idéologie et pragmatisme', in Brogiolo and Ward-Perkins (1999), 195–209.
Gawlikowski, M. (1989), 'A residential area by the South decumanus', in Zayadine (1989), 107–36.
——(1992), 'Installations omayyades à Jérash', *Studies in the History and Archaeology of Jordan*, 4: 357–62.
——and Musa, A. (1986), 'The church of bishop Marianos', in Zayadine (1986*a*), 137–53.
Geremek, H. (1981), 'Les *Politeuomenoi* égyptiens sont-ils identiques aux *bouleutai*?', *Anagennesis*, 1: 231–47.
——(1990), 'Sur la question des *boulai* dans les villes égyptiennes au Ve–VIIe siècles', *JJP*. 20: 47–54.
Gianfranceschi, I., and Ragni, E. L. (1996), *L'area di santa Giulia: Un itinerario nella storia, la domus, le capanne langobarde, il monastero, il tesoro* (Brescia).
Giardina, A. (ed.) (1986), *Società romana e impero tardoantico*, iii. *Le merci. Gli insediamenti* (Rome/Bari).
——and Schiavone, A. (eds.) (1981), *Società romana e produzione schiavistica*, i. *L'Italia: Insediamenti e forme economiche*; ii. *Merci, mercati e scambi nell mediterraneo* (Rome/Bari).
Glaube, H., and Wirth, E. (1984), *Aleppo, historische und geographische Beiträge zur baulichen Geltung, zur sozialen Organisation und zur wirtschaftlichen Dynamik einer vorderasiatischen Fernhandlungsmetropole* (Wiesbaden).
Glick, Th. F. (1996), *Irrigation and Hydrolic Technology: Medieval Spain and its Legacy* (Aldershot).
Glucker, J. (1978), *Antiochus and the Late Academy*, Hypomnemata 56 (Göttingen).
Goffart, W. (1982), 'Old and new in Merovingian taxation', *Past and Present*, 96: 3–21.
Goldman, H. (1950), *Excavations at Gözlü/Tarsus* (Princeton).
González, A. C. (1998), 'From the Roman to the Arab: The rise of the city of Murcia', in Marín (1998), 205–16.
González, J. (1986), 'The *Lex Irnitana*: A new copy of the Flavian municipal law', *JRS* 76: 147–243.
Goodchild, R. (1979), *Libyan Studies*, ed. J. Reynolds (London).
Gorecki, J. (1991/2), 'Antike Fundmünzen in Limyra', *Jahreshefte des Östr. Archäolog. Inst.* 61: 185–7.
Gorges, J.-G. (1979), *Les Villas hispano-romaines* (Paris).
Grabar, O., Holod, R., Knudstad, J., and Trousdale, W. (1978), *City in the Desert: Qasr al-Hayr East*, 2 vols. (Cambridge, Mass.).
Graf, F. (1997), 'Camels, roads and wheels in Late Antiquity', in *Donum Amicitiae = Electrum*, 1 (Cracow), 43–9.
Greatrex, G. (1997), 'The Nika riot: A reappraisal', *JHS* 117: 60–86.

Greene, K. (1986), *The Archaeology of the Roman Economy* (London).

Greenwalt, C. H., Ratté, C., and Rautman, M. L. (1993), 'The Sardis Campaigns 1988 & 1989', *AASOR* 51: 1–43.

——————(1995), 'Sardis Campaigns 1992 & 1993', *AASOR* 53: 1–36.

Grégoire, E., and Kugener, M.-A. (eds.) (1930), *Marc le Diacre, Vie de Porphyre, évêque de Gaza* (Paris).

Gregory, T. E. (1979), *Vox Populi: Popular Opinion and Violence in the Religious Controversies of the 5th Century A.D.* (Columbus, Ohio).

Grierson, P. (1960), 'Coinage and money in the Byzantine Empire, 498–c.1090', *Settimane di Studio del Centro Italiano di Studi sull'alto Medioevo,* viii (1961), 411–53.

Gros, P. (1985), *Mission archéologique française à Carthage: Byrsa*, iii. *La Basilique orientale et ses abords*, Collection de l'école française de Rome 41/3 (Rome).

Grünewald, M. E. G. (1974), *Spätantike Herrschaftsvillen in den nordwestlichen Provinzen des römischen Reiches* (Vienna).

Gui, I., Duval, N., and Caillet, J.-P. (1992), *Basiliques chrétiennes d'Afrique du Nord*, pt. I. *Inventaire de l'Algérie* (2 vols.) Études Augustiennes: Antiquités 129 (Paris).

Gurt, J. M., and Ripoll, G., with Chavarría, A. (2000), *Sedes Regiae-Regna Barbarica 400–800 d.C.* (Barcelona).

————and Fernández, C. G. (1994), 'Topografia de la antigüedad tardía hispánica, reflexiones para una propuesta de trabajo', *Antiquité tardive* II, 161–80.

Guyon, J. (1985), *Inscriptions chrétiennes de Marseilles, Alpes-Maritimes et Narbonnaise* II, Mémoires de l'École Pratique des Hautes Études (Sciences historiques et philosophiques) (Paris).

——(1991*a*), 'From Lugdunum to Cenvenae: Recent work at Saint-Bertrand-de-Comminges (Haute-Garonne)', *JRA* 4: 89–122.

——(1991*b*), 'Actes du XIe Congrès International d'Archéologie Chrétienne', *JRA* 4: 431–41.

Haas, C. (1997), *Alexandria in Late Antiquity: Topography and Social Conflict* (Baltimore/London).

Haldon, J. F. (1990), *Byzantium in the Seventh Century* (Cambridge).

——(1994), '*Aerikon, aerika*: A reinterpretation', *Jahrbuch der österreichischen Byzantinistik* 44, Herbert Hunger zum 80. Geburtstag (Vienna), 135–42.

——(1995), 'Seventh century continuities: The *Ajnâd* and the "Thematic Myth"', in Averil Cameron (1995), 379–423.

——(1999), 'The idea of the town in the Byzantine empire', in Brogiolo and Ward-Perkins (1999), 1–23.

Halsall, G. (1995), *Settlement and Social Organization: The Merovingian Region of Metz* (Cambridge).

——(1996), 'Towns, societies and ideas: The not so strange case of the Roman and early Merovingian region of Metz', in Christie and Loseby (1996), 234–61.

Hanfmann, G. M. A., with Mierse, W. (1983), *Sardis from Prehistoric to Roman Times* (Cambridge, Mass.).
Hanson, R. P. C. (1985), 'Transformation of pagan temples into churches in the early Christian centuries', in *id.*, *Studies in Christian Antiquity* (Edinburgh), 347–58.
Harding, L. (1949), 'Recent work on the Jerash forum', *Palestine Exploration Quarterly*, 81: 12–20.
Hardy, E. R. (1932), *The Large Estates of Byzantine Egypt* (New York).
Harmand, L. (1957), *Un aspect social et politique du monde romain, le patronat sur les collectivités publiques des origines au Bas-Empire* (Paris).
Harries, J. (1992*a*), 'Christianity and the city in Late Roman Gaul', in Rich (1992), 77–98.
——(1992*b*), 'Rome and the barbarians: A climate of treason', in J. Drinkwater and H. Elton (eds.), *Fifth Century Gaul: A Crisis of Identity* (Cambridge), 298–308.
——and Wood, I. (1993), *The Theodosian Code* (London).
Harries, Jill (1994), *Sidonius Apollinaris and the Fall of Rome* (Oxford).
Harris, W. V. (1989), *Ancient Literacy* (Cambridge).
Harrison, D. (1993), *The Early State and the Towns: Forms of Integration in Lombard Italy AD 68–74* (Lund).
Harrison, R. M. (1963), 'Churches and chapels in central Lycia', *Anat. St.* 13: 117–51.
——(1979), 'Nouvelles découvertes romaines tardives et paléobyzantines en Lycie', *CRAI*: 229–39.
Harvey, A. (1989), *Economic Expansion in the Byzantine Empire* (Cambridge).
Harvey, S. (1988), 'Syriac Historiography and the Separation of the Church', *Byzantion*, 58: 295–302.
Hassan, F. A. (1981), *Demographic Archaeology* (London).
Heather, P. (1991), *Goths and Romans* (Oxford).
——(1996), *The Goths* (Oxford).
Heinzelmann, M. (1976), *Bischofsherrschaft in Gallien, zur Kontinuität römischer Führungsschichten vom 4. bis zum 7. Jahrhundert, soziale, prospographische und bildungsgeschichtliche Aspekte*, Beiheft Francia 5 (Munich).
——(1988), 'Bischof und Herrschaft vom spätantiken Gallien bis zu den karolingischen Hausmeiern. Die institutionellen Grundlagen', in F. Prinz (ed.), *Herrschaft und Kirche*, Monographien zur Geschichte des Mittelalters 33 (Stuttgart), 23–82.
——(1990), 'Studia sanctorum', in C. Lepelley *et al.* (eds.), *Haut Moyen-Âge: Culture, éducation et société*, Études offertes à Pierre Riché (Paris), 105–38.
Hellenkemper, H. (1994), 'Early church architecture in southern Asia Minor', in K. Painter (ed.), *Churches Built in Ancient Times: Recent Studies in Early Christian Archaeology* (London).
Hendy, M. F. (1985), *Studies in the Byzantine Monetary Economy, 300–1450* (Cambridge).

Hendy, M. F. (1988), 'From public to private: The western barbarian coinages as a mirror of the disintegration of late Roman state structures, *Viator*, 19: 29–78.

Herlihy, D. (1978), *The Social History of Italy and Western Europe 700–1500*, Variorum no. IV 'The Carolingian Mansus', *EcHR* 13 (1960): 78–89.

Herman, E. (1942), 'Die kirchlichen Einkünfte des byzantinischen Niederklerus', *OCP* 8: 378–442.

Hernández, M. C. (1998), 'The social structure of al-Andalus during the Muslim occupation (711–55) and the founding of the Umayyad monarchy', in Marín (1998), 51–83.

Hild, F., and Hellenkemper, H. (1990), see *Tabula Imperii Byzantini* = *TIB*.

Hillgarth, J. N. (1980), 'Popular religion in Spain', in James (1980), 1–60.

——(1986), *Christianity and Paganism 350–750* (Philadelphia).

Hill, D. R. (1971), *The Termination of Hostilities in the Early Arab Conquests AD 634–56* (London).

Hill, S. (1996), *The Early Byzantine Churches of Cilicia and Isauria* (Aldershot).

Hillenbrand, R. (1999), 'Anjar and early Islamic urbanism', in Brogiolo and Ward-Perkins (1999), 59–98.

Hirschfeld, Y. (1992), *The Judaean Desert Monasteries in the Byzantine Period* (New Haven).

Hitti, P. K. (1916; repr. 1966), *The Origins of the Islamic State*, a translation of Baladhuri's History (New York).

Hobley, B. (1986), *Roman and Saxon London: A Reappraisal* (London).

Hodges, R., and Bowden, W. (1998), *The Sixth Century: Production, Distribution and Demand*, The Transformation of the Roman World vol. 3 (Leiden/Boston/Cologne).

——and Hobley, B. (eds.) (1988), *The Rebirth of Towns in the West 700–1050* (London).

——and Whitehouse, D. (1983), *Mohammed, Charlemagne and the Origins of Europe* (London).

——Gibson, S., and Mitchell, J. (1997), 'The making of a monastic city: The architecture of San Vincenzo al Volturno in the ninth century', *PBSR* 65: 233–86.

——Saraçi, G., *et al.* (1997), 'Late Antique and Byzantine Butrint', *JRA* 10: 206–34.

Hohlfelder, R. L. (ed.) (1982), *City, Town and Countryside in the Early Byzantine Era* (New York).

——(1992), 'An introduction to coin finds at Caesarea', *JRA Suppl.* 5: 167–8.

Holm Nielsen, S., Nielsen, I., Anderson, F. G. (1986), 'The excavation of Byzantine baths in Umm Qeis', *Annual of the Department of Antiquities of Jordan*, 30: 219–32.

Holum, K. G. (1992), 'Archaeological evidence for the fall of Byzantine Caesarea', *BASOR* 286: 74–85.

——(1996), 'The survival of the bouleutic class at Caesarea in Late Antiquity', in Raban and Holum (1992), 615–27.

——and Hohlfelder, R. L. (1988), *King Herod's Dream: Caesarea on the Sea* (New York).

——and Raban, A. (eds.) (1992), *Caesarea*, see under Raban, A., and Holum, K. G. (eds.).

——Avner, R., and Patrich, J. (eds.) (forthcoming), *Caesarea Papers*, ii: Herod's temple, the praetorium and granaries, the later harbour, a gold coin hoard and other studies, Journal of Roman Archaeology Supplement (Ann Arbor).

Homés-Fredericq, D., and Hennessy, J. B. (eds.) (1989), *Archaeology of Jordan*, II.i–ii, *Field Surveys and Sites, A–K, L–Z* (Louvain).

Hommes et richesses dans l'empire byzantin, tome i. *IVe–VIIe siècle* (Paris/ Lethielleux 1989).

Hommes et richesses dans l'empire byzantin, tome ii. *VIIIe–XVe siècle* (1991), ed. V. Kravari, J. Lefort, and C. Morrisson (Paris).

Honigmann, E. (1951), *Évêques et évêches monophysites d'Asie antérieure au VIe siècle*, CSCO CXXVII subsid.17 (Louvain).

Hopkins, K. (1978), 'Economic growth and towns in Classical Antiquity', in P. Abrams and E. A. Wrigley (eds.), *Towns in Societies* (Cambridge), 35–77.

——(1980), 'Taxes and trade in the Roman Empire (200 BC–AD 400)', *JRS* 70: 101–25.

Hopkinson, N. (ed.) (1994), *Studies in the Dionysiaca of Nonnus*, Camb. Phil. Soc. Suppl. Vol. 17 (Cambridge).

Hornickel, O. (1930), *Ehren und Rankprädikate in den Papyrusurkunden* (Giessen).

Humphrey, J. H. (1980), 'Vandal and Byzantine Carthage', in J. G. Pedley (ed.), *New Light on Ancient Carthage*, 85–120 (Ann Arbor), 85–120.

——(1986), *Roman Circuses: Arenas for Chariot-racing* (London/Berkeley).

——(1988), *The Circus and Byzantine Cemetery at Carthage*, i (Ann Arbor).

——(ed.) (1991), *Literacy in the Roman World*, JRA suppl. 3 (Ann Arbor).

Humphries, M. (1999), *Communities of the Blessed: Social Environment and Religious Change in Northern Italy, c.250–400* (Oxford).

Hunt, D. (1993), 'Christianising the Roman Empire: The evidence of the Code', in Harries and Wood (1993), 143–58.

Hurst, H. R. (1994), *Excavations at Carthage, the British Mission*, ii/1, *The Circular Harbour* (Oxford).

——and Roskams, S. P. (1984), *Excavations at Carthage*, i/1. *The Avenue du président Habib Bourguiba* (Sheffield).

Huxley, G. L. (1977), 'The second dark age of the Peloponnese', *Lakonikai Spoudai*, 3: 84–110.

Ibach, R. D. (1987), *Hesban*, v. *Archaeological Survey of the Hesban Region* (Berrien Springs).

Ibrahim, M., Sauer, J., and Yassine, K. (1976), 'The East Jordan Valley Survey 1975', *BASOR* 222: 41–66.

Jaeger, H. (1960), 'Justinien et l'episcopalis audientia', *Nouv. Rev. Hist. Droit Franc. et Étr.*, 4 sér., 38: 214–62.

Jäger, H. (ed.) (1987), *Stadtkernforschung* (Cologne).

Jäggi, C., Meier, H. R., and Brenk, B., with a contribution by I. Kehrberg (1997), 'New data for the chronology of the early Christian cathedral at Gerasa: Third interim report', *Annual Department of Antiquities of Jordan*, 41: 311–20.

James, E. (ed.) (1980), *Visigothic Spain: New Approaches* (Oxford).

——(1988), *The Franks* (Oxford).

Jankuhn, H., Schlesinger, W., and Steuer, H. (eds.) (1973–4), *Vor und Frühformen der europäischen Stadt im Mittelalter*, 2 vols. (Göttingen).

Jarnut, J. (1982), *Geschichte der Langobarden* (Stuttgart).

Jeffreys, E., Jeffreys, M., and Scott, R. (eds.) (1986), *John Malalas*, Byzantina Australiensia 4 (Melbourne).

——*et al.* (1990), *Studies in John Malalas* (Sydney).

Johnson, A. C., and West, L. C. (1949), *Byzantine Egypt: Economic Studies* (Princeton).

Johnson, S. (1983), *Late Roman Fortifications* (London).

Jones, A. H. M. (1940), *The Greek City from Alexander to Justinian* (Oxford).

——(1949), *Constantine the Great and the Conversion of Europe* (London).

——(1960), 'Church finance in the fifth and sixth centuries', *Journ. Theol. Stud.* NS 11: 84–94.

——(1964), *The Later Roman Empire 284–602* (Oxford).

Jones, J., *et al.* (1988), *First Millennium Papers: Western Europe in the First Millennium AD*, BAR S401 (Oxford).

Jongmann, W. (1991), *The Economy and Society of Pompeii* (Amsterdam).

Jouffroy, H. (1986), *La Construction publique en Italie et dans l'Afrique Romain* (Strasbourg).

Kaimio, M., and Koenen, L. (1997), 'Report on the decipherment of Petra papyri', *Annual of the Department of Antiquities of Jordan*, 41: 459–62.

Kaiser, R. (1979), 'Steuer und Zoll in der Merowingerzeit', *Francia*, 7: 1–18.

——(1987), 'Civitas und Bischofsitz', in Jäger (1987), 247–78.

Karayannopulos, J. (1958), *Das Finanzwesen des byzantinischen Staates* (Munich).

Karlin-Hayter, P. (1993), 'Où l'abeille butine, la culture littéraire monastique à Byzance aux VIIIe et IXe siècles', *Rev. Bénédictine*, 103: 90–116.

Karwiese, S. (1985), *Anzeiger der österreichischen Akademie der Wissenschaften*, Phil. Hist. Klass. 122, 135–43.

——(1986), *Anzeiger der österreichischen Akademie der Wissenschaften*, Phil. Hist. Klass. 123, 85–91.

——(1995*a*), 'The church of Mary and the temple of Hadrian Olympius', Koester (1995), 311–19.

——(1995*b*), *Gross ist die Artemis von Ephesus, die Geschichte einer der grossen Städte der antiken Welt* (Vienna).

Kaster, R. (1988), *Guardians of Language: The Grammarian and Society in Late Antiquity* (Berkeley).

Keay, S. J. (1988), *Roman Spain* (London).

——(1991), 'New light on Tarraco', *JRA* 4: 383–97.

——and Díaz-Andreu, M. (1997), *The Archaeology of Iberia: The Dynamics of Change* (London).

Keenan, J. G. (1973), 'The names of Flavius and Aurelius as status designations in later Roman Egypt', *ZPE* 11: 33–63.

——(1974), 'The names of Flavius and Aurelius as status designations in later Roman Egypt, Part 2', *ZPE* 13: 283–304.

——(1981), 'On village and polis in Byzantine Egypt', *Proc. XVI Int. Congr. of Papyrology*, 479–85.

——(1983), 'An afterthought on the names of Flavius and Aurelius', *ZPE* 53: 245–50.

——(1984), 'Aurelius Apollos and the Aphrodito village elite', *Atti VII Congr. Int. di Pap.*, 557–83.

——(1985), 'Notes on absentee landlordism in Aphrodito', *BASP* 22: 137–69.

Kehrberg, I., and Ostrasz, A. A. (1997), 'A history of the occupational changes at the site of the hippodrome of Gerasa', *SHAJ* 6: 137–67.

Kelly, J. N. D. (1995), *Golden Mouth: The Story of John Chrysostom* (London).

Kempf, K. (1964), 'Untersuchungen am Trierer Dom 1961–63', *Germania*, 42: 126–41.

Kempf, S. J. (1968), 'Grundrissentwicklung und Baugeschichte des Trierer Doms', *Das Münster*, 21: 1 ff.

Kennedy, David L. (1997), 'Aerial archaeology in Jordan: Air photography and the Jordanian Southern Hawran', *Studies in the History and Archaeology of Jordan*, 6 (Amman), 77–86.

——(1998*a*), 'The identity of Roman Gerasa: An archaeological approach', *Mediterranean Archaeology*, 11: 39–69.

——(1998*b*), 'The surface remains of Umm El-Jimal and its surroundings', in B. De Vries (1998), 39–90.

Kennedy, H. (1985*a*), 'From Polis to Medina', *Past and Present*, 106: 3–27.

——(1985*b*), 'The last century of Byzantine Syria', *Byzantinische Forschungen*, 10: 141–83.

——(1992), 'Antioch from Byzantium to Islam and back again', in Rich (1992), 181–98.

——(1996), *Muslim Spain and Portugal: A Political History of al-Andalus* (London/New York).

Kent, J. H. (1966), *Corinth*, viii/3. *The inscriptions 1926–1970* (Princeton).

Kent, J. P. C. (1981), *Roman Imperial Coinage*, viii. *AD 337–64* (London).

——(1994), *Roman Imperial Coinage*, x (London).

Kern, O. (1900), *Die Inschriften von Magnesia am Mäander* (Berlin).

Keydell, R. (1961), 'Mythendeutung in den *Dionysiaka* des Nonnos', *Gedenkschrift für Georg Rhode*, ed. G. Radke (Tübingen), 105–14 = R. Keydell, *Kleine Schriften 1911–76* (Leipzig, 1982), 523–32.

Keys, D. (1999), *Catastrophe: An Investigation into the Origins of the Modern World* (London).

Kienast, D. (1962), 'Der Münzlauf von Ankara, Studien zu Besondertheiten des Geldumlaufs im Ostteil und Westteil des Imperiums', *JNG* 12: 65–112.

King, G. R. D. (1982), 'Preliminary report on a survey of Byzantine and Islamic sites in Jordan (1980)', *ADAJ* 26: 85–95.

King, G. R. D. and Cameron, Averil (1994), *The Byzantine and Early Islamic Near East*, ii. *Land Use and Settlement Patterns* (Princeton).
——*et al.* (1983), 'Survey of Byzantine and Islamic sites in Jordan: Second season report (1981)', *ADAJ* 27: 385–436.
King, P. D. (1972), *Law and Society in the Visigothic Kingdom* (Cambridge).
Kirsten, E. (1954), 'Chorbischof', *RAC* 2: 1105–14.
——(1958), *Die byzantinische Stadt*, Berichte zum XI Internationalen Byzantinisten Kongress München 1958 (Munich), i. 1–48.
Klingshirn, W. (1985), 'Caesarius of Arles and the ransoming of captives in Sub-Roman Gaul', *JRS* 75: 183–203.
——(1994), *Caesarius of Arles: The Making of a Christian Community in Late Antique Gaul* (Cambridge).
Knapp. R. (1992), *Latin Inscriptions from Central Spain* (Berkeley).
Koenen, L. (1996), 'The carbonised archive of Petra', *JRA* 9: 177–91.
Koester, H. (ed.) (1995), *Ephesos, Metropolis of Asia*, Harvard Theological Studies 41 (Valley Forge, Pa.).
——(ed.) (1998), *Pergamon City of the Gods,* Harvard Theological Studies 46 (Valley Forge, Pa.).
Kopecek, T. A. (1974), 'The Cappadocian fathers and civic patriotism', *Church History*, 43: 293–303.
Kraeling, C. H. (1938), *Gerasa, City of the Decapolis*, Amer. School of Oriental Research (New Haven).
Kraemer, C. J. (1958), *Excavations at Nessana*, iii (Princeton).
Krause, J.-V. (1987), *Spätantike Patronatsformen im Westen des römischen Reiches* (Munich).
Krautheimer, R. (1980), *Rome: Profile of a City* (Princeton).
Kravari, V., Lefort, J., and Morrisson, C. (eds.) (1991), *Hommes et richesses dans l'empire byzantin*, ii. *VIIIe–XVe siècle* (Paris).
Krüger, J. (1990), *Oxyrhynchos in der Kaiserzeit* (Frankfurt am Main).
Kuehn, C. (1995), *Channels of Imperishable Fire: The Beginnings of Christian Mystical Poetry and Dioscoros of Aphrodito* (New York).
Laistner, M. L. W. (1967), *Christianity and Pagan Culture* (Ithaca, NY).
Lamberton, R. (1989), *Homer the Theologian: Neoplatonist Allegorical Reading and the Growth of the Epic Tradition* (Berkeley).
Lampinen, P. (1992), 'The coins, preliminary report', in Vann (1992), 169–72.
Lane Fox, R. (1986), *Pagans and Christians* (Harmondsworth).
Lang-Auinger, C. (1996), *Hanghaus 1 in Ephesos, der Baubefund = Forschungen in Ephesos* VIII.3 (Vienna, 1996).
La Rocca, C. (1989), 'Plus ça change, plus c'est la même chose: Trasformazioni della città altomedievale in Italia settentrionale', *Società e Storia*, 45: 721–8.
——(1992), 'Public building and urban change in northern Italy in the early medieval period', in Rich (1992), 161–80.
La Rocca Hudson, C. (1986), ' "Dark Ages" a Verona. Edilizia privata, aree aperte e strutture pubbliche in una città dell'Italia settentrionale', *Archeologia Medievale*, 13: 31–78.

Lassus, J. (1977), *Les Portiques de Antioche* (Princeton).

Leclercq, H. (1948), 'Chorévêques', in Cabrol and Leclerq, *Dictionnaire d'archéologie chrétienne et de liturgie*, iii. 1423–52.

Lefebure, M. G. (1907), *Recueil des inscriptions grecques chrétiennes d'Égypte* (Cairo).

Lefort, J. (1991), 'Population et peuplement en Macédoine orientale IX–XV siècle', in Kravari, Lefort, and Morrisson (1991), 63–82.

Lehmann, C. M. (2000), 'The governor's palace and warehouse complex, west flank (areas KK7–9, CV, 1993–95 excavations)', in Holum, Raban, and Patrich (forthcoming).

—— and Holum, K. G. (2000), *The Greek and Latin Inscriptions of Caesarea Maritima*, Caesarea Reports, vol. i (Boston).

Leipoldt, J. (1903), *Schenute von Atripe und die Entstehung des nationalen ägyptischen Christentums*, Texte und Untersuchungen XXV.1 (N.F.X.1) (Leipzig).

Lemerle, P. (1963), 'La Chronique improprement dite de Monemvasie: Le Contexte historique et légendaire', *REB* 21: 5–49.

—— (1971), *Le Premier Humanisme byzantin* (Paris); translated into English as Lemerle 1986, see below.

—— (1979), *Agrarian History of Byzantium from the Origins to the 12th Century* (Galway).

—— (1979–81), *Les Plus Anciens recueils de miracles de S. Demetrius*, i. *Le Texte*; ii. *Commentaire* (Paris).

—— (1986), *Byzantine Humanism the First Phase*, tr. Helen Lindsay and Ann Moffatt, Byzantina Australiensia 3 (Canberra).

Lenzen, C. J., and Knauf, E. A. (1987), 'Beirt Ras/Capitolias, a preliminary evaluation of the archaeological and textual evidence', *Syria*, 64: 21–46.

Lepelley, C. (1979–80), *Les Cités de l'Afrique romaine au Bas-Empire*, 2 vols. (Paris).

—— (1992), 'Permanences de la cité classique et archaïsmes municipaux en Italie au Bas-Empire', in M. Cristol *et al.* (eds.), *Institutions, société et vie politique dans l'empire romain au IVe siècle ap. J.-C.*, Mélanges d'histoire de l'antiquité tardive offerts à A. Chastagnol (Rome), 353–71.

—— (ed.) (1996), *La Fin de la cité antique et le début de la cité médiévale de la fin du IIIe à l'avènement de Charlemagne* (Bari).

—— (1998), 'Le Patronat épiscopal au IVe et Ve siècles: Continuités et ruptures avec le patronat classique', in Rebillard and Sotinel (1998), 17–33.

Lestocquoy, J. (1953), 'Le Paysage urbain en Gaul', *AESC* 8: 159–72.

Levick, B., Mitchell, S., Potter, J., and Waelkens, M. (eds.), coins by Nash, D. (1988), *Monuments from Aezanitis*, *MAMA* IX (London).

—— —— —— —— (eds.)(1993), *Monuments from Appia and the Upper Tembris Valley*, *MAMA* X (London).

Levine, L. I., and Netzer, E. (1986), *Excavations at Caesarea Maritima 1975, 1976, 1979: Final Report*, Quedem 21 (Jerusalem).

Lewin, A. (1991), *Studi sul la città imperiale romana nell'Oriente tardoantico*, Biblioteca di Athenaeum 17 (Como).

Lewin, A. (1995*a*), *Assemblee popolari e lotta politica nelle città dell'impero romana* (Florence).

——(1995*b*), 'Il mondo dei ginnasi nell'epoca tardoantica', *Atti del X Convegno Internazionale dell'Accademia Romanistica Constantiniana* (Naples), 623–8.

Lewis, A. R. (1976), 'The dukes of the regnum Francorum, AD 550–751', *Speculum*, 51: 381–410.

Lewitt, T. (1991), *Agricultural Production in the Roman Economy*, BAR Int. 568 (Oxford).

Liebeschuetz, H. (1967), 'Western Christian thought from Boethius to Anselm', in A. H. Armstrong (ed.), *Cambridge History of Later Greek and Early Medieval Philosophy* (Cambridge), 538–639.

Liebeschuetz, W. (1959), 'The finances of Antioch in the fourth century AD', *BZ* 52: 344–56 = Liebeschuetz (1990*b*), ch. 12.

——(1972), *Antioch: City and Imperial Administration in the Later Roman Empire* (Oxford).

——(1973), 'The origin of the office of the pagarch', *BZ* 66: 38–46 = Liebeschuetz (1990*b*), ch. 17.

——(1974), 'The pagarch: City and imperial administration in Byzantine Egypt', *JJP* 18: 163–8 = Liebeschuetz (1990*b*), ch. 18.

——(1979), *Continuity and Change in Roman Religion* (Oxford).

——(1985), 'Synesius and municipal politics in Cyrenaica in the 5th century AD', *Byzantion*, 55: 146–64 = Liebeschuetz (1990*b*), ch. 14.

——(1986), 'Why did Synesius become bishop of Ptolemais?', *Byzantion*, 56: 180–95 = Liebeschuetz (1990*b*), ch. 15.

——(1990*a*), *Barbarians and Bishops: Army, Church and State in the Age of Arcadius and Chrysostom* (Oxford).

——(1990*b*), *From Diocletian to the Arab Conquest: Change in the Late Roman Empire* (Great Yarmouth).

——(1991), 'Hochschule', *RAC* 15: 858–911.

——(1992*a*), 'A. H. M. Jones and the *Later Roman Empire*', *Bulletin of London Institute of Archaeology*, 29: 1–8.

——(1992*b*), 'The end of the ancient city', in Rich (1992), 1–49.

——(1997), 'Cities, taxes and the accommodation of the barbarians: The theories of Durliat and Goffart', in W. Pohl (ed.), *Kingdoms of the Empire: The Integration of Barbarians in Late Antiquity*, i, ESF Project the Transformation of the Roman World (Leiden), 135–51.

——and Kennedy, H. (1988), 'Antioch and the villages of Northern Syria in the 4th–6th centuries AD', *Nottingham Medieval Studies*, 32: 65–90.

Lieu, S. N. C. (1985), *Manichaeism* (Manchester).

Life of Nicholas, see under Sevcenko, I., and Sevcenko, N. (1984).

Lifshitz, B. (1957), 'Une inscription byzantine du Caesarée en Israel', *REG* 70: 118–33.

——(1961), 'Inscriptions grecques de Césarée en Palestine', *Revue Biblique*, 68: 115–26.

Lightfoot, C. S. (1998), 'The survival of cities in Byzantine Anatolia: The case of Armorium', *Byzantion*, 68: 56 ff.
Lilie, R.-J. (1976), *Die byzantinische Reaktion auf die Ausbreitung der Araber* (Munich).
——(1995), 'Araber und Themen. Zum Einfluss der arabischen Expansion auf die byzantinische Militärorganisation', in Averil Cameron (1995), 425–60.
Lizzi, R. (1989), *Vescovi e strutture ecclesiastiche nella città tardoantica*, L'Italia Annonaria nel IC–V secolo D.C. (Como).
——(1990), 'Ambrose's contemporaries and the Christianisation of Northern Italy', *JRS* 80: 156–73.
——(1998), 'I vescovi e i *potentes* de la terra: Definizione e limite del ruolo episcopale nelle due *partes imperii* fra IV e V secolo d.C.', in Rebillard and Sotinel (1998), 81–104.
Lloret, S. Gutiérrez (1993) 'De la *ciuitas* a la *madîna*, destrucción y formación de la ciudad en el sureste de Al Andalus' *IV Congreso de Arqueología Medieval Española,* i (Alicante), 13–35. Translated into English as: 'From *Civitas* to *Madína*: Destruction and formation of the city in the south-east al-Andalus—the archaeological debate', in Marín (1998), 217–63.
Longo, A. A. (1990), 'Siracusa e Toarmina nell'agiografia italogreca', *Rivista di studi bizantini e neoellenici*, NS 27: 33–54.
Loseby, S. T. (1992*a*), 'Bishops and cathedrals: Order and diversity in the fifth century urban landscape of Southern Gaul', in Drinkwater and Elton (1992), 144–55.
——(1992*b*), 'Marseilles: A late antique success story', *JRS* 82: 165–85.
——(1996), 'Arles in Late Antiquity: Gallula Roma Arelas and urbs Genesii', in Christie and Loseby (1996), 45–70.
Lotter, F. (1971), 'Antonius von Lerins und der Untergang Ufernorikums: ein Beitrag zur Frage der Bevölkerungs Kontinuität im Alpen-Donau-Raum', *Historische Zeitschrift*, 212: 265–315.
Luca, G. de (1984), *Altertümer von Pergamum* XI.4 (Berlin).
MacAdam, H. I. (1994), 'Settlements and settlement patterns in Northern Transjordania', in G. R. D. King and Averil Cameron (1994), 49–94.
MacCoull, L. S. B. (1988), *Dioscorus of Aphrodito: His Work and his World* (Berkeley).
MacDonald, B. (1980), 'The Wadi al-Hesa Survey 1979: A preliminary report', *Annual of the Department of Antiquities of Jordan*, 24: 169–83.
——(1981), 'The Wadi al-Hesa Survey', *Biblical Archaeologist*, 44: 60–1.
Macias, A. C. (1988), *El libro de las vidas de los santos padres de Mérida* (Mérida).
MacKenzie, M. M., and Roueché, C. (eds.) (1989), *Images of Authority: Papers presented to Joyce Reynolds on her 70th birthday* (Cambridge).
McKitterick, R. (ed.) (1990), *The Uses of Literacy in Early Mediaeval Europe* (Cambridge).
McLynn, N. B. (1994), *Ambrose of Milan* (Berkeley).
MacMullen, R. (1982), 'The epigraphic habit in the Roman Empire', *AJP* 103: 233–46.
——(1986), 'The frequency of inscriptions in Roman Lydia', *ZPE* 65: 237–8.

McNeill, W. H. (1976), *Plagues and Peoples* (New York).
McNicoll, A. W., Edwards, P. C., *et al.* (1992), *Pella in Jordan*, ii (Sydney).
——Smith, R. H., *et al.* (1982), *Pella in Jordan*, i (Canberra).
Macrides, R., and Magdalino, P. (1988), 'The architecture of ekphrasis: Construction and context of Paul the Silentiary's ekphrasis of Hagia Sophia', *BMGS* 12: 47–82.
Maehler, H. (1974), BGU XII, *Papyri aus Hermupolis* (Berlin, 1974).
Maier, J.-L. (1973), *L'Épiscopat de l'Afrique romaine, vandale et byzantine* (Rome).
Majcherek, G. (1997), 'Roman and Byzantine houses from Kōm el-Dikka (Alexandria)', *Topoi*, 1951: 133–45.
Mango, C. (1975), 'The availability of books in the Byzantine Empire AD 750–850', in *Byzantine Books and Bookmen* (Washington), 29–46.
——(1980), *Byzantium: The Empire of New Rome* (London).
——(1985), *Le Développement urbain de Constantinople IVe– VIIe siècles* (Paris).
——and Dagron, G. (eds.) (1997), *Constantinople and its Hinterland* (Aldershot).
Mango, M. M., and Bennett, A. (1994), *The Sevso Treasure*, Art Historical Description and Inscriptions, Methods of Manufacture and Scientific Analysis, JRA Suppl. 12 (Ann Arbor).
Mann, J. C. (1983), *Legionary Recruitment and Veteran Settlement during the Principate*, ed. M. Roxan, London Institute of Archaeology Occasional Papers 7 (London).
——(1985), 'Epigraphic consciousness', *JRS* 75: 204–6.
Mannoni, T. (1989), 'General remarks on the changes in techniques observable in the material culture of the first millennium in North-West Italy', in Randsborg (1989), 152–5.
Marazzi, F. (1998), 'The destinies of late Antique Italy: Politico-economic developments', in Hodges and Bowden (1998), 119–59.
Marc le diacre (1930), *Vie de Porphyre, évêque de Gaza*, ed. and tr. H. Grégoire and M.-A. Kugener (Paris).
Marín, M. (ed.) (1998), *The Formation of al-Andalus*, Part 1. *History and Society*, The Formation of the Classical Islamic World 46 (Aldershot).
Markus, R. (1990), *The End of Ancient Christianity* (Cambridge).
——(1997), *Gregory the Great and his World* (Cambridge).
Marrou, H. I. (1938), *Saint Augustin et la fin de la culture antique* (Paris).
——(1955), *Histoire de la éducation dans l'antiquité*, 3rd edn. (Paris).
Martin, A. (1998), 'L'Image de l'évêque à travers les "canons d'Athanase": Devoirs et réalités', Rebillard and Sotinel (1998), 59–70.
Martin, J., and Quint, B. (eds.) (1990), *Christentum und antike Gesellschaft* (Darmstadt).
Martindale, J. R. (1992), *The Prosopography of the Later Roman Empire* iii A–iii B (AD 527–641) (Cambridge).
Maspero, J. (1912), *L'Organisation militaire de l'Égypte byzantine* (Paris).
Mateos Cruz, P. (1995), 'La cristianización de la Lusitania (ss. IV–VII): Extremadura en época visigoda', *Extremadura Arqueológica*, 4: 239–63.

Mathisen, R. W. (1984), 'The family of Georgius Florentius Gregorius and the bishops of Tours', *Medievalia et Humanistica*, NS 12: 83–95.
——(1992), 'Gallic visitors to Italy, business or pleasure?', in Drinkwater and Elton (1992), 228–38.
——(1993), *Roman Aristocrats in Barbarian Gaul* (Austin, Tex.).
——and Sivan, H. S. (eds.) (1996), *Shifting Frontiers in Late Antiquity* (Aldershot).
Matthews, J. F. (1975), *Western Aristocracies and the Imperial Court AD 363–425* (Oxford).
Mattingly, D. J. (1995), *Tripolitania* (London).
——and Hayes, J. (1992), 'Nador and fortified farms in North Africa', *JRA* 5: 408–18.
——and Hitchner, R. B. (1995), 'Roman Africa, an archaeological review', *JRS* 85: 165–213.
——and Lloyd, J. A. (eds.) (1989), *Libya: Research in History, Archaeology and Geography* (London) = *Libyan Studies*, 20.
Mazor, G. (1987–8), 'The Bet Shean Project', *Excavations and Surveys in Israel*, 6: 7–23.
Mazzarino, S. (1951), *Aspetti Sociali del Quarto Secolo* (Rome).
Meiggs, R. (1973), *Roman Ostia*, 2nd edn. (Oxford).
Merschen, B., and Knauf, E. A. (1988), 'From Gadara to Umm Qais', *Zt. d. deutschen Palestina-Vereins*, 104: 128–32.
Metcalfe, D. M. (1967), 'How extensive was the issue of folles during the years 775–820?', *Byzantion*, 37: 270–310.
Meyer, E. A. (1990), 'Explaining the epigraphic habit in the Roman Empire: The evidence of epitaphs', *JRS* 80: 74–96.
Mietke, G. (1999), 'Stephen Hill, *The Early Byzantine Churches of Cilicia and Isauria*' (review), *BZ* 92: 120–4.
Millar, F. (1993), *The Roman Near East 31 BC–AD 337* (Cambridge, Mass.).
Miller, J. M. (1979), 'Archaeological survey of central Moab', *BASOR* 234: 43–52.
Millett, M. (1990), *The Romanization of Britain* (Cambridge).
——(1991), 'Pottery, population or supply patterns? The *Agger Tarraconensis* Approach', in Barker and Lloyd (1991), 18–26.
Miltner, H. (1936), 'Epigraphische Nachlese in Ankara', *JÖAI* 30: 9–96.
Mirkovic, M. (1997), 'Dioskoros als *syntelestes*', *Akten des 21 internationalen Papyrologenkongresses, Berlin 1995*, Archiv für Papyrusforschung Beiheft 3 (Stuttgart/Leipzig), 696–705.
Mitchell, S. (1982), *Regional Epigraphic Catalogue of Asia Minor,* ii. *The Inscriptions of North Galatia*, BAR Int. 135 (Oxford).
——(ed.) (1983), *Armies and Frontiers in Roman and Byzantine Anatolia*, British Institute of Ankara Monograph 5, BAR Int. 156 (Oxford).
——(1989–90), 'Archaeology in Asia Minor 1985–89', *JHS Archaeological Report*, 36: 83–131.
——(1993), *Anatolia: Land, Men and Gods in Asia Minor*, i. *The Celts and the Impact of Roman Rule*; ii. *The Rise of the Church* (Oxford).

Mitchell, S. (1995), *Cremna in Pisidia* (London).
——and Waelkens, M. (1998), *Pisidian Antioch: The Site and its Monuments* (London).
——with French, D., and Greenhalgh, J. (1982), *Regional Epigraphic Catalogue of Asia Minor*, ii. *The Ankara District, the Inscriptions of North Galatia*, BAR Int. 135 (Oxford).
——Owens, E., and Waelkens, M. (1989), 'Ariassos and Sagalassos', *Anatolian Studies*, 39: 63–77.
Mitford, T. B. (1950), 'Some new inscriptions from early Christian Cyprus', *Byzantion*, 20: 128–32.
Mittmann, S. (1970), *Beiträge zur Siedlungs und Territorialgeschichte des nördlichen Ostjordanlandes* (Wiesbaden).
Mochi Onory, S. (1933), *Vescovi e città (sec IV–V)* (Bologna).
Modéran, Y. (1993), 'La Chronologie de la vie de saint Fulgence de Ruspe et ses incidences sur l'histoire de l'Afrique vandale', *MEFR*, Antiquité, 105: 135–88.
Mols, R. (1954–6), *La Démographie historique des villes d'Europe du XIV au XVIII siècle* (Paris).
Momigliano, A. (1990), *The Classical Foundations of Modern Historiography* (Berkeley).
Morley, N. (1996), *Metropolis and Hinterland: The City of Rome and the Italian Economy* (Cambridge).
——(1997), 'Urban systems in Roman Italy', in H. M. Parkins (ed.), *Roman Urbanism: Beyond the Consumer City* (London), 42–58.
Morony, M. G. (1984), 'Landholding and social change: Lower al-'Iraq in the early Islamic period', in Tarif Khalidi (ed.), *Land Tenure and Social Transformation in the Middle East* (Beirut), 210–22.
——(1987), 'Grundeigentum im frühislamischen Irak', *Jahrbuch für Wirtschaftsgeschichte*, 135–47.
Morris, R. (1995), *Monks and Laymen in Byzantium 843–1118* (Cambridge).
Morrison, C. C. (1980), in J.-P. Sodini, G. Tate, *et al.*, 'Déhès, Campagnes I–III (1976–78)', *Syria*, 1–304.
Morrison, C. (1989), 'Monnaie et prix', in *Hommes et richesses dans l'empire byzantin*, i (Paris), 239–60.
——and Lefort, J. (organisateurs) (1989), *Hommes et richesses dans l'empire byzantin*, i. *IVe–VIIe siècles* (Paris/Lethielleux).
Mrozek, S. (1973), 'A propos de la répartition chronologique des inscriptions latines dans le haut empire', *Epigraphica*, 35: 355–68.
——(1978), 'Munificentia privata in den Städten Italiens in der spätrömischen Zeit', *Historia*, 27: 355–68.
Mulder, N., and Guinée, R. (1992), 'Survey of the terrace and western theatre area in Umm Qais', *ARAM* 4: 387–406.
Müller-Wiener, W. (1986), 'Von der Polis zum Kastron, Wandlungen der Stadt im ägäischen Raum von der Antike zum Mittelalter', *Gymnasium*, 93: 435–75.
——(1989), 'Bischofsresidenzen des 4.–7. Jahrhunderts im östlichen Mittelmeerraum', *Actes XI Congr. Int. d'Arch. Chrét.* (Rome), i. 651–709.

Murray, A. (1986), 'The position of the *grafio* in the constitutional history of Merovingian Gaul', *Speculum*, 64: 787–805.

Nehlsen, H. (1972), *Sklavenrecht zwischen Antike und Mittelalter, germanisches und römisches Recht in den germanischen Rechtsaufzeichnungen*, Göttinger Studien zur Rechtsgeschichte 7 (Göttingen).

Netzer, E., and Weiss, Z. (1995), 'New evidence for Late Roman and Byzantine Sepphoris', *JRA* Suppl 14: 164–76.

Nielsen, I. (1990), *Thermae et Balnea: The Architecture and Cultural History of Roman Baths*, i. *Text*; ii. *Catalogue* (Aarhus).

Nodes, D. J. (1993), *Doctrine and Exegesis in Biblical Latin Poetry*, Classical and Medieval Texts, Papers and Monographs published by F. Cairns, 31 (Leeds).

Noll, R. (1963), *Das Leben des heiligen Severin* (Berlin).

Northedge, A. (ed.) (1992), *Studies on Roman and Islamic Amman*, i. *History, Site and Architecture* (Oxford).

——(1994), 'Archaeology and the new urban settlements in early Islamic Syria and Iraq', in G. R. D. King and Averil Cameron (1994), 231–65.

Nöthlichs, K. L. (1972), 'Zur Einflussnahme des Staates auf die Entwicklung eines christlichen Klerikerstandes', *JAC* 15: 136–53.

——(1989), 'Kirche, Recht und Gesellschaft', in *L'Église et l'empire au IVe siècle*, Entretiens Fondation Hardt 34 (Geneva), 251–99.

——(1996), *Das Judentum und der römische Staat*, Minderheitenpolitik im antiken Rom (Darmstadt).

Oleson, J. P. (1996), 'Artifactual evidence for the history of the harbour of Caesarea', in Raban and Holum (1996), 359–80.

——Fitzgerald, M. A., Sidebotham, A. N., *et al.* (1994), *The Harbour of Caesarea*, ii, BAR Int. 599 (Oxford).

Orlandis, J. (1987), *Historia de España: Época visigoda (409–711)* (Madrid).

Ormrod, W. M., and Lindley, P. G. (eds.) (1996), *The Black Death in England* (Stamford).

Ostrasz, A. A. (1989), 'The hippodrome of Gerasa, a report of excavation and research 1982–87', in Zayadine (1989), 51–77 = *Syria* 66: 51–77.

Oswald, F., Schaefer, L., and Sennhauer, H. R. (1966), *Vorromanische Kirchenbauten* (Munich).

Ovadiah, A. (1970), *Corpus of Byzantine Churches in the Holy Land* (Bonn).

——and Gomez de Silva, C. (1981–4), 'Supplementum to corpus of Byzantine churches in the Holy Land', *Levant*, 13 (1981), 200–61; 14 (1982), 122–70; 16 (1984), 129–65.

Pack, E. (1998), 'Italia', *RAC* 18: 1049–1202.

Palet, J. M. (1997), *Estudi territorial del Pla de Barcelona, segles II–I a.C. X–XI d.C.* (Barcelona).

Palmer, A. (1990), *Monks and Masons on the Tigris Frontier: The Early History of Tur 'Abdin* (Cambridge).

——(1993), *The Seventh Century in the West–Syrian Chronicles* (Liverpool).

——and Rodney, L. (1988), 'The inauguration anthem of Hagia Sophia in

Edessa and a comparison with a contemporary Constantinopolitan kontakion', *BMGS* 12: 117–67.
Palol, P. de (1966), 'Demografía y arqueología hispánicas, siglos IV–VIII, Ensayo de cartografía', *Boletín del Seminario de Estudios de Arte y Arqueología*, 32 (Valladolid), 5–67.
——(1967), *Arqueología cristiana de la Espana romana, siglos IV–VI* (Madrid).
——(1968), *Arte hispánico de la época visigoda* (Barcelona).
——(1969), 'Demography and archaeology in Roman Christian and Visigothic Hispania', *Classical Folia*, 23.1: 32–114, 23 maps, New York.
——(1992), 'Transformaciones urbanas en Hispania durante el Bajo Imperio: Los ejemplos de Barcino, Tarraco, y Clunia. Transcendencia del modelo en época visigoda: Toledo', in *Felix temporis Reparatio,* Atti del Convegno Archeologico Internazionale: 'Milano capitale dell'Impero Romano' (Milan), 381–94.
——(1996), *Estudis d'antiguitat tardana oferts en homenatge al professor Pere de Palol i Salellas*, ed. J. M. Gurt i Esparraguera *et al.* (Barcelona).
Parenti, R. (1994), 'Le tecniche costruttive fra VI e X secolo: Le evidenze materiali', in Francovich and Noyé (1994), 479–96.
Parker, A. J. (1992), *Ancient Shipwrecks of the Mediterranean and the Roman Provinces* (Oxford).
Parkins, H. M. (ed.) (1997), *Roman Urbanism: Beyond the Consumer City* (London).
Paroli, L., and Delogu, P. (eds.) (1993), *La storia economica di Roma nell'Alto Medioevo alla luce dei recenti scavi archeologici*, Atti del Seminario Roma 1992 (Rome).
Patlagean, E. (1977), *Pauvreté économique et pauvreté sociale à Byzance, 4e– 7e siècles* (Paris).
Patrich, J. (1995), *Sabas, Leader of Palestine Monasticism: A Comparative Study* (Washington).
——(1996), 'Warehouses and granaries in Caesarea Maritima', in Raban and Holum (1996), 146–76.
——(2000), 'A government compound in Roman-Byzantine Caesarea', *Acts of the Twelfth World Congress of Jewish Studies, Jerusalem 1997* (Jerusalem), 35–44.
——*et al.* (forthcoming), 'The governor's palace and warehouse complex (areas KK, CC, NN, May 1993–December 1995 excavations', in Holum, Raban, and Patrich (forthcoming).
Patterson, J. R. (1991), 'Settlement city and elite in Samnium and Lycia', in J. Rich and A. Wallace Hadrill (eds.), *City and Country in the Ancient World* (London), 147–68.
Paul, G. (1996), 'Die Anastylose des Tetrapylons in Aphrodisias', in C. Roueché and R. R. R. Smith (eds.), *Aphrodisias Papers* III (Ann Arbor), 202–14.
Paverd, F. van de (1991), *St John Chrysostom: The Homilies of the Statues* (Rome).
Pentz, P. (1992), *The Invisible Conquest: The Ontogenesis of Sixth and Seventh Century Syria* (Copenhagen).
——(1997), *Hama, fouilles et recherches de la fondation Carlsberg 1931–38*, iv/1. *The Medieval Citadel and its Architecture* (Copenhagen).

Percival, J. (1942), 'The fifth century villa: New life or death?', in Drinkwater and Elton (1992), 156–64.

Perry, S. G. F. (1881), *The Second Synod of Ephesus* (Dartford).

Petit, P. (1955), *Libanius et la vie municipal à Antioche au IVe siècle aprés J.-C.* (Paris).

Petrikovits, H. V. (1981), 'Die Spezialisierung des römischen Handwerks: 2, Spätantike', *ZPE* 43: 285–306.

Picard, J. C. (1988), *Le Souvenir des évêques: Sépultures, listes épiscopales et cultes des évêques en Italie du Nord dès l'origines aux Xè siècle* (Rome).

Piccirillo, M. (1989), 'Gruppe episcopali nelle tre Palestine e in Arabi', *Actes du XIe Congrés International d'Archéologie Chrétienne 1986*, i (Rome), 459–502.

——(1992), 'Les Problèmes résolus et les questions posées par les très premières campagnes de fouilles à Um -Rasas Kastron Méfaa: La Fin de la civilisation urbaine au Jordanie', *SHAJ* 4: 343–6.

——(1993), *The Mosaics of Jordan* (Amman).

Pietri, L. (1983), *La Ville de Tours du IVe au VIe siècle: Naissance d'une cité chrétienne*, Coll. de l'école française de Rome 69 (Paris).

Piganiol, A. (1947), *L'Empire chrétien (325–395)* Paris.

Pohl, W. (1988), *Die Avaren: Ein Steppenvolk in Mitteleuropa 567–822 n.Chr* (Munich).

——with Reimitz, H. (1998), *Strategies of Distinction: The Construction of Ethnic Communities 300–800* (Leiden).

Porath, Y. (1996), 'The evolution of Caesarea's south-west zone: New evidence', in Raban and Holum (1996), 105–29.

Porphyry (1969), *The Cave of the Nymphs in the Odyssey (De antro nympharum)*, revised text and translation by the seminar in Classics, State University of New York, Buffalo, Arethusa Monograph 1.

Potter, T. W. (1979), *The Changing Landscape of Southern Etruria* (London).

——(1995), *Towns in Late Antiquity: Iol Caesarea and its Context* (London).

Poulter, A. (ed.) (1983), *Ancient Bulgaria*, Papers presented to the International Symposium on the Ancient History and Archaeology of Bulgaria, 2 vols. (Nottingham).

——(1990), 'Nicopolis', *Current Archaeology*, 121: 37–42.

——(1992*a*), 'The use and abuse of urbanism in the Danubian provinces during the Later Roman Empire', in Rich (1992), 99–135.

——(1992*b*), 'Nicopolis ad Istrum, the anatomy of a Graeco-Roman city', in H.-J. Schalles, H. von Hesberg, P. Zanker (eds.), *Die römische Stadt im 2. Jahrhundert N.Chr* (Cologne), 69–86.

——(1995), *Nicopolis ad Istrum: A Roman, Late Roman and Early Byzantine City, Excavation 1985–92*, i (London).

Prévot, F. (1984), *Les Inscriptions Chrétiennes*, Recherches archéologiques franco-tunisiennes à Mactar V, l'école française de Rome 34 (Rome).

Prinz, F. (1965; repr. 1988), *Frühes Mönchtum im Frankenreich. Kultur und Gesellschaft in Gallien am Beispiel der monastischen Entwicklung (4.–8. Jahrhundert)* (Munich/Paris).

Prinz, F. (1971), *Klerus und Krieg im frühen Mittelalter* (Stuttgart).
——(1973), 'Die bischöfliche Stadtherrschaft im Frankenreich vom 5. bis zum 7. Jahrhundert', *Hist. Zeitschr.* 217: 1–35.
Pseudo-Dionysus of Tel-Mahrē (1996), *Chronicle Part III*, tr. with notes and intro. by W. Witakowski, Translated Texts for Historians 22 (Liverpool).
Raban, A. (1996), 'The inner harbour of Caesarea, archaeological evidence for its gradual demise', in Raban and Holum (1996), 628–60.
——and Holum, K. G. (eds.) (1996), *Caesarea Maritima: A Retrospective after Two Millennia* (Leiden/New York/Cologne).
Raddatz, K. (1973–4), 'Recopolis eine westgotische Stadt in Kastilien', in Jankuhn, Schlesinger, and Steuer (1973–4), i. 152–62.
Radt, W. (1988), *Pergamon: Geschichte und Bauten, Funde und Erforschungen einer antiken Metropole* (Cologne).
Randsborg, K. (ed.) (1989), *The Birth of Europe: Archaeology and Social Development in the First Millenium*, Analecta Romana, Instituti Danici Suppl. 16 (Rome).
——(1991), *The First Millennium AD in Europe and the Mediterranean: An Archaeological Essay* (Cambridge).
Rashev, R. (1983), 'Pliska—The first capital of Bulgaria', in Poulter (1983), ii. 255–68.
Rasson, A.-M., and Seigne, J. (1989), 'Une citerne byzantino-omeyyade sur le sanctuaire de Zeus', in Zayadine (1989), 117–51.
Rathbone, D. (1990), 'Villages, land and population in Graeco-Roman Egypt', *Proc. Camb. Phil. Soc.* 36: 100–42.
——(1991), *Economic Rationalism and Rural Society in Third Century AD Egypt: The Heroninos Archive and the Appianus Estate* (Cambridge).
Rautman, M. L. (1986), 'The decline of urban life in sixth century Sardis', in *The 17th International Byzantine Congress, Washington 1986: Abstracts of Short Papers* (New York), 285.
——(1995*a*), 'A Late Roman town-house at Sardis', *Asia Minor Studien*, 17 (Bonn), 49–65.
——(1995*b*), 'Two late Roman wells at Sardis', *AASOR* 53: 37–84.
Rebillard, É. (1998), 'Augustin et le rituel épistolaire de l'élite sociale et culturelle de son temps: Élements pour une analyse processuelle des relations de l'évêque et de la cité dans l'Antiquité tardive', in Rebillard and Sotinel (1998), 127–52.
——and Sotinel, C. (eds.) (1998), *L'Évêque dans la cité du IVe au Ve siècle: Image et autorité*, Collection de l'école française de Rome 248 (Rome).
Reece, R. (1992), 'The end of the city in Roman Britain', in Rich (1992), 136–44.
Rees, B. R. (1952), 'The defensor civitatis in Egypt', *JJP* 6: 73–102.
——(1953–4), 'The curator civitatis in Egypt', *JJP* 7–8: 83–105.
Rémondon, R. (1953), *Papyrus Grecs d'Apollônus Anô* (Cairo).
——(1959), 'Papyrologie et histoire byzantine', *Ann. Un. Sar.* 8: 91 ff.
——(1961), 'Soldats de Byzance d'après un papyrus trouvé à Edfou', *Recherches de Papyrologie*, 1: 41–93.
——(1965), '*PHamb* 56 et *PLond* 1419: Notes sur les finances d'Aphrodito du VIe au VIIIe siècle', *CE* 40: 401–30.

——(1966), 'L'Égypte au Ve siècle de notre ère', *Atti dell'XI Congr. Int. di Papirologia* (Milan), 135–48.

——(1971), 'Le Monastère Alexandrin de la Metanoia: Était-il bénéficiaire du fisc ou à son service', *Studi in onore di Eduardo Volterra*, v (Milan), 771–81.

——(1972), 'Bibliographie de R. Rémondon', *CE* 47: 295–8.

Rey-Coquais, J.-P. (1977), *Inscriptions grecques et latines découvertes dans les fouilles de Tyr 1963–74*, i. *Inscriptions de la nécropole*, Bulletin du Musée de Beyrouth 29 (Beirut).

——(1995), 'Textiles, soie principalement, et artisanat du textile dans les inscriptions grecques du Proche Orient', *Studies in the History and Archaeology of Jordan*, 5: 77–81.

Rheidt, K. (1991), *Die Altertümer von Pergamon XV*, die Stadtgrabung, ii. *Die byzantinische Wohnstadt* (Berlin).

——(1998), 'In the shadow of Antiquity: Pergamum and the Byzantine Millennium', in Koester (1998), 395–413.

Rich, J. (ed.) (1992), *The City in Late Antiquity* (London).

——and Wallace-Hadrill, A. (1991), *City and Country in the Ancient World* (London).

Richards, J. (1980), *Consul of God: The Life and Times of Gregory the Great* (London).

Riché, P. (1957), 'La Survivance des écoles publiques en Gaule au Ve siècle', *Le Moyen Age*, 63: 421–36.

——(1962), *Éducation et culture dans l'occident barbare, 6e et 7e siècle* (Paris).

——(1965), 'L'Enseignement du droit en Gaule du VIe au XIe siècle', *Ius Romanum Medii Aevi*, 1.5b: 1–21.

——(1972), 'L'Enseignement et la culture des laïcs dans l'occident précarolingien', *Settimane di Studi* 19 (Spoleto), 231–51.

——(1976), *Education and Culture in the Barbarian West*, a translation by J. J. Contreni of Riché 1962 (South Carolina).

Riddle, J. M. (1991), 'Oral contraception and early term abortifacients during Classical Antiquity and the Middle Ages', *Past and Present*, 132: 3–32.

Ripoll, G. (1989), 'Características generales del poblamiento y la arqueología funeraria visigoda', *Espacio, Tiempo y Forma*, Revista de la Facultad de Geografía e Historia, Serie I.2 Prehistoria, 389–418.

——(1991*a*), *La ocupación visigoda en época romana a través de sus necrópolis (Hispania)*, Col·lecció de Tesis Doctorals Microfitxades, no. 912, Universitat de Barcelona, Barcelona.

——(1991*b*), 'Materiales funerarios de la Hispania visigoda: problemas de cronología y tipología', in P. Périn (ed.), *Gallo-Romains, Wisigoths et Francs en Aquitaine, Septimanie et Espagne*, Actes des VIIe Journées Internationales d'Archéologie Mérovingienne, Toulouse 1985 (Rouen), 111–32.

——(1993), 'La necrópolis visigoda de El Carpio de Tajo: Una nueva lectura a partir de la topocronología y los adornos personales', *Butlletí de la Reial Acadèmia Catalana de Belles Arts de Sant Jordi*, 7–8: 187–250.

——(1998*a*), 'The arrival of the Visigoths in Hispania: Population problems at the process of acculturation', in Pohl, with Reimitz (1998), 153–87.

Ripoll, G. (1998*b*), *Toréutica de la Bética (Siglos VI y VII D.C.)* (Barcelona).
——and Arce, J. (forthcoming), 'The transformation and end of the Roman villae and domus in the West, IV.–VIII. centuries', in Christie, Gauthier, and Brogiolo (forthcoming).
——and Brown, K. R. (1993), 'Visigothic art', in *The Art of Medieval Spain AD 500–1200*, Metropolitan Museum of Art, New York; H. N. Abrams (New York), 41–69.
——and Velázquez, I. (1995), *La Hispania visigoda del rey Ataúfo a don Rodrigo*, Historia de España (Madrid).
Robert, L. (1948), 'Epigrammes relatives à des gouverneurs', *Hellenica*, 4: 34–114.
——(1958), 'Inscriptions grecques de Side en Pamphylie, époque impériale et bas empire', *R Ph* 32: 15–53.
Robinson, C. F. (ed.) (1998), *A Medieval Islamic City Reconsidered: An Interdisciplinary Approach to Samarra* (Oxford).
Robinson, D. M. (1924), 'A preliminary report on the excavations at Pisidian Antioch and at Sizma', *AJA* 28: 435–44.
Rocca Hudson, C. La (1986), 'Dark Ages a Verona: Edilizia privata, aree aperte e strutture pubbliche in una città dell'Italia settentrionale', *Archeologia Medievale*, 13: 31–78.
Rochow, I. (1976), 'Die Heidenprozesse unter den Kaisern Tiberius II Konstantinus und Maurikios', in F. Winkelmann and H. Köppstein (eds.), *Probleme der Herausbildung des Feudalismus* (Berlin), 120–30.
——(1991), 'Der Vorwurf des Heidentums als Mittel der innenpolitischen Polemik in Byzanz', in M. Salamon (ed.), *Paganism in the Later Empire and Byzantium* (Cracow), 133–56.
Rodríguez, A. R., Molinos, M., and López, M. C. (1991), 'Settlement and continuity in the territory of the Guadalquivir valley (6th century BC–1st century AD)', in Barker and Lloyd (1991), 29–36.
Rodziewicz, M. (1984), *Alexandrie*, iii. *Les Habitations romaines tardives d'Alexandrie* (Warsaw).
Roques, D. (1987), *Synésios de Cyréne et la Cyrénaique du Bas-Empire* (Paris).
Roueché, C. (1979), 'A new inscription from Aphrodisias and the *πατὴρ τῆς πόλεως*', *Gr. Rom. Byz. Stud.* 20: 173–85.
——(1989*a*), *Aphrodisias in Late Antiquity* (London).
——(1989*b*), 'Floreat Perge', in MacKenzie and Roueché (1989), 205–28.
Roueché, C. M. (1993), *Performers and Partisans at Aphrodisias* (London).
Rouche, M. (1974), 'La Matricule des pauvres: évolution d'une institution de charité du Bas-Empire, jusqu'à la fin du Haut Moyen Age', in M. Mollat (ed.), *Études sur l'histoire de la pauvreté* (Paris), i. 83–110.
——(1979), *L'Aquitaine des Wisigoths aux Arabes 418–781* (Paris).
Rouillard, G. (1928), *L'Administration civile de l'Égypte byzantin* (Paris).
Rousseau, P. (1985), *Pachomius: The Making of a Community in Fourth Century Egypt* (Berkeley).
Rudé, G. (1952), *Paris and London in the 18th Century* (London).

——(1964), *The Crowd in History* (London).
Ruggini, L. (1961), *Economia e società nell'Italia annonaria*, rapporti fra agricoltura e commercio dal IV al VI sec. dC (Milan).
Russell, J. (1982) 'Byzantine instrumenta domestica from Anemurium', in Hohlfelder (1982), 133–64.
——(1986), 'Transformations in early Byzantine urban life: The contributions and limitations of archaeological evidence', in *XVIII International Byzantine Congress: Major Papers* (La Rochelle, NY), 131–54.
——(1987), *The Mosaic Inscriptions of Anemurium* (Vienna).
Sack, D. (1989), *Damaskus, Entwicklung und Struktur einer orientalischen Stadt* (Mainz).
Saliou, C. (1994), *Les Lois des bâtiments, recherches sur les rapports entre le droit et la construction privée du siècle d'Auguste au siècle de Justinien* (Beirut).
——(1996), *Le Traité d'urbanisme de Julien d'Ascalon (VIe siècle)*, Travaux et Mémoires Monographies 8 (Paris).
Salway, B. (1994), 'A survey of Roman onomastic practice', *JRS* 84: 124–45.
Sánchez Albornoz, C. (1943), *Ruina y extinción del municipio Romano en España e instituciones que le reemplazan* (Buenos Aires).
——(1971*a*), *Estudios Visigodos*, Istituto Storico Italiano per il Medio Evo: Studi Storici fasc. 78–9 (Rome).
——(1971*b*), 'Extinción y olvido del municipio hispano-romano', in Sánchez Albornoz (1971*a*), 104–47.
——(1971*c*), 'Ruina del municipio hispano–romano en España e instituciones que le reemplazan', in Sánchez Albornoz (1971*a*), 51–103.
Saradi, H. (1988*a*), 'The demise of the ancient city and the emergence of the medieval city in the Eastern Roman Empire', *Echos du monde classique*, 32 NS 7: 365–401.
——(1988*b*), 'L'Enregistrement des actes privés (*insinuatio*) et la disparition des institutions municipales au VIe siècle', *Cahiers des Études Anciennes* (Canada), 21: 117–30.
——(1994), 'The dissolution of urban space in the early Byzantine centuries: The evidence of imperial legislation', in N. G. Moschonas (ed.), *Hommage à D. A. Zakynthus*, Symmeikta 9 (Athens), 295–308.
——(1995), 'Evidence of barter economy in the documents of private transactions', *BZ* 88: 405–18.
——(1997), 'The use of ancient spolia in Byzantine monuments: The archaeological and literary evidence', *International Journal of the Classical Tradition*, 3: 395–423.
——(1998), 'Aspects of early Byzantine urbanism in Albania', in *ΟΙ ΑΛΒΑΝΟΙ ΣΤΟ ΜΕΣΑΙΩΝΑ* (*The Albanians into the Middle Ages*), Proceedings of the International Symposium on 'The Medieval Albanians' 1996, Institute of Byzantine Research of the National Centre of Research (Athens), 81–130.
Sartre, M. (1982), *Inscriptions Grecques et Latines de la Syrie*, xiii/1, *Bostra* (Paris).
——(1985), *Bostra des origines à l'Islam* (Paris).
——(1991), *L'Orient romain* (Paris).

Sartre, M. (1993), *Inscriptions Grecques et Latines de la Syrie*, xxi/4, *Inscriptions de la Jordanie* (Paris).

Sauvaget, J. (1941), *Alep, essay sur le développement d'une ville syrienne des origines au milieu du XIXe siècle* (Paris).

——(1949), 'Le Plan antique de Damas', *Syria*, 26: 314–58.

Schäfer, C. (1991), *Der Weströmische Senat als Träger antiker Kontinuität unter den Ostgotenkönigen 949–540 AD* (St Katharinen).

Scherrer, P. (1995), 'The city of Ephesus from the Roman period to Late Antiquity', in Koester (1995), 1–25.

Schick, R. (1995), *The Christian Communities of Palestine from Byzantine to Islamic Rule* (Princeton).

Schlunk, H., and Hauschild, Th. (1978), *Hispania Antiqua: Die Denkmäler der frühchristlichen und westgotischen Zeit* (Mainz).

Schmidt, H. F. (1957), 'Das Weiterleben und die Wiederbelebung antiker Institutionen im mittelalterlichen Städtewesen', *Annali di storia del diritto*, 1: 85–135.

Schmiedt, G. (1974), 'La città scomparse e città di nuova formazione in Italia in relazione al sistema di communicazione', *Topografia urbana e vita cittadina*, Settimana di Studio XXI (Spoleto), 505–607.

Schubert, W. (1969), 'Die rechtliche Sonderstellung der Dekurionen Kurialen im der Kaisergesetzgebung des 4–6 Jhs', *Zeitschrift für Rechtsgeschichte*, Röm. Abt. 86, 287–331.

Schulz, A. (1992), 'Ariassos eine hellenistisch römische Stadt in Pisidien', in E. Schwertheim (ed.), *Forschungen in Pisidia*, Asia Minor Studien 6 (Bonn), 29–41.

Schwertheim, E. (ed.) (1992), *Forschungen in Pisidia*, Asia Minor Studien 6 (Bonn).

Scott, J. A. (1987), 'Sardis in the Byzantine and Turkish eras', in E. Guralnick (ed.), *Sardis 27 Years of Discovery* (Chicago), 74–87.

Scott, R. (1990), 'Malalas' view of the classical past', in G. Clarke, B. Croke, R. Mortley, and A. Nobbs (eds.), *Reading the Past in Late Antiquity* (Rushcutters Bay), 146–64.

Seeck, O. (1919), *Regesten der Päbste und Kaiser für die Jahre 311–476* (Stuttgart).

Segal, A. (1995), *Theatres in Roman Palestine and the Provincia Arabia* (Leiden).

Segal, J. B. (1970), *Edessa the Blessed City* (Oxford).

Seigne, J. (1986*a*), 'Jérash sanctuaire de Zeus', *Revue Biblique* 93: 239–47.

——(1986*b*), 'Recherches sur le sanctuaire de Zeus à Jérash (Octobre 1982–Décembre 1983)', in Zayadine (1986*a*), 29–105.

——(1989), 'Monuments disparus sur photographies oubliées du sanctuaire de Zeus et autres monuments de Jérash', in Zayadine (1989), 99–116.

Seitz, K. (1892), *Die Schule von Gaza* (Heidelberg).

Selb, W. (1967), 'Episcopalis audientia von der Zeit Konstantins bis zur *Novella* XXXV Valentinians III', *ZRG RA* 84: 162–217.

Sevcenko, I., and Sevcenko, N. (1984), *The Life of Nicholas of Sion* (Brookline, Mass.).

Shahid, I. (1984), *Byzantium and the Arabs in the Fourth Century* (Washington).
——(1989), *Byzantium and the Arabs in the Fifth Century* (Washington).
Shanzer, D. (1986), *A Philosophical and Literary Commentary on Martianus' Capella's De Nuptiis Philologiae et Mercurii* (Berkeley/Los Angeles).
Shboul, A., and Walmsley, A. (1998), 'Identity and self-image in Syria-Palestine in the transition from Byzantine to early Islamic: Arab, Christian and Muslim', *Mediterranean Archaeology*, 11: 255–87.
Sherwin White, A. N. (1973), *Roman Citizenship*, 2nd edn. (Oxford).
Sidebotham, S., and Wendrich, W. (1998), *Berenike 96: Report of Excavation at Berenike* (Leiden).
Sijpesteijn, P. J. (1986), 'Five papyri from the Michigan collection', *ZPE* 62: 133–7.
——(1987), 'The πατὴρ τῆς πόλεως and the papyri', *Tyche*, 2: 171–4.
Sirks, A. J. B., Sijpesteijn, P. J., and Worp, K. A. (1996), *Ein frühbyzantinisches Szenario für die Amtswechslung in der Sitonie*, Die griechischen Papyri aus Pommersfelde, mit einem Anhang über die Pommersfelder Digesten Fragmente und die Überlieferungsgeschichte der Digesten, Münchener Beiträge zur Papyrusforschung 86 (Munich).
Sivan, H. (1988), 'The appropriation of Roman law in barbarian hands: "Roman-barbarian" marriage in Visigothic Gaul and Spain', in Pohl, with Reimitz (1988), 189–203.
——(1992), 'Town and country in late antique Gaul: The example of Bordeaux', in Drinkwater and Elton (1992), 132–43.
Sjöström, I. (1993), *Tripolitania in Transition: Late Roman and Early Islamic Settlement* (Avebury).
Skinner, G. W. (1977), 'Regional urbanization in 19th century China', in G. W. Skinner (ed.), *The City in Late Imperial China* (Stanford, Calif.), 211–49.
Small, A., and Buck, R. J. (1994), *The Excavations of San Giovanni di Ruoti*, i. *The Villa and its Environment* (Toronto/Buffalo/London).
Smith, R. H., Day, L. P., *et al.* (1989), *Pella of the Decapolis*, ii. *Final Report on the College of Wooster Excavation in Area IX, the Civic Complex, 1979–85* (Wooster).
Smith, R. R. R., and Ratté, C. (1996), 'Archaeological Research at Aphrodisias in Caria', *AJA* 100: 5–33.
————(1997), 'Aphrodisias', *AJA* 101: 1–22.
Sodini, J.-P. (1984), 'Le Habitat urbain en Gréce à la veille des invasions', *Villes et Peuplement dans l'Illyricum Protobyzantin*, Collection de l'école française de Rome 77 (Rome), 341–97.
——(1993), 'La Contribution de l'archéologie à la connaissance du monde byzantin, IVè–VIIè siècle', *DOP* 47: 139–84.
——(1995), 'Habitat de l'antiquité tardive 1', *Topoi*, 5: 151–218.
——(1997), 'Habitat de l'antiqité tardive 2', *Topoi*, 7: 435–577.
——and Tate, G. (1980), 'Déhès (Syrie du Nord), Campagnes I–III (1976–78)', *Syria*, 57: 1–303.

Sodini, J.-P. and Villeneuve, E. (1992), 'La Passage de la céramique byzantine à la céramique omeyyade en Syrie du Nord, en Palestine et Transjordanie', in Canivet and Rey-Coquais (1992), 195–218.

Sorabji, R. (1983), *Time, Creation and the Continium* (London).

——(1987), *Philoponus and the Rejection of Aristotelian Science* (London).

Sotinel, C. (1998), 'Le Personel épiscopal: Enquête sur la puissance de l'évêque dans la cité', in Rebillard and Sotinel (1998), 105–26.

Spandel, R. (1957), 'Dux und Comes in der Merowingerzeit', *Savigny Zeitschrift für Rechtsgeschichte*, 74: 41–84.

——(1965), 'Bemerkungen zum frühfränkischen Comitat', *Savigny Zeitschrift für Rechtsgeschichte*, 82: 228–91.

Spiesser, J.-M. (1984), *Thessalonique et ses monuments du IVe au VIe siècle* (Paris).

Stahl, W. H. (1971), *Martianus Capella and the Seven Liberal Arts* (New York).

Stein, E. (1919), 'Beiträge zur Geschichte von Ravenna in spätrömischer und byzantinisher Zeit', *Klio*, 16: 40–71 = Stein (1968), 359–84.

——(1949), *Histoire du Bas Empire*, ii (Brussels).

——(1968), *Opera Minora Selecta* (Amsterdam).

Steinwenter, A. (1956), 'Die Stellung der Bischöfe in der byzantinischen Verwaltung Egyptens', *Studi in onore di Pietro de Francisci*, i (Milan), 75–99.

Stern, S. M. (1970), 'The constitution of the Islamic city', in A. H. Hourani and S. M. Stern (eds.), *The Islamic City*, Papers in Islamic History 1 (Oxford), 25–50.

Stevens, S. T. (1989), 'The circus poems in the Latin Anthology', in J. H. Humphrey (ed.), *The Circus and Byzantine Cemetery at Carthage*, i (Ann Arbor), 152–78.

Strategius (Antiochus) Monachus (1960), *La Prise de Jérusalem par les Perses en 614*, ed. and tr. G. Garitte, CSCO 203 (Louvain).

Stratos, A. N. (1968), *Byzantium in the Seventh Century*, i. *AD 602–34* (Amsterdam).

Stroheker, K. F. (1970), *Der senatorische Adel im spätantiken Gallien*, 2nd edn. (Darmstadt).

Tabula Imperii Byzantini = *TIB* published as *Denkschriften der österr. Akad. der Wissenschaften* from 1976:

Vol. i, J. Koder and F. Hild, *Hellas und Thessalia* (1976).

Vol. ii, F. Hild and M. Restle, *Kappadokien* (1981).

Vol. iii, P. Soustal with J. Koder, *Nicopolis und Kephallenia* (1981).

Vol. iv, K. Belke, with M. Restle, *Galatia und Lykaonien* (1984).

Vol. v, F. Hild and H. Hellenkemper, *Kilikien und Isaurien* (1990).

Vol. vii, T. Drew-Bear, *Phrygien und Pisidien* (1990).

Tarradell, M. (1977), 'Les Villes romaines dans l'Hispania de l'est', in P.-M. Duval and E. Frézouls (1977), 97 ff.

Tate, G. (1989), 'Les Campagnes de Syrie du Nord', in *Hommes et richesses dans l'empire byzantin*, i. *IVe–VIIe siècle* (Paris), 163–86.

——(1992), *Les Campagnes de la Syrie du nord, IIe au VIIe siècles*, i, Bibl. archéologique et historique 133 (Paris).

Tchalenko, G. (1953–8), *Villages antiques de la Syrie du Nord: Le Massif du Belus à l'époque romaine*, 3 vols. (Paris).

Teodor, T. G. (1984), 'Origines et voies de pénétration des slaves au sud du Bas-Danube (VIe–VIIe siècles)', in *Villes et Peuplement dans l'Illyricum Proto-byzantin*, Collection de l'école française de Rome 77 (Rome), 63–84.

Testini, G., Cantino Wataghin, G., and Pani Ermini, L. (1989), 'La cattedrale in Italia', *Actes du XI Congrès International d'Archéologie Chrétienne* (Rome), 1–231.

Thébert, Y. (1987), 'Private life and domestic architecture in Roman Africa', in Paul Veyne (ed.), tr. A. Goldhammer, *A History of Private Life* (Cambridge, Mass./London), 313–409.

Thomas, C. A. (1981), *Christianity in Roman Britain to AD 500* (London).

Thompson, E. A. (1969), *The Goths in Spain* (Oxford).

——(1979), 'Gildas and the history of Britain', *Britannia*, 10: 203–26.

——(1984), *St. Germanus of Auxerre and the End of Roman Britain* (Wadebridge).

——(1990), 'Ammianus Marcellinus and Britain', *Nottingham Medieval Studies*, 34: 1–15.

Timm, S. (1985), *Das christlich-koptische Ägypten in arabischer Zeit*, iii (Wiesbaden).

Trombley, F. R. (1987), 'Korykos in Cilicia Trachis: The economy of a small coastal city in Late Antiquity (saec. V–VI)', *Anc. H. Bull.* 1: 16–23.

——(1993), 'Byzantine Dark Age cities', in *ΤΟ ΕΛΛΗΝΙΚΟΝ, Studies in Honour of Speros Vryonis Jr.*, ed. J. Slangdon, S. W. Reinert, and others (New York), 429–49.

——(1993–4), *Hellenic Religion and Christianization AD 320–529*, 2 vols. (Leiden).

——(1994), 'Religious transition in sixth century Syria', *Byzantinische Forschungen*, 20: 153–95.

——(1997), 'War and society in rural Syria c. 502–613 AD: Observations on the epigraphy', *Byzantine and Modern Greek Studies*, 21: 154–209.

Tsafrir, Y., and Foerster, G. (1987–92), 'The Bet Shean project', *Excavations and Surveys in Israel*, 6: 25–43; subsequent reports in *ESI* 7–8 (1988–9), 15–23; *ESI* 9 (1989–90), 120–8; *ESI* 11 (1992), 3–32.

————(1997), 'Urbanism at Scythopolis-Bet Shean', *DOP* 51: 85–146.

Ulbert, T. (1989), 'Bischof und Kathedrale, 4.–7. Jahrhundert archeologische Zeugnisse', *Actes du XIe Congrès International d'Archéologie Chrétienne 1986*, i (Rome), 429–57.

Valenti, M. (1996), 'La Toscana tra VI e IX secolo: Città e campagna tra fine dell'età tardoantica ed altomedioevo', in Brogiolo (1996), 81–106.

Van Dam, R. (1985), *Leadership and Community in Late Antique Gaul* (Berkeley/London).

Van der Vliet, J. (1993), 'Spätantikes Heidentum in Ägypten im Spiegel der koptischen Literatur', in D. Willers *et al.* (eds.), *Riggisberger Berichte*, i (Riggisberg), 99–130.

Vann, R. L. (ed.) (1992), *Caesarea Papers*, i, JRA Suppl. 5 (Ann Arbor).

Van Ossel, P. (1985), 'Quelques apports récents à l'étude de l'habitat rural gallo-romain dans la région mosane', *Les Études Classiques*, 53: 79–96.

Van Ossel, P. (1992), *Établissements ruraux de l'antiquité tardive dans le nord de la Gaule*, Gallia supplement 51 (Paris).

Varinholu, E. (1988), 'Inschriften von Stratonikeia in Karien', *Epigraphica Anatolica*, 12: 79–128.

Velkov, V. (1962), 'Les Campagnes et la population rurale en Thrace aux IVe–VIe siècles', *Byzantinica Bulgarica*, 1: 31–66.

Vetters, H. (1997), 'Zur Baugeschichte der Hanghäuser', *Forschungen in Ephesos* VIII.1 (Vienna), 12–28.

Vie de Théodore, see under Festugière, A.-J. (1970)

Villeneuve, F. (1988), 'Prospection archéologique et géographie historique: La Région d'Iraq al-Amir (Jordanie)', in P.-L. Gatier *et al.* (eds.), *Géographie Historique au Proche Orient* (Paris), 257–88.

Vismara, G. (1967), Edictum Theoderici, *Ius Romanum medii aevi*, pt. I, 2b. aa. a (Milan).

Vittinghoff, F. (1958), 'Zur Verfassung der spätantiken Stadt', *Studien zu den Anfängen des europäischen Städtewesens*, Vorträge und Forschungen (Konstanz-Lindau), 11–39.

Vives, D. J. (1969), *Inscripciones cristianas de la España romana y visigoda* (Barcelona).

Voegtli, H. (1993), *Die Fundmünzen aus der Stadtgrabung von Pergamon*, Pergamenische Forschungen 8 (Berlin).

Von Falkenstein, V. (1989), 'Die Städte im byzantinischen Italien', *MEFR* (MA) 101–2: 401–64.

Von Gerkan, A., and Krischen, F. (1928), *Milet* I.9: Thermen und Palaestren (Berlin).

Von Halban, A. (1899, 1901, 1907), *Das römische Recht in germanischen Volksstaaten*, 3 vols., Untersuchungen zur deutschen Staats- und Rechtsgeschichte (Breslau).

Vööbus, A. (1958–60), *A History of Ascetism in the Syrian Orient*, 2 vols. (Louvain).

Vriezen, K. J. (1992), 'The centralised church in Umm Qais (Gadara)', *ARAM* (Oxford), 4: 371–86.

Waage, D. B. (1952), *Antioch on the Orontes*, iv. *Greek, Roman and Crusader Coins* (Princeton).

Waelkens, M. (1993), *Sagalassos* I, First General Report on the Survey 1986–89 and Excavations 1990–91 (Louvain).

—— and Poblome, J. (1993), *Sagalassos* II, Report on the Third Excavation Campaign 1992 (Louvain).

—— —— (1995), *Sagalassos* III, Report on Fourth Excavation Campaign 1993 (Louvain).

—— —— (1997), *Sagalassos* IV, Report on Survey and Excavation Campaigns 1994 and 1995 (Louvain).

Wallace-Hadrill, A. (1994), *Houses and Society at Pompeii and Herculaneum* (Princeton).

Walmsley, A. G. (1992*a*), 'Fihl, Pella and the cities of North Jordan during the Umayyad and Abbasid periods', *SHAJ* IV (Amman), 377–84.

——(1992*b*), 'The social and economic regime at Fihl (Pella) between the 7th and 9th centuries', in Canivet and Rey-Coquais (1992), 249–61.

Walmsley, A. (1996), 'Byzantine Palestine and Arabia', in Christie and Loseby (1996), 125–58.

Ward-Perkins, B. (1978), 'Luni, the decline and abandonment of a Roman town', in Blake, Potter, and Whitehouse (1978), 313–21.

——(1984), *From Classical Antiquity to the Middle Ages: Urban Building in Northern and Central Italy AD 300–850* (Oxford).

——(1988), 'The towns of northern Italy: rebirth or renewal', in Hodges and Hobley (1988), 16–27.

——(1997), 'Continuists, catastrophists and the towns of post-Roman northern Italy', *PBSR* 65: 157–76.

——(1998), 'The cities', *CAH* 13: 371–410.

——(1999), 'Re-using the architectural legacy of the past, *entre idéologie et pragmatisme*', in Brogiolo and Ward-Perkins (1999), 225–32.

Wataghin, G. Cantino (1989), 'L'italia settentrionale', in P. Testini, G. Cantino Wataghin, and L. Pani Ermini, 'La cattedrale in Italia', *Actes du XIe Congrès International d'Archéologie Chrétienne 1986* (Rome), 5–229.

——(1996), 'Quadri urbani nell'Italia settentrionale: Tarda antichità e alto medioevo', in Lepelley (1996), 239–71.

——(1999), 'The ideology of urban burials', in Brogiolo and Ward-Perkins (1999), 147–80.

Watson, A. (1983), *Agricultural Innovation in the Early Islamic World AD 700–1100* (Cambridge).

Watson, P. (1992*a*), 'Byzantine occupation in areas III & IV', in A. W. McNicoll, P. C. Edwards, *et al.* (1992), 163–81.

——(1992*b*), 'Change in foreign and regional economic links with Pella in the seventh century AD: The ceramic evidence', in Canivet and Rey-Coquais (1992), 233–47.

Watt, J., and Trombley, F. (1999), *The Chronicle of Joshua the Stylite*, Translated Texts for Historians Series (Liverpool).

Webster, L., and Brown, M. (1997), *The Transformation of the Roman World* (Berkeley/Los Angeles).

Weidemann, K. (1970), 'Zur Topographie von Metz in der Römerzeit und im frühen Mittelalter', *Jahrb. R.-G. Mus. Mainz*, 17: 147–71.

Wenskus, R. (1961), *Stammesbildung und Verfassung: Das Werden der frühmittelalterlichen Gentes* (Cologne).

Whitby, Mary (1985), 'The occasion of Paul the Silentiary's ekphrasis of S. Sophia', *Cambridge Quarterly*, 36: 215–28.

——(ed.) (1998), *The Propaganda of Power: The Role of Panegyric in Late Antiquity* (London/Boston/Cologne).

Whitby, Michael (1986*a*), 'Procopius and the development of the Roman defences in Upper Mesopotamia', in P. Freeman and D. Kennedy (eds.),

The Defence of the Roman and Byzantine Near East, ii, BAR S297 (Oxford), 713–35.
Whitby, Michael (1986*b*), 'Procopius' description of Dara', in P. Freeman and D. Kennedy (eds.), *The Defence of the Roman and Byzantine Near East*, ii, BAR S297 (Oxford), 737–83.
——(1988), *The Emperor Maurice and his Historian, Theophylact Simocatta and Balkan Warfare* (Oxford).
——(1991), 'John of Ephesus and the pagans: Pagan survivals in the 6th century', in M. Salamon (ed.), *Paganism in the Later Roman Empire and in Byzantium* (Cracow), 111–31.
——(1995), 'Recruitment in Roman armies from Justinian to Heraclius (ca.565–615)', in Averil Cameron (1995), 61–124.
——(1998*a*), '*Deus nobiscum*: Christianity, warfare and morale in Late antiquity', in M. Austen, J. Harries, and C. Smith (eds.), *Modus Operandi* (London), 191–208.
——(1998*b*), 'Evagrius on patriarchs and emperors', in Mary Whitby (1998), 321–46.
——(1999), 'The violence of the circus factions', in Keith Hopwood (ed.), *Organised Crime in Antiquity* (London), 229–53.
——and Whitby, Mary (1986), *The History of Theophylact Simocatta*, an English translation with intro. and notes (Oxford).
————(eds.) (1989), *Chronicon Paschale 284–628 AD*, tr. with notes and intro., Translated Texts for Historians 7 (Liverpool).
Whitcomb, D. (1992), 'Reassessing the archaeology of Jordan in the Abbasid period', *SHAJ* IV (Amman), 385–9.
——(1994), 'The misr of Ayla, settlement at al-'Aqaba in the early Islamic period', in G. R. D. King and Averil Cameron (1994), 155–70.
Whittow, M. (1990), 'Ruling the late Roman and early Byzantine city', *Past and Present*, 129: 3–29.
——(1996), *The Making of Orthodox Byzantium, 606–1025* (London).
Wickham, C. (1981), *Early Medieval Italy* (London).
——(1984), 'From the Ancient World to Feudalism', *Past and Present*, 103: 3–36.
——(1988), 'Marx, Sherlock Holmes and Late Roman Commerce' (review of A. Giardina (ed.), *Società romana e impero tardoantico*, iii. *Le merci. Gli insediamenti*), *JRS* 78: 183–93 = Wickham (1994), 77–98.
——(1989), 'Italy and the early middle ages', in K. Randsborg (ed.), *The Birth of Europe: Archaeology and Social Development in the First Millennium*, Analecta Romana, Instituti Danici Suppl. 16 (Rome), 140–51 = Wickham (1994), 99–118.
——(1994), *Land and Power*, Studies in Italian and European Social History, 400–1200 (London).
——(forthcoming), 'Trade and exchange, 550–750: The view from the West', in Averil Cameron (ed.), *The Byzantine and Early Islamic Near East*, vol. 5 (Princeton/Darwin).

Wieacker, F. (1955), *Vulgarismus und Klassizismus im Recht der Spätantike*, Sitzungsberichte d. Heidelberger Akad. d. Wissenschaften, phil. hist, Kl. 1955.3 (Heidelberg).

Wightman, E. M. (1978), 'The towns of Gaul with special reference to the North-East', in M. W. Barley (ed.), *European Towns, their Archaeology and Early History* (London), 303–14.

——(1985), *Gallia Belgica* (London).

Wilkinson, T. J. W. (1990), *Town and Country in S.E. Anatolia: Settlement and Land Use at Kurban Höyük* (Chicago).

Willers, D., *et al.* (1993), *Riggisberger Berichte* 1, Begegnungen von Heidentum und Christentum in Egypten, Abegg Stiftung (Riggisberg).

Wilson, R. J. A. (1996), *Sicily under the Roman Empire: The Archaeology of a Roman Province 36 BC – AD 535* (Warminster).

Wipszycka, E. (1970), 'Les Confréries dans la vie religieuse de l'Égypte chrétienne', *Proceedings of XII Int. Congr. of Papyrology* (Toronto), 511–25.

——(1971), 'Les Reçus d'impôts et le bureau de comptes des pagarchies au VIe–VIIe siècles', *JJP* 16–17: 105–16.

——(1972), *Les Resources et activités économique des églises en Égypte du IVe au VIIIe siècle*, Papyrologia Bruxellensia 10 (Brussels).

——(1998), 'L'attività caritativa dei vescovi egiziani', in Rebillard and Sotinel (1998), 71–80.

Wirth, E. (1974), 'Zum Problem des Bazars (suq, qarsi.): Versuch einer Begriffsbestimmung und Theorie des traditionellen Wirtschaftszentrum der orientalischen Stadt', *Der Islam*, 51: 203–60; 52 (1975): 6–46.

——(1975), 'Die orientalische Stadt. Ein Überblick auf Grund jüngerer Forschung zur materialen Kultur', *Saeculum*, 21: 49–54.

Wiseman, J. (1984), 'The city in Macedonia Secunda', *Villes et peuplement dans l'Illyricum protobyzantin* (Paris), 289–313.

Wolf, H. (1991), 'Die Kontinuität des städtischen Lebens in den nördlichen Grenzprovinzen', in Eck and Galsterer (1991), 287–318.

Wolff, S. R. (1991), 'Archaeology in Israel', *AJA* 95/3: 489–538.

Wolfram, H. (1987), *History of the Goths,* a new and completely revised edition of the German version of 1979, tr. Th. J. Dunlap (Berkeley).

Wood, I. (1990), 'Administration, law and culture in Merovingian Gaul', in McKitterick (1990), 63–81.

——(1993), 'The Code in Merovingian Gaul', in Harries and Wood (1993), 159–77.

——(1994), *The Merovingian Kingdoms 450–751* (London).

Wood, J. (1992), 'The fortifications', in Northedge (1992), 105–27.

Worp, K. A. (1994), 'A check list of bishops in Byzantine Egypt', *ZPE* 100: 283–318.

Wright, R. (1982), *Late Latin and Early Romance in Spain and Carolingian France* (Liverpool).

Wright, W. (1882), *The Chronicle of Joshua the Stylite* (Cambridge).

Wulf, U. (1994), 'Der Stadtplan von Pergamum', *Ist. Mitt.* 44: 135–74.

Yegül, F. (1986), *The Bath Gymnasium Complex at Sardis* (Cambridge, Mass.).
——(1992), *Baths and Bathing in Classical Antiquity* (Cambridge, Mass./ London).
Zacharias of Mytilene (1903), *Vie de Sévère*, ed. and tr. M.-A. Kugener, *PO* 2/1 (Paris), 7–115.
Zayadine, F. (1986*a*) (ed.), *Jerash Archaeological Project*, i. *1981–1983* (Amman).
——(1986*b*), 'The Jerash project for excavation and restoration, a synopsis with special reference to the work of the Department of Antiquities', in Zayadine (1986*a*), 7–28.
——(1989) (ed.), *Jerash Archaeological Project*, ii. *1984–88* (Paris) = *Syria* 66.
Zeumer, F. (1898–1902), 'Geschichte der westgotischen Gesetzgebung', *Neues Archiv*, 23: 419–56; 24: 39–122; 26: 91–149.
Zeumer, K. (1886), *Formulae Merowingici et Karolini Aevi*, *MGH*, Legum sectio 5 (Hanover).
——(1902), *Leges Visigothorum*, *MGH* Leges 1.1. (Hanover).

INDEX

Abasikron, Egyptian governor 270–2
Abbasid dynasty 295, 297, 298, 300, 304, 310, 314
abbots 66, 68–70, 120
Abila, Palestine 297
Abusan, Egypt 270 n, 271
Acindynus, crypto-pagan of Harran 263 n
actuarii 205, 206
Adana, Anatolia 52
Adonis, loved by Aphrodite 227
Aegina, Greece 285
Aemilia, Italy 95
Aemilianus 136
Aemilianus, bishop of Vercellae 157
Aezanitis, Anatolia 14 n, 45
Africa *see* North Africa
Agali monastery, Spain 336
Agathias, writer 243
Agobard, bishop of Lyons 363
agonothetes 203, 204, 205
agora 36–7, 39, 56, 58
agriculture 68, 71, 73, 196 n, 295, 315, 379–84, 392–3, 409–10
Aguntum, Balkans 76
Aisāilīlūn, Egyptian grandee 275, 279
Aix en Provence, Gaul 384
al-Qadisiya, Mesopotamia 311
Alamundarus, Arab chieftain 265–6
Alaric, Visigothic chief 16, 321, 322
Alaric II, Visigothic king 21, 128
Albi, Gaul 88
Alboin, Lombard king 379
Aleppo, Syria 84n, 313, 412
Alexandria, Egypt:
  bishops 116, 141–2, 143–4, 146–7, 167, 174n
  civic finances 170–1, 180n
  coins 45, 46n
  curial government 109n, 114n, 174
  disorder 214, 217, 255, 256, 258, 260, 262, 271n, 281
  education 15
  shows 205, 206n, 208
  urban decline 40, 305, 314
Amalfi, Italy 127, 375
Ambrose, bishop of Milan 141, 143, 155
Amiens, Gaul 84 n
Ammaedara *see* Hadrumetum
Amman, Jordan 64, 298, 299, 303, 308, 314 n
Ammianus, writer 325 n
amphitheatres 30, 58, 97, 99, 204 n, 373
Ampurias, Spain 134
Anastasiopolis, Anatolia 113
Anastasius, bishop of Antioch 174 n, 268
Anastasius, emperor:
  and Balkans 77
  building programmes 300
  and factions 213 n, 254
  finances 167
  legislation 19, 55–6, 149
  in panegyrics 240
  and post-curial government 107–8, 150, 401
  reforms of coinage 23, 44
Anatolia:
  bishops 32, 42, 142–3, 148, 155
  Christianity 48, 291–2, 404
  churches 32, 34, 41–2, 46, 48, 51, 52, 146, 414
  coins 23–4, 43–6
  depopulation 292
  deurbanization 34, 40, 43, 155
  evacuations 378
  fortified settlements 292
  monasteries 291
  plague 69, 392
  resettlement 292–3, 317
  trade 45–6, 282, 305
  urban decline 30–54, 103, 291–5, 399, 400, 410, 411, 413–14, 415
  villages 63, 291, 293–4
Anatolius, governor of Osroene 263–4
Anatolius, *principalis* 115
Ancyra, Anatolia 44–5, 113, 292
Andarchius 319 n
Andronicus, governor of Libya 142
Anemurium, Anatolia 39 n, 42, 52
Angers, Gaul 132
Anglo-Saxons 11, 103
Angoulême, Gaul 88, 131
Anjar 308, 310 n
Ankara *see* Ancyra
Annauni tribe 345
annona 152, 158, 206 n, 385, 386, 394, 411
Antaeopolis, Egypt 65, 67, 109 n, 172 n, 178–81, 188, 190
Anthemius, emperor 156
Antinoopolis, Egypt 109, 145, 193 n
Antioch, Pisidia 41, 52

Antioch, Syria:
  bishops 142–3, 145, 153, 263, 269
  buildings 37, 40, 414
  coins 24, 45, 46n, 294n
  depopulation 52
  disorder 207, 214, 217, 249n, 251n, 253, 254, 255–6, 273
  factions 207, 251n, 253, 254
  fortifications shortened 51n
  government 14n
  invasions 283
  in Malalas 238
  monasteries 67, 68–9
  religion 243, 254, 256, 263, 265–6, 273
  shows 206, 208, 219n
  urban change 37, 40, 51, 52, 56, 72, 295, 412
  villages (interrelation) 71–3
Anulinus, proconsul of Africa 140–1
ἀνυταί 123
Apamea, Syria 37, 55, 56, 228, 258–9, 266, 283, 305n, 314n
Aphrodisias, Anatolia 36–7, 39, 48, 178n, 215, 236n, 260, 302
Aphrodito, Egypt 65, 67, 68, 145, 178, 179–81, 184n, 185n, 186n
Apions, Egyptian family:
  in civic government 116, 188–9, 191, 192, 194, 195, 196
  influence 185, 200, 201n, 206
Apollinaris, bishop of Ravenna 159
Appion, bishop of Syene 144
Apulia, Italy 381
apūlon 199, 200n, 279
aqueducts 16, 39, 41, 52, 95
Aquincum, Balkans 77
Aquitaine, Gaul 20, 86, 131, 318–19
Arabia (now mainly Jordan):
  under Arab rule 32, 303–4
  churches 72, 298, 304, 414
  classical survivals 30, 32, 59, 311
  coins 24, 298
  inscriptions 13, 14n
  plague 73n
  trade 57, 282
  urban change 54–63, 297–8, 304–5, 413–14
  villages 64, 72, 73, 298, 304
Arabs:
  administration 91–2, 308, 375
  agreements with Empire 292, 293
  agricultural advances 315
  compared with Germans 315–16
  confederations 316, 354
  desert palaces 310
  ethnic identity 316, 361n, 367, 404
  government 91–2, 124, 282, 407n
  impact on cities 289, 303–4, 307, 308, 310–11, 314–15, 406, 416
  Islamic city 41, 308, 310–11, 406, 416
  in North Africa 376–8
  in Palestine 400, 414
  raids into Anatolia 43, 54, 290n, 294–5, 404–5
  reasons for success 405–8
  relations with locals 144, 282, 306–8, 316–17, 367
  religion 316, 354
  settlements in Roman Near East 308–14
  in Spain 91–2, 375–6, 383
  in Syria 412, 414
  taxation 66, 282, 407n
  tolerance 307–8
Arcadia, Greece 286
Arcadius, emperor 204n
archaeology:
  ambiguity of evidence 9, 300, 304, 377, 388–90, 396, 397
  evidence of ethnic culture 359–60
  field surveys 388–90, 396, 397
  see also coins; pottery
ἄρχοντες 66, 106, 110n
Arethusa, Mesopotamia 148
argentarii (silversmiths/money-changers) 59, 268
  purchase *solidi* 56
Argos, Greece 237, 370
Arianism 160, 316, 354–5
Ariassus, Anatolia 41, 42, 52
aristocracy:
  bishops from 82, 86, 88, 161
  in Egypt 66, 181–98, 199, 200, 201
  in Gaul 86, 91–2, 93, 361
  provincial 86, 91–2, 97–8, 105n, 200, 280–1, 360–1, 407
Arles, Gaul 84, 85, 88, 162–4, 384n
Armenia 403n
Armorium, Anatolia 292
army:
  and bishops 153, 269
  bucellarii 190, 200–1
  finance 175, 281–2, 283
  garrisons 84, 194–5, 279, 281–2, 407–8
  Islamic 308, 310, 316, 317
  political influence 211–12, 269, 279, 281
  recruitment 6, 345, 350–1, 363–6, 403
  and Roman citizenship 345–6
  wages 23, 152, 206n
  weakness 279, 288, 317n, 366, 407–8
Arras, Gaul 84n
Arsinoe, Egypt 188, 194–5, 200
Arycanda, Anatolia 37
Ascra, Greece 287

Asemus, Balkans 288 n, 407 n
Asia Minor *see* Anatolia
Asterius, count of the East 268
Asturias, Spain 338
Athens 15, 37, 110 n, 236 n, 237, 287, 294, 343 n
  academy closed 242
Athos, Greece 293
Athrībis, Egypt 274, 275, 279
Attila, Hun king 77, 144
Augustanus Laurentius *(vicus),* Italy 381
Augustine, Saint 99n, 142, 143n, 149–50, 155, 219n, 225, 245, 337
Aurelian, praetorian prefect 144 n
Ausonius, poet 321 n
Autun, Gaul 84
Auxerre, Gaul 88
Avars 119, 246, 284–5, 288, 290 n, 291, 379
Avitus, bishop of Vienne 319 n
axiomatikoi see honorati
Aykelāh Revolt, Egypt 255, 257, 269–72, 276, 279
Ayla, Jordan 310

Baalbec, Syria 263, 266
Badajoz, Spain 376
Baetica, Spain 15 n, 72 n, 89–90, 136, 336, 383
Baghdad, Mesopotamia 63, 304, 308, 311, 412
Balkans:
  Christianity 155
  deurbanization 5, 76–7, 91, 284–91, 369, 378
  evacuation of population 278, 288–9, 290
  fortified settlements 51, 76, 80, 288–9, 376, 413
Banu Qasi, Visigothic origin 367
barbarians:
  aristocracy 86, 91–2, 93, 361
  assimilation of locals 366–7, 403
  impact on cities 10–11, 76, 77, 86, 90–2, 308, 314–15, 392
  imperial policy 290, 316, 354
  intermarriage 352–3
  literacy 318, 320, 362 n, 402
  retention of ethnic identity 362–3
  rise to power 351–2
  Roman citizenship 351, 352
  settlement 5, 10
  in social change 352, 353–68
  see also under individual peoples
Barcelona, Spain 89 n, 90, 134
Basil, Saint, bishop of Caesarea 141, 152 n, 225
Basileius, *quinquennalis* 110 n
basilicas 29, 34, 84, 85, 97, 101
Basilicata, Italy 381, 385
Basiliscus, emperor 258
Basques 11, 88, 378
Basra, Mesopotamia 308, 311
baths 30, 34, 39, 61, 97, 99, 117, 180, 373, 377
Beauvais, Gaul 84 n
Beja, Spain 92
Belalis Maior, North Africa 101
Belisarius, general 116, 133, 350, 364
Ben, Egypt 270
Benevento, Italy 375
Benjamin, bishop of Alexandria 174 n
Berbers 316, 366, 377–8
Berenice, Red Sea port 45
Beroea, Syria 313
Berytus, Syria 15, 147, 231, 235–6, 237, 244 n, 412
Bet Shean *see* Scythopolis
Béziers, Gaul 384
Birecik, Mesopotamia 295
Birtha Castra, Mesopotamia 148
bishops:
  in administration of cities 110–12, 116, 137–9, 144–5, 148–55, 156–9, 160–7, 199, 401
  in Anatolia 32, 42, 110–12, 142–3, 148, 155
  building programmes 6, 41, 148–9, 155
  charity 4, 151, 155, 218–19, 349
  in city survival 6, 11, 89, 92, 95–6, 375–6
  as conciliators 152–3, 155–6, 158, 165–6
  in disorders 147–8, 257–8, 262, 263, 267 n, 268–9, 271, 274–5, 276
  distinction from secular office 150–1, 168
  duty of prayer for community 11, 140–1, 375–6
  in Egypt 116, 145–7, 148, 154, 198, 199
  election 113, 120, 141
  in Italy in 6th century 155–9
  leadership in emergencies 144, 283
  legal role 139–40, 151–3
  in Merovingian Gaul 86, 88, 89, 130, 138, 155, 161–6, 166
  and monasteries 88, 89, 146, 147
  moral responsibilities 138–9, 142, 151, 155, 157, 162–3
  in North Africa 155, 159–60, 167
  palaces 32, 36, 37
  as patrons in and of cities 137, 142–5, 148, 156
  persecution of pagans 57, 143–4, 155, 163 n, 262, 263
  privileges 139, 141
  relationships with kings 130, 156, 160–2, 165, 166–7
  rise to power 138–67
  in Syria 138, 144, 145
  taxation role 134, 135, 152, 160–1
  at Thessalonica 116, 119–20, 121

bishops *(cont.)*:
  in Visigothic Spain 92, 155, 160–1, 166
  in West compared with East 124, 130, 141–2n, 154–5
Bithynia, Anatolia 12, 293
Blues and Greens 97, 117, 205–8, 211–17, 251, 253–5, 258–9, 274–6, 404
Boeotia, Greece 286
Bologne, Gaul 84n
Bonakis, general 274, 279
Bonosus, general 273, 279
books 231–9, 322–30
Bordeaux, Gaul 84, 85, 131
Bostra, Syria 54, 55, 57, 59, 61, 62, 64
bouleutai see councillors
bouleutēria see *curiae*
Bourges, Gaul 84, 131, 415
Brad, Syria 63n
Braulio, bishop of Saragossa 338, 339n
Brescia, Italy 370–1, 374, 395
Breviarium of Alaric 21–2, 127–8, 134, 355, 357
Britain 7n, 76, 103, 369, 378, 411, 415
Brixia, Italy 364
Bruttium, Italy 382
buildings:
  building regulations 40, 144, 152
  converted 29–30, 36, 37, 49, 61, 89, 93, 302, 305n
  encroaching 29, 39, 40, 42, 58, 61, 62, 90, 99, 100, 102, 302, 304, 371
  finance 170, 171, 173, 179, 180, 401
  Islamic 298, 303–4, 311, 315, 370–3, 375, 377
  materials reused 34, 39, 41, 59, 85, 90, 370–3, 396
  mud-brick 43n
  reduced availability of sophisticated techniques 387–8
  retreat from classical monumentality 3, 14, 85, 94, 95, 99, 302, 373, 396–7
  wooden 40, 102, 369, 371, 372, 387, 390, 395, 398
Bulgars 119, 286, 291
Burgundians 362, 363
Būsīr, Egypt 270
Butrotum, Albania 288

Caesarea, Cappadocia 51
Caesarea, Palestine 24, 52, 57, 58–9, 172n, 204n, 303, 304–5
Caesarius, bishop of Arles 161, 162–4, 319, 335
Cahors, Gaul 131
Cairo, Egypt 305, 308, 310, 311
Cairouan (Qayrawan), North Africa 311, 377
Calama, North Africa 101
Calliopius, praetorian prefect 149n
Campania, Italy 16, 72n, 97, 364, 381
Campsa, Italy 364
Candidianus, *comes civitatis* 106
canon 175
Cantabria, Spain 90, 136
Capitolias, Palestine 55, 297
Cappadocia, Anatolia 51, 68, 123n
Carnutum, Balkans 77
Cartagena, Spain 376
Carthage, North Africa:
  abandoned 377
  shows 204, 205, 209n, 219, 402
  trade 386
  urban change 17, 97–101, 386
Cassian, Saint John 320
Cassiodorus, historian 21, 96n, 126, 128, 156–7, 333
Cassiopeia 226, 228–9
Castille, Spain 90
Catalonia, Spain 338, 386
Catania, Sicily 96, 125
cathedrals 36, 46, 51, 62
Centcelles, Spain 92
Ceraitae, Anatolia 42
Cercadilla, Spain 92
Chalcedonism 69, 249, 257–60, 265–6, 268, 276, 283, 404
Chalcis, Syria 314n
Chalon-sur-Saône, Gaul 84, 88
Châlons-sur-Marne, Gaul 84n
chariot races 91, 148, 180, 204, 205, 207, 209, 218, 220
Cherchel *see* Iol Caesarea
Cherson, Crimea 124
Childebert, Merovingian king 131
Childebert II, Merovingian king 131, 165
Chilperic, Merovingian king 133, 164n
Choba, North Africa 101
Choricius, orator 229–30
Chosroes II, Persian king 273, 306
Christianity:
  asceticism 67–70, 397–8, 412
  and cities 4, 6, 10n, 11, 30, 223, 247–8, 412, 414–15
  and Greek literary culture 223–48
  inscriptions 13, 14, 15, 16–19, 55, 61–2, 73
  and Islam 101, 305–8, 316–17, 375–6, 377
  and Latin literary culture 318–41
  morality 226, 228–9, 232, 239
  Orthodox *see* Chalcedonism
  and pagan imagery (coexistence) 225–32, 239, 240, 241, 321, 330–1, 402
  paganism suppressed 3, 143–4, 145, 147, 155, 163n, 224, 241–3, 260–9

and social change 349, 411–12
in villages 63, 66, 67
see also Arianism; bishops; Chalcedonism; churches; clergy; monasteries; Monophysitism
Christodora, Egyptian lady 275, 279
Christodorus of Coptus, writer 234
Chromatius, bishop of Aquileia 155
Chrysaphius of Constantinople 206
Chrysostom, Saint John 218–19, 225, 346
Church *see* clergy
churches:
in Anatolia 32, 34, 41–2, 46, 48, 51, 52, 146, 414
in Arabia 57, 61–2, 304, 414
building 18, 41, 52, 56, 57, 61–3, 372, 374
conversions 36, 41, 46, 93, 95
in countryside 62–3, 71, 94
demolished 62, 101–2
in Egypt 145–6
in fortified settlements 76, 80, 84, 85, 86, 96, 101, 159
in Gaul 18, 85, 86, 102
in Italy 18, 95, 102, 372, 374, 397
in Jordan 298, 299
in North Africa 18, 100
in Palestine 51, 57, 299, 300, 414
in Spain 18, 94, 102
in Syria 57, 414
in villages 62–3, 64, 71, 94
Cilicia 13, 54, 64, 73, 114, 148, 217, 249 n, 290
cities:
abandoned 7, 95–6, 101, 287–91, 310 n, 311, 377, 378–9, 381
change in East 30–74, 284–317, 400, 409–16
change in West 74–103, 369–79, 382–3, 384, 386, 389–90, 393–9, 401, 414–16
Christianized 4, 6, 10 n, 11, 30, 223, 247–8, 412, 414–15
citizenship 342–3, 349–50, 403
city-fortress new model 77–82, 96, 289, 376, 383 n
civic finance 122, 170–5, 177, 178–81, 197 n, 202, 401
civic leadership 191–201, 278–9
consumer city? 8, 411
definition 2–3, 5–6, 63, 396
Islamic 41, 308, 310–11, 406, 416
in Malalas 238
migration into country 65 n, 73, 97, 102, 393, 411
military role 48, 59, 175, 194–5
in Nonnus 234–7
policing 191–2
population *see under* population
self-government 2–3, 116–20, 131–3, 157, 270, 272, 277–82, 405–8
urbanization 10, 412
villages (interrelationship) 63, 70–2, 73
city centres:
decline 39, 46, 74, 76, 94, 98–9, 101, 369, 373
restructured 32–4, 36–7
city states:
definition 2, 63
in Eastern Empire 103
government 2–3
under Roman Empire 2–3, 7–8, 411
in Western Empire 86, 91–2, 103, 130–1
cives 132–3, 134
civil service 173, 179, 181, 198–9, 280, 282, 411
Claudian, poet 234, 321–2
clergy:
anti-paganism 3, 143–4, 145, 147
charity 4, 140, 141–2, 146, 150, 151, 155, 349, 401
duties 66, 140–1
educational influence 4, 94, 166, 319–20, 402
financial resources 140, 150, 153–4, 167
imperial grants 140, 141–2, 150, 154, 167, 168
legal responsibilities 149–50, 319–20, 339
literary tradition 225, 320
moral responsibilities 138–9, 150, 151, 162–3, 167
organizations 146–7, 167
political influence 106, 107, 119, 121, 198, 349
and the poor 4, 140, 141, 202, 401
shows censured 4, 91, 117, 145, 204, 218–19, 224
see also Christianity
Clermont-Ferrand, Gaul 84, 85, 415
climate 409–10
Clunia, Spain 89, 90
Clysma (Suez) 172 n
Code of Euric 20, 21, 357, 358
Code of Justinian 19, 104, 177
Code of Recessuinth 21
Code of Theodosius 19, 21, 128
coins:
Ephesus 244
as evidence 23, 24–5, 43–6, 408–9
Gerasa 298
payments in kind 409
Petra in seventh century 294, 298
Sardis 45
uneven distribution 45

collectarii 56
Colluthos, pagarch of Antaeopolis 193
Cologne, Germany 83, 84, 166
colonnades 29, 39, 40, 56, 58, 76
comes civitatis 55, 91, 126–7, 128, 130, 164
Conimbriga, Spain 89n, 90, 92, 376
Constans II 292
Constantine, emperor 3, 12, 138, 139–42, 167
Constantine Porphyrogennetus 290
Constantinople:
  Christianization 241–2, 246, 247
  disorder 214, 215, 217, 243, 250–1, 252–3, 254, 255–6, 263–6
  education 244, 402
  factions 206, 207, 216n, 217, 251n, 254, 277, 278
  mint 46
  monasteries 68
  paganism 143–4, 242–3, 263–5
  plague 243
  shows 205–6, 207, 253
Cordova, Spain 74n, 90, 92, 136, 311, 338, 375, 383
Corinth, Greece 12, 18, 37, 287, 288, 294
Corippus, writer 240
corn-buyers *see* σιτώνης
Corteolona, Italy 374n
Corycus, Cilicia 18, 55, 107–8, 146
Cosa, Italy 380, 392
Cosmas, leader of the Blues 272
Council of Chalcedon *see* Chalcedonism
councillors (decurions, curiales):
  Anastasius' reforms 108–9
  of Bostra 59
  compared with notables 113, 121, 125, 150
  competition 104, 173, 174, 203, 401
  of Corycus 55–6
  duties 121, 126, 127, 135–6, 174–5, 181, 189, 193–4, 197n
  in Egypt (sixth century) 193
  financial obligations 135–6, 174–5, 178, 203
  in Italy (sixth century) 126–8
  no longer commemorated 14, 32, 110, 117
  no longer responsible for city 104–5
  record-keeping 121–2, 131, 136
  shows 203, 206, 208
  tax collection by 10, 123, 126, 127, 130, 134, 174, 181, 187–8
  wealth of 10, 22, 105, 109, 193, 196
countryside:
  churches 62–3, 71, 94
  depopulation 292, 379, 394
  mid-Byzantine revival 291, 297, 299
  migration from cities 73, 97, 102, 393, 411
  monasteries 67–70, 89, 94, 102–3, 283
  revival under Arabs 315
  tax collection 65, 67, 178–9, 184–5, 186
  transformation 5, 96, 287, 293, 379–84, 389–90, 392–4, 397
  see also villages
craftsmen 18, 55, 56, 73, 117, 277, 289, 374, 387, 397
Cremna, Anatolia 42, 52
Crete 109, 286
Croats 290
curatores 55, 107, 110, 126, 131, 150, 180, 192–5, 199
curiae 4, 29, 32, 36–7, 104, 109, 121, 128
curiales see councillors
cursus publicus 179, 189–90
customs duties 171, 172, 177, 205
Cyprus 293
Cyril, bishop of Alexandria 143–4, 147
Cyrus, bishop of Alexandria 154
Cyzicus, Anatolia 45, 217, 292–3

Dacia, Balkans 285
Dalmatia, Balkans 76, 77, 96, 285
Damascius, philosopher 260
Damascus, Syria 63, 303–4, 311, 313, 314, 412
Danube region 76–7, 82, 284–5
Daphne, Syria 263, 267
Daras, Mesopotamia 149n
Dardania, Balkans 285
Datius, bishop of Milan 157
decurions *see* councillors
defensores:
  duties 111, 116, 122, 126, 131, 149–50, 199
  election 55–6, 107, 110, 112–13, 126, 135, 149
  in *Variae* 125
Déhès, Syria 24, 71
Demetrius of Thessalonica, Saint 117, 118, 119–20
demilitarization 279, 317n, 366, 403
δημόσιον λογιστήριον 186, 188, 190n, 197n, 390–2, 393–4
depopulation 53n, 72, 292, 305n, 378, 379, 390–2, 393–4, 409–10
Dertona, Italy 157
desert palaces 310
deurbanization 29, 34, 202, 284–6, 289–90, 378, 411
Dioclea, Balkans 290
Diocletian, emperor 3, 12, 123
Dionysiaca (Nonnus) 231–7, 238, 239, 326
Dionysius, bishop of Edessa 306, 307
Dioscorus, bishop of Alexandria 146–7, 258
Dioscorus of Aphrodito (poet) 66–7, 193, 230
disease *see* plague
disorder:
  anti-pagan 143–4, 147, 241–3, 249, 254–5,

260–9, 281, 407
in Eastern Empire 206n, 214, 215, 217, 249–83, 404, 406–7
factional 117, 206n, 213, 214–15, 217, 249–57, 258–9, 404, 406–7
religious 249, 255, 256, 257–60, 265–6, 276, 282–3, 404, 406–7
Djebel Zawiyé, Syria 63n
documents *see* papyri
Domentianus, general 255
Donatism 159, 336, 337
Dracontius, poet 330–2
Durostorum, Balkans 77
Dyrrhachium, Balkans 285

earthquakes 52, 56, 62, 241, 243, 267, 283, 297, 303
Eastern Empire:
deurbanization 34, 284–6, 289–90, 378
disorder 206n, 214, 215, 217, 249–83, 404, 406–7
late Late-Antique boom 54–63, 102, 288, 289n, 314–15, 414, 416
regionalism 30, 46, 170, 278–82
resettlement of Balkans 290–3, 303, 308, 310, 314, 317
resettlement under Arabs 303
urban change 30–74, 284–317, 400, 409–16
economy:
consumer city? 7–8
Empire and economy 10, 385–6, 411
evidence of coins 43–6
impact of natural causes 409–10
impoverishment 397–9
inbuilt self-destruction? 392–4
not a single economy 409
problems of economic change 9–10
of villages 71, 72, 73, 379–82
Edessa, Mesopotamia 106–7, 116, 148, 208, 217, 246, 263, 305–7
Edict of Theoderic 20–1
education 4, 166, 223–4, 244–5, 318–20, 333, 334, 402, 412
Egara, Spain 134
Egypt:
administration breaks down 191, 197–8, 202
aristocracy 278–81
army 279, 288n
bishops 116, 141–2, 143–4, 146–7, 148, 154, 198, 199
bureaucracy 180, 190, 198–9, 280
Christianity 143–4, 145–6, 232, 317
churches 145–6
civic finance 169–202, 197n
civic leadership 192–6, 198–201
civil service 173, 179, 181, 198–9
disorder 214, 255, 257, 260, 262, 269–72, 274–6, 276
factions 251–2, 254n, 255, 257
guilds 171, 190, 194
'houses' 66, 181–98, 199, 200, 201–2, 270, 272
Islam 310
landowners 66, 105, 181–98, 199, 200, 201
monasteries 68, 69, 145–6, 147, 186, 190, 232, 258, 259
movement into country 73, 310
paganism 260, 262
plague 391
policing 191–2
population of cities 73, 84n, 169n
shows 206, 207n, 208, 219n
taxation 67, 109, 124n, 171–2, 173–4, 177, 178–9, 182–5, 187–9
trade 282, 305
villages 64–5, 66–7, 73
women in office 188, 194–5
ἐκλήπτορες 123
El-Bara, Syria 63n
El Rabacal, Spain 92
Els Munts, Spain 92
Elusa, Palestine 63n
embolē 66, 179, 186, 190
Emerita, Spain 136
Emesa, Syria 24, 56, 412
Emona, Balkans 76
emperors:
acclamations 208–9, 217, 218
deposed 211–12
and factions 207, 210, 211–13, 214, 254, 257, 272, 278
support for Church 48, 139, 140–1, 225, 247, 411–12
emphyteutic leases 174
Ennodius, bishop of Ticinum 333
Ephesus, Anatolia 24, 32–4, 37, 44, 49, 51, 177n, 218, 292, 294
epigraphic habit *see* inscriptions
Epiphania, Syria 56
Epiphanius, bishop of Ticinum 156
Erythrae, Anatolia 37
Esbeita, Palestine 63n
Étang de Berre, Gaul 384
Etenna, Anatolia 52
Etruria, Italy 380–1
Eugenius, bishop of Toledo 332, 336, 338, 340n
Eulogius, bishop of Alexandria 271
Eunapius, writer 325n
Eunomius, count of Tours 164n
Euric, Visigothic king 20, 156

Eusebius, bishop of Tarraco 91, 140, 220n, 238
Eutropius, bishop of Valencia 336n
Eutychius, bishop of Constantinople 265
Evagrius, historian 108, 262–3, 268
exactores 123, 187–8, 209
exactorikē taxis 187–8

factions:
  disorder 117, 206n, 213, 217, 249–57, 258–9, 314–15, 404, 406–7
  finance 205–6, 401
  history and functions 97, 122, 204, 205, 207–10
  political influence 206–7, 211–18, 271–2, 273, 274–6, 277–8, 404
Fatimid dynasty 295, 300, 304
Ferrara, Italy 96n
Firmicus Maternus, writer 326
fiscus Barcinonensis 134–5
Flavian, bishop of Antioch 142–3, 145
Florence, Italy 372
food shortages 254n, 255, 409–10
fora 34, 41, 287
fortifications *see* walls
Franks:
  assimilation 161, 362, 363, 367
  culture 318, 361
  ethnic identity 316, 362–3, 367
  intermarriage 356n
  in Italy 364
  legislation 133–4, 319n
  monasteries 88–9
Fravitta, *magister militum* 352n
Fréjus, Gaul 384
Fructuosus, bishop of Braga 336n
fundus 183–4

Gadara, Palestine 55, 297
Gaeta, Italy 375
Gainas, *magister militum* 351
Galatia, Anatolia 63, 67–8, 293
Galilee, Palestine 64, 299
Gallaecia, Spain 38n, 356
games *see* shows
Gascony, Gaul 7n
Gaul:
  bishops 86, 88, 89, 155, 161–6, 166
  churches 85–6, 102
  civitates 6–7, 86, 88, 131, 134, 166
  countryside 384
  education 318–19, 320
  government 86, 88, 127–34
  inscriptions 15, 18
  under the Merovingians 130–4, 161–70
  monasteries 85, 88–9
  population 83–5
  shows 88, 219–20
  taxation 129, 130, 131n
  trade 384, 415
  villas 129
  under the Visigoths 20, 21, 86, 127–9, 161, 354, 355
Gaza, Palestine 15, 113, 143n, 226
Geiseric, Vandal king 144
gentiles 353
George of Pisidia 245, 340
Gerasa, Arabia:
  under Arab rule 297–8, 303
  coins 24
  inscriptions 14, 59, 61, 201n
  urban change 51, 54, 55, 57, 59, 61–2, 148, 204n, 297–8, 303–4, 314n
Germanic peoples 5, 124, 138, 316, 352, 353–4, 363, 398, 402
Germanicia, Anatolia 292
Germanus 212
Gerona, Spain 134
gesta municipalia 131
Ghassanids 316, 414n
Golan Heights, Palestine 299
Gortyn, Crete 109
Goths 289, 291 *see also* Ostrogoths; Visigoths
governors, provincial 12, 16, 39, 95, 112, 115, 122–3, 152, 206, 209, 272
Grado, Italy 18
'grandees' of Edessa 91–2, 107, 152, 188
Gratian, emperor 176
Greece 5, 7n, 15, 80, 219n, 237, 284–91, 293, 369
Greens and Blues *see* Blues and Greens
Gregory, bishop of Antioch 153, 255, 263, 267, 268–9, 281
Gregory, Saint, bishop of Nazianzus 225
Gregory, Saint, bishop of Nyssa 225
Gregory, Saint, bishop of Tours 86, 129, 130, 132–4, 161, 164–6, 334, 335, 340
Gregory the Great, Pope 127, 154, 158, 246, 319, 334
guilds 114, 171, 190, 194, 204, 205, 277
Gundovald, Merovingian king 131
Guntram, Merovingian king 131, 133n, 165

habitatores 111n, 113–15
Hadrian I, Pope 397
Hadrianopolis, Anatolia 111–12, 151
Hadrumetum, North Africa 101
Haïdra, North Africa 17, 100n, 377
Hama *see* Epiphania
harbours 59, 100
Harran, Mesopotamia 263n
Hauran, Syria 54, 64, 65–6, 297, 310n
Heliopolis, Syria 110n

Helladius, bishop of Toledo 336
Hemmaberg, Austria 76
Heracleopolis, Egypt 116, 194, 195
Heraclius, emperor 160, 211, 213 n, 255, 272, 274–6, 290, 306, 408 n
hermits 67–70, 412
Hermopolis, Egypt 84 n, 105 n, 109, 145–6, 169 n, 185, 188 n, 193 n, 197 n
Hesychius Illustris 49, 234–5
Hilary, bishop of Arles 335
Hippo, North Africa 149–50
hippodromes 61, 204, 207
Hippolitus, loved by Phaedra 226, 227
Homs *see* Emesa
honestiores 346, 347
honorati 12, 55, 105, 106, 107, 110, 112 n, 125, 126, 128–9, 150, 156–7
Honoratus, Saint 88, 320
Honorius, emperor 149, 321
Hostegesis, bishop of Cordova 375
'houses' in Egypt 22, 66, 181–98, 199, 200, 201–2, 270, 272
housing 42, 88, 90, 99, 302, 369–73, 399 *see also* mansions; villas
humiliores 346
Huns 76, 77
ὑποδέκται 123, 179, 189 n
Hypatia, philosopher 143, 147
Hypatius, usurper 213 n

Iamblichus, philosopher 325, 326
Ibas, bishop of Edessa 148, 208, 217
Ibn al-Qutiya family, Visigothic origin 367
Iconium, Isauria 110 n
icons 246–7
Ildefons, bishop of Toledo 336, 338
Ildibadus, Gothic king 365, 366
Illus, Isaurian general 260
Illyricum, Balkans 117, 285
incastellamento 96, 382–3, 393
industry 7 n, 8, 89, 297–8, 384–6, 387–8, 393
inscriptions:
  Christian 13, 15, 16–19, 45 n, 55, 73, 148–9, 400
  epigraphic habit 11–19
  as evidence of Persian invasion 414 n
  as evidence of political change 12–14, 18, 38–9, 55, 94–5, 111–12, 116–17, 302 n, 400
  on tombstones 11, 13, 16–18, 43 n, 55, 73
  in villages 13, 54–5, 56, 65, 66, 73
Iol Caesarea, North Africa 101–2, 369, 371, 377
Iraq *see* Mesopotamia
Irni, Spain 345
Isaac, Egyptian governor 270–2
Isacius, bishop of Jerusalem 273
Isaiah, bishop of Edessa 306
Isauria 39, 42, 54, 64, 110 n
Iscia, Balkans 285
Isidore, bishop of Seville 91, 323, 336 n, 337, 338–40, 360–1
Islam 11, 283, 290, 307–8, 316–17, 404
Italica, Spain 74 n, 89, 376, 383
Italy:
  agriculture 379–82, 392–3
  bishops 95–6, 144, 155–9
  Byzantine 18, 109, 114, 124, 127, 197, 200, 395
  castelli 96, 382–3, 393
  churches 95, 102, 372, 374, 397
  classicism survives 76
  countryside in decline 379–83, 389–90, 392–3, 397
  education 333, 334
  fortified settlements 95, 96, 288–9
  Frankish invasion 364
  impoverishment 95, 379, 385, 390, 394, 395–9, 411
  industry 384–6, 387–8
  inscriptions 15, 16, 18, 94–5
  'liberation' from Goths 95, 157, 350–1, 363–6, 375, 394–5, 403 n
  literature 319, 333–4
  under the Lombards 77, 95, 157, 361, 371, 375, 379, 395
  militarization 124, 127, 200 n
  monasteries 158, 159, 333–4, 371, 374
  under the Ostrogoths 15, 18, 38, 102, 125–7, 128 n, 156, 350–1, 363–7
  plague 391, 392, 395
  population 127, 373–4, 393, 395, 397
  shows 219
  taxation 125 n, 126, 127
  trade 375, 384–6, 388–9, 395 n
  urban change 15, 94–7, 157–8, 369–74, 395–9, 415
  villas 96, 97, 372, 385, 392–3, 395–6

Jacob, notable of Aykelāh 270–2
Jerome, Saint 225
Jerusalem 57, 58, 66, 67, 216 n, 273, 299, 303
Jews 143, 215, 247, 254, 256, 273, 282, 340–1, 363 n, 407
John, bishop of Constantinople 267 n
John, bishop of Ephesus 48, 242–3, 262–3, 268
John, bishop of Gerona 337
John, bishop of Niciu 197–8, 199, 214, 251, 257, 269–72, 273, 276
John, bishop of Thessalonica 117 n, 119
John, duke of the Thebaid 230
John, governor of Alexandria 274

John IV, pope 285
John of Damascus 307
John the Almsgiver, bishop of Alexandria 259n
John the Augustalis 270–1, 272
John the Cappadocian, praetorian prefect 252, 253
Jordan 63n, 122, 297, 298–9, 303, 305, 310, 314, 317, 400
Judaea 64
Julian, bishop of Toledo 338
Julian, emperor 175, 230, 325
Julian of Ascalon 40n
Julius Africanus 238
Justin I, emperor 211, 254
Justin II, emperor 213n, 251n, 267
Justinian, emperor:
  building programme 15, 61, 102, 123, 148, 410
  and Christianity 137, 141n, 150–1, 154, 168, 219
  Christianization of literature 240–1, 243–4
  and factions 213, 216n, 254
  finance 123, 167, 170–5, 205n
  legislation 12n, 19, 104, 108, 150–1, 154, 170–5, 198, 205n
  and post-curial government 111, 112, 122, 280, 401
  shows 219
  suppresses paganism 48, 241–3, 260, 265
  wars 77, 95, 157, 160, 350–1, 363–6, 375, 394–5, 403n
Justinian 3, general 267
Justinian II, emperor 292–3
Justus, bishop of Toledo 336

Keos (Greek island) 286
Keszthely-Fenékpuszta *see* Valcum
Khirbat al Samra, Arabia 298
Klagenfurt, Austria 76
Kom Obo, Egypt 148
kontakion 241
kopiatai 123
Korykus *see* Corycus
κτήτορες see *possessores*
Kufa, Mesopotamia 311

La Cocosa, Spain 92
Laconia, Greece 286
Lakhmids 316
Lambaesis, North Africa 100
landowners:
  councillors become a minority 22, 105
  Egyptian estate archives 22
  'immunity' 130
  impoverishment 395–6
  privileges 8, 129
  profitability of estates 186n
  sources of wealth 184, 196, 197, 392–3
  tax collection by 67, 123, 129, 182–5, 187
  unequal division of property 182n
  see also 'houses' in Egypt
Laodicea, Syria 112, 412
Laon, Gaul 88
law schools 236, 237, 244
Lawrence, bishop of Milan 156
Le Mans, Gaul 131
Leander, bishop of Seville 336n, 337, 338
Lebanon *see* Syria
Leges Visigothorum 357, 358
legislation:
  bishops' role 139–40, 142, 145
  building regulations 40, 144, 152
  codification 19, 20–2
  and ethnic identity 356–9
  Farmers Law 293–4
  Ostrogothic 20–1
  on property 105, 106–7, 109, 129, 173–4, 175–8, 183–5, 293–4
  to protect *curiae* 104–5, 108, 128
  and Roman citizenship 343–5, 349, 357
  Visigothic 20, 21–2, 127–8, 134, 356–8, 361n
lektikarioi 123
Leo, emperor 42, 106, 213n, 258
Leo II, emperor 211
Leo III, emperor 157n
Leo the Great (Pope) 144
Leo VI, emperor 109
Leodegar of Autun 319n
Leontius, house of 191
Leovigild, Visigothic king 136n, 160, 356, 357
Leptis Magna, North Africa 101
Lérins monastery, Gaul 88, 320
Lex Romana Visigotorum see *Breviarium of Alaric*
Libanius, writer 104, 145, 237
Liber Iudiciorum 20
Lienz *see* Aguntum
Liguria, Italy 38n, 95, 156, 364, 366, 375, 378
literacy 224, 318, 320, 335, 402
literature 25, 223–48, 319–41, 402
λογευτής 201n, 307
λογιστής see *curatores*
Lombards 77, 95, 157, 318, 361, 371, 375, 379, 395
Lombardy, Italy 375
Lorca, Spain 376
Lucania, Italy 382
Luitprand, Lombard king 374n
Luni, Italy 371
Lupus, *principalis* 110n
Lusitania, Spain 15n, 89–90, 336, 356

Luxorius, poet 97
Lycaonia, Anatolia 68
Lycia, Anatolia 42–3, 64, 69
Lydia, Anatolia 63
Lydus, John 108, 242n, 243
Lyons, Gaul 84, 85

Macedonia 17, 96, 117n, 413
Macrobius, writer 323–7
magister militum 59, 61, 281
magistrates 14, 110, 126, 137
Mainz, Germany 415
maiores 127
Maktar, North Africa 17
Malalas, John 108, 207, 212, 234, 237–9, 243, 250–1
Mampsis, Palestine 63n
mandylion 246
mansions 36, 37, 56, 97–8, 100, 305n, 370, 399
Manūf, Egypt 274, 275, 278–9
Marcellus, bishop of Apamea 57, 143n
Marche, Italian region 378
Marcian, emperor 207, 213n, 253–4
Marcian, prefect 279
Mardites 292
Marinus, praetorian prefect 108
Mark the Deacon 113
Marmoutier monastery, Gaul 88, 320
Marriage of Philology and Mercury (Martianus Capella) 326, 327–30
Marseilles, Gaul 88, 384
Marsyas 226
Marthanes, dux 217
Martianus Capella, poet 323, 326, 327–30
Martin, bishop of Braga 319n
Martin, Saint, bishop of Tours 7, 88, 164, 165, 320
Masona, bishop of Merida 160
Massala, Sicily 96
Mauretania, North Africa 167
Maurice, emperor 69, 211–12, 213n, 251, 255, 263n, 405
Megara, Greece 38n
Melkites *see* Chalcedonism
Memphis, Egypt 311
Menas, notable of Aykelāh 270–2
Menas, general 255
Menas, leader of the Greens 272
Menas, pagarch of Antaeopolis 194n
Menas, scribe 274–5
Merida, Spain 74n, 89n, 90, 92, 376
Merovingian dynasty 21, 84, 86, 89, 102, 130, 161, 166, 334
Meseta, Spain 90–1, 356, 359
Mesopotamia:
  under Arab rule 289
  bishops 144, 148
  persecution of paganism 281
  religion 317, 404
  urban decline 289, 295, 310–11, 314, 400, 414
Metanoia monastery, Egypt 186, 190
Methana, Greece 286
Metz, Gaul 83n, 85, 86, 399
migration 73, 97, 102, 285, 314
Milan, Italy 219, 371–2, 402
Miletus, Anatolia 34n, 37n, 49–51, 54
Minturnae, Italy 381
Moesia, Balkans 285
monarchy 5, 86, 124, 138, 166–7, 358, 397, 398
monasteries:
  agricultural production 68, 293, 333
  in Anatolia 67, 68–9, 291
  and bishops 88, 89, 146, 147
  as economic centres 89, 333
  educational influence 94, 333, 336–7
  in Egypt 68, 69, 145–6, 147, 186, 190, 232, 258, 259
  in Gaul 85, 88–9
  influence of 66, 68–70, 89, 94, 103, 333
  in Italy 158, 159, 333–4, 371, 374
  in Jordan 299
  in North Africa 94, 337
  in Palestine 66, 67, 69–70, 258
  in Spain 94, 336–7, 394
  in Syria 67, 258, 259
  in villages 67–70
Monemvasia, Greece 285, 288n
Monophysitism:
  centred on monasteries 70, 147
  definition 249
  in disorders 255, 257–60, 263, 265–6, 268, 270–1, 276, 282–3, 306
Monza, Italy 374n
Mopsuestia, Anatolia 114, 115, 116
mosaics 58, 85, 92, 97–8, 100, 225, 226–9, 299, 300
mosques 298, 375, 377
Mousaius, house of 191
Murcia, Spain 376
Musaeus, writer 233–4
Mylasa, Anatolia 172n
mythology 224, 226–9, 232–4, 236, 240, 323, 330–1

Naissa, Balkans 284, 286
Nantes, Gaul 84
Naples, Italy 115n, 116, 127, 133, 167, 385
Narbonne, Gaul 84, 384
Narses, general 207, 272–3, 364, 365n, 379

Nea Paphos, Cyprus 226, 228–9
Neapolis, Palestine 204 n
Negev, Palestine 54, 63 n, 64, 66–7, 122, 299
Neoplatonism 325–6
Nepos, emperor 156
Nessana, Palestine 63 n, 66–7, 122, 300
Nicaea, Anatolia 292
Nicagoras, archon 110 n
Nicetius, bishop of Trier 415
Nicetius, general 275
Nicholas of Sion 69
Niciu, Egypt 274, 275
Nicomedia, Anatolia 45
Nicopolis, Greece 287
Nicopolis ad Istrum, Balkans 51, 77–80, 289
Nika Riot, Constantinople 213 n, 215, 241, 250, 252–3, 254, 256
nomikoi 244
Nonnus, poet 231–7, 326
Noricum, Balkans 76, 378–9
North Africa:
  agriculture 315
  under Arab rule 9–10, 332–3, 376–8
  bishops 144, 149, 155, 159–60, 167
  Byzantine 100–1, 332
  Christianity 100, 101, 145, 155, 377
  churches 18, 100
  classicism survives 74
  factions 97
  fortifications 51–2, 100–1
  inscriptions 15, 17, 18, 97
  literature 319, 330–3
  monasteries 94, 337
  population 100, 378
  shows 97, 219
  trade 305, 384–6, 388–9
  urban change 15, 97–102, 369, 376–8, 386
  under the Vandals 160, 319, 386, 394
notables:
  councillors compared 113, 121, 125, 150
  election 55–6, 107, 110–11, 112–13, 126, 135, 149, 150, 164
  in Merovingian Gaul 131–4
  no legal definition 120
  problems of leadership and collective action 115–16, 198–201, 278–80, 406–7
  in provincial assemblies 38, 125–6
  regional groups 281–2
  rise of 107–8, 110
  titles 112, 114–15, 197 n
  who were they? 111–16, 125–6
notaries 127
Nova Justinianopolis, Anatolia 292–3
Novae, Balkans 77
Novellae (Justinian) 19, 104, 170–5
Novellae (Theodosius) 21
numerarii 134–5, 152 n
Numidia, North Africa 100, 167, 172 n

Odoacer, Germanic king 76, 156, 379
Odysseus allegorized 228
Oescus, Balkans 77
οἰκήτορες see *habitatores*
οἶκοι see 'houses' in Egypt
Olympia, Greece 288
Olympic Games 206, 207 n, 254 n
Olympiodorus, historian 325 n
Ombi, Egypt 109
Opsikion, Anatolian theme 292
Optimus, bishop of Antioch 41
Orange, Gaul 384
ordines see councillors
Orestes, prefect of Egypt 144 n
Origines, encyclopedia of Isidore of Seville 338–40
Orihuela, Spain 376
Orleans, Gaul 84, 88, 131
Orphism 325–6
Ostrogoths:
  assimilation of locals 363–7
  and bishops 156–7
  coins 23
  ethnic identity 364–7
  in Italy 15, 18, 38, 102, 125–7, 128 n, 156–7, 350–1, 363–7
  legislation 21, 358 n
  numbers 357 n, 364
  warrior culture 318, 322
Oxyrhynchus, Egypt:
  Christianity 147, 230–1
  'houses' 116, 183, 187, 188–9, 191, 194, 195, 196–7, 200
  population 169 n
  villages 73

paganism:
  Christian attacks 3, 143–5, 147, 155, 163 n, 224, 231, 241–3, 249, 260–9, 281, 307, 404, 407, 410
  images tolerated 225–32, 239, 240, 241, 321, 330–1, 402
  in literature 225, 229–32, 324–7, 329–30
    see also mythology
  morality 138 n, 232, 322
pagarchs 135 n, 180, 188–9, 193, 195, 197 n, 199, 201, 270 n
paididaskaloi 244
palaestra 42
Palermo, Sicily 383
Palestine:
  under Arab rule 303–4, 400, 414
  bishops 141
  Christianity 258, 267, 307

churches 51, 57, 299, 300, 414
classicism survives 30, 32
coins 24
disorder 249 n, 267, 272–4
inscriptions 13, 14 n, 55, 65–6, 302 n
monasteries 66, 67, 69–70, 258
plague 73 n
population 53 n, 57, 305 n
resettlement 303, 308, 310
trade 282, 305n
urban change 54–63, 297, 300, 302–5, 308, 310, 313, 314, 400, 410, 412, 413–14
villages 14 n, 54, 64, 66–7, 72, 73, 299–300
Palladius, writer 323
Pamphylia, Anatolia 13
Pannonia, Balkans 77, 80, 285
Panopolis, Egypt 69, 232
Paphlagonia, Anatolia 111–12
papyri:
end of civic documents 22, 122
from Nessana 66, 300
from Petra 62 n, 109 n, 304 n
from Ravenna 126
parabalani 146–7, 167
Paris, Gaul 84, 85, 86, 131
Paschal Chronicle 251
pater civitatis 110, 111, 112, 116, 124, 172, 180, 192, 193
Patras, Greece 110 n, 285, 286, 288
patria 234–5
patriarchs *see* bishops
Paul, bishop of Merida 337
Paul, prefect of Samnud 275
Paul the Silentiary 237 n, 240–1, 243
Paulinus 267 n
Pavia, Italy *see* Ticinum
Pednelissus, Anatolia 52
Pella, Palestine 55, 297, 303, 304–5
peregrini 343, 344, 347
Pergamum, Anatolia 34 n, 37 n, 39, 46–8, 51, 292, 294
Persians:
deportations 52, 56, 72, 289 n, 295, 305 n, 409, 410
in Egypt 283
favour Monophysites 259, 283, 306
invade Anatolia 42, 43, 48–9, 53, 54
in Mesopotamia 144, 259, 273–4
reasons for success after 600 405–8
in Syria 56, 144, 266, 283, 414
wars 52–3, 288, 404–5, 408 n
Pessinus, Anatolia 113
Peter, bishop of Edessa 148 n
Peter Mongus, bishop of Alexandria 147, 174 n, 262
Petra, Arabia 62, 109, 122, 174 n, 304–5
Philadelphia *see* Amman
Philae, Egypt 148
Philippicus, general 269
philoponoi 147
Philoxenus, house of 191
Phlegethius, proconsul of Ephesus 218
Phocas, emperor 117, 212, 213, 249, 251, 255, 272, 274–6, 405
Phocas, praetorian prefect 242
Phoenicia *see* Syria
Photius, Roman commander 267
Phrygia, Anatolia 54, 63, 73, 293
Picenum, Italy 95
Pisander of Laranda 233
Pisidia, Anatolia 41, 52, 63, 68 n, 73, 293
Placcus, bishop of Gerasa 61
plague 52–4, 62, 69, 71, 72, 73 n, 243, 283, 392, 395, 409–10
Plato, prefect of Constantinople 206
Poetovio, Balkans 77
poetry 229–30, 231–7, 240–1, 243, 245, 319, 321–2, 330–2, 334
Poitiers, Gaul 84, 85, 131–2, 133 n, 415
politeuomenoi see councillors
Pomerius, grammarian 319
Pontus, Anatolia 12
popes 137, 157, 158
population:
boom reversed 42–3, 57, 291–2, 293
city average (Egypt) 169
decline in cities 5, 7, 46, 48–9, 52, 83, 100, 374
does not give city status 2
effect of plague 52–4
estimates (Gaul) 83–5
Italy 373, 390–2, 395
see also depopulation
Portugal 92, 356 n
possessores 110, 111, 112, 113–15, 125–6, 127, 150, 183–4, 280
pottery:
as evidence of urban decline 45 n, 49, 52, 287, 304, 369, 384–6, 388–9
manufacture 89, 297–8, 385, 387, 393
trade 49, 282, 294, 305, 369, 384–6, 388–9, 394
prefect of the *plebs* 264 n
Priene, Anatolia 294
primates 111, 112, 113, 114
principales 112, 113, 126
Priscian, orator 108, 240
Proclus, philosopher 326
Procopius, historian 15, 38 n, 53, 213, 242 n, 250, 365–6
Procopius of Gaza, sophist and theologian 226, 240

προεώδρία 192, 193, 196
protectores 55, 113
Proterius, bishop of Alexandria 258
πρωτεύοντες 111, 112–13, 124, 280
Protogenes, teacher 244
Provence, Gaul 17, 76, 88, 318–19, 384
provinces:
  aristocracy 86, 91–2, 97, 199–201, 280–1, 360–1, 407
  assemblies 12–13, 38, 122–3
  bureaucracy 3, 105, 180, 190, 198–9, 280
  capitals 12, 13, 37–9, 115
  governors *see* governors, provincial
  regionalism 30, 46, 124, 159, 170, 202, 278–82, 350–1, 353–68, 413
  Roman citizenship 343–50, 351, 352, 361
prytaneia 29, 34
public spectacles *see* shows

Qayrawan, North Africa *see* Cairouan
Quwaysma, Jordan 298–9

Ratiaria, Balkans 77
Ravenna, Italy:
  bishops 159
  buildings 102, 372–3
  education 319
  government 109, 114, 115, 117n, 126, 127
  shows 219, 401–2
  urban decline 372–3, 395n
Reccared, Visigothic king 355
Recopolis, Spain 82
Regensburg, Germany 76–7
regionalism 30, 46, 124, 159, 170, 278–82, 350–1, 353–68, 413
res privata 170n, 176, 177
Rheims, Gaul 84n, 85
Rhodes 216n
Rihab, Arabia 298
riots *see* disorder
Rioya, Spain 338
riparii 179, 191, 192, 193n, 195
roads 52, 71, 100, 299n, 373
Romanos, poet 241, 243–4
Rome, Italy:
  churches 285, 374
  industry 385
  plague 391
  popes 137, 157, 158
  population 374n
  shows 204, 205, 206, 207n, 219, 401
  urban decline 16–17, 373
Rougga, North Africa 102
Rugi, barbarian tribe 365
ruralization 58, 283, 362

Sabas, Saint 69–70
Sabratha, North Africa 101
sacrae largitiones 172n, 176, 177, 179
Sagalassus, Anatolia 40n, 46n, 52
Saintes, Gaul 84
Salerno, Italy 375
Salona, Balkans 285, 290
Salvian, priest 219
Samaritans 267, 282
Samarra, Mespotamia 311
Samnium, Italy 16, 381
Samnud, Egypt 274, 275
San Canzian D'Isonzo, Italy 18
Santiago de Compostela, Spain 376
Sao Cucufate, Spain 92
Saragossa, Spain 90, 91
Sardica, Balkans 284, 286
Sardinia 127
Sardis, Anatolia 23, 37, 43–4, 45, 48–9, 51, 243, 292, 294
Saturnalia (Macrobius) 323–7
Saturnia, Italy 380
Savaria, Balkans 77
Sbeitla, North Africa 17
Scarbantia, Balkans 77
schools 223, 224, 242, 244, 318, 320, 336, 402
Sclavenes *see* Slavs
scriniarii 123
Scythopolis, Palestine 24, 51, 55, 57, 58, 169n, 204n, 300–3, 304–5
Seleucia in Pieria, Syria 112, 412
Selge, Anatolia 52
senators 128
seniores 127, 132
Senlis, Gaul 84n
Sens, Gaul 84, 131
Sepphoris, Palestine 303
Septimius Severus, emperor 233
Serbs 290
Serena, wife of Stilicho 321, 322
Sergius, bishop of Birtha Castra 148n
Sergius, bishop of Constantinople 246
Servitanum monastery, Spain 336
Sessa Aurunca, Italy 381
Sétif, North Africa 377
Severinus, Saint 378–9
Severus, bishop of Antioch 219n, 260
Seville, Spain 74n, 89n, 90, 375, 383
Shenoute of Atripe 69, 232
shops 29, 40, 43–4, 58
shows:
  administration 203, 205–8, 209–10, 253, 256
  and Christianity 4, 91, 117, 145, 148, 204, 224
  finance 97, 179, 180, 203, 205–7, 401

imperialization 203, 205–8, 209–10, 278 n
performers 203–4, 205, 207
political influence 207, 208–9, 210–18, 268
survival 88, 91, 117, 122
see also factions
Sia, Anatolia 42
Sicily 5, 96–7, 125, 157, 285
Side, Anatolia 54
Sidonius, bishop of Mainz 84 n, 415
Sidonius Apollinaris, bishop of Clermont 131, 161, 321 n, 362
Sigbert, Merovingian king 131–2
Simeon Stylites the Elder 70
Sinduni tribe 345
Sinuessa, Italy 381
Sirmium, Balkans 77, 288, 379
Siscia, Balkans 77
Sisebut, Visigothic king 91, 219 n, 332, 338
Sisenand, Visigothic king 336 n
Sitifs, North Africa 101
σιτώνης 110, 111, 116, 150
Slavs 11, 117 n, 118, 119, 284, 288, 291, 292
social change 5–6, 73, 255–6, 276–82, 346–50, 352, 353–68, 408, 409–12
Socrates, historian 138
Soissons, Gaul 84, 86
Spain (Hispania):
agriculture 383
Arab conquest 316, 317 n, 366, 367–8
Arab grandees of Visigothic descent 91–2
Arab rule 91–2, 311, 313, 338, 375, 383
Arianism 160
assimilation of Goths and provincials 357, 360–2, 363
bishops 92, 152 n, 155, 160–1, 166
Christianization 91, 94, 155, 160
churches 94, 102
countryside changing 383
decurions 135–6
education 336
estates 93–4
fortified settlements 90, 413
inscriptions 15, 17, 18
literature 319, 332, 336–40
monasteries 94, 336–7, 394
shows 91, 219–20
taxation 131 n, 134–5
trade 386, 394
urban change 15, 76, 89–94, 97, 102, 375–6, 383, 393–4, 415
villas 92–3, 129, 394
under the Visigoths 15, 21, 90–2, 93–4, 134–6, 160, 166, 354–63, 367
Spalatum, Balkans 290
Sparta, Greece 237, 288
St. Sophia, Constantinople 237 n, 240–1
Stilicho, commander in chief 321–2, 351
Stobi, Greece 289–90
Strategius the Monk 251
στρατηλατεία 194–5
Stratonicea, Anatolia 110 n
streets 29, 39, 40, 41, 43, 58, 373 n
suburbanization 6, 34, 42, 46–8, 80, 84, 85, 159
successor kingdoms *see* monarchy
Sufetula, North Africa 101
σύμμαχοι 200
συντελεστής 182–4, 185
Synesius, bishop of Ptolemais 142, 144
Syracuse, Sicily 96
Syria:
under Arab rule 289, 303–4, 317, 412, 414
bishops 138, 144
Christianity 57, 147, 307, 308, 317
churches 54, 57, 414
classicism survives 30, 32
coins 24
depopulation 53 n
deportations 52, 56, 72, 289 n, 295, 305 n, 409, 410
disorder 258, 259–60, 266, 272–4, 281
evacuations 290, 305
inscriptions 13, 14 n, 55, 65–6, 414 n
monasteries 67, 258, 259
Persian invasions 56, 144, 266, 283, 414
plague 52–4, 62, 71, 72, 283
regionalism 281
religion 258–60, 283, 404
resettlement by Arabs 308, 310
shows 206, 219 n
trade 282
urban change 54–63, 295, 305, 308, 310, 311, 313, 314, 400, 405, 410, 412, 413–14
villages 54, 56, 64, 65–7, 70–2, 73, 295, 297, 314
wealthy families 307, 308

Tarraco, Spain 15 n, 17, 89, 90, 91, 92, 134, 383, 393, 394
Tarragona *see* Tarraco
Tarsus, Cilicia 206 n, 216 n
Taurini family 196 n
tax collection:
autopragia 65, 67
by councillors 10, 123, 126, 127, 129, 130, 134–5, 174, 181, 187–8
difficulty in collecting 401
by others 108, 123, 130
see also taxation in Egypt
in villages 65, 67, 178–9, 184–5, 186
taxation:
under Arabs 407 n
and bishops 134, 135, 152, 160–1

taxation (*cont.*):
customs duties 171, 172, 177, 205
in Egypt 67, 109, 124n, 171–2, 173–4, 177, 178–9, 182–5, 187–9
'immunity' 130, 164n, 167
in kind 66, 160, 179, 186, 190
see also *annona*
land tax 173–4, 182–5
preassigned to expenditure 171–2, 177, 178–9, 180, 201, 407
for shows 179, 180, 205, 401
ταξεῶται 123
Tebessa, North Africa 377
technology 387–8
temples 5, 30, 34, 36, 46, 57, 61, 95, 147
Teurnia, Austria 76
theatre claques 208, 210, 217
theatres 39, 41, 58, 61, 76, 99, 207, 218, 220n
Thebaid, Egypt 109, 145
Thebes, Greece 237, 288
Thecla, Saint 225
Theodemir, Visigothic leader 313, 367, 376
Theoderic, Ostrogothic king 20–1, 96, 119, 125, 156, 205n, 206n, 219
Theodolinda, Lombard queen 374n
Theodore, bishop of Alexandria 274
Theodore, bishop of Niciu 275, 279
Theodore, bishop of Sykeon 67, 68–9, 70n, 113
Theodore, prefect 274
Theodore, official in Osroene 263–4
Theodoret, bishop of Cyrrhus 148
Theodorus, pagarch of Oxyrhynchus 194n
Theodosian Code 19, 21, 128
Theodosius, *comes civitatis* 106
Theodosius, son of Maurice 212, 274n
Theodosius I, emperor 142–3, 143
Theodosius II, emperor 144, 171, 206, 207, 211, 253, 256
Theodosius Zticca of Constantinople 206
Theodulf of Orleans, writer 338
Theon, house of 187, 191, 192
Theophanes, Saint 251
Theophilus, bishop of Alexandria 143–4, 147
Theophilus, emperor 124
Theophilus, governor of Merada 279n
Theophilus, Roman commander 263, 267
Theophylact Simocatta, historian 245, 274, 340
Thérouanne, Gaul 84n
Thespiae, Boeotia 287
Thessalonica, Greece 116–20, 249n, 284, 285
Theveste, North Africa 101
Thomas, bishop of Amida 149n
Thrace 80, 292, 293, 413
Thuburbo Maius, North Africa 100
Tiberias, Palestine 57
Tiberius, emperor 213n, 265, 267
Tiberius II 123
Ticinum (Pavia), Italy 38n, 156, 157, 219
Timagenes, house of 187, 188, 192, 194, 195–6
Timothy Aelurus, bishop of Alexandria 174n, 258
Toledo, Spain 91
tombstones 11, 13, 16–18, 43n, 55, 73, 293, 298n, 339n
Tongeren, Gaul 84n
Torre de Palma, Portugal 92
Totilla, Ostrogothic king 350n, 351, 364, 365
Toul, Gaul 84n
Toulouse, Gaul 84
Tours, Gaul 6–7, 84, 131, 133–4, 164–6
trade:
caravan 315
between city and villages 71
collapse of 9–10, 59, 294, 369, 395n
Mediterranean 9–10, 88, 313, 375
North Sea 415–16
pottery 49, 282, 294, 305, 369, 384–6, 388–9, 394
Red Sea 283
regionalized 282
stimulated by transfer of tax 10, 385–6
Trapezont, Anatolia 148, 292
Tribonius, *quaestor* 252
triclinium 37, 214
Tridentum, Italy 345
Trier, Gaul 17, 83, 86, 415
Trieste, Italy 18
Tripolitania, North Africa 45, 64, 72
Troesmus, Balkans 77
Tuliasses tribe 345
Tunisia, North Africa 305n, 311, 378
Tur Abdin, Mesopotamia 259
Tuscany, Italy 95, 364, 372, 382, 395
Tyre, Syria 235–6, 412

Umayyad dynasty 63, 295, 298, 303, 304, 308, 310, 400, 416
Umm al-Jimal, Jordan 57, 63n, 297
Umm el Rassas, Jordan 299
Uraias, Ostrogothic chief 366
urbanization 9–10, 40n, 96, 289n, 399

Valcum, Balkans 80
Valencia, Spain 90, 376
Valens, emperor 141, 176, 244
Valentinian, emperor 176
Valentinian I, emperor 149
Valentinian III, emperor 204n

Vandals:
army 366
assimilation of locals 366
and bishops 144, 160
in city survival 10–11, 18, 97–8, 100, 289, 291
coins 23
culture 322, 332
in North Africa 18, 97–8, 100, 144, 160, 386, 394
Vegetius, writer 323
Venantius Fortunatus, bishop of Poitiers 319, 334, 340
Venetia, Italy 95, 364, 366
Verdun, Gaul 84n
Verona, Italy 364, 371
Victor, archon 110n
Vienne, Gaul 17, 84, 319
villages:
in Anatolia 63, 64, 72–3, 291, 293–4
in Arabia 62–3, 72, 73, 298, 304
ascetic movement 67–70
autopract 65, 67
Christianization 63, 66, 67
churches 62–3, 64, 71
in decline 71–4, 287, 293, 295, 299–300, 409
definition 2, 63
economy 71, 72, 73
government 65–7
gsur system 64
independence 65–7, 73
inscriptions 13, 54–5, 56, 65, 66, 73
in Jordan 298–9
relationships with city 63, 70–2, 73
see also city states
villas 92–3, 96, 97, 102, 129
Viminacium, Balkans 77
vindices 108, 123, 135n, 172, 174n, 201, 307
Visigoths:
Arab conquest 316, 317n, 366, 367–8
army 366
assimilation of locals 357, 360–2, 363, 366
and bishops 160, 166
Christianization 160, 319, 354–5, 362
culture 318, 332, 337–8, 355, 356, 358, 359–60, 361–2, 363
ethnic identity 354–62, 363, 366, 367, 403
in Gaul 20, 21, 86, 127–9, 131, 354, 355
intermarriage 355, 356–7, 361n
Islamic conversion 367, 375–6
legislation 20, 21–2, 127–8, 134, 355, 356–8, 361n
numbers 357
in Spain 15, 21, 90–2, 93–4, 134–6, 160, 166, 319, 336–8, 354–63, 367
Vitalian, pope 109
Vitalis, bishop of Ravenna 159
Vittigis, Ostrogothic king 365

walls:
area enclosed
Africa 101
Gaul 82–4
Germany 86
Spain 90
late defences
Bostra 61
Ephesus 34
Italy 95–6
Marseilles 88
Miletus 49
Palestine 58
Pergamum 48
Regensburg 77
problem of dating late walls 49–52
in restructured cities 34, 76
shortened 51–2, 77, 287, 292, 305
Western Empire:
compared to East 102–3, 155, 202, 314–15, 340–1, 415–16
Witzia, Visigothic king 367
women as officeholders 188, 194–5

xenophobia 215

Zacharias of Mytilene 260
Zeno, emperor 42, 207, 213n, 241n, 254, 260, 262
Zoilos, πρωτοπολίτης 124
Zosimus, historian 325n